DATE			

Winds of Change
Economic Transition in Central and Eastern Europe

DANIEL GROS AND ALFRED STEINHERR

Winds of Change

Economic Transition in Central and Eastern Europe

LONGMAN
London and New York

Longman Group UK Limited,
Longman House, Burnt Mill,
Harlow, Essex CM20 2JE, England
and Associated Companies throughout the world.

*Published in the United States of America
by Longman Publishing, New York*

First published 1995
ISBN 0 582 102715 CSD
ISBN 0 582 102707 PPR

British Library Cataloguing-in-Publication Data

A catalogue record for this book is
available from the British Library

Library of Congress Cataloging-in-Publication Data

Gros, Daniel, 1955–
Winds of change : economic transition in Central and Eastern Europe / Daniel Gros and Alfred Steinherr.
p. cm.
Includes bibliographical references (p.) and index.
ISBN 0–582–10271–5 : £35.00. — ISBN 0–582–10270–7: £17.99
1. Europe, Eastern—Economic conditions—1989– 2. Former Soviet republics—Economic conditions. 3. Europe, Eastern—Economic policy—1989– 4. Former Soviet republics— Economic policy.
I. Steinherr, Alfred. II. Title.
HC244.G695 1995
338.947—dc20 95–18415
CIP

Set by 8 in Times 10/12pt
Printed and bound in Great Britain by Bookcraft (Bath) Ltd.

'To the memory of my father: in his life (1900–1994) he witnessed both the rise and the fall of communism in Europe.'

Daniel Gros

'For my parents who lost their youth in the darkest chapter of European history, but have lived to see the prospect of a new Europe.'

Alfred Steinherr

Contents

Preface

Sir Brian Unwin
President
European Investment Bank

Five years have elapsed since in 1989, Europe's *annus mirabilis*, the gates were opened for Eastern Europeans. Expectations of a better life in the countries beyond the old Iron Curtain were never higher than immediately after the fall of the Curtain.

Since then we have all – in the East and in the West – become wiser and, by necessity, more patient. Even in Eastern Germany, where unification made prospects most promising, reality seriously sobered initial dreams. In Hungary and the Czech and Slovak Republics stabilisation has now been successfully completed, while in Poland notable progress has been achieved. Elsewhere, with the exception of the Baltic States, the picture is more sombre. The ugly heads of national rivalries and of archaic political management are still being raised in many countries. The lifting of the communist propaganda veil also uncovered primitive production structures more resembling those of developing countries than those of the industrial countries of Western Europe. The challenges for political and economic reforms in those countries are – alas – far greater than those in Central Europe.

This book is an important attempt to provide a comprehensive view of the economic heritage of these reforming countries, of the reforms that are necessary, both from a theoretical and a practical viewpoint; and of the responsibilities of the West. In order to ensure that the book is not quickly outdated by the rapid evolution of policies, the authors have concentrated on issues of lasting interest. Moreover, I am sure, many of the issues addressed in this book, such as: was German monetary integration at a 1:1 exchange rate a mistake? Is the disintegration of Yugoslavia or the Soviet Union costly in economic terms? Why has Russia failed so far to stabilise its economy? Are workers worse off than under the old regime? – are issues that will serve as textbook examples even in 10 years' time.

Part I offers a historic review of the rise and decline of communism set against Marx's theoretical claims. It demonstrates that the Marxist theoretical baggage offered an attractive vision with great propagandistic potential but little help in practical matters. On the contrary, several Marxist precepts turned out to be a serious handicap, such as the neglect of interest rates justifying large-scale capital intensive projects, or the classification of the social value of goods leading to a neglect of services. In practice, communism tried to catch-up with the leading industrialised nations by using exploitation of labour as the main vehicle, and in that process it became crucial to gain time and disregard costs that were not helpful to catching up. Shabby production, accident-prone equipment and a deteriorating environment commanded little attention as these factors did not show up in plan targets or Net Material Product figures.

There was just one period when communism recorded remarkable economic achievements: during the initial big push by Stalin during the 1930s, culminating in record achievements during the war years. This experience proved that, given a clearly defined goal and the right incentives, the Soviet economy was able to perform at top level.

To many Westerners the rapid disintegration of communism during the 1980s still remains a puzzle. Why then? And why so rapidly? It was, of course, a confluence of factors, but a few were of outstanding importance. One was certainly the renaissance of the market economy under US President Ronald Reagan and the British Prime Minister Margaret Thatcher and their uncompromising attitude towards the Soviet Union. The economy of the Soviet Union was stagnant and unable to pick up the challenge of 'Star Wars'. After the difficulties in Afghanistan, Soviet generals were doubly humiliated and ready to accept economic reforms, a readiness shared by growing parts of the disgruntled, consumption-constrained Soviet population. But why was economic performance declining? Apart from the exhaustion of the labour surplus, the plan-induced inefficiencies in resource allocation and the permanent management and incentive problems, the command economy was still better suited for traditional large-scale industrial production than for service activities which tend to dominate the creation of value-added in advanced economies.

Part II examines in detail the measures needed to get out of the swamp of inherited socialist production structures. The authors argue convincingly that the debate about the optimal strategy for reform, big bang versus gradualism, is misplaced. There is no alternative to tackling all inherited problems at once, even though some measures produce immediate results (price liberalisation, foreign trade liberalisation) and others require years to come to fruition (privatisation, legal reforms, financial sector reforms). And apart from structural reforms all transition economies need a stabilisation programme, both to deal with the inherited monetary overhang and the on-going pressure on prices resulting from the dire straits of state-owned enterprises after price reform and trade liberalisation.

The authors rightly stress the need to try to identify the entire population with the reforms and to provide an effective income support. Their prescription is to distribute housing and a share of the productive stock to the population at large.

In their proposals for financial sector reforms the authors take a resolutely Continental view with which I am not sure I am always in full agreement. They argue that building a liquid and well-functioning capital market suitable for corporate finance and governance takes too much time. The only alternative is universal banking, which has a respectable track record in Germany and other continental European countries. For government financing, however, they propose rapid development of short-term and long-term public debt instruments to decouple monetary policy from fiscal policy.

Part III reviews the issues for reforms in Germany, the Visegrad countries and former Yugoslavia, while Part IV deals with the disintegration of the Soviet Union and reforms in Russia. The choice of countries covered reflects the objective difficulties faced by the much larger group of former socialist countries. In a sense the easiest case is that of East Germany, having become overnight part of Germany and of the European Union. While the instantaneous integration into a developed economy, with its capital market, price system and legal framework, was undoubtedly an advantage, it also posed problems. The highly protective social and legal framework of advanced Western European countries is claimed by some observers to be responsible for the inflexibility of their labour markets and for a very high natural unemployment rate. For East Germany the combination of the Western *acquis social* with too rapid wage convergence has made catching up particularly difficult, despite the massive financial and resource transfers provided by West Germany.

The Visegrad countries have succeeded to different degrees in macroeconomic stabilisation. One aim of macroeconomic reform was to achieve a competitive exchange rate to facilitate their export reorientation. As a result labour costs in these countries are among the lowest in Europe and exports are booming. Foreign direct investments are flowing in at a prudent pace, encouraged by the relative economic stability achieved so far. Among the important remaining tasks is completion of the very difficult privatisation process and the complex reform of the tax system.

Yugoslavia, before its tragic explosion, had attracted great attention in the West because it had experimented with a middle-of-the-road approach, in between the Western and the socialist camps. It developed a system of labour management more attractive than a command economy and perhaps even capable of adaptation to Western management practices. The analysis in this chapter shows, convincingly in my view, that labour management failed because the overall decisions still came down the party line and there was no market for property rights. Overall, Yugoslavia performed better than most socialist economies, but still suffered from the same causes of decline during the 1980s.

The analysis also brings out clearly the fact that the different parts of Yugoslavia never formed a well-balanced and integrated economic space. It is, therefore, not surprising that some successor states see their future as small independent states joining the EU. The more difficult question is, of course, what about the others?

Some of the problems of Yugoslavia can be found amplified in the former Soviet Union (FSU). The countries of the FSU are, of course, much poorer than their neighbours to the west and single party dictatorship and economic centralisation are more solidly engrained. Russia, in the centre, has to overcome the deep psychological shock of its loss of presumptive world power (and of being the centre of an empire) and the other countries of the FSU are faced with sorting out nationality problems, overcoming the extreme specialisation and therefore dependency which developed over the last 60 years in the FSU, and building up their own institutions and in some cases living without implicit (e.g. via cheap oil prices) or explicit subsidies.

Russia has not so far been able to stabilise its economy, like many other successor states of the FSU, but unlike the Central European countries and, to some extent, the Baltic States. The chapter on Russia provides some new insights into several, much-commented-on, special features of reforms. For example, it shows that the extreme increase in inflation after price liberalisation, which was a surprise to Western advisers, could have been foreseen by a more careful analysis of velocity (nominal GDP/money supply). Indeed, since 1987 velocity declined substantially in the Soviet Union whilst prices were kept under control. Velocity in 1992 was therefore substantially below its equilibrium and only became corrected when prices were freed.

Similarly, the concern about rapid growth of inter-enterprise debt was due to a confusion between stocks and flows. The situation in Russia never seemed to have been worse than, for example, that in Poland. This chapter also makes several other interesting points. For example, if Russia could effectively collect taxes on exports, its fiscal deficit would disappear. Or, the absence of a reasonably efficient financial sector, together with the presence of highly volatile inflation, produces extraordinarily high income transfers, away from workers to financial intermediaries.

Although it has no mandate to make finance available for projects in the FSU, the European Investment Bank, as one of the world's largest multilateral lending institutions, is determined to assist the process of reform and reconstruction in Eastern and Central Europe with all its experience and within its financial possibilities. It operates in close cooperation with the Commission of the EU and with the other multilateral institutions. The Bank has financed projects in all five Central and Southern European countries, in former Yugoslavia and in the Baltic States. By the end of 1993 funds of ECU 1,705mn were committed in support of a total of 39 projects. On a sectoral basis 30 per cent of EIB loans went to transport, 19 per cent to telecommunications, 14 per cent to energy and 36 per cent to industry. The EIB has also recently been asked by the Council of Ministers to continue its work in 11 countries of Eastern and Central Europe within a new ceiling of ECU 3bn over the next three years.

Part V of this book is also of considerable interest to me as President of the European Investment Bank. It deals with the question: what can the West do for Eastern countries? I very much subscribe to the view and analysis of the authors that finance by itself is, in general, of only secondary importance. Of course, in specific instances of national distress or during periods of rapid build-up of the capital stock, foreign financing has an important role to play. But under normal circumstances it is not so much the capital contribution as the technical expertise and transfer of know-how that is of importance. For the European Investment Bank the prime objective is to assist in a rational choice of projects cementing the economic future of reforming countries in an open environment.

In this respect the discussion of the optimal size of the EU is of special interest. As the authors rightly point out, the question is not only whether candidates are ready for entry, it also concerns the ability of the Union to adapt its decision-making processes and its support mechanisms (notably, the agricultural policy and structural funds). As the negotiations with the applicant EFTA countries have shown, these are not easy issues and in the foreseeable future it seems unlikely that the Union will expand beyond the Visegrad countries. But this does not mean that the Union's influence stops there. A free trade area, as proposed in Chapter 16, from the Atlantic to the Pacific, is surely the most effective support for developing Eastern Europe.

One sector of key strategic importance for the development of Russia is energy. Russia needs to develop energy production and reduce its energy consumption to levels closer to those in market economies in order to make available an exportable surplus to pay for its restructuring. It cannot possibly do this without Western technology transfer and financial investments. For Western Europe a secured supply of Russian oil and gas will be essential in order not to become dependent once more on Middle Eastern supplies. For that reason the European Energy Charter launched by Dutch Prime Minister Lubbers is of key importance. The EIB has been charged to help manage a Euratom Facility to contribute to reducing the risk of nuclear pollution in

Eastern Europe and the FSU – a considerable risk for Western Europe. The nuclear pollution risk illustrates very vividly the interest of Western Europe in assisting reforms in Eastern Europe.

While representing the personal views of the authors, this book draws on a wealth of experience in the European Investment Bank and elsewhere to address one of the most critical issues facing Western Europe – and indeed, the world – today. As you would expect from Alfred Steinherr and Daniel Gros, it constructs its themes on a rigorous analytical base, and it provides a wealth of material for the professional and academic economist. But at the same time the authors succeed in presenting their discourse in a clear and easy-going style that should attract a larger audience and appeal to anyone with an interest in comparative economic systems and in the reforms in Eastern and Central Europe in particular. We all owe them a debt of gratitude and I wish this volume every success.

Acknowledgements

In writing this book we were fortunate enough to be able to count on the support of many people. They are too numerous to be all mentioned here, but we would still like to express our appreciation for the help we received from some of them. Maureen Thibaut-McCaw typed several drafts with great efficiency and made sure that we were always working on the latest version. Koen Schoors, Guy Vandille and Anna Castallo provided the research assistance that is behind most of the data we present. Gérard Duchêne and an anonymous referee gave us useful comments; we have to apologise for not following all of their suggestions. Gerd Schwartz, Mark Stone and Tessa van der Willigen were the authors of the first draft of Chapter 11. They are not responsible for what we made out of their material. The editorial staff at Longman who accompanied this project cheerfully through all of its delays, for which we take full responsibility.

Finally, Daniel Gros thanks the Centre for European Policy Studies (CEPS) for its supportive environment. The TACIS and PHARE programmes of the European Commission also provided crucial support for Daniel Gros by financing several projects that allowed him to concentrate on developments in the CIS and other reforming economies.

PART ONE

THE RISE AND DECLINE OF COMMUNISM: AN OVERVIEW

K. Marx:
"Tut mir leid Jungs!
War halt nur so'ne Idee von mir . . ."

Introduction

Today, communism appears to many as a historic stupidity and, without a shadow of a doubt, capitalism has victoriously emerged as the dominant paradigm. Such a view is too short-sighted and conditioned by the recent demise of communism. It neglects at least two points. First, the *realisation* of any theory always differs from the *theoretic model* which, at any rate, captures only part of societal organisation. History and the distribution of social and political values interfere with the economic model. For example, only under very restrictive assumptions could it be claimed that, say, colonial capitalism was superior to Soviet communism. Second, because the working class suffered from unbearable misery during the take-off phase of the now successfully developed capitalist countries - a misery still prevalent throughout the developing world – the Marxist vision gave hope to large fractions of society of both developed and developing countries, a hope that capitalism was unable to provide. And, despite the current universal popularity of capitalism, we can be sure that the capitalist paradigm will again be challenged some time in the future.

There were times (before the Second World War and during the Cold War) when the West did not feel totally assured about its superior economic and military force and when a communist bush fire in poor parts of the world was feared. Western Europe, for geographic reasons, was concerned about Soviet aggression and its democracy felt internally weakened by Moscow-supported communist parties.

The Soviet view of communism was the prescribed model everywhere in the Soviet block. The need for incentives was, however, sometimes recognised and temporary concessions were granted; for example, in strongly Catholic Poland, where farming largely remained in private hands and dissidents met with more tolerance than in other East European countries. Hungary, too, was allowed, after its abortive revolution in 1956, to embark on a more relaxed economic policy, which included incentives for workers and greater powers for middle management in agriculture and industry. But when Czechoslovakia seemed to be heading towards the dismantling of single-party rule in 1968 and to be espousing other 'bourgeois democratic' heresies, Soviet and Warsaw Pact troops marched in and restored communist order.

In all countries where communist parties took over government, single-party 'democracy' with dictatorship by the proletariat was the final outcome. But even in Western countries with strong democratic traditions and mature economies Moscow-sponsored communist parties played a role, although their influence has waned of late. Figure 0.1 summarises the situation in Western Europe in the 1970s at the height of that influence. At that time there were about 60 million Communist Party members in some 90 countries across the globe. While the party was not allowed in all countries in the West, it nevertheless achieved a membership of 3 million and more. The largest Western Communist parties were those in Italy (1.8 million) and France (.6 million).

The main issue addressed in Part I is whether communism failed because it was based on a model, in some sense inappropriate, or whether the particular Soviet incarnation was at fault. We shall argue that the model serves not too badly in special circumstances such as the initial economic take-off in the terminology of Rostow (1960), but fails hopelessly in a mature economy. Moreover, the Soviet brand of communism – the only one actually implemented – suffers from the weight of Russian history and particularities that would have dragged down any approach – as witnessed by the current difficulties in reforming the Russian economy and introducing capitalism.

Chapter 1 elaborates those features of communist rule which were inherited from Tsarist Russia: the centralisation of power and the need for ideology, the key role of the military and the imperial aspirations, the emphasis on heavy industry and the neglect of agriculture, and so on. In fact, according to Marxist theory, the socialist revolution should not even have occurred in Russia but instead in a more developed country such as Germany. The very start therefore contradicted theory as did much in the later evolution. Chapter 1 shows, moreover, that the new regime was not equipped with a blueprint for running a communist society and instead had to proceed by trial and error, up to the very end.

What then was the basic equipment of the new regime? Marx provided both a critique of capitalism, whose principle arguments are reproduced in Chapter 1, and a vision of a communist future in the 'long run', but not much for the interim period.

Marx taught the ultimate and inevitable collapse of the capitalist order and its replacement by a classless communist one. Under communism, the state itself would be abolished and society would be governed by the principle 'from each according to his ability, to each according to his needs'. But there would be a transitional stage – Marx called it socialism[1] – which would be ruled by the principle 'from each according to his ability, to each according to his work'. Under socialism, the victorious workers, the proletariat, would exercise a form of dictatorship to ensure that socialism could be applied without obstruction from whatever 'capitalist attitudes' society might not yet have succeeded in getting rid of.

Marx had little concrete to say on how this proletarian revolution would come about. That job was left to Lenin – who is the major architect of pre-Stalinist communism (Marxist–Leninist) – and others.

One big controversy throughout most of the 70 years of communist rule in the Soviet Union centred on the 'party of the new type' that Lenin helped to build up. Lenin argued for the creation of a centralised, tightly disciplined revolutionary party. This was criticised by his rival in the Russian revolutionary movement, Leon Trotsky (1861–1940) until he eventually aligned himself with Lenin's ideas.

The Revolution of 1917 was a watershed. All across Europe, during the late nineteenth century, reformists had been grouping themselves into a body whose direct descendant was the Socialist International. The revolutionaries joined the Communist International (Comintern) which Lenin had set up in Moscow in 1919. Lenin's principle of 'democratic centralism' – or compulsory adherence to central party policy – became the model for Communist parties everywhere else. So did the one-party Soviet State established by Lenin and Trotsky and completed by Stalin. The key features of that state were:

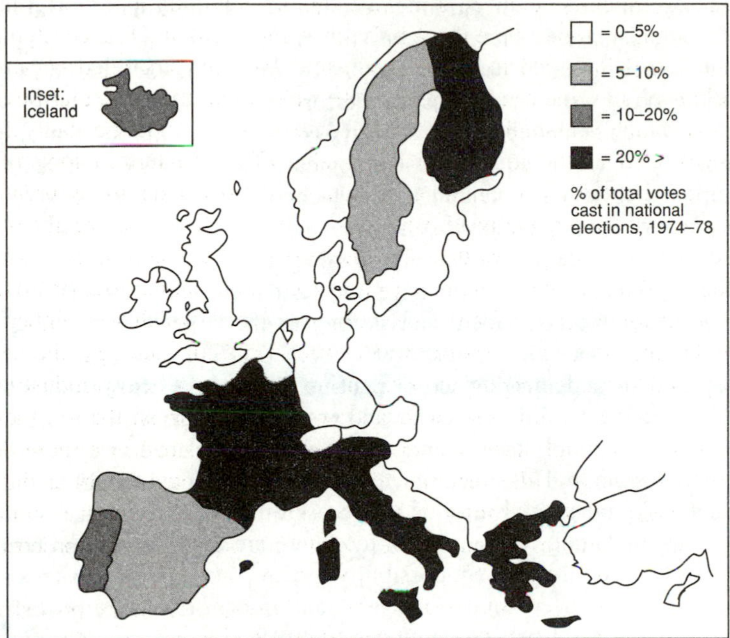

Note: The lowest numbers of seats held by Communists in national parliaments, 1974–78 was 0 (UK, Ireland, W. Germany, Austria, Norway, Denmark). The highest, with 228 out of 630, was Italy.

FIG. 0.1 Communists in non-communist Europe: western communist parties' strength in national elections, 1974–78.

- total control of the state by the ruling party, with complete power of political initiative and decision-making reserved for the inner leadership and ultimately the party leader alone;
- the absence of any real legal limitation on state power (despite a constitutional façade) with the state identified with the party;
- monopoly party control over all forms of social organisation;
- monopoly party control over all channels of communication, with the right to impose censorship and to mould public opinion.

As for economic management, the revolutionary regime followed Marx's instruction to expropriate to a large extent and improvised a 'war economy' (compulsory requisitions) during the post-Revolution turmoils. Most interestingly, the following phase, called the New Economic Policy (NEP), returned to greater decentralisation, cooperative organisation and a larger role for small-scale private ownership. When the NEP failed to produce satisfactory results, a political power struggle developed between those in favour of more decentralisation, privatisation and opening up to the outside world (it is interesting to ask what communism would have become had they won their case) and those opting for the opposite. Unfortunately and dramatically, the latter, spearheaded by Stalin, won. Stalinism turned into one of the most repressive 'totalitarian systems' (Arendt 1951), forcing the economy into the straightjacket of centralised planning, with vast forced savings, inhumane penalties for deviation from imposed norms, concentration on development of heavy industry and collectivisation of all economic activity, with virtual extermination of the kulaks (wealthy peasant class). In a narrow sense Stalin was successful: at the expense of sacrificing most contemporaries (either in labour camps or simply by frustrating their claim to a constant or rising share in output) a large investment effort guaranteed rapid output growth during the 1930s which helped to resist the Nazi assault. The victorious war turned Stalin into a national hero, rekindled socialist ideological zeal and thus helped reconstruction and development of Soviet nuclear and space technology – still at the cost of maintaining the vast part of the population in misery.

One lesson of this period is that communism was able to rally forces not only against external threats but also to achieve internal targets (industrialisation) as long as belief in the system was sustained and as long as the target was a simple one (e.g. double steel output). But this approach was doomed to fail over time. As the system did not allow a shift in demand to satisfy pent-up demands by citizens, support waned. And, equally important, whilst the command system can cope with standard industrial production (steel), it simply cannot evolve into a more modern economy serving complex consumer demands. This inherent contradiction on its own would already explain the incapacity of fundamental reforms unsuccessfully attempted by all successors of Stalin up to and including Gorbachev. In fact there are other barriers to reforms. The most important is the difficulty (impossibility?) of reconciling monoparty communist leadership with a more decentralised incentive and information system. One particular illustration of the conflict between political control and economic needs is the treatment of foreign trade and investments. Highly desirable from an economic point of view, it could not be accepted beyond narrow limits for fear of loss of control.

After this *tour d'horizon* of the history of the Soviet Union from an economic point of view in Chapter 1, Chapter 2 drills down on the key economic institutions of the Socialist economy: the plan, the contractual and implicit incentives, property rights (or lack thereof), and the financial system. The aim is to show how the system functioned and why it was bogged down by features that could not be removed.

The chapter also discusses two permanent policy priorities not dictated by socialism in itself which, perhaps curiously, turned out to be fatal in the end: the option of autarkic development and the goal of catching up with the West. The first policy choice was dictated by political concerns (a strategy abandoned by China in 1978) and the second, extensively analysed in Chapter 3, by the conviction that socialism could only survive and dominate the world if it could win the Darwinian race in terms of material production. Because it became clear in the 1980s that it had lost the race, which communists themselves singled out to be decisive,[2] Soviet communism disappeared – but left the sad inheritance of a highly polluted racetrack scattered with industrial junk, and with people so abused that the race will not be forgotten for a long time. Was it the model? Was it the Soviet incarnation? Certainly both joined hands to produce disaster. China proves that communism paired with economic reforms and foreign trade can perform remarkably well. But it does not prove that communism can and will survive.

Notes

1. In this book we use interchangeably the terms 'socialism' and 'communism' as has become the custom.
2. In fact, they fell victim to Marx's theory that for a *capitalist* society 'to accumulate is to conquer the world of social wealth . . .' (Marx 1933: 649).

CHAPTER ONE

From pre-war Russia to the fall of communism: an overview

Il était donc une terre où l'utopie était en passe de devenir réalité. D'immenses accomplissements déjà nous emplissaient le coeur d'exigence. Le plus difficile était déjà fait, semblait-il, et nous nous aventurions joyeusement dans cette sorte d'engagement pris avec elle au nom de tous les peuples souffrants. Jusqu'à quel point, dans une faillite, nous sentirions-nous de même engagés? Mais la seule idée d'une faillite est inadmissible.

(André Gide, *Retour de l'U.R.S.S.* 1936)

Ever since the socialist takeover in Russia a debate has been raging about the profundity of the changes imposed on Russian society.[1] Expropriation of 'individual owners of the means of production' and even of non-directly productive assets (e.g. housing), the role of government in establishing production plans, in taking responsibility for their execution and in setting prices and wages seem to suggest that society was radically changed from top to bottom. However, looking back on Russia's history since Peter the Great, we find that many features of Russian pre-Revolutionary society survived and indeed were sometimes reinforced after the Revolution. The Soviet Union remained an empire with its border problems and nationality conflicts, and continued to police its population severely. Democracy was as absent and repression as regular after as before the Revolution. State organisation remained highly centralised and the problems of the periphery were, as always, ignored, misunderstood and repressed. Within the imperial borders the conflict between town and country was as acute in the 1930s as in the seventeenth century. The leadership remained divided between imperial expansion eastwards or westwards, and between opening up or closing up to foreign, mostly Western, influences. The empire invariably rooted its strength in strong ideological grounds: in pre-Revolutionary days in absolute monarchy and religion and afterwards in the Marxist framework. Both regimes, each claiming to pursue a superior mission, had expansionary goals for which a strong and influential military was necessary. The need to equip the military, more than the desirability of improving the welfare of citizens, was in each case the driving force behind industrialisation.

A demonstration of these continuities scales down the historic importance of the communist revolution. Many features of developments in the Soviet Union which could be regarded as resulting from communist rule may well have emerged under a different regime altogether. However, while it would not do to ignore these historic continuities, neither should we fatalistically assert that the communist regime was already dormant in the genes of Russian history.

To clarify these points we recall the salient features of Russian history in Section 1 before going on to outline the socialist takeover in Section 2. The New Economic Policy which ended the search for a workable model of socialist economic management and then gave way to the Stalinist command economy is discussed in Section 3.

The end of the NEP was a turning-point. From the First Five-Year Plan on, a system developed which the world has identified with the communist model: totalitarian in its political structure, and with a command economy as the economic complement. The Stalinist reorientation is discussed in Section 4. When the regime was at its zenith, its totalitarian perfection basked in the flush of victory over the Nazi aggressor and served as a general model for export. However, towards the end of the Stalinist era, the country was left saddled with enormous unresolved problems arising from changes in the system to accommodate greater participation in decision-making, from the fading of the 'Stalingrad effect' of an invincible world power and, above all, from the need to reform the economy, in spite of a growth record never achieved before or thereafter.

Section 5 then analyses the unsuccessful attempts by Khrushchev to push through these badly needed reforms. His failure to deliver precipitated a loss of credibility for the USSR as a world power, and reactionary forces rallied round Brezhnev to organise restoration (Section 6).

Stationary conditions under Brezhnev bottled up to what became an explosively pressing need for reform in all spheres of Soviet social, political and economic life. When Gorbachev lifted the lid off these repressed needs he was soon engulfed by a tidal wave of demands for reform. Section 7 demonstrates that partial reforms soon proved inadequate in light of the delays accumulated in dealing with complex and inter-dependent issues of economic reform, individual freedom and repressed nationalism. Section 8 then claims that the failure of Soviet-type communism was endogenous and had little to do with the personalities of the men actually in charge. But it had a lot to do with the ingredients inherited from Russian history that contributed decisively to the Soviet realisation of communism.

1. Key features of Russian history up to the Socialist Revolution

Russia has always been something of an unknown quantity in Europe's western reaches. It has been considered as retarded and brutish, but also at times as a powerful and awe-inspiring foe. History and space produced a number of remarkable constraints for Russia which survived even the 70-odd years of communist rule. This brief historical synopsis highlights some of these constraints.

A good starting point to illustrate this is Peter the Great, the founder of the pre-Revolutionary Russian State, who brought the Middle Ages to a close during his reign from 1689 to 1725. It was he who provided the first impetus towards industrial revolution in Russia, chiefly in order to supply his need for a powerful navy and army.

In 1697 Peter set up the first foundry and cannon factory in the Urals with the aim of breaking his dependence on supplies from Sweden. At the time of his death there were 12 metallurgical factories in the Urals and the Russian metal-working industry had become the largest in Europe. Half of these factories belonged to the state, the other half to the ennobled bourgeoisie and the old Stroganov aristocracy. A more efficient tax administration was set up to help finance his ventures, a head tax was implemented and domestic textile and steel production were heavily protected.[2]

Peter's unsurpassed achievement (or act of folly) was, of course, the foundation of the new capital of St Petersburg. Construction commenced in 1703, draining resources in a way for which the poorly developed Russian economy was ill-prepared. He brought in large numbers of European experts (architects, engineers, scientists, officers and administrators) to westernise Russia. This demanded such a gigantic effort that the country was still reeling under its effects when Catherine the Great came to power in 1762.

Peter the Great had imperial ambitions that strangely resembled those of the Soviet Union 250 years later. He fought a long drawn-out war with Sweden for more than 20 years in a bid to extend his influence over the Baltics. By securing access to the Baltic Sea and the Black Sea, Peter the Great helped to elevate Russia to the position of first continental European power. He failed, however, in his quest to modernise Russia sufficiently to set it on a sustainable path of modernisation and growth – as did the communists.

A second attempt at modernisation was made by Catherine the Great. In 1766 she set up a Commission to prepare a Code fixing the rights and obligations of the nobility and of ordinary citizens. The result was hailed as the most liberal work of eighteenth century Russia and was applauded by Diderot and Voltaire alike. Catherine herself had contributed personal writings inspired by Montesquieu and Beccaria. However, the project was put on ice and then finally discarded. After failing to implement changes, and after facing open rebellion, she turned much more traditionalist and set to completing Peter's work in embellishing St Petersburg and expanding the empire, aided and abetted by an endless inflow of foreign experts. Both Peter's and Catherine's achievements were only made possible by a massive transfer of know-how from Western Europe, a transfer that the communists could not and did not wish to perpetuate. In Chapters 2 and 3 it is shown that this turned out to represent a major handicap.

After the war of liberation against Napoleon, Alexander I focused Russia's energies during the first half of the nineteenth century on territorial expansion rather than economic reform. The perennial key questions for nineteenth century Russian development were: are better incomes from agriculture needed to generate internal demand, or should agriculture be taxed more heavily to generate investable surplus? (Export-led growth was not retained as an alternative given the large size of the country.) Should serfs be freed or not for the benefit of more rapid development? (This debate was raging at the same time in the United States.) Should the state take the lead in industrial development by investing massively in infrastructure or should the aristocracy be induced to take the lead? Such questions were not fundamentally different from those debated in other countries at a comparable level of development. The real problem was that no consistent answers were forthcoming until the 1890s.

The economy stagnated during the first half of the nineteenth century and industrialisation did not take off until well into the second half of the nineteenth century, after Tsar Alexander II had set free the serfs in 1861. It then took another 30 years to generate a powerful spurt of industrialisation. The delay is hardly surprising, for even if the freeing of the serfs had been expressly designed to set industrialisation in motion, the country simply lacked the administrative, legal and physical infrastructure for an industrial take-off. In particular, communications between the vast stretches of empire were poor and enormous capital resources were needed to build modern means of communication (railways) in what was the largest country on earth.

The under-developed domestic market was seen as one of the greatest inhibiting factors for growth. In the 1890s the state attempted to manage development in such a way that the growth of peasant demand for industrial goods would no longer be a pre-requisite of successful industrialisation. On the contrary, the prevailing view finally was to curtail that demand in order to increase the share of national output available for investment. This also meant increased exports and better chances of larger and cheaper loans from abroad. It was a policy that was to be confirmed in the twentieth century under communist rule, with one regrettable difference: foreign trade and investment were kept at bay.

The Russian state put the peasantry under very considerable fiscal pressure. In the closing years of the 1890s, Russian agriculture produced less bread grain per capita than had been the case three decades earlier. With a growing population and increased exports, domestic availabilities fell sharply. A central principle of governmental policy was to absorb a larger share of the peasants' output rather than to stimulate that output.

Industrialisation in Russia was also conspicuous for the sheer size of both individual plant and individual enterprise – indeed this was also a prominent feature of later developments in the Soviet Union.[3]

The average annual rate of industrial growth during the 1890s was around 8 per cent, a remarkable success that compares favourably with the growth of other catching-up countries in Western Europe at that time. The very speed of the transformation, however, made for maladjustments of various kinds. The discrepancy between industry on the march and relatively stagnant agriculture was perhaps the most crucial of those tensions.

The years between the 1905 Revolution and the outbreak of World War I were also a period of fairly rapid growth of industry in Russia (some 6 per cent per annum), even though the rate of change lagged behind that of the 1890s. During those years industri-alisation could no longer be the primary concern of government. Wars and revolution had greatly strained budgetary capabilities. Railway building continued, but on a much reduced scale. Nothing underscores more clearly the government's change of mind than Stolypin's reforms in 1906 and 1910. The essence of the 1906 reform was that any peasant could demand a share of the village land, and by 1917 more than half of all peasant households held their land in hereditary tenure. However, a law of 1910 restricted the amount of land any one peasant could acquire by purchase.

Unfortunately, as observed by Voltaire in his *Histoire de l'Empire de Russie sous Pierre le Grand*, then, and again and again, in Russia *tout vient trop tard*. It was left to the regime that finally emerged from the 1917 Revolution, generated in the misery of war and the shame of defeat, to create a different set of conditions and to blend them with some of the old ingredients of Russian economic history into the strange and powerful infusion of Soviet industrialism.

What, then, were the constants of Russian history, preserved under communism? First of all, its relative separateness from the rest of the world, punctuated by occa-sional openings to accelerate development.[4] Second, a definite imperialist thrust to extend its power in Europe and Asia. This territorial expansion created a permanent conflict between the centre and the periphery and among the various nationalities subjugated by the Russians. The communist regime persuaded the world that the nationalities problem had been definitively solved and that a new species – Homo Sovieticus – had been invented. It was only when the empire disintegrated that the nationalities conflict came to the surface again and all its gory consequences with it.[5]

Third, there was never such a thing as democracy in this vast country either before or after the socialist revolution. Prior to the Revolution, central power was propped up by the Church and afterwards by communist ideology. The administration considerably tightened its grip on the country after the communist takeover but the centralised administration before and after the takeover failed to treat other nationalities on an equal basis and integrate them.

Fourth, specific sectoral misallocations were repeated over and again. A permanent victim of development was agriculture, whose terms of trade were always unfavourable. The lack of investment in infrastructure has also generally fallen more heavily on the countryside and agricultural producers were ever marginals, both before 1861 (the year of their liberation from serfdom) and after.

And last but not least, there was the importance attached to the military and the vast resources poured into defence.

2. The Socialist Revolution in Russia

The Bolsheviks came to power in 1917. Although revolutionary fervour spread from its St Petersburg base across the country, it was unable to prevent the empire from breaking up. The USSR was founded by the Treaty of 30 December 1922 signed by Russia, Belorussia, Ukraine and Transcaucasia. The principle of 'self-determination' was highly debated and allowed the Baltic states to gain independence. Lenin was squarely opposed to federalism but determined to save the old empire. That is why he accepted bilateral treaties between Russia and independent republics. The Constitution of 1924 was the consecration of the union of sovereign states with equal rights.[6]

With hindsight, much Marxist thinking – the intellectual luggage of European revolutionaries at the turn of the century – appears faulty and half-baked, but in the early part of the twentieth century it was a formidable, sweeping piece of work that takes its place even to this day as one of humankind's most influential achievements. Yet the economic tools were largely inspired by and in agreement with classical economics, mainly Ricardian thinking, not much of which (e.g. the theory of value, the theory of growth) has survived the scrutiny of contemporary minds.

A decisive shortcoming of the Marxist tool-kit is that it mainly provided a critique of capitalism without proposing a blueprint for a socialist society.[7] It was therefore a more useful instrument for an opposition party than for a party responsible for running a country. The new leaders' task was also complicated by the lack of empirical demonstrations. For want of guidance they turned to the history of developed countries, remembering that 'the industrially more developed country represents to the less developed country a picture of the latter's future' (Marx 1933: Preface).

How useful, then, was the Marxist tool-kit to revolutionaries? Despite its shortcomings, it was undoubtedly of outstanding value for several reasons. To begin with, it provided a 'scientific' explanation of 'expropriation' and hence a moral justification for revolutionary activists and 'for expropriating the expropriators' (see Box 1.1). Second, it offered a theory of crisis that seemed germane to capitalism. Combating a system as imperfect as capitalism, beset by 'fundamental contradictions' and ultimately 'doomed to fail',[8] became a logical necessity, justified both morally and by reason of workers' class interests.

Box 1.1 Basic Marxist concepts: the theory of exploitation

Marx starts his theory of exploitation from the following postulates:

1. The class structure of capitalist society essentially consists of two classes: the bourgeois class that owns, and the proletarian class that does not own.
2. By virtue of the position of these two classes in the productive process, their interests are necessarily antagonistic.
3. The resulting class struggle provides the mechanism that triggers the propensity of economic evolution to change social organisation.

It needs to be explained why Marx saw the interests of the bourgeois and proletarian classes as antagonistic (why cannot both benefit from economic progress?) and how these laws of social evolution are liable to change social organisation.

According to Marx, in capitalist society labour is a commodity. Hence its value is determined in the same way as the value of any other commodity, that is, by the amount of labour necessary to produce it. Although today the labour theory of value is discredited, Marx was simply subscribing to the Ricardian elaboration, a serious contribution to classical economics which was not as shocking to his contemporaries as it is to us today.

The amount of labour socially required to reproduce labour consists of the food, shelter, entertainment, and so on, that is needed to sustain a socially defined 'minimum vital'. Suppose it takes four hours of work to reproduce a worker. These 'reproduction costs' are considered as variable capital (v), because they require outlays by the employer. Suppose that the worker is made to work 10 hours. Then, because capitalists only pay the minimum vital, they realise a surplus (s) of six hours and s/v is the rate of exploitation. Because the workers do not receive the full value of their work (10 hours), they are exploited. Hence the antagonistic interests of the two groups, workers and capitalists.

This line of reasoning presents some obvious flaws. What is the 'minimum vital' empirically and what keeps labour's income down at the cost of reproduction? A growing economy creates more jobs and more competition for workers, and puts upward pressure on wages so that workers also benefit from growth.

Marx saw the world differently. He observed the extreme misery of the urban unemployed and the vast under-employment in traditional sectors and he saw this as a permanent feature of capitalist society. The 'reserve army of labour' kept

continued

Box 1.1 *continued*

wages down to a minimum through competition for employment, which tallied with the views of classical economists. Whilst growth created new jobs, technological progress and increasing mechanisation meant that machines were replacing workers and swelling the ranks of the reserve army.

Any temporary decline of the reserve army, rising wages, and reduced profitability necessarily ends in a calamitous new crisis:

> But if one were to attempt to clothe this tautology [that crises are caused by the scarcity of solvent consumers] with a profounder justification by saying that the working class receive too small a portion of their own product, and the evil would be remedied by giving them a larger share of it, or raising their wages, we should reply that crises are precisely always preceded by a period in which wages rise generally and the working class actually get a larger share of the annual product intended for consumption. From the point of view of the advocates of 'simple' common sense, such a period should rather remove a crisis. It seems, then, that capitalist production comprises certain conditions which are independent of good or bad will and permit the working class to enjoy that relative prosperity only momentarily, and that always as a harbinger of a coming crisis. (Marx 1933: II 475–76)

From today's vantage-point Marx can be accused of having failed to understand the employment creation and income gains from technical progress and associated rising demand, but it must be borne in mind that many Western intellectuals championed socialist ideas as a humanely attractive alternative to the pallor of early capitalist development and that even today many still perceive technical progress as a threat to employment. Also the devastating European wars were attributed to economic interests not only by Marxists.[9] For more than half a century communist ideology could '*embraser les coeurs au feu du verbe*' (Pushkin, *Prophète*) in developed and developing countries alike, for the promise of a better and more peaceful world.

The Marxist prediction of the inevitable evolution of capitalism towards socialism did not materialise because the analysis was faulty. In fact what happened was that the less developed countries turned out to be far more (socialist) revolution-prone than their rich capitalist counterparts. The main reason is indubitably that the process of accumulation benefited labour in a measure not anticipated by Marx (see Box 1.2). During the last 50 years and in virtually every country in the world, the share of labour in national income has not declined (see World Bank, *World Development Report*, 1994) and incomes have been multiplying, so that labour has benefited from growth at least proportionately. In addition employed labour has been able to accumulate wealth so that the distinction between the entrepreneur-capitalist and the worker only 'owning his arms' has become blurred.

Box 1.2 Basic Marxist concepts: the theory of accumulation

Marx, like all classical economists, assumed that workers consume all of their wages. The steadily growing surplus accruing to capitalists is used for two purposes, namely for capitalists' consumption and for accumulation. Accumulation itself is not equal to investment in the modern sense of the word, since part of it serves to employ additional variable capital (additional workers) and only the balance adds to the stock of constant capital. Part of accumulation is therefore consumed by workers.

The analysis starts with a two-sector model of the economy. Sector I produces the means of production (capital goods like machines and raw materials like cotton) and Sector II goods for consumption. In Sector I one then has:

$$c_1 + v_1 + s_1 = w_1 \qquad [1]$$

where c_1 is the constant capital (machines, raw material) used up in the production of goods in Sector I; v_1 is variable capital (the cost of labour) used up; s_1 is the capitalist's surplus and w_1 is output.

The same holds true for Sector II:

$$c_2 + v_2 + s_2 = w_2 \qquad [2]$$

Now, the economy as a whole cannot use up more means of production than are being produced by Sector I:

$$c_1 + c_2 = c_1 + v_1 + s_1 \qquad [3]$$

and workers and capitalists together cannot consume more than is produced by Sector II:

$$v_1 + s_1 + v_2 + s_2 = c_2 + v_2 + s_2 \qquad [4]$$

Equations [3] and [4] are not independent and reduce to

$$c_2 = v_1 + s_1 \qquad [5]$$

Equation [5] provides the conditions for simple reproduction, that is, a stationary equilibrium. In such a state of equilibrium the constant capital used up for the production of consumption goods is equal to variable capital and surplus in the production of capital goods. Accumulation only occurs when capitalists stop consuming all their surplus and re-invest part of it. Market forces, in the Marxian view, compel capitalists to do just that, so that accumulation is a defining feature of capitalism.

Success in a capitalist society consists in accumulating capital. 'To accumulate is to conquer the world of social wealth, to increase the mass of human beings exploited by him, and thus to extend both the direct and the indirect sway of the capitalist' (Marx 1933: 649). In fact capitalists have no choice. Competition never sleeps and technological progress does not stop and wait for them. In neo-

continued

Box 1.2 *continued*

classical economics it is argued that investors are driven by the prospect of higher return. Profit is also important for the Marxist capitalists who know, however, that they are destroying themselves, since their accumulation reinforces the tendency of the rate of profit to fall. The rate of profit is defined as:

$$s/(c + v) \qquad [6]$$

that is, surplus over total capital. Because surplus is only created by labour, any investment in fixed capital therefore lowers the profit rate and increases the 'organic composition of capital' $c/(c+v)$. This is what Marx called 'the fundamental contradiction of capitalism'.

> On the other hand, the fall in prices and the competitive struggle would have given to every capitalist an impulse to raise the individual value of his total product above its average value by means of new machines, new and improved working methods, new combinations, which means to increase the productive power of a certain quantity of labour . . . The depreciation of the elements of constant capital itself would be another factor tending to raise the rate of profit. The mass of the employed constant capital, compared to the variable, would have increased, but the value of this mass might have fallen. The present stagnation of production would have prepared an expansion of production later on, within capitalistic limits. And in this way the cycle would be run once more. One portion of the capital which had been depreciated by the stagnation of its function would recover its old value. For the rest, the same vicious circle would be described once more under expanded conditions of production in an expanded market, and with increased productive forces. (Marx 1933: III 297–99)

During the first half of the twentieth century capitalism was quite dynamic and, particularly in the richest countries, it did not look as though it were about to expire (except during economic recessions such as the Great Depression). Happily, Marxists came up with the theory of 'retarding factors'[10] (see Sweezy 1942 and Griffith and Gurley 1985). Some of these factors were seen to destroy even such virtues of capitalism as were associated with competitive capitalism, so that capitalism in its advanced form was destined to become dominated by monopolies and close association with the state and so to degenerate into imperialism. The working class therefore faced two enemies: the capitalists and their agents, the institutions of state.

Although the theory suggested the ultimate breakdown of capitalism without the proletariat having to strike a single revolutionary blow, the outlook was by no means certain in light of these retarding factors. Hence an active revolutionary endeavour was needed to stop prolonging the process. Ideally, on the basis of this analysis, the overthrow of capitalism should have started in England, France or Germany, not in retarded Russia. Why then did it happen in Russia?

A first clue is provided by the controversy between Kautsky and Lenin on the question of whether socialism can take the parliamentarian route. By shelving the revolutionary goals Kautsky accepted an initial opposition role for the Socialist Party in Germany. Ever since that day, the Socialist Party has been a major actor on the German political stage, fully accepting the rules of democratic society. Such a role was certainly not foreseen by Marx and it did not have the same potential in countries like Russia with a much less developed middle class and a much less numerous industrial proletariat.

We can therefore turn the Marxist prediction on its head: socialist revolutions are less likely in the most advanced capitalist economies than in the least developed countries, as the latter offer limited scope for democratic evolution. In 1987, according to Kornai (1992), 35% of the world population lived under communist rule. Most countries were poor relatives of Western Europe and the United States both before and after communist power took over, so that the share of these countries in world output was less than 15% (see Collins and Rodrick 1991).

Casual empiricism and the data in Kornai (1992) indeed suggest that all socialist revolutions occurred in poor countries, with the exception of Eastern Europe. There, however, socialism was not the result of an internal revolutionary process but was imposed by the Soviet Union. All non-imported socialist revolutions seem to have the following features in common. The countries are poor and have not yet embarked on industrialisation and income distribution is highly biased in favour of a small class of land-owners. The political structure is non-democratic and the mass of the impoverished population is deprived of political rights. In some cases external or internal wars unsettle the existing order. As a result, an alternative is sought for a despised and exploitative political system. Socialist ideology provides a 'scientifically' argued critique, associates economic malfunctioning with the political system and offers the perspective of utopia. All the existing value systems can easily be put aside, as 'The ruling ideas of each age have ever been the ideas of its ruling class' (Marx and Engels 1930). No value system therefore has eternal validity and religion is an instrument of the existing dominant class and the 'opium of the people'.

All these characteristics of a disintegrating society were present in Russia. After the peace of Brest-Litovsk the Russian economy was shattered, the aristocracy, law and order discredited, and the empire's outskirts in open rebellion. Even patriotism had evaporated so that the Marxist idea of identification with one's class, as against one's country, came close to reality. This was not the case in Western Europe where patriotism was flying high in the victorious countries.[11] The only major country where the empire, the state and the ruling classes were thoroughly discredited was Russia. As in Germany, millions of unemployed, armed discharged soldiers without a job crowded into the towns dissatisfied, restless and ready to overthrow what remained of the old regime. Even if Marx had never written a line, a social revolution would have been in the Russian air.

But as it happened, his analysis was there for the taking. It was not directly applicable as such, since the context was significantly different. The communist utopia of a classless society, without a command structure, without a state and everything in common ownership, simply could not be implemented straight away. Also, lacking widespread popular support, a structure was needed to spread the gospel, to extend and preserve power. This structure was to be provided by the Communist Party. Because the country's administration emerged from the war in tatters, the first important task for the party was to assert its power and to take a firm hold of the administrative reins.[12]

In addition to the traditional tasks of government, the communist regime immediately took control of the economy. Unfortunately, the party's economic management came on top of ever more extensive 'government of the people', which made the overall responsibility that much heavier. For those tasks the new regime had neither the blueprint nor the capital, the skills or general popular support.

Immediately after the takeover, the communists set up the Glavki-system. Glavki was a department of the Supreme Economic Council which organised nationalisation and production on an industry-by-industry basis. All firms within a given industrial sector were brought under the umbrella of a glavki. As early as 1920, at the eighth Soviet Congress, enterprises rose in revolt against the excessive concentration of decision-making in the Glavki-system, foreshadowing the NEP and repeated reforms in later years under Khrushchev and Gorbachev.

The 1918–20 period was conditioned by the civil war which brought its own special problems. The way production was organised was dubbed 'war communism'. Lenin said in 1921: 'War communism was thrust upon us by war and ruin. It was not, nor could it be, a policy that corresponded to the economic tasks of the proletariat. It was a temporary measure' (quoted in Dobb 1939: 123). The main issue during the years of war communism was the treatment afforded agricultural production. With hyperinflation rife, peasants refused to deliver and government saw coercion as the only way out of the conundrum. The surplus produce of each peasant farm was subjected to requisitioning. The same was true in industry but as industry had already been nationalised in the immediate aftermath of the takeover, requisitioning of industrial surplus production was formally less shocking. The collection of agricultural surpluses and their allocation to army, industry and the main distribution points for workers' rations were organised by the Commissariat of Supplies (*Narcomprod*).

From the start the new regime faced two formidable political challenges: to gain control inside the country and to fend off feared interventions from outside, as the communist take-over of Russia met with strong internal opposition backed by foreign forces. Civil war broke out in 1918 and lasted until 1920.[13]

Lenin was aware of the difficulty for communism of surviving in a world surrounded by capitalist countries. That is why he attached great importance to social revolution in Germany. When these hopes were dashed in 1921, the theory of peaceful coexistence was developed to cope with the weakness of the Soviet military, to economise time and to justify acceptance of support by capitalist countries.

The way in which the Communist Party organised itself and gained control in Russia was often repeated under very similar conditions elsewhere. In order not to get lost in details, it may be preferable to limit the discussion to stylised facts.

Political leadership and economic management is assumed by the Communist Party, which identified with the state. 'Democracy' is exerted through party elections at different levels: local, regional, central. Former political institutions are eliminated right away; the administration is reorganised and staffed with party cadres.

'Expropriation of the expropriators' begins at once. Part of the factories, banks, and other institutions are taken into state or collective ownership. Work starts immediately on centralising production and distribution. The most important of the measures of redistribution is to confiscate the estates of the landowners and divide them among the landless and the poor peasants.

Due to the disruptive effects of post-war economic turmoil, one of the most immediate tasks is to ensure that food is distributed fairly. Rationing is introduced, so that basic foodstuffs at accessible prices become available to the poor as well. Black marketeers who try to side-step the rationing system are prosecuted and socially disgraced. In fact, they often serve as scapegoats for economic difficulties. High prices or insufficient supplies are blamed on speculative activities which, to prove the point, are much more harshly punished than in capitalist societies.

No matter how serious the economic problems, a campaign of education covering the entire population is set into motion, free basic health care for all is promised, and holidays for children are organised to gain popular support.

Numerous attributes of the revolutionary period are understandable in the light of prior events and readily explained by them. No less understandable is the fact that this period can only be transitional, since many of the factors that sustain the system are temporary and since only in a few cases do revolutionary fervour and self-sacrifice last a lifetime. It becomes vital for society to encourage people to perform well by dispensing material rewards and, as they are limited, to resort to penalties.

Once all the wealthy have had everything possible confiscated from them, the scope for that kind of redistribution is exhausted. Production is set back by events preceding and following the revolution and by the confusion of transition. In the Soviet Union, industrial production in 1920 had fallen to little over 20% of the 1917 level.[14] The realisation dawns that production, not confiscation, is the way to continue improving the population's material position.

But delivering the promises of a better life is now hindered by anarchy, lack of law and order and arbitrary local actions. No society, whatever its nature, can function without some degree of discipline. There is a growing demand for order to be restored.

All these altered circumstances prepare the ground for the country to step beyond the socialist revolutionary-transitional system. The spirit of revolutionary heroism gradually fades as the new system becomes institutionalised and bureaucratic, and life returns to 'normal'. The desire for a return to normal was very evident after war communism ended and the New Economic Policy (NEP) was in the making.

3. The new economic policy

The call for a new economic policy came most forcefully from three sectors: industrial firms chafing at excessive concentration; trade unions complaining of lack of freedom of action; and agriculture bent under the yoke of requisitioning

With discontent in the countryside and industrial production paralysed by lack of supplies, Lenin realised the need to turn the peasants into allies again. Groping for a workable solution in the absence of an available blueprint, requisitioning was abandoned and replaced by a proportional tax on all production exceeding subsistence level. On the industry front, the NEP laid the groundwork for commercially autonomous units called 'trusts', into which smaller enterprises were federated. Private trading and markets were allowed again. When the NEP was brought in, small businesses were denationalised and a census taken in 1923 indicates that about 12% of workers were employed in private enterprise at that time.

However, from the very beginning all enterprises suffered from under-funding and were forced almost exclusively to rely on self-financing. When the State Bank reopened in November 1921 it was likewise short of resources. Hyperinflation was rampant during 1921 and 1922 and the rouble was devalued twice. A new rouble was created after the second devaluation, equal to 1 million old roubles, and the price level was 200 000 times that of 1913. Barring measurement errors it therefore seems likely that the new rouble was heavily undervalued. Anyhow, this provided the basis for a hard-rouble policy. In 1923 the State Bank started to issue the chervonetz rouble with a partial gold cover (but not convertible into gold).

During the scissors crisis of 1923–24 (see below), the purchasing power of the chervonetz rouble contracted substantially. Kondratiev explained this trend in terms of the sharp increases in the price of industrial goods due to supply shortages. The government attached more importance to the monopoly power of state industry and pressured trusts to lower their prices on pain of being refused new credit lines, setting maximum selling prices and opening up markets to imports. Some of these threats were less than convincing since the government lacked the foreign exchange with which to pay for imports.[15]

Faced with these problems, a plea was made in October 1923 to revert to tighter planning by the 'Declaration of the Forty-Six', drafted by Preobrazhensky and supported by Trotsky. At the other end of the spectrum Bukhanin, Rykov and trade union leader Tomsky argued in favour of opening up to foreign investors and dropping the state's foreign trade monopoly. The issue was not settled immediately and had to wait for a more deep-seated change in power relations, leading to the end of the NEP.

As to the agricultural question, the 1917 Revolution redeemed the ancient hopes of the Russian peasantry by letting them seize the land of the gentry. In addition, after the end of the civil war and when the NEP compromise was put into operation, the peasants found themselves greatly relieved of obligations towards the state as compared to pre-war years. At last, the 'internal market' deemed necessary for endogenous growth seemed to have become a reality.

Lenin had refused to choose a development model favouring either industry or agriculture. In his view, a view which became the basis of the NEP, agricultural and industrial development should go hand in hand. In re-establishing heavy industry the first purpose should therefore be to supply agriculture with the equipment it needed; and support was to be given to small-scale rural industry. Private ownership was to be maintained in small manufacturing and service industries and in agriculture.

If the revolution had effected nothing besides a change in the position of the peasantry, agricultural output might have grown slowly but steadily and the rate of growth in industry would perhaps have slightly exceeded that in agriculture with a massive transfer of under-employed farm workers into industrial centres. Stronger peasant demand was bound to effect a change in the composition of Russian industry with greater stress laid on the 'light' industries.

Box 1.3 The economics of price scissors

The term 'price scissors' refers to the prices of industrial goods in relation to those of agricultural goods. This term originated in the Soviet debate in the aftermath of the October Revolution about how to raise resources required to finance industrialisation. This debate is still going on today with equal pertinence in less developed countries (LDCs).

The following famous graph (Fig. A) shows why the relative price movement during 1922–24 has been referred to as first a closing and then an opening of price scissors:

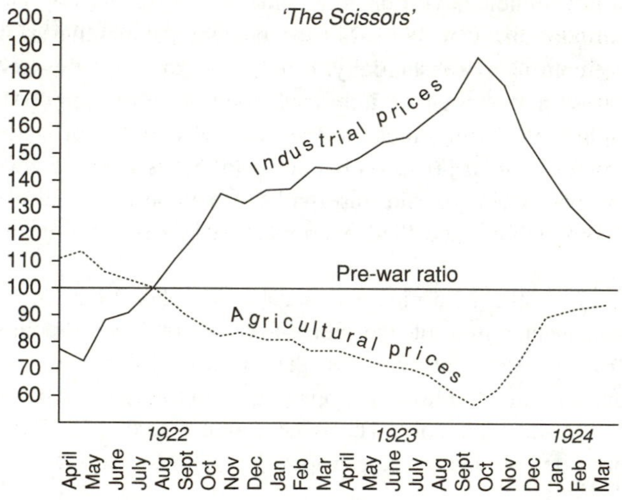

FIG. A Relative movements of the retail prices of agricultural and industrial goods, according to Gosplan: general trend removed. 1913 ratio between agricultural and industrial prices = 100
Source: Dobb (1939)

The main contribution to this debate comes from E. Preobrazhensky. He based his analysis on an explicit model of a peasant sector coexisting with a state-controlled industrial sector. His two main propositions are*:

1. turning the internal terms of trade against the peasantry increases the total savings funds in the economy; and
2. the urban workers need not necessarily suffer from that.

The first proposition is of central importance because it asserts the feasibility of using the (internal) terms of trade as an effective instrument for the accumulation of capital.

Sah and Stiglitz (1992) have shown Proposition 1 to be valid because lower agricultural prices necessitate a lowering of the urban wage which, in turn,

continued

Box 1.3 *continued*

increases the investable surplus of the state. Proposition 1 is independent of the price elasticity of the surplus sold by the rural sector. A decrease in the relative price of agricultural goods will lead to a greater decrease in the surplus sold by the rural sector if the price response of the rural surplus is higher. This, in turn, will require a larger curtailment of urban demand for agricultural goods. This larger decrease in the urban wage necessarily increases the investable surplus of the state by a larger amount.

Sah and Stiglitz claim that Proposition (2) is incorrect: a price squeeze of agriculture hurts industrial workers just as much as it hurts farmers. However, this issue is still not settled. For example, Baland (1993) argues that Sah and Stiglitz's assumption that consumers are not rationed and that market equilibrium prevails throughout the economy neither corresponds to the historic context nor to Preobrazhensky's modelling. Relaxing these assumptions leads to the confirmation of the validity of Preobrazhensky's second proposition.

Empirical studies by Ellmann (1975, 1987) show that during the First Plan period most of the accumulation came from industry and not from agriculture. During that period the main policy tool was coercion rather than terms of trade.

* Preobrazhensky formulated two further propositions: a smaller stock of industrial capital
(3) necessitates the state putting a greater squeeze on the peasants; and
(4) implies that the profit from the industrial sector would be a smaller fraction of the total investable surplus.
Both propositions are correct under mild conditions. See Sah and Stiglitz (1992).

However, the revolution also established an iron grip on large-scale industry. During the NEP period, the old antagonistic interests opposing industry and the peasantry re-emerged in the so-called 'scissors crisis': in the fact that the government-dominated industry had insisted upon terms of trade that were unfavourable to agriculture. Nor was there any sign of a shift toward more emphasis on the consumer-goods industries. If anything, toward the end of the NEP the share of heavy industry in total output was somewhat larger than before the war.

Through most of the NEP period the high rate of industrial growth camouflaged the fact that little had changed. As long as the problem was to rebuild pre-war industry, largely using pre-war equipment and pre-war labour and technicians, the incremental capital–output ratios were very low and the rapid increases in the supply of consumer goods kept discontent at bay. But the situation was bound to change as Russian factories approached pre-war capacity and further rises in output began to require much more sizeable investment outlays.

This, no doubt, was a crucial and critical moment in the economic history of Soviet Russia. Adjusting to a lower rate of industrial growth would have been difficult under any circumstances. In the specific Soviet conditions of the late 1920s it was aggravated by political factors. To prevent too steep and too sudden a fall in the rate of industrial growth, much higher savings were needed. To increase the rate of taxation carried the threat of resistance; and after the experience of the scissors crisis, when the prices of industrial supplies to the peasantry had had to be lowered in relation to farm prices, an industrial price hike was hardly within the range of practical politics. The legacy of the NEP, with its low taxes, downward pressure upon the industrial terms of trade and failure to provide for a timely shift in the composition of industrial output in favour of consumer goods, expressed itself in a situation of inflationary pressures where too large a volume of (low) peasant purchasing power bore down upon an even smaller volume of available consumer goods.

With hindsight it is interesting to compare the NEP with reforms in China after the Mao years. Chinese reforms during 1978–81 gradually liberalised prices for agricultural goods with the result that production and productivity increased sharply. Higher rural incomes generated savings that could be used for investment in industry, more specifically in the small and medium sized town and village enterprises. Why did the NEP not yield comparable positive results? A major reason is that Russia was already more industrialised in the 1920s than China in the 1970s and that agriculture was therefore of lesser importance. Industrialisation favoured heavy industry and there was no institutional support for light industry at local level, directly absorbing the agricultural surplus. Dramatically it took more than 50 years for a demonstration of what could have been done, although the results would have been less spectacular in Russia, for the reasons already mentioned and because total savings were much lower than in China before reforms started.

The economic crisis that followed marked the end of the NEP period. It was at the same time a political crisis of the very first magnitude that brought Stalin to the helm. The inability to maintain food supplies to the cities and the growing resistance of millions of peasants seemed set to spell doom to the Communist Party dictatorship. Without further fundamental changes in the country's economic structure, the conditions for a resumption of industrial growth looked inauspicious.

On the eve of the First Five-Year Plan (1926–31) state and collective farms together supplied less than 2% of the total grain crop and covered little more than 1% of the area under cultivation. Although the harvest of 1925–26 was exceptionally good, only 14% of the total harvest was marketed compared with 26% before the war. The prime reason was indubitably the fact that farm prices remained unfavourable, not that the kulaks refused to deliver, as was officially claimed. Indeed, 85% of production fell on middle and small peasants and only 15% on the kulaks. In November 1926 the 15th Party Congress took the historic decision to base the Soviet industrialisation process on large-scale farming on cooperative lines. The decision to strengthen the state's grip over the economy by extending its direct control, by setting up a planning system and by restricting individual ownership further ended the NEP and paved the way for a complete change of direction: Stalinism.

4. Successes and abuses of the Stalinist era

The NEP became bogged down in serious difficulties which were crying out to be resolved. Either the system had to edge closer to a market economy or else it needed to establish its own clear-cut organised planning solution. Stalin and his supporters opted for the '*Flucht nach vorne*' designed to extend nationalisation to all productive property and to set in place an integrated planning and command machinery. But in order to do this they first had to impose their views, a task greatly facilitated by the power-void left by Lenin's death in 1924.

Agricultural output in 1928–29 was catastrophic in spite of severe penalties.[16] This made it easy for Stalin to pin the blame on the kulaks and to forge ahead with his plans for reorganisation. The Stalinist reorientation was completed with Stalin's speech of 23 June 1931 in which he condemned the egalitarianism of earlier revolutionary days, and argued against the promotion of workers to positions of higher responsibility as well as pleading for a wider pay range.

Drastic measures were taken in September 1932 to reverse the sharp decline in productivity (28% between 1928–30): generalised introduction of the internal passport and compensation on a piece-work basis. Stalin's reward for these moves came at the 14th Party Congress in 1934 when he was proclaimed 'leader of the working classes of the whole world, incomparable genius of our era' and, more simply, 'the greatest man of all times and all people'.

The all-out emphasis placed by Stalin's development strategy on heavy industry at the expense of agriculture and consumers generally sparked rapid urbanisation. The population in some urban centres sky-rocketed with five or sixfold increases in the space of just a few years: Dniepropetrovsk in the Ukraine, Sverdlovsk (Yekaterinburg) in the Urals, or Novosibirsk in Siberia.

This massive drift from the land was at the root of numerous difficulties: poor work discipline, alcoholism, hooliganism and delinquency. To stem the tide of degeneracy, the 'work booklet' was copied from Nazi Germany and in 1940 the working week was adjusted from six days of seven hours to seven days of eight hours. Severe penalties were introduced to foster discipline, including labour camps and the death penalty, which remained in force until 1956. The pay scale widened to a factor of 10 between unskilled workers and Stakhanovite worker heroes. For the average worker the real wage declined by 40% during the 1930s despite much tougher work standards. Farmers were not even granted an internal passport and so remained yoked to their *kolkhoze* (collective farms) just as the serfs had been. By the end of the 1930s the number of citizens imprisoned in labour camps was estimated at between 3.5 and 10 million.

In retrospect, the threat to the continuation in power of the Soviet regime during the 'great reorientation' in 1928–31 seems blurred by the indubitable successes achieved subsequently. But the threat was a real one indeed, and it was under pressure of this danger that Stalin embarked upon the gamble of the First Five-Year Plan, commenced in 1926 but with its execution delayed until 1928. Viewed as a short-run measure, the declared, but never achieved, purpose of the First Five-Year Plan was to right the industrial imbalance through an increase in consumer goods output based on an increase in plant capacity.[17] It was a daring scheme if one considers that to bring it off meant accepting a further, albeit temporary, worsening of the situation as an even larger share of national income was deflected into investment and away from consumption. Again, in the best Russian tradition, it was to be a race against time. If the Soviet government could keep peasant resistance down for the relatively short period of a few years, it might be able to offer them sufficient quantities of consumer goods at not-too-unfavourable terms of trade, and so head off the dangers and put village/city relations on a new and sounder footing.

Not unlike the imperial government in the wake of the 1905 revolution, Soviet leadership was keenly aware of the peasants' hostility to itself. Like its imperial predecessors, it was anxious to find or to whip up a modicum of support in the villages in hopes of facilitating its task in the difficult years ahead. Following suitable adjustments, the collective farms had originally been intended to serve as models to put new heart into the peasant masses. As long as the number of collective farms was kept small, the state would be able to offer sufficient assistance, so that membership of the collective farms would carry real advantages.

These high hopes were dashed, however, for the peasants put up far more resistance than expected. The peasantry which had emerged victorious from the Revolution and the civil war had very little in common with the docile masses of the imperial period. The bitter struggles that followed developed a logic of their own. The dogged defence by the peasants of the revolutionary land seizures evoked an all-out offensive by the government.[18] The peasants went down in defeat (and suffered losses of life by the millions through persecution and during the famines of 1932–33) and widespread, though still incomplete, collectivisation followed (see Table 1.1).

Collectivisation supplied an unexpected solution to the disequilibrium which darkened the last years of the NEP and marked the actual starting-point of the great change in Soviet economic policies. But it also profoundly changed the face of the government's industrialisation plans. Once the peasantry had been successfully forced into the collective farming machinery, once it became possible to extract a large share of agricultural output in the form of 'compulsory deliveries' without bothering overmuch about the *quid pro quo* in the form of industrial consumer goods, the difficulties of the late 1920s were shaken off. The government emerged with its hands freed. There was no longer any reason to regard the First Five-Year Plan as a self-contained, brief period of rapid industrialisation, and the purpose of industrialisation was no longer to

TABLE 1.1 The collectivisation of Soviet agriculture

Year	Collective farms (thousands)	Peasant households collectivised of total number of households (per cent)	Gross agricultural production (index)	Livestock production (index)
1913	—	—	96	87
1918	1.6	0.1	—	—
1928	33.3	1.7	100	100
1929	57.0	3.9	93	87
1930	85.9	23.6	88	65
1931	211.1	52.7	84	57
1932	211.1	61.5	76	48
1933	—	—	82	51
1934	—	—	86	52
1935	245.4	83.2	99	74
1936	—	—	93	76
1937	—	—	116	83
1938	242.4	93.5	107	100

Source: Gregory and Stuart (1986)

relieve the shortage of consumer goods. A programme of perpetual industrialisation through a series of five-year plans was now on the agenda. What had in the earlier stages been conceived of as a brief intermezzo turned into another great spurt of industrialisation, the greatest and longest in the history of the country's industrial development.[19]

This reorientation in favour of industry was also considerably eased by what was initially a favourable response in agriculture. Whereas agricultural production had fallen by about one quarter between 1928 and 1932 and Stalin's reforms uprooted the peasantry, causing the famine of 1932–33 with an estimated three to five million victims, it now rallied and went up by nearly one half between 1932 and 1937 (see Table 1.1), although at the end of the period it was still barely above the 1913 level.

The Second Five-Year Plan (1933–37) was more successful. It was more carefully prepared than the first, building on experience gained, and its implementation went more smoothly. It consolidated rapid growth and gave marginally more importance to light industry.

The Third Five-Year Plan took off in 1938 but soon had to be revised to accommodate stepped-up defence efforts. In 1940 the allocation for defence was double the 1938 figure and by 1941 it had tripled. Defence and investment together accounted for over 50% of national income in 1940.[20]

The war robbed the USSR of the fruits of its (considerable) growth in the 1930s and the production of consumer goods especially plummeted. In 1946, it was 40% down on the already very low pre-war level. The western part of the USSR emerged from the war a wasteland of wrecked factories, mines, railways, towns and villages. Most of its livestock had been slaughtered (see Table 1.2) and 25 million people were left homeless.

During the war four million people joined the Communist Party, which reached a membership of 5.7 million in 1945. Of the country's 9.5 million workers only 2.5 million had already formed part of the workforce in 1940. With this rejuvenation also came a rise in the level of education. Nevertheless, the difficulties of converting the war economy, the loss of skilled labour during the repression of the 1930s and the vast war losses meant that industrial production sustained a drop of 17% in 1946.

Early in 1946 Stalin projected a trebling of pre-war coal and steel output in the course of the next three Five-Year Plans, a goal which was effectively achieved in 1960. But converting the war economy to peace-time conditions was no easy task. Industrial production topped the pre-war level for the first time in 1948, but at a heavy price: the maintenance of arms production at high levels and continued emphasis on heavy industry rather than restructuring them to suit a peace-time economy.

Table 1.2 Livestock in the former USSR *(million head)*

	1929	1941	1946	1951	1954	1955	1960	1964
Cattle	66.8	54.5	47.6	57.1	55.8	67.1	74.2	85.4
Pigs	27.4	27.5	10.6	24.4	33.3	52.1	53.4	40.9
Sheep and goats	114.6	91.6	70.0	99.0	115.5	142.6	144.0	139.5
Horses	36.1	21	10.7	13.8	15.3	14.2	11.0	8.5

Source: Dobb (1966)

Indeed, Stalin had launched a two-tier development plan in 1947: first, to turn the USSR into the world's dominant military power, and, second, to 'transform nature'. Gigantic schemes to create an internal sea in Siberia and to reduce Siberia's temperature by redirecting cold currents from the Pacific were developed but fortunately never materialised.[21]

The speed of post-war recovery was yet again the result of catching up and of victory-inspired identification with the system. Full employment of a smaller labour force was quickly reached as a large proportion of the male population had been killed in the war. Moreover, only 20% of the 2.3 million homeward-bound prisoners-of-war were reincorporated into Soviet society. The remainder were regarded as a threat to the system since they had been abroad and were able to compare. They were shut up in labour camps that still housed millions of people, comparable to the late 1930s.[22]

Taking advantage of victory, Stalin introduced profound changes with an imperialist overtone, reinforcing his dictatorial powers, and cutting the Soviet Union off from the Western world, despite the joint war effort. In a speech on 24 May 1945, Stalin defined the Russian people as the ruling people of the USSR, putting an end to the notion of the Russians as *primus inter pares*. In so doing he reverted to the pre-revolutionary idea which saw the Russians as the civilising and protective race.[23]

Economic performance in the Soviet Union and the socialist countries in Eastern Europe was, of course, adversely affected by Stalin's decision to draw down an 'iron curtain',[24] which deprived the socialist bloc of eligibility for Marshall Plan funding[25] and of participation in the European Payments Union, in trade arrangements, in the World Bank and the IMF and later, in the European regional arrangements that eventually gave birth to the European Community. These negative effects were not immediately apparent, but they put a severe strain on the division of labour, on technological transfer and on outside pressure for incessant improvement, impairing the longer-run growth potential.[26] For the long-run implications of the choice of an autarchic development, see Chapter 2.

The apparent success of the Soviet experiment in terms of rapid growth lasted throughout the Stalin years and was frequently hailed as proof of the efficiency of the 'socialist' system: 'It is doubtful whether in any previous age so profound a change affecting so large an area of the world's surface has ever occurred within such a narrow span of time' (Dobb 1966).[27]

On the other hand, there was always a good deal of unwillingness to accept the Soviet presentation of rapid growth of its industry because it clashed with the prevailing Western assumption of the fundamental inefficiency of socialism. With hindsight, Western reassessment of Soviet growth proves these sceptics right. Moreover, there was always the contradiction between an enormous increase in the volume of industrial output on the one hand and, on the other, a level of real wages which in the early 1950s was still substantially below that of 1928, with peasants' real income registering an even greater decline. By forcibly holding down consumption in the population at large and by letting the area of consumer goods output take the brunt of errors and miscalculations in the planning process, the Soviets succeeded in channelling capital and human resources into capital formation, thereby assuring the rapid growth of the only segment of the economy in which it was interested. In so doing Soviet leaders rigorously applied the Marxist law of accumulation by political choice rather than economic necessity, at the cost of continued frustration of Soviet citizens' demand for consumer goods.

5. Castles in the sand: Khrushchev's reforms

Like other totalitarian systems, Stalinism assumed an aura of eternity while it lasted. But the sufferings which this regime institutionalised provoked strong reactions that became more open when Stalin left the stage.[28] The first reform efforts under Khrushchev were stifled and succeeded by the Brezhnev restoration which bottled up the subsequent attempts at reform under Gorbachev.

When Khrushchev assumed the leadership after Stalin's death in 1953, Soviet citizens expected wide-ranging reforms to improve their living conditions and to redress a situation where the *nomenklatura* had become the new exploiting class of a refurbished (state) capitalism. Stalin had successfully created a non-fascist version of the totalitarian state. According to the German-American philosopher and authority in totalitarianism, Hannah Arendt, the Soviet Union became a totalitarian state under Stalin, not before, and it ended with his death.

The 20th Congress of the Communist Party of the Soviet Union opened on 14 February 1956 and became a turning point. Khrushchev embarked on a number of revisions of Stalinist principles with far-reaching consequences. The first was a prudent start with de-Stalinisation, criticising the personality cult of Stalin, the perversions of his 'democratic centralism' and the illegality of his prosecutions. This part of a report, which leaked to the West, encouraged reform-minded leaders in Central Europe and contributed to the uprising in Hungary that same year. Khrushchev also underlined the importance of *détente*, recognising that confrontation between the communist and capitalist blocks was not a historical necessity and that a pacific coexistence was desirable. Going one step further, Khrushchev recognised that the modalities of socialist construction could vary from country to country. This was a serious break with the Stalinist tradition, opening up the possibility of a pluralist socialist camp. Again, reformers in Poland and Hungary felt encouraged.

The reaction of the conservative members of the Politburo was virulent and the Central Committee issued a very watered-down version of Khrushchev's speech. Their position was strengthened by the uprisings in Poznan and Budapest which Khrushchev was forced to quell.

Khrushchev set out on his economic reforms with commendable zeal. His first target was agriculture – once again. Farming was in a state of chaos, the *kolkhozes* were in dire need of equipment, and production was sagging. Khrushchev pushed through an increase in prices for agricultural goods and smoothed heavy industry's ruffled feathers by stepping up investments in machinery for the agro-sector. Unfortunately, he also launched a major campaign to extend farming to hitherto virgin territories, armed with the necessary agro-chemistry and the enthusiastic help of young pioneers. In the space of three years, the area of land under cultivation increased by 30%.

Initial results were positive and output went up by 25% during the first three years. But with the intensive use of fertilisers and excessive irrigation in delicate soils, by 1963 production in these newly developed areas had fallen by 65%. A further reason for these agricultural troubles was the attempted reorganisation of the *kolkhozes* into federations which failed for lack of popular support and straitened financial circumstances.

Khrushchev desperately tried to break up the extreme centralisation of the decision-making process. His proposals were repeatedly voted down before being accepted by the Supreme Soviet in May 1957. Eleven industry ministries were closed down and authority was reorganised on regional lines (*sovnarkhozes*).[29]

While he stumbled in his internal reforms, Khrushchev did score some successes on the external policy front, albeit coupled with bad luck and some resounding failures. During 1953–56 Khrushchev nurtured improved relationships with China and Yugoslavia, pursued *détente* with the Western powers and sought greater influence in the Third World.[30]

In this way Khrushchev successfully pursued de-Stalinisation both at home and abroad.[31] But like Gorbachev in later years, he found to his cost that ugly or no, Stalinism still possessed its own iron logic. Most annoying to Khrushchev was that the waning of Stalinist monolithic power encouraged insurrection among freedom-minded Central Europeans, strengthening the old guard and seriously impairing his position.

Khrushchev's final undoing was his failure to come to terms with President Kennedy in Vienna in 1961 and his subsequent defeat in the Cuban missile crisis in 1962. It vindicated Mao's early opposition to peaceful coexistence. In reply to a searing critique of Khrushchev's policy by Mao in the *People's Daily* in 1960 entitled 'Vive Leninism', Khrushchev stopped Sino-Soviet cooperation on a nuclear bomb and pulled Soviet experts and advisers out of China. This brought about a split in the socialist camp and Romania ended up siding with China. By the time Khrushchev left the scene not many of his reforms had survived.

6. Brezhnev's restoration of the socialist idyll

After Khrushchev's fall in 1964, the next 20 years have been described variously as 'the era of developed socialism', 'the era of consolidation' or 'the years of stagnation'. Stalin and Khrushchev had fought administrative sclerosis, the former through institutionalised terror and the latter through legal means and reforms. Brezhnev for his part made a glorified principle of 'stability and continuity'.

Khrushchev had hardly departed when the administration was recentralised in 1965. The *sovnarkhozes* were abolished, the industrial ministries shut down by Khrushchev put back in business and new centralised state committees created (*Gostsen* for prices, *Gosnab* for supplies, *Gostekhnika* for new technologies, and so forth). The enterprise reform, which had taken economist Liberman years to prepare, was codified in 1965, but abandoned in 1970. After initial improvements it failed to effect any lasting changes in the incentive system. Alongside the production targets, sales targets were introduced as a way of reducing excessive stocks. Part of the surpluses were to be left for the enterprise to dispose of at their discretion and the bonus for exceeding plan targets was raised. The new team built up a formidable gerontocracy (the average age of cadres went up by 10 years during that era) and nepotism flourished as never before in the USSR.[32]

Khrushchev had proclaimed the need for a new constitution to codify the creation of a 'state of the entire people'. The new constitution was finalised in 1977 and strengthened the leading role of the party. The myth of the ever-imminent coming of communism was abandoned (this state of communism was defined as a situation of abundance of goods and hence the disappearance of both economics and the state) and a new creed set up in its stead, that of 'developed socialism'. The urgent need for economic reforms 'immediately' to remedy the generalised shortages was recognised but this indefinitely delayed the disappearance of the state. For the time being the promotion of law and order headed the agenda, and a fresh attempt was to be made at improving efficiency and reliability in the administration. Citizens were to be even more closely involved with public administration (in *kolkhozes* and enterprises), and an all-out effort was made to reach consensus on the bases of Soviet society (party and bureaucratic interests). Fundamental policy choices such as the reorientation of economic priorities, decentralisation, clientism versus the promotion of top performers, party principles versus technocratic values, and so on were never discussed in the open. As the real problems were never aired, no reform went very far and public morale became increasingly disillusioned and passive.

Soaring world oil prices in 1973 and the more than tenfold increase in the market price of gold during the early 1970s proved a substantial windfall for Soviet export earnings, limited, however, to the relatively small exports outside the Comecon (the socialist countries' trade system). In this respect the Soviets treated their vassals with generosity, renouncing sharp terms of trade gains. Between 1972 and 1976 imports of Western capital goods were multiplied by a factor of four. New hope was pinned on these imports to effect a transfer of technology and to increase productivity. The results were disappointing, however, as the real problems (resource allocation, management incentives) were never tackled (for more details, see Chapter 2). In a desperate bid to increase productivity a set of decrees redefined performance standards in great detail, but all that this produced was yet more confusion and inefficiency.

When the Brezhnev team took up the reins of power, agriculture was in a very frail condition. From the outset Brezhnev gave top priority to farming – for the first time in Soviet history – and increased its funding (up to 20% of total investment funds). Yet due to the earlier failure of extensive farming methods the need for grain imports kept on rising, and this required foreign currency funding. Whereas agriculture had always been exploited for the benefit of industry, under Brezhnev it turned into a heavy mortgage on the entire economy. Despite high investment, productivity in agriculture declined dramatically during these years, as shown in Chapter 3.

Agricultural prices were raised every five years, but never enough to protect agricultural terms of trade. Farm workers were issued with internal passports (which had been taken from them in 1938) and got rid of their second-class citizen status. The size of private plots doubled and the ceiling on the number of privately owned farm animals was abolished. Agricultural workers were also granted the same social security benefits as industrial workers. Yet none of these measures sufficed and they came too late to stop the haemorrhage of the countryside.

In 1982 the persistence of problems in agriculture triggered yet another rather desperate reform: the creation of the agricultural production complex (APK). Under this organisational reform, all state farms, *kolkhozes* and upstream and downstream agro-enterprises in a given district were lumped together. Again, results were disappointing as it merely meant additional layers of decision-making being heaped on top of existing ones, a move not calculated to alleviate administrative unwieldiness. As in industry, collective work groups (brigades) were introduced with work-sharing and revenue-sharing arrangements. These had even more limited success than in industry, as many local cadres were concerned about the reconstitution of family cells.

The problem was that neither peasants nor local party cadres had been willing to trust and cooperate with the state since the brutal collectivisation measures of the 1930s. Although a considerable financial effort was made during the Brezhnev years to accelerate agricultural development, results were disappointing. It was not so much investment funding which was at fault, but rather the planning system and the way in which individual peasants were dissociated from the fruits of their labour. When Brezhnev died, agriculture was still in the same sorry state it had been when Stalin died, but its collective cost had sky-rocketed.

Other economic sectors also showed signs of decline: the rate of growth dropped markedly, capital productivity and investments slumped, as did private consumption, and unfinished constructions began to be visible everywhere.

The slowdown in the growth of the working population[33] put a stop to growth based on expansive methods. (See Chapter 3 for details.) With the military work discipline of the Stalin years, the parking of peasants without passports in *kolkhozes* and the reserve pool of female workers all gone, the only way to grow was to increase labour productivity. But it was in this area that all reforms failed and where Brezhnev's neo-conservative (some called it neo-Stalinist) approach had nothing to offer. A famous study by the Academician T. Zaslavskai, known as 'The Novossibirsk Report', in 1983 concluded that the origins of crises lay in the system's inability to make efficient use of the human and intellectual potential of Soviet society.[34] While this was nothing new in the USSR, what was different was that it was now happening in a more advanced and more educated society with higher aspirations.[35]

During 1975–85 the system's inability to accommodate dialogue at a time when more sophisticated means of communication were beginning to make information about the malfunctioning of the system more generally available spawned a crescendo of manifestations of dissent, and ultimately led to the need for *Glasnost*. Among the most important were: ethnic and religious movements (Catholics in Lithuania, the Jewish community, a Moslem resurgence); the cultural dissent of the young, attracted to Western values; non-conformist works of art; an ecological movement opposed to plans for diverting Siberian rivers to Central Asia and to the pollution of Lake Baikal and the Aral Sea; demonstrations against the war in Afghanistan; and criticism of economic management by young technocrats in distant Siberian research outfits.[36]

Brezhnev's restoration idyll came under fire from the reforms instituted by 1968 in Czechoslovakia. The reform package proposed to replace the command planning system by a plan spelling out guidelines and incentives, more autonomy for enterprises, a more important role for the market and more self-management by workers in firms. Brezhnev's solution was to invade Czechoslovakia with a Warsaw Pact army.[37]

A second and even more important challenge to Soviet control reared its head in Poland. In 1970 a jolting increase in consumer prices drove workers onto the streets of Gdansk in numbers unprecedented in a socialist country. Workers who could not vote with their voice, voted with their feet (they 'chose to exit', to use Hirschman's term). For the next ten years, Polish policy was laxist, avoiding overdue reforms and raising living standards by borrowing abroad. When the rate of foreign borrowing had to be slowed down in 1980 new price hikes became necessary, provoking new and even more massive demonstrations and strikes: the government was forced to admit an independent labour union, Solidarnoc.

The Polish situation in the 1970s was quite different from previous troubles in Poznan, Budapest or Prague. After the reforms instituted by Gierek, the Poles no longer had any faith in reforms from the top down. Solidarnoc was the first counterweight to the party to emerge in any socialist country. Confronted with this new situation, it became risky for the USSR to intervene and hope to keep loss of human life within bounds and its already tainted leadership image unscathed.

By contrast, during the 1970s relations between the USSR and Western powers improved dramatically, notwithstanding the threat coming from the new and powerful nuclear missiles aimed at Western Europe, the famous SS-20. A series of treaties normalised relations with West Germany. US President Nixon visited Moscow in 1972 and 23 agreements were concluded to facilitate co-operation in a range of areas, including trade. Between 1971 and 1976, US and German exports to the USSR increased by a factor of eight. Nevertheless, the USSR did not obtain the most-favoured-nation clause, which the US Congress made conditional upon the liberalisation of emigration of Soviet citizens of Jewish origin.[38]

The invasion of Afghanistan in December 1979 confirmed the impression of many observers in the West that détente was lop-sided and that both economic co-operation and military concessions had to be rethought. US President Reagan promised to do so and by launching 'star wars' he set to creating major difficulties for the pursuit of Soviet external policy in the 1980s.

7. The impossibility of reform: Gorbachev's failed illusions

Brezhnev died on 12 November 1982. His successors Andropov and then Tchernenko left no mark on history. The real change was ushered in with Gorbachev in 1985. Contrary to conditions under Khrushchev, reforms were no longer the province of a handful of reformers within the party. The whole nation was aware of the system's shortcomings and avid for a radical overhaul. It was not at all inclined to settle for mini-moves. At stake were the principle of accumulation and of tight regulation of the economy, the need to improve the dismal quality of consumer products and to narrow the distance between the people and the command levels.

The catchwords which signposted the change from preceding eras before and after the socialist revolution were glasnost, uskorenie and perestroïka.[39]

At the outset these slogans were really no more than a much-needed semantic change. But, starting with semantic concessions and, as usual, with criticism of past mistakes, the dynamic forces developed a dialectic of their own that had not been anticipated. Soon people found it was possible to debate issues outside the party's Holy Grail: the party was overtaken by events. De-Stalinisation was truly completed during this period, when for the first time criticism was no longer stopped dead in its tracks by party interests.[40]

The first reform proposals took their inspiration from the 'Novossibirsk Report' already mentioned above. Reformers rallied round the ideas of A. Aganbeguian, L. Albakine, F. Burlatski and T. Zaslavskaia and agreed to focus primarily on enterprise reform, with a view to making firms more independent and more responsible. The law on enterprise of 30 June 1987 came into effect on 1 January 1989 and featured many of the reformers' ideas. In practice, however, the administration was in no great hurry to change relationships (after all, they received the enterprises' surpluses and stood to forfeit the power that went with control of these firms).

A law dated 19 November 1986, which was rounded out on 26 May 1988, facilitated private ownership for small crafts and trades and in the service activities. Initially taxation on such activities was prohibitively high, but in due course taxes were brought down. By 1990 some 10 000 small private enterprises (called co-operatives) had sprung into being and half a million people were registered as 'independents'. Actually these estimates are on the low side, since the number of people employed in the underground economy during that year is estimated at close to 15 million.

In agriculture, leasing contracts were introduced running for periods of up to 50 years. Response was rather timid to begin with and official prices for agricultural output were not adjusted sufficiently to make private investment worthwhile.[41]

Gorbachev was much more successful on the foreign policy front. On 8 December 1987 he signed an agreement to destroy medium-range missiles with detailed provisions for mutual control. He also put an end to Soviet intervention in Afghanistan. Unilateral retreat was announced in February 1988 and completed early in 1989.[42]

Another landmark in 1989 was the onset of liberalisation in Eastern Europe. Gorbachev had realised that the Soviet Union was now in too weak a position domestically to maintain its iron grip on Eastern Europe and understood that it would be better to concentrate on internal reforms. For the first time in Soviet history the imperial aspirations were identified as too costly and ranked below the aim of sustaining Party control. In July 1990, the Soviet Union agreed to German reunification, in a move which put a final end to World War II and to the division of Europe into two camps. It heralded the start of a process to redesign the economic map of Europe, the implications of which are discussed in the concluding chapter, Chapter 16.

When the Soviet Union fell apart in late 1991, none of the essential components of reform had been implemented. Among the many reform plans, the famous '500 days programme', drawn up by a group led by Professor Shatalin, came closest to embracing all the elements of a comprehensive reform. Although 500 days might be considered a rather protracted 'big bang', still even this long transition period looked pretty ambitious to anyone aware of the enormous number of decisions that would have had to be taken.

Why, then, were none of these programmes implemented? There are at least two fundamental replies. First, and foremost, political structure and economic management were only one side of the coin. The other was the Soviet empire, openly challenged by the republics seizing their historic opportunity. As a result the 'war of laws' developed, under which each republic passed a declaration of sovereignty stating that its laws would take precedence over Union law, whereas the Union government insisted that Union law should take precedence. Second, Gorbachev still attempted to save the basic socialist structure of the economy, ready to reform it substantially, not abandon it.

The macroeconomic destabilisation that developed in the absence of a credible reform programme was a clear sign of fatal crisis which is further analysed in Chapter 13. One explanation for the rapid disintegration is that the Soviet Union operated a system of incentives and controls and of fixing objectives which, although never efficient, worked somehow. When the system itself was put into question by perestroïka, the incentive and command structure began to crumble. The effects of disintegration were all the more negative because the system was excessively centralised. The process of disintegration was further hastened by the uncertainty created when expectations of sweeping changes in the system were repeatedly disappointed.

Expectations of liberalisation or of a regime change also made it possible for people to air their disagreements and enabled the open assertion of conflict, something few people had experienced in a lifetime. The malfunctioning of the Soviet economy had always to some extent been due to lack of motivation and passivity in work commitment. This passivity had increased and become more open and pronounced. Strikes were no longer only (not even mainly) motivated by wage claims; they pursued, first of all, political demands for some sort of reform – decentralisation of power, more individual freedom, and so on. What was often branded as 'sabotage' was in fact simply a way of moving away from a strict enforcement system to one of fewer controls and greater individual responsibility. Such a transition phase is necessarily disorganised, contradictory, and bad for production levels. Particularly worrisome in the Soviet case was the extent of disagreement at all levels and the fact that the structures of the old regime – the party, the KGB and the military-industrial complex[43] – still had enough power to block or even overturn reforms. The process of liberalisation was therefore a drawn-out one and indeed was never more than a complicated compromise. The more time went by the greater grew the risk of complete destabilisation and of hyperinflation, and the extent to which compromises had to be accepted made even the long-term gains appear doubtful.

The party was clearly unable to make the difficult choices needed to check destabilisation. It never got beyond crisis management. As resources grew scarcer the various groups in society and in different parts of the administration were pitted against each other in a fierce battle for power and resources – the Union vs. the republics, the military vs. civilians, industry vs. agriculture, the various industrial sectors vs. one another, and so forth.

Enterprises got into dire financial straits in the process, since the credit mechanism was not designed to cope with rapid changes in domestic and foreign prices. In this way even fundamentally sound firms encountered difficulties for lack of payments or credit lines. In many cases the inter-enterprise credit system was stretched to the limit to ensure survival and the State helped by printing money. The absence of export credit facilities, in particular, and of traditional trade patterns represented a serious bias against exports and the breakdown of foreign exchange allocations made it very difficult to maintain traditional import patterns. Because the Soviet structure of production was highly specialised and lacked sufficient elasticity of substitution, import cuts created bottle-necks, stopped domestic production, and fed back into reduced exports. Chapters 13 and 14 provide more in-depth analysis.

8. The fall of communism: inevitable?

Socialism lasted for over 70 years and reached the height of its extension and glory after World War II until the 1980s. Not so long ago, few Western observers would have dared to predict the vertiginous decline of communism that culminated in the liberation of Eastern Europe and the break-up of the Soviet Union during 1989–91.

But, writing in 1976, the dissident Andrei Amalrik put the question: 'Will the Soviet Union survive 1984?', which suggests that to some insiders at least the signs of decline were apparent well before the actual fall. Economic factors played an important and probably decisive role, as has been exhaustively argued in this chapter. This view is sustained by the analysis of the slowdown of growth in Chapter 3. But it is equally certain that other factors contributed significantly to the ultimate collapse, in particular to its timing, without being essential causes. In eschewing reform of the politico-administrative system, communism signed its own death-warrant. And partial reforms as attempted by Gorbachev just did not work. Rather, they sped up the fall.

It was an illusion to believe that the political system could be reformed without touching the economy. And as the Chinese are slowly realising, the reverse is equally foredoomed. Once information flows more freely and citizens are better informed and free to express themselves, they can no longer be kept in check as meek economic robots. They will fight for better living conditions and for the Western consumer nirvana.

As the Chinese experience has demonstrated, partial economic reforms can be very successful.[44] But liberalisation of some but not all markets creates new contradictions such as underpricing of controlled goods (and restraining their supply) and generating huge income differentials ('capitalist speculation and exploitation'). Pressure builds up to extend the scope of reforms until little is left of the command economy. And with resources allocated, goods produced, and income distributed by the market it is hard to see what would be left of communism.

Why then did the system survive for over 70 years? Earlier in this chapter it was argued that the downfall of communism could easily have occurred sooner, indeed much sooner, or later. 1918–21 were the years when the options were still wide open and virtually anything was possible: a return to a non-socialist society, or choice of a different type of socialism. The period of the NEP was one of trial and error with co-operative forms of organisation and agriculture left to individual and co-operative producers. The big and decisive turning-point came during the Stalinist take-over (1929–33), with the establishment of the command economy, the extermination of the kulaks, collectivisation of agriculture and acceleration of forced savings to speed up industrialisation. World War II placed the country and the survival of its system in jeopardy by external aggression. In their fight for survival, the Soviets and their system achieved one of their outstanding successes. Victorious Stalinism flourished in the first flush of this success. Since the beginning the aspirations of workers for a larger share of income, of consumers for more choice and higher quality and of nationalities for more independence remained oppressed and represented a permanent, latent powder keg, although in terms of a more egalitarian distribution of income the system achieved a success that contributed to its longevity. See Chapter 3.

It was during the years in which the system had reached maturity (1970–80) that problems not only built up but came out into the open and could no longer be ignored. Revolutionary enthusiasm having faded, there was nothing to take its place so as to keep citizens in high spirits, no sufficient progress in welfare to keep them committed to the socialist goal.

As the economy progressively ran out of steam and became less able to pick up the technological and managerial challenge, the problems bedevilling the system started to surface. The Chernobyl disaster in 1986 brutally demonstrated the lack of technological quality and control and the administration's inability to prevent such accidents and to deal openly with such accidents as did occur.

The Soviet Union had its own Vietnam: with the war in Afghanistan, esteem for the army that had emerged victorious from World War II, and which was believed to be the most powerful army in the world, took a serious knocking. Possibly even more portentous was US President Reagan's 'Star Wars' gauntlet flung down in the race for technological supremacy. At the latest at that moment, the Soviet leadership realised that its economy was not powerful enough to enable it to stay in the running. Even military leaders then put their weight reluctantly behind economic reform.

All this was happening at a time when the level of education had increased sufficiently for the people to spot the contradictions of official propaganda, and when telecommunications improved their access to information.

In 1985, when Gorbachev launched perestroïka and insisted on glasnost, the world from a Soviet perspective must have appeared wholly strange. In the USSR, little ever changed for the better and there was no hope in sight. Beyond Soviet borders, Europeans were positioning to create an integrated market spanning a continent, Reaganite and Thatcherite reforms sparked fresh enthusiasm for capitalist exploits in the US and even in Europe. While Japan continued its rapid growth, it was outdone by the performance of the Asian tigers and China (with the help of a little bit of capitalism).

So, during the 1980s economic, political and social factors joined forces in speeding up the end. With the benefit of hindsight, it could be said that what disintegrated never made much sense. Politically, the USSR remained an empire of the 19th century burdened with problems of over-extension and the difficulties of integrating a large array of nationalities. Militarily, the country overreached itself and bled itself white trying to stay in the military race. It was brought to bay when economic growth slowed down, the military aura became tarnished and Eastern Europe had to be let off the hook. And ideologically, the system forfeited belief in its Utopian claims by failing to demonstrate the French writer Anatole France's 19th century claim that in the midst of the duress of the industrial revolution 'le Socialisme c'est la bonté et la justice'.

The fall of communism and the disintegration of the Soviet Union may not have been inevitable. But the forces that built up over time became so formidable that the outcome cannot be attributed to chance, but must be understood as the logic of events.

Notes

1. See Carrère d'Encausse (1991), Dobb (1939, 1966), Gregory and Stuart (1986), Werth (1990).
2. To tighten his control over the nobility and to enlist the educated classes for state service an aristocratic hierarchy (*tsin*) was established with rank depending on the state function assumed. Every nobleman had to serve either in the military or in the civilian administration. It was made quite easy for the educated middle classes to work their way into the nobility on merit alone. This tended to thin the already meagre ranks of the middle class still further, so that the rise of the bourgeoisie in Russia to form a powerful political class was nipped in the bud. The Russian nobility on the other hand soon became the most numerous in Europe, even on a per capita basis.
3. For one thing, nineteenth century technology (iron and steel, heavy equipment) typically

favoured large plant, and to accept the most advanced technology also meant accepting larger and larger plant. The state, in its promotion of industrial establishments, showed remarkably little interest in small business. A small number of large enterprises were easier to promote than a large number of small ones and bureaucratic corruption tended to reinforce a tendency that was already present for economic reasons. Given the lack of managerial staff, larger plant and businesses made it possible to spread the thin layer of available talent over a larger part of the industrial economy. See Gerschenkron (1962).

4. This seclusion slowed down technological transfer, excluded the country from the gains of the international division of labour, and perpetuated inefficiencies. Chapters 2 and 3 provide theoretical and empirical evidence.
5. For a detailed discussion see Carrère d'Encausse (1991).
6. The separation of Church and State had already been carried out in 1918, a circumstance which augured ill for the Communists as the Patriarch of the Russian Church promptly pronounced anathema against them.
7. Marx did, however, go beyond analysis and elaborated on proletarian revolution in *The Communist Manifesto* and participated in the foundation of the Communist International in 1864.
8. The main contributors to the 'breakdown theory' were Bernstein (1899), Grossmann (1929), Kautsky (1902), Luxemburg (1922) and Tugan-Baranowsky (1901).
9. Even after a long trip to the USSR in 1936, André Gide remained convinced that some aberrations observed were only regrettable human errors which did not put in question the whole enterprise. The quote at the beginning of this chapter illustrates the enthusiasm and hopes of Western leftists for the success of the Russian Revolution.
10. Retarding factors fall into two categories: those which tend to raise the rate of growth of consumption relative to the growth of the means of production (population growth, unproductive expenditures and state expenditures, imperialistic conquest of markets on the periphery) and those which reduce the disruptive consequences of the growth in the means of production, that is the declining rate of profit (new industries, wasteful investments, monopolisation).
11. Nor was it true in Germany, where the socialists had sided with their country during the war (the *Dolchlegende* attempted to discredit this), a stand that produced the schism of the International Movement. After the war the Germans – including the socialists – closed ranks in convincing themselves that the war was not lost on the battlefield and that patriotism was still an honourable sentiment.
12. That was a formidable task. In 1917 the Communist Party had 40 000 members, no more than a handful of professional revolutionaries given the size of the country. Of course there were supporters outside the party. But there were only 8 million industrial workers in a country with a population of 150 million. Clearly, support was most substantial in the cities and from the outset the countryside was left aside.

    With such a small revolutionary group that still boasted only 115 000 party members in 1918 and 250 000 in 1921, control could only be assured using existing cadres in the administration, army, and industry. This led to the creation of a dual structure which has been maintained ever since. The party planted secretaries in industry, political commissaries in the army and the administration, whose task was to control the class enemies inherited from the old regime, who could not be eliminated because of their skills, which the party members lacked.
13. The new communist government financed the war and met other pressing expenditure largely through inflation. In 1919 the inflation rate tripled and in 1920 quadrupled again. At the end of the civil war the purchasing power of a rouble was just 1% of what it had been three years earlier in October 1917. Wage payments were partially protected through payments in kind. In 1918, 50% of wages were paid in kind, in 1919, 75% and in 1920, 90%.

14. Data mentioned in this chapter are taken from the traditional studies of the Soviet economy: Dobb (1966), Gregory and Stuart (1986), Nove (1969), Ofer (1987). These data cannot be considered as iron-clad and have not resisted current re-examination, although it is still difficult to make a choice among the more recent re-assessments. For a comprehensive discussion see, for example, Easterly and Fischer (1994).
15. Austria and Germany, which found themselves in a very similar position, were saved in 1922–24 by foreign loans, while the USSR obtained only very little foreign funds.
16. Both agricultural and industrial production fell markedly in 1928. The system then developed a new, highly meretricious way of explaining away calamities and more worldly bungling. In April 1928 industrial sabotage was discovered (read: staged) in the Chakhty region. The trial created the myth of sabotage instigated by foreign capitalist interests, a very useful addition to the stock of enemy portraits for explaining problems such as the kulak menace and the right-wing peril.
17. For a detailed discussion see Dobb (1966).
18. The Molotov Committee divided kulaks into three categories. The first, of about 60 000 families, were considered as counter-revolutionaries, and the second, of about 150 000 families, as abusive exploiters. Both groups were arrested and transferred to Siberia. Their property was confiscated. The third group was composed of kulaks loyal to the regime. They were transferred to the confines of their regions.
19. By decreeing the collectivisation of agriculture and forcing through a policy of rapid industrialisation, Stalin sought to increase the Soviet Union's economic capabilities as quickly as possible. In that way, he assumed he would be able to broaden the Soviet Union's foreign policy and military options. He also assumed that the initial emphasis on rapid industrial growth of the heavy industrial sector would eventually make possible a significantly improved standard of living and a richer agricultural development. In effect, this was an implicit social contract between Stalin and the Soviet people: sacrifice and suffering now for what was to be a stronger country with abundance later. This forced-draft policy did indeed increase Stalin's foreign and military alternatives, but it did not bring the promised affluence for Soviet consumers. If anything, the Stalinist model seemed to be incapable of satisfying consumer needs (Goldman 1983: 88).
20. The emphasis in investment shifted markedly to the chemical, machinery and transport sectors east of the Ural mountains. Just before Nazi Germany assailed the USSR, and in the first months of the war, plants in the western part of the USSR were dismantled and shipped east of the Urals. Over 70% of Leningrad's industrial equipment was evacuated in this way and altogether 12 million people (half of the population of industrial centres such as Kiev and Kharkov) followed suit. Despite the difficulties of reorganisation on this scale, Soviet production of tanks and aeroplanes surpassed that of Germany no later than the summer of 1943. Had the USSR lacked industrial maturity and organisation it would not have been possible to produce up to 2,000 planes and 2,000 tanks a month, more than Germany. Even qualitatively speaking the T-34 tank compared well with the German Tiger tank and the Il-1 fighter was claimed to be superior to the Me-109.
21. Stalin's return to the vast – by now megalomaniac – projects of the 1930s ran into considerable opposition. The chief of Gosplan, Voznessensky, attempted a more balanced plan and was duly executed in 1949.
22. Werth (1993), on the basis of data accessed only after the disintegration of the Soviet Union, is able to correct previous estimates. Solzhenitsyn had estimated that at the end of Stalin's era there were 10 million people in the gulags. The correct number is 2.5 million. To this number need to be added 2.7 million 'special workers', that is deported nationalities (Caucasians, Balts, Germans); 800 000 people executed; and those that died in the camps: in 1942 alone 250 000.
23. Stalin restored the civilian and military titles (in 1946, the People's Commissaries became

Ministers) which Lenin had regarded as the incarnation of the bourgeois state and had therefore decided to abandon. The Red Army of Workers and Peasants became the Soviet Army and the Bolshevik Party the Communist Party. Yet more important than changing names was the change in the role of the party. Stalin ruled single-handedly and ignored the party. Between March 1939 and October 1952 no party congress was held; between February 1947 and October 1952 the Plenum did not meet; and the Politburo never met in full. Stalin operated, illegally, with restricted sub-commissions. Major decisions such as the approval of the 5th Plan were taken by the Politburo in a matter of minutes, waiving all discussion for fear of incurring Stalin's displeasure. At the same time, he launched into an exhaustive rewriting of Russian history and science. Most discoveries and mathematical theorems have been credited to Russian scientists in the USSR ever since.

24. Churchill coined this expression in March 1946 in a talk at Fulton (Missouri).
25. Czechoslovakia and Poland had already agreed to participate in the International Conference in Paris held in July 1947 to discuss the particulars of the Marshall Plan. Soviet pressure forced them to withdraw.
26. As Stalin could not hope for transfers from the Western world, he proposed from a very early date to exact large reparation payments from Germany. The United States and in particular Foreign Secretary Marshall had not forgotten Keynes's analysis of the implications of the reparation payments after the First World War and refused to go along with this. This meant that East Germany had to shoulder the burden of reparation payments to the USSR all on its own, considerably slowing down its own reconstruction effort.
27. Dobb further notes: 'The story of the economic development of what at first was Soviet Russia and since 1923 has been the USSR holds a special interest for our times for two main reasons. Firstly, it provides the first case in history of a working-class form of State (under the slogan of the "dictatorship of the proletariat") . . . But secondly, it affords a unique example of the transformation of a formerly backward country to a country of extensive industrialisation and modern techniques at an unprecedented tempo: a transformation unaided by any considerable import of capital from abroad, but effected under the guidance and control of a national economic plan, instead of the conditions of laissez-faire and atomistic capitalist enterprise which characterised the classic industrial revolutions of the past.'
28. It is perhaps difficult in the 1990s to understand that during his lifetime, Stalin was widely admired by Western intellectuals. To quote just one, the Brazilian writer Jorge Armado, member of the Brazilian CP and known for his humanity and generosity: 'When I heard of Stalin's death I cried as if my own father had died. The next day when I met my comrades in Santiago de Chile they all had put on black ties' (Le Nouvel Observateur, 5–11 August 1993: 72).
29. Some major successes were achieved in advanced technology. The chief Soviet breakthroughs that indeed hoisted the USSR to a level that began seriously to worry the West consisted in mastering H-bomb technology and in securing a temporary lead in space technology with the launching of Sputnik in 1956.

    Khrushchev also attempted to give a little more freedom to artistic expression in the USSR. Here, however, he failed the first test. When Boris Pasternak was awarded the Nobel Prize for Literature in 1958 for a novel he had finished in 1955, he was forced to turn down the prize. *Dr Zhivago* was resented as anti-Soviet and even anti-Russian and had over-stepped the bounds of cultural liberalism. In 1962 however, Krushchev backed up a novel by an unknown writer, Alexander Solzhenitsyn's *One Day in the Life of Ivan Denisovich.*
30. An agreement was signed with China in 1953 in which the USSR granted assistance for the construction of 146 large industrial complexes. The USSR agreed to evacuate Port Arthur and Dairen and to discontinue its activities in Manchuria. The CCP obtained an upgrading of its status in the international movement to virtually equal the role

of the CPSU. In particular, the need for cooperation was recognised and China was given a leading role in the Third World.

Motivated by the urge to improve external relations, a Yugoslav–Soviet reconciliation took place in 1955. The Joint Declaration of 2 June 1955 recognised that 'the policies of military blocs increase international tension' and that 'development of peaceful co-existence requires the co-operation of all States, without taking into account ideological and social differences'. More remarkably still, 'questions of internal organisation, social systems and different forms of socialist development exclusively regard the people concerned'. Without making the slightest concession on its neutrality, Yugoslavia in addition obtained sizeable Soviet economic assistance.

31. Following the establishment of diplomatic relationships with the Federal Republic of Germany, remaining war prisoners were released. Also under Khrushchev gulag convicts were released in large numbers.
32. Brezhnev and Kosygin shared power until the mid-1970s, although they represented different political choices. Brezhnev gave priority to heavy industry, defence and agriculture and after 1972 to the development of Siberia. Kosygin thought it was essential to modify this conservative ordering and to shift priority to the consumer goods sector. The uprising in Czechoslovakia in 1968 established a disconcerting correlation between consumer welfare and political claims that told against Kosygin's views. As America stepped up its war commitments in Vietnam the balance swung in favour of Brezhnev and a rekindling of the defence effort. From that time on, the army played a dominant role in setting economic priorities, favouring heavy industry and the military-industrial complex. On 7 May 1976 Brezhnev became a Marshall of the USSR. The appearance of the General Secretary in military uniform symbolised the convergence of military and party interests.
33. Between 1960 and 1970 the fertility rate dropped by 7% and the mortality rate by 3%. Similarly, the structure of the population changed considerably: the Muslim population which had represented 10.7% of the total population in 1959 accounted for 16% in 1979.
34. The report was secret and only discussed in restricted circles of the Academy of Science and the Party. As so often in those days, a copy was leaked to the West.
35. Against this backdrop of crisis, dissenting groups gained in popularity. Several movements can be discerned in the 1960s which are collectively referred to as the 'democratic movement'. A first such movement might be called 'authentic Marxism–Leninism', whose leaders were Roy and Joures Medvedev. They were convinced that Stalin had deformed the true Marxist–Leninist ideology and that a return to source was needed. The second movement was represented by Sakharov's 'liberalism', a pairing of Western democracy with socialist principles. The third was Solzhenitsyn's equally nebulous ideology, combining Christian or moral values with Slav traditions and Russian soul-searching. This 'democratic movement', despite its resonance abroad, remained marginal at home. Its major success, with considerable long-term consequences, was that in the space of just a few years (1967–73) the question of human rights in the USSR became a major international issue, going on to play a crucial role in the CSCE (the Conference on Security and Cooperation in Europe) when this took off in 1973.
36. The Brezhnev years were not very happy ones in terms of external relations either. The Soviet leadership was seriously challenged within the socialist camp by Cuba and by China's greater revolutionary fervour. Both severely criticised the USSR for not intervening more openly in the Vietnam war. In 1965 China demanded a public denunciation of the USSR by socialists worldwide. Fortunately for the USSR, China embarked on its cultural revolution in 1966 and became completely embroiled in its domestic affairs.
37. The subsequent 'normalisation' in Czechoslovakia resulted in closer cooperation among East European States both in military and economic terms. Apart from the Warsaw Pact and Comecon, a host of inter-State institutions was created to coordinate transport, energy

and chemical supplies and so forth. In fact, their real purpose was to help to extend Soviet control over their 'brother states'. This 'limited sovereignty' was part of the so-called Brezhnev doctrine of 'proletarian internationalism'.

38. In 1972, SALT 1 (Strategic Arms Limitation Talks) came to an agreement and in 1974 it was agreed to pursue SALT 2, which was finally signed in 1979. Détente reached its zenith in 1972–75 and 1975 was enshrined in the ratification of the Conference on Security and Co-operation in Europe (CSCE) by all European countries, Canada and the United States.
39. Glasnost can be defined as 'rendering public what was hidden'. Behind that slogan was an appeal for an open discussion of the economic situation, of the crisis in the party, which was indistinguishable from the Administration and incapable of imparting new vigour to the evolution of society, and above all of the ideological crises which no official echelon was yet willing to admit openly. In adopting the slogan 'glasnost', Gorbachev promised to reduce controls and to improve access to information. He also repeatedly declared that 'glasnost is healthy criticism of shortcomings, not an assault on Socialism and its values'.

    Along with glasnost there was the call for 'uskorenie': the speeding-up of economic development fuelled by continuous reforms. And to top it all, 'perestroïka' was a call to restructure just about everything.
40. Glasnost obviously also created new problems or rekindled old ones. The old arguments between 'Slavophiles' and 'Westerners', between 'liberals' and 'apparatchiks', between 'Stalinists' and 'non-Stalinists', to name but some, once again reared their troublesome heads. One in particular has turned into a major and dramatic issue: the problem of nationalities, which had been stifled for too many years.
41. A detailed account of perestroïka and its failure is given in Goldman (1991).
42. The Soviet troops had suffered 13 000 casualties and 40 000 injuries. According to Podnieks's film: 'Is it easy to be young?', the Afghan war was as unpopular in the Soviet Union as the Vietnam war had been in the United States.
43. The expression is Eisenhower's, the object was the questionable symbiosis between US military and industrial interests – its chief consummation was in the USSR.
44. See Chapter 4 for an analytic review.

CHAPTER TWO

The institutional design of socialist economies

Every year humanity takes a step towards Communism. Maybe not you, but at all events your grandson will surely be a Communist.

(N.S. Khrushchev, 1956)

This chapter describes how the Soviets solved the problem of organising a socialist economy, partly inspired by Marxist theory and for the rest motivated by the concrete problems in hand coupled with the communists' determination to stay in power and, at least at an early stage, inspired by Faustian ambition. This Soviet model, which itself underwent drastic changes under Stalin, became the blueprint inflicted on other socialist countries by Soviet 'assistance'. 'Assistance' notwithstanding, all socialist countries deviated from the Soviet standard to some extent, but the differences were never so great as to result in significantly modified performance. The only exception to this rule occurred in those socialist countries which severed their ties with the Soviet Union, namely China and Yugoslavia.

Institutional design followed from the priorities of socialist *Realpolitik*: self-sufficiency and state control over the economy and growth. Section 1 sets out the theme. The major institutional characteristics of Soviet socialism are collective ownership of virtually all property rights on physical and human capital (Section 2) and replacement of the market as the coordinating mechanism by state planning (Section 3). Most of the problems rife in socialist economies go back to these two institutional innovations. Monopolisation of the economy and giganticism are the result of both collective ownership and planning, irresponsibility and lack of incentive spring from the absence of individual ownership rights and too rigid principal–agent relationships; shabby goods and want of variety stem from lack of competition, itself a consequence of strict planning; and so on. The role of the state in comprehensively allocating resources rendered superfluous well-developed financial markets – which assume the allocative function of savings to investment in market economies (Section 4).

1. Policy priorities of socialism

The Soviet system made three far-reaching fundamental policy choices which have since become hallmarks of the socialist system, although they are not inherent features.

The first key policy choice favoured national self-sufficiency in order to become independent of the capitalist class enemies. This target – which was never fully realised – was also backed up by an industrial strategy of import substitution still in vogue among developing countries around the world until recently. Given its geographic size and its huge population, this objective was certainly more easily defensible in the Soviet Union than elsewhere. The decisive reasons for pursuing a policy of autarky were, however, military and political. The economic disadvantages, illustrated in Box 2.1, tended to be neglected. Throughout its lifetime, the Soviet leadership was perpetually concerned with intervention by foreign powers bent on gratifying the desire of the 'revanchists' to halt the march of socialism. And unfortunately Hitler proved them right. For the same reason, the Soviet leadership always banked on the worldwide spread of socialism and Lenin once expressed the fear that if Germany did not turn socialist then the socialist future of the Soviet Union itself was in danger.

Box 2.1 The cost of not trading 'ideas'

Open economies trade both goods and 'ideas'. Ideas are partly embodied in goods and can be copied at low cost, a fact that, for example, made Japan rich. But particularly in modern economies, 'ideas' relate to 'how to do business'. This requires foreign direct investment and foreign management. For example, in the 1980s US automobile producers have re-learnt from Japanese production in the US and joint ventures how to produce more efficiently.

The Soviet Union had opted for basic autarchy of the Comecon bloc. Although some trade with the non-Comecon countries had taken place, this trade was limited to specific categories of goods (e.g. wheat) and the West refused exportation of certain high-tech equipment for strategic reasons. This restriction of trade deprived the Soviet economy of the traditional gains from international trade, which can be very substantial. But possibly more important for economic development than the trade in 'objects' is the trade in 'ideas'. As argued by Romer (1993), the notion of a technology gap contains both an 'object gap' (infrastructure, production plants) and 'idea gap' (know-how about production, packaging, distribution, marketing, inventory control, quality control, worker motivation, etc.). Reconstruction of a revolution- or war-ridden economy is more concerned with 'objects' whilst the modern economy is more dependent on 'ideas'. Ideas develop more naturally in an advanced and competitive economy than in a poor and tightly controlled one. But the advantage of a retarded economy is to be able to fill the 'idea gap' through a (usually cheap) transfer, as ideas do not have opportunity costs (wheat shipped to the Soviet Union cannot be consumed any longer in the exporting country; a computer programme transferred can still be used unimpaired). The big disadvantage of the Soviet bloc was, therefore, the choice of cutting itself off from the idea-transfer out of fear of polluting socialist ideas, a disadvantage that became more important over time.

Can one get a notion of the importance of this choice? Not in precise terms.

continued

Box 2.1 *continued*

> But a feel can be obtained from the success of the Chinese partial reforms. China today is still a more distorted economy than, say, India. To explain China's successes since the opening up of 1978 purely on the grounds of partial internal reforms is therefore not convincing and does not do full justice to the significance of the enormous inflows of direct foreign investments. Investors from Hong Kong and Taiwan provided more than 60 per cent of all foreign investment in China, setting up and operating business in China, thereby supplying expertise in marketing, management, training and technology. Without this transfer of 'ideas' the Chinese success would be a miracle.
>
> *Source:* Romer (1993) and Bateman and Mody (1991).

The second policy choice – related to but not dictated by the institution of collective ownership – was to allocate resources by using the price mechanism only as a secondary support instrument. Ideally, the communists would have preferred to allocate resources in a way entirely circumventing markets and prices. They quickly found this to be impossible. Workers receive wages which they will spend by optimising the benefits from their purchases. These benefits will depend on the price and availability of goods. As in capitalist economies with widespread state intervention, the communists used an administered price system to allocate resources according to principles other than demand and supply. Thus, while markets did not determine prices, prices still played a key role and in some cases markets reappeared as part of a highly developed underground economy in an otherwise plan-driven command economy. According to the Shatalin Commission, the underground economy accounted for about 20 per cent of the former Soviet Union's GDP by the late 1980s.

The third and not unrelated policy choice was rapid growth on top of an apparently lexicographic ordering of preferences. This is investigated carefully in Chapter 3. It was the need to demonstrate success and it was military aspirations that made growth the top priority. But there were other reasons as well. The planning process clearly found it easier to deal in quantitative than in qualitative targets. And the growth rate is the most easily measurable and visible quantitative indicator. Finally, the greater the waste generated in the production of investment goods, the greater the inefficiency of investment decisions, the more widespread the bottlenecks of essential technological supports and the closer to full employment the economy moves, the less growth potential there will be for a given amount of savings. Hence the need to step up forced savings in an attempt to preserve growth.

2. The absence of property rights

In capitalist societies the various forms of private ownership (individual ownership, limited liability partnerships, cooperatives) develop and gain ground basically as a result of spontaneous economic processes, backed up by a legal system which protects private ownership and enforces private contracts. Though there are times when state regulations give a greater boost to capitalist ownership, it certainly cannot be said that it is the state which has organised the development and stabilisation of capitalism.

By contrast, the creation of state ownership is not the result of spontaneous processes but of revolutionary action by the party-state. The cornerstone of the Marxist–Leninist party programme is 'expropriation of the expropriators', in other words, the ordering of society on the basis of public rather than private ownership. Above all, socialism, its establishment and maintenance, are not just instrumental to other, ultimate values, but an intrinsic ultimate value in their own right: to guarantee the survival of socialism in power. Socialism differs from capitalism first and foremost in that it replaces private ownership with public ownership; hence the elimination of private ownership and the establishment of public ownership are an intrinsic value as well. Of course, productivity is also expected to be higher than under capitalist ownership. But there is already vast intrinsic value in that the capitalists are no longer exploiting the workers and the workers are no longer subordinate to the capitalists.[1] Moreover, and in practice most importantly, the property managed by the bureaucracy is the essential constituent of that bureaucracy's power.

It is on this precise point that cardinal differences exist between the Marxist–Leninist action programme and the programmes of other brands of socialism, such as the Social Democrats. In the Social Democratic view, forms of public ownership of production and distribution have only instrumental value. They cannot be avoided but they should be implemented only insofar as they further the values regarded as intrinsic: primarily welfare, social justice and individual freedom. Private ownership need not necessarily be abolished where it serves these intrinsic values better than nationalisation could. One problem with which communist governments were confronted when putting collectivisation into practice was judging how far they could go. What matters according to Marxist theory is ownership of the means of production. But whereas there is no difficulty in applying this principle to industrial concerns, small trades and crafts are another matter. And what about small farming as compared to the latifundia? What about poultry farming as compared to extensive livestock breeding? Consumer durables are not means of production but possibly signs of personal wealth. If a car can be privately owned, what about a home or even several homes? Each socialist country drew the line according to its own lights. Yugoslavia went furthest in recognising the incentive problems of state ownership. Yugoslavia's self-management formula and worker ownership will be discussed separately in Chapter 12.

Individual work effort and performance is also highly dependent on the property rights structure. In capitalist economies fortunes are made on new ideas in the scientific or marketing sphere, on the right investment decisions at the right time, or on the ability to spot unsatisfied needs. The prospect of netting exceptional returns is a powerful stimulus and prods people into thinking, into trying out new ideas, and into taking risks. In socialist economies there are no such dynamic forces at work because property rights do not exist.

In socialist societies property rights, in this case basically individual property rights (a particular person has an idea, develops a product, and so on), are not accepted since all capital belongs to society. Unfortunately, this concept is never nailed down with any precision. Which society are we talking about? The present generation or future generations? How is social wealth distributed in the event of the socialist society breaking up? This lack of clarity lies at the root of at least two serious problems.

First, if ownership is not clearly defined then property belongs to all and hence to none. Typically, nobody feels responsible for maintaining capital. This is precisely what happened to the USSR's reproducible capital (housing, factories) and to its non-reproducible capital (mineral resources, the environment).

Second, if and when such societies terminate their communist 'social contract', what happens to the capital? If property rights had been clearly defined (never mind rightly or wrongly), there would have been no need for the debate now raging in former socialist countries about whether to privatise through selling off assets or through handouts, or not at all. In short, the need for writing Chapter 8, summarising the privatisation debate and its initial conditions, would not have arisen.

3. The role of planning and administrative control

Marx held that capitalism manages to establish a high degree of organisation within the firm, but produces anarchy in the market. Socialism by contrast avoids the anarchy which results if individual decisions are not coordinated by granting power to the state to organise the economy centrally on a national scale. Marxist thinkers did not bother to work out the nitty-gritty nor the pitfalls of nationwide economic planning. Planning as it developed in socialist countries was the outcome of trial and error in the Soviet Union in the early years.

Plans range from the short-term to the medium-term, usually from one to five years. The one-year plan is the operational tool; the five-year plan lays down a set of targets which are crucial in steering investment.

The most fleshed-out part of the plan is the input–output matrix that serves to define production targets.[2] These are set by sector and for key products which may run into several hundreds or indeed thousands. Material balances are prepared for the allocation of key products. Typically, the residual factor is final consumption, after the intermediary uses are satisfied as fully as possible to avoid production constraints elsewhere. Any shortfalls not absorbed by consumption mean that large parts of the plan may have to be rebalanced.

Part of final output is intended for investment, which is granted priority in carrying out the plan and may even receive import allocations. Other sectors with preferential access to imports are exports. Foreign trade balances are drawn up with either imports or foreign financing facilities balancing the current account.

A major chapter addresses targets for technological achievements. Labour allocations are relatively straightforward and the whole exercise is rounded off with a financial plan for the state budget and the banks. Pricing policy plays a less important role but price guidelines do form part of the plan document.

The plan cannot specify the details of production and allocation for millions of individual products. It operates on the aggregates described. Disaggregation takes place first by addressees, that is, the different ministries and/or agencies. Each ministry in turn controls several directorates, each of which administrate a sector or sub-sector. The directorate then allocates its plan for the individual firms it controls. The plan it transmits to a firm is *compulsory*. It is often a very elaborate document running into thousands of figures.

Although the plan passes comments from the top down, some provision is made for reactions and comments by subordinate levels. It is a phase of intense bargaining with the 'industrial lobbies' keen on softening plan targets. After some to-ing and fro-ing, the plan is finalised in the aggregate and transformed into an order to the firm. Implementation of the plan is then reported from the bottom up. During the preparatory and executive stages of the plan there is also extensive horizontal coordination among the various ministries responsible.

The planning process is one of extraordinary complexity and keeps a giant bureaucracy in business. Yet it is not so much the hordes of bureaucrats involved that is of importance: in capitalist societies the staff employed by firms, and the combined number of staff from all firms, in forecasting demand and planning production may be equally large. It is the concentration of information processing and the inefficiency that give rise to concern.

Schumpeter (1968) considered 'the creative destruction' of the competitive process as the central virtue of market economies. The competitive process is a highly selective one in which only the fittest survive. In a planned economy this process is totally aborted as the creation of new firms and the closure of inefficient ones is decided by the higher echelons of bureaucracy. This then raises the question: what motivates bureaucrats to seek high performance in their area of responsibility? Owing to the complexity of the planning process some misallocation can scarcely be avoided. Nevertheless, if bureaucrats, managers and workers were handed the 'right' incentives, then even a planned economy could mimic competitive equilibrium as demonstrated by Oskar Lange (1936). Although Lange's solution remains theoretically unassailable in a static analysis, it does raise the key question of how bureaucrats or productive agents are motivated in a socialist system.

In a socialist firm the management is typically chosen by the bureaucracy on grounds that include professional merit among other values such as political reliability. Managers never have a free hand in implementing the plan directives they receive. The superior bureaucracy makes regular inspections and party secretaries exercise important control functions within the firm.

Moving down the hierarchical ladder, incentives become scarcer and the importance of penalties increases. At managerial level there is an array of incentives and penalties. Direct income plays a much less important role than in capitalist economies. However, material benefits do matter: mainly easier access to rationed goods and services such as cars, homes, dachas and the like. Power and prestige are somewhat more prized than in capitalist countries, as income is less differentiated.

Some incentives are fairly typical for the socialist context. For years many party members acted with complete faith in their socialist utopia. As was demonstrated at specific times (the years immediately following the socialist revolution, the war years), socialist ardour can be a powerful propelling force. The trouble is that when belief in the political and moral values of the system wanes – as was undoubtedly the case during the Brezhnev and Gorbachev years – performance may fall off as sharply as it was thrust upward in more stirring times.

On the disciplinary front, socialist systems wield a much more fearsome clout than the capitalist economies where typically, the worst that can befall an individual is dismissal. Imprisonment, forced labour or execution for sabotage of the plan are some of the harsher penalties in the socialist workers' paradise.

From an economic viewpoint, two features of the socialist system stand out in sharp relief. First, penalties and incentives serve mostly to stiffen discipline and there is no direct link with performance. Second, at best they enforce a 'satisfactory' level of performance – but fail to generate 'best' results. As the penalties for failing a plan target are not commensurate with the benefits of exceeding it (workers and managers have no claim to more than a minimal share of the residual income), there is no incentive to surpass targets. Moreover, the system generates total aversion to risk for the reasons just given. Clearly, then, over-achievement, initiative or any other deviation from established procedure are sheer folly in such a system. Specific features of the socialist system which at times seem strange to Western observers likewise become crystal clear when viewed against this incentive background. In a situation where supplies of raw materials and intermediate inputs are irregular, risk-averse managers will hoard as much as they can whenever supplies are available, irrespective of cost.[3]

The same is true for capital and labour. An over-equipped factory may not produce cost-effectively but it is less hampered in fulfilling plan targets if some of its machinery breaks down. And indeed, excessive investment and very high ICORs (incremental capital–output ratios) were typical of the Soviet Union.

Another pronounced bias is excessive use of inputs. As shown in Chapter 16, the use of energy per unit of output in the socialist countries was between twice and four times that in OECD countries. The use of transport, for geographical reasons and because of the planners' disregard for decentralisation, was four to ten times as high per unit of output.

Labour is a two-fold problem: at plant level, staff is not easily increased or disciplined, and motivation is often low. As there is no real labour market to speak of, obtaining additional staff by administrative procedure is a time-consuming process. With only small income differentials for workers, the chief source of flexibility in terms of compensation is in non-pecuniary benefits, such as shirking. Managers are considered good managers and will face fewer problems from the workers if they are not too demanding. So they put in for higher-than-strictly necessary staff quotas to make sure plan targets are met and staff are kept quiet.

These arguments also exemplify that within the apparently monolithic, centrally planned economy considerable bargaining takes place. Each institution issues overstated signals to superior bureaucratic levels to obtain easier targets and more inputs, and requires maximum service from its own lower levels. Horizontally the same is true: each firm bargains for maximum credit, investment, labour and inputs and strives to minimise its supplies to other firms.

One feature that is easily understood in the light of the complexity of the planning process is the planners' concentration on quantitative priority tasks (aggregate growth, production targets for strategic products, export targets). It is clearly impossible to hit thousands of detailed targets or even to specify qualitative targets unambiguously. To satisfy top decision-makers and for propaganda reasons all efforts are centred on the priority tasks, never mind if the cost is out of all reasonable proportion. Priority allocations for defence purposes are a prime example of the irrelevance of cost.

What all these situations have in common are ill-specified incentives and an information problem. The aggregate plan largely disregards consumers' needs; firms have no idea what the quantity and quality of its inputs will be or what ultimate fate lies in store for its outputs; ministries ignore the exact 'production function' of firms because it pays to cheat, and so on.[4] Box 2.2 illustrates the problem in a game-theoretic framework.

Box 2.2 Incentive problems for planners and workers in a game-theoretic framework

		Response by firms in terms of quality and maintenance	
		high	low
Plan targets in terms of output	high	10,4	7,5
	low	6,7	4,9

FIG. A Pay-off matrix

As argued in the text the planner is more successful in setting quantitative targets (say, number of tractors produced) than in enforcing qualitative standards. At any rate, performance of the planner is evaluated mainly on the basis of output growth. When the firm receives exacting plan targets it will feel under increased strains and will attempt to adjust by reducing quality standards, plant maintenance and spare parts production.

Figure A illustrates the pay-offs for different outcomes of a 'game' played between the planner and, say, the plant manager. For each outcome (level of production and level of quality) there is a pay-off for the planner (the first number) and a pay-off to the plant manager (the second number). If there were no conflict between these two agents there would be no game: both would pick the same outcome. But, as argued in the text, there is typically a conflict: the planner set output targets too high for the manager's taste who then reacts by letting quality drop so that the outcome is socially sub-optimal.

The numbers in the pay-off matrix are chosen so as to reflect these features and are assumed to be additive. The equilibrium outcome is a high volume production target paired with low quality, that is the pay-off (7,5).

The disincentives for workers can also be illustrated with a game, known in game theory as 'the prisoner's dilemma'. The pay-off at Fig B below assumes that workers receive a pay unrelated to their individual performance (which is an exaggeration) and a bonus for collective output. As a consequence of this pay structure each worker is best off when he or she gets away with doing nothing at all (enjoying shirking) and all the others work hard to generate a bonus. When all the workers work hard they get the largest possible bonus but suffer from hard

continued

Box 2.2 *continued*

work. Therefore they achieve a lower individual pay-off than in the first scenario. Unfortunately, if all try to be smart then nobody tries hard any longer and, so, all are miserable. And this is indeed the equilibrium outcome: the pay-off (20,20).

efforts furnished		Worker II: high	Worker II: low
Worker I	high	50,50	10,60
	low	60,10	20,20

FIG. B Pay-off matrix: the prisoner's dilemma

The planners always had a preference for large projects. In many cases the belief in economies of scale has proved astonishingly long-lived. Economies of scale arguments were used to justify the largest *kolkhozes*, hospitals, universities, power plants and white elephants in the world. For many goods there existed only one, or a small number of, producers. This contrasts sharply with studies in Western economies which find that only a handful of activities bring together the conditions for a natural monopoly. In most activities the cost curve is U-shaped with minimum average costs attained at fairly small scales of production.[5] For that reason, and to offer diversity, most economic sectors in the West see a great number of firms competing with each other.

Developing countries usually assign less urgency to maintaining existing capital than to new investments. The same is true in socialist countries. Maintenance requires a skilled workforce and service companies which according to socialist principles do not produce value. In addition there is much more prestige associated with a new plant or machine than with merely maintaining old ones.

A closely related problem is the neglect of complementary but minor production, including spare parts. If an enterprise produces, say, tractors, then its plan target is a certain output of tractors. Spare parts are clearly of lesser concern as they would only reduce the production capacity available for the production of tractors. For a tractor to be useful, different types of agricultural tools need to be on offer as well as fuel. But peripheral tools are not as visible targets as the number of tractors produced and so are not always made available. Western observers have often wondered why Soviet agriculture should suffer from inadequate tool supplies given that the number of tractors per hectare exceeds that in most Western countries. And what is so visible in agriculture also hampers industry, which suffers from frequent and long production stoppages due to lack of input deliveries, machines in need of repairs and so on.

This lack of balanced, integrated planning shows its worst effects – bad as the resulting malfunctioning of the economy is already – in another area which is also a problem in capitalist economies: the neglect of the environment. Again, in principle it should be easier to avoid harmful environmental effects in a planned economy than in a market economy driven by capitalist sharks pursuing their own interests and closing their hearts to the woes of others. Since the distinction between private cost (the firm discharging harmful waste saves the cost of destroying it) and social gain (society suffers from the toxic discharges) evaporates in a socialist system (in principle, citizens own the productive assets but property rights are unfortunately not clear on that score), a comprehensive planning process would weigh the cost of pollution-avoidance in the production sector against the damage caused to citizens (both present and future generations) in terms of health, aesthetic pleasure and access to unspoiled nature. That a poor country should have a higher rate of pollution than a rich one is no doubt perfectly rational: the opportunity cost of non-pollution is higher (starving people tend to be less concerned about clean air than wealthy people) and the economic value of human beings lower on productivity grounds. In the case of the Soviet Union the size of the country is an additional factor allowing it greater environmental largesse than a more densely populated smaller country. Nevertheless, even when allowing for these factors the degree of pollution in socialist countries is such that it can only be explained by a lack of policy concern.[6]

Feshbach and Friendly (1992) argue that: ‘Most damaging of all to nature, the planning system treated all natural resources – land, water, mineral deposits and forests – as state property, virtually as a free good, the cost of which to the user was either minimal or nil’.

4. The financial system

Box 2.3 explains why finance was considered by Marx to be redundant. Before looking at what the limited role of money has brought about, we need to describe what this role consists of and which are the institutions in charge of the flow of funds in socialist economies.

Box 2.3 Marxist monetary theory

In Marx’s view monetary exchange was one of the vices of capitalism, yet he had very little to say about monetary economics. He observed that in primitive barter economies commodities were exchanged against other commodities (C – C). When money appeared on the economic scene it was used to facilitate exchange: producers would sell their commodities for money which was then used to buy

continued

Box 2.3 *continued*

other goods for consumption (C – M – C). The exchange values of the initial and the final 'C' were identical, as money was only a convenience in exchange economies. The use values, of course, were different or there would have been no reason for trade.

In a capitalist economy production requires investment. Capitalists hire labour and buy intermediate products (C) against money (M), and sell their output at M^1 $(M - C - M^{1)}$. Clearly, $M^1 - M > 0$ because capitalists will only produce if they can make a profit. And equally clearly $(M^1 - M)/M$ is nothing else than the profit rate. Hence we need not dwell on this famous formula, as it is not really a theory of money, but just another term for profit, or, as argued by Marx himself, a theory of value.

A socialist economy, Marx argued, would return to direct allocation and exchange of goods without monetary intermediation. This seemed to him more 'natural'. He was equally suspicious about interest rates and considered them as usury on grounds that recall St Thomas Aquinas. As a result interest rates never played the role in socialist planning that they did in capitalist economies, as witnessed by the tendency to over-invest and to over-capitalise production not only in terms of a poor country but even when compared to advanced economies.

In actual fact, however, socialist countries have remained monetised. To do away with money proved another utopian pipe dream. Still, money plays a much more limited role in these countries than in capitalist economies. To that extent some steps toward the utopian goal of a money-free economy have been made. But in practical terms the only result has been another (and no small) contribution to the inefficiency of the system.

BANKING

The banking system in socialist economies is entirely state-owned. It consists of several organisations: the central bank and various specialised banks (an investment bank, sectoral banks – for example a bank for agriculture, a foreign trade bank, a savings bank for the general public). The specialised banks are nominally independent, but in fact they are regulated by the central bank; indeed, the regulations are so binding that one may regard the banking system as a monobank.[7]

Banks in socialist countries constitute a centralised, hierarchical machine vested with the prerogatives of official authority. Banking is a branch of the bureaucracy, and the central bank, as the body running it, lacks even nominal autonomy, since it is subordinate to the government, whose instructions it has to obey.

The central bank of a socialist country issues money. In addition however, it fulfils a function which in capitalist economies is taken care of by the commercial banks: it handles the entire credit supply of both the state and state-owned firms. Each state-owned firm keeps an account at the central bank. Precise rules govern the amount of cash a firm may keep and what it may be used for. All other balances must be placed in the firm's account at the central bank. Nor can the firm as 'owner' of the money dispose freely of the cash it has deposited in the bank, which is drawn upon almost automatically, according to a system of centrally set ordering, to cover the various kinds of expenditure.

Accounts are divided into various 'sub-accounts' between which there is no free flow of money. Money intended to cover the purchase of materials and semi-finished products cannot be used to pay wages; money for wages cannot be used for materials, and so forth. Money balances are 'earmarked'. The problems raised by this system after the disintegration of the FSU are extensively discussed in Chapter 13.

The money earmarked for investment is segregated from all other funds including, for instance, expenditure connected with material inputs for day-to-day production. In certain countries and at certain times segregation occurs at the central bank; elsewhere and at other times the financing of investment is undertaken by the investment bank (i.e. the arm of the central bank specialising in investment).

In view of all this, money fails to represent a 'universal means of exchange'. The national currency is 'not convertible' within the country: 'investment money' cannot be converted into 'materials money' or 'wages money', or vice versa, even within the state-owned sector. This 'internal non-convertibility' heightens the rigidity of economic activity and not seldom prevents rational substitution between the factors of production.[8]

This applies even more to conversion between the national currency and foreign currencies. All financial relations with the outside world are strictly centralised into the hands of the central bank or its 'arm', the foreign trade bank. Money is non-convertible; conversion is restricted by general regulations and detailed, case-by-case adjudication.

The integrated banking sector has a complete picture of firms' monetary transactions. Never before has such full, centralised information on the movement of money been available under any previous social system. Yet in actual fact, this huge mass of information is barely used to serve the integrated management of the economy.

It is a convention of direct bureaucratic control to entrust the banking system with the monitoring of inventories. The information basis required derives from the provision of short-term credits, which also provides the means of intervening in a crude and slipshod way. If a firm is judged according to a variety of empirical norms to be overstocked, the bank limits the availability of working-capital credits. More importantly, it sends inspectors round and issues admonitory reports to the firm's superior bodies. This function might as well be performed by an 'inventory-monitoring office'. It is a piece of plain bureaucratic coordination that is none of a real bank's business, which is to provide market coordination and to engage in commercially motivated activities.

Another arm of the monobank deals with transactions by the general public. There, and only there, may citizens keep their bank accounts. Banking services to the general public are meagre and backward. Apart from accumulating cash, the only legal way of investing money is in a savings deposit. Citizens may apply to this monopoly savings bank for credit to build their own homes and, in certain countries and at certain times, to make instalment purchases of certain durable consumer goods. The scale of the credit taken up by households is insignificant by comparison with capitalist economies.

The banking system pays interest on deposits and charges interest on loans. All interest rates are centrally set and there is no differentiation for risk as all firms are state-owned and cannot fail. The rates are usually very low, and real interest rates have all too frequently been negative if hidden rather than official inflation is taken into account.

Remarkable from a Western point of view is the fact that the only financial assets in socialist economies are bank deposits. By definition, there are no ownership rights, but equally there are virtually no negotiable debt instruments such as bonds. Business and government obtain all their financial needs from banks and, occasionally, from abroad. Apart from their foreign debt, the socialist governments have no outstanding debt other than the money supply (in a broad sense, including savings deposits).

THE INTEGRATED FINANCIAL SYSTEM

Figure 2.1 (p. 54) shows a diagram of the socialist financial system, where the banking sector is aggregated into the central bank (the 'monobank'). The system is particularly simple because financial assets other than cash and deposits simply do not exist. Because banks and non-financial enterprises belong to government, all these sectors (government, central bank and firms) can be aggregated into one public sector account. This aggregation shows that the net wealth of the economy is equal to the net money supply held by households (cash plus deposits less bank debt).[9] While straightforward, this point is nonetheless of the utmost importance to the privatisation debate. The cancellation of debt for enterprises is a matter internal to the government sector and therefore mainly an accountancy problem.

In socialist economies the deficits run up by the central government budget have always been modest. Figure 2.1 shows why. Whether it is the government or the enterprise sector that is in deficit is immaterial: the deficits of either are indeed perfect substitutes. The measures needed to reform the financial sector of formerly socialist economies are developed in Chapter 9.

5. Conclusions

Politically and ideologically motivated choices of autarky and state control over the economy deprived the socialist economies of the institutions that are the hallmark of Western economies: markets, private ownership. Instead they had to rely on social ownership and state planning. The inefficiencies that are inherent in this institutional set-up were analysed in this chapter.

Some consequences of this institutional set-up were not obvious from the beginning. The difficulties, such as institutional organisation experiences in the non-industrial sector, were not perceived as long as the goal was to develop industry, starting from heavy industry. But agriculture and services are more difficult to deal with in a command economy and repeated reforms only resulted in failure.

The choice for autarky was not dictated by socialist principles but became desirable to avoid 'capitalist contamination'. Unfortunately, the cost of not benefiting fully from international trade, particularly trade in 'ideas', increased even more as basic needs were satisfied and as the economy in the 1960s was ready to become more sophisticated.

In the West a major regulator of resource allocation is the financial market, with shareholders acting as 'corporate governors'. The severe under-development of socialist

Central Bank			
Assets		**Liabilities**	
Loans to:		Deposits by:	
households	100	households	2,500
firms	3,000	firms	200
governm.	1,500	governm.	300
		cash in circ.	1,700
	4,600		4,600

Government			
Assets		**Liabilities**	
Deposits	300	Bank debt	1,500
Net debt	1,200		

Firms			
Assets		**Liabilities**	
Deposits	200	Bank debt	3,000
Net debt	2,800		

Public sector*			
Assets		**Liabilities**	
Loans to:		Deposits by:	
households	100	households	2,500
		cash in cir.	1,700
Net worth of assets	4,100		

Households			
Assets		**Liabilities**	
Deposits	2,500	Bank debt	100
Cash	1,700		
		Net wealth	4,100

* Public sector = government and banks and firms

FIG 2.1 The integrated financial system of a socialist economy

financial markets made mandatory savings necessary, failed to regulate resource allocation and to control corporate performance.

This lack of control shows up clearly in the excessive accumulation of capital under conditions of low and declining marginal returns to capital. And the absence of a proper evaluation of the cost of resources resulted in large-scale production of goods with 'negative value-added'. The over-emphasis on growth in the absence of institutions controlling the allocation of factors of production has resulted in a *débâcle*, and ultimately the fall of communism, that deserves separate treatment in the next chapter.

Notes

1. Bettelheim (1968) proposed to answer the question of whether a society is on the road to socialism by another question: namely, does the working class hold power?
2. Planning gave priority to physical units of measurement which were, however, aggregated into monetary units in a Monetary Plan (sectoral cash flows), a Treasury Plan and a Foreign Exchange Plan.

3. According to OECD data, during the period 1981–88 inventories as a proportion of GDP averaged 2.7 per cent in the USSR as compared to 0.4 per cent in the OECD countries.
4. This problem was first identified and analysed in depth by Hayek (1935).
5. For a summary of empirical estimates of economies of scale, see Emerson *et al*. (1988).
6. Despite lower industrial output per head in socialist countries, air pollution is much higher. According to United Nations (1987) data, sulphur oxides amounted to 300 kg per head of population in East Germany compared with 42 kg in West Germany.
7. Lenin envisaged that: 'A single state bank, the biggest of the big, with branches in every rural district, in every factory, will constitute as much as nine-tenths of the socialist apparatus. This will be countrywide book-keeping, countrywide accounting of the production and distribution of goods.' Lenin [1918] (1964: 106).

   In 1986, prior to moves toward a two-level banking system, the Soviet state banking system (Gosbank and the specialised banks) employed 406,300 people (Garetovskii 1989: 10). This is very little compared to capitalist economies, where employment in banking represents on average close to 5 per cent of aggregate employment. See Gilibert and Steinherr (1989).
8. This use of the term 'internal non-convertibility' refers to restrictions applied to bank accounts and should be distinguished from the macroeconomic internal convertibility concept: currency can be used for settlement of claims with residents but not with non-residents.
9. Net wealth in a capitalist society is equal to money supply and government debt held by households and firms.

CHAPTER THREE

The obsession with growth

*Faust (erblindet): Was ich gedacht, ich eil es zu vollbringen;
Des Herren Wort, es gibt allein Gewicht. Vom Lager auf, ihr Knechte! Mann für Mann! Laßt glücklich schauen, was ich kühn ersann! Ergreift das Werkzeug! Schaufel rührt und Spaten! Das Abgesteckte muß sogleich geraten. Auf strenges Ordnen, raschen Fleiß Erfolgt der allerschönste Preis; Daß sich das größte Werk vollende, genügt ein Geist für tausend Hände.*

(Goethe, *Faust* Part 2, Act 5)

This chapter evaluates the major concern and ultimately failure of communism: to catch up with the economic advance of the West. Section 1 discusses the motivation underpinning the major policy objective, common to all socialist economies at all times, namely their excessive emphasis on growth.

Despite the inter-temporal injustice which heavily penalised the first generations under socialism through very high forced savings, later generations did not reap the benefits of their forebears' sacrifices. Socialist economies seemed doomed to fail in their bid for sustained growth and be quite unable to let their citizens enjoy the fruits of sacrifice and labour.

Section 2 deals with the preliminary issue of measurements, as Soviet accounting standards are not easily reconcilable with Western practices. Section 3 starts from a growth-accounting framework and shows the contributions of the accumulation of factors of production (labour, capital, land) and of productivity growth. If the Soviet economy had been able to put its immense accumulation of productive factors (extensive growth) to efficient use, it would have been at the top of the world's growth league. Unfortunately they were not. Section 4 overviews the successes and failures of Soviet communism and Section 5 concludes.

1. Growth: the overriding plan objective

As we have repeatedly pointed out, socialism has only been developed in poor countries. In all poor countries, catching up with advanced nations is a top policy priority. socialist revolutionaries came to power on a promise to achieve exactly that (and to redistribute income in favour of the working classes). Faith in the feasibility of catching up is solidly backed up by Marxist theory. Clearly, then, in the view of socialist regimes, catching up would be proof of the superiority of socialism and would also substantiate the socialist leaders' legitimacy. It is worth recalling Stalin's claim in 1947 that he would catch up with Western economies within 10 years[1] – a claim repeated by Khrushchev 10 years later when he said the Soviet Union would overtake the United States in another 10 years – and Mao's desperate bid in 1957 to achieve the 'Great Leap Forward' and to catch up with the United States within 15 years.[2] These claims were not totally unrealistic. Until the late 1950s, the era of rapid Soviet growth and of the successful Sputnik launch, the main question among Western scholars was: when would the USSR overtake the US? At that time, specialists like Bergson (1961) did not exclude the possibility that this might be quite imminent. Now we know that catching up did occur but only in capitalist economies, notably in East Asia and in China after the 1978 opening-up policy.

Owing to the backwardness of economic conditions, to the shortages of virtually all goods and services and to human nature which always strives for more, the growth objective is easily passed down the hierarchical echelons and shared by all economic agents. While it is easy to understand that catching up receives undivided popular support, it is much harder to fathom how investment decisions are actually made. None of the mechanisms used in capitalist economies are available. At the aggregate level, in capitalist countries savings and investments are brought into balance by adjustments of the real rate of interest and of expected income. Individual investment projects are judged on the basis of investment costs (inclusive of financing cost), production costs and expected revenues discounted at the appropriate interest rate. Apart from expected sales not one of these variables is relevant for investment decisions in a socialist economy.

Because government controls investment spending, public sector consumption and wage payments, investment and savings are no longer independent decisions. Once wages are set, the remaining national income is at the disposal of the integrated public sector for consumption or investment purposes. Savings out of wage incomes represent 'voluntary' savings and are additional to the 'involuntary' or forced savings from the integrated budget. As a result the total amount of savings in socialist countries tends to be far above the levels in capitalist economies and is more easily manipulated by policy-makers.[3]

The share of investment is much lower than total national savings in socialist countries as military expenditure is much higher (estimated at about 15 per cent but possibly as high as 25–30 per cent of GDP[4]) than in capitalist countries (5–6 per cent of GDP in the United States and less in Japan and Western Europe). Thus, for the Soviet Union or China the total savings rates might be above 50 per cent of GDP (of which some 30 per cent is used for investment and some 20-30 per cent for defence). These data suggest that aggregate investment, in general, is maximised in line with the overall growth priority, subject to a level of consumption that the population will accept short of open rebellion. If the ultimate gauge of performance is growth of output, not social utility, the return on investment is of secondary importance.[5] But even output may not have been the prime objective of planners. Ofer (1987) argues that the goal was to maximise growth of GNP less consumption, that is, growth of investment and of military expenditures. Measured that way, Soviet achievements appear much more favourable. The same view is expressed by Berliner (1966): 'But if we are to capture faithfully the aims of the Soviet elite, then we must accord first place to military defence, and derivatively to heavy industry, as the aim of economic development.'

Confronted with virtually unlimited demand for investment funds and no price mechanism to regulate its allocation, administrative rationing is imperative. A first important decision springs from political priorities: the resources needed for defence, production targets of key strategic products and so on. Now bargaining sets in. Each firm belongs to a ministry that becomes its political advocate. The firm may be one that produces inputs needed in another industry and so they form a coalition to improve their bargaining position.

There is definitely a hierarchy of interest groups. The power of each group is correlated with its size in terms of output, its strategic position in the output structure and its strategic importance for the political priorities. For example, the military-industrial complex and the KGB have doubtlessly been the most powerful interest groups of all, and for a long time their claims went unchallenged and untouched.

As a rule it is difficult to turn down a request for investment out of hand. All firms have some administrative and political support; furthermore, administrations are better at 'satisfying' through acceptable compromises than in making difficult and risky choices. As a result, no investment project meets with a flat refusal and decisions are a very long time in the coming. Funds are spread thin over all projects with underfunding the inevitable result. This generates hiccups, delays and indeed sometimes projects grind to a complete halt before they are ultimately completed. Due to very long approval and completion times and to the dissipation of funds, projects more often than not are technologically obsolete by the time they are completed and their cost is many times what it would have been had they been carried out without hindrance or delay.[6]

While bargaining and power relationships certainly influence the choice of investments and the investment process itself, the planning process has developed a system of priorities. These priorities concern the sectoral structure of the economy and within sectors, certain types of products.

Among the productive activities top priority goes to industry, which has always been regarded as the engine of economic development. It leaves agriculture behind, but farming in turn does better than services.[7] By and large, a lack of balance in development strategy is not to be condemned as such. Hirschman (1958) and Streeten (1959) have argued that a poor country simply cannot tackle everything at once and that it would be wise to concentrate on a few key sectors that are able to pull along connected activities. Due to their upstream and downstream linkages progress in these sectors will spread to others, aided by the incentive effects of imbalances in technology and incomes. What is questionable, however, is a strategy that by design maintains an unbalanced approach for generations, and hinders the spread of investment flows into other areas of economic activity.

In the realm of industrial activity there are priorities by sector and by type of product. Investment goods prevail over consumer goods[8] and as investment is seen as the prime condition for growth, investment goods receive the highest priority. The development of heavy industry has been singled out as the basis for successful growth since way back before the Revolution. Because large quantities of steel are used in the production of machinery (and mechanisation is the road to greater productivity and technological progress) and, incidentally, in arms production, the iron and steel sector and heavy equipment always played a special role. This role was most ruthlessly developed by Stalin,[9] but has been maintained ever since. According to one statistical source, the share of heavy industry in total investment in industry between 1917 and 1976 amounted to 84 per cent.[10]

Table 3.1 confirms the allocation bias in favour of industry and capital-intensive agriculture to the detriment of housing and the service sector. This can hardly be due to Soviet citizens' preference for spending so much less (in proportion) on housing than Western consumers. This biased structure with its excessive emphasis on heavy industry has been blamed for stagnation in the 1980s and, in particular, for the technological slow-down. See Gomulka (1986) and Ofer (1987).

In this section the growth fixation of socialism has been stressed. Our next step must be to find out what results this strategy actually produced. One might expect that, with growth given such overriding precedence over consumption and the quality of life, socialist countries would have out-performed Western countries on that score at least, as in the Olympic games. Unlike the world of sports, however, there is a major obstacle in comparing growth performance: the problem of measurement to make the data internationally comparable.

TABLE 3.1 Sectoral distribution of capital stocks, 1987 (*percentages*)

	Agriculture	Industry	Agriculture and industry	Dwellings	Other
Soviet Union	14.2	32.2	46.4	18.6	35.0
Industrial market economies	5.0	23.4	28.4	35.9	35.6
United States	2.8	22.4	25.2	45.6	29.2
Finland	7.5	19.9	27.4	33.8	38.8
Germany, F.R.	3.6	20.1	23.7	44.2	32.1

Source: USSR-Soviet data; industrial economies-OECD data. Easterly (1993).

2. Measuring growth

Table 3.2 provides some measures of historic growth performance in the Soviet Union, both on an official and on an adjusted Western basis. Several interesting facts emerge from these data. Average growth during the twentieth century was virtually identical for the former Soviet Union and the United States. If one takes the period 1929–87, in order to exclude the pre-socialist, war and NEP years, then the Soviet Union did better by one percentage point, despite World War II which benefited US but harmed Soviet growth. As can also be seen from Table 3.2, the official figures considerably exaggerate growth. The question is, is this a coincidence or is it a systematic feature of Soviet statistical endeavour?

On an adjusted basis the Soviet growth record is not exceptional by Western standards but, until 1970 at least, was quite respectable. Two periods of rapid growth occurred from 1922 to 1940 and from 1950 to 1960 (in fact, from 1946 to 1960). Growth rates close to 10 per cent are typical for capitalist economies emerging from depression or war, as witnessed by the growth rates of European and some Asian countries in the 1950s. Each of the two periods of rapid growth in the Soviet Union was preceded by a war period during which production plummeted.[11] When peace and

TABLE 3.2 Economic growth in the Soviet Union and in the United States (average annual rate)

	Soviet Union official NMP	Soviet Union revised NMP	US GDP
1900–13		3.5	4.0
1913–21	− 10.7	−10.7	1.5
1922–40	15.3	8.5	2.5
1941–50	4.7	-0.6	4.5
1951–60	10.3	9.3	3.2
1961–70	7.0	4.2	3.7
1971–80	4.9	2.1	2.8
1981–85	3.6	0.6	3.1
1986–89	2.7	n.a.	3.0
1900–87	—	3.3	3.2
1929–87	—	4.0	3.0

Source: Commission of the European Communities (1990)

order were restored, unemployed, work-eager labour was in abundant supply, as was capital stock which, at least in part, only needed to be repaired and brought back on stream.

We are forced to conclude that on the basis of adjusted growth evaluation and notwithstanding its tremendous growth effort, the Soviet Union never succeeded in matching the best Western performances. Before explaining why, we need to make sure that the official data are indeed over-estimated and that the adjusted data offer a more reliable basis for comparison.

Official statistics suffer from measurement errors (which include neglect of the underground economy), over-reporting by plant managers and political manipulation, but this is hard to verify. Major biases are, however, created by the conceptual treatment of value creation. First, the Marxist distinction between productive and non-productive activity creates a sizeable difference between Western national income accounting and material product accounting. Net material product (NMP) does not include most services. This at any rate under-estimates GDP and is likely to over-estimate growth. Because services receive a lower priority in the socialist growth process, their growth rate over long time spans is definitely lower than growth in the 'productive' sphere. Hence, if services were included, this would increase GDP but might lower the overall growth rate.

Another major distortion is created by the pricing system. The prices of many industrial products are over-valued in relation to agriculture and services. Because they also enjoy a higher growth rate, the upward bias in their weight (which depends on the *value* of output) tends to bias upwards the aggregate growth rate. A similar bias results from hidden inflation. GDP deflators used are the official price indexes which are under-estimates of true price trends, even though there were periods of pronounced price adjustments (see Table 3.3). What is presented as the real rate of growth may, in fact, be closer to a nominal rate of growth.

Finally, the statistics fail to reflect changes in the quality of products. Western statisticians also find it difficult to take into account quality changes but approximations are

TABLE 3.3 Official price index in the Soviet Union: long time series

Period	Average annual change of official retail prices (percentage)
1928–37	20.5
1938–40	5.9
1941–47	18.1
1948–57	−8.2
1958–76	0.0
1971–75	−0.1
1976–80	0.6
1981–85	1.0
1986–89	2.1

Source: For the period 1928–75: D.M. Nuti (1986, pp. 42–44). From 1976: United Nations (1990, p. 136).

used much more systematically than in socialist economies. Moreover, the problem with Western statistics is that they tend to take only partial account of quality improvements so that GDP figures under-estimate the true figures. By contrast, socialist statistics fail to take account of declining quality so that NMP figures overstate the true index. For a detailed discussion of statistical and conceptual problems with socialist national accounts, see Bergson (1991), Desai (1986) and Ofer (1987).

3. Factors contributing to growth

'Extensive growth' refers to the accumulation of the factors of production (labour, capital, land) and 'intensive growth' to increases in the productivity of production factors.[12]

Box 3.1 summarises the factors contributing to economic growth: labour, capital (both physical and human), land and factor productivity.

Box 3.1 A framework for explaining growth

A stylised explanation of growth starts from the technological constraints captured by an aggregate production function :

$$Y = TF\,(K, N, L) \qquad (1)$$

where Y is aggregate output, F a production function and T a measure of technological efficiency, that is, total factor productivity (TFP). For a given level of T, the function F gives the amount of output that can be produced by efficiently using the primary factors of production, that is, the available stock of capital (K), of labour (N) and of land (L). F gives the potential output rather than actual

continued

Box 3.1 *continued*

output on the assumptions of full use of available production factors and efficient organisation of firms and markets.

Relation (1) is easily transformed into relation (2) in terms of growth rates:

$$y = at + bk + cn + dl \qquad (2)$$

where y, t, k, n, l are the growth rates of Y, T, K, N and L. Relation (2) is useful to organise thoughts about growth. If technology and the quality of factors of production remained constant, then output growth would be a linear function of the accumulation of factors of production. Socialists call this the 'extensive' method of growth. Disembodied technological progress is captured by t and embodied technological progress by higher productivity of the primary factors of production. Together they represent the 'intensive' method of growth in socialist parlance.

Disentangling the contributions to growth of accumulation and of technological progress is not easy. In traditional growth accounting pioneered by Denison (1962), the primary production factors were taken as such and all technological progress (and possibly economies of scale) were captured by t, treated as a residual. As shown in the text, computations of t depend strongly on the assumed production function F and, depending on that choice, give contradictory results.

Equation (2) neglects financial and pricing constraints. It is therefore necessary to derive a sustainable equilibrium growth rate.

Assuming that savings represent a constant fraction of national product, that the labour force grows at the exogenous rate n and technological progress is labour-augmenting at the exogenous rate m, then the neo-classical steady-state growth path (Solow 1956) is described by:

$$y^* = (n + m)\, k/s \qquad (3)$$

Equation (3) provides a useful, even if somewhat unexpected insight: the equilibrium growth rate is exclusively determined by $n + m$, that is, the exogenous rates of growth of the labour force and of technological progress. The savings rate which determines gross investment has no effect on equilibrium growth but only on the level of national product and on the growth rate during the catching-up period.

Equation (3) is derived on the assumption that the economy uses its resources efficiently so as to operate on its production function surface. Moreover, in this neo-classical model economy policy can only affect the level of income but has no effect on the growth rate.

The literature on endogenous growth (Romer 1986, 1987, 1990; Lucas 1988; Barro 1989) has developed models in which policies can generate important effects on equilibrium growth. In these models the traditional assumptions of constant returns to scale, the dependence on non-reproducible factors of production and diminishing returns to each factor are variously relaxed and the role of

continued

Box 3.1 *continued*

investment in human capital is developed. Barro (1989) and Sala-i-Martin (1990) have shown how tax rates can distort savings decisions and thereby lower the growth rate, while tax-financed government services can potentially raise productivity and growth. King and Rebelo (1990) have shown how differences in tax rates can generate large differences in growth rates.

The policies pursued by socialist economies are therefore more usefully discussed in a model of endogenous growth to avoid under-estimating their negative effects on growth performance. Easterly (1993) has attempted to estimate the growth effects of distortionary policies in socialist economies and arrives at sizeable effects of the misallocation of capital.* Because distortions are pervasive he is led to conclude:

> While the model is highly stylised, it provides insight into the need for radical reform in socialist economies – for a 'Big Bang'. Radical reforms will encounter strong political resistance, but so will partial reforms. The question is why carry out politically costly partial reforms that bring little benefit when a radical reform with not much higher political costs can revolutionise the economy?

* According to the results obtained by Easterly, the under-investment in housing (keeping all other distortions constant) is responsible for lower growth of 0.29 per cent a year, or for a loss of output of 19 per cent over six decades. Similarly, the effect of over-investment in industry and agriculture on the growth rate is estimated at 0.16 per cent over six decades. The loss of output from this global distortion alone amounts to 10 per cent of output.

LABOUR ACCUMULATION

Socialist planners had banked on maximising labour mobilisation. Data in Ofer (1987) suggests that from 1928 to 1985 population increased at an average annual rate of 1.3 per cent, the number of employed by 1.9 per cent and hours worked by 1.8 per cent. In this way the growth in labour contributed not only to GNP but also to the growth of GNP per capita. When the Soviets came to power, unemployment in urban centres was high and so was under-employment in agriculture. Up to World War II, there was no shortage of unskilled labour (see Table 3.4.) and the investment strategy served to equip the available excess labour supply. This is a major reason for the growth sustained during the 1920s and 1930s. Misallocation of investment was less important as all capital was in short supply and could be put to good use. What was lacking was skilled labour, in particular in management. It took the regime at least until the 1950s to replace the trained elite inherited from the Tsarist regime and offset the losses suffered during World War II.

The loss of human capital throughout the history of the Soviet Union was one of the highest in world history and inflicted incalculable economic costs. When the socialists took over in 1914 the country suffered from the loss of human lives during World War I. Socialist reorganisation of the society withdrew traditional cadres from their responsibilities, in effect reducing their social utility dramatically. Some of the greatest

TABLE 3.4 Growth of the workforce in the Soviet Union

Year	Workforce* (in millions)	Period	Average Annual Growth Rate of Workforce (%)
1927	11.3	—	—
1932	22.8	1927–32	15.1
1937	27.0	1932–37	3.4
1950	40.4	1937–50	3.1
1955	50.3	1950–55	4.5
1960	62.0	1955–60	4.3
1965	76.9	1960–65	4.4
1970	90.2	1965–70	3.2
1975	102.2	1970–75	2.5
1980	112.5	1975–80	1.9
1985	117.8	1980–85	0.9
1989	115.4	1985–89	−0.5

Source: Kornai (1992)
* Excluding *Kholkoz* members

talents emigrated before and after the internal war between the progressive (red) and reactionary (white) forces. Whilst all numbers are highly uncertain, about one to two million Russians emigrated between 1917 and 1925, the intellectual elite of the country. During the famine of 1933, 3–5 million people died and the kulaks were executed, put into labour camps, or transferred to distant regions to carry out low productivity tasks.

Millions ended up in gulags or were executed during the Stalin years. At the death of Stalin, 2.5 million were in gulags (Werth 1993). World War II cost an estimated 20 million Soviet lives and of returning war prisoners, 1.5 million were executed or deported. After Stalin's death over a million Jews and dissidents emigrated. This extensive and continuous destruction of people, including the intellectual elite of the country, is above all a human tragedy, but also an immense economic cost which can be appreciated by the huge gain realised by immigration countries such as the United States.

In order further to augment the available labour force, particularly during the war and thereafter, the socialist economies achieved exceptionally high participation rates in the labour force. In 1980 the Soviet participation rate, measured as a ratio of all those working to the population aged 15–64, was 86.9 per cent, compared to 66.5 per cent in the OECD and 70.9 per cent in the United States (Ofer 1987). Much of this higher participation came from a higher female participation than in capitalist countries (see Table 3.5). If one disregards the marginal disutility of work then, even in a labour-abundant country, it makes sense to stretch working time to the maximum acceptable level. As so often, Marx's analysis of the capitalist system was applied with a vengeance by socialists. He had argued that the only limit to capitalist exploitation of workers was the physiological need to rest in order to keep the variable capital (labour) intact. Working conditions in capitalist countries throughout the nineteenth century were indeed dismal, but they were no better in the Soviet Union, at least until the 1960s.

TABLE 3.5 Activity rate of women in the age group 40–45: an international comparison

	1950	1970	1985
Socialist countries			
Bulgaria	78.6	88.5	93.3
Czechoslovakia	52.3	79.9	92.4
East Germany	61.9	79.1	86.1
Hungary	29.0	69.4	84.7
Poland	66.4	79.5	84.7
Romania	75.8	79.5	85.1
Soviet Union	66.8	93.2	96.8
North European countries	30.9	53.8	71.1
West European countries	34.5	46.4	55.6
South European countries	22.4	29.7	37.1

Source: ILO and Kornai (1992)

Note: The countries covered are Austria, Belgium, France, West Germany, the Netherlands, Switzerland, Luxembourg, United Kingdom (Western Europe); Greece, Italy, Malta, Portugal, Spain (Southern Europe); Bulgaria, Czechoslovakia, East Germany, Hungary, Poland, Romania, Soviet Union (socialist countries); the Scandinavian countries (Northern Europe). Regional averages are unweighted.

As long as there is unemployment and the participation rate can be increased, equation (3) in Box 3.1 suggests that the contribution of labour to growth is a dominant factor.[13] But at some time or other this potential is exhausted. It then needs to be replaced by qualitative improvements in labour skills. The absence of competitive conditions, the lack of a market for services and of differential wages seriously hampered the development of skills, so that socialist economies suffered more from the labour constraint of a fully employed economy than capitalist economies.

CAPITAL ACCUMULATION

Table 3.6 provides a comparison of official and Western estimates of growth rates of output per worker and of capital per worker. Overall, both data sources confirm that the capital–output ratio has been increasing during the entire period 1928 to 1987. The Soviet capital stock has been growing since 1928 at an annual rate of 7 per cent (and at 7.5 per cent if the Second World War years are excluded) until 1985. Extensive growth (i.e., rising capital–output ratio) is doomed to be slowed down by diminishing returns and implies that the investment ratio has to increase over time. Indeed, the Soviet investment ratio doubled between 1950 and 1975 (Ofer 1987). The level reached by the capital–output ratio in the USSR in the 1980s was among the highest in the world (Easterly and Fischer 1994). Thus, although many countries exhibit increasing capital–output ratios over time (Japan is a prime example, also the EU), the USSR was an extreme case.

So extensive growth contributed to the slowdown of Soviet growth after the 1950s. Furthermore, as argued below, the translation of extensive growth into diminishing returns was, by Western standards, extremely pronounced. The reason was a very low elasticity of substitution between labour and capital.

TABLE 3.6 Soviet growth data, 1928–87

Period	Industry, official	Industry, Western	Total economy, Western
Growth rates of output per worker, alternative estimates			
1928–87	6.3%	3.4%	3.0%
1928–39	12.5%	5.0%	2.9%
1940–49	0.1%	−1.5%	1.9%
1950–59	8.9%	6.2%	5.8%
1960–69	5.7%	2.8%	3.0%
1970–79	5.2%	3.4%	2.1%
1980–87	3.4%	1.5%	1.4%
Growth rates of capital per worker, alternative estimates			
1928–87	6.2%	3.2%	4.9%
1928–39	11.9%	6.5%	5.7%
1940–49	1.5%	−0.1%	1.5%
1950–59	8.0%	3.9%	7.4%
1960–69	6.1%	3.4%	5.4%
1970–79	6.3%	4.1%	5.0%
1980–87	5.6%	4.0%	4.0%

Source: Western data is based on Powell (1963, 1968), CIA (various years), Kellogg (1989). Easterly and Fischer (1994).
Note: Growth rates are logarithmic least-squares estimates.

LAND

The third factor of production is land, which serves as shorthand for agricultural land, forests, minerals and so on. Land under cultivation increased by 0.8 per cent on average during 1928–83 (Ofer 1987), reflecting territorial acquistions in 1939, and Khrushchev's Virgin Land Programme during the 1950s. The Soviet Union is particularly well-endowed with natural resources although geographical dispersion, vast distances and climatic hardships lower the economic value of available natural resources. Because prices bore no relation to production costs, relative scarcity and interest rates, the Soviet economy exploited nature (woods, water, soil, mineral wealth) excessively.[14] This policy bias produced the present situation which Feshbach and Friendly (1992) describe as follows:

> In the last decade of the 20th century, there are no leading industrial cities in the Soviet Union where air pollution is not shortening the life expectancy of adults and undermining the health of their children. The growth that made the USSR a superpower has been so ill-managed, so greedy in its exploitation of natural resources and so indifferent to the health of its people, that ecocide is inevitable.

In fact, the socialist system generated and fell victim to a major inconsistency in managing their natural resources.[15] If the rate of interest (the expression of the inter-temporal time preference) is high, then a society prefers to transfer more to future generations than when the rate of interest is low. The high level of forced savings reflects very considerable concern on the part of socialist planners for the welfare of future generations and is inconsistent with low real interest rates, that is, it is inconsistent with time preferences that give priority to the present. Several generations of Soviet citizens have been sacrificed since the 1920s in order to build up an industrial power basis to enrich future generations. By the same token, low rates of interest and high concern for future generations should have been reflected in great care for natural wealth and a low pace of exploitation of mineral resources. In fact, however, the Soviets exploited their mineral resources and nature recklessly.

Such an inconsistency can only occur in a context where interest rates do not matter and where prices do not reflect costs and demand. As argued in Chapter 16, the best productive sites for oil and many other minerals are already exhausted and the marginal cost of production now makes many resource sites uncompetitive even at world market prices. The same is true for agriculture in certain parts of the former Soviet Union. Considerable investments will be needed to bring ecological conditions in over-used areas back into balance.

FACTOR PRODUCTIVITY

The data in Table 3.6 summarise the growth of output and capital per worker. These are the basic data for the estimation of total factor productivity (TFP). In Table 3.7 the results obtained from assuming a Cobb–Douglas production function are reproduced. Labour's share is set equal to 0.6 and capital's share equal to 0.4 (a rather conventional assumption for developing countries). The estimations are carried out for the different data sets of Table 3.6. Independently of the source used, there is a strongly declining trend of TFP growth after the 1950s, whilst the 1950s stand out as a period of exceptional growth. Thus, the explanation for the growth slowdown would be a combination of extensive growth, implying diminishing returns on capital, and a declining productivity growth. Also of interest is the contradiction between the results obtained from official Soviet data and Western revisions for the 1930s. Official data show extraordinary growth of TFP, whilst Western GNP data imply negative growth rates. As to sectoral contributions, it is remarkable that TFP growth in industry was positive until the 1980s (and the war-ridden 1940s). Even during the 1980s the negative TFP growth in industry was below the negative growth for GNP. This implies that the slowdown in productivity was most pronounced in the non-industrial sector. As industry accounts for an abnormally high share of GNP (as services were underdeveloped), the negative contribution of the non-industrial sector is strikingly high. As suggested by Easterly and Fischer (1994), agriculture was the main culprit with a negative rate of productivity growth of 4 per cent p.a. during 1970–90.

Weitzman (1970, 1983) questions the validity of a Cobb–Douglas approximation and claims that the assumption of a unit elasticity of substitution is untenable in the Soviet context. He concludes that a CES production function with an elasticity of 0.4 fits the data better than the Cobb–Douglas production function.

Easterly and Fischer (1994) estimate a CES production function and recalculate TFP growth rates for 1950–87 (assuming Hicks-neutral technical progress). They find elasticities of substitution as low as 0.13 for the industrial sector and 0.4 for GNP on Western data for the period 1950–87. For the entire data range 1928–87, elasticities of substitution are higher but not statistically significant, so that we neglect these results and focus on those for 1950–87.

The rate of substitution in Table 3.8 is much lower than those estimated for Western

TABLE 3.7 Total factor productivity growth rates, alternative series, USSR

Period	Western estimates industrial sector	Official industrial sector	Western estimates GNP
1928–40	1.7	7.2	−1.2
1940–50	−1.1	1.7	−0.2
1950–60	6.1	4.1	1.3
1960–70	1.9	3.4	−0.1
1970–80	2.4	1.7	−0.8
1980–87	−0.1	1.1	−1.2

Source: Easterly and Fischer (1994).

TABLE 3.8 Elasticities of substitution and TFP growth with estimated CES functions

	Western estimates industrial sector	Official industrial sector	Western GNP
For 1950–87 sample:			
Elasticity of substitution	0.13*	0.40*	0.37*
TFP growth in:			
1950–59	2.40%*	3.72%*	1.09%*
1960–69	2.36%*	3.60%*	1.10%*
1970–79	2.51%*	3.74-%*	1.16%*
1980–87	2.43%*	3.62%*	1.09%*
For entire sample period, 1928–87:			
Elasticity of substitution	0.22	0.45*	0.81
TFP growth in:			
1928–39	−1.38%	0.72%	−0.52%
1940–49	−0.72%	0.51%	−1.32%*
1950–59	0.36%	1.48%*	−0.21%
1960–69	0.40%	1.27%	−0.15%
1970–79	0.43%	1.38%	−0.18%
1980–87	0.37%	1.328%	−0.33%

Source: Easterly and Fischer (1994)
* indicates elasticity of substitution significantly different from one or TFP growth rates significantly different from zero.

countries and even lower than those obtained for developing countries. This implies that extensive growth resulted in abnormally high diminishing returns to capital.

As can also be seen from Table 3.8, the CES approach implies that TFP growth remained fairly constant at around 2.5 per cent for industry and 1 per cent for GNP on Western data. There are therefore two possible ways of interpreting the Soviet growth slowdown. One, supported by the Cobb-Douglas approach, is declining marginal returns to capital due to extensive growth combined with declining productivity growth. A second and statistically more appealing explanation, based on a CES approach, puts all the weight on extensive growth with very sharply decreasing returns to capital.

This, of course, makes one ask: why was extensive growth not corrected and why was the elasticity of substitution so abnormally low?

The answer to the first question is much more straightforward than the answer to the second. The traditional mechanism of a market economy where investments need to generate a return superior to the cost of capital did not operate in the Soviet Union. The problem was the absence of a proper pricing mechanism.

The answer to the second question is more of a conjecture. Under the planning system additional equipment did not displace workers. Employment in productive units has been relatively stable so that more capital generated more under-employment but not less unemployment. Furthermore, the optimal mix of factors of production in terms of skill requirements and support services was rarely achieved. Planning consisted above all in adding more equipment, not in restructuring the optimal mix.

4. Failures and achievements

We shall start this section on the positive side, as the regime also produced some positive achievements. The Soviets' overriding priority, as in other developing countries, was growth, but propelled by the need to demonstrate the superiority of the communist regime. Western revisions of the official Soviet growth records demonstrate that the official data vastly exaggerate the growth rate. Nevertheless, growth during the 1950s was remarkable and during the 1930s and 1960s respectable. The 1920s record can be pardoned by the turmoils of the civil war and the groping for a model to organise the economy. Similarly the 1940s suffered from World War II. The ultimate failure of the system was, however, the dramatic slowdown of growth during the 1970s and 1980s. The reasons are reviewed below.

The system was able to generate full employment rapidly and maintain it over time. This is still perceived today by the citizens of the FSU as a success. The price for this 'success' was, of course, quite high: under-employment and a very low growth of consumption. The share of consumption (in current prices) declined from 73 per cent in 1928 to 64 per cent in 1950 and 55 per cent in 1980 (Ofer 1987). Consumption here includes household consumption and communal services, such as education and health. The share of consumption in the Soviet Union was therefore below levels in the West by at least 10 percentage points.

Another (partial) success was income distribution, not as egalitarian as claimed by communist ideology but still less skewed than in market economies. Box 3.2 provides details.

Box 3.2 Income distribution in the Soviet Union

Incomes in the USSR were radically equalised in the earliest post-Revolutionary years, but have become progressively more unequal ever since. There have been three cycles of contraction and expansion of inequality. The initial one occupied essentially the first decade after the Revolution, thus embracing first the years of War communism and then those of the NEP. The second cycle occurs during the

continued

Box 3.2 *continued*

first two decades of five-year plans and war under Stalin. Having become extraordinarily marked by the early post-Second World War years, inequality in pay had again tended to decline afterwards.

In the USSR, the period 1932–33 was one of extensive famine, which affected especially the rural population. It is not clear how, if at all, the millions of so-called kulaks and their families, who were being deported from the countryside at the time, are treated in data such as shown in Table A. Farm income per capita was still well below that of the non-farming population at the time of Stalin's death, but has risen markedly in relation to the latter since then.

Calculations in Bergson (1984) indicate that inequality of wages in 1928 tended to be less than that in the United States in 1904, though not as markedly so as between the USSR in 1928 and Russia in 1914.

TABLE A: Urban and rural food consumption per capita USSR, 1928 and 1932 (kilograms)

Item	Urban		Rural	
	1928	1932	1928	1932
Bread, grains	174.4	211.3	250.4	214.6
Potatoes	87.6	110.0	141.1	125.0
Meat and lard	51.7	16.9	24.8	11.2
Butter	2.97	1.75	1.55	0.7

Source: Nove (1969, p. 177)

Under Stalin income inequality increased to reach its pinnacle in 1946. A decade later, however, it had markedly decreased. The decline continued until around 1968. At that time inequality measures were comparable to those of the most egalitarian income distributions in capitalist countries such as Sweden. More recently there has been something of a reversal, though the inequality still does not compare with that of 1956, let alone that of 1946.

In contrast to the Western experience, high incomes did not appear to be perpetuated on any scale through inheritance in the USSR, though the inter-generational transmission of such wealth as was privately owned was permitted. Children of elite personnel and of better-placed individuals generally, however, were inordinately represented in admission to higher educational institutions. They also appear to have been over-represented in posts such as their parents occupied.

There is considerable difference in average earnings between the Soviet republics and there is no clear evidence that this has become less over time. In the late 1980s there was, in fact, a sharp widening of the gap with Russia.

In the official Soviet view, Soviet society was destined to become fully egalitarian. That followed at once from Marx's famous scheme of post-Revolutionary

continued

Box 3.2 *continued*

social evolution. Thus the USSR was admittedly still in Marx's egalitarian 'lower' stage but was seen as bound to advance in time to his egalitarian 'higher' one. Confronted by the Soviet experience, one imagines, Marx himself might have been surprised at how protracted the lower stage was proving to be, and disconcerted by currents manifestly at odds with attainment of the higher one.

The results for the USSR cannot be taken as applying equally to all socialist economies. There is considerable variety across countries (and across time, as already seen for the Soviet Union). Czechoslovakia had the lowest degree of earnings dispersion, followed by Hungary and then Poland. Table B summarises the statistical information in the form of Gini coefficients and percentiles.

TABLE B: Earnings distribution in 1986–87 All full-time workers (male and female)

	Gini	P_{10}	P_{25}	P_{75}	P_{90}	P_{95}	P_{90}/P_{10}
Czechoslovakia 1987	19.7	63.2	78.3	125.8	154.6	173.4	2.45
Hungary 1986	22.1	62.0	77.9	128.7	163.9	192.5	2.64
Poland 1986	24.2	60.9	77.6	129.3	169.1	206.5	2.77
USSR 1986	27.6	55.7	72.1	136.4	182.8	–	3.28
Great Britain 1986	26.7	55.7	72.9	135.3	179.7	217.3	3.23

Note: P_{10} denotes the earnings of the bottom decile relative to the median, expressed as a percentage. P_{90}/P_{10} is the decile ratio.

The Gini coefficient is half the expected absolute difference in incomes, relative to the mean, between any two persons drawn at random from the population. A Gini coefficient of 30 per cent, for example, implies that the difference, on average, between the incomes of two persons is equal to 60 per cent of the population's mean income.

A graphical interpretation can be given using the Lorenz curve. The Lorenz curve is constructed by imagining everyone lining up in order of their income and then calculating their share of total income.

If all incomes were equal, the Lorenz curve would follow the diagonal. A measure of inequality is therefore the surface between the diagonal and the Lorenz curve. The Gini coefficient is equal to the ratio of this surface to the area of the triangle OAB.

GDP per capita is a standard measure of welfare which neglects, however, income distribution. One way of taking into account the desirability of a more egalitarian income distribution is to compute per capita income times (1-Gini).

continued

Box 3.2 *continued*

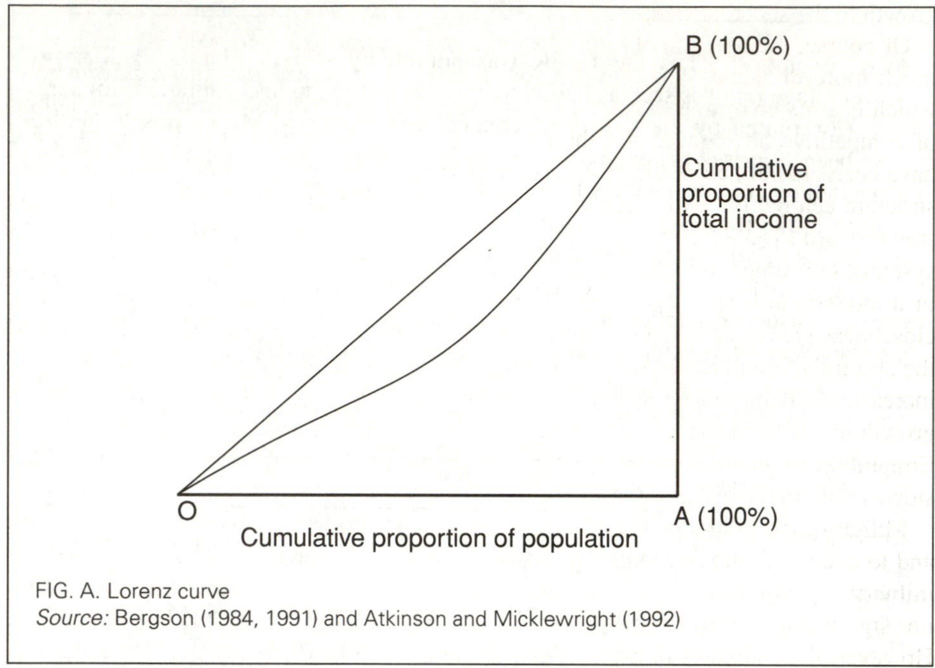

FIG. A. Lorenz curve
Source: Bergson (1984, 1991) and Atkinson and Micklewright (1992)

We now turn to the slowdown of growth during the 1970s and 1980s. Some insights can be gained from an international comparison, as certain factors (world demand, extensive growth) affected other countries as well. Easterly and Fischer (1994) use the Western data from Table 3.6 and World Bank data on per capita growth for 102 countries. Over 1960–89 Soviet per capita growth was, in fact, slightly above the global average, but well below the upper range performers.

Given the strong accumulation of productive factors (capital, labour) in the Soviet Union, it is desirable to control for these factors to derive information about the efficiency of the growth process. Running a regression of per capita growth on the standard growth determinants (initial income, population growth, schooling and the investment to GDP ratio), Easterly and Fischer show that the growth performance, once one takes these factors into account, was dismal. Secondary education and the investment ratio are near the top of the sample distribution. Had the Soviet economy operated like the average of the sample, it would have had one of the highest growth rates. Or, in other words, Soviet per capita income in 1989 was only half of what it would have been if it had performed according to the sample average during 1960–89. As it turned out, 'the Soviet economic performance conditional on investment and human capital accumulation was the worst in the world over 1960–89' (Easterly and Fischer 1994).

What then are the reasons for the slowdown of growth during the 1970s and 1980s? There is no single explanation although it all boils down to the regime's objectives (autarky, military superiority, restrictions on individual freedom) and institutions (planning, social ownership), as examined in Chapter 2.

Worldwide growth declined during 1970–90, but less than growth in the Soviet Union. As the Soviet Union remained virtually closed and benefited rather than suffered from the oil price increases, there is no negative feedback of slower world growth to the socialist camp.

Of course, the absence of wide-ranging foreign trade had other effects which were much more dramatic. The transmission of technological and managerial know-how, which is a major source of gains from international trade, in addition to the signalling of competitive advantages and the real value of resources was cut off. This may not have been crucial before the 1970s as the Soviet Union built up a traditional economic structure centred on heavy industry. But it became a crucial shortcoming for the next step forward to an advanced economy. Human skills, market knowledge, distributional systems, consumer satisfaction, rapid change, development of services are all features of a modern, advanced economy for which the Soviet Union was not geared up and closedness prevented it from importing 'ideas'. See Box 2.1 in Chapter 2. Because of the system's failure to respond positively to these challenges the labour force became increasingly demotivated so that the country suffered both from a slowdown in the growth of the labour force for demographic reasons and a lower average performance. Emigration of the most highly trained ethnic group, the Jewish population, and of dissidents only made matters worse.

Military expenditure increased in a vain attempt to stay at par with the United States and to cope with the Afghanistan adventure. Some economists have used the share of military expenditure in GDP as an explanatory variable in growth regressions and find no significant contribution to slower growth (see Easterly and Fischer 1994). However, the estimates of Soviet defence expenditure do not usually include the real cost of the military-industrial complex whose cost, as argued in Section 3.1, is closer to 25–30 per cent of GDP than to the 15 per cent usually advanced. The argument that sustained military efforts have contributed significantly to the growth slowdown can therefore not be put aside, although quantification still needs to be made.

The major explanation for the slowdown in growth was extensive growth, as shown in the previous section, with a dramatic decline in returns to capital and, more controversially, a slowdown in total factor productivity. They, in turn, are the consequences of the planning system, the absence of a price regulator and the closedness of the economy.

5. Conclusions

The superiority of socialism under the guidance of the USSR had been proclaimed by the Soviet leadership ever since the victory at Stalingrad. We have highlighted the contradictions and failures of the system. What, then, are the real or perceived successes of the Soviet Union?

An empire that matched Europe's mightiest fell to pieces in 1917. What was subsequently reconstructed by the Soviets became one of the two largest military powers the world has known, equipped with an ideology which gave hope to the Third World. Its technological exploits were remarkable though limited to specific goals mainly in areas related to the military. Economically, its track record is less impressive yet not without its successes. Unemployment (unlike under-employment) became a thing of the past, and citizens' basic educational and economic needs were satisfied. Income distribution was less uneven than in capitalist countries, although reality fell significantly short of Marxist goals. But still, it is nevertheless hardly surprising that there are many today who regret the mediocre but stable conditions of Soviet times.

After World War II, socialism benefited from its participation in the victory over Nazi Germany and its elevation to world power rank. While this undoubtedly bought Soviet citizens self-confidence and demonstrated the Soviet Union's potential capacity to become a world leader, it was the beginning of the end. The country's one besetting constraint had always been a lack of skilled labour. After World War II, a power base expanded within the Soviet State that absorbed the best and the brightest: the military-industrial complex.[16] This complex achieved world-class performance, catching up with US nuclear domination and at times even taking the lead in space technology. But while the US could afford such costly aspirations, the USSR could not. The best scientists, engineers, managers and the best machines and raw materials were poured into the military-industrial complex. Between 20 and 30 per cent of GDP was funnelled into that sector, and the rest of the economy had to be content with the leavings.

Lack of competition inside the economy, protection from foreign trade and limited access to Western high technology increasingly hindered growth as technological development accelerated and the international division of labour in the West deepened. The effectiveness of investment gradually declined, and white elephants became the most prolific Soviet species. Making the right investment choices becomes more essential in a mature economy than in a closed, under-developed economy. Therefore, the same procedures that had worked reasonably well during the initial stages of development grew increasingly inadequate. In particular the cut-off from the trade in 'ideas', which did not hold back the post-war reconstruction effort, stifled the economy increasingly and aborted its attempt at promotion into the class of 'modern' economics. Extensive growth resulted in dramatically diminished returns to capital during the 1970s and the 1980s, a process that could not be stopped as planning ignored such signals and there was no pricing system for the allocation of capital.

The overall growth rates of output were respectable since they were usually above those of the developed market economies. However, they were achieved at a very high price in terms of consumption that had to be sacrificed. The output statistics (which suggested that the former Soviet Union had slightly narrowed the distance to the US) turned out to be misleading once the borders were opened. The verdict of consumers and the markets showed that Soviet output was worth much less than was assumed in the statistics. In the 1980s it was estimated that Soviet income per capita was about 50 per cent of that of the US. When the markets were allowed to value the output of Russia (one of the better parts of the FSU) the result was that income per capita turned out to be about 10 per cent of the US level, about the same level as Turkey. In this perspective it becomes understandable why, by the end of the 1980s when the growth potential of socialist economies was exhausted, citizens despaired because they could only look back in anger, received no comfort in the present and saw no promise in the system's future.

Mephistopheles's reply to Faust's request for progress reports on his glorious environmental project: ('mit jedem Tage will ich Nachricht haben, wie sich verlängt der unternommene Graben') could have been written for this chapter:

> 'Man spricht, wie man mir Nachricht gab,
> von keinem Graben, doch vom Grab.'

Notes

1. Berliner (1966) quotes an earlier call by Stalin from 1931: 'We are fifty or a hundred years behind the advanced countries. We must make good the distance in ten years. Either we do it or they crush us.'
2. This hope and naivety persisted until the Brezhnev years, despite mounting evidence that things just were not working out that way. Here is an example of the kind of utopian visions still marketable in the socialist countries in the 1950s and 1960s: 'Our table will be covered with the best nature can offer: prime meat and milk products, the best of the orchard, strawberries and tomatoes at a time when they are not yet ripening on our fields, grapes in winter and not only when in abundance in autumn. As socialists we know perfectly well that in the socialist camp an excess of food products will be available by 1965. . . . To imagine that future abundance in the retail outlets, mighty and ever-growing waves of food and specialities from the four corners of the earth, of clothes and shoes of marvellous new materials, of kitchen appliances and working machines, cars big and small, handicrafts and jewellery, cameras and sports equipment . . .' Walter Ulbricht, *Unsere Welt von Morgen*, Berlin: Verlag Neues Leben, 1961 (author's translation). To forecast in 1961 for 1965 such a paradise, which in fact is more a description of conditions in the developed capitalist world in the 1990s, is quite incomprehensible after 40 years of unsuccessful attempts in the Soviet Union.
3. Another use of the term 'forced savings' refers to the lack of goods available for expenditure so that agents are 'forced to save'. This concept is examined in Chapter 5.
4. Estimates by Brada and Graves (1988) and Steinberg (1987) range from 12 to 16 per cent of GNP. But as we now know, GNP was vastly over-estimated at more than 50 per cent of US GNP and therefore the share of defence was under-estimated. These studies neglect, moreover, the resource cost of the military-industrial complex, absorbing the best brains and material resources for which no correct opportunity cost is imputed. Connected areas of nuclear and space technology are also not fully accounted for in these studies. If the strength of the Soviet army was comparable to the United States, then the 5 per cent defence budget of the US, which enjoys a GDP at least 5 times that of the USSR, must translate into a share of Soviet defence in GDP of at least 30 per cent.
5. 'The system stressed production for production's sake. Whether the goods were actually used by a purchaser was immaterial. Presumably someone would find a use for them sooner or later. Since everything always seemed to be in short supply, it was usually sooner. Therefore, the system put a premium on good production engineers who knew how to prevent production breakdown, issue a steady flow of supplies and maximise the production process. Those who excelled at quality control or sales served no purpose and thus, more often than not, were flushed out of the system. Inevitably, economic growth became the chief gospel of the Soviet Union, and Gosplan became its chief prophet' (Goldman 1983: 32).
6. According to Judy and Clough (1989) about 25 per cent of the projects completed during the first part of the 1980s had been on the drawing-board 10 to 20 years earlier. Projects take up to 5 times as long to complete as in Western economies. These delays became longer over time.
7. Marxist theory insisted on the distinction between 'productive' and 'non-productive' activities, with the latter comprising most services. As a result, services receive very low ranking in the scale of investment priorities. It is of course true that many services can manage without major investment outlay, but as independent businesses (hairdressers, restaurants, bars, street peddlars, repair shops, etc.) are not built up in socialist economies, such services remain under-developed. Other services such as financial intermediation are altogether unavailable, partly for ideological reasons. Finally, some of the more

investment-intensive services such as housing, tourism, health and education, remain seriously under-developed because they are firmly stuck at the lower end of the scale of priorities. See Aganbegian (1989)

8. This distinction is close, but not identical, to that between class-one and class-two production in socialist parlance. Class-one produces means of production, that is, investment goods plus raw and semi-finished materials.
9. In the 1920s, during the NEP, there was extensive discussion among party members about the optimal growth strategy. Stalin was certainly much influenced by Preobrazhenskii who adopted Marx's theory of primitive capitalist accumulation to the socialist context (this is another illustration of our general point that Marxist political theory of capitalism found application in socialist economies). To realise a 'big push', consumption must be cut back to free resources for investment (forced savings). The prices for agricultural products must be lowered and those of industrial products raised, as explained in Box 1.3 of Chapter 1. Agriculture needs to be collectivised to free labour for industrial expansion. Investment is thus concentrated on industry and, as consumption is set back, on heavy industry. Ironically, Preobrazhenskii and many of his disciples fell prey to Stalin's furore, who then applied their ideas with a brutality not foreseen by his intellectual forebears.
10. Statistika, Moscow (1977) p. 436 as quoted by Kornai (1992: 173).
11. We shall see below that even the revised estimates of Table 3.2 are on the high side. In fact, the Soviet Union had only one period of rapid growth, namely, during the 1950s.
12. Extensive growth is defined by Ofer (1987) more restrictively as a rising capital–output ratio and is used in this sense in the rest of this chapter.
13. The coefficients of the primary factor of production in equation (2) of Box 3.1 are the distributive shares in output. The coefficient of labour is, on average, about three times as large as the coefficient of capital.
14. In Western terminology, the real problem was wrong prices, in particular of the rate of interest. A standard result of non-renewable natural resources theory is that in equilibrium the price must increase by the rate of interest. That is, it pays to sell a resource now if the future price increases at a rate below the rate of interest. By contrast, if the price of the resource increases at a rate above the rate of interest, then the resource should be left in the ground. In equilibrium, the increase in the price of the resource needs to equal the rate of interest.
15. In Soviet national accounting there were no capital charges other than depreciation and rents on land and natural resources were introduced only after 1966, and then only half-heartedly.
16. Before World War II, defence made large claims on heavy equipment but not on the country's best scientists, engineers and managers. Increasing technological sophistication shifted requirements over time to absorb an increasing share of human capital.

References to Part I

Aganbegian, A.G. (1989) *Inside Perestroïka*, Harper and Row, New York.

Amalrik, A. (1970) *Will the Soviet Union Survive until 1984?*, Harper and Row, New York.

Arendt, H. (1951) *The Origins of Totalitarianism*, Harcourt Brace Jovanovich, New York.

Atkinson, A.B. and **Micklewright, J.** (1992) *Economic Transformation in Eastern Europe and the Distribution of Income*, Cambridge University Press, Cambridge.

Baland, J-M. (1993) The Economics of Price-Scissors: a Defence of Preobrazhensky, *European Economic Review*, January.

Barro, R.J. (1989) *A Cross-country study of growth, saving and government,* NBER Working Paper No 2855, National Bureau of Economic Research, Cambridge, Massachusetts.

Barro, R.J. (1990) *Public finance in models of economic growth*, in J. Bhagwati et al. (eds.) *Trade, Balance of Payments, and Growth,* Papers in Honour of Charles P. Kindleberger, North Holland, Amsterdam.

Bateman, D.A. and **Mody, A.** (1991) *Growth in an Inefficient Economy: a Chinese Case Study*, World Bank, Washington, D.C.

Bergson, A. (1961) *The Real National Income of Soviet Russia Since 1928*, Harvard University Press, Cambridge, Massachusetts.

Bergson, A. (1984) Income inequality under Soviet socialism, *Journal of Economic Literature*, September.

Bergson, A. (1991) The USSR before the fall: how poor and why?, *Economic Perspectives*, Fall

Berliner, J.S. (1966) The economics of overtaking and surpassing, in H. Rosovsky (ed.) *Industrialisation in Two Systems: Essays in Honor of Alexander Gerschenkron*, Wiley, New York.

Bernstein, E. (1899) *Die Voraussetzungen des Sozialismus und die Aufgaben der Sozialdemokratie*, J.H.W. Dietz, Stuttgart.

Bettelheim, C. (1968) *La transition vers l'économie socialiste*, F. Masper, Paris.

Brada, J.C. and **Graves, R.L.** (1988), Slowdown in Soviet defence expenditures, *Southern Economic Journal*, **54**, pp. 969–84.

Bukharin, N.I. (1926) *Der Imperialismus und die Akkumulation des Kapitals*, Verlag für Literatur und Politik, Vienna and Berlin

Bukovski, V. (1990) *USSR: de l'utopie au désastre*, Robert Laffont, Paris.

Carrère d'Encausse, H. (1991) *La gloire des nations ou la fin de l'Empire soviétique*, Fayard, Paris.

CIA (1982) *USSR: Measures of Economic Growth and Development*, US Government Printing Office, Washington D.C.

CIA (various years) *Handbook of Economic Statistics*, US Government Printing Office, Washington D.C.

Collins, S.M. and **Rodrick, D.** (1991) *Eastern Europe and the Soviet Union in the World Economy*, Institute for International Economics, Washington D.C.

Commission of the European Communities (1990) *Stabilisation, Liberalisation and Devolution: Assessment of the Economic Situation and Reform Process in the Soviet Union*, European Economy no 45, Brussels.

Denison, E.F. (1962) *The Sources of Economic Growth in the United States and the Alternatives Before Us*, Committee for Economic Development, New York.

Desai, P. (1986) *The Soviet Economy: Efficiency, Technical Change and Growth Retardation*, Blackwell, Oxford.

Dobb, M.H. (1939) *Political Economy and Capitalism*, International Publishers, New York.

Dobb, M.H. (1966) *Soviet Economic Development since 1917*, Routledge and Kegan Paul, London.

Easterly, W. (1993) How much do distortions affect growth?, *Journal of Monetary Economics*, November.

Easterly, W. and **Fischer, S.** (1994) The Soviet economic decline: historical and republican data, NBER Working Paper no.4735, National Bureau of Economic Research, Cambridge, Massachusetts.

Ellmann, M.J. (1975) Did the agricultural surplus provide the resources for the increase in investment in the USSR during the first Five Year Plan?, *Economic Journal*, **85**.

Ellmann, M.J. (1987) *Collectivisation and Soviet Investment in 1928-32 Revisited*, Working Papers, University of Amsterdam.

Emerson, M. *et al.* (1988) *The Economics of 1992*, European Economy, no 35, Brussels.

Engels, F. [1878] (1975) Anti-Dühring, in K. Marx and F. Engels, *Collected Works*, Vol. 25, International Publishers, New York, pp. 5–309.

Feshbach, M. and **Friendly, A.** (1992) *Ecocide in the USSR*, Basic Books, New York.

Garetovskii, N.V. (1989) Voprosy sovershenstvovaniia bankovskoi sistemy (Issues in perfecting the banking system), *Deng'i i Kredit*, **11**, pp. 8–16.

Gerschenkron, A. (1962) *Economic Backwardness in Historical Perspective*, Harvard University Press, Cambridge, Massachusetts.

Gilibert, P-L. and **Steinherr, A.** (1989) *The Impact of Financial Market Integration on the European Banking Industry*, Centre for European Policy Studies, Brussels.

Goldman, M. (1983) *USSR in Crisis. The Failure of an Economic System*, Norton, New York.

Goldman, M. (1991) *What went wrong with Perestroika?*, Norton, New York.

Gomulka, S. (1986) *Growth, Innovation and Reform in Eastern Europe*, University of Wisconsin Press, Madison, Wisconsin.

Gregory, P.R. and **Stuart, R.C.** (1986) *Soviet Economic Structure and Performance*, Harper and Row, New York.

Gregory, P.R. and **Stuart, R.C.** (1989) *Comparative Economic Systems*, 3rd ed., Houghton Mifflin, Boston, Massachusetts.

Griffith, K. and **Gurley, J.** (1985) Radical analyses of imperialism, the Third World and the transition to socialism, *Journal of Economic Literature*, September.

Grossmann, H. (1929) Die Änderung des ursprünglichen Aufbauplans des Marxschen 'Kapital' and ihre Ursachen, *Archiv für die Geschichte des Sozialismus und der Arbeiterbewegung*, **XIV**, (2), pp. 305–8

Hayek, F.A. (ed.) (1935) *Collectivist Economic Planning*, Routledge and Kegan Paul, London.

Hilferding, R. (1923) *Das Finanzkapital*, Wiener Volksbuchhandlung, Vienna.

Hirschman, A.O. (1958) *The Strategy of Economic Development*, Yale University Press, New Haven, Connecticut.

Hirschman, A.O. (1970) *Exit, Voice and Loyalty*, Harvard University Press, Cambridge, Massachusetts.

International Monetary Fund, The World Bank, Organisation for Economic Cooperation and Development and **European Bank for Reconstruction and Development** (1991), *A Study of the Soviet Economy*, Organisation for Economic Cooperation and Development, Paris.

Judy, R. and **Clough, R.** (1989), *Soviet computer software and applications in the 1980s*, Hudson Institute, Working Paper H1-4090-P, Bloomington.

Kautsky, K. (1899, 1901–2) Krisentheorien, *Die Neue Zeit*, **XX**, (2), pp 37–47, 76–81, 110–18, 133–43

Kellogg, R.L. (1989) Inflation in Soviet investment and capital stock data and its impact on measurement of total factor productivity, CIA Office of Soviet Analysis, Washington, DC.

King, R. and **Rebelo, S.** (1990) Public policy and economic growth: developing neo-classical implications, *Journal of Political Economy*, October.

Kornai, J. (1986) The soft budget constraint, *Kyklos*, **39** (1), pp. 3–30.

Kornai, J. (1992) *The Socialist System – The Political Economy of Communism*, Princeton University Press, Princeton, New Jersey.

Lange, O. (1936, 1937) On the economic theory of socialism, *Review of Economic Studies*, October, February, **4** (1,2), pp. 53–71, 123–42.

Lenin, V.I. (1932) *The State and Revolution*, International Publishers, New York.

Lenin, V.I. (1933) *Imperialism*, International Publishers, New York.

Lenin, V.I. ([1918] (1964) Can the Bolsheviks retain state power? in V.I. Lenin, *Collected Works*, Vol. 26, Progress, Moscow; pp. 87–186.

Liberman, E.G. [1962] (1972) The plan, profit and bonuses, in A. Nove and D.M. Nuti (eds.) *Socialist Economics*, Penguin Books, Harmondsworth, pp. 309–18

Lucas, R.E. (1988) On the mechanics of economic development, *Journal of Monetary Economics* **22**(1), pp. 3–42

Luxemburg, R. (1922) *Die Akkumulation des Kapitals. Ein Beitrag zur ökonomischen Erklärung des Imperialismus*, Vereinigung Internationaler Verlags-Anstalten, Berlin.

Maddison, A. (1989) *The World Economy in the 20th Century*, OECD, Paris.

Marx, K. (1905–10) *Theorien über den Mehrwert*, 3 vols., edited by Karl Kautsky, J.H.W. Dietz, Stuttgart.

Marx, K. (1911) *A Contribution to the Critique of Political Economy*, Charles Kerr, Chicago, Illinois.

Marx, K. (1933) *Capital*, 3 vols., Charles Kerr, Chicago, Illinois.

Marx, K. (1966) *Critique of the Gotha Programme*, International Publishers, New York.

Marx, K. and **Engels, F.** (1930) *The Communist Manifesto*, M. Lawrence, London.

Naughton, B. (1992) Implications of the state monopoly over industry and its relaxation, *Modern China*, January.

Nordhaus, W.D. (1990) Soviet economic reform: the longest road, *Brookings Papers on Economic Activity*, no 1, pp. 287–308.

Nove, A. (1969) *An Economic History of the USSR*, Penguin, London.

Nove, A. (1981) A note on growth, investment and price indices, *Soviet Studies*, **23**, (1) pp. 143–145

Nuti, M.D. (1986) Hidden and repressed inflation in Soviet-type economies: definitions, measurements and stabilisation, *Contributions to Political Economy*, **5**, pp. 37–82.

Ofer, G. (1987) Soviet economic growth: 1928–1985, *Journal of Economic Literature* **25**, (4), pp. 1767–1833.

Powell, R.P. (1963) Industrial production in A. Bergson and S. Kuznets, (eds.) *Economic Trends in the Soviet Union*, Harvard University Press, Cambridge Massachusetts.

Powell, R.P. (1968) The Soviet capital stock and related statistical series for the war years, The Economic Growth Centre, Yale University, New Haven, Connecticut.

Ricardo, D. (1887) *Principles of Political Economy and Taxation*, G. Bell and Sons, London.

Romer, P.M. (1986) Increasing returns and long-run growth, *Journal of Political Economy*, **94**, pp. 1002–37.

Romer, P.M. (1987) Growth based on increasing returns due to specialization, *American Economic Review*, **77**(2) pp. 56–62.

Romer, P.M. (1989) What determines the rate of growth of technological change?, Working Paper Series, WPS 279, World Bank, Washington, D.C.

Romer, P.M. (1990) Endogenous technological change, *Journal of Political Economy*, **98**.

Romer, P.M. (1993) Idea gaps and object gaps in economic development, *Journal of Monetary Economics*, December.

Romer, P.M. (1994) New goods, old theory and the welfare costs of trade restrictions, *Journal of Development Economics*.

Rostow, W.W. (1960) *The Stages of Economic Growth*, Cambridge University Press, Cambridge.

Sah, R. and **Stiglitz, J.E.** (1992) *Peasants versus City-dwellers*, Clarendon Press, Oxford.

Sala-I-Martin, X. (1990) Lecture Notes on Economic Growth II, *NBER Working Paper* no.3564.

Schumpeter, J.A. (1968) *The Theory of Economic Development. An Inquiry into Profits, Capital, Credit, Interest and Business Cycles*, Harvard University Press, Cambridge, Massachusetts.

Solow, R. (1956) A contribution to the theory of economic growth, *Quarterly Journal of Economics*, **70** pp. 65–94.

Steinberg, D. (1987) Estimating total Soviet military expenditures: an alternative approach based on reconstructed Soviet national accounts in C.G.Jacobsen (ed.) *The Soviet Defence Enigma:* Estimating Costs and Burdens, Oxford University Press, New York.

Streeten, P. (1959) Unbalanced growth, *Oxford Economic Papers*, new series, June, **11** (2), pp. 167–90.

Sweezy, P.M. (1942) *The Theory of Capitalist Development*, Modern Reader, New York.

Tugan-Baranowsky, M. (1901) *Studien zur Theorie und Geschichte der Handelskrisen in England*, G. Fischer, Jena.

United Nations (1987) *Environment Statistics in Europe and North America. An Experimental Compendium*, United Nations, New York.

United Nations (1990) *Economic Survey of Europe in 1989–1990*, United Nations, New York.

Weitzman, M.L. (1970) Soviet postwar economic growth and capital-labor substitution, *American Economic Review*, **60**, (5) pp. 676–692.

Weitzman, M.L. (1983) Industrial production in A. Bergson and H.S. Levine (eds.) *The Soviet Economy: Toward the Year 2000*, Allen & Unwin, Boston, Massachusetts.

Werth, N. (1990) *Histoire de l'Union Soviétique*, PUF, Paris.

Werth, N. (1993) Goulag, les vrais chiffres, *L'Histoire*, **169**, September.

World Bank (1994) *World Development Report,* World Bank, Washington, D.C.

PART TWO

TRANSITION AND RECONSTRUCTION

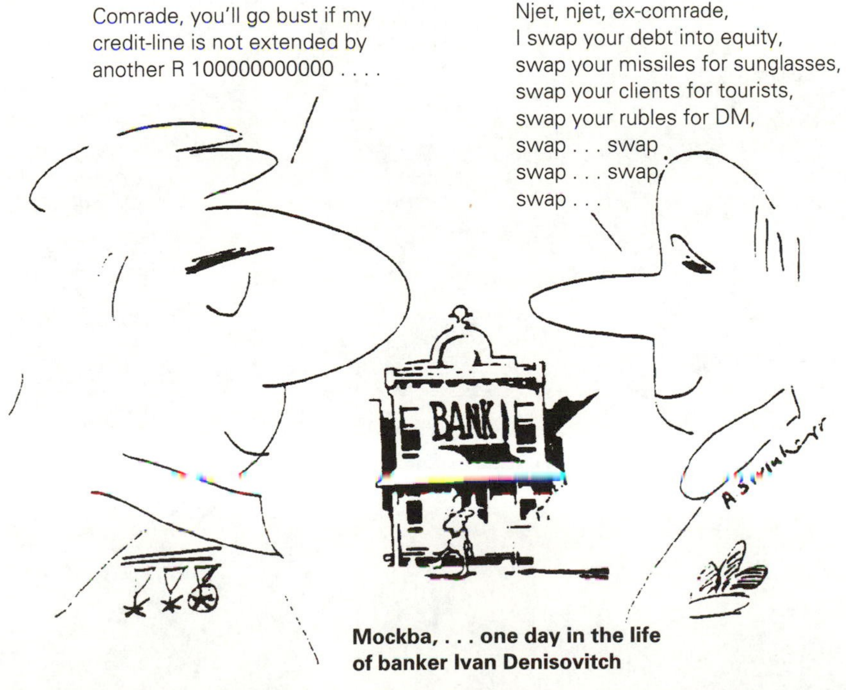

Mockba, . . . one day in the life of banker Ivan Denisovitch

Introduction

The six chapters that follow discuss the difficulties of reforming the former socialist economies with the aim of preparing them for accelerated growth and convergence to Western living standards. Although all reforms are inter-dependent, we have tried to separate them into coherent sub-groups for ease of discussion.

Chapter 4 sets out by assessing the scope and time-frame of reforms and argues in favour of a comprehensive – instead of a fine-tuned sequential – reform programme. Price reforms are discussed in Chapter 5. Chapter 6 makes a plea for opening up the reforming economies (REs) to foreign trade in order to benefit from export-led growth. Chapter 7 investigates the ways to stabilise the macroeconomic situation in REs through appropriate monetary, fiscal and exchange rate policies. Chapter 8 turns to privatisation and Chapter 9 focuses on reform of the financial sector.

A particular difficulty for reforms is presented by the fact that whilst general objectives are clear (to catch up with the economic performance of market economies), there does not exist a definite view yet in these countries on how to achieve them. As *The Economist* (24–30 March 1990, p. 22) puts it: 'Hundreds of books have been written on the transition from capitalism to communism but not the other way. There is no known recipe for unmaking an omelette'.

The scope of the necessary reforms assumes the dimension of revolution and a complete change of regime. To signal clearly and credibly this regime change and ensure its irreversible nature, a complete revision of the constitution, laws and institutions in these countries is required. On that basis, reforms would achieve an altogether different significance, a definite departure from 'the road to serfdom' and an unbinding of the creative forces of Prometheus.

The main elements of the necessary economic reforms identified in these chapters comprise the following.

Price reform

Reform of the price structure is the cornerstone of internal reforms. Ultimately prices will be determined in line with world market prices. If prices, or a large set of prices, for goods of social or national importance remained bureaucratically fixed, then the other elements of economic reform would not make much sense. The bad experiences of Hungary, Poland and Yugoslavia with a neither-plan-nor-market system support this thesis. In order to avoid a damaging burst of inflation, the liberation of controlled prices and removal of producer subsidies has to be complemented by monetary and fiscal discipline, the establishment of a new market-conformable tax system and better incentives for saving, that is, a positive real interest rate, to maintain savings close to current levels of forced savings. To use Kornai's (1986) term, 'soft budget constraints' generate waste and need to be replaced with binding constraints. Capitalism can and does have a human face, but it cannot afford to reward benefits independently of performance or need.

A historic opportunity . . .

In spite of the difficulties to be faced by Eastern European countries in their restructuring effort, there are grounds for optimism. As brilliantly demonstrated by Olson (1982), big leaps can only occur in the aftermath of destruction of an ossified and non-performing system. Indeed, success breeds its own long-term decline through protection of acquired privileges, cartelisation of interest groups and reduced incentives to innovation and risk-taking. Natural disasters, economic depression, revolution and war destroy outlived structures and protect interest groups that would not have yielded otherwise. In history, major dynamic rebirths only occurred after catastrophic destructions.

Like Western Europe after World War II, Eastern European countries now have the historic opportunity to create *ex novo* optimal economic and social institutions and thereby free their latent energies. They have the human capital that distinguishes them from LDCs and makes rapid reconstruction possible. The factor endowment of Eastern European countries is quite similar to that of Western Europe after World War II or to that of some Asian NICs. Moreover, they can avoid policy choices demonstrated as erroneous by experience and leapfrog those Western countries whose oligarchic and inward-looking politico-institutional framework has not had the chance to be dynamited away.

The readiness of Western governments and industry to assist reforms provides potential support never offered in history to this extent. This support is financial, but even more important it provides market access and technology transfer in a wide sense (political, legal, management, financial expertise and production technology through co-operation and joint ventures). This support will be forthcoming all the more forcefully, the more determined the reforms. This is already a major argument for rapid and drastic reforms.

. . . for a 'big-bang' reform

Gradual reforms have the intuitive appeal of not rocking the boat and tackling problems measure for measure in a logical order. Experience shows, however, that such a logical ordering is not possible (or impossible to follow for political reasons) and that, during the transition from one system to another, contradictions develop which may cause performance to deteriorate even further and reinforce conservative forces.

The step-by-step process and the possibility of learning-by-doing, that is, reversing mistaken policies, are often considered as the major advantages of gradualism, but more often than not these advantages are decisive drawbacks. Partial steps introduce new inconsistencies. For example, partial price reforms are likely to distort resource allocation even more seriously, a problem well known in the theory of second-best and in actual experience from Hungary to China. Learning-by-doing is a slow, costly and not necessarily converging process towards the ultimate goal. It increases uncertainty and confuses long-term decisions, spanning a time frame during which institutions and policies are likely to change in an unpredictable way, and thereby consumes credibility. Last, but not least, a gradual transition process brings about the danger that the *nomenklatura* would – sooner or later – regain its powers and produce a Kafkaesque metamorphosis. Any unsuccessful reform may be worse than no reform at all. Therefore a complete reform package, with constitutional rules restricting the government's freedom in monetary matters, is the best insurance and provides an institutional framework which minimises uncertainty for planning the future. However, to carry out a comprehensive reform, broad-based political support is required. If such support is not available then there might be no real choice and all that is achievable will be uneven, gradual measures.

A 'big-bang' approach may have an unpleasant ring about it. It may therefore be necessary to give a definition. The essential feature is comprehensiveness, immediacy and irreversibility. Reforms need to be firmly anchored in new constitutions, laws and institutions. Their elaboration and creation requires time. However to generate a coherent final structure, an overall concept is needed from the start. Such an approach does not exclude putting at times the cart before the horse, such as the introduction of hard budget constraints before enterprises have been privatised. In this respect one can remain Marxist and let the economic infrastructure determine its superstructure response.

Property rights

The supply responses to price reforms and effective control over use of national resources might remain weak unless the restrictions on private property rights of the means of production are relaxed. Property rights are the fundamental defining elements of any organised society. Introduction of private property therefore requires constitutional anchoring. But not only the laws have to be changed to make private ownership economically viable. The practical guarantee of equal treatment of private and state-owned companies is no less important. This implies free access to the labour, capital and goods markets for the private sector.

Privatisation creates the opportunity to develop a well-functioning capital and money market rapidly. Such markets have never existed in centrally planned economies and there is a lack of experienced native specialists. Joint ventures with Western banks and non-banking financial firms would prove particularly helpful for speedy introduction of an efficient banking system, stock markets and modern financial services.

Financial markets

In several Eastern European countries a two-tier banking system is being created and privatisation of banks is being pushed ahead. Reform of banking is a key issue and is to be carried out as early as possible and independently of the chosen reform strategy. When government stops regulating funds, an efficient mechanism must be created to make savings attractive and allocate resources efficiently. Banks are the only economic agents able to assume an efficient allocation of resources and develop adequate financial instruments during the transition period, provided that macroeconomic policies succeed in a coherent framework. Eastern European countries lack experience, technology and market connections and therefore joint ventures, or the direct taking of stakes in Eastern European countries' domestic banks, are the obvious solution. We do not recommend special incentives, such as tax advantages, to foreign or joint ventures. Tax incentives are costly and poor substitutes for fair rules and a stable economic and institutional environment. Because it takes times to develop financial markets, banks have to assume wide-ranging tasks (universal banking).

Currency convertibility

The three main elements of internal liberalisation (price reform, macroeconomic stabilisation and privatisation) have to be complemented by external liberalisation aiming at an outward-looking development approach. A removal of non-tariff barriers, most notably the abolition of export and import quotas and the state monopoly over foreign trade, should help to undermine the domestic monopoly of some state-owned companies and introduce more competition in the internal market. But a uniform *ad valorem* tariff could yield substantial revenues and give some protection (declining over time) to industries that cannot finance the adjustment in the still under-developed financial markets.

The integration of Eastern European countries into the international division of labour according to their comparative advantages also requires a convertible currency, at best full convertibility, but at least for current account transactions. For most Eastern European countries the first step has to be the introduction of a uniform foreign exchange rate. Convertibility in most countries requires drastic devaluations when prices are liberalised and repressed inflation becomes open, as already experienced in most Eastern European countries. The error of Western European countries during the late 1940s, namely the maintenance of over-valued exchange rates, needs to be avoided.

Because flexible exchange rates generate too much instability and exert too little constraint on domestic policies, the exchange rate must be fixed. Convertibility may then remain limited to current account transactions. A price reform in the tradable goods sector would derive from (current account) convertibility. Capital account convertibility needs, however, to be rapidly established in order to facilitate foreign direct investments. To ease opening-up the capital account we see a two-tier exchange market as a second-best policy in those countries where stabilisation is incomplete.

How long will the transformation period be?

Fischer and Gelb (1991) made an assessment of the time that it would take for some reforms to be completed. They estimate that most reforms would take at least a few years but some would take longer. 'Institutional reforms' and 'large scale restructuring and privatisation' would take more than 10 years. The reform of the public finances was not included, but it is unlikely that it can be completed within a decade.

The fact that different sectors will require different times to be successfully transformed implies that the process cannot be a smooth one. On the contrary, it will be a very bumpy one. The staggered completion of institutional changes will create uncertainty. Economic agents will continually face the possibility that each step might not be followed by the next one required. In some cases the option value of waiting will become particularly high.

An important aspect of the transformation process that has not received the attention it deserves is the complementarity or inter-dependence of institutions and skills in a modern economy. The various components – institutions, industries, professional skills – support and feed each other. In planned economies, the planners tried to anticipate and cope with this inter-dependence directly, but, as we now know, they often failed badly. In a market economy the required skills and institutions develop on their own on the basis of competition, with some governmental assistance and, at times, some governmental hindrance.

As the centrally planned economies attempt to reincarnate themselves into market economies they will come to require some of these skills. For example, the restructuring of the commercial banks and of public enterprises, or the introduction of a fully fledged tax on the profits of the enterprises, will require accounting and managerial skills not available in these countries and that cannot become available in sufficient quantities in the short or even in the medium run. This deficiency will inevitably slow down the transformation process and increase the chances of derailments. It will also require that, in order to economise on these skills, the institutions that are created, especially at the beginning, must be the simplest possible. Thus transplanting sophisticated Western institutions to these countries without major adaptations will not do. This particular problem must be kept in mind as we discuss future developments of financial and fiscal institutions.

The staggered introduction of institutions' reforms also implies that at any one time the spotlight of reform will be on a particular social group, be this the workers or the managers of particular enterprises or the managers of commercial banks. As is well known, the most difficult reforms to carry out are often those which increase the general welfare at the immediate cost of particular groups (managers of enterprises, workers in particular industries, etc.). These groups will have a strong interest to organise themselves politically and will try to oppose some of the changes. In a democratic environment they have the freedom to articulate and defend their views. It will take strong and enlightened governments and a great deal of public explanation of the need for reform to keep the process going.

Lessons from Western European reconstruction

Independently of the reform package chosen, Eastern European countries will be confronted with extraordinary adjustment difficulties. Forty years of socialism have created economic and political structures that cannot be amortised with a stroke of the pen. It is also useful to remember that not all non-socialist European countries (e.g.

Greece) have performed significantly better. So, on what does economic success depend in the end? A clue is provided by the fact that since World War II the most successful countries in post-war reconstruction were not those best endowed with capital initially (by history, Marshall Plan or otherwise) but rather those that had the largest initial gap to fill, had a well-trained labour force and had espoused market principles and the competitive challenge of foreign trade early and seriously. This experience suggests that Eastern European reconstruction is not primarily a question of external financial support, although, as argued in Chapter 15, reforms in the FSU would greatly benefit from a new Marshall Plan. Much more important is a drastic reform of the national economy which can only be undertaken with a constitutional reform to establish what Montesquieu defined as '*l'esprit des lois*'. If that is done then Western funds and technology will be attracted to an extent unimaginable and impossible after World War II. Official aid will, of course, be useful, but not quintessential, as argued in Part V.

Another lesson is that Eastern European countries should opt for 'export-led growth'. This implies growth in foreign trade (and not the mercantilist concept of an export surplus). Only if Eastern European countries restructure their economies by specialising within the international division of labour and by importing equipment and consumer goods that make producers efficient and consumers happy, will they be able to narrow the gap. If not they will have to struggle to prevent the gap from becoming increasingly wider as is the case with some non-socialist, non-market oriented countries in Western Europe.

CHAPTER FOUR

Scope and timing of reform

You cannot act in life as with dice that you throw again

(Antiphon, *Fragments,* 8)

After the political revolution of the late 1980s which eliminated 'Soviet' power there was, and still is, strong popular pressure for swift and tangible economic progress. This puts political leaders throughout Central Europe and the former Soviet Union (FSU) in a quandary. It is quite impossible for them to do economic battle on all fronts at once and they are woefully aware that it might be years before basic living conditions change palpably for the better. Their problem, was, and still is, to set priorities and develop a consistent plan for social change and economic development. In other words, they have to decide on the speed and sequencing of reforms. The lively academic and political debate of this issue suggests that an economically compelling sequence of reforms is by no means easy to establish. There is, however, broad consensus on the ultimate objectives and on the inter-dependence between the essential moves on the battleground of reform.

The ultimate goal in all cases is to mould a democratic society propelled by a successful market economy. Some Central European countries, in particular Poland, Hungary, the Czech and Slovak republics, are already quite advanced in this respect, but they are both more ambitious and more concrete. They aim at full reintegration into the political, cultural and economic mainstream of Europe which for them also implies membership of the European Community in the not-too-distant future. Success for them means setting out to catch up with Western Europe.

The countries of the FSU face a much more complex problem: they first have to forge new constitutions, they need to transform or dissolve over-centralised structures and sort out their relations with other successor states and with the outside world from scratch. While the Central European countries need 'only' prepare themselves for a return to the European fold, the FSU has no comparable model or goal to strive for. In a fundamental sense, therefore, the FSU stands alone. The challenge facing it is to minimise the risks of a lapse into dictatorship, economic chaos or internecine war. Economic collapse and receding prospects of restored law and order, full employment and prosperity in the tolerably near future all put the success of reforms in the balance. The goals for these countries need to be defined more modestly. This may be difficult, particularly because the Soviet Union was one of the powers that could have fatally influenced the destiny of the world. To accept a more humble role is not easy and will always be resented by political groups attached to the 'glorious past'. The fate of the Weimar Republic is a serious warning.

After the political 'big bang' in Poland almost all countries opted, at least intellectually, for a comprehensive package of reforms. Not unexpectedly, as the initial results of the efforts were disappointing (high inflation, drop in production, etc.) in a number of countries (Russia, Ukraine, some of the Baltics), in 1992–93 political movements emerged in these countries that called for more gradual reforms. However, the new leaders that emerged in Russia (Chernomyrdim), Ukraine (Kuchma) and Lithuania (Brasauskas) with programmes to slow down the reform pace did in fact continue them. We believe that they did this because they recognised that partial reforms may be worse than no reforms at all. For example, as long as prices are controlled, production will stagnate. But price liberalisation alone, without macroeconomic stabilisation, can lead to hyperinflation; macroeconomic stabilisation, in turn, needs the support of fiscal and financial reform. In the end, everything is linked to everything else: a market economy is an indivisible mechanism that grinds to a halt if any one of the essential elements described below is missing. To slow down the pace of reforms after some controls have been dismantled is like pausing in the middle of a river because it is difficult to cross: making a pause in mid-stream means that one is much more likely to be rushed away in the rapids.

The remaining half of the crossing is, however, at least as difficult. This is the effective implementation of the reforms. The difficulties that arise in the implementation of reforms have often been overlooked. But a reform programme that remains on paper can make things even worse than no reform at all.

The problems that arise in the implementation of reform programmes vary from country to country. They depend on the strength of the administrative machinery inherited by the reformers, the overall political situation and the popular support for reforms. Differences in these factors are in our view more important in explaining the huge differences in the fate of the reforms in Central and Eastern Europe than differences in the intellectual concepts behind the reforms. The Czech Republic and Russia might serve as the two extremes.

In the Czech Republic (and the Czechoslovak state before) the reforms were successful mainly because there existed an efficient and honest administration that did implement the new laws as intended, state managers were effectively controlled by the government prior to privatisation and the newly created fiscal administration was able to produce enough revenues to balance the budget. Moreover, strong support from most political parties and the population at large made the reforms credible in the sense that the perceived risk of reversal or macroeconomic destabilisation was close to zero. Putting the Czech–Slovak issue aside, the political spectrum was, and still is, quite centralised and strong centrifugal tendencies are absent.

Contrast this to Russia: since in the Soviet Union all power came from the party, which was organised mainly at the union level, the Gaidar government of the Russian republic, which was committed to a big bang, could not rely on an effective administrative machinery. Moreover, the first Russian parliament, the 'Supreme Soviet', was dominated by representatives of the old order (army and the military-industrial complex) that were bound to lose from reforms. As a result the decision-making power of the government was neutralised and reforms were not implemented. With the old order in shambles the result was chaos. This explains why during the first year of the reforms, the Russian government could achieve only price liberalisation. Without parliamentary support and any bureaucratic apparatus the government lost control over state-owned enterprises and the new tax system brought in only a fraction of the revenues that were needed. One result was total macroeconomic destabilisation. Another result, (and a further cause of macroeconomic destabilisation) was that state enterprises did not adjust; they just kept producing the old goods with the same techniques while they were financed by cheap credit from the Central Bank. Moreover, there was no widespread popular support for quick structural reforms, partially because of the lack of success of the reforms. There were thus continuing debates about the desirable speed of reform and a reversal of the reform strategy was always possible. In other words the programme was not credible.

To be successful a reform plan must thus take into account political and economic reality. A plan that can be executed successfully in Czechoslovakia is not necessarily a good recipe for Russia.

The real world difficulties in implementation are also the reason why some sequencing of reforms is unavoidable. Some steps need more preparation and take more time to implement than others. Prices and external trade can be liberalised quickly. But privatisation and the creation of a fiscal administration take more time.

Another way to express the same idea is that any reform programme comprises both 'negative' and 'positive' steps, measures to dismantle old and create new structures. Destroying first and creating afterwards produces chaos in the interim. Yet, as creating always takes longer than destroying, some disorder is unavoidable in the transition. What amount of chaos is created by destroying first, and what amount of chaos can be tolerated, varies from country to country.

The discussion has so far been abstract because the main elements of reform have not yet been analysed. It will therefore be useful to discuss first what steps need to be taken and only then return to the question of how they should be taken, that is, to what extent it is possible and advisable to reform step by step. We therefore return to this issue in Sections 5 to 7 at the end of this chapter. Sections 1 to 4 discuss the individual components of reforms.

As mentioned in the introduction to Part II the main elements of economic reforms are: (1) price reform or rather price liberalisation (Section 1); (2) external liberalisation (Section 2); (3) privatisation and extensive creation of property rights (Section 3); and (4) macroeconomic stabilisation (Section 4). Before arguing for a comprehensive approach to reform we now briefly discuss each of these elements in turn. The main point we wish to make here is that all these elements are intimately linked and that reformers have a unique historic opportunity for Schumpeterian 'creative destruction'.

1. Price liberalisation

Reform of the price structure is the cornerstone of internal reforms. Prices must be determined by 'scarcity', that is, by the market. If prices, or a large set of prices, for goods of social or national importance remain bureaucratically fixed, then the other elements of economic reform do not make much sense. The bad experiences of socialist Hungary, Poland and Yugoslavia which had a 'neither-plan-nor-market' system at different points in time support this thesis.

Technically, price liberalisation is easy to implement: the government just announces that henceforth all households, enterprises and so forth can set their own price. The real difficulty is political, as inevitably price liberalisation entails income redistribution.

Price liberalisation must also be accompanied by the freedom to trade, that is, people have to be able to buy low and sell high. Freedom for commerce is essential to ensure that the goods that are produced reach those consumers that have the best use for it. In the very first phase of the transition this is the only efficiency gain that is available because even under the most favourable circumstances enterprises need time (months, if not years) to produce different products and to become more efficient.

In order to avoid a damaging burst of inflation, the liberation of controlled prices and removal of producer subsidies have to be complemented by monetary and fiscal discipline, and the establishment of a new market-conformable tax system. We discuss this issue separately in Chapter 7.

It should perhaps be pointed out here that price reform per se cannot be a cause of inflation. If subsidies and production taxes are eliminated simultaneously, this should not affect the overall price level. Some prices would go up (foodstuffs, rents), while others would go down (many tradable industrial goods). What happened in the ex-GDR (this is discussed in Chapter 10) is a case in point: only months after the Deutschmark was introduced in July 1991 (a move accompanied by a comprehensive price reform), the overall price level had already dropped from the previous year's level. But, price reform can transform repressed inflation into open inflation if there is a monetary overhang, as discussed in Chapter 7.

Price liberalisation (coupled with freedom for commerce) is initially often difficult to sustain politically. As the old distribution system breaks down, a few well-connected individuals will become rich very quickly because they know where the scarce goods can still be obtained at low prices. Over time a new market-based distribution system will evolve and profits in that sector will stabilise at the normal rate. But in the beginning very high profits from this apparently unproductive activity might cause popular resentment.

2. External liberalisation

For tradable goods price liberalisation means world market prices. This is again easy to achieve in theory: all that is needed is to liberalise foreign trade completely. A stroke of the pen could just eliminate all restrictions to export and import. However, in reality the solution is not that easy, neither economically nor politically. While economists generally agree that all quantitative restrictions should be eliminated immediately there are respectable arguments for retaining or instituting some tariffs.

One argument is that tariffs can yield substantial revenues for the government. A simple calculation can show that this can be an important source for a government that has to create a new fiscal system from scratch and will thus have only a very uncertain revenue base at the beginning of the reform process.

Another argument for retaining some tariffs comes from 'second best' considerations. It could be argued that some of the state owned industries need temporary protection to prevent them from failing all at the same time because the capital market is too under-developed to finance temporary losses of firms that are potentially viable in the long run. How much protection is needed according to this argument depends obviously on the level of the real exchange rate. A very depreciated real exchange rate reduces the need for tariff protection and *vice versa*. Trade policy during the transformation should thus be discussed together with the exchange rate regime.

Another reason why the exchange rate regime needs to be discussed together with trade policy is that external liberalisation is not meaningful unless the domestic currency becomes convertible at least for trade transactions.

We return to these issues in more detail in Chapter 6. At this point we just wish to point out that trade policy is one of the main elements of the overall reform package.

3. Property rights and financial markets

Price liberalisation can only stimulate the production (as opposed to the distribution) of scarce goods by the private sector if individuals and enterprises can engage in this activity and own factors of production. In Germany this is called *Gewerbefreiheit*, that is, the right for anybody to engage in any economic activity. This freedom is thus another indispensable ingredient of any transformation programme. *Gewerbefreiheit* can also be achieved at the stroke of a pen. To be effective, however, it must be accompanied by private ownership of factors of production. The supply responses to price reforms will thus remain weak unless the restrictions on private property rights of the means of production are eliminated.

But private ownership is no more than a starting point. What counts are the rights and obligations attached to ownership and how stable they are expected to be. Property rights are the fundamental defining elements of any organised society. See Box 4.1.

In agriculture the main factor is land. The possibility of owning land is taken for granted in the West and in Central Europe. To re-establish the unlimited freedom to own, sell and buy land did not represent any problem in this part of the world. However, in Russia and some other CIS states with a different tradition this issue has not yet been settled.

In industry the main factor is physical capital (human capital has always been privately owned although the attached property rights, i.e. the freedom to choose a profession or employment, were severely limited under communism). Private ownership of factors of production and the possibility of hiring labour are thus essential ingredients of a market economy.

Box 4.1 Property rights

Property rights are most developed in market economies but private ownership is neither a necessary nor a sufficient condition for well-developed property rights. It is not necessary because control is more important (being in control of a strip of forest in Northern Siberia is considerably more important than having an

continued

Box 4.1 *continued*

ownership claim). Nor is it sufficient: private ownership in an area controlled by the Mafia or, for example, by bureaucracy such as the one in India before the 1990 reforms prevent its usefulness. Property rights concern ownership, legal duties and rights associated with it, proof of ownership and duration of ownership. Property rights may be challenged by force (burglar or foreign army), by the state (requisitioning or taxes), by time (patent protection, natural decay, lease expiration), by social evolution (rising wages or rights for labour participation may reduce the value and control of capital), or by conflicting property rights (the right to a clean environment diminishes the value of a polluting plant). The clearer property rights are defined, the less conflict a society faces and the more stable the political structure, the more valuable are property rights. Property rights are essential for economic development and many historians and economists today reinterpret the causes of the take-off of the British economy in the eighteenth century much more in terms of innovations in property rights that originated in the Netherlands than in terms of the technological revolution which was facilitated by the property rights innovation.

What have property rights got to do with growth?

First, property rights tend to diminish transaction costs in production, storage, transportation and sales. Banditry in any form discourages economic activity or makes it more expensive through purchase of security devices and forces. Today, in Russia or Southern Italy, such costs are potentially very high.

Second, lack of durable property rights discourages long-term investment. Russian farmers or Western oil prospectors are unlikely to invest long term, not knowing how rights to land-ownership will evolve or which authorities can durably grant a natural resource exploitation right, under what kind of fiscal obligations.

Third, for investors to pool resources by investing in a public company, the residual rights of the shareholders must be clear and the limits of the rights of other parties (state, labourer) must be legally binding or politically calculable. For the lack of such conditions public companies have not been successful even in pre-communist Russia or China.

Fourth, there is no incentive for innovation if there is no protection of property rights of innovations (patents and copyrights).

Fifth, trade and finance can only develop efficiently if there are solid property rights. In the absence of such rights one may still produce, say, gold, hide it, transport it and trade it when an opportunity arises, all at a very high cost. But to trade on the basis of book entries, to hedge the price risk on the future market or to sell short requires crystal-clear and highly elaborated property rights, which facilitate cutting transaction costs, allowing hedging of risks and thereby increasing the return/risk trade-off and the incentive to invest in this activity.

This being said, it would be wise to design political institutions best suited for the development of reliable property rights. History and political theory are, however, unclear on this issue. Classical thinkers and Marx agreed that democracy is

continued

Box 4.1 *continued*

a threat to property. Thomas Macaulay pictured universal suffrage as 'the end to property and thus of all civilisation' and Marx agreed that democracy inevitably 'unchains the class struggle'. The modern theory of political decision-making points to other weaknesses of democracies and stresses rent-seeking activity, that is, distribution of income to buy elections in favour of the majority. But then, as argued by Olson (1991) autocrats cannot credibly commit themselves. Moreover, what matters even more is that the durability of an autocratic regime is not credible. Dictators usually announce a 1,000 year regime, but history falls significantly short of this.

Nevertheless, and in particular in countries in transition, a strong state is required to settle conflicting claims. Unfortunately a strong state, if not anchored with a large segment of the society (as in some successful Asian countries) is itself a threat to private property rights.

But not only the laws have to be changed to make private ownership economically viable. The practical guarantee of equal treatment of private and state-owned companies is no less important. This is again a question of implementation which cannot be answered in abstract.

This much is obvious. However, the real problem arises with the ownership of the existing stock of capital. Since at the beginning of the transition all land, buildings and machinery is owned by the state, the private sector would be able to develop only very slowly (through the accumulation of capital) unless a large part of the state-owned capital is transferred quickly into private hands.

Privatisation (of land and capital) is thus a crucial part of the transition programme. However, experience has shown that privatisation is different from price liberalisation and *Gewerbefreiheit*. The latter two can be achieved at the stroke of a pen, but privatisation is a process which takes considerable time. Experience in a number of post-socialist countries has shown that it is comparatively easy to privatise quickly small enterprises (essentially shops and restaurants) and small agricultural plots because the new owner can immediately assume effective control over the enterprise. Also the fact that this small enterprise privatisation frequently only changes the nature of the property rights contract (typically from lease-holder or employed worker to owner-worker), without calling for complicated reassignments of rights and redistribution, creates a favourable and largely non-conflictual political backing.

Privatisation of large enterprises (the majority of all manufacturing units had more than 100 employees under the socialist regime) is much more difficult: the state and existing management lose control and therefore rents; employees fear loss of employment or loss of shirking; and society at large is worried about the *nouveaux riches*. Also from an economic viewpoint efficiency is not ensured by mere privatisation; as formal ownership does not necessarily imply also effective control. This problem exists also in market economies and it has never been fully resolved. Different countries have developed different institutions to deal with corporate governance: that is, the fact that it is difficult for a large number of shareholders to control effectively the management of large enterprises.

For these practical reasons large-scale privatisation takes time. Since there exist many different approaches to privatisation we have devoted a large part of Chapter 8 to this issue.

Intimately linked with the privatisation of the existing state-owned stock of capital is the question of the organisation of financial markets. Indeed to privatise means to sell capital, so that privatisation helps to create a capital market. If it is well done an efficient capital market will develop rapidly. Such markets have never existed in centrally planned economies and there is a lack of experienced native specialists. But privatisation cannot really proceed in a void. If there are no banks and no other institutions that can provide capital for investments the government will *de facto* continue to dominate the economy. Privatisation must thus go hand in hand with financial market reform. This is why we discuss privatisation and financial market reform in this light in Chapter 9.

4. The remaining role of the government: price stability and an efficient fiscal system

Even if *Gewerbefreiheit* and the other elements of a market economy mentioned so far are established, a private sector will not emerge if the monetary and fiscal systems are not reformed. Confiscatory tax rates are equivalent to a formal prohibition of private ownership and must thus be abolished. However, with the establishment of a market economy the state does not disappear. It still has to produce some public goods (defence, police, justice, etc.) and it therefore has to levy some taxes. It is thus not possible to simply eliminate old taxes, instead, a new 'market conform' fiscal system needs to be created.

Another task for the government is to maintain a stable macroeconomic environment. The example of the Latin American countries shows that high and variable inflation rates have very damaging effects on investment and growth. While a private sector can work even in almost any macroeconomic circumstances growth will really start only if investors can rely on a minimum of macroeconomic stability. This minimum requires a stable inflation rate. History demonstrates, however, that it is near to impossible to stabilise the inflation rate at levels much higher than a few percentage points. It is therefore more practical to aim at price stability. Price stability can only be achieved if the fiscal accounts are more or less balanced. This is difficult to achieve at the beginning of the transformation process because expenditures continue to be high and the new fiscal system might not yield immediately all the potential revenues.

5. Comprehensive reform versus step by step and 'learning by doing'

We have shown so far that a functioning market economy needs a number of institutions that are all linked and do not function well in isolation. This, in our view, is the main argument for a comprehensive, or 'big-bang', approach: at the very beginning a comprehensive set of new ground rules should be laid out signalling an irreversible and clear-cut regime change with a new constitution and legal system, redefined property rights and redesigned economic institutions. In essence what is needed is a new social contract based on the rule of law.

The fundamental problem is thus not simply to change some rules of the game but rather to change the nature of the game that is played. The entire legal structure in a centrally planned economy is in fact inappropriate in a market economy: the constitutional, civil, business, commercial and social laws must all be tailored to a different economic and social order. A market economy can only work if the doctrine that *salus publica suprema civitatis lex est* becomes as clear to leaders in Central Europe and the Soviet Union as it was to Kant.

Integrating new laws into old legal structures is not good enough. Such a course would create confusion and convince neither citizens nor outsiders (foreign lenders, investors and traders). The entire legal structure has to change and the state itself must subject itself to the rule of law, or confidence in the reform programmes will be short-lived. To ensure domestic peace, a social contract is needed: a new constitution has to be accepted implicitly or explicitly by the majority of people. Property rights must be clearly defined to boost incentives, long-term commitments and 'book-entry trading' and the whole judicial set-up constructed so as to guarantee that these rights will be respected in the long term.

Recognising that reforms need to be comprehensive does not imply, however, that all reforms must absolutely be implemented at the same instant.

We have emphasised in this chapter the linkages between price reforms, privatisation, financial market reforms, fiscal reforms and the legal framework (contract law, property rights, banking regulations, tax legislation and the like). Some of these reforms take relatively little time (say, revising a law), others may take years (the creation of an efficient banking system). This serves to reinforce our preference for an all-embracing, comprehensive reform, but it hardly implies that every single thing has to be changed on the spot. The government needs to set priorities for its agenda and thus there will be some sequencing of reforms.

The sequencing problem has been extensively studied in the analysis of the structural adjustment of developing economies. While some rules of thumb have emerged, a more important lesson of theoretical studies and of practical experience is that linear sequencing of individual policy changes is not the right approach.

One aspect of the sequencing issue is often overlooked, namely the sequencing of political and economic reforms. By comprehensive reforms we mean, as argued above, that law and order needs to be established with the greatest urgency, in step with economic reforms. We are not advocating the need for the immediate establishment of democracy. Opponents of this view could argue that democracy is a basic human right. Whilst agreeing with this view, we are not convinced that democracy will lead, at any level of economic development and at any level of societal dissent, to a desirable outcome. A second argument often advanced in favour of democracy is that it favours development. We see democracy rather as a long-term goal. However, there is no clear causal link between democracy and economic growth, as demonstrated in Box 4.2. At certain stages of economic development and of national consent or dissent, democracy may not be a practical choice. It is quite natural that democracy was easily reintroduced into the Czech and Slovak Republics, Hungary and Poland, but not so easily in Romania, Bulgaria, Ukraine, Russia and other parts of the FSU.

Box 4.2 Is democracy good for growth?

The recent Western assumption that democracy is good for growth has been questioned by the success of several Asian economies that lack democratic institutions.

Clearly, democracies cannot work well in societies with a low level of development and very deep internal conflicts, as demonstrated by Arrow's 'Impossibility theorem'. Asian societies with a very exceptional homogeneity of cultural values such as work ethics, and starting out from extreme poverty, might not have benefited from more democracy. On the other hand, it is well documented that growth is favourable to democratic institution building. See Huber *et al.* (1993).

Some order seems at any rate preferable to total anarchy. Olson (1993) sees considerable progress when roving bandits become sedentary because they will then stop destroying capital and realise that in order to maximise their revenue they must limit predatory action, provide some protection and order. This is traditionally the behaviour of war-lords and, in modern times, of the Mafia.

Historically, sedentary bandits turned into fiefdom chieftains and autocrats of more structured society. What then is better for economic development, an autocratic or a democratic regime?

Box 4.1 argued that on the basis of property rights the issue cannot be settled. Moreover, at a very low level of economic development or with a high degree of social dissent, the choice may not be available: only an autocratic regime may be able to impose law and order. Perhaps Russia falls into that category.

Two arguments can be evoked in favour of autocratic regimes: first, dictatorship insulates the state from particularist pressures and, second, democracy undermines investment. As demonstrated by Becker (1983) interest groups in democracies compete for rents. The outcome is inefficient as lobbying is wasteful, as income transfers cause dead-weight losses and as the state is induced to be time-inconsistent. Democracy is bad for investment because unions and the government representing labour interests strive for current consumption, at the cost of savings and investment. Clearly, these arguments are not watertight. For a critique see Przeworski and Limongi (1993). The most powerful counter-argument is, of course, that autonomous rulers are predatory.

Figure A illustrates the relationship between political regimes and economic performance. Assume that output, or the growth of output, (y) is a function of the tax rate as depicted by curve y. At very low levels of taxation, output is stimulated by taxation or, rather, by the use of taxes for financing law and order, a social safety net, and physical infrastructure. After some point ($t>t_2$) higher tax rates discourage growth.

continued

Box 4.2 *continued*

Fiscal revenue is $T=t.y$ so that for given y, T increases when t increases. However this increase slows down when $t>t_2$ and T starts to decline when $t>t_1$. In the graph the curve T is known as the 'Laffer curve'. It is to be noted that with these assumptions the maximum of y is necessarily obtained for a value of t smaller than the one at which T attains its maximum.

Anarchy would be close to point $t=0$: no revenue is available for law and order. That is still better than the outcome of banditry at $t=1$: bandits 'tax' all revenue and therefore production breaks down completely.

A 'bureaucratic' regime (the communist regime) is likely to operate close to $t=t_1$: at this point total fiscal revenue is maximised and thereby the power of the bureaucracy whilst output is sub-optimal. A market economy or a 'benevolent' dictator (or the autocratic Asian regimes) would operate at point $t=t_2$ where they maximise output (or its growth). A dictator, by contrast, might maximise the fiscal residuum, that is, the difference between output and the cost of the public sector (the vertical distance between curves y and T). The outcome would be at $t=t_3$ where output is again sub-optimal.

Does this approach describe reality? It seems it is only partially confirmed by empirical studies. (For a survey of the empirical literature on the relationship between political regimes and growth, see Przeworski and Limongi 1993.)

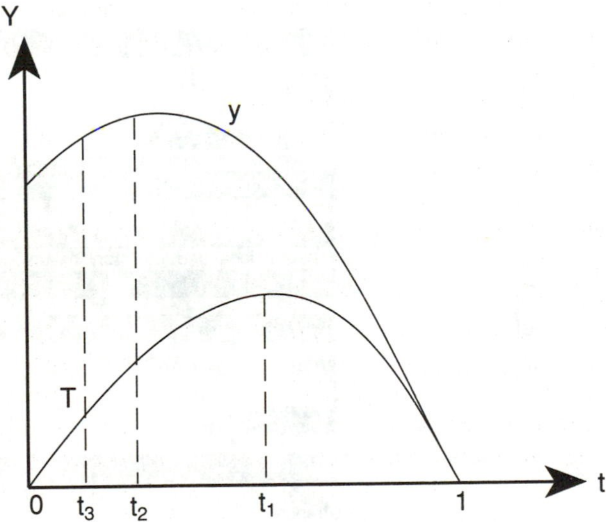

FIG. A Political regimes and economic performance

6. A 'typical' reform package

The actual stepping-stones of reform will vary according to the state of the economy, to the level of popular tolerance for the disruptions that are sure to accompany reform, and to the political situation. In order to be more concrete we show briefly the prototype reform for a representative European socialist economy with initial conditions close to those of Poland and Czechoslovakia.

The order of priorities reflects the time and effort needed to achieve these goals. We put macroeconomic stabilisation first because in countries with high inflation and non-sustainable balance-of-payments deficits, the government will have to devote a lot of effort to macroeconomic stabilisation provided, of course, that prices and foreign trade have been liberalised. How tough the programme will be and what will be the range of accompanying structural reforms will depend on the magnitude of the initial imbalances and on how much voters can be expected to swallow. A new government, or a government with broad-based support for radical change, has considerable room for manoeuvre, but this is hardly likely to last. It should therefore use the brief space of time available to push through tough measures which it may be impossible to impose later on. Countries that do not enter the reforms with macroeconomic imbalances have the advantage that they can concentrate immediately on the more long-run issues like privatisation.

Figure 4.1 highlights how much needs to be done right at the start. Virtually all the reforms, or preparations for them, must be launched quickly, even if they take a decade to implement. Of course, Fig. 4.1 exaggerates the precision of the process, and makes no allowance for the inevitable setbacks that must occur in any economic reform programme.

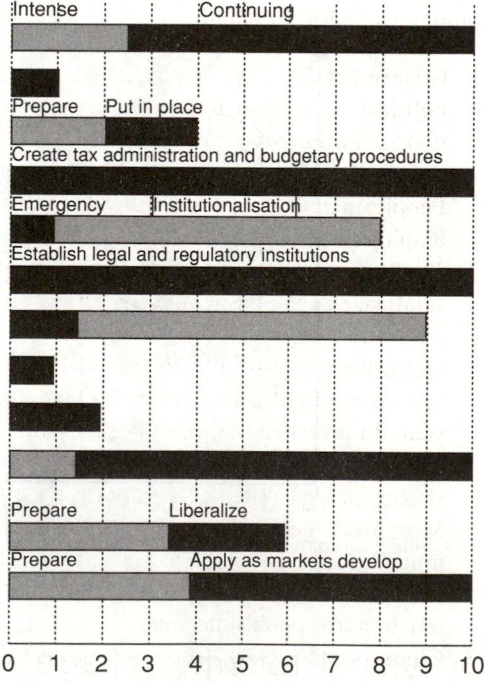

FIG. 4.1 Sequencing of reform
Source: Adapted from Fischer and Gelb (1991)

There is another vital element that does not show up in Fig. 4.1. A government that sets out on the road to reform with a clear idea of what it wants to achieve and with a popular mandate to forge ahead is bound to be more successful than a government and a society that are not sure of what they want. The outlook is decidedly better for those countries which agree on the need to move to a normal, private market economy.

7. Theoretical arguments for gradualism

In addition to China's successful example – synthesised in Box 4.3 – there are also some theoretical arguments in favour of gradualism. These do not represent a comprehensive body of theory, but suggest interesting, albeit highly controversial, possibilities.

Box 4.3 China and the case for gradual reforms

Is the comprehensive approach the only one that works? The case against this view is illustrated by China's remarkable success in achieving gradual reforms. We argue that the Chinese experience is not a useful example for Eastern Europe as even a superficial analysis of the causes for the unrivalled success in China reveals. The appendix to this chapter gives the details of the arguments that can be summarised in four points.

1. Eastern Europe has already had its political Big Bang. China has not. The political revolution has swept away the old control machinery and this makes it impossible to control parts of the economy – not in some areas or in a few selected sectors, but across the board throughout the system. People in Eastern Europe now expect a degree of freedom of choice, of employment, of consumption incompatible with gradual reform.
2. The key sector in China is farming. It is highly labour-intensive, and the small size of the basic unit makes farming a natural candidate for quick liberalisation. In fact the 'gradual' reforms in China quickly liberalised a sector that employed more than half of the population. In this sense China had more of a big bang than the Eastern European countries where it took years to privatise big industrial enterprises which produce almost all of the output. The absence of financial markets, which leads to a self-finance constraint, is also much less important in this highly labour-intensive sector. Moreover, the Chinese tradition of family or clan, and occasionally communal, support constitutes a sort of informal capital market. In Eastern Europe farming is much less important for the overall economy and also much more capital-intensive.
3. China decentralised decision-making to provincial and communal authorities which embarked on development of local industry on a competitive

continued

Box 4.3 *continued*

basis. These township and village enterprises are not privately owned but behave very much like privately owned firms. The increasing share of non-state enterprises is not the result of privatisation of existing state-owned enterprises (SOEs), but rather the result of more rapid growth of non-state enterprises.

4. The very diverse and little integrated structure of the Chinese economy facilitated a regional differentiation of conditions for foreign trade and investment. Success of the 'open economic zones' generated ever-increasing demands for similar status across the country. In this respect gradualism was extremely successful as it allowed experimentation and avoided abrupt disruptions of the existing structure.

Compared to China – which, like the FSU, already before 1978 had savings in excess of 30 per cent of GDP – industries in some of the European socialist economies, especially in Russia, are much more developed. The financial needs of Russian industry absorbed the lion's share of savings, whereas in China this was not the case. Comprehensive reform of the industrial sector is a necessary condition for the success of wider economic reform. Russia is too heavily industrialised (in 1989 the share of industry in GDP was 45.6 per cent in Russia, as compared to 44.2 per cent in Germany, and industry's share of total employment was 30.9 per cent, as compared to 30.2 per cent in Germany. Such an economic structure would be suitable had Russia a similar level of efficiency to that of Germany.), as Sachs (1991) argued, since industry accounts for close to half of GDP compared to 30 per cent in 1992 in Turkey which has a comparable *per capita* income. Structural changes of such magnitude require time.

Dewatripont and Roland (1991) show that economic reforms face serious political constraints. They demonstrate that the usual approach to Pareto-improving reforms with compensation payments can be misleading. Under normal circumstances, the efficiency gain generated by a shift to the market should be sufficient to compensate potential losers, even after taking into account transition costs and the potential distortionary effects of compensation schemes. If this is the case, institutional change supported by appropriate compensation schemes would be Pareto-improving, and any resistance to change would remain unexplained, at least if one assumes that agents are rational. The required compensation payments may, however, prove much more costly to the government if it cannot observe the potential losses suffered by different categories of agents (workers, managers, civil servants), especially in the case of hidden rents which are prevalent in socialist countries. They might prove still more costly if, in addition, agents do not believe that the government can commit itself to scheduled inter-temporal compensation schemes.

In their model, these two authors consider a workforce which is heterogeneous in terms of relative opportunities outside their current jobs. The situation just prior to restructuring is characterised by low productivity and excessive employment in a range of sectors. Moves towards allocative efficiency imply a major shift to higher productivity and massive lay-offs and labour reallocation during transition. As the government cannot distinguish between individual agents, it can only achieve the desired outcome via an exit bonus and wage increases, inducing workers with the best relative outside opportunities to leave. Reform plans are proposed by the government, which is assumed to be in control of the reform agenda, although subject to political constraints. They also assume that a majority of workers (or even unanimity) is required to approve a reform plan prior to implementation. The potential compensations might prove to be a heavy drain on the state budget. A trade-off appears between allocative efficiency and the financial cost of reform. Political acquiescence to full-scale reforms, implying massive redundancies overnight, can command a high price in terms of exit compensation. Partial reforms, with only those workers with the highest relative outside opportunities being laid off, will generally cost less, but will be inferior in terms of allocative efficiency.

Hence the result that gradualism is advantageous when political acceptance of full-blown and immediate reforms implies excessively costly compensation. But because gradual reforms only produce results over time, governments face a credibility problem. If they can pre-commit to their reform plans, partial reforms could be preferable to immediate complete reforms since the saving on compensation payments outstrips the allocative loss it implies. But if the government cannot commit itself in advance to its own reform plans, maintaining partial reforms is not time-consistent: once a partial reform has been implemented and workers with the best relative outside opportunities have left, it becomes optimal for the government to offer a new plan where, again, individuals with the best relative outside opportunities among the remaining workers leave. Allocative efficiency is thereby achieved gradually, at a financial cost which is lower than the one that accompanies a Big Bang reform – at least as long as agents fail to learn from experience, which is a very strong assumption.

Is democratic decision-making an obstacle to reform? A government in control of its reform agenda can win majority approval for plans which end up hurting majority interests inter-temporally. The general idea is that the government can, through holding out a credible threat of future reforms, extract today concessions from the group which will be in the minority tomorrow, and use their votes to hurt another group of individuals today. This suggests that a democratic government which has the necessary legitimacy to be in full control of the reform agenda may in large part circumvent the political constraints that might plague the implementation of efficiency-enhancing reforms, and win acceptance for transition measures which are painful for a majority of the population. So it is not impossible, albeit very difficult, to carry out wide-ranging reforms that harm the interests of large or powerful groups in a democratic society.

8. Rules versus discretion

Dewatripont and Roland (1991) focus on the role of credibility in achieving majority support for reform. However, the point is more general. Lack of credibility constitutes a major obstacle to successful transformation in many respects. To acquire credibility, policy-makers must demonstrate that they are willing to operate a fundamental policy change. Calvo and Frenkel (1991b) argue that the adoption of firm rules within a solid policy framework, rather than the practice of discretion, may reduce the perception of arbitrariness and strengthen confidence in the policy-making process.

The advantages of rules (especially those that are simple and not excessively state-contingent) over discretion are particularly marked when policy-makers start paying more heed to market signals. In this setting, discretionary action may be counter-productive, since the structure of prices and other market signals reflects the prevailing distortions, and discretionary action is therefore likely to be guided by the wrong signals. Simplicity is especially desirable where policy-makers and the civil service are untested. Furthermore, a clear statement favouring rules over discretion could go a long way in signalling a basic change in the policy regime. The key challenge, however, is how to make such a statement credible.

The issue of credibility is two-pronged and applies to both the economic programme and policy commitments. The economic programme should be practicable, hold up under professional scrutiny and reflect the experience and lessons gained from previous episodes. Policy commitments for their part should not be susceptible to the 'time inconsistency' problem, the temptation to change policy direction in mid-course. Policy-makers make explicit or implicit statements which influence private sector response. In this sense, policy-makers are the 'dominant players' in the economic arena. The private sector moulds its economic behaviour on expectations in connection with the present and future course of government policy. As time goes by the authorities, observing the behaviour of the private sector, may be tempted to depart from previously announced policy intentions which have governed the private sector's actions. This is the well-known 'time inconsistency' problem which may hamper the credibility of policy commitments.

The two elements of credibility – of the economic programme and of policy commitments – are inter-dependent. For example, the more credible the economic reform programme, the greater the likelihood of policy commitments facing 'time inconsistency' problems. This is because a credible transformation programme has short-term hardships virtually built-in and is liable, therefore, to generate political pressure and provoke interest groups into lobbying for mid-course changes, which may give rise to 'time inconsistency'. The private sector may actually anticipate this in the earlier stages of the economic transformation process, and adjust its behaviour accordingly. If this occurs, market operators may end up paying excessive attention to the near term and discount longer-term prospects – and so generate a sub-optimal inter-temporal allocation. To prevent this, policy-makers may find it useful to tie their own hands. This can be done in a variety of ways, ranging from clear, measurable political promises, the adoption of internal legal constraints (e.g. a ban on central bank financing of government budget deficits), external legal constraints (e.g. through international agreements such as membership of GATT), to the adoption of a programme negotiated with an international institution.

What is the alternative? When all is said and done, the only practical choice is between rather arbitrary, contradictory and slow sequencing on the one hand and a comprehensive approach on the other.

9. Conclusions

As we have argued already, we are in favour of a comprehensive approach. Yet there are circumstances in which the adoption of a rapid and comprehensive reform package is impeded by lack of political support, thereby undermining credibility. Without credibility, the 'first-best' programme may have to be jettisoned, since lack of credibility is tantamount to distortion. The theory of 'second best' then comes into play, precisely the point made by Dewatripont and Roland. In other words, choices may at times need to be made as to the appropriate pacing and sequencing of reform measures. There is no general blueprint for this, as the theory of second best by definition implies that optimal pacing and sequencing depend on circumstances, themselves of course highly fluid notions reflecting the diversity of historical background, economic, legal and political institutions and entrepreneurial tradition. We can offer only a few considerations.

Since the economic transformation programme stands or falls with credibility, it is imperative for the measures implemented early in the sequence to have broad-based political support. This is most likely to be forthcoming if the reforms throw off positive and visible results quickly, and if the appropriate 'safety nets' needed to protect the weaker members of the community are in place. That is why, for example, economic transformation programmes adopted by high-inflation countries (like Poland in 1990) should throw their full weight behind achieving macroeconomic stabilisation.

Another argument for a big bang is that it offers the opportunity to begin with a clean slate in financial terms through a currency reform. As we pointed out in Chapter 2, bank claims on enterprises and enterprise debt cancel out in the integrated public sector accounts of socialist countries. Cancelling their debt claims would have been absolutely no problem for the banks. Indeed, the value of deposits would have found its counterpart in claims on the government for an amount decided by the terms of the currency reform.

In a big bang it would thus be possible to cancel all enterprise debt, which anyway resulted from the old, arbitrary system so that privatisation would not be held up by over-indebtedness of firms. Moreover, the banking system would not have to carry non-performing loans on its books so that it would be able to build up capital and perform competitively.

With gradual reforms this is not possible. Serious sectoral imbalances will develop. Banks hold large amounts of non-performing assets and by a whim of history, that is, the timing of reforms, some enterprises are up to their ears in debt while others have been more fortunate. Once partial reforms are well under way and many firms have already gone independent or private, it is too late for a general currency reform.

Moreover, if the economy is subject to strong inflationary pressures an even more radical approach could be taken: a currency reform would eliminate the 'monetary overhang' without creating an inflationary spiral.[1]

Our basic tenet is in perfect agreement with the 'Ten Commandments for Reforms', as formulated by the Czech Prime Minister, Vaclav Klaus (*The International Economy*, Sept./Oct.1993):

1. It is impossible to centrally plan the origin and rise of a market economy.
2. There is absolutely no way to avoid the transformation shakeout of non-viable economic activities.
3. Start with a heavy dose of restrictive macroeconomic policy which prepares the ground for price and foreign trade liberalisation.

4. Having withstood requests for help, for bailout, for subsidies, for modernisation and demonopolisation of state-owned firms, the government must initiate a rapid and comprehensive privatisation process.
5. The delicate task is to find the right moment for the shift in macroeconomic policy – from the restrictive one to the neutral or, perhaps, even the expansionary one.
   No transforming economy has reached the stage where it would be appropriate to release fiscal and monetary controls and start Keynesian-like demand-expanding policies.
6. The inevitable price shock which follows price deregulation must be pre-announced, pre-explained, defended and 'survived'.
7. The economy cannot be restructured without a comprehensive shift in the property rights structure. To expect a change in economic agents' behaviour without privatisation is unwarranted and never happens.
8. The basic reform strategy should be based on a maximum degree of sharing of non-trivial transformation.
9. The role of foreign aid in the transformation process is marginal at most.
   What we really need from the rest of the world is not aid; it is trade and exchange. By exchange I mean symmetrical relations based on the principles of equivalence.
10. It is absolutely necessary for the reformers to believe in the success of the reforms. The preconditions for success are: credible programmes, not populism; realism, not false promises; optimism and self-confidence, not pessimism.

Note

1. Of course, a currency reform by itself does not solve all problems; in particular, it does not solve the corporate governance problem.

Appendix: Gradual reforms pay off in China[1]

Since changing economic tack in 1978, China has brought about one of the most dramatic improvements in human welfare of all times. With GNP growth averaging some 9 per cent a year, China's economy quadrupled during 1978–94, a performance comparable to the likes of Japan, Taiwan and South Korea during their fastest quarter-century of economic growth. In 15 years, China's foreign trade (exports plus imports) has grown to some $200 billion, up from a mere $21 billion in 1978, at a time when growth in the 'rich' world has been decidedly torpid.

Communist China's reforms have been a mix of sometimes highly contradictory ingredients. However, by and large, the country has followed its East Asian neighbours. The main elements of the reform have thus been: land reforms geared to boosting rural incomes, transfer of profits and labour from farming to industry; high savings rates to finance industrial investment, low taxes; increasing competition in the home market and openness to foreign influence. There is no cut-and-dried formula for this last element. It tends to consist of a combination of foreign prices, goods, investment and technology, the prime objective being to bring world standards to the local economy. China's reformers have managed to do so, albeit at the cost of enormous contradictions owing to the coexistence of a market and a command economy, at times straining the very fabric of reform.

China has its fair share of weaknesses as a result of the coexistence of command and private sectors: corruption, political interference and the temptation to override market signals. These are perceived as being so entrenched that many people believe it is impossible to reform a communist economy gradually. Big bangs do not appeal to the Chinese, who call their own method of reform 'crossing the river by feeling the stones underfoot'. The thrust of the Chinese economists' argument against quick comprehensive reform is that it has the same defect as central planning: it forces governments to take too many big decisions on questions that it knows precious little about, such as how to sequence reforms or how to privatise. They much prefer to experiment cautiously, letting different regions and different companies try different things. If they work, extend them. If not, bury them.

So far, the argument is running strongly China's way. What has made gradualism work in China, and can it work elsewhere?

The secret of China's success lies in its use of competition in many guises. At grass-roots level this works surprisingly well – enough for China to hold its own among its East Asian neighbours – but in its half-reformed state the economy is full of contradictions and strains, and the murkiest area concerns the role of government.

REFORMS IN AGRICULTURE

The first of China's three waves of reform concentrated on freeing farmers from the commune system. A market economy in food was created, initially by freeing prices for most foodstuffs except grain and eventually by abolishing the agricultural communes as the unit of production and replacing them with what were to all intents and purposes family farms. The results were impressive: grain output grew by a third in six years, cotton almost trebled, oil-bearing crops more than doubled, fruit production went up by half. Real incomes in the countryside, helped by rapid growth of small-scale town and village enterprises, grew even more spectacularly, registering a three-fold rise in just eight years. Chinese farmers were granted long-term leases but not full ownership. This is not too detrimental as Chinese agriculture is very labour-intensive and does not require long-term investments. However, rural infrastructure has deteriorated markedly as property rights remain fuzzy.

Per capita farming output in China had not increased at all between the mid-1950s and 1978, year one of the reforms, and then in the early 1980s, real value-added in agriculture went up by 7 per cent annually while the number of people working the land went down. This made everyone in China, be they food producers or food consumers, quickly and palpably better off. It laid the groundwork for sustained growth of agricultural output and generated the surplus of rural savings needed to finance industrialisation. Politically, where the reforms scored was that they captured this surplus, not by milking the countryside dry, as Stalin had done, but by making farmers richer. No need for political persuasion: three quarters of China's population were won over to reform with a minimum of fuss.

LIMITED OPENING-UP TO FOREIGN TRADE

The second plank of the early reforms was less sensational, but no less significant. China's 'open-door policy' began by eliminating central government monopoly over foreign trade. Four experimental 'special economic zones' were set up, three in Guangdong province next door to Hong Kong, the other in Fujian province across the straits from Taiwan. These were intended to draw in foreign capital, companies and expertise – mainly, as their locations show, from the ethnic Chinese businesspeople of Hong Kong and Taiwan. The open-door policy has been China's ticket to prosperity, just as export-led growth has been to the Asian tigers.

REFORMS IN INDUSTRY

The spin-off of rural reform was enhanced political clout for its perpetrators, who now had their hands free to concentrate on other targets. Starting in 1984 it was industry's turn. A lot has been accomplished in two rounds of reform (1984 and 1987), although the central difficulty with state-owned industry has still not been tackled.

The flow of goods passing through the hands of the planners is gradually diminishing. In 1978 some 700 producer goods were allocated by the Plan; by 1991 the number had fallen below 20. Almost none of the inputs or outputs in the rapidly growing non-state sector are now covered by the Plan. But, as an industrial survey by the Chinese Academy of Social Sciences shows, even the state-owned firms are affected. By 1989, as much as 56 per cent of input purchases fell outside the Plan orbit and almost 40 per cent of output sales. Today, almost 60 per cent of coal, 55 per cent of steel and 90 per cent of cement production is distributed by the market rather than the Plan.

It will therefore come as no surprise that prices are beginning to reflect true scarcity situations. The government introduced a two-track pricing system in the mid-1980s which, although it gave the green light to some corruption as intermediaries bought at low state prices and sold at high market prices, at least introduced market pricing into the system. Moreover, it is spreading. Most factory managers use market prices as reference for marginal decisions (because, provided the state quota accounts for less than all the inputs and outputs, the cost of an extra unit of input and the price of an extra unit of output are fixed by the market). This is of importance: economic decisions achieve allocative efficiency at the margin whilst intra-marginal decisions only affect rents. That is, it is nice for a manufacturer to obtain a certain amount of subsidised raw materials. But if this quantity falls short of the desired quantity at market prices then the optimal size of production will be determined by the price of the raw material in the market. The government has now cut the number of raw material inputs subject to price controls, which brings the proportion of prices that are market-set, by value of sales, to 75 per cent. Moreover, since mid-1991 the government has taken advantage of a period of price stability to raise state prices for some commodities, such as coal and grain, closer to market levels.

Competition has spread through the economy from many sources. Although some springs from foreign trade and investment, the real motor is inter-provincial rivalry released by the decentralisation of economic power. Each and every Chinese province has been transfixed by the success of Guangdong, whose real GDP has grown by a staggering 13 per cent a year for the past 14 years. Proximity to Hong Kong has, of course, been an incomparable advantage, but had it not been for Guandong's pro-business government and minimal state control of firms, Hong Kong would have kept its economic distance. With this glittering example in mind, the provinces are now trying to outdo one another in drawing foreign investment and designing and implementing the most attractive models of reform.

The biggest competitive impetus of all, however, has come from the growth of small industries, mainly in the countryside, that are not owned by the central government but are not exactly private either. These 'collectives' have spread like wildfire through China, competing vigorously with each other and with the state firms, too.

Not surprisingly, the Chinese economy is taking on an ever less socialist hue, and indeed its industrial structure now looks far more like that of its geographical neighbours than that of its erstwhile ideological brothers in Russia and Eastern Europe. Chinese industrial output relies heavily on a vast army of small firms totally absent from the scene in the former Soviet Union.

Growth is virtually the prerogative of smaller firms. In 1978, just before the reforms began, state-owned firms accounted for 78 per cent of China's industrial output. The state share has shrunk by more than two percentage points a year ever since, and now stands at just over half of total output. The Chinese government reckons that it will have fallen to 25 per cent by 2000. If agriculture and services are taken into account, the state's share of Chinese output is already no more than 25 per cent: considerably less than in some West European countries.

A singular feature of the Chinese experience is that the private sector has managed to grow without access to bank or state credit. China's private entrepreneurs have to rely on self-finance (supported by the extended family and communal arrangements). This is an encouraging example of McKinnon's self-finance proposal which is discussed in Chapter 9.

The most telling change in reformist China is how much more efficient the economy has become. In the two decades prior to reform, China's real GDP grew by a respectable 5–6 per cent a year, but 'total factor productivity' did not increase much, if at all. The vast bulk of China's pre-reform growth stemmed from adding more inputs, especially capital, not from using either more efficiently. With savings and investment rates as high as China's – both run at around 35 per cent of GDP – economic growth can be bought for a long time this way, but not for ever, as we demonstrated in Chapter 3.

1978 proved a watershed in productivity terms. By one calculation, total factor productivity in China's state firms rose by almost 2.5 per cent a year during the 1980s, a far cry from zero growth in the pre-reform years (Jefferson *et al.* 1992). Non-State firms for their part managed 5 per cent a year. In both cases, productivity growth picked up speed as the decade progressed.

There are other signs that the Chinese economy is becoming more competitive and efficient. Profitability in state and non-state industries is declining at the same time as productivity is going up. Returns in the state and non-state sectors are beginning to converge. The range of profit rates across industries is likewise narrowing – from 7–98 per cent in 1980 to 8–23 per cent in 1989. All this suggests an overall reduction in monopoly power and profits and a levelling-out of returns across regions, industries and companies (Naughton 1992). The state-owned firms have also improved the incentive structure along capitalist lines and managers can now be fired. In gathering political support for his reforms in the early 1980s, Deng Xiaoping said he was aiming to build 'socialism with Chinese characteristics'. It is now obvious that he has been building capitalism with Chinese characteristics.

The dangers with gradual reform are, however, also well illustrated by the changing fortunes of the agricultural and industrial sectors. During the first 10 years of the reforms agricultural incomes rose more rapidly than incomes in the state sector, generating discontent in the latter. The initial villain of the reforms was the '1,000 Yuan farmer',[2] at a later stage joined and replaced by entrepreneurs and traders in the liberalised sector. Corruption became widespread as civil servants made key decisions for allocating licences and goods produced in the state sector, but could not officially obtain benefits from the growth process. The Tian-an-men reaction was about political costs of liberalisation, traditional communist values and, by no small extent, about income distribution. In the meantime, thanks to spreading liberalisation, industrial and urban income growth have caught up with agriculture and discontent is now spreading in the countryside. The next social clash seems to be already programmed.

REFORM OF GOVERNMENT

With farming and industry both firmly launched on a growth and efficiency path, the 14th Congress of the Chinese Communist Party decided in October 1992 that the time had come for a third round of reforms. For all of China's progress in creating a market economy for firms, government performance continues to lag behind. On the agenda are difficult tasks such as streamlining the administration, reforming the fiscal sector, revamping the financial system and redesigning monetary policy. Inflation is becoming a serious source of concern and the instruments for global, as compared to firm-specific, monetary and fiscal policy do not yet exist.

Notes

1. This Appendix is based on Blejer *et al.* (1991), the *Economist* (1992), Harrold (1992).
2. Some farmers were reported to earn 1,000 yuan per month, or about 10 times the income of a middle-ranked civil servant.

CHAPTER FIVE

Price liberalisation

'What is a cynic?' 'A man who knows the price of everything and the value of nothing'
(Oscar Wilde, *Lady Windermere's Fan*, Act III)

Price liberalisation is the cornerstone of all internal reforms, and there is broad consensus on this point. Only market-determined prices send out the scarcity signals that enable a market economy to work properly. This is now so much taken for granted that there is no longer any serious discussion about this issue. However, price liberalisation is sometimes delayed and in many countries it is not complete even now. Apart from interest group pressure one fundamental problem is that, even for highly intelligent people like Oscar Wilde, prices and values appear to be different norms. This is why we discuss briefly in this chapter the reasons why price reform has not always been extended to all sectors and why it was delayed, for example, in the FSU by almost a year.

We argued in Part I that, theoretically, planning in a socialist country could replicate the equilibrium obtained in a market economy. If this were all that there was to it, the case for price liberalisation would not really be important. However, we also showed that in the reality of socialist systems prices had a different meaning. Subsidies artificially lowered raw material prices, whereas taxes added to the prices of transformed goods. At the retail level, subsidies once again interfered to bring the price of basic foodstuffs down. As a result, effective taxation was high for manufactured and some consumer goods, low for intermediate ones and negative for raw materials, energy and some basic consumer goods. Moreover, many goods were not available at their official price. Queuing time and connections were thus more important for consumption than the official price.

The key difficulty of price reform is its timing. If prices are liberalised before a large part of the economy is privatised and restructured, consumers might not be much better off. With the high degree of specialisation in socialist economies, many enterprises are, in fact, monopolies. It has therefore been argued that freeing their prices might then be detrimental to consumers and only increase producer rents. We argue below that this danger has been exaggerated and should not be used as an excuse for delaying widespread price liberalisation.

Price signals have the function of steering resource allocation. But as long as property rights are not settled there is no incentive for managers of state-owned enterprises (SOEs) to control costs (e.g. wages or capital costs), to divest established activities and redirect resources to other uses. Finally, the freedom to trade and to set prices in an environment where property rights are vague – and therefore legal enforcement uncertain – encourages rent-seeking activities in the twilight zone between legality and illegality or even completely outside the law.

This dilemma is unavoidable as privatisation, promulgation of the supporting laws and translation into corresponding civil behaviour take considerable time. To retard price liberalisation until the successful completion of the privatisation process is therefore also not a practical option. The only way out is to speed up privatisation as much as possible, to reinforce the accountability and control of SOEs in the meantime, and to design incentive constraints to SOEs that come close to those of privatised firms. Also the monopoly power of SOEs can very effectively be reduced through rapid opening to foreign competition. In this respect the experience in the Visegrad countries is quite encouraging.

We retain the conviction that complete price liberalisation should be part of the first steps. Section 1 shows that this measure should yield substantial benefits. However, price liberalisation also creates problems. We turn to the most important ones in the remainder of this chapter. In Section 2 we discuss the – in our view largely apparent – fall in real wages that followed price liberalisation in all reforming countries in Central and Eastern Europe. Section 3 then asks whether price liberalisation can be a cause for inflation. Section 4 turns to the issue of demonopolisation. Section 5 concludes with some considerations concerning the link between price liberalisation and the rest of the reform programme.

1. Efficiency gains from price reform

Why undertake price reform? The obvious answer is that price reform yields economic gains. We will discuss the nature and the size of these gains in a short- to medium-run context in order to find out the impact price reform can have at the beginning of the reform process. We thus concentrate on the adjustment in consumption that can be immediate once prices change, as it takes much more time to change production. The other parts of the reform package aim at providing the right environment for firms so that they are restructured and new investments can take place. They will thus take much more time to have an impact 'on the ground'. The efficiency gains in consumption are thus the only ones that are available immediately and so are important in maintaining popular support for the reforms.

How large can the efficiency gains from price liberalisation be if only consumptions can adjust? Imagine a closed economy in which there are queues for most goods. Before price liberalisation each household consumed up to the point where the total cost (price plus waiting time) was equal to the marginal utility it could get from consuming this good. The marginal utility was presumably different from the marginal cost of production (at the level of production decided by the planners). After price liberalisation markets clear so that queues are eliminated (and the price is equal to the marginal utility for consumers). While each individual household can adjust the consumptions of each particular good, all households together can only consume in the aggregate the same amount as before if production does not adjust instantaneously. Before production has adjusted, the elimination of queues[1] is thus the main welfare gain from price liberalisation. If trade liberalisation is also among the first measures, as we advocate, this argument is, of course, valid only for so-called non-tradable goods because for all tradable goods an excess domestic supply can be exported and an excess of domestic demand can be satisfied through imports. For goods that are tradable consumption can then adjust in the aggregate even if production is initially sluggish to react. For these goods the domestic price is determined by the world market and the world market price represents the marginal cost for the economy. After price liberalisation marginal cost will thus equal marginal utility. With price liberalisation consumers will reorient their consumption pattern increasing demand for goods whose prices fall and decreasing demand for goods whose prices increase (e.g. oil). The lower consumption of the latter pays for an increase in imports of the former and other goods.

However, even for non-tradables there should be gains that go beyond the elimination of queues. After price liberalisation consumers should be able to find, within their budget, the product they prefer. People who prefer potatoes should no longer end up with onions and *vice versa* for those preferring onions.

Since consumers will reduce their consumption of goods with a low marginal utility and increase consumption of goods with a high marginal utility, this reorientation of consumption (and implicitly trade) must make them immediately better off.

Over time production can begin to adjust. And if production can change, aggregate consumption of non-tradables can also change. This yields additional welfare gains that are illustrated in Box 5.1. The basic economic mechanism is that before price liberalisation marginal utility in consumption was not equal to marginal cost of production. A net gain is available to producers and consumers for any increase in the production (and consumption) of a good for which marginal utility exceeds marginal cost.

Box 5.1 The welfare gains from price reform

Price distortions can arise only if there are trade restrictions or explicit taxes and subsidies. As a result they have consequences for consumers, producers and the treasury. Four typical situations are illustrated. Fig. A is the simplest one. It depicts a short-run period during which domestic supply cannot change, but the goods are tradable at a fixed international price, $\bar{p}$. Before the reforms the domestic price was kept low through subsidies, at p_1, with the result that consumption expanded to c_1. When subsidies are eliminated and the equilibrium price $\bar{p}$ is established, producers will gain (surface $p_1ae\bar{p}$) and consumers will lose (surface $p_1be\bar{p}$). The treasury saves its subsidies equal to twice the triangle *abe*. Hence the net social gain is equal to the triangle *abe*. In Fig. B the domestic market is closed to imports and the price is fixed at p_1, but supply is somewhat elastic. Production at level q falls short of the equilibrium level $\bar{q}$ and for that reason there is queuing which has an implicit cost (in terms of nuisance and uncertainty). The cash price is p_1 whilst the effective price, inclusive of the queuing

continued

Box 5.1 *continued*

cost, is p_2. The total value of the time lost in queuing is the area abp_2p_1. Suppose now that following liberalisation the price moves to the equilibrium price $\bar{p}$. Then consumers gain $\bar{p}ebp_2$ and producers gain $p_1ae\bar{p}$. The total welfare gain is p_1aebp_2, that is the sum of saving queuing costs and of the triangle gains to consumers and producers through higher production.

Suppose next that imports are liberalised and that the price of imported goods is p_3, below the domestic post-liberalisation price $\bar{p}$. This time not everybody will gain. As illustrated in Fig. C, consumers gain a further $p_3ge\bar{p}$ whilst producers lose $p_3fe\bar{p}$, leaving over a net gain equal to fge.

Figure C has dealt with the case where the price of domestic goods is above the marginal cost of domestic production and above the world market price. In Fig. D the opposite case is depicted where domestic prices are subsidised (the subsidy per unit of output is equal to the distance between p_2 and p_1). The cost of the subsidy to the treasury is p_1abp_2. When the subsidy is eliminated the price increases from p_1 to $\bar{p}$ and the quantity produced declines from q to $\bar{q}$. Consumers now lose $p_1ae\bar{p}$, producers lose $\bar{p}ebp_2$ and the treasury saves p_1abp_2 so that the net welfare gain is abe.

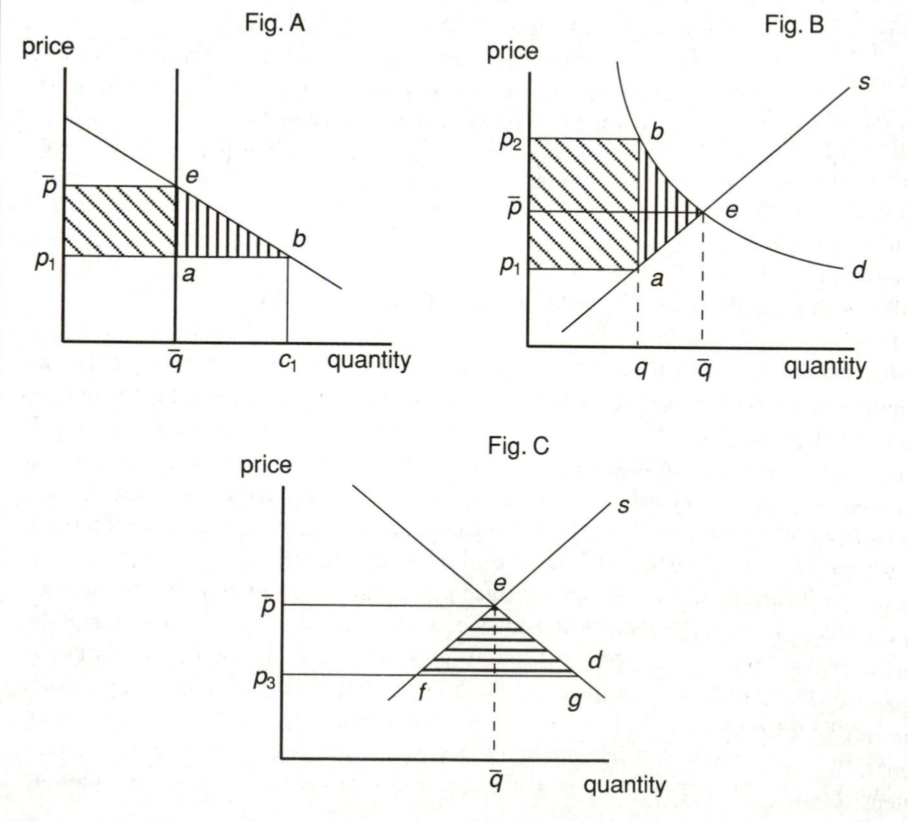

continued

Box 5.1 *continued*

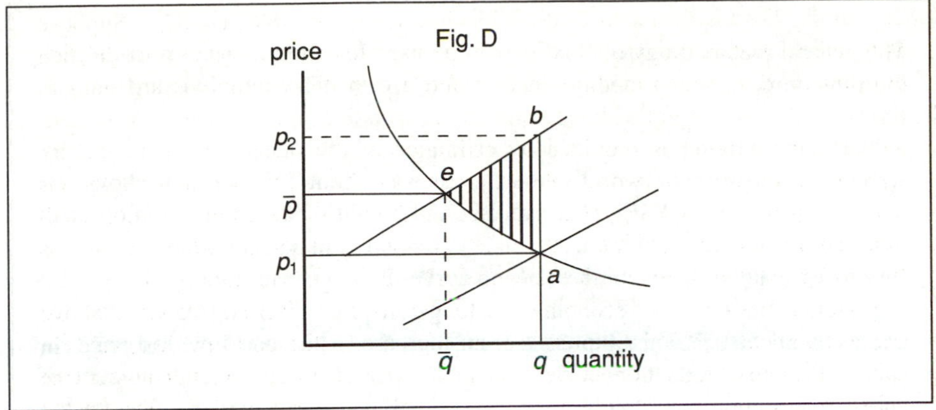

Reducing the consumption (and production) of previously over-priced goods and *vice versa* for under-priced goods thus yields net welfare benefits to society. How large are these gains? No comprehensive estimate has been attempted so far. It would anyway be not only very difficult, but also conceptually wrong to just add 'triangles' from all different markets. The fact that distortions are omnipresent makes it conceptually difficult to measure the gains from price liberalisation. The demand curve for any one product is affected by the prices of other products. A simultaneous change of all prices could thus shift the entire aggregate demand curve and lead to other effects which could potentially outweigh the direct effect from the change in the price of the particular product concerned.

Empirical studies of Western economies using the 'triangles' methodology that represent the welfare gains in Box 5.1 have usually found that the welfare gains from eliminating particular taxes or other distortions are not very large (relative to national income). However, this might be due to the fact that these studies usually consider relatively small distortions that exist in particular sectors of the economy which account only for a small fraction of national income. This should be different in socialist economies where the distortions are large and permeate the entire economy.

While it seems impossible to give a precise estimate of the welfare gains from overall price liberalisation it is still possible to estimate the order of magnitude of the gains in some sectors. We propose to do this using one of the most important distorted sectors of the economy under socialist planning, that is, energy. Box 5.2 below shows that liberalising prices in this sector alone should, in the long run, lead to welfare gains in the countries of the FSU equivalent to at least US$ 60–135 billion, or more than 10 per cent of income of these countries even if their GDP is estimated generously. Since the intensity of energy use was about the same in the other Central and Eastern European countries, one can assume that for most former socialist countries in Europe the welfare gains from liberalising this sector are similar as a proportion of income.

Box 5.2 The welfare cost of under-pricing energy

The general methodology of Box 5.1 can be used to estimate the cost of the single most important commodity: energy. We use in this example data from the FSU.

The starting point is provided by estimates of the under-pricing of energy which indicate that the world market price was about 150 per cent above the domestic price in the FSU. This indicates the height of the triangle. In order to estimate the base of the triangle, that is, the reduction in consumption, it is necessary to estimate the shape of the demand curve. Econometric studies for the West suggest that in a market economy the long-run price elasticity of demand for energy is about 0.5. This implies that an increase in the price by 150 per cent should lead to a reduction in demand of 75 per cent. The overall amount of energy production can also be measured. Applying world market prices to the individual components oil, gas and electricity, this yields a total value of the FSU energy production of about US$ 240 billion p.a. in the years up to 1990.

The triangle welfare gain, due to the change in consumption, is equal to the triangle *abe* under the demand curve in Fig. A of Box 5.1. This area is given by: one half of (the absolute value of) the product of the change in demand and the change in price (i.e. 0.5 × change in quantity × change in price).

Since only the elasticity of demand is known (elasticities link proportional changes in price to proportional changes in demand) it is necessary to translate the absolute changes in proportional or percentage terms. The welfare gain is then equal to half the proportional change in price times the proportional change in quantity times the value of initial production.

With the numbers mentioned this yields: 0.5 × 1.5 (increase in price) × 0.75 (fall in demand) × US$ 240 billion = US$ 135 billion. If the distortion in the FSU is assumed to have been 'only' 100 per cent the estimated welfare gain would still be US$ 0.5 × 1 x 0.5 × 240 billion = US$ 60 billion.

In order to relate this dollar figure to FSU income one has to estimate the value of the FSU economy. Generous estimates put the GDP per capita in the FSU at about US$ 2 500 to 3 000. The first estimate of the welfare loss is thus considerably above 10 per cent of GDP. Given that the actual combined GDP of Russia and the other ex-FSU republics was in 1992–93 much lower than the estimate used here, the welfare gain might turn out to be more than 10 per cent of national income even for the second estimate. However, since the demand elasticity refers to long-run effects, it might still be appropriate to use the higher GDP estimate.

Source: Gros and Jones (1991)

The welfare gains calculated in Box 5.2 represent a lower boundary since they take into account only the consumers' surplus. In order to obtain the overall welfare gain one would have to add the producers' surplus illustrated in the other figures of Box 5.1. However, this would require more information about the energy production conditions in the FSU. The important point about these calculations is not so much the precise number, but the order of magnitude. For example, the potential welfare gains calculated here for only one sector, of 10 per cent of income, are a multiple of the gains the European Community expects from the internal market programme.

The demand elasticity used here refers to the long run. In the short run it is much more difficult to economise on energy. This implies that in the very short run the welfare gains will be much smaller. Studies of demand for energy in the West indicate that it takes 10 years for the adjustment to be complete. If one accepts this and assumes that the adjustment is evenly spread over time, the welfare gains from price liberalisation in the energy sector would be 'only' 1 per cent of GDP in the first year, 2 per cent of GDP in the second, and so forth. However, even though the initial gains are more modest, but still substantial, there is no reason to delay price liberalisation because the adjustment will start only if prices change (and are expected to remain free).

The welfare effects of sectoral exemptions to price liberalisation are thus likely to be substantial. Experience has shown, however, that there are three sectors which are often, at least temporarily, exempted from price liberalisation, namely foodstuffs, housing and energy.[2] The underlying argument is always one of income redistribution: higher prices of these goods will make parts of the population worse off and that is often deemed socially unacceptable. Since the above-mentioned sectors cover a large part of overall consumption and since their demand is rather inelastic in the short run, the income effects can indeed be large for those parts of the population that do not receive higher prices for their production, mainly pensioners and state employees.[3] However there are always better ways of achieving the desired redistributive effect than to fix the price of these goods at a distorted level. We show this briefly with respect to the three sectors mentioned above.

FOOD

In the case of foodstuffs one way to avoid the redistribution of income that goes with price liberalisation would be to offer direct income support to people in need. Alternatively vouchers, which give the right to buy certain foodstuffs at low prices (presumably in a limited number of state stores), could be issued which, if transferable, would maintain the scarcity signal of prices. All Central European countries and the FSU anyway have such vast agricultural resources that farm prices are bound to remain low, always assuming that no time is lost and farming is liberalised and privatised outright.

The main problem for post-socialist agriculture is the food-processing industry. A number of studies have shown that under socialism food processing was particularly inefficient. In some cases food processing even subtracted value (see, for example, Hughes and Hare 1992). Inadequate domestic food processing is the main reason why most post-socialist countries spend a large part of their total hard currency earnings (about 30 per cent) on high value Western food (sweets, yoghurts, etc.).

HOUSING

Continued rent protection would freeze the housing market in its current sorry state. Since construction is potentially an important source of unskilled jobs, such a policy would make no social sense either. If it is felt that the redistributive effect of an unavoidable (and economically appropriate) increase in rents must be tempered, the answer might be to give current occupants the opportunity of buying their homes at an income-related price. Once private ownership is secure, rents and house prices set by the market will ensure that construction can take off, and owners will have an interest in renovating their homes. Unemployed workers would then have something useful to do. In post-war Western Europe, the unemployed contributed significantly to rebuilding the housing stock destroyed by war.

ENERGY

We have already discussed the exceptional importance of the energy sector. It is exceptional because the level of production is high, reflecting endowments and the emphasis of central planners on heavy industry and the fact that planners apparently also assigned a low shadow price to energy.[4] At the level of the consumer, the price of energy (petrol, electricity), in terms of other tradable goods, was much lower than in the West. The upshot of all this was that the use of energy per unit of output was several times higher in the post-socialist countries than in the West.[5] This implies that proper pricing of energy is both economically more important, and politically more difficult, than in the West.

Increasing prices for household heating is of course very difficult in countries where badly insulated apartments have no individual meters (as in the FSU area). However, energy (in the form of gas, oil or electricity) is a homogeneous product, which has a well-defined world market price. The shadow price of energy can thus be measured easily in terms of hard currencies. This holds for energy-importing as well as for energy-exporting countries (for the latter, such as Russia, gas and oil are often the only products which can be sold on the world market).

The real exchange rate of most post-socialist countries is usually at a very low level in the period immediately following the reforms. This implies that world market prices for energy lead to massive price increases in terms of non-tradables. For example, in Russia the cost of heating would be several times the rental cost and higher than the income of many pensioners if electricity and other forms of energy were priced in hard currency. This is why energy price liberalisation was so much delayed. The solution to this political problem would have been to allow households to consume a certain fixed amount (e.g. 50 per cent of previous consumption) at low prices and to charge world market prices for the rest so that at the margin consumers would pay the appropriate price.[6] This would allow the country still to reap the welfare benefits calculated above.

A further argument against the continuation of price controls is that once prices are set at the political level it becomes very difficult to change them and keep them at least constant in real terms. Governments are often tempted to use the controlled prices to slow down inflation. A good example is Russia where energy prices (petrol, household electricity) were kept constant in nominal terms for months while inflation was running at 20–30 per cent per month (annual rates of over 500 per cent). One result was that the price of electricity was at times 100 times lower than in the West (at market exchange rates). This mechanism magnifies the distortions caused by continuing price controls.

The capital market represents a special problem for price liberalisation and we reserve Chapter 9 for an extensive discussion. Maintaining low nominal interest rates, which imply negative real returns once inflation is correctly measured, means that credit will have to be rationed. Otherwise everybody would ask for credit, buy durable goods and repay the credit by reselling the goods once prices have increased enough. Maintaining low nominal interest rates can then even accelerate inflation.

Nevertheless, applying the general principle of price liberalisation by totally freeing interest rates also leads to problems. The credit or capital market has some peculiarities that make it difficult to argue that interest rates should simply be freed and the banking system be given free rein to lend. First of all, there is no (commercial) banking system at the outset of the reforms. Second, even if interest rates are freed, state-owned firms, which do not yet face a real budget constraint, will simply offer to pay higher interest rates than everybody else and thus obtain the lion's share of credit at any price. It has even been argued that the distortions in the capital market will be so severe that entire sectors should be excluded from obtaining credit from the banking system (McKinnon 1991). We discuss this issue in more detail in Chapter 9.

2. Price reform and inflation

The main purpose of price reform is to allow the market to determine *relative* prices. Changes in relative prices do not necessarily imply that the general price level increases or that there is inflation: some prices might go up (foodstuffs, rents), while others go down (many tradable industrial goods). However, there are two reasons why price decontrol might have an impact on the general price level: (1) the monetary overhang; and, (2) the elimination of subsidies. In reality price liberalisation led to a jump in the general price level in all reforming countries but in some countries the price level stabilised after the initial jump whereas in others prices continued to increase, that is, there was inflation.[7] The main reason for the high inflation rate that emerged in some countries of Eastern Europe was, of course, the lax monetary policy followed by these countries. This is a macroeconomic issue that will be discussed in Chapter 7. In this section we only briefly analyse how wage indexation can magnify the initial jump in the price level and possibly transform a jump in the price level into an uncontrollable inflation.

A MONETARY OVERHANG

A monetary overhang, discussed in more detail in Chapter 7, arises if the government pumps more money into the economy than households can spend given the available supply of goods and the fixed prices. Before price liberalisation, queues are the rationing mechanism that distributes the available supply of goods. After price liberalisation all households will try simultaneously to get rid of a large part of their excess cash balances. The only way they can succeed in the aggregate is when the price level rises up to the point where the real value of the money actually held (the nominal amount does not change with price liberalisation) corresponds to the real balances households (and enterprises) need to finance their current transactions (plus any precautionary savings). However, once the price level has risen to this new equilibrium level there is no reason why it should keep on rising. In other words price reform *per se* cannot be a cause of continuing inflation. Price reform can bring repressed inflation (the mirror image of the monetary overhang) into the open and thus cause a jump in the general price level. However, inflation, in the sense of a continuing increase of prices, will arise only if the government injects more money into the economy or if wages are indexed. As discussed in Box 5.3, wage indexation can indeed have a magnifying effect on the jump in the price level that is required to eliminate the monetary overhang. However, the elimination of the monetary overhang requires only a change in the level, not continuing inflation.

Box 5.3 Wage indexation and price liberalisation

Assume that before the reforms workers received on average a wage rate that would have allowed them to buy more than total production at the price fixed by the planners. This can be represented by the equation:

$$w_{t-1} = (1 + x)\, p_{t-1} \qquad [1]$$

where x denotes the extent to which 'official' wages exceed productivity. Of course, after price liberalisation even state-owned enterprises will no longer pay workers more than what they produce. Instead, even state-owned enterprises will have to charge a mark-up to cover their other costs. This is represented by:

$$p_t = (1 + m)\, w_t \qquad [2]$$

where m denotes the proportional mark-up rate. These two equations imply that measured real wages have to fall with the reforms:

$$(w_t / p_t) / (w_{t-1} / p_{t-1}) = 1 / (1 + x)(1 + m) \qquad [3]$$

The size of the fall in measured real wages depends on the product of the excess wages and mark-up used by firms after price liberalisation. The initial increase in the price level does not have an independent influence on the fall in real wages.

If there is no wage indexation the story stops here. Price liberalisation implies a fall in real wages because they have to reflect productivity, not because prices rise. In principle the adjustment of real wages to reality could have been achieved by a fall in wages, at unchanged prices. The reason for the overall price increase must therefore be sought elsewhere, namely in monetary developments. In Chapter 7 we discuss how a monetary overhang necessitates a once and for all increase in the price level.

Wage indexation can, however, have a pronounced impact in this context because it provides a dynamic feedback between wages and prices. Assuming there is a lag in the indexation mechanism, wage indexation can be represented by:

$$w_{t+1} - w_t = \alpha\, (p_t - p_{t-1}) \qquad [4]$$

where the parameter α denotes the strength of wage indexation. If $\alpha = 1$ there is full wage indexation; $\alpha = 0$ implies no indexation.

continued

Box 5.3 *continued*

This link between wages and prices implies that the price level cannot be constant after the initial jump. Inflation will thus continue for some time after price liberalisation. How long will inflation persist and will it eventually disappear? Using equation [2] and setting $m = 0$ for simplicity one finds that inflation (or rather the first difference in the price level) n periods after the reform is equal to:

$$p_{t+n} - p_{t+n-1} = \alpha^n (p_t - p_{t-1}) \quad [5]$$

This shows that, as long as α is smaller than one, inflation will gradually diminish over time. However, the *cumulative* jump in the price level will be much higher than the initial jump that was necessary to correct the monetary overhang. If one compares the price level at infinity, when inflation has ended, to the initial price level one obtains:

$$p_{t+n} - p_t = (p_t - p_{t-1}) / (1 - \alpha) \text{ for } n \to \infty \quad [6]$$

If $0 < \alpha < 1$ this implies that the overall increase in the price level has to be much larger than the one that is initially necessary to eliminate the monetary overhang. With 50 per cent wage indexation prices will rise by double the price jump caused by the monetary overhang; and with 80 per cent indexation the initial jump is amplified by a factor of 5. Wage indexation will thus magnify the initial jump in the price level. With full indexation inflation gets out of control since $1/(1-\alpha)$ goes to infinity.

Of course, these continuing increases in the price level will result in a higher demand for money. They can thus happen only if the central bank accommodates them by increasing the money supply. But this is a macroeconomic problem common to all countries that want to combat inflation. Price stability might at times require a suspension of wage indexation.

THE ELIMINATION OF SUBSIDIES

A second reason why price liberalisation might affect the general price level is often said to arise from the need to accompany price decontrol by an elimination of producer subsidies and arbitrary consumption taxes. If subsidies and consumption taxes are eliminated simultaneously the net effect on the budget should be zero. If the net effect is not zero, for example if the government, on average, subsidised consumption goods, the government can reduce wage taxation by the amount that was used before to finance consumption subsidies. However, in this case there might be a small net effect on the price level, just as when consumption taxes are increased in the West.

However, there is again no reason why the initial jump should lead to sustained inflation which will arise only if the money supply expands continuously. All this implies therefore is that the liberation of controlled prices and removal of producer subsidies has to be complemented by monetary and fiscal discipline, and the establishment of a new market-conformable tax system. We discuss this issue separately in Chapter 7.

We have argued so far that price liberalisation *per se* should not be a cause for continuing inflation. It should at most have an impact on the overall price level. Has this been borne out by experience? The high rates of inflation that accompany the transition in Central and Eastern Europe seem to contradict this hypothesis. A closer look reveals, however, that price reform cannot be held responsible for this (see Fig. 5.1).

What happened in the ex-GDR is a case in point: only months after the Deutschmark was introduced in July 1991 (a move accompanied by a comprehensive price reform), the overall price level had actually dropped from the previous year's level; subsequently it rose again in steps when administrative prices were increased and wages rose closer to the West German level. In Czechoslovakia we also see that whilst price liberalisation led to an initial jump in the price level there was no sustained increase in prices.

The developments in Poland and Russia were quite different. In both countries there was an initial jump in the price level (over 250 per cent in the case of Russia, about 70 per cent for Poland), but the price level continued to increase after the initial jump (January 1992 in Russia and January 1990 in Poland). However, as shown in Chapters 7 and 14, the subsequent inflation in both countries cannot be ascribed to price liberalisation; instead it resulted from monetary financing of large fiscal deficits (in Russia) and some inflation inertia due to wage indexation.

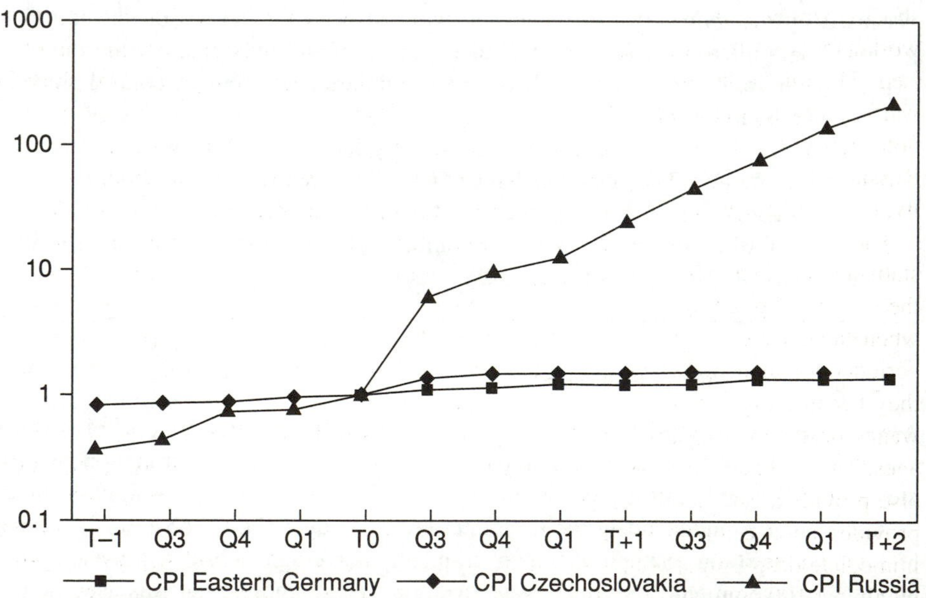

FIG 5.1 Price liberalisation: three different experiences
Source: own calculations based on RET (Russia), IFS (Cze) and Bundesbank (E Germany); logarithmic scale, T0 = 1.

3. Price reform and wages

After price liberalisation, reported real wages (i.e. nominal wages deflated by the consumer price index) usually fall by a substantial amount. For example, in Poland real wages dropped by almost 40 per cent in the first month of the shock therapy; in Russia the fall was even more pronounced: in January 1992 measured real wages fell to almost one fourth of the December 1991 level (see Chapter 14). The remarkable fact is, however, that this fall in real wages did not lead to social unrest.

The main reason why the apparent reduction in real wages did not lead to social unrest was that the wages deflated by the 'full' price to consumers, that is, the price plus waiting cost, did not fall necessarily by the same amount and might even have increased. Production did not fall overnight when prices were liberalised. Households must thus have been able to buy, on average, the same bundle of goods as before price liberalisation. Workers, who constitute the majority of all households, should not be worse off than the average since there was no 'capitalist' class that could have gained at their expense. The only 'capitalist' under socialism, the government, did gain from price liberalisation through more revenues from state owned enterprises that could charge higher prices. This revenue allowed the government to finance the elimination of subsidies without increasing taxes.

Sachs (1993) provides evidence that in the case of Poland consumption (of workers and the population in general) actually increased for major items after real wages started to fall. He also argues that most of the fall in real wages immediately following price liberalisation was a correction of the unsustainable increase in wages before the shock therapy started in 1990. These wage increases might actually have made workers worse off since they only resulted in longer queues before prices were liberalised. The mirror image of this argument relates to the gains from the elimination of waiting time that constitute the first benefit from price liberalisation. It is surprising to note, however, that measured real wages fell not only in countries like Poland and Russia, where they had previously increased substantially despite a fall in productivity, but more generally throughout all Eastern Europe (see Chapter 11).

The thesis that the drop of real wages following price liberalisation was only a statistical artefact implies in principle that after price liberalisation wages deflated by the consumer price index should be at about the same level as they were in the past when there were no queues. Unfortunately, it is difficult to find a good comparison period since there were always shortages in the socialist system. But one can see that they became much worse during the late 1980s. One should therefore compare real wages post-liberalisation to real wages during a recent period with minimum shortages. This is done carefully for a number of countries in Koen and Phillips (1993) who also provide a detailed analysis of price liberalisation in Russia. They argue that 1987 provides an acceptable base year. Their analysis shows that in Russia, where the immediate drop in real wages was most dramatic, measured real wages had increased by almost 100 per cent up to the end of 1991 (compared to 1987) as wages increased much more than official prices. This was clearly not sustainable since in the meantime production, and productivity (since employment was constant), had fallen considerably. The average Russian could see this also quite clearly in the state-owned shops which were almost completely empty at the end of 1991. Against this background a radical fall in measured real wages was unavoidable. The actual fall of three-fourths in January 1992 probably overshot the equilibrium, but already by June 1992 real wages were almost back to the 1987 equilibrium. Since at that time there were no longer any appreciable shortages the real purchasing power of wages in Russia must have exceeded the earlier level because in 1987 there were still important shortages. In other reforming countries the changes are less dramatic, but real wages generally recovered quickly and returned in most cases close to the pre-extreme shortages equilibrium.

The argument that at unchanged production effective real wages cannot have declined is thus supported by the data. However, this argument is valid only for the very short run because in all post-socialist countries production did fall within one year of the reforms by 20 per cent or more. This suggests that some reduction in real wages might have taken place after all since the pie available for distribution was shrinking. The official data on the decline in production have to be taken with caution, however, because production by the 'informal', now legal, private sector was not immediately included in the official statistics of 'socialist production'. The reported 'socialist' production did not include the activities of the emerging private sector that, in countries like Poland, did immediately contribute a substantial fraction of overall income. Berg and Sachs (1992) even claim that if under-reporting is taken into account more than half of the reported fall in production is a statistical artefact.

One could even argue that the decline in production that took place in response to price liberalisation might have actually increased welfare. One reason is that, at world market prices, a number of industries might have produced negative value-added. Closing down these industries can only increase overall welfare although measured production would fall. Moreover, a reduction in the production of military hardware should also not be construed as a negative development.

There is, however, also evidence that some reduction in valuable production has taken place in most post-socialist countries. Several studies, for example, Hughes and Hare (1992), Duchene and Gros (1994), have shown that the decline of production was not related systematically to the change in profitability after price liberalisation (and

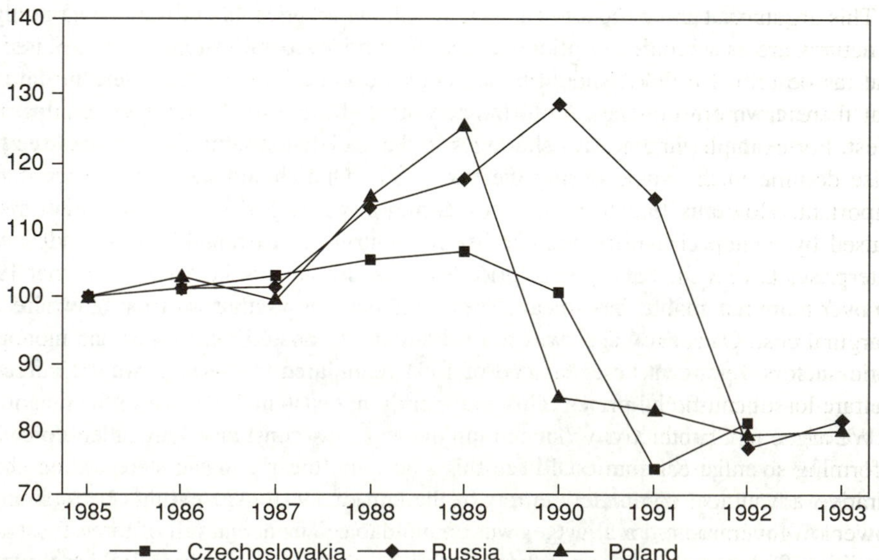

FIG 5.2 Price liberalisation and 'real wages' Real wage index (1985 = 100)
Source: own calculations based on, IFS (Poland and Czechoslovakia) and RET (Russia). Date of price liberalisation: 1.1.90 for Poland; 1.1.91 for Czechoslovakia; 1.1.92 for Russia.

foreign trade reform), as one would think it would if it were mainly due to an elimination of negative (or low) value-added industries. Moreover, even in Russia, branches of industry that worked intensively for the military did not, on average, experience a greater output decline than others. But the decline in intra-FSU trade seems to have affected the magnitude of the output decline. It is often asserted that the collapse of CMEA (or COMECON) trade was also a major factor in the output decline in Central Europe, but this has not been documented through systematic studies.

Over time there has thus probably been some reduction in welfare-relevant production because of the macroeconomic problems discussed below. Some reduction in real wages might thus have taken place initially. However, it would be wrong to interpret this necessarily as a fall in welfare or standard of living. In most countries the efficiency gains in consumption, production and trade will have more than outweighed the limited fall in welfare-creating production. Only countries like Albania or Ukraine which fell into complete macroeconomic instability (or Armenia and Georgia which were involved in civil wars) are likely to have suffered a serious fall in living standards.

4. Price liberalisation and demonopolisation: the importance of international competition

In a number of countries it was argued that prices could not be freed until the economy had been demonopolised because price liberalisation might simply substitute state-administered monopolies with private monopolies. This argument was used as late as 1993–94 in Ukraine to delay price liberalisation.

This argument can be valid only if the distortions caused by (private) monopolistic structures are as important as those caused by the 'socialist' pricing structure. Recall that, as described in Part I, the planners tended to emphasise economies of scale so that there are more products produced by only one or a few enterprises than in the West. For example, in the FSU in 209 out of 334 industrial products one single enterprise dominated the market.[8] The danger of monopolistic pricing is thus potentially important. However, there are at least two reasons to believe that the distortions caused by monopolistic structures should be limited. For example, if all (industrial) enterprises have a similar degree of monopoly power they will all use a similar mark-up over marginal cost so that in equilibrium the relative prices correspond to (relative) marginal cost. Of course, this does not yield the correct relative price of the monopolistic sectors versus the competitive sector (agriculture, services), but it limits the welfare losses caused by monopolistic structures.

We argue in Chapter 6 that opening up the economy must be regarded as critical to reforming socialist economies. But opening up is not only a way for exploiting comparative advantage, it is also the most efficient means for curtailing the monopoly power of governments and large corporations. Price liberalisation is not only a precondition for trade reform and currency convertibility, there is also a link in the other direction. Implementing price liberalisation in the context of a marketless economy is difficult, as shown by the experience of Russia. In the absence of proper market structures and real competition, and given the monopolistic structure of the economy (shortages and a small number of producers), relative prices, once freed from state control, will not go quickly to the equilibrium level that equates marginal utility to marginal cost of production.

Foreign markets and prices bring not only information, and the competition of foreign goods. External liberalisation under a fixed exchange rate also produces downward pressure on domestic prices (provided the exchange rate is not set too low, as argued in the next chapter). This is a prime consideration for reformers, who fear the inflationary developments that could result from price liberalisation in a context of shortages and 'monetary overhang' accumulated by the population. Opening up to foreign markets can therefore be invaluable in reducing internal monopoly power and stabilising prices.

There are, of course, sectors in which international competition cannot replace the lack of domestic competitors. In these cases 'normal' anti-monopoly legislation and regulation will have to be used. The same holds true for the case of the so-called natural monopolies, such as local power supplies, trains, and so forth. Since these enterprises will anyway remain in state hands for the foreseeable future even a disorganised government with a weak administrative structure should be able to prevent the worst abuses in this area.

If all this is done there is no need to delay price liberalisation until an effective competition legislation has been established.

5. Conclusions

While the need for price reform was recognised very early there was hesitation everywhere.

The main political problem with price liberalisation (coupled with freedom for commerce) was initially that, as the old distribution system broke down, a large segment of the population had to pay higher prices and a few well-connected people made fortunes in emerging markets. Over time a new market-based distribution system evolves and profits in that sector stabilise at the normal rate. But in the beginning very high profits from this apparently unproductive activity did cause popular resentment.

The decision to liberalise prices is, in a sense, the easy part, the harder part is how to get the beneficial effects on the production side. This is not as straightforward because price reform will not work in that area unless firms face 'hard budget constraints'. Without this financial discipline, the managers of firms might just continue to produce the same old goods instead of adjusting production to the new market conditions. The contrasting fortunes of Russia and Poland illustrate this. In both cases price liberalisation came long before privatisation. But in Poland SOEs faced tight financial constraints and started to adjust immediately, as can be seen from the export boom that followed the reforms. In contrast, Russian SOEs received almost unlimited subsidies in the form of cheap credit and did not adjust production to the same extent (see Chapters 11 and 14 for more details). Under these conditions managers will collude with workers to raise wages without limits, triggering an inflationary spiral. Chapter 9 discusses some further aspects of how to establish effective financial discipline (bankruptcy laws, etc.) and effective corporate governance.

Price reform, then, is only the beginning. Moreover it is fraught with real, although transitory, political problems. The main political problem is the apparent dramatic drop in the standard of living that results from the need to adjust wages to productivity. Theoretical considerations and the data suggest that this decline was only apparent. The fact that in no country has there been a popular movement to re-establish broad based price controls indicates that the welfare gains predicted by economists must have been real.

Notes

1. The elimination of queues is a tangible saving in time for everybody. However, with market clearing prices people with a higher monetary income (but less time to spare to wait in line) will be better off relative to people with a lower monetary income (and more time to spare), e.g. pensioners. The overall economic efficiency gains from price liberalisation will thus be unevenly distributed across the population.
2. Even a reformer with a historic reputation for his pro-market convictions skidded on this point: 'I am convinced that the best solution is to proceed from a currency reform to a market economy with prices set by the market. Of course, in practice, we would not do that (especially not for food, rents and coal), but the trend is the correct one.' Ludwig Erhard, the father of the German miracle, on 14 January 1948.
3. In socialist economies the accumulation of real or financial assets was very limited. Therefore, people were unable to fall back on accumulated savings to bridge difficult times. Safeguards for their incomes are therefore even more necessary than in Western economies.
4. We explained in Part I that socialist planners assigned a low price to energy because neither capital costs, environmental nor depletion costs were properly valued and the model of growth chosen was based on cheap inputs (labour and material inputs).
5. See Gros and Jones (1991) for further details.
6. A reminder: to ensure efficiency in allocating resources prices need to be market prices only at the margin. That determines the amount of production or consumption, independently of the subsidised price of intra-marginal quantities. They only have redistributive – and not allocative – effects.
7. In China there has been more inflation since prices became gradually liberalised starting in 1978. However, it is not easy to disentangle the effects of price liberalisation from those of excess demand. In comparison to other fast-growing economies in Latin America or Asia, the inflation record in China does not appear to be worse.
8. See IMF *et al.* (1991) cited by Bennet and Dixon (1993: p. 2).

CHAPTER SIX

External liberalisation

The doors of heaven and hell are adjacent and identical.

(Nikos Kazantzakis, *The Last Temptation of Christ*)

The external aspects of reform are no less important than the domestic ones – not only for the obvious reason that access to the know-how accumulated by the market economies promises huge gains in productivity – but also because in an open economy, domestic policy is constrained. Domestic prices and interest rates cannot durably deviate from world market conditions without serious repercussions or even a return to autarky. The exchange rate regime, the level of the exchange rate and the 'openness' of the country (as measured by the level of tariff and non-tariff protection of domestic activity, convertibility rules and so on), therefore have central importance for the domestic reform process itself. History demonstrates that policy-makers tend to be reluctant to open the door to foreign trade, often perceived as a door to hell. Only during the 1980s have more and more countries opened up and discovered that it can be a door to heaven.

We start the discussion of the external aspects of the reforms in Section 1 with the liberalisation of external trade and the desirability of some temporary external protection. Section 2 assesses the contribution trade can make to economic growth, as this is after all the main purpose of external liberalisation. Section 3 analyses briefly to what extent international capital transactions should also be liberalised. Section 4 then turns to the related question of convertibility and the exchange rate regime. Section 5 summarises.

1. Trade liberalisation

We have already emphasised in Chapter 4 the link between price and trade liberalisation. One without the other does not make sense. Moreover, trade liberalisation is easy to achieve: all that is needed is a stroke of the pen that eliminates all restrictions to export and import. However, in reality the issue is a more complex one because for trade liberalisation one can make a good case for gradualism. While economists generally agree that all quantitative restrictions should be eliminated immediately there are respectable arguments for retaining or instituting some tariffs. Completely free trade has never existed and over time progress has been achieved only gradually throughout the world, through a succession of difficult and drawn-out GATT rounds.

If one takes into account how trade was repressed and regulated in socialist economies it becomes clear that to liberalise foreign trade a number of practical steps must be taken. The most pressing of these would be to abolish the state monopoly on foreign trade, unifying the exchange rate so that all exporters and importers transact at the same rate, eliminating all quantitative restrictions (or converting them at least into tariff equivalents); and moving to unrestricted foreign exchange convertibility for current account transactions.

There is no need to provide special arguments for the abolition of the state monopoly concerning foreign trade. The rationale for exchange rate unification is also clear. It eliminates the many different implicit export taxes (usually on energy and other material inputs) and import subsidies (usually on so-called 'essential' imports). One immediate result is that the domestic currency prices of these goods rise to the world levels.[1] In the short run, producers in manufacturing would have an incentive to begin economising on energy and other material inputs.

The unified exchange rate can transmit world market prices to the economy only if exporters and importers actually have access to foreign exchange. This is why 'current account convertibility' for residents is an additional required step. We discuss later in this chapter the macroeconomic implications of this and also the extent to which non-residents should be allowed to hold domestic currency abroad.

The net effect of the initial steps is 'only' to convert implicit protection by direct controls into explicit protection by tariffs – possibly still rather high tariffs. The final step is to decide on the appropriate level of the explicit protection. We argued in Chapter 5 for complete price liberalisation and completely free trade is, at least in the longer run, the appropriate complement to price liberalisation. However, during the transition period some tariff protection should be maintained through a modest uniform *ad valorem* import tariff in the 20 to 40 per cent range.

Why temporary tariff protection? One argument is that tariffs can yield substantial revenues for the government. A simple calculation shows that this can be an important source for a government that has to create a new fiscal system from scratch and will thus have only a very uncertain revenue base at the beginning of the reform process.[2]

An order of magnitude of the potential revenue can be calculated easily. For a country with a ratio of imports to GDP of about 30 per cent (e.g. Hungary in 1992), a tariff of 25 per cent would yield a revenue of about 7.5 per cent of GDP. Since total government revenues have usually been around 40 to 50 per cent in the transforming economies, this implies that tariffs could easily provide between 15 and 18.75 per cent of total government revenues. This would actually not be outside the range spanned by the experience of a number of other 'emerging' countries, as shown in Table 6.2.

TABLE 6.1 Trade dependence of some Eastern and Central European countries during 1992

	Imports (in % of GDP)	Exports (in % of GDP)
Czech Republic	38.4%	32.7%
Hungary	31.6%	29.6%
Poland	17.8%	14.6%
Russian Federation	41.7%	47.7%

TABLE 6.2 Share of central government revenue from taxes on international trade

	Share of revenue %
Argentina	25.5
Ecuador	14.3
Thailand	19.1
Turkey	5.1
USA	1.5

Source: International Monetary Fund, Government Finance Statistics Yearbook, 1992
Note: 1990 data

As Table 6.2 shows, tariffs account for a significant proportion of government revenue in some countries with a similar *per capita* revenue as the transforming economies in Europe. The proportion of revenue derived from tariffs in slow-growing Argentina was similar to that in fast-growing Thailand. In richer countries, represented here by the US, tariff revenues are usually negligible. However, richer countries have a mature tax system and can obtain the revenue they need more easily through 'normal' taxes.

The fiscal argument would suggest that the degree of tariff protection, and its reduction over time, should be a function of the fiscal 'needs' of the government. We discuss the latter extensively in Chapter 7.

Another argument for retaining some tariffs comes from 'second best' considerations. It could be argued that some of the 'senile' state-owned industries need temporary protection to prevent them from failing all at the same time. According to McKinnon (1991) and Hughes and Hare (1992), many industries in Eastern Europe would show negative cash flows (and sometimes even negative value-added) at world market prices in the short run, that is, before input combinations and product quality can be adjusted. Hence a devaluation coinciding with the move to free trade would simply raise material input prices in tandem with the prices of finished goods and negative cash flows would persist. Moreover, with incomplete financial markets firms with negative cash flow (but positive value-added) today might go bankrupt even if they are perfectly viable and competitive in the long run when the scale of production and the input mix are adjusted. Because manufacturing absorbs a very high proportion of the East European labour force and firms with a negative value-added constitute a large fraction of all firms, a wholesale collapse of the industrial fabric would lead to huge unemployment.

Given the fundamental long-run uncertainty about substitution in production, product quality and equilibrium real factor costs, McKinnon (1991) underlines the need for a system of interim protection that would initially sustain the profitability of most existing manufacturing and processing output. If this protection is progressively scaled down over several years, it would allow market mechanisms to winnow out the inefficient industries from those that are ultimately viable under free trade.

How much protection is needed according to this argument obviously depends on the level of the real exchange rate. A very depreciated exchange rate reduces the need for tariff protection if under-valuation can be sustained and *vice versa*. Trade policy during the transformation should thus be discussed together with the exchange rate regime (see below).

Another reason for temporary tariff protection is that at the beginning of the reforms there is likely to be a pent-up demand for foreign goods that is likely to exceed proceeds from exports plus the available foreign exchange reserves. Protectionism, however, is manifestly a second-best solution to the problem of excess demand for foreign goods. As stressed by Bofinger (1990) among others, the underlying reason for such excess demand is that excess consumption by some agents is not financed by private capital flows but by the central bank, that is to say, monetary policy (at the given exchange rate) is too lax. So the first best answer to excess demand for foreign goods is 'hard' macroeconomic policies that force 'hard' budget constraints on the private sector.

We therefore retain only two justifications for temporary protection. The first is the need to provide domestic producers with temporary protection so that some can restructure. In this sense tariffs are needed because the domestic capital market does not yet function and thus cannot finance temporary losses. The second justification is the tariff revenue. A tariff, like all other taxes, causes distortions, but in the absence of an efficient domestic fiscal system this might be the only tax that can really be levied.

However, given these aims, it is still important to cut distortion of domestic resource allocations down to a minimum. The best solution would be a flat uniform (*ad valorem*) tariff between, say, 20–40 per cent to start with. It is difficult to defend these numbers on purely economic grounds, but experience suggests (see Table 6.3) that within this range the beneficial effects (tariff revenue and maintaining domestic activity) exceed the negative effects in terms of distortionary costs and evasion activities by traders. The uniform rate ensures that there are no distortions for resource allocation among tradable goods.

Opening up economies to international trade also partially solves another problem, namely that even when reforms are complete, many firms will still be the only domestic suppliers of certain products. Strong international competition should prevent domestic monopolists from using their monopoly power to charge higher-than-world-market prices (see Lipton and Sachs 1990), as was argued in Chapter 5.

We are aware of the fact that tariff protection is very much a second best approach but this is the world we are living in. An import tariff raises the real exchange rate and therefore hurts export industries. If one abstracts from inter-temporal considerations

TABLE 6.3 Shares of output in industries with negative value-added (at quality adjusted world prices)

	Share of output
Bulgaria	50.8%
Czech Republic	34.8%
Hungary	34.6%
Poland	8.4%
USSR	22.3%

Source: Hughes and Hare (1992)

one can go one step further: simple arguments can show that an import tariff is equivalent to an export tax (tariff). The equivalence can be established if one takes into account that for a small country that cannot affect world market prices the import tariff increases the price of imported goods, relative to exported goods. An export tariff, at given world market prices, lowers the price of the exported good at home, relative to the imported good. Lowering the price of one good relative to another, or increasing the other price leads, of course, to the same relative price.[3]

This equivalence between export and import tariffs is revealing. It shows that perhaps the most important side-effect of trade protection is the reduction in the growth of trade, both imports and exports. This is crucial because export-led growth is the only way Central and Eastern European countries can hope to catch up with Western standards of living. This is another reason why the protection we advocate for the transition has to be temporary and modest.

The Central European countries are in the fortunate position that for general political reasons they have already bound their hands by signing the new style Association Agreements with the European Community. These agreements provide for the establishment of a (bilateral) free trade area between the EU and the country in question by the end of the century. Although this 'hub and spoke' approach is not ideal from a theoretical point of view, these agreements have the immense advantage that they give traders the virtual certainty that at the end of the 10-year transition period these countries cannot have any import tariffs (on manufacturing goods) on exports originating from the Community and *vice versa*.[4]

The European Community (or rather the European Economic Space which comprises EFTA as well) provides more than 46.5 per cent (in 1992) of the imports of the Central European countries and is the market for almost 90 per cent of their exports of manufacturing goods. The six Central European countries that have signed the Association Agreements (Czech and Slovak republics, Hungary, Poland, Bulgaria and Romania) have thus *de facto* opened their economy to international trade and, conversely, have gained access to the huge market on their doorstep.[5]

We would suggest that these countries should retain a uniform tariff of 40 per cent that would be cut by four percentage points each year so that it would be eliminated within 10 years. A similar policy should be followed by the former Soviet republics.

Liberalising foreign trade should bring efficiency gains so that everybody could be better off. However, if the initial price structure is quite different from world market prices trade reform also implies large shifts in income distribution. The main redistributive effect has come from the repricing of (initially Soviet, then) Russian energy exports. The Soviet Union sold relatively cheap energy and other material inputs to East European economies in return for manufactured goods of lesser quality than those traded in Western markets.

The Central European countries and most former Soviet republics lost the subsidies for their material inputs. However, Central European countries suffered much less from the negative value-added (at world market prices) syndrome, despite the fact that their extensive manufacturing and agricultural industries had become addicted to cheap material inputs – particularly energy. In fact, some of them were able to sell their manufactures to the West. The examples of Poland, Hungary and Czechoslovakia are encouraging. Within the space of just a few years they have managed to redirect their exports from the CMEA area to competitive Western markets. See Table 6.4 below.

TABLE 6.4 East European countries' share of the OECD market (percentage change of market share over the period)

	Bulgaria	Czechoslovakia	Hungary	Poland	Romania
1979–1989	−18.5	−44.0	−7.8	−32.3	−46.3
1986–1989	−19.9	0.9	1.5	−23.5	−27.8
1989–1992	59.10	82.4	36.4	49.2	−55.1

Source: OECD (various years)

Trade liberalisation by Russia thus caused considerable adjustment problems. However, trade liberalisation *vis-à-vis* the West does not seem to have caused important adjustment problems in Central Europe. On the contrary, the West, especially the Community, reacted with an unprecedented opening of its market allowing the 'hard currency' exports from some countries to double in the space of a few years. We now discuss the contribution of trade to growth. The situation of the oil importing former Soviet republics is described in Chapter 13.

2. The gains from trade: trade and growth

The experience with trade liberalisation in the West suggests that the static efficiency gains from trade liberalisation in terms of the standard welfare 'triangles' are probably small.[6] It is often claimed that the dynamic gains are more substantial. These dynamic gains, are, however, difficult to measure, and one is bound to rely on broader means. We therefore review below the experience of Southern European countries which maintained highly protected markets and widespread state interventions until they joined the EU. Before describing the sequence of these countries it is useful to recall the starting point for Central and Eastern Europe.

Prior to 1989, Central and East European trade was predominantly conducted within the socialist bloc[7] (see Fig. 6.1). This inward concentration became even more marked in the 1980s, accounting for about 60 to 70 per cent of Central Europe's foreign trade by 1988. Until the demise of CMEA all these trade flows were managed bilaterally and subject to one- or five-year horse-trading between governments. The data for 1992 show convincingly that not much time is required to redirect trade. Industrial countries already account for two-thirds of the exports (and imports) of Central European countries.

The inward concentration of CMEA member countries' trade was accompanied by a loss of market shares outside this protected area. All Central European countries lost market shares in the 10 years prior to 1989 as shown in Table 6.4. However, since 1989 the reforms have led to a strong reversal of these trends (except for Romania), as can be seen in the last row of Table 6.4.

Gros and Gonciarz (1994) show that the distribution of trade of the Central European countries is now already quite close to that of European Union countries of similar size. In this very partial sense these countries are now already well integrated into the Western European economy. Chapters 15 and 16 discuss what this implies for the future of these countries and for Europe in general.

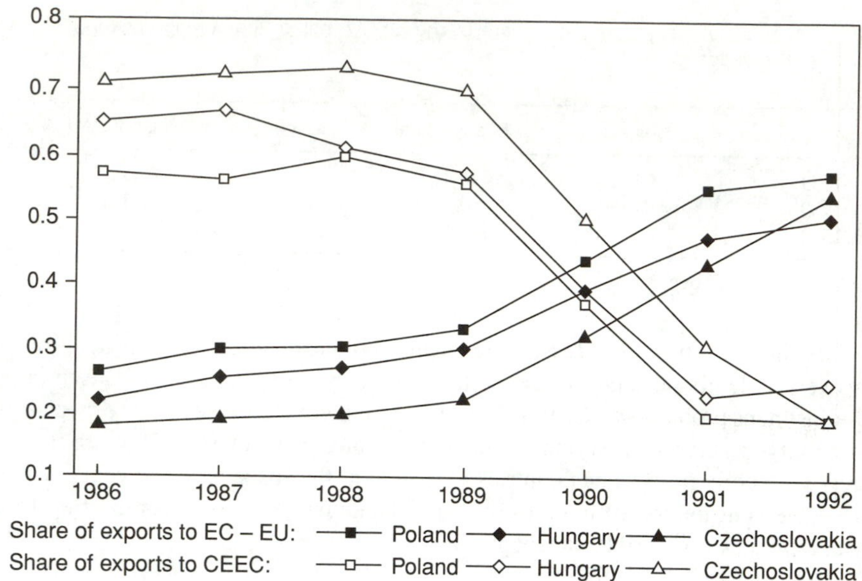

FIG 6.1 Central Europe: redirection of exports

Figure 6.2 shows that not only has the share of Europe increased, but the total value of exports has grown quickly. In the case of Poland and Czechoslovakia exports more than doubled between 1989 and 1992. The much worse performance of Russia (discussed in more detail in Chapter 14) is also apparent here.

Steinherr and Perée (1992) argue that the experience of some Southern European countries, which joined the European Community in the 1980s, probably offers useful hints as to the conditions required for successful economic transformation. In the case of the Southern European EU members the trade barriers that had to be eliminated were, of course, modest in comparison to the transformation that went on in Central and Eastern Europe. In this sense one would expect much larger effects of trade liberalisation in Eastern Europe.

As observed by Sachs (1993), in the early 1950s Poland, as the poorest of the three Visegrad countries, had a *per capita* income comparable and, by some accounts, even exceeding that of Spain. By 1988 Spain's *per capita* income was five times the Polish level. The most important difference between these two countries – closed to the outside world and predominantly agricultural in the early 1950s – is that, starting in the mid-1950s, Spain opened up increasingly with the hope of joining the European family. This opening up also prevented the economic structure from ossification, helped to expand services and to attract foreign investment. What holds for Poland is also true for the Czech and Slovak Republics and Hungary, which in the 1950s were much more advanced than Spain (and all three Visegrad countries were very much ahead of Portugal which has surpassed them all in the meantime).

Consider now the development of the world market shares of the most recent members of the EU, which are reported in Table 6.5 and compared with the same indicator for two Asian NICs. Between 1970 and 1990, the latter managed to double their share of the world market every 10 years. The performance of Spain, Portugal and Greece over that same period falls well short of that mark: Greece and Portugal sustained a cut

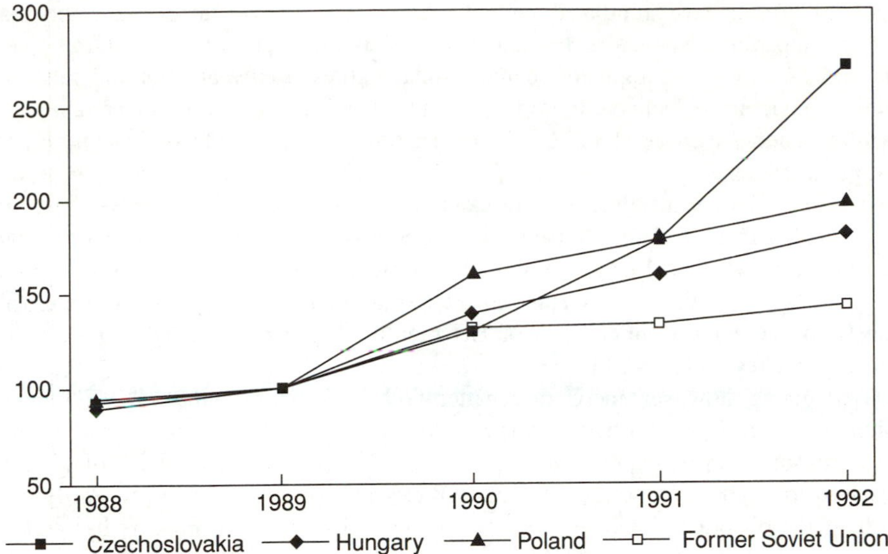

FIG 6.2 Central European exports to EC. 1989 = 100
Source: DOT, import data of EC-EU

TABLE 6.5 World market shares*

	Spain	Portugal	Greece	South Korea	Taiwan
1970	1.2	0.42	0.44	0.48	0.50
1985	1.5	0.36	0.40	1.67	1.38
1990	2.0	0.53	0.30	2.11	2.02

* Measured by the ratio of the sum of exports and imports of the country in question to the sum of world exports and imports
Source: IMF (various issues)

in their share of the world market between 1970 and 1985, while Spain registered only a very modest gain.

The picture has changed dramatically, however, since they joined the European Community. Spain and Portugal, who became members in 1986, have increased their world market share by 35 per cent and 45 per cent respectively. Greece, on the other hand, which joined in 1981, was unable to capitalise on her closer EU links during the 1980s and has watched her market share shrink by about one-third. The Greek experience is a clear warning that integration into the EU or, more generally, opening up to foreign trade, is no guarantee of success by itself. As described in Larre and Torres (1991), the difference in the speed of catching up between the Iberian countries and Greece is mainly due to the latter's inability to deal with supply-side deficiencies. The stimulative effect of the lifting of customs barriers has been offset by failure to restructure the productive sector.

In Spain and Portugal, the lifting of customs barriers was accompanied by industrial adjustment to reflect comparative advantages. With more competition from outside, structural reforms have stimulated the reallocation of productive factors to sectors that have a comparative advantage. In Spain production and exports of agricultural products and of transport equipment soared whilst textiles, footwear, oils and fats and metal manufacturing declined. In Portugal, with much lower labour costs, certain manufactured goods, such as clothing, benefited from integration whilst agriculture and textiles suffered.

To gain additional insights, we will examine the Spanish and Portuguese cases in more detail. Table 6.6 depicts changes in the geographic distribution of their foreign trade between 1981 and 1990. Prior to their joining the European Community in 1986, there had been no significant change in their trade patterns, except for an upturn in exports to the EU (in anticipation of EU membership) and a general lowering of exports to the rest of the world.

After joining, however, these trade patterns changed considerably. The EU share, which accounted for about half of Spain's exports in 1985, has since leapt to around two-thirds of Spanish exports. In the case of Portugal, the EU share of exports increased from about 60 per cent to nearly three-quarters of total exports. Partly as a result of the oil price slump in 1986, the geographic pattern of imports has shifted even more dramatically than that of exports in the Community's favour. It is clear from Table 6.6 that EU membership has produced strong trade-creation effects with the European Community and, possibly, some trade-diversion effects away from other countries.[8]

In addition to the changing geographic structure of trade flows, the product mix of exports and imports alike underwent significant changes in the course of the 1980s, as shown in Table 6.7. The most notable changes occurred in the realm of manufactures.

TABLE 6.6 Geographic structure of Spanish and Portuguese foreign trade (in percentage of total exports or imports)

		Spain Exports			Spain Imports	
	EU	Other industrial countries	Rest of the world	EU	Other industrial countries	Rest of the world
1981	45.9	15.4	38.7	29.5	21.9	48.6
1985	53.4	19.3	27.3	37.9	20.7	41.4
1990	64.9	13.1	21.9	59.1	20.2	20.7
1992	70.7	11.4	17.9	60.3	18.1	21.6
		Portugal Exports			Portugal Imports	
1981	56.5	21.9	21.6	44.9	24.2	30.9
1985	62.5	23.1	14.4	45.99	21.9	32.2
1990	73.5	17.6	8.9	69.1	14.8	16.2
1992	73.2	15.8	11.0	73.7	12.8	13.4

Source: EUROSTAT (1991) and own computations

As trade barriers went down and growth in the Iberian countries picked up, imports of manufactured goods soared. There was nothing odd about this, given the change in relative prices. Investment goods have also taken a larger share of imports, as the relatively antiquated production structure of the late 1970s was upgraded to broaden and deepen productive capacity in response to the challenge of foreign competition. The rapid growth of foreign trade, shown in Table 6.5, was sustained by remarkable growth of trade in manufactured goods, both on the import and the export side. Outdated economic structures, low starting incomes and the general disadvantage of being latecomers on foreign markets are not, therefore, in themselves a barrier to success.

As the benefits of improved production capacity only emerge in time, the adjustment process has led to current account deficits. Since 1987 they were over 3 per cent of GNP in 1990 in the case of Spain and over 1 per cent in Portugal. This current account handicap has not created any financing problems. Autonomous long-term credits and foreign direct investments have more than fully funded the deficit. Owing to the improved prospects accompanying closer European integration, foreign firms have increased their investments in Spain massively.

Spain and Portugal clearly benefited from catching up as described in Box 6.1: asset values and labour costs compared favourably to those in Northern Europe until recently, attracting foreign investment, enjoying an internal demand explosion and rapid GDP growth. But there is a difference: although richer, Spain had an unemployment rate of 22 per cent when it entered the Community whilst Portugal only had 8.8 per cent unemployment in 1985. Since then employment in Spain has grown at a rate of over 3 per cent per year until the current recession and productivity grew at a meagre 1 per cent on average. In Portugal, employment grew by less than 1 per cent on average, but productivity soared at an average of about 4 per cent. Both catching-up

TABLE 6.7 Product composition of Spanish and Portuguese foreign trade (as percentage of total exports or imports)

	Spain Exports			Spain Imports		
	Food and beverages	Raw materials and fuel	Manufacture	Food and beverages	Raw materials and fuel	Manufacture
1981	16.9	9.7	73.3	8.7	53.8	37.5
1985	12.4	12.9	74.7	7.9	47.0	45.1
1990	13.0	9.1	77.9	9.7	18.0	72.3
	Portugal Exports			**Portugal Imports**		
1981	10.5	18.7	70.8	13.9	33.1	53.0
1985	8.1	14.8	77.2	15.3	54.0	30.7
1990	6.7	13.0	80.4	15.4	26.9	57.6

Source: EUROSTAT (1991)

countries therefore achieved a growth of GDP in excess of 4 per cent – well above the Community average growth of about 3 per cent during 1985–91.

Box 6.1 From rags to riches: the catching-up hypothesis

After 1780 it took Britain 58 years to double its real income *per capita*; it took America 47 years from 1839; Japan did it in 34 years after the Meji reforms; and it took Korea 11 years from 1966. The later a country has become industrialised, the faster it has caught up. Britain's industrial revolution was a slow process because it was driven by industrial and technological innovations that absorbed resources and took time to develop. 'Catching up' has been much easier.

The more backward a country, the greater the scope for fast growth by copying the leaders. America's GDP per head was already 75 per cent of Britain's before it started its industrial expansion. In 1950 East Asian countries' GDP *per capita* was only 10 per cent of America's, even when adjusted for purchasing power· The poorer the country, the larger the pool of potential workers; the harder people will try to improve their lot; and the cheaper tends to be the labour cost component. Cheap labour and a nascent capital stock ensure high returns for capital, attracting both domestic savings and foreign investment.

During the nineteenth century the European continent to a great extent copied British technology. East Asia has also done so during their catching up. To adopt new technologies three ingredients are necessary: heavy investment in both physical and human capital and availability of a market. East Asian countries have invested in excess of 33 per cent of their GDP, roughly double the European level (in the European Community an average of 19 per cent in recent years). In addition much of the recent success of Asian countries has been based on investment in education. America's catching up benefited from the massive expansion of its domestic market. Asian countries could not rely on their domestic market and had to opt for an export drive. Korea's and Taiwan's exports account for 31–40 per cent of GDP.

Today's laggards benefit from a market increase in technological transmission, more readily available from foreign direct investment, the existence of an international capital market financing transitory deficits and a worldwide decrease in protectionism. So their chances of benefiting from 'catching up' are better than ever. Nevertheless, most countries have not succeeded in catching up. What is the fundamental difference between fast-growing East Asian countries and stationary poor countries elsewhere? The preconditions are precisely the institutional changes discussed here in Part II: appropriate property rights, a stable legal and administrative environment, trade with the rest of the world, and so on.

What lessons can be drawn from this discussion for Eastern Europe? Will its productive sector be able to restructure itself so as to face the challenge of foreign competition with some confidence? If the experience of Spain, Greece, and Portugal is any guide, there is reason to believe that the most promising policy option for Eastern Europe is 'export-led' growth, that is, restructuring based on comparative advantage, acceptance of an initial trade deficit as industry and infrastructure are rebuilt, and ultimate repayment of the accumulated debt through trade surpluses. Moreover, the length of the transition period and the cost of adjustment can be reduced if a number of specific conditions are met.

Counter-examples are also available to reinforce the points just made. Greece is trailing behind despite massive Community support because it is unable to restructure from within. Even more telling and appalling is the Argentinean example: one of the richest countries in the world in the 1920s, it has fallen to a level comparable to Central European countries. The reasons are clear: excessive protection of traditional activities for a long time; extensive price controls and provision of free social services; lack of social consensus to control fiscal and monetary policies; uncertain property rights at the mercy of regime changes, and so on.

Export-led growth also ensured the success of the fast-growing Asian tigers, even more successfully than in the Southern European countries. This raises the question whether Eastern European countries should not opt for an 'Asian strategy' instead of a free-trade approach with Western Europe. At first it is not clear what an 'Asian strategy' is: among the Four Tigers, Korea, Taiwan and Singapore developed with heavy government involvement, whilst Hong Kong espoused market principles; Korea opted for a big industrial concern strategy whilst the others let small and medium-sized enterprises prosper; Korea and Taiwan were highly protectionist in the early stages which is not an option for countries with an association agreement with the EU. The real secret of the Asian approach is not export-led growth based on protected domestic markets, but high rates of savings combined with a strong social consensus about the need to work hard.

The experience of Spain and Portugal seems to suggest that the massive import requirements attending adjustment of the productive sector might to a large extent be funded by foreign loans and direct investments. However, it is doubtful that Eastern Europe will obtain financing on a similar scale unless it provides investors with guarantees that they can repatriate their profits. We would argue that the crucial factor is the prospect of EU membership.

EU membership is important at several levels. First, the Southern European countries, by joining the European Community, were not only opening up their economy to foreign competition, but they were also given easier access to the large European market. As things stand at present, the associated countries of Central Europe (Poland, the Czech and Slovak Republics, Hungary, Romania and Bulgaria) have all obtained an agreement that should give their manufacturing products free access to the EU within five years.

Second, and more importantly, direct investment has flowed into Spain and Portugal because the economic and political environment became stable and the economies were catching up. EU membership was the decisive factor that transformed some Southern European countries with a history of dictatorships, revolutions and frail young democracies, into safe bets. The prospect of EU membership could have the same effect for some Central European countries. At present it seems that only three Visegrad countries (Poland, the Czech Republic and Hungary) stand a chance of joining the Community.

3. Liberalisation of the capital account

We argued in the preceding subsection that trade liberalisation requires 'current account convertibility',[9] that is, exporters and importers have to be able to buy and sell foreign exchange for their transactions. 'Current account convertibility' thus makes the domestic currency convertible only for trade, or other 'current' transactions. A much debated question is whether foreign currency should also be made available for capital account transactions.[10]

Why should trade transactions be free (subject at most to a uniform tariff) whereas capital transactions are restricted? The main issue here is macroeconomic stability and the state of the domestic capital market. In a first best world there would be no need to impose restrictions on capital movements. However, as we argue repeatedly in these chapters, the creation of an efficient domestic capital market is the part of the overall reform that might take the most time. Transition countries are thus likely to be for some time in a second best world, in the sense that the domestic capital market is not working well.

In many reforming economies macroeconomic stabilisation was delayed. In these cases interest rates were often kept very low; much lower than the rate of inflation or the rate of depreciation of the currency that could be reasonably expected. Russia provides the best example of this situation: in 1992–93 interest rates on the interbank market and those charged by the Central Bank of Russia, were about 100 to 200 per cent p.a. while inflation was running at 2,000 per cent and the exchange rate was depreciating at a similar rate. Under these circumstances anybody with access to credit could make a huge profit by just investing the proceeds in foreign exchange. This was clearly not in the interest of the country as a whole since the government was at the same time desperately seeking new money on the international capital market. For the individual concerned it was, of course, completely rational to invest in the world capital market (and thus give a credit to foreigners). But the country as a whole lost from these operations because the social return for Russia would have been much higher if this capital had been invested at home. Prohibition of foreign exchange transactions not related to foreign trade can avoid this loss. Of course, it would be better still for the country to raise nominal interest above the inflation rate. In that case there might not be a massive capital outflow and hence no need for prohibition.

Another, related circumstance under which limitations on capital movements can be justified, arises when budget constraints on some sectors of the economy are not yet hardened. For example, large enterprises, that are nominally owned by the state, but *de facto* no longer under its control might have access to the banking system under the assumption that they are 'too large to fail'; these enterprises might also borrow large sums that they invest abroad. If the country as a whole is at the same time refused additional credit from abroad this type of operation reduces social welfare.

There can thus be situations in which it is not in the interest of the country to permit full capital account convertibility. The first best would, of course, be to eliminate the distortions on the domestic capital market. However, this might not always be feasible immediately. If these capital market distortions cannot be eliminated, a second best measure remains to limit capital account convertibility. These limitations will, in practice, always be circumvented through over-billing of imports, under-billing of exports and many other ways. Effectiveness is always curtailed.

McKinnon (1991) claims that not until the domestic capital market has been fully liberalised, with well-defined financial and fiscal constraints on firms and individuals firmly in place, such that unrestricted borrowing and lending at equilibrium domestic interest rates becomes a working proposition, can the domestic currency of any one socialist economy be safely made fully convertible into foreign exchange on capital account. Many years hence, he argues, individuals and enterprises – including joint ventures with foreign firms – might possibly be allowed to choose freely between domestic and foreign sources of finance. But this must be the last, rather than the first, step in the optimum sequencing of liberalisation.

The experience of a number of Latin American countries that liberalised their economies during the 1980s also suggests that capital account liberalisation should wait (see Box 6.2). In these countries premature liberalisation of capital movements led to large capital inflows that drove up the real exchange rate and thus increased unemployment. When the capital inflows dried up the exchange rate depreciated and domestic banks were unable to service their debt. This presented the government with a choice: risk the collapse of the domestic banking system or take over the banking system and its foreign debt. All governments chose the latter and therefore ended up with much more foreign debt than they had intended, even in Chile where the government had always pretended that foreign borrowing by private agents should be of no concern for public policy. This experience has led to the near consensus that current account liberalisation should come before capital account liberalisation.[11]

Box 6.2 Capital account liberalisation: the Southern Cone failure

Opponents of an early liberalisation of capital account transactions often point to the problems faced by Argentina, Chile and Uruguay – the Southern Cone countries – during their reforms in the late 1970s and early 1980s. All three countries had extensively reformed and liberalised their domestic financial system and removed capital controls (Chile only partially). As a result of removing ceilings on interest rates, of publishing future exchange rates (*tablitas*) and of a more rapid than expected decline in inflation rates, real interest rates became highly volatile and rose to levels as high as 30 per cent for extended periods of time. These rates attracted foreign capital inflows causing the exchange rates to appreciate. The real effective exchange rate of Argentina trebled between 1977 and 1981; doubled in Uruguay and increased by 50 per cent in Chile. The trade accounts deteriorated so dramatically (reinforced by backward wage indexation in Chile and lax fiscal policy in Argentina) that all three countries had to abandon the reform.

This experience still receives conflicting interpretations. In particular it is evident that the course of events as described above could have been avoided. First, the strong increase in the real interest rate could have been curbed by more expansionary monetary policy. Second, fiscal policy could have been tightened to

continued

Box 6.2 *continued*

control inflation and also contribute to lower interest rates. The combined effect of this policy mix (tight fiscal policy and expansionary monetary policy) would have kept inflation and the exchange rate below the actual rates. Nevertheless, it needs to be recognised from this experience that the government needs to dispose of considerable sophistication and flexibility to cope with a possible perturbation through capital inflows. If, as in Russia, the budget deficit is not under control then a capital inflow may serve to finance the budget deficit and slow down reforms. Appreciation may kill worthwhile projects whilst government invests in or keeps alive white elephants.

But even under such circumstances capital-hungry Eastern European countries would do better with a liberalised capital account than with rigid and comprehensive capital controls. Our preferred approach is to use a two-tier exchange market during transition. If the Southern Cone countries had operated such a scheme their trade performance would not have suffered from the capital inflow and local business would have benefited from the availability of foreign capital.

Source: Edwards and Teitel (1986); Mathieson and Rojas-Suarez (1993).

However, even as a second best, limits on capital movements have a drawback: they need to be enforced. By contrast, full convertibility has one big advantage: it does not require any controls. Countries with a sound macroeconomic balance should thus move to capital account convertibility. Latvia is a good example. It would have been difficult for the authorities of this country to control capital movements when the country re-emerged from the FSU because the government had to be organised from scratch. Moreover, the government was able to balance its books quite quickly and hard budget constraints were effectively imposed on state-owned enterprises. This is why in this case it was sensible just to lift all controls on foreign exchange transactions, which is tantamount to capital account convertibility.

We advocate a different position that imposes no quantitative controls on capital movements because this type of restriction can have a strong negative impact on foreign investment that is really needed for the reconstruction of the European East. We would propose a dual exchange rate regime that deflects the potential capital market distortions mentioned above on a separate market. Since this solution has to be discussed together with the exchange rate regime, we now turn to this issue.

4. Currency convertibility and the exchange rate regime

When liberalisation started in 1989–90 it was often argued that an immediate move to (current account) convertibility was not possible because the countries concerned (Poland in the first instance) did not have enough foreign exchange reserves. However, subsequent events proved that this argument was wrong. Provided the exchange rate is low enough convertibility does not require large reserves. Indeed, a purely floating exchange rate does not need any support in terms of foreign exchange reserves. However, for reasons discussed below almost all reforming countries opted for a fixed exchange rate.

If the exchange rate is fixed, the central bank plays the role of seller or buyer of last resort by tapping or building up net external assets. Except in the case of full monetary union where the exchange rate is irreversibly fixed, monetary authorities may change the parity in order to adjust to external disequilibriums. When the exchange rate is flexible, and determined by market forces, the central bank refrains from intervention of any kind. Whether or not there are restrictions on foreign exchange operations does not matter in this case. It follows therefore that currency convertibility is largely independent from exchange rate arrangements, which have their own far-reaching implications.

Once full convertibility[12] has been accepted the government needs to choose the exchange rate regime. The classic options regarding the exchange rate regime are: a free float, a fixed but adjustable peg and a dual exchange rate system combining the first two options. More extreme solutions have also been proposed and adopted: see the currency board solution chosen by Estonia discussed in Chapter 14.

The free-floating option has gained little support from economists. The governments of former socialist countries must guarantee, amongst other conditions, stability and, in particular, reduce uncertainties about their exchange rates if they want to increase external trade and attract foreign investment. With the limited financial instruments that are available flexible exchange rates are likely to create an uncertainty for traders that cannot be hedged as easily as among other currencies with more developed financial markets. No country in Eastern Europe has refrained from interventions in the foreign exchange markets. Even in Latvia, which formally had a free float, the central bank intervened heavily to slow down the appreciation of the Lat.

We prefer fixed but adjustable exchange rates. During the transition period they have to be supported by capital controls, otherwise the exchange rate commitment could be undermined at any time by speculative flows, owing to political uncertainties that cannot be eliminated during the transition.[13]

Our proposed solution for the transition is therefore an intermediate regime between fixed and flexible exchange rates, that is, a dual exchange system. This solution is economically equivalent to fixed exchange rates with varying capital levies on capital transactions.[14] In such a system, current account transactions are treated at the controlled, and usually fixed, exchange rate, while financial funds flow in and out of the country at a freely flexible exchange rate. Such a system was introduced temporarily in Poland and Romania.

The underlying aim of such a system is to shelter the domestic real economy from external and domestic financial shocks. At the micro level capital can flow in and out of the country in pursuit of the most favourable return/risk trade-off. However, at the macro level there can be no net capital flows unless the central bank chooses to intervene in the market for capital account, that is, financial transactions. The free, financial rate has to adjust in such a way that the capital account is always in equilibrium. In such a system the domestic monetary authorities do not have to react to financial shocks from the outside. The system redirects automatically the burden of adjustment to the financial exchange rate instead of the domestic interest rate. The current account exchange rate can be kept constant, thereby maintaining stability for the relative prices of goods and services, provided domestic prices are stable.

In fact, by imposing a varying tax on capital transactions (equal to the flexible gap between the controlled and uncontrolled exchange rates), such a system reduces the substitutability between domestic and external assets, without erecting any barrier to capital flows at the individual level. This imperfect substitutability confers some latitude on domestic monetary authorities. In practice, however, the latitude of the domestic monetary authorities is limited because the spread between the controlled and the uncontrolled rates is constrained by the impossibility of a leak-proof separation of both exchange market compartments.[15] After reflection this is an advantage rather than a disadvantage: when the free rate moves far away from the fixed rate then it is unlikely that the fixed rate is still an appropriate rate. This tension would suggest the need for a fixed rate adjustment and policy-makers cannot sustain the fixed rate at the wrong level for too long.

An essential feature of the dual exchange system is that there cannot be any net capital inflow or outflow unless the central bank decides to intervene in the financial exchange market. The central bank is therefore released from financing net capital imbalances but has to support current account disequilibriums.

Such a regime should, however, be strictly temporary. Given the flexibility inherent in such a system, it would be straightforward to wind it down gradually by eliminating the implicit capital controls through a commitment to keep the spread between the two rates within certain limits that are reduced over time. Belgium operated a dual-exchange rate system for over 40 years with considerable success. Its discontinuation in 1991 was not even noticed by market participants.

Two decisions are of overriding importance in fixing the (commercial) exchange rate. First, the choice of currency to which the national currency is pegged and, second, the rate for the peg.

This second choice is mainly an empirical question and we wish only to stress that the frequent error of maintaining an over-valued exchange rate needs to be avoided. In this respect, West European experience after World War II is a good lesson: growth resumed only when over-valuation ended and was highest in those countries with currencies close to or below purchasing power parity rates. See the Appendix to this chapter for a review of post-war European policies.

By far the majority of countries maintain fixed exchange rates with respect to one or a basket of currencies. About 30 to 40 currencies are pegged to the SDR, members of the EMS are pegged to the Ecu, and about 30 other currencies are pegged to a basket *sui generis*. Specific (*sui generis*) baskets are constructed with a view to composing an exchange rate target as an average of bilateral exchange rates, weighted by foreign trade structure. The more intensive trade relationships are with any given country, the more important is the relevant bilateral exchange rate. However, specific baskets have serious shortcomings in their function as exchange targets. The first is that trade flows are only one aspect, capital flows are another of equal importance and the geographic pattern of trade and capital flows are usually not highly correlated. A second shortcoming for countries forced to establish credibility is that a specific basket is not directly observable and, in fact, some central banks make an effort not to reveal the exact basket construction. The market, therefore, finds it difficult to evaluate the course of exchange rate policy and its ability to remain on track. In addition, if the basket was known and a stable exchange rate in terms of the basket was expected, prudent reserve management would require holding foreign exchange positions that replicate the basket to minimise foreign exchange risk.

Because of these difficulties or shortcomings, many countries opt for a standard basket such as the SDR or the Ecu. The latter has a decisive advantage over the former, in that it is a traded currency and widely diversified financial instruments in Ecu do exist. Moreover, the predominant part of foreign trade of Eastern European countries is already concentrated on the EEC and this share is likely to increase over time. See Chapter 16 for a prospective analysis of future trade flows between East and West Europe.

Under fixed exchange rates, a small country can, at best, only achieve the monetary stability of the currency to which it is pegged. It can, of course, do worse. This constraint suggests that if a country aims at monetary stability then it should peg to a stable currency that becomes the anchor for its national monetary system. The DM or the Ecu would therefore be much more promising than, say, the US dollar, both for considerations of stability and trade structure.

5. Conclusions

External liberalisation is a necessary complement to internal price liberalisation. We argue that the benefits of external liberalisation are substantial and that the magnitude of the benefits also depends on the quality of capital markets. Trade liberalisation provides the economy with the 'right' price signals. Exposure to world prices helps to demonopolise the economy, to enhance competition and to improve the allocation of resources. However, in adjusting to the removal of protection, even 'good' and economically viable firms may require credit-lines to bridge restructuring. The adoption of 'hard budget constraints' eliminates the automatic financing of enterprises' deficits by the government. Without sufficient access to capital markets, such 'good' firms may be forced out of business, thereby reducing the benefits from trade liberalisation. Moreover, in attempting to protect themselves, the 'good' but endangered enterprises may be tempted to join the 'bad' and economically non-viable enterprises in lobbying against trade liberalisation, thereby reducing the likelihood that liberalisation will be adopted. These considerations imply that the benefits from, and support for, trade liberalisation can be significantly enhanced by the early development of domestic capital markets.

The state of the domestic capital market also determines whether or not capital account convertibility should be allowed immediately. Most economists, inspired by historical experience, argue that full convertibility, including capital account operations, is a much less urgent concern than current account convertibility. Once a stabilisation programme is successfully implemented, the need for foreign capital in those countries suggests, however, that full convertibility may be beneficial. We propose as an interim solution a two-tier exchange market that combines a fixed rate for current account transactions with a freely floating rate for capital account transactions. No administrative controls on individual capital operations are required in this case. The Visegrad countries have made enough progress in stabilisation and the creation of domestic capital markets no longer to need a dual exchange rate. However, in other

Eastern European countries, notably Russia, this would still be an appropriate step forward.

Notes

1. The revenue position of the government would be greatly enhanced if it retained a full claim on the profits or surpluses being generated by natural resource-based industries at the higher domestic prices. For that it need not retain ownership. Appropriate taxes can transfer the natural rents to the government.
2. Typically, the uniform tariff rate that maximises tariff revenues is higher than the rate that maximises welfare of consumers and producers through international trade. For a small economy and abstracting from distortions this optimal rate is zero.
3. Formally this can be shown by observing that with an *ad valorem* import tariff of t, the domestic price ratio is: Pimp(1+t)/Pexp. With an *ad valorem* export tariff of t the domestic price ratio is Pimp/(Pexp/(1+t)), which is equivalent to the result under an import tariff. See Lerner (1939).
4. See Gros (1991).
5. We do not discuss in this chapter the role of the West in the transformation in Central Europe; this is done in Chapter 11. However, we would like to note here that these Association Agreements, although they can be criticised in many detailed points, are a significant contribution to the long-run success of the East European transition to market economy because they open up a huge market for exports from this region and commit these countries to an outward-looking strategy.
6. See Emerson *et al.* (1988) and the references cited therein.
7. As trade within the CMEA was conducted in transferable rubles, which are not convertible, aggregation of global trade flows depended heavily on the implicit exchange rate used in the analysis. The figures in Fig. 6.1 should therefore be interpreted with care and are best seen as a rough guide for analysing the change in East European trade patterns.
8. Yugoslavia was the first socialist country that managed to change the geographic distribution of its foreign trade within a few years. In 1982, 45 per cent of its exports went to the CMEA countries and only 21 per cent to the EU. In 1988, 39 per cent of exports went to the EU and only 26 per cent to the CMEA zone (see Gros and Steinherr 1991a).
9. Internal convertibility refers to the right of residents freely to acquire foreign exchange; external convertibility gives to non-residents the right to convert domestic currencies; both may be subjected to specific conditions or limitations so that convertibility is called restricted or limited.
10. The external liberalisation of the smaller Central and East European countries was supported by bridging finance from the international agencies. But accepting official bridging finance based on strict conditionality is not tantamount to a general relaxation of controls over private capital movements.
11. Since the early 1980s capital controls again became universal in Latin America. It is estimated that the illegal accumulated capital outflows are roughly equal to Latin America's foreign debt. We could therefore argue that the problem of massive inflows is more easily manageable and more welfare-enhancing than the outflow of capital which takes place when there are controls.
12. Transitional arrangements for increased convertibility between Central European countries and the Soviet Union are not discussed here. For a discussion of the desirability of a transitional East European Payments Union, see Bofinger (1990) and Kenen (1990). These authors stress the limited usefulness of such a payments union if the FSU is not a member, because trade within the European ex-CMEA countries accounts for only a small fraction

of their global trade. Fostering trade inside this group of countries is therefore less important than eliminating impediments to trade with the rest of the world by a rapid return to convertibility. However, inclusion of the FSU completely changes the complexion of the problem, as is shown in Chapter 13.

13. The only way Central European countries could maintain a fixed exchange rate (with a convertible currency) without capital controls is by adopting the currency board solution or by joining a monetary union. See Bofinger (1990) and Box 7.4 in Chapter 7.
14. For an assessment of dual exchange rates, see Decaluwe and Steinherr (1976).
15. For an analysis of the effects of arbitrage between the two exchange-rate markets, see Gros (1988).

Appendix: The importance of trade for post-war reconstruction in Western Europe

Foreign trade has been an engine of growth for Western Europe since the early 1950s, starting out after the war from conditions that bear resemblance to those in Eastern Europe today, particularly in the FSU: insufficient and obsolete capital stock, underemployment paired with availability of skilled workers, prices out of line with economic reality, efforts at economic planning for reconstruction, insufficient domestic capital and low levels of foreign exchange reserves. Of course, many things were also different. World capital markets, and therefore access to private foreign borrowings, were virtually non-existent, the world economy was less integrated and standards of living were much lower.

In this Appendix, we review succinctly the immediate post-war experience because it provides several practical lessons. For details see Kaplan and Schleiminger (1989). First, despite widespread belief to the contrary, Marshall Plan aid was not in fact a decisive factor and we shall argue in Chapter 15 that, today, Western financial resources are certainly helpful but not decisive for rapid growth in Eastern Europe. Second, the most critical factor was the return to competitive conditions for resource allocation within the international division of labour. Many countries that were unwilling to reform the state's dominating role and open up fared less well in post-war growth. Third, until 1949 all European countries, to different degrees, maintained over-valued exchange rates with serious consequences: slow development of foreign trade, continuing domestic interventionism, and delayed return to convertibility. Fourth, those countries that moved most decisively to an international division of labour achieved remarkably quick returns to (partial) convertibility, full employment and high growth. This is what is happening now in Central Europe, but not in the FSU, and for which a Marshall Plan II might be necessary, as argued in Chapter 15.

The very fact that large parts of the capital stock of Europe had been run down, or destroyed, during the war while complementary factors of production, that is, skilled and unskilled labour, were readily available, should have made private trans-Atlantic investments highly profitable. Unfortunately, an efficient and developed international capital market did not exist. Nor did reconstruction plans convey clear messages as to the evolution of the institutional framework. Therefore, the reverse happened and on a net basis Europe transferred capital to the comparatively capital-abundant United States.

The economic policies of West European countries after the war provide the explanation for this development. Internally, these policies were rooted in the continuation of war-time controls over production and prices of major goods and the financing of expansionary demand policies by money creation.

Externally, these policies were complemented by severe over-valuation of European exchange rates *vis-à-vis* the US dollar until 1949 (Fig. 6.A.1). This over-valuation served to make imports of capital goods and food that were considered as 'essentials' cheaper in terms of domestic currency but made exports too expensive. In addition, European governments were reluctant to admit openly the consequences of their internal inflation by abandoning pre-war parities. The resulting severe shortage of foreign exchange forced European governments to keep their currencies inconvertible. Over-valuation not only limited the growth of cross-Atlantic trade by discouraging European exports, it impeded growth of intra-European exchanges of goods and services as well. In addition, each country attempted a mercantilist approach to increase exchange reserves. Because only the US dollar promised stability and only the United States had a complete range of products to offer, every European country had an incentive to accept no currency but dollars in exchange for its goods. Due to the severe shortage of money that could be used as a store of value and medium of exchange in transactions between currency areas, Europe turned to barter trade, that is, to an extensive network of bilateral agreements specifying in detail the quantities and values of goods to be exchanged.

The consequences were a grossly inefficient allocation of available resources, an inherent bias against the division of labour among countries and failure to attract private resources for reconstruction and growth from outside.

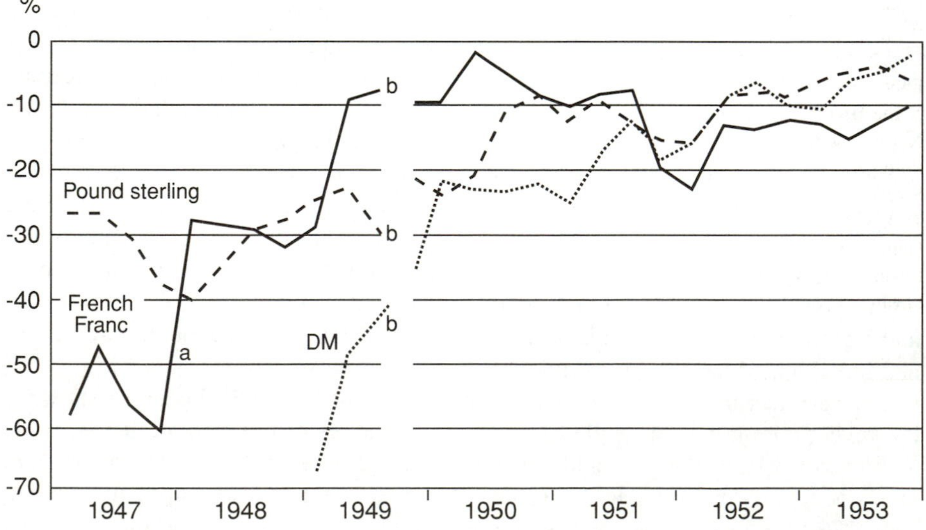

FIG 6.A.1 Overvaluation of major West European currencies, 1947–1953
Source: Kostrzewa et al (1989)

The most visible direct result of these policies was the European balance of payments crisis of 1947. The monetary expansion at over-valued exchange rates, the ill-fated British attempt to make the pound sterling convertible at the untenable pre-war parity and the temporary absence of Europe's traditional supplies caused a high level of dollar imports and discouraged exports and inflows of private capital at the same time. In 1947, Western Europe lost one third of its gold or dollar reserves.

The details of the European Recovery Programme were elaborated in negotiations between the United States and West European governments. Marshall Plan expenditures started in April 1948 and by 1949 had reached their peak. The economic impact of the Marshall Plan has recently been the subject of lively debate, and the traditional view that this massive transfer of resources made a considerable contribution to the economic recovery of Western Europe has been contested. A comparison of the aid receipts of individual countries (as a percentage of their GNP) and their economic performance as measured by the growth of GNP and exports reveals no clear picture. A statistical analysis (Spearman rank correlation) shows only a weak and insignificant positive correlation between aid receipts as a percentage of GNP and the growth of exports and especially GNP in the 1948–53 period (Table 6.A.1).

TABLE A.6.1 Marshall Plan aid and economic performance

	Aid receipts in m $*	GNP 1950 in bn $	Annual Real Growth Rates (1948–1953)			
			GNP	Industrial production	Exports	Gross capital formation†
Austria	703.5	2.430	8.66	12.82	22.30	16.87
Belgium–Luxembourg	324.8	7.052	3.87	2.92	8.71	3.66
Denmark	271.2	3.348	3.79	3.96	15.46	7.46
France	2862.6	29.090	4.26	4.47	17.08	0.56
West Germany	1317.2	23.310	13.32	20.37	50.09	20.12
Greece	773.7	2.185	9.01	14.69	17.76	4.55
Italy	1253.5	15.165	6.05	9.96	8.68	11.79
Netherlands	980.6	4.976	5.18	7.63	23.89	2.96
Norway	263.6	2.720	3.34	7.26	7.54	3.61
Portugal	41.6	1.398	3.71	–	4.87	1.98
Sweden	82.1	6.520	3.59	2.48	7.54	2.11
Turkey	213.1	2.300	7.39	8.36	12.81	–
United Kingdom	2690.7	37.337	2.71	4.03	4.40	2.92
Ireland	146.5	1.086	3.07	7.78	12.92	6.00
Iceland	29.3	(0.110)	1.63	–	0.71	–
All recipients‡	11954.0	139.027	5.27	7.71	13.3	–

* Total expenditures, adjusted for the reallocation of aid via bilateral drawing rights 1948/49.

† 1948-1953 average (gross capital formation: 1948–1952 average), in per cent

‡ Excluding the working capital of the European Payments Union which amounted to 350 m dollars.

Spearman rank correlation coefficients between aid receipts in per cent of GNP and (i) GNP growth: 0.179 (26.2); (ii) export growth: 0.358 (9.5); (iii) growth of industrial production: 0.544 (2.7), growth rate of gross capital formation: 0.275 (18.2); in brackets: probability of non-correlation (in per cent).

Source: Kostrzewa et al. (1989)

The basis for the allocation of Marshall Plan funds among the recipients was a country's balance of payments situation *vis-à-vis* the dollar area, not an evaluation of investment needs or of how the resources could be employed most productively. This is a general drawback of trade – as compared to investment – financing. The major recipients of Marshall Plan aid in absolute terms, namely Britain and France, were exactly the two countries who went through recurrent balance of payments crises in the 1950s. On the other hand, West Germany – which had suffered a net outflow of resources in the post-war period if war reparations and the costs of military occupation are deducted from the Marshall Plan payments and the further assistance which the country had received until 1952 – experienced an unprecedented export boom, rapid accumulation of foreign reserves and outstandingly high rates of economic growth whilst achieving price stability.

The actual improvement in the European payments position which took place while the Marshall Plan operated can be largely attributed to the devaluations of European currencies against the dollar in September 1949. German exports grew rapidly due to the abolition of central planning and most price controls in conjunction with a drastic currency reform to eliminate the monetary overhang ('repressed inflation') in June 1948; and the stepwise relaxation of restrictions on foreign trade. The exchange rate remained under-valued during the 1950s and West Germany's share in world exports rose more than eightfold between 1947 and 1952. This helped to reduce the need for Western Europe to import from the US, thereby maintaining better foreign trade balances. Impressive as these figures are, the re-emergence of West Germany was still hampered by the fact that firms had to rely predominantly on their own earnings to finance investments, as internal and external capital markets were under-developed.

Overall, the Marshall Plan cannot be counted as a relevant lesson. As capital markets were not as complete as today, there was little alternative to official lending. Aid payments were useful and decreased hardship but also relieved European governments of the need to correct their economic policies in a way which would have made possible a much earlier return to convertibility. Instead, it encouraged the majority of European governments to continue with their internal policies of economic planning and demand expansion.

Externally, most countries of Western Europe could thus afford learning-by-doing and take the long road to trade liberalisation and currency convertibility. Due to reluctance on both sides of the Atlantic to devalue European currencies sufficiently, the 'dollar gap' retarded the removal of barriers to international trade and payments for more than a decade. Although, under the prevailing economic policy conditions, the Marshall Plan was indeed helpful for many countries, West Germany's *Wirtschaftswunder* demonstrates that a shift in economic policies along the lines of its reforms of June 1948 might have been even more beneficial. In the case of such a change, a short-term infusion of public funds might have been a good thing to ease the transition period. Aid would, however, have been less necessary.

The slow return to convertibility is also full of lessons about what to do and what to avoid. In the first years following World War II, Western European countries maintained their non-convertible currencies and imposed tight trade restrictions, aimed at limiting exports of 'essential' goods, encouraging exports of 'goods of lesser importance', encouraging imports of essential goods, and limiting imports of goods of lesser importance.

Since all the countries were basically in the same economic situation, they all had the same protectionist attitude, which obviously could only lead to a contraction in their international trade and a slow reconstruction process.

The first trial solution aimed at encouraging trade flows between European countries took the form of a system of bilateral agreements. These stipulated that the partner countries would limit their exports of essential goods and, at the same time, their imports of less scarce and 'non important' products. On the financial side, these agreements set up mutual credit lines within the limits of which the net positions arising from bilateral transactions did not require actual settlement by the central banks.

Another attempt consisted of re-establishing the convertibility of one currency: in July 1947, sterling was again made convertible for the current transactions of the balance of payments: non-residents were allowed to use the payments received in this currency to settle current transactions with almost all countries. This experience was short-lived, as huge amounts of sterling were sold for dollars (for reasons given in the previous section).

Finally, a multilateral clearing system (European Payments Union) was proposed in December 1949 to ease, at least in its first stage, the problems arising from the non-convertibility of the currencies. This system came into force in July 1950, with the purpose of improving the industrial network of the European countries, the well balanced development of trade, and eventually reaching the goal of convertibility of currencies for current account transactions.

With a few exceptions, this was achieved in December 1958; as, in the meantime, the debtor countries had been gradually able to repay their debt, the system was abolished on the same date.

CHAPTER SEVEN

Macroeconomic stabilisation

In order to draw a limit to thinking, we should have to be able to think both sides of this limit.
(L. Wittgenstein, *Tractatus Logico-Philosophicus,* Preface)

The socialist countries managed their economy by keeping a tight grip on the microeconomic unit: firms, workers and consumers. They did not need (or at least felt they did not need) any global instruments to steer aggregate demand (fiscal expenditures and the fiscal deficit), to control overall liquidity (monetary policy), to direct the distribution of revenues (incomes policy) or to stabilise the exchange rate (exchange market intervention). Once the transition to a market economy has started, such instruments had to be created and policy-makers had to learn how to use them.

Experience has shown that the most dangerous phase comes during the beginning of the transition, when the old controls no longer operate (prices and wages have been liberalised) but the new macroeconomic tools are not yet in place. In this vacuum, compounded by uncertainty about the future, temporary disruptions in the production process, loss of traditional export markets and a long list of related problems, chances are high that inflation will go out of control. When this happens all the other parts of the reform programme are threatened as well. One therefore has to draw a limit and consider both sides of it, the cost of hyperinflation and chaos, on the one hand, and the cost and temporary hardship of stabilisation, on the other. Hyperinflation is generally defined as inflation of 50 per cent per month or more. By this definition hyperinflation is a rare phenomenon; but among reforming countries Poland, ex-Yugoslavia (Serbia) and the Ukraine have already experienced hyperinflation at some point. Russia and some other CIS states have come close to it.

The chapter looks at the most important threats to macroeconomic stability during the transition phase.[1] If the transformation of socialist into market economies could be achieved instantaneously macroeconomic stabilisation in Central and Eastern Europe would require exactly the same steps as elsewhere in the West. However, we will show that macroeconomic stabilisation of an economy 'in transition' to a market economy is somewhat different because the factors that constitute the dangers are different.

We begin this chapter with an analysis of the 'so-called' monetary overhang, which was considered an obstacle to price liberalisation at the very beginning of the reforms in most Central and Eastern European countries. We then address two dangers for macroeconomic stabilisation that are specific to economies in transition: first, how to assert some control over nominally still 'state-owned' enterprises, which in fact no longer follow the orders of the state; second, fiscal reform, or how to obtain enough revenues for the state so that the recourse to the inflation tax can be limited. Finally we turn to the external aspects of stabilisation, namely, how to use the exchange rate to provide a nominal anchor.

1. The monetary overhang

In a number of socialist countries the so-called 'monetary overhang' (see Box 7.1 for an explanation) was seen as a serious obstacle to price liberalisation because, it was argued, after price liberalisation consumers would suddenly spend all their accumulated excess cash balances and this would lead to inflation. It would have been more appropriate to speak of a jump in the price level, but the discussion was usually in terms of inflation. Price liberalisation led, indeed, in all cases to a jump in the price level. However, the size of the initial jump differed greatly, from about 50 per cent in the CSFR to over 250 per cent in Russia. There were also great differences in terms of the subsequent performance: prices stabilised in some countries (CSFR, Latvia), but in Russia and to some extent Poland prices continued to increase rapidly even after the initial jump.

The inflationary pressures that did in fact persist in most, but not all, post-socialist countries after the initial price shock were thus not due only to the combination of price liberalisation and monetary overhang. Theoretical considerations and empirical evidence suggests that the main cause of continuing inflation were lax financial policies, in turn due to a lack of control over SOEs and an inefficient fiscal system.

Table 7.1 Countries in transition: consumer prices (annual % change)

	1989	1990	1991	1992	1993
Czechoslovakia*	1.4	10.8	57.7	10.8	20.8
ex-GDR					
Hungary	17.0	28.9	36.4	23.0	22.5
Poland	251.1	585.8	70.3	43.0	35.3
Russia†	2.3	5.6	92.7	1353.0	895.9

* Data for Czech Republic in 1993
† Data for USSR in 1989
Source: IMF, World Economic Outlook

Box 7.1 Monetary overhang

A monetary or liquidity overhang is defined as an excess stock of cash or savings deposits (and the sight deposits of firms) because the population has been 'forced to save'. If one speaks of an 'overhang' one first has to establish that the actual holdings are somehow excessive. A monetary overhang is usually diagnosed if the actual ratio of cash (or savings deposits) to income exceeds that observed in market economies.

There are two reasons why the ratio of cash or financial assets to income may be much larger in socialist than in market economies. They are basically dissimilar, and only if we understand the difference between the two can we predict with some confidence what might happen during stabilisation.

The first reason is excess demand and rationing, in particular in goods markets. This may prompt consumers to hold both a large volume of goods ('buy when you can, not when you need') and of cash (so as to be able to seize the opportunity of buying things). Such behaviour is well documented not only for consumers, but also in the case of East European firms, which tended to carry unusually high levels of raw materials and goods in process to avoid breaks in production.

The second, more widely emphasised reason is forced saving, or the fact that consumers are not able to spend their money on what they want. A closer analysis suggests, however, that 'forced savings' are likely to be temporary and will arise only under extreme conditions if one takes a microeconomic point of view (the incentives faced by an individual household), but from a macroeconomic point of view very different conclusions emerge.

At the *microeconomic* level it makes sense to speak of forced savings only if *all* prices are fixed and *all* goods are rationed, because only under these circumstances would people be forced to save what they could not spend anywhere. But even in the worst days of the Soviet Union, some goods were in fact available and there was a thriving black market, operating at market-clearing prices, for a range of products. Households could then always find some goods on which to spend 'excess' savings. Forced savings should then only be temporary since if people do not expect shortages to ease, there is no reason for them to keep saving, since tomorrow will be no different from today.

In other words, sustained forced saving means either that many people are incurable optimists, or that they have no access to the black market (including the black market for foreign exchange), or that they have no use at all for the goods available at market-clearing prices. Only when liberalisation is actually in the air does it make sense to build up an excess balance. But why should the public accumulate domestic currency (in cash or ill-remunerated deposits) when it has to expect that the prices of most goods will go up? On the contrary their attempt to spend just before price reform ensures that the queues will get even longer (and the shelves even emptier), as could be observed in the Soviet Union towards the end of 1991.

continued

Box 7.1 *continued*

The reasoning so far looked only at the incentives of individual households to accumulate savings. However, the term 'forced savings' does make sense from an economy wide, or *macroeconomic* point of view. The underlying cause for the monetary overhang is a mismatch between wages and the amount of goods available at the state-controlled price level. In many socialist economies the sum of all wages in the economy exceeded the available supply of goods at the price level fixed by the government. Imagine a socialist economy with 1,000 workers that produces 1,000 widgets (one per worker, per unit of time). The government fixes the price of each widget at one (ruble). However, workers receive a salary of 2 (rubles); the total salary mass is thus 2,000 (rubles). Workers will try to spend all their salary, but on average they will not be able to do so since only one widget *per capita* is on sale in the shops. (On average, of course. Some workers with better connections might be able to get two widgets, others might have to do without.) At the aggregate level the population is therefore 'forced' to save the difference between the total wage bill and the value of the total supply of goods sold through state stores. Trade, even at market clearing prices, between households does not affect the aggregate equilibrium since the only way cash can go back to the government is via the state-owned stores or savings accounts.

At the aggregate level households are thus 'forced' to save. However, they will do this only if prices and expectations are such that each individual household does so voluntarily. Expectations about the future become crucial in this respect: if households perceive that the supply of goods (especially consumer durables) will increase in future they will want to put part of their income into savings accounts until the goods arrive. If they expect the shortages to increase, they will bid up prices on the black market to the point where they are indifferent, at the margin, between consuming black market goods or saving the money after all.

How large was the monetary overhang in the various Eastern European countries? In most socialist economies planners were able to keep the difference between the wage bill and the value of the available consumer goods relatively small. This should not have been difficult since there was little pressure for higher wages and the monetary value of the supply of consumer goods could be calculated easily. However, in most socialist countries the growth rate of money (cash and savings deposits) exceeded that of nominal income a little and even small flows can accumulate to considerable stocks over time. Households might have been quite content to accumulate considerable savings during the 1960s when growth was still satisfactory. However, as growth slowed and turned into stagnation (see Chapter 11) during the 1980s expectations changed and households were willing, or rather forced, to keep their savings balances only because queues got longer and longer. Moreover, as *perestroika* proceeded in the USSR and political control became weaker in some Central European countries workers demanded and obtained higher wages. The final straw came when price liberalisation was imminent. At that point one had to expect that prices were going to increase and people were willing to stand in line (or bribe shop employees) up to the point where the value of the time lost in the queue (or the bribe) was equal to the difference between the current price and the expected future price. At that point the stock disequilibrium became very large. This is why the so-called monetary overhang did indeed represent a serious problem in a number of countries. Figure 7.1 shows the ratio currency to NMP for the few countries for which long-term series are available. This graph shows that in the FSU disequilibrium was clearly building up, but that the problem was much less severe in the CSFR and there was no change in the currency/NMP ratio in the ex-GDR.

Widespread rationing, queues and a large price differential between official prices and black markets are a sure indicator of a monetary overhang, but it proved extremely difficult to estimate the size of the jump in the price level that was required to eliminate the overhang. In all countries the increase in the price level that followed price liberalisation was larger than expected. The biggest error was made in Russia where the IMF estimated an overhang of about 50 per cent (in 1991) whereas prices jumped by almost 300 per cent in January 1992.[2] See Chapter 14 for details.

When price reforms became imminent it became imperative to have numerical estimates of the jump in the price level one could expect after price liberalisation. Most analysts relied on estimates of the demand for money that one could expect after price liberalisation which could then be compared to the existing money stock. In practice these estimates started from an analysis of the observed ratio of money (cash or financial assets) to income. This ratio, also called velocity, was quite high in most socialist economies compared to market economies because of the macroeconomic 'forced savings' explained above: the governments printed more money but without giving households the opportunity to buy more from the state sector. If one makes certain

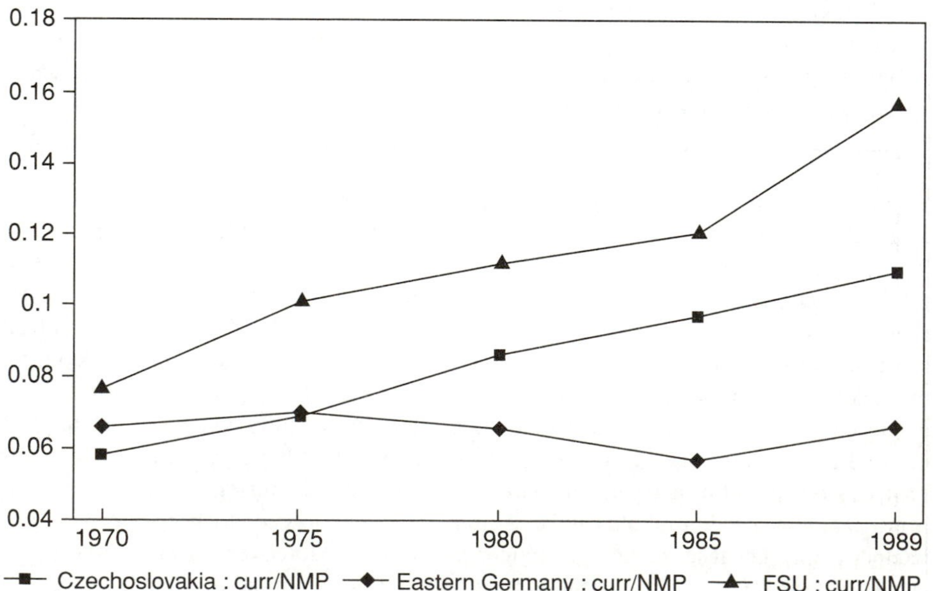

FIG 7.1 Monetary overhang; three Eastern European experiences
Source: World Bank (Czechoslovakia); Bundesband (East Germany), Ministry of Finance (Russia)
Note: Results for 1989 could be distorted by inflation. Calculation of avg(currency)/NMP showed that inflationary distortion was of minor importance

assumptions about velocity after the reform, one can then calculate the jump in the price level necessary to attain an equilibrium. Box 7.2 explains in more detail how this approach can be implemented.

How was it possible that most estimates were so wrong? Many relied on sophisticated models of the demand for financial assets that work quite well over the long run in developed market economies. However, these models proved useless to predict the behaviour of households in transitional economies who had basically only three assets: cash, savings deposits and foreign currencies. Velocity of savings deposits, which are an imperfect substitute for foreign exchange, turned out to be rather variable and there were important cross-country differences as shown in Fig. 7.2 below. Chapter 14 discusses in more detail the case of Russia which had the largest one-month jump in prices and compares it to the Polish experience. It is shown there that for the short run dynamics one could have made more accurate predictions if one had relied on the velocity of cash instead of that of savings deposits (M2). This is also confirmed by a comparison between Figs 7.1 and 7.2. The first is correlated with the price jump after price liberalisation (none in the ex-GDR, 50 per cent in the CSFR and 250 per cent in Russia), whereas the second is not.

Box 7.2 Money and prices: the classic approach

The 'classic' approach to the relationship between money and prices starts with a definition of the velocity of circulation of money.

$$V \equiv PQ/M \tag{1}$$

where P indicates the price level, Q aggregate production or sales, and M money. The three bars (instead of the usual two used in equations) indicate that (1) is a definition and not a relationship that is obtained only in equilibrium. The actual value of velocity can be calculated whether or not the economy is in equilibrium and whether or not the economy is market-based or centrally planned.

Different values of V can be calculated for different definitions of money (cash, M1, M2, etc.). Here we are interested in the behaviour of velocity of cash because the way cash is used by householders does not change greatly even with radical reforms.

In a command economy the authorities control (at least in theory) P, Q and M. They can thus implicitly also determine V whose value is, in principle, irrelevant for them.

The definition of velocity becomes, however, an *equilibrium relationship* if we consider a market economy and assume that production is determined by factors, such as the endowment with capital and labour that are independent of the quantity of money in circulation. The authorities can still determine M (nothing else, especially not P). Moreover, the way households manage their cash balances can then determine velocity, V, so that the price level, P, becomes the variable that has to adjust.

For market economies V is typically quite stable over time. There are considerable cross-country differences that reflect different payment patterns due to

continued

Box 7.2 *continued*

differences in the use of cash machines, bank accounts, and so on; but they are not important if one wants to consider the evolution over time in one given country.

The relationship (1) was used extensively to predict the amount of the required jump in prices after price liberalisation. If prices were controlled at time t, but free at time $t + 1$ the jump in prices should be equal to:

$$\frac{P_{t+1}}{P_t} = \frac{(V_{t+1}/V_t)(M_{t+1}/M_t)}{(Q_{t+1}/Q_t)} \tag{2}$$

If one is interested in the behaviour of prices immediately after price liberalisation, say after one month, one can neglect changes in Q, as changes in aggregate production take time to materialise. Even in the worst case output did not fall by more than 2 to 5 per cent per month in the immediate post-reform phase. Moreover, there is no reason why the government should print more money when it liberalises prices. For the first months after price liberalisation one can thus assume that $Q_t + 1/Q_t$ is approximately equal to one. Likewise $M_t + 1/M_t$ should also be close to one. (If it is not, part of the jump in prices is due to the increase in money, not price liberalisation.)

This implies that an economist wanting to predict the jump in the price level upon price liberalisation needs 'only' to predict by how much velocity will increase. It is in this area that very important misjudgements occurred.

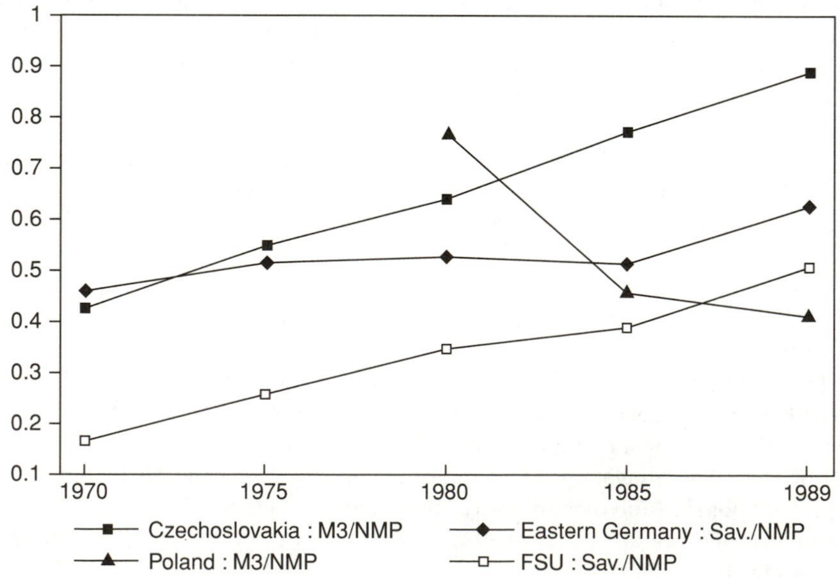

FIG 7.2 Monetary overhang: financial asset holdings in four Eastern European countries
Source: World Bank (Czechoslovakia and Poland); Bundesbank (East Germany), Ministry of Finance (Russia)
Note: There is no important inflationary distortion except for Poland. Therefore we used AVG(M3)/NMP for Poland

However, while the exact size of the overhang was not known *ex ante* the reformist governments knew that they had to face this problem. They had a range of options: from explicit or implicit confiscation (implicit being through inflation) to consolidation. *De facto* confiscation was the approach that was actually followed in most countries (except in Germany), but we discuss briefly others as well.

Explicit confiscation by declaring *part* of the outstanding stock of money to be no longer legal tender was likely to be politically risky, as shown by the experience of the ill-fated attempt by the Ryshkov government of the FSU to withdraw certain high denomination ruble notes from circulation in early 1991. This approach was never again seriously considered. Currency reform, that is, confiscating the *entire* stock of money, is the fast way of getting rid of the overhang. The German monetary reform of 1948 is one example of how this method has been used successfully in the past, especially when implemented as part of an all-round scheme to deal with hyperinflation. But there is a catch. Since the 'incidence of the tax' associated with monetary reform is not distributed evenly across the population, the political support needed for a successful implementation of the tough follow-up policies may fall off. Governments may then be forced into income policies to provide social safety nets and hopefully drum up some political support. As emphasised by Calvo and Frenkel (1991a), the income policies that have to go with confiscation will reduce economic efficiency; the net advantage of confiscation might thus be reduced.

In between explicit confiscation and consolidation are measures that involve a reduction in liquidity, that is, they make it more difficult for households to spend their money, for example by freezing savings deposits for a number of years. To what extent this approach is different from confiscation depends, of course, on the (real) interest rates paid on these deposits during the time they are frozen. At the other end of the spectrum is consolidation which can be achieved by making money, that is, domestic liquid assets, attractive enough to households so that they want to hold the entire stock. The obvious way is to increase the rate of interest paid on domestic currency deposits. This should induce households to hold these assets (i.e. M2 or M3) instead of trying to use them right away to buy goods.

In choosing this last approach of raising the interest rate on bank deposits, governments are taking their chances in budgetary terms, at least while banks are still government-owned or government-backed. Bank deposits are to all intents and purposes public debt, and the interest on deposits may be regarded as public-debt service. Viewed from this angle, credit and budget policies are closely linked, and a rise in the deposit rate will need to be financed through new taxes. Whether or not consolidation is possible depends on the ability of the tax system to generate the necessary tax revenue, and on the distributive and efficiency implications of the associated 'incidence of the tax'. In this respect the situation in transforming economies is very different from that of post-war stabilisations. In Germany in 1948 the pre-stabilisation money-to-GDP ratio was considerably higher than the ratios in Central Europe or Russia (including or excluding savings accounts). Consolidation was clearly not an option in Germany at that time because paying a real interest rate of 2–3 per cent would have cost 10–15 per cent of GDP. It might have been an option in Central Europe and the countries of the FSU where this ratio was close to 1.

Instead of enticing people to hold large liquid balances, the government might also achieve a reduction in liquidity by enticing people to exchange their money balances for other assets, such as assets sold by the government on the open market. In Eastern Europe, the elimination of monetary overhang through open market sales was made difficult by the lack of conventional financial instruments and poorly developed capital markets. At the start of the reforms, it was often thought that the most promising way of absorbing excess liquidity would have been to sell off the housing stock and SOE. This was discussed in depth (especially in the FSU), but not carried out on a large scale anywhere. The receipts from the sale of housing and of those enterprises that could be sold quickly turned out to be too small to have a real effect on the monetary overhang. There were also other reasons: in Chapter 8 we argue for reasons of speed of privatisation and of social justice against selling the available capital stock (and in favour of a currency reform).

Implicit confiscation through an upward jump of the price level was the course of (in)action actually chosen by most governments in Central and Eastern Europe. As discussed above the main concern was then the required jump in prices. It turned out to be difficult to predict how households would reorganise their assets and change their consumption behaviour. *A priori*, however, it was clear that a variety of considerations would have to come into play as outlined already in Blanchard *et al.* (1990). The main considerations are that in response to the removal of microrationing, people want to run down their stock of hoarded goods and reduce their cash holdings. They do this by shifting from cash to interest-yielding assets, and by consuming the goods they were hoarding, thus for a while reducing their consumer demand. In response to the removal of macrorationing, they want to decrease their stock of financial assets and so bump up consumer demand. But, with the outlook for the future highly unsettled, they may also want to save, to prepare against future contingencies. How people behave at this juncture is thus difficult to predict. In general, the macroeconomic environment and the nature of the financial instruments available should be the main factors.

What happened in reality was that the future course of inflation was the chief source of uncertainty and lack of inflation-proof assets did prompt people to plump for consumption rather than saving. The demand for financial assets thus fell dramatically in countries where inflation was not brought under control, but even in these cases the holding of cash turned out to be quite predictable.

2. Sources of destabilisation

All reforming countries had to deal with the monetary overhang. They chose just to liberalise prices and the result was a jump in prices. In some cases this was the end of the story. For example in Czechoslovakia prices rose by about 25.8 per cent[3] when prices were liberalised in January 1991, but during the remainder of the year inflation fell to about 1 per cent per month and stayed at that level during 1992 and 1993. In this case price liberalisation led mainly to a jump in the level of prices. However, this turned out to be the exception, rather than the rule. In most other reforming countries the first years were characterised by macroeconomic problems in the form of rising fiscal deficits and substantial inflation rates. In Russia the initial jump in the price level was followed by monthly inflation of about 20 per cent per month and fiscal deficits in excess of 10 per cent of national income. Russia is an extreme example, but most reforming countries had similar problems.

What were the root causes of macroeconomic destabilisation? The destabilisation that took place in Eastern Europe during the last days of the *old* regime arose because the declining political regime could not constrain unrealistic income aspirations. This situation fuelled inflation in two ways. First, it had a direct impact on the financial position, leading to budget deficits and monetisation. Second, the government, not keen for political reasons to countenance the economic contraction needed to reconcile income claims, instead accommodated wage and price increases through monetary expansion and so set the stage for a wage–price spiral.

Under the post-socialist regimes similar difficulties arose. But the visible, proximate cause for inflation was different from case to case. For the transforming economies there were three main dangers for macroeconomic destabilisation: (1) enterprises that do not accept a tight budget constraint, (2) workers who do not accept the apparent decline in real wages that comes with price liberalisation and demand wages that exceed productivity, and (3) a fiscal deficit that explodes because profit transfers from SOE decline. The first two dangers are briefly discussed immediately below. The last one is discussed at some length in Section 3 because it turned out to be a major problem in most reforming countries.

The first danger for stabilisation arose in most transforming economies immediately after price liberalisation when enterprises stopped paying each other. This situation leads to a chain accumulation of so called inter-enterprise arrears as firms that are not paid by their clients are in turn unable to pay their suppliers. If this process becomes widespread the price level can no longer be controlled by monetary policy since enterprises could finance any level of transactions by using inter-enterprise arrears instead of money.

The danger from the accumulation of inter-enterprise arrears was thus that these arrears would become so widespread that enterprises could use them as a substitute for money. In a certain sense the managers of the largely still state-owned enterprises had an interest in such a process because that would free them of the budget constraints that had, in principle, also to be introduced with the reforms. The main goal of managers initially was to ensure that they were able to pay wages (possibly at a high level) and maintain the social services formerly provided by enterprises. However, there were also countervailing forces since all the individual enterprise managers still had an interest in trying to be paid by their clients, while at the same time not paying their suppliers. It was often difficult to enforce payment from customers because bankruptcy laws did not exist in some countries and even where they existed they were not enforced on a large scale. The only sanction available to creditors was just to cut off supplies. Firms that were physically linked to their clients (e.g. producers of gas and oil through pipelines) could thus do little to enforce payments. It is not surprising that they ended up being the main net creditors, especially in Russia, and their clients became the main beneficiaries of the arrears phenomenon. However, a large proportion of the arrears was also owed to the government (theoretically the owner of these firms!).

Calvo and Corricelli (1993b) point out that there is an external effect in the arrears phenomenon in the sense that for each individual enterprise the cost of incurring arrears, that is, the cost of not paying a bill, is a function of what other firms do. Consider a situation in which most enterprises pay on time. In this case it will not be too difficult for the creditor firm to put pressure on the few recalcitrant debtors, cutting off supplies and even initiating bankruptcy proceedings. Moreover, a non-paying firm cannot expect to be bailed out by the government because the presumption that it is not profitable is strong if all other firms pay. All this will be different when most firms do not pay their bills. Under these circumstances it will be difficult for the creditor firm to put pressure on the debtor. Cutting off supplies does not help because nobody is paying anyway. Initiating bankruptcy proceedings will be difficult because the courts would not be able to handle thousands of cases and because the non-payment of bills might not be accepted as a cause for bankruptcy proceedings if it was common and if the debtor enterprise could claim that it could not pay because it was owed money by other enterprises. Finally, when arrears are widespread firms can expect that the government will bail them out because the political costs of wholesale failures would be prohibitive.

The cost of not paying should thus be high when the arrears phenomenon is limited and it should be low when arrears are widespread. This suggests that two equilibria might exist: a low arrears equilibrium in which firms pay their bills because the cost of not paying is high; and a high arrears equilibrium in which few firms pay because the cost of not paying is negligible.

In the high arrears equilibrium enterprises effectively no longer have a budget constraint (consumers still have one because they have to pay in cash). An ever-increasing chain of inter-enterprise arrears would thus not only threaten macroeconomic stabilisation, but the cornerstone of all reforms – the introduction of hard budget constraints. This is why the emergence of arrears caused considerable anxiety among policy-makers. Romania seems to illustrate this point, as shown by Khan (1993).

It was also recognised early (see e.g. Begg and Portes 1992) that inter-enterprise arrears also exist in developed Western market economies, where they are called suppliers' credit. The latter can be an efficient market mechanism that substitutes for bank credit because in some cases suppliers might know the financial conditions of their clients better than a bank. The real question was thus whether the arrears that arose in the transforming economies were of a similar nature or whether they went beyond this voluntary extension of suppliers' credit. Since there were vast differences in the experience of different countries it is not possible to assert globally that the extreme arrears equilibrium outlined above was avoided. With hindsight it is clear, however, that the problem was in most other cases less severe than initially thought.

The experience of Poland is instructive because the problem was most acute *before* the reforms were implemented (the level of arrears, as a proportion of GDP, peaked at 18 per cent at the end of 1989). Once the reforms were implemented arrears declined to about one half of this value. In this case the reforms apparently created a credible budget constraint. In other countries, however, the arrears started to grow with the implementation of reforms. Apart from Romania, the most spectacular case was Russia. In mid-1992 the stock of arrears was equivalent to the GDP of Russia during that period. If one assumes that for each ruble of GDP (which is a value added concept) there are two rubles of transactions between enterprises, then during the first half of 1992 every second transaction was not paid. This comes close to the bad equilibrium of a generalised 'no payment' environment without a budget constraint.

However, it turns out that the impression that 'IED (inter-enterprise debt) attained truly epic proportions' (Rostowski 1993) in Russia was based on a confusion of stocks and flows. While the flow (i.e. the increase of inter-enterprise debt) was very large initially, the level did not get out of hand. At its peak, at the end of June 1992, the stock of inter-enterprise debt was equivalent to about 20 per cent of GDP (June 1992 at annual rate). After June 1992 Russian IED declined in real terms so that even at its peak IED cannot have been much more important in Russia than in Poland. For more details of the Russian experience see Chapter 14.

A second danger for stabilisation that arose in many instances was that workers did not accept the (largely) apparent cut in real wages that came with price reform. This raises the issue of income policies in the form of price and wage guidelines.

3. State-owned enterprises: a roadblock to fiscal stabilisation?

Once liberalisation gets under way, a serious fiscal problem typically arises because the formal central planning machinery is progressively weakened as decision-making and effective property rights pass to the still state-owned enterprises themselves, and perhaps to a newly enfranchised private or cooperative sector. Price controls may or may not be removed in this transitional period. The government is in effect surrendering its tax base by relinquishing control over state property. As the old taxation system was implicit rather than explicit, there is no formal tax collection service at the beginning of the transition that can claw back revenue from entities no longer under government control.

Profits from SOEs were one of the major sources of revenue for the government. This source was subject to very large fluctuations in the initial transition period. Immediately after price liberalisation most SOEs increased their profits because many of them were monopolies. Governments were often able to obtain part of these profits because they still conserved some effective control over SOEs at the outset of the reform. This effect was important in Poland and Russia. Increased profits from SOEs allowed the budgets in these two countries to be roughly balanced during the first few months after price liberalisation. However, as competition (especially from imports) increased, and as workers also demanded higher wages the profits of SOEs fell. Moreover, the control of the government over managers fell and some of the most profitable SOEs were privatised. For all these reasons transfers of profits to the budget fell sharply after the first few months were over.

Of course, the transfer of some property away from direct government control is only the tip of the iceberg. There are other factors that hasten the decline in revenue. Central and local governments do not just sit back and let liberalisation run away with all their traditional industrial firms. They will, on the contrary, try to hang on to as many of these as possible. Yet as soon as goods and service markets are given a freer rein, the government's revenue position suffers. Industrial enterprises face new competitive challenges from newly enfranchised private or cooperative firms and, possibly, from freer imports. The industrial profit base contracts as the monopoly positions of the old SOEs are undermined.

As revenue declines, the pressure increases on governments to slash expenditure. Since government-financed investment expenditure is usually the first casualty, local governments, in particular, press the banks to lend to the firms they own or control to finance their infrastructure investments.[4] Not only does this foster unhealthy fiscal competition among parts of the government to whom control over enterprises means fiscal revenue, but, in addition, the forced extension of bank credit undermines monetary control. We return to this issue below.

With the transition to a market economy the government thus loses one of its most important sources of revenues. But, as mentioned above, in the very short run the reforming government typically experiences a windfall gain as revenues from profit taxes soar because initially prices increase by more than salaries. The experience of the first years in Russia confirms this, as shown in Table 7.2 which refers to the consolidated government, that is, the central and local governments together.

If profits decline because wages go up the government should receive higher wage (income) taxes that should offset the loss of profit taxes. However, it appears that this was not the case in Russia since profit taxes made up almost 80 per cent of all direct taxes throughout the period. Household income tax never accounted for more than 20 per cent of the profit tax (or about 20 per cent of GDP).

In Poland the fall in profit taxes was even more striking: between 1990, the first year of the reforms, and 1991 the revenue from income tax fell by over 8 percentage points of GDP (from 14 per cent of GDP to 5.8 per cent, see Chapter 11 for more details).

The data presented in Table 7.2 do not capture two other important elements of the short-run developments on the fiscal side that have been mentioned:

1. We argued that the central government that is responsible for setting macroeconomic policies has to take the interests and possible reactions of local governments into account. This emerges most clearly in the case of Russia where about 44 per cent of all government revenues were raised at the local level; for profit taxes the proportion was even above 60 per cent. In Poland local government levels were much less important, they accounted for only about 12 per cent of all government expenditure and receipts.
2. Another development concerns the expenditure that supports SOEs. During 1992 the Russian government received a total of 1,567 billion rubles in profit taxes, 8.7 per cent of GDP, but during that same period it spent 2,059 billion, about 11 per cent of GDP, under the heading 'national economy', half of which constituted subsidies.[5] Since the economy was still dominated by SOEs in 1992 most of

TABLE 7.2 Profit taxes in Russia

Year	Profit taxes (in R bn)	Total revenue (in R bn)	GDP (in R bn)	as % of GDP	
				Profit taxes	Total revenues
1992	1566.8	5327.6	18064.3	8.7	29.5
1993	16773.5	41449.1	162300.0	10.3	25.5
1994	18007.5	60012.0	245000.0	7.4	24.5

Source: 1992 and 1993: Ministry of Finance of Russian Federation
1994: average of first two quarters in 1994 for profit tax/GDP
1994: data first half year for total revenues/GDP

> these subsidies must have gone to the state sector. Moreover, since almost all the profit taxes must also have come from SOEs, the '*net*' revenue from profit taxes (i.e. net of expenditure on subsidies received by SOEs directly from the budget, which were about 1,000 billion) was only about 500 billion rubles, about 3 per cent of GDP and less than 10 per cent of all government revenues.[6] In Poland the subsidies that survived during the first year of the reforms were also substantial since they were equivalent to about 50 per cent of the revenue from income taxes.

Thus the initial fiscal honeymoon did not last. Wages quickly recovered most of the ground lost relative to prices and profits therefore declined rapidly. Moreover another dangerous development arose once the initial boom in profits was over: in some cases the 'soft budget constraint' threatened to reappear.

Just before the onset of reforms, once central planning was dismantled but the uncodified tax system based on the seizure of accumulated enterprise surpluses was not, managerial incentives came to grief. The syndrome of the 'soft budget constraint' was worse than ever: firms making incipient losses received subsidies for their pains (including cheap credit) while 'successful' firms were stripped of their surpluses. In addition, the government was in such dire need of revenue that it could not keep itself from intervening at random in order to extract more surpluses, a task considerably facilitated when enterprises' highly visible deposits with the state bank would be (re)frozen or seized. The transition from this situation to one where banks lend only for viable projects and the government takes only a clearly identified part of profits requires some time.

Loss-making enterprises continue to borrow from the state bank, refuse to pay taxes or do not pay their suppliers to avoid lay-offs, contributing to the loss of control over the money supply. A further complication is that once planning controls are removed, profitable enterprises will be anxious to spend the cash balances they could not previously touch lest they be seized or refrozen, adding to inflationary pressure. Luckily, however, this is only a once-and-for-all effect.

Another problem is that the productivity of physical capital – both fixed assets and inventories of inputs and goods – typically falls immediately after the reforms. As attractive monetary assets, whether liquid cash, or time deposits bearing a positive real rate of interest, are not usually on offer, newly liberalised firms will over-bid for storable material inputs, foreign exchange, capital goods and so forth. In effect, decentralised enterprises will carry 'excess' inventories of all kinds as substitute monetary stores of value (McKinnon 1991). The problem arises from the starting point for reforms that was in many cases catastrophic.

It was often alleged that managers of SOEs would constitute a roadblock for reforms because they would not understand how to operate under market conditions and because their own interests were threatened by privatisation. The first argument is difficult to assess *a priori*. SOEs worked or used to work in an environment that was, in a certain sense, even more difficult than a Western market because supplies were erratic and workers could not always be disciplined. The limited evidence available from Poland, which managed to increase exports to the West by over 50 per cent during the first years after the reforms, suggests that, indeed, SOE managers were able to operate in a market economy since over 70 per cent of exports came from SOEs.[7] The second argument is clearly rather weak since any competent manager (who was not politically compromised) must have reckoned that his or her income could only increase in a market economy. Pinto *et al.* (1993) suggest furthermore that the performance of SOEs in Poland was much better than often expected. Interviewed, managers repeatedly did not express fundamental opposition to the reforms and did not object to the principle of hard budget constraints.

This confirms that the crucial element in determining the performance of enterprises is the hard budget constraint. In Poland the availability of cheap credit diminished sharply at the outset of the reforms. Since it took the banking system some time to become competitive, and competent enough to be able to distinguish between good and bad borrowers, large SOEs continued for some time to have privileged access to credit. But even this did not last for more than one year. In contrast, in Russia, during the 12 to 18 months of transition, SOEs had ample access to cheap credit that came ultimately from the central bank. Under these conditions it is not surprising that little adjustment took place. SOEs cannot therefore threaten stabilisation if the central banks reign in overall credit expansion and if there is some discipline in the banking sector.

4. Fiscal and monetary destabilisation

We have shown above that the reforming governments had to face a serious fiscal problem. But the interesting question is whether the fiscal problems led to inflation. *A priori* one would expect this to be the case since fiscal and monetary policy are closely intertwined. The latter often serves to finance fiscal deficits and the former exerts an influence on aggregate demand in a way which may contradict the monetary objectives. A truly independent central bank, in control of monetary policy and responsible for regulating banks and financial markets, could, in principle, achieve sustained price stability. But granting independence to a central bank is one thing and maintaining it another. It is not enough merely to wave the constitutional wand: unwavering political and popular support are indispensable to continued independence. In the long run, independent central banks should not find it more difficult to achieve price stability than their Western counterparts. In the short run, the task is much more complex.

The problem for the central bank is that, in the very short run, the public sector has no alternative to monetary financing and reforms might seriously destabilise fiscal revenues, at least until revised tax laws succeed in broadening the tax base. In time, as growth picks up and the new tax system comes into full swing, these transitory deficits will evaporate. They can therefore be regarded as specific to a once-and-for-all change of regime, and a one-off financing method is justified. One such opportunity is to sell off housing and land to citizens with payments spread out over the years, as with mortgage financing. To encourage sizeable down-payments, a variable but positive real interest rate could be imposed without great difficulty on a scale sufficient to stabilise the initial budget.

However, this solution was not adopted anywhere on a large scale. The main danger then arises from fiscal deficits not financed by the sale of bonds to the public. When this happens, the central bank will be unable to resist pressure to cover part of the deficit through the printing press. Experience has shown, however, that the amounts that can be raised through such an 'inflation tax' come to little more than 3–4 per cent of GDP in the long run (see Fischer 1982). Since money demand is sensitive to high inflation rates, there is a strong 'Laffer curve' effect beyond certain thresholds (i.e. beyond inflation rates of 20–30 per cent, the revenue from inflation tax declines rapidly). Attempts to finance even larger deficits lead to hyperinflation (because they destroy the base for the inflation tax). See Box 7.3.

The experience of the reforming countries has, however, been extremely varied on this account. As discussed in more detail in Chapter 14, Russia financed more than 15 per cent of GDP from this source, but in Central European countries the scope of the inflation tax has been more modest. Moreover, the link between deficits and inflation was not as strong as one would have expected.

Table 7.3 reports the data for Poland, Hungary and Russia and shows that there was no direct link between the fiscal deficit and inflation once the reforms were under way (the pre-reform years shown in the case of Poland and Russia should not be taken into account since with an administered price system fiscal and monetary policy cannot be expected to have a direct impact on prices). Poland is an interesting case because during the first three years following the 'big bang' of 1990 the officially recorded fiscal position of the government continued to deteriorate as it went from a small surplus in 1990 to a deficit of about 4 per cent of GDP in 1991 whereas inflation declined from 95 per cent in 1990 to 70 per cent in 1991 and 43 per cent in 1992. The Polish case is intriguing because of the clear inverse relationship between fiscal deficit and inflation. Hungary is somewhat different in that there is no clear direct relationship at all between fiscal position and inflation.

How can these facts be reconciled with the general presumption that the root cause of inflation is monetary financing of a fiscal deficit? The last column of Table 7.3 shows that monetary financing indeed took place on a very large scale.

TABLE 7.3 Fiscal policy and inflation

	Fiscal balance in % GDP	Inflation CPI annual % change	Seigniorage in % GDP
Poland			
1989		251.1	23.4
1990	+0.4	585.8	9.2
1991	−3.8	70.3	2.5
1992	−6.0	43.0	4.0
Hungary			
1989	−0.1	17.0	3.4
1990	−4.9	28.9	7.9
1991	−7.4	36.4	10.3
1992		23.0	0.9
Russia	−15.0		
1991*	−3.5	92.7	
1992	−9.7	1353.0	21.03
1993		859.9	10.65

* Data for Former Soviet Union
Source: Fiscal balance: UN, ECE, *Economic Survey for Europe* 1992–1993; RET, various issues
Inflation: IMF, *World Economic Outlook*, various issues
Seigniorage: Gros and Vandille (1994) and own calculations

Monetary financing can essentially take two forms: printing of additional cash, or requiring commercial banks to hold more reserves with the central bank. The column entitled 'seigniorage' shows the sum of these two forms of monetary financing as a ratio of GDP. The values that appear in this table are extraordinarily large in relation to those even in highly inflationary market economies. As shown in detail in Chapter 14, the main reason why seigniorage was so high in Hungary is that, during the first years following the reforms, the reserves of Hungarian commercial banks with the central bank increased considerably. In Poland (and Russia) the cash component contributed about half of the total, but another reason why seigniorage was so high in Russia was that the slow payments system forced banks to keep large zero-interest-bearing reserves at the central bank.

Box 7.3 What is seigniorage and how much can the government get?

Seigniorage is the flow of expenditure the government can finance by creating additional 'money' through the central bank. How much can the government finance in this way? It is an important source of government revenues in most post-socialist countries.

The 'money' created by the central bank is the monetary base, that is, the sum of bank notes (and coins) and the required reserves that commercial banks have to hold with the central bank. The 'tax base' for the seigniorage (also called the inflation tax) is thus the demand for base money. Denote the monetary base by H_t and assume that the demand for monetary base (in reality mostly cash) is proportional to nominal income and a decreasing function of inflation. In analytical terms this can be written as:

$$H_t = kY_t P_t (1 - \delta\pi_t) \qquad [1]$$

where k represents the reciprocal of the velocity of circulation if there is no inflation (denoted by π_τ). Y_t denotes national income in real terms and P_t the price level.

Seigniorage is the *change* in the monetary base. It is thus equal to $(H_t - H_{t-1})/P_t$. Using [1] seigniorage S_t in real terms is given by:

$$S_t/P_t = [kY_t P_t (1 - \delta\pi_t) - kY_{t-1} P_{t-1} (1-\delta\pi_{t-1})]/P_t \qquad [2]$$

Assuming we are considering the short run when income can change very little, we can set $Y_t - Y_{t-1}$ and seigniorage as a proportion of income will be equal to:

$$(S_t/Y_t P_t \equiv s_t = k [(P_t - P_{t-1})/P_t - \delta (\pi_{t\_}(P_{t-1}/P_t)\pi_{t-1}] \qquad [3]$$

Since $\pi_t \equiv (P_t - P_{t-1})/P_t$ this equation implies that if the rate of inflation is to remain *constant*, (i.e. formally $\pi_t = \pi_{t-1}$) seigniorage revenue as a proportion of income is equal to:

$$s = k\pi - \delta\pi^2 \qquad [4]$$

continued

Box 7.3 *continued*

This implies that the proportion of income that can be financed by seigniorage is an inverted quadratic function of inflation and thus goes down with very high inflation rates. The maximum seigniorage is given at the point where $ds/d\pi - 0$, that is, where $k = 2\delta\pi$. This implies that $\pi_{s \text{ is max}} = k/2\delta$. The maximum seigniorage is then given by:

$$s_{max} = k^2/2\delta - \delta(k/2\delta)^2 = k^2/4\delta \qquad [5]$$

How much this could be in reality can be calculated approximately by using assumptions that are broadly representative of middle income market economies. Assume that the ratio of money demand to income at zero inflation is about 0.1 (corresponding to a velocity of circulation of 10) and that the semi-elasticity of money demand with respect to income is about 0.1. This implies that the maximum amount of seigniorage the government can earn at a *steady* rate of inflation is 2.5 per cent of income (at an inflation rate of 50 per cent). Attempts to obtain more will lead to hyperinflation. Inflation rates above 50 per cent will only diminish the real seigniorage the government obtains, because the public economises on its holdings of money. This illustrative example refers only to the long run when inflation is anticipated. In the short run the revenue from seigniorage might be much higher because the government sometimes increases the supply of money more quickly than the public adjusts its expectations.

Reality is, of course, more complicated than these formulas. In Russia, for example, money demand was apparently not very sensitive to inflation so that initially seigniorage was much higher than the maximum calculated here.

The risk of 'wage-push' inflation is particularly high while industry is for the most part still awaiting privatisation, since public sector managers will not like private owners putting up strong resistance to wage claims which are not justified by productivity gains. As Lipton and Sachs (1990) point out, there is no market mechanism during transition to ensure wage restraint in the public sector. So until private ownership spreads, wage restraint can only be enforced at the political level and then only if the government enjoys widespread popular support.

5. The external anchor

In the socialist regime prices were fixed administratively. But this way to achieve (at least superficially) stability no longer works in the transition. In a market economy price stability demands a nominal anchor. In principle there are two ways of anchoring prices: through the money supply or through the exchange rate.

As our previous discussion has shown, during transition it is extremely difficult for the central bank to resist pressure from government to monetise the deficit. The only possible improvement would consist in rendering the central bank independent and in anchoring this independence in the constitution. This is no guarantee for success, particularly as public opinion may turn against the central bank and make it responsible for economic hardships, but could be helpful. The other innovation needed to decouple monetary policy from fiscal policy is to create a market for government paper.

If stabilisation is successful and inflation is wiped out, people will be willing to hold money again and demand for money will go up. At a given price level, increased demand for money would require a one-off increase in nominal money supply to accommodate rising demand. How to engineer such an increase without making it look like a resumption of money growth obviously again raises the issue of credibility. Yet if the money supply is not increased, very high interest rates will have to be contended with for some time. Moreover, we showed previously that during transition velocity is highly unstable, so that it is difficult to estimate the money supply growth that is compatible with price stability.

The main alternative anchoring option – fixing exchange rates – is also fraught with difficulties. The possibility that policy laxity can *ex post facto* be corrected through a devaluation can never be excluded. Even if this does not happen, capital controls are used to soften the disciplinary effect of fixed exchange rates and give domestic policy makers considerable freedom. The constraint of a fixed rate on monetary policy will then only be felt when the competitivity gap becomes sizeable. And as the disciplinary device is imperfect, fixed exchange rates with capital controls (the situation almost everywhere in Eastern Europe) present major risks. The first is that as long as the outcome of stabilisation is in the balance, very high nominal (and, if prices are stable, *ex post facto* real) interest rates may be required in defence of the exchange rate. And if prices continue to rise for a while, the real exchange rate will steadily appreciate. Corrective devaluation halfway into the stabilisation programme also raises questions as to credibility and risks fuelling inflation. In fact, a precondition for successful nominal anchoring is a monetary and fiscal reform without which the nominal exchange rate will quickly have to be abandoned.

In view of these dangers, it is wise to initially fix the exchange rates at an under-valued level. This creates room for some slippage in competitivity, and avoids immediate credibility problems. In addition, under-valuation gives a boost to exports and makes imports more expensive. The reorientation of production to the external sector is thereby facilitated. As shown in Chapter 11, all Central European countries strove for an under-valued exchange rate.

Of course, under-valuation should not be pushed too far. One obvious cost is the lower terms of trade that most of the time result from under-valuation. Another possible problem is the destabilisation of domestic inflation brought about by the feedback of devaluation on domestic prices. As argued in Chapter 11, this was a problem Poland had to face in 1990–91.

One way of tying the policy-makers' hands more seriously is to give up the freedom of using monetary policy – thereby convincingly constraining fiscal deficits to non-monetary financing – and exchange rate policy. This can be done by adopting the 'currency board' solution, that is, by making domestic currency equivalent to a chosen foreign currency and anchoring this decision in the constitution. Estonia has implemented this option and has locked its currency to the Deutsche Mark (DM). Price stability was achieved by Estonia within less than one year. For technical details see Box 7.4.

Box 7.4 The currency board solution

How does such a system work? The monetary authority announces that it is ready to exchange unlimited amounts of foreign currency into domestic currency at the announced rate (8 kroons for 1 DM in the case of Estonia). This will be credible if the foreign currency reserves are equal in value to the sum of all the liabilities of the monetary authorities (i.e. cash and deposits of banks). The monetary authority also announces that it will create additional currency only against foreign currency receipts. Variations in the domestic money supply are then exclusively caused by net in- or outflows of foreign exchange. What currency should be the anchor? Estonia chose the DM. The best anchor is the currency most widely used in the country's foreign trade and offering the price stability to be copied.

The monetary authority ('the currency board') holds its assets exclusively in liquid interest-earning foreign assets in the anchor currency. Its liabilities are restricted to the 'monetary base', that is, cash in circulation and deposits by banks (including required reserves). As the monetary base is only a small share of all deposits and savings accounts, typically 20–40 per cent, the required foreign exchange backing is not very large relative to the overall money supply and GDP. It usually corresponds to about 10 per cent of a year's income.

One important difference between the clear currency board approach and a fixed exchange rate is thus that the balance sheet of the 'currency board' does not contain advances to government and holding of government debt instruments. This would be somewhat different if, at the starting point, foreign exchange reserves were insufficient. The rules could then be modified as follows. Some of the initial money supply would be backed up by credits to the government. Any *increase* in the money supply would, however, have to be fully backed up by foreign exchange and, over time, government credit would have to be replaced by foreign exchange holdings according to a binding rule drawn up in advance.

The requirement that only the monetary base is to be covered with foreign exchange holdings, and not the entire money supply, takes into account the fact that the monetary base corresponds to currency in its strictest sense. Interest earning deposits are close substitutes for both monetary and financial instruments. As long as banks incur a resource cost of collecting and remunerating deposits they are forced in a competitive banking market to allocate these funds rationally. Clearly, independence of commercial banks and competition, enhanced by the presence of foreign banks, are essential ingredients.

Could the foreign exchange constraint cause insufficient liquidity? Suppose that, due to initial foreign exchange scarcity, there is a lack of domestic liquidity. Banks would have to borrow abroad to satisfy their clients. With the credibility achieved by the reform, and as long as the quality of banks' balance sheets remains intact, they will be able to borrow foreign exchange, convert at the board and obtain liquidity in domestic currency.

continued

Box 7.4 *continued*

The currency board, as any central bank, would have the benefit of domestic seigniorage: its assets are remunerated whereas its liabilities are not (or only partly on bank deposits). The social cost of foreign exchange backing is also very low: private banks borrow foreign exchange abroad which is reinvested by the currency board in international markets. The cost is equal to the spread between interest rates paid and received which should be equal to a small premium for differences in liquidity and risk. The social benefit can however be enormous in terms of monetary stability and hence a better base for sustainable growth.

6. The sustainability of stabilisation and the need for social safety nets

Stabilisation programmes notoriously fall short of expectations because there are simply too many things that can go wrong, as illustrated by Lipton and Sachs (1990) in the case of Poland. Achieving or maintaining budget balance can be political suicide and where some fiscal correction does take place, this may be in the shape of emergency taxation via high real prices for public-sector goods rather than broad-based fiscal reform. Prices and wages go on rising and in the end force monetary accommodation to avoid too profound a contraction of the economy. And, when stabilisation does succeed, the need to restrain inflation often engenders deep economic contraction.[8]

Can post-stabilisation economic depression be avoided? In principle, the answer is yes, as argued by Blanchard *et al.* (1990), but in practice it requires a combination of several happy circumstances. Once the initial transformation shock is over, in theory, all that is required is a change in taxation and spending structures, typically, the elimination of the inflation tax offset by a cutback in subsidies. As a rule, we do not think of tax changes as a major contractionary factor. The cut in subsidies to consumers will scale down disposable income, and the cut in subsidies to firms (which firms have to compensate for by increasing prices) will reduce real wages. But if the subsidy cut and the inflation tax are of equal magnitude to start with, real income, that is, income including losses on money balances, will be unchanged. There may be distributive effects, with income distribution moving away from, presumably, the poorest people, those who held the least money and bought the most subsidised goods. These effects are unlikely to be substantial or imply a major downturn in demand. By the same token, the removal of distortions and the improved climate overall might be expected to induce firms to invest more and reassure consumers as to the future and so to spend more. This optimistic view does not, however, reckon with four crucial factors in Eastern Europe.

First, uncertainty about the future does not disappear with the inception of a stabilisation programme. Once the first relief caused by temporary stabilisation wears off, scepticism comes back with a vengeance. Even the best stabilisation programmes sometimes fail and firms will probably prefer to wait and see which way the wind blows rather than embark on an investment spree.

Second, inflation may not come to a dead halt either, owing to the coordination problems outlined above or because the stabilisation programme is not perceived as wholly credible. In that case, developments will depend on the choice of nominal anchor. In the event of a fixed exchange rate, for example, suspicion of the programme and the odds of devaluation later, may have to be paid for in very high interest rates to defend the exchange rate, and these may in turn affect demand and lead to contraction.

Low credibility leads to expectation of devaluation, contraction and abandonment of the programme, which, in turn, make the programme less likely to succeed. High credibility may be self-sustaining as promises are being delivered.

Third, the initial shock which triggered the process to start with may not yet have worn off. In that case, unless workers and firms have learned about inflation the hard way and can be persuaded to agree on the distribution of income between profits and wages, unemployment is the only way of keeping wages and prices consistent with price stability. Otherwise, all that stabilisation can achieve is to set the clock ticking again.

Finally, stabilisation also has repercussions for the supply side itself. Certain unprofitable firms may not be able to weather the changes brought about by the removal of subsidies and the revamping of price structures, and if closed, lessen the economy's ability to respond to demand in the short run.

All these risks are a potential threat to sustained stabilisation. Success depends on the overall consistency and credibility of the stabilisation programme and the political support it receives. For widespread political support a safety net is required.

In choosing among alternative safety nets, it should be borne in mind that there is no way of protecting all segments of society. A comprehensive reform programme may involve sacrifices by a substantial share of the population and therefore needs to be seen as fair and efficient. Furthermore, in designing the mechanism through which the safety net operates, the introduction of new distortions should be avoided to the utmost. In this regard, the safety nets should not interfere with the incentives to work, save and invest, nor should they tamper with monetary and exchange rate policies. Rather, allowance should be made for them in the budget and they should be effected through income transfers.

The safety net we strongly prefer is a give-away privatisation programme that provides citizens with real assets to compensate for the reduction in income streams. Such assets may be used as collateral for borrowing in bad times, making saving less mandatory, and their maintenance and improvement (e.g. of the housing stock) allows under-employed workers to minimise the opportunity cost of under-employment. The details are developed in the next chapter. For the design of an overall programme the experience with stabilisation in Latin America provides a useful reference. See Box 7.5.

Box 7.5 Lessons from Latin America

Many Latin American economies have suffered for decades from high and volatile inflation and low and volatile growth. Many socialist economies are comparable to Latin America in terms of economic and institutional developments: widespread (although declining) state ownership of resources and intervention in managing the economy, uncertain property rights, high foreign indebtedness,

continued

Box 7.5 *continued*

under-development of market institutions, and high protection of domestic activity against foreign competition. As a result of a high inflation record, distortions of the tax system and indexation of contracts have become widespread. During the 1980s several Latin American countries commenced with wide ranging reforms. Chile and Mexico successfully stabilised their economies and achieved remarkable recoveries of their financial health and of their growth record. Bolivia, in contrast, achieved stabilisation, but its economy remained stagnant.

Chile went through two stabilisation episodes. The first one, during 1973–77, was a closed economy stabilisation including a drastic fiscal adjustment and control on money growth. Three-digit inflation persisted up to 1977 despite a sharp recession starting in 1975 with a 13 per cent drop in GDP. The second stabilisation, during 1978–82, centred on the exchange rate, resulted in a large real appreciation and was unable to bring domestic inflation down to foreign inflation, mainly because of sustained wage indexation.

The main lessons of the Latin American experience can be summed up as follows:

1. The reliance on a major price level jump to eliminate the monetary overhang proves to be costly. In Chile in 1973 expectations of inflation became high and chaotic, with economic agents adjusting their prices in anticipation of expected further inflation. These expectations, compounded with a nearly full indexation of the economy, lengthened the path towards price stability enormously. A monetary reform would have resulted in a smoother and less traumatic transition.
2. An important component of *fiscal adjustment* is to create a tax system that is not vulnerable to inflation itself. The sophisticated inflation adjustment clauses introduced to the Chilean tax system in late 1974 greatly helped Chile to eliminate the public sector imbalances.
3. Efforts to *de-index the labour market* – delinking wage increases from past inflation – should be maintained throughout the stabilisation programme. In Chile the return to full backward-looking indexation in late 1976 added considerable inertia to the inflationary process.
4. An *exchange rate-based stabilisation programme*, where the nominal exchange rate is either pegged, or its rate of change is predetermined at a rate below ongoing inflation, carries a serious danger of provoking a major over-valuation. This suggests then that in instances when exchange rate pegging becomes part of the anti-inflation programme, the initial starting point should be one of under-valuation as in Mexico in 1988.
5. The most important goal of the adoption of a predetermined nominal exchange rate as part of a stabilisation programme is to alter the dynamics of the inflationary process. A *credible adoption of an exchange rate* rule will reduce the degree of inertia in the system. A comparison between the Chilean and Mexican cases shows that while in the former the adoption of

continued

Box 7.5 *continued*

the exchange rate rule did not affect the inertial forces built into the system, in Mexico the degree of persistence in inflation was significantly reduced. The main difference in these two experiences is that in Mexico the exchange rate rule was supplemented with other incomes policies to gain greater credibility.

6. In Chile and Mexico it took a long time to achieve *sustained growth*. Stabilisation, clarity in tax and property rights rules, and a low but positive real rate of interest were the key to obtaining a strong investment response but it took years to get these three elements in place.
7. In Chile and Mexico a primary commodity accounted initially for about three-quarters of exports. With the opening up of the economy and the accompanying real devaluation, a large *supply response* was obtained in both cases. A high rate of growth of non-traditional exports reduced the export share of copper in Chile and the export share of oil in Mexico to below 50 per cent.

Source: Edwards (1991), Corbo (1992)

7. Conclusions

The inherited destabilising feature of reform economies was the monetary overhang. Slow introduction of a hard-budget constraint of SOEs, itself feeding back into a fiscal disequilibrium financed by monetary expansion has been a subsequent destabilising factor.

Our analysis of the various means of eliminating the monetary overhang reveals that in all cases the private sector ends up being taxed by the full amount of the overhang, one way or another. In deciding the policy response to the monetary overhang, the government must recognise that the various solutions differ where the 'incidence of the tax' is concerned, not in overall effect.

Once the monetary overhang is eliminated the major sources of destabilisation are income claims by all segments of society (wage earners, firms, government) which, when added up, are inconsistent with available resources. This problem is made all the more difficult during transition as resources are reallocated and remunerations are reset closer to market conditions, at times giving rise to very large changes. Unfortunately, during this spin of the wheel, budgets are still softly monitored. If the government cannot impose hard budget constraints on SOEs then workers will not be faced with hard-bargaining firms and the increase in wage costs with spillover into lower tax revenues or higher subsidisation demand by firms. And as long as the financial sector is not reformed the budget deficit has to be financed through money creation.

What can be done in such a situation? First of all, these dangers to stabilisation illustrate once more the need to advance as quickly as possible on all reforms: tax reforms, privatisation, financial sector reforms and so on.

Second, for a broadly based stabilisation programme widespread popular support is needed. This support can be strengthened if the programme is perceived as efficient, promising rapid success, and fast, so that hardship and later gains are shared by all. For that reason we favour give-away privatisation of housing and a share of the productive assets on an equal basis. Much more problematic are specific income policies such as wage indexation, which often make the control of inflation harder.

Third, at least small countries may obtain credibility by tying their politicians' hands through an external anchor. An extreme form of external anchor is adoption of a 'currency board'; much less constraining would be a fixed exchange rate. Large countries, perhaps unfortunately, do not easily accept tying their hands (in this political sense Russia is a large country although it is not in an economic sense). It must find the domestic political support for stabilisation, or else stabilisation will not work. This dilemma is perhaps best illustrated by the present situation in Russia analysed in Chapter 14.

Notes

1. Chapters 4, 5, and 6 dealt mainly with microeconomic issues, although micro- and macroeconomic issues are closely inter-woven, both in the sequencing of reforms and because macroeconomic policies rely on a functioning microeconomic framework.
2. Prior to the reforms many economists specialising in Soviet economies had, of course, produced estimates of the monetary overhang. Some of the estimates relied on the difference between controlled and free prices for food (in those countries where there existed small markets for privately produced food). This approach assumed in general that eventually the price level would be somewhere in between the controlled and the free prices. However, it turned out that the overall price level went straight to the free price level.
3. See United Nations (1992).
4. This could be observed in all East European countries, particularly in those with less centralised structures, such as the FSU and Yugoslavia.
5. See *Russian Economic Trends*, 1993.
6. However, in Russia the subsidies that went through the budget were actually secondary to those coming from another source, namely the Central Bank of Russia; this is discussed in more detail in Chapter 14.
7. In 1990 Polish exports were helped by a special effect: in that year the FSU continued to supply energy at below world market prices. Some of this energy was re-exported embodied in finished products such as fertilisers.
8. The German stabilisation of 1923 was followed by a sharp but short-lived contraction, with unemployment (of union workers) rising to 23 per cent in a matter of months and then falling to 8 per cent after only a year.

Appendix: Reform of the fiscal sector

The fiscal systems in socialist countries were simple and effective. None of the confrontational clashes that envenom relations between taxpayers and tax administrators in the West occurred under this system. A highly effective mechanism, it was able to generate levels of taxation unheard of in most industrial countries. With the introduction of a market economy all the prerequisites of this system disappear since (1) prices and wages are liberalised; (2) private sector activities, that cannot be directly controlled, grow; (3) methods of payment change; and (4) taxes are supposed to be neutral for resource allocation. All this sharply reduces the information available to tax inspectors whilst increasing the confrontational nature of tax collection: tax evasion will have come to stay. A whole new statutory tax system and a new tax administration will have to be built up almost from scratch, calling on skills (accounting and legal) that previously were not needed. It is clear that this change will take many years to complete.

East European reformers need to tailor the existing institutional set-up to the changing role of government and to define its scope. According to Tanzi (1992), the five building blocks of public finance reform are the establishment of a new tax administration and new budgetary institutions and reform of the tax system, public spending and social security systems.

SETTING UP A NEW TAX ADMINISTRATION AND REFORM OF THE TAX SYSTEM

The reforming economies are absolutely crying out for new, modern tax administrations. Under the new order there will be millions, not thousands of taxpayers and the tax administration will need all the information it can get to cope with conditions of liberalised prices and no production quotas. To compound its problem, economic transformation will increase the proportion of total income originating precisely in that part of the economy that is most difficult to tax, to wit, the service sector and small-scale public-sector activity.

The new system should be simple and easy to administer. Anything requiring complex administrative procedures or a large number of taxpayers filing returns is doomed to failure. Clearly, then, simply transplanting Western tax systems *en bloc* must be ruled out. A global income tax, for example, always a favourite in many Western economies, would have disastrous results in the early stages of reform. It does not easily lend itself to widespread withholding at source (especially when accompanied by highly progressive rates) and would entail large-scale filing of returns and complex administrative procedures with which the East European countries simply cannot cope at this point. What they should be looking for is a system based on income taxes with relatively low rates, which minimise filing and rely on withholding at source for wages, interest and possibly dividend incomes. The same principles can be brought to bear on value-added taxes with multiple rates and zero-rating of some goods. Here, reformers must bear in mind the close link that exists between the exemption threshold and administrative simplicity: a low threshold means more taxpayers and more administrative complications. The snag is that many of the reforming countries are anxious to become part of Europe and will attempt to develop tax systems that are compatible with those of their future partners. A worthwhile objective in itself, it should not be achieved by cloning the European tax system. Simplicity and compatibility are not mutually exclusive.

REFORM OF SOCIAL SECURITY ARRANGEMENTS

At a time when many of the reforming countries are reeling under severe unemployment shocks, social security is an area of special concern. In many of these countries, social security taxation is so high as to be unsustainable in the longer run, yet their systems are in many cases actually making large losses. In a market economy, if employers are forced to shoulder a social security burden as heavy as in some of the former socialist countries, this can only give strong incentives to underground economic activity to evade payment.[1] Furthermore, such high taxes on labour will inevitably have an impact on the optimal capital/labour mix. With taxes on labour and subsidies for capital, there is a very real risk of excessive substitution of labour through capital and unemployment. A major overhaul of the entire social security system is a pressing agenda item in all reforming countries. In practice, they may have to increase the retirement age, subject would-be pensioners to closer scrutiny, especially for disabilities, and generally reduce the number of beneficiaries and the level and coverage of benefits.

SETTING UP A MODERN BUDGETARY SYSTEM AND REFORM OF PUBLIC EXPENDITURE

Under central planning, there was no budget office in the sense understood in market economies. Allocations for a certain amount of social spending by the relevant ministries were made by the planning office, with only limited input from the spending ministries, and leaving much of the responsibility for providing social services for workers and their families to the state enterprises themselves. In a market economy, firms will no longer do this, shifting the burden to the spending ministries which will face correspondingly increased financial needs. Budgetary decisions will have to be made bearing in mind resource availability and efficiency criteria. The budget office must establish a close link between total budgetary appropriations for the budget year and expected government revenue, both of which are in turn influenced by developments in the economy. It must develop good forecasting techniques to assess the impact of the economy on revenue and expenditures. It must also closely scrutinise the results of public spending in order to maximise its welfare impact and keep a tight rein on costs. A unified budget format encompassing the full range of programmes would turn the budget into a useful policy tool. To cut a long story short, a modern budget office must be established. As in other areas, this objective will take many years to accomplish.

And last but not least, a large pool of highly skilled people hitherto employed in military and civilian administration can be released and retrained to staff the emerging tax administration or try their luck in the new private sector.

Note

1. For the connection between high social security taxes and the underground economy, see Tanzi (1992).

CHAPTER EIGHT

Privatisation

Men that hazard all do it in the hope of fair advantages: a golden mind stoops not to shows of dross.

(Shakespeare, *The Merchant of Venice* II, vii, 18)

In Eastern Europe, the success of Western economies is perceived so overwhelmingly that market-based capitalism appears as the only widely shared objective for social organisation. History has shown that a market economy based on private property performs much better than socialism. Yet the theoretical support for the transformation of non-market economies into capitalist ones is less solid than is often assumed.

It is worrisome that the widely acclaimed general equilibrium results which form the basis for the allocation efficiency of a market economy falter when real-world features of imperfect information and incentive problems are taken into account. With lop-sided and incomplete information, equilibrium may cease to exist and, if it does, it may not prove to be market-clearing (Stiglitz 1987). In the absence of a complete set of futures markets, that is, incomplete financial markets, entry and exit decisions need to be made on the basis of expectations about the behaviour of other agents, so that each agent needs a model of the whole economy. These results have led Arrow (1987) to conclude, 'the superiority of market over centralised planning disappears. Each individual agent is in effect using as much information as would be required for a central planner'. In the Appendix to this chapter we therefore discuss some alternatives to capitalist ownership. These doubts about the superiority of capitalism on theoretical grounds are not just irrelevant abstract considerations of academic economists. They point to the fact that in reality capitalism has to work in an imperfect world as well. This implies that the creation of a market economy through privatisation has to proceed carefully to ensure that the unavoidable market imperfections are minimised. Following Churchill one could say that capitalism is a very bad system, except that it is a lesser evil.

Section 1 therefore proposes a careful analysis of the institutional requirements for privatisation. Section 2 discusses the difficulties of valuing firms in reforming economies. A strong plea is made in Section 3 for give-away privatisation as contemplated in several East European countries. Section 4 summarises the redistribution effects of privatisation and Section 5 concludes.

Privatisation requires financial resources, markets and institutions to monitor firms and to trade ownership rights, and a solution to the bad debts held by banks. We relegate discussion of these problems to Chapter 9 and focus this chapter on the questions of why and how to privatise firms.

1. The goals of privatisation and restructuring

A privatisation programme, whatever its complexion, should set out to achieve a range of objectives. First and foremost, privatisation should be viewed as an instrument for promoting efficiency by creating an incentive-based economy. Second, privatisation should lead to a distribution of ownership that is accepted as fair. This is important because otherwise political support for the reforms could diminish and turn into a general climate of resistance to change. Third, the privatisation process should serve the creation of a market structure compatible with the expectations of a decentralised and ultimately democratic society.[1] Private ownership is necessary to achieve separation of political and economic decisions and in this separation lies the scope for efficiency and stability gains.

The first aim, increased efficiency, cannot be achieved at the stroke of a pen through a change of ownership. West European experience clearly shows that ownership *per se* is not really the issue. Indeed, if enterprises are to be compelled to behave more efficiently, they must face competitive pressures in markets with rational prices and hard budget constraints (Newbery 1991a). Therefore, as shown by Vickers and Yarrow (1988), the major determinant of success in transforming the performance of state-owned enterprises (SOEs) is not just ownership, but the entire economic environment in which they operate.

The success of privatisation hinges on owners' ability to monitor managers' performance properly. A firm is the result of incomplete contractual arrangements under asymmetric and incomplete information (Coase 1937). Except in the case of the owner-manager, all enterprise structures are subject to some form of principal–agent problem. Hence, it is important to design an incentive scheme such that the agent's (manager's) best interest is secured by doing what benefits the principal (owner) most. A perfect solution to the principal–agent problem would be an incentive mechanism in which agents maximise their own utility or income when their actions maximise the principal's utility or income. Such perfect conciliation of the agent's and the principal's objectives is nevertheless impossible under most ownership structures.

In a market economy, many forms of organisation exist side by side. These range from the owner-manager enterprise structure that characterises most small firms, where the principal and the agent are one and the same person, to the unit trust (institutional investors) structure, where the ultimate owners only own the firm through the intermediation of the trust which is responsible for monitoring managerial performance.

We already agreed in Part I that the major pitfall in East European social organisation has been faulty principal–agent relationships. It may be true, as Lange (1937) has argued, that a planner could replicate the price vector of a competitive equilibrium (although, in practice, this would not make sense). But the incentives and penalties for managers at the micro level are not the same, hence the production response to a given set of prices is not the same either.

The principal–agent conundrum is not only a microeconomic problem. It has often been noted, for example in Lipton and Sachs (1990), that wage-earners in reforming economies are not confronted with principals who effectively oppose wage increases or reduction in work efforts. Failure to address this problem can lead to macroeconomic destabilisation, as is becoming clear in Russia.

In the early period following privatisation, the stock market is also unlikely to provide enough discipline to ensure the strict control of large firms.[2] The most promising corporate governance mechanism is likely to be a combination of widespread shareholdings assisted in their role of principals by institutions acting on their behalf. There is some choice as to the type of institution. One choice will be discussed in Chapter 9, namely the creation of universal banks. Another institution acting as a principal is the unit trust (investment funds). A further guarantee for the efficiency of the principal's role should be sought by allowing foreigners to participate in the management of institutional funds, as advocated by Tirole (1991).

2. Valuing firms

The valuation of firms in reforming economies is considerably more complex than in mature market economies, as their future viability and performance is hard to assess in a highly unsettled environment. The difficulties are summarised in Box 8.1.

Box 8.1 Determining the firm's value

In order to sell, a value first needs to be assigned to the firm. Improved accounting methods are a necessary, but far from sufficient, condition for this, as the value of a firm is the discounted value of its expected future profit stream (P_t):

$$V(k) = \Sigma b^t E(P_t), \quad [1]$$

where b is the discount factor and E the expectation operator. Value $V(k)$ has very little in common with the book value of a firm. In some circumstances it may represent a lower limit for the price, P_v, at which the firm can be sold:*

$$V(k) \leq P_v \leq V(k/i). \quad [2]$$

Although $V(k)$ is an estimate with a considerable margin of error, a risk-neutral seller without cash-flow constraints would not accept a price below $V(k)$. When the sum of the parts is worth more than the total, then a purchaser would be ready to pay more than $V(k)$, and sell off parts of the firm thus acquired.† Similarly, if there are synergies between firm k and acquirer i, then $V(k/i)$, the value of firm k to i, exceeds $V(k)$. The only way to exploit condition [2] is to organise open and well-advertised bidding procedures.

In order to put the valuation exercise into perspective and to focus on the major determinants of the firm's value in East European conditions, it is helpful to consider the elements that determine the profitability of firm k as follows:

continued

Box 8.1 *continued*

$V(k) = f$ (product, production structure, initial conditions (A) [3]
market structure . . . (B)
output and factor prices, taxes . . . (C)
macroeconomic environment . . .) (D)

For the sake of exposition the various arguments of the function *f(.)* are ordered from (A) to (D) in ascending order of scope from the microeconomic level (A), to the market (B), and the macroeconomic level (C and D). Of course, the various factors generally overlap. But it is important to note that the firm only controls part of factor (A) (as history and one-off policy decisions are beyond its control); the evolution of economic structure, in particular openness, determines factors (B) and (C); and macroeconomic policy, the credibility of the domestic government, and shocks originating inside and outside the national economy are behind factor (D).

* Condition [2] could be violated in distorted markets, that is, firms may be sold at prices below their intrinsic value. As argued by Sinn and Sinn (1991), if competition among potential purchasers is restricted and if sales are forced through in a short time by an agency that is not itself wealth-maximising, prices could even become negative.

† It is often claimed that state trusts need to be dismantled before privatisation can proceed. While this is true in the case of monopolies in the non-tradable goods sector, it should not be regarded as mandatory in other cases. First, foreign trade liberalisation will dramatically reduce the power of national monopolies. Second, conglomerates are likely to become unbundled after privatisation, thus realising an arbitrage gain. Experience in developed countries also indicates that large companies very often restructure their peripheral activities before selling them off.

Source: Steinherr and Perée (1992)

INFORMATION AND INITIAL CONDITIONS

One difficulty for privatisation (factor A in Box 8.1) refers to the firm's ability to combine various inputs economically to produce goods or services that will be bought by customers. It therefore refers to the X-efficiency of the firm. Privatisation, which is the key to transformation at this level, is expected by means of a coherent set of incentives and constraints to enable the firm significantly to increase its economic efficiency.

Current production structures and initial conditions before restructuring are the legacy of the old economic order. As discussed in Part I, central planning has consistently emphasised potential economies of scale and favoured the creation of mega-firms facing little or no competition on the domestic market. Despite a higher average investment rate than in industrial economies, the productive sector has been unable to achieve significant productivity gains. The low level of technological progress encapsulated in new investments, massive over-staffing, obsolete working practices, and poor-quality capital stock suggest that there is plenty of scope for a drastic reduction of X-inefficiency.

Another typical feature common to East European SOEs was their autarkic production strategy. Chronic input shortages and poor distribution prompted firms to produce as many of their own manufacturing components as possible. Although this was not really compatible with the desire of the planners to maximise the use of economies of scale, local managers had little choice but to try to overcome the unreliability of supplies this way. Under these circumstances no sub-contracting or service sector and thus no medium-sized business sector could develop. Bearing in mind that sub-contracting, medium-sized businesses and services are the very instruments of flexibility that have helped the industrialised world to adapt to economic change, the former socialist countries have a lot to make up. Almost all large socialist manufacturing firms will thus not only have to restructure their core business, but also spin off ancillary activities which in the past occupied a large part of their workforce.

The high indebtedness of SOEs is another key feature of initial conditions in the East European business world. Concrete ways of dealing with this problem will be discussed in Chapter 9.

MARKET STRUCTURE: IS THERE A NEED FOR COMPETITION POLICY?

Another factor difficult to assess (factor B in Box 8.1) concerns the effect of industry structure. In reforming economies many large SOEs face no domestic competition at all, simply because there are few or no firms which produce the same kind of product. For the FSU it is estimated that for two out of three products one single plant was the main supplier (Bennett and Dixon 1993). This situation was due to the fact that SOEs were generally highly integrated both vertically and horizontally – mostly for the reasons outlined above rather than because of any economic rationale. The peculiar production structure that led to this monopolistic market structure will, of course, change over time, but in the meantime the market structure will remain different from that in the West. It needs a drastic overhaul if privatisation is to generate the full advantages of competition.

This has important implications for privatisation since public or private monopolies behave in much the same manner, namely as monopolies (Vickers and Yarrow 1988). From the discussion in Chapter 5 it should be borne in mind that for most products monopolies can only exist by the grace of government. If governments do not want them to exist, the most effective means of ensuring competitive behaviour is for them to introduce a measure of 'contestability' through foreign trade. Furthermore, as already argued in Chapter 5, if all firms had the same degree of monopoly power then they would all charge the same mark-up on marginal cost so that relative prices would not be different from a competitive economy. Monopoly power therefore creates a problem mainly if it is spotty, that is, if some firms enjoy large monopoly power and others little or none at all.

There are two main ways of avoiding uncompetitive market practices: regulation and openness. In the particular case of Eastern Europe, regulation is the more debatable method, chiefly because the authorities' decision-making prerogatives are in danger of being captured by interest groups. The recommendation of the classical maxim 'competition where possible, regulation where necessary' is the safer alternative. For the tradable goods sector, competition can be ensured by liberalising foreign trade, as was argued in Chapter 5. Only sectors that for technical constraints cannot be exposed to foreign competition (e.g. the electricity grid) are in need of regulation. Nevertheless, since a fair and sound regulatory system is never easy to design, contestability should be promoted in preference to regulation wherever possible.

Product markets are not the only ones that should be made competitive. A well-functioning labour market is also crucial to successful restructuring. Since substantial unemployment must be reckoned with, at least in the short term, the whole reform process could be in jeopardy if firms' employment choices were put in a strait-jacket. Unless employment levels are adjusted, productivity gains will be minimal, and the reallocation of labour across the economy and the acquisition of new skills made more difficult. Liberalisation of the labour market will meet with dogged resistance on the part of workers unless the overall reform package is perceived as fair and credible and offers a solid safety net, as was argued in Chapter 7. Experience shows that during the first year or two of reforms unemployment rises only slowly, suggesting that initially restructuring is *de facto* quite limited and labour is kept on the pay-roll even when output declines strongly.

MACROECONOMIC UNCERTAINTY

Given the highly uncertain environment in which firms – domestic and foreign – will have to operate, macroeconomic instability presents awesome risks. The longer it takes the authorities to establish credibility, to temper the surrounding uncertainty and to stabilise the economy, the slower adjustment will be. As demonstrated by Dixit (1989), uncertainty can be a powerful disincentive to grasping investment opportunities. Indeed, in a turbulent environment, there is strong pressure on potential entrepreneurs to delay even attractive projects, if part of the investment is irreversible.[3]

A 'wait and see' attitude by investors is an optimal response to uncertainty. Indeed, when a potential investor has to decide whether or not to go ahead with a project, he or she is faced with three options: to invest now, not to invest at all, or to keep the investment opportunity open for future reference. It is this third possibility which makes the investment opportunity resemble a call option. If the excess rate of return of the investment over the opportunity cost of capital is not high enough to compensate for risk, it is optimal not to exercise the option and to wait and see how economic conditions evolve. Investment will therefore not be forthcoming unless the option is sufficiently deep in the money. Furthermore, Dixit's calculations show that the excess current return necessary to induce investment is a positive function of both the level of uncertainty and the degree of investment irreversibility. Even for small amounts of uncertainty and irreversibility, the premium required to undertake the investment project can be considerable. Macroeconomic uncertainty thus not only increases uncertainty about the value of the firm, it also reduces the amount of investment potential all private owners (domestic or foreign) will undertake.

This discussion clearly shows that the valuation of East European firms is fraught with enormous difficulties. Therefore, the attempt to sell at once most large companies directly to domestic and foreign investors is likely to lead to rock-bottom prices. Another reason why it is difficult to sell large enterprises rapidly is that domestic savers will not be able to bid large amounts if they have to pay in cash. The flow of savings from domestic savings is limited for each time period and quite small relative to the value of the stock of capital of the entire economy. Sinn and Sinn (1991) stress this effect in their analysis of the sell-off of SOEs in the former GDR. However, since the new *Länder* accounted for only 10 per cent of the overall German GDP there is no problem in the German case, except that most firms are not bought by East Germans (see Chapter 10). It is clear that any attempt to sell 100 per cent of the capital stock of an economy within a short period, say a year, must decrease prices close to zero. The only way out of this conundrum would be to allow investors to pay later, that is, for the government to accept IOUs in exchange for the control over the assets of the SOEs. But this would entail major risks. Since it will always remain uncertain to what extent investors will actually pay up later (they have every interest in taking the assets and running), this approach can only be a partial or occasional solution to the stock/flow problem.[4]

The lack of insufficient domestic savings can be overcome by selling SOEs to foreigners. The potential of a 'sell-out' to foreigners has, however, been strongly resisted everywhere. Politically it has turned out unacceptable to sell a large portion of industrial assets, notably the 'jewels', to foreigners for the fear of loss of national control. Foreign investors anyway would have bought in most countries only at rock-bottom prices since the risk of a reversal of reforms or a future (re) nationalisation can never be eliminated. In the Central European countries which are to become members of the EU, these problems have been at least partially overcome. But in the countries of the FSU, which have just become independent, the desire to safeguard 'sovereignty' proved too strong. These are the main reasons for discarding the one-by-one send off approach and for the need to search for other solutions outlined in Section 4 and in the Appendix.

Authors such as Van Long and Siebert (1991) have modelled the transition from a socialist to a market economy as a shock to prices and therefore to output and the value of the firm, generating a J-curve performance response.[5] This is certainly correct, although the downturn in production everywhere in Eastern Europe resembles more an L-curve. The risk of a J or an L-curve adjustment is that labour unrest could jeopardise the reform package, so that firms would be bankrupted before they ever got within sight of the delayed recovery. In privatisation terms, firms would be sold off 'for a song'.[6]

3. The case for give-away privatisation

We have argued so far that it is not possible to sell quickly all SOEs on a one-by-one basis. This raises the question whether it is preferable to drop the one-by-one approach or maintain it but accept a slower pace of privatisation.

What matters most on both economic and political grounds is that the privatisation process should be swift and comprehensive.[7] The attitude taken by the SOEs themselves will be paramount in determining the success of adjustment in Eastern Europe, because SOEs inevitably dominate industry in the short run. At the outset of the reforms the ownership structure will certainly not be ideal, but if managers and workers know that privatisation and a competitive environment are around the corner they will start immediately to adjust (provided they are prevented from running off with the firm's assets). A clear, realistic timetable for reform is thus crucial in ensuring that the SOE responds from the beginning to market signals.

Experience has shown that the transitional phase, in which the economic incentive system associated with central planning has been jettisoned but no market economy is yet in place, is the most dangerous phase. In the resulting fog of uncertain property rights and effective lack of management supervision, it is child's play for managers to dispose of enterprise assets for their personal benefit, bringing decapitalisation and collapse of the production process in its wake.

Of course, a rapid change of ownership structures also has a price. One of the consequences will be a sharp increase in unemployment as the newly privatised firms shed excess labour and become more efficient. Another possible consequence is a highly skewed redistribution of income which, in turn, might produce a political backlash. These consequences may well arise, but there are steps to mitigate the cost of transition by retaining some of the alternatives mentioned below.

Moreover, one also has to consider the cost of a more soft-pedalling alternative. What would be wrong with, say, privatising a handful of firms every now and again, so that it would be several years before a substantial proportion of firms would have moved to the private sector? The state would then continue to control most of industry and one could argue that this would be like in some West European countries where the privatisation drive of the 1980s left public sector enterprises in partial charge of certain industrial sectors. The hitch in this argument is that public sector companies in the West are always a small part of the overall economy and have to reckon with market signals if they are to hold their own *vis-à-vis* private enterprises. They operate in an established market economy with all the trappings of financial markets, ownership structures and control machinery firmly in place. In some Latin American countries state ownership was more pervasive than in Western Europe and the price in terms of bad economic performance was also correspondingly higher. Countries like Argentina stopped growing for 50 years and resumed growth only in the wake of structural reform and extensive privatisation programmes.

The gradualist and piecemeal approach would also mean that the least efficient enterprises would be the last to leave the public sector arena, if indeed they were sold off at all. This is amply illustrated by the Treuhand experience discussed in Chapter 10. The point is that such enterprises are both large and numerous. They would constitute a significant drain on public sector finances for some time to come as it would be politically costly to close them down.

Given the pitfalls of standard privatisation procedures in Eastern Europe, a number of alternative proposals have been put forward. These typically rely on some sort of distributive scheme involving the free distribution or sale at a nominal charge of a share of the ownership in SOEs to private citizens. This would obviate the need for valuing enterprises, a task of Herculean proportions, as was argued above.

We now elaborate in some detail a proposal already submitted in Gros and Steinherr (1990). Table 8.1 summarises other proposals of a similar kind, differing only in institutional details.

Whenever a large public-sector company is privatised, its capital would be divided into a number of shares for the government to give away.[8] There are two ways of doing this, which are not mutually exclusive and could therefore be combined:

1. The number of shares is set equal to the number of eligible citizens, with everybody receiving one share, either directly or indirectly, as part of a national investment fund.
2. The number of shares is set equal to the number of workers in the firm, each of whom receives one share.

TABLE 8.1 Comparison of give-away privatisation proposals

Proposal	Structure of ownership	% of ownership	Management supervision	Mechanism of privatisation
Free distribution to workers and citizens (Gros and Steinherr 1990)	Banks and holding companies Direct ownership Government	50 30 20	Banks and holding	Free distribution
Citizens' shares (Feige 1990)	Citizens Central governments Republics	50 10 20	Mainly private and foreign owners	Citizen shares sold at under-valued prices; private shares auctioned with right of first refusal to workers and managers
Financial intermediaries (Frydman and Rapaczynski 1991)	Citizen-owned mutual funds	100	Private intermediaries that bid for the enterprises they would like to acquire	Free distribution of vouchers to the public; intermediaries' funds sell stock to the public in exchange for vouchers used to bid for enterprises in a series of auctions
Financial intermediaries (Lipton and Sachs 1990)	Citizen-owned mutual funds Pension funds Banks Workers Managers Government for later privatisation	20 20 10 10 5 35	Competing mutual funds that overlap in the same firms, banks and eventually a 'stable core' of private investors that will acquire shares from the government	Free distribution except for sale to private investors at a later stage
Privatisation companies (Blanchard *et al.* 1990)	Citizen-owned holding companies	100	Holding companies, themselves controlled by competition, government supervision, and the use of performance-based compensation	Free distribution of shares in holding companies to all citizens
Self-management	Workers and managers	100	Current employees acquire rights to profits and assets of enterprises; ownership rights non-transferable	Legal structure in Hungary and Poland allowed some 'spontaneous' privatisations by current management

Under the first alternative each citizen would receive one share in the form of a book entry. Over time, as privatisation progressed, each citizen would hold an increasingly diversified portfolio. Obviously, not all citizens would be interested in holding all the shares they received and an informal market would therefore quickly be established. This would provide the basis for an over-the-counter market which could eventually blossom into an organised stock exchange. An investor wishing to obtain control over a company would have to acquire shares at market rates or with a take-over proposal. Whether the investor was a resident or a non-resident would then be a question of secondary importance. Citizens, as shareholders, would decide about each sale to foreigners, whether to cash in now rather than later – or not at all – as in a referendum, with the clear advantage that each citizen would have the same endowment of 'voting' rights (one share). A possible sell-out to foreigners could not be criticised because it would not be a decision taken by the old or a new *nomenklatura*.

Such a privatisation programme would be flexible enough to accommodate worker participation, if desired, by combining it with the second alternative. Instead of strengthening union power along the lines of the German *Mitbestimmung*, workers could be allocated shares in their firm, which would give them voting rights and a stake in the firm's results. Needless to say, there should be no ban on disposing of such shares, so as to allow for better risk diversification. This is important if privatisation is not to lead to full workers' control over firms which, as evidenced by the Yugoslav experience, may carry its own special brand of inefficiency.

One implication of such a scheme would be that all workers would receive shares in all firms scheduled for privatisation, plus a special allocation of shares in their own firm. Public sector employees would be excluded from that allocation. Economically speaking, the firm-specific allocations might be likened to a risk premium, since the risk of bankruptcy or lay-offs is higher in the private sector. Moreover, as the public administrations inherited from the old system present a bad case of hypertrophy anyway, some sort of incentive to leave public sector employment might help to trim them down.

Finally, it might be a good idea, for a limited time, if governments maintained a minority share of 10–30 per cent. The government could in this way make sure there is no abuse during the restructuring phase. The countervailing power of worker/shareholders and of outside shareholders represented by banks should suffice to prevent the government from pursuing objectives too antagonistic to long-term value maximisation. Moreover, the government would automatically receive a part of future profits. All shareholders, including the government, would participate even in profits that are hidden from (initially imperfectly administered) corporate taxes as share values over time would reflect these hidden profits.

Privatisation along these lines offers several attractive advantages, in particular:

1. It would be consistent with social justice. In fact, the concept of 'social ownership of the means of production' would for the first time have real, as opposed to rhetorical, meaning. And since the social contribution made by each individual would be impossible to assess for purposes of share allocation, there should be no discrimination and everybody should simply be granted one share.
2. It has definite political appeal in that it creates a tabula rasa. The new order would start with social capital distributed equally to all. Capitalism would then also be perceived as a system with the potential not only for greater dynamism but even for greater social justice than the defunct 'social ownership'. This is a notion much prized in Western Europe, where privatisation often aims at spreading share ownership as widely as possible. It might be argued that citizens owning a portfolio of shares in national industry turn into convinced 'capitalists' and recognise its 'human face'.

3. Private ownership, if widely distributed at the starting-point, is liable to command stronger support than alternative property rights proposals. Recent difficulties with privatisation everywhere in Eastern Europe confirm this view. The right of governments to privatise, the prices negotiated, the neglect of workers' interests (and more generally those of the general public) have all run into fierce criticism.
4. For privatisation purposes no prior assessment of the value of the firm would be necessary. That job would be taken on at a subsequent stage by the stock exchange. Nor would the decision to privatise have to be made at the stroke of a pen. Companies could be privatised one by one, or in large batches at a time, whichever was deemed most appropriate.

A major objection to all variants of the give-away solution is that it deprives governments of the revenue that would be generated by selling off state firms. In theory, selling state firms and redistributing the revenue to citizens in the form of lower taxes or better services amounts to the same thing. In practice, however, governments could retain privatisation revenues to limit the deficits they usually run during the transition.

A more important counter-argument is that, taking the stock markets of some non-socialist countries (e.g. Greece, Portugal) as reference, it seems doubtful that much revenue would be sacrificed For example, in Greece and Portugal the entire stock market capitalisation is equal to 8 per cent and 14 per cent respectively of (annual) GDP decades after the introduction of market-based economies. Privatisation revenue in the Central European countries is unlikely to come to even this much, since existing capital stock is often close to worthless under the new price structure that is about to emerge. However, even if we accept these figures as an upper limit, they still indicate that a privatisation scheme, based on one-by-one sales of SOEs which might have to be spread over as much as a decade, is unlikely to bring in more than 1 per cent of GDP per year in revenues. Furthermore, against these limited revenue gains one has to set the efficiency loss brought about by continuing government management of a large slice of industry.

The experience in the ex-GDR analysed in Chapter 10 shows that it is even possible that the net revenue from privatisation is negative if the seller (Treuhand) insists on employment guarantees.

Any privatisation scheme adopted must face the fact that some firms are downright unprofitable and cannot survive even with price reform and new management. Such firms are best closed down. Parts of industry do, however, have a chance of survival with efficient management and a rational price structure. Even if not immediately profitable, the present value of such firms might be quite high after reform. However, as argued above, it is impossible for outsiders to determine exactly the prospects of each firm. But if the state 'gives firms away' their actual worth is irrelevant, and it makes the task of closing down firms without a future that much easier. It would be impossible to sell such firms at a positive price and they would have to remain under state control with old-fashioned and wasteful 'soft budget' constraints. If they are privatised, however, shareholders will find it is no use keeping them going and will advocate closure.

Privatisation should also be a blessing to developing stock market operations. Of course, the entire population cannot be expected to exert effective control over the companies it collectively owns. In this respect, the problem is no different from that of large Western companies with hundreds of thousands of shareholders. A system of proxy-voting exercised by private banks and specialised financial companies would have to be instituted. Foreign banks, investment brokers and portfolio managers could play a key role in managing these widely held shares and in developing stock markets and efficient stock market control over corporate resource allocation and strategy. We discuss these issues in more detail in Chapter 9.

The whole point of privatisation is to achieve better control over the productive sector. Diffuse share ownership carries the risk of leaving effective control in the hands of the existing *nomenklatura*. That is why it is important that voting rights be exercised effectively until stock market control is established – a process that will require time. One solution might be to set up financial investment companies entitled to acquire shares, up to certain limits, in a restricted number of firms (e.g. one firm per industry). Citizens and the state would jointly own these financial companies or, alternatively, they could be privately owned and would manage shares directly owned by citizens.

The 'citizens' shares' approach faces the problem that, given the large number of shares that must be issued, each single share will be worth very little. For example, in a country with 10 million voters, a share in a company worth 100 million dollars would itself be worth a mere ten dollars. Even on efficient Western stock markets, the fixed cost of a transaction is high. This implies that the citizens' shares approach would have to be confined to large companies or that the shares of all firms in the same industry would have to be bundled into one investment certificate. The contractual 'workers' shares' approach could be applied more easily to small firms, whose real value would be difficult to establish and which are not easily managed by governments.

4. The redistributive effects of privatisation

The major redistributive impact of privatisation is expected to fall on governments as SOE used to be an important source of revenue for government budgets, as described in Chapter 7.

The proposals outlined above each offer their own solutions. Some (Feige, Gros and Steinherr, Lipton and Sachs), assume that central government would retain a minority share on a temporary or permanent basis to provide a source of revenue that would reduce reliance on other taxes. The appeal of this scheme is that from the point of view of fiscal theory, share ownership is probably the least distortionary way of raising revenue open to any government. Free distribution of property does not necessarily entail a commensurate loss of assets, because it stands in for other expenses the government would have faced. This is particularly true of social safety net spending and the recapitalisation of financial intermediaries floundering in deep financial waters.

All privatisation proposals have important implications for income and wealth distribution as well as for private savings. In so far as consumers anticipate efficiency gains from better-defined property rights, share handouts are a way of increasing private wealth on strictly egalitarian lines and of cushioning the social impact of rapid economic change and the concomitant rise in unemployment.[9] The distributive effect is in fact an important political objective, since the sale of State assets would probably be coldly received as serving the purposes of the old communist *nomenklatura* and black marketeers. Also, depending on the nitty-gritty of the scheme adopted, individual citizens would find themselves in possession of a nicely diversified share portfolio taking in the whole spectrum of industrial activity. This would considerably reduce the entrepreneurial risk to individuals lacking the expertise and financial know-how to manage their portfolios.

The provision of a well-diversified portfolio is considered in some proposals, with a view to ensuring that the distributive aspect of privatisation benefits all citizens. Of course, consumers would be able to adjust their portfolio in time, but many may choose not to take any action. In most proposals, enterprises would in fact be grouped in such a way as to produce well-diversified portfolios. If asset composition is perceived as too risky, consumers are likely to become frustrated about the blessings of privatisation and pressure may build up to bail out less successful intermediaries.

5. Conclusions

Experience in all countries, East and West, shows that privatisation of SOEs is a politically sensitive issue, including the fear of 'carpetbagging' by foreigners. It also poses numerous technical difficulties (how to value firms in a transition environment) and faces macro constraints (the lack of domestic savings), and therefore requires a great deal of time. But this raises serious problems in the meantime for the effectiveness of reforms. Indeed, in all reforming countries it has become all too obvious that reforms are quite limited in increasing the efficiency of the economy as long as SOEs are not submitted to hard budget constraints. Whilst it is not inconceivable to submit SOEs to hard budget constraints – and, as shown in Chapter 11, in the Visegrad countries some progress has been achieved in this respect – it is very difficult. Big firms are large employers and therefore too big to fail in view of the political weight they can represent. Nor can managers of SOEs to be privatised at some time in the future easily be given the incentive to act like capitalist managers.

These difficulties with a quick case-by-case privatisation, on the one hand, and with the introduction of hard budget constraints if privatisation were to take a long time, on the other hand, lead us to support give-away privatisation. This can be done quickly, as no evaluation of firms is necessary, and fairly (no carpetbagging by foreigners or domestic profiteers). As for the corporate governance problem, solutions are available in the form of intermediaries (funds, banks) which hold the shares of privatised enterprises, with citizens having participation rights in the funds.

So far, no Eastern European country has opted for a global give-away privatisation plan. But many countries have adopted partial give-aways for a share of assets to be privatised. For a country-by-country record, see Chapters 10 and 11 and Frydman *et al.* (1992). The desire to sell large concerns for cash and, in some cases, doubts about the corporate governance issue of give-away programmes have led all countries to a mixed approach, spread over time: retaining for the time being some enterprises considered as key enterprises in state ownership (banks, energy, telecommunications, railways, etc.); selling case-by-case some profitable SOEs and closing down others; creating a temporary parking lot in the form of a holding for SOEs to be privatised (the Treuhand model); converting debt into equity and thus making banks own SOEs; and give-away coupon programmes. As a result hard budget constraints operate on some firms but not on all and restructuring is seriously slowed down.

Notes

1. It is therefore essential to privatise not only SOEs but also real estate, shops and small enterprises. This part of the privatisation process is much easier than privatisation of SOEs and we therefore do not dwell on this issue. We would, however, favour give-away privatisation of dwellings (against continuation of inflation-adjusted rent payments serving as purchase instalments) and shops, allowing for cooperative set-ups.
2. Even in developed market economies the effectiveness of owner control of firms is debatable. For a very positive assessment of the US experience, see Jensen (1988); for a more reserved evaluation of the German variety, see Steinherr and Huveneers (1992). Furthermore, as convincingly argued by Eckaus (1990), it is important to appreciate how long it took US stock markets to become respectable and useful in their present roles.
3. This may explain why the bulk of investment by nationals and foreigners alike currently concentrates on trading companies and plant needing little new fixed investment.
4. Some of these problems have marred the Treuhand approach of selling SOEs at lower prices in exchange for promises to invest and maintain negotiated employment levels. See Chapter 10.
5. Because the value of the firm is the present value of future profits, the J-curve effect of restructuring economic activity is compatible with a rise or fall in the firm's value during transition. As it is inconceivable that all firms would be generally worse off under market conditions, some stand to gain and others will lose. Yet, as financial markets are not perfect anywhere, and least of all in Eastern Europe, the J-curve effect does matter. That is why it is so important to ease the debt burden right from the start. With real assets rendered less valuable or worthless by the cessation of the socialist mode of production, the debt structure needs to be taken away as well. Taking a forward-looking approach to evaluate firms, as in Box 8.1, suggests that many more firms should be able to weather the J-curve effect and aspire to a normal self-supporting structure in the long run.
6. Additional difficulties encountered in lightning sales at prices close to the value of the firm are discussed in Sinn and Sinn (1991).
7. It has indeed been suggested that the difficulties faced by the 1990 Balcerowicz Plan in Poland were at least partly due to the absence of privatisation. See Lipton and Sachs (1990) and Frydman and Rapaczynski (1991).
8. The privatisation of smaller firms along these lines may become unmanageable. For such reasons, plans to distribute coupons which could be realised rapidly have been extensively discussed in Czechoslovakia but have been shelved for the time being.
9. As argued in Chapter 10, the drama unfolding in East Germany is largely due to the fact that citizens in the East were despoiled of their property rights so that they are reduced to bargaining for higher transfers and wages.

Appendix: The case for alternatives

Public ownership in the narrow sense of state control of firms is not indispensable to a relatively egalitarian distribution of the economy's surplus. Public ownership, in a wider sense, can be designed to ensure that the distribution of company profits is decided by democratic political process – yet firms are controlled by agents who do not represent the state. In most developed economies, mechanisms exist to influence both the allocation of resources and the distribution of income. A mix of state-supported research programmes, Japan's MITI-type industrial policy, state ownership of sensitive sectors (energy, communications, transport, education), subsidies and taxes are used to steer allocation and distribution. What the East European experience has shown is that a system of pervasive state control of firms, coupled with the absence of markets, simply does not work. Some claim that competitive markets are the lifeblood of an efficient and vigorous economy, but that full-scale private ownership is not necessary for competition and markets to function successfully.[1] Contrary to popular belief, however, this claim has not yet been disproved by either history or economic theory. The wholesale failure of the socialist experience in Eastern Europe as well as in countries like Sweden or France supports the conjecture but is not proof that all its constituent elements are useless.

The main problem with public ownership as traditionally practised is the inefficiencies associated with the failure to separate political from economic criteria in resource allocation and in company decision-making. (The 'soft budget constraint' is an instance of this failure.) Crucial decisions concerning the entry and exit of firms and the selection, promotion, and dismissal of managers have all too often remained the prerogative of the all-powerful Party *nomenklatura*. Sachs (1991) claims, on the basis of recent experience in Poland, that market socialism involving 'liberalisation without privatisation' is particularly pernicious, because it gives managers and workers in public firms autonomy without responsibility, which not infrequently leads to their teaming up to cannibalise the firm's assets. This could mean two things: either that crucial incentive and agency problems in the management of public firms have to be addressed, or that this is impossible in a social market economy.

We now go on to summarise a proposal for a social market economy as put forward by Bardhan and Roemer (1992). It involves taking firms out of the state's orbit, without granting individual citizens unlimited private property rights in them. Citizens will have rights to firms' profits, but they will not be able to capitalise these profit streams. Managements will be monitored by the banks responsible for financing the firms' operations and, in some cases, by other firms in the same financial group, rather than by individual partners or through the sale of shares.

The proposal therefore combines the role of banks in financing and monitoring firms, as will be argued in Chapter 9, with the notion of widespread, uniform distribution of ownership to ensure more egalitarian distribution as advocated in this chapter. This approach seems quite attractive and susceptible of practical implementation. Why?

First, Western-style capitalism – particularly the American brand – is unlikely to be practicable in Eastern Europe. The institutions of Western capitalism, including its legal, political, and economic infrastructure, have taken many years to mature and some of them are not easily replicable. In fact, the bank-centred organisation described in Chapter 9 is a way of mitigating this historical handicap. It was the under-development of capital markets in late nineteenth-century Germany that led banks to become heavily involved in the financing and management of industrial concerns. Even in the case of Japan, as Horiuchi (1989) points out, the banking system owes its existence to the highly imperfect financial markets and economic uncertainties of the immediate post-war period.

It is hard to sustain that income distribution on capitalist lines is the only arrangement consistent with efficiency. If we compare Japan and some European countries with very high marginal taxation levels to the United States, we find that in order to work, entrepreneurial functions do not require the very considerable drain on the social surplus that corporate capitalists usually exact, and that inherited wealth does not serve a useful social purpose.

Furthermore, a more egalitarian distribution of profits may also lead to fewer of the public 'bads' associated with many of capitalism's less endearing features. Several examples spring to mind, not least pollution.

In a capitalist society, the political economy operates as follows. Citizens regulate the level of the public 'bad' – say, pollution – in the voting booth. A traditional median-voter approach as in Roemer (1991) yields the result that a more egalitarian distribution of income could generate higher levels of the optimally produced public 'bad'.

The following line of reasoning reaches the opposite conclusion: a large shareholder suffers a smaller than average share of pollution since he or she can set up residence away from the site of production and pollution, and receives a higher than average share of profits. The shareholder is therefore more inclined to accept pollution than the average citizen. Moreover, large shareholders are powerful: they fund political parties and, more generally, are influential in steering the political process. So it would not be surprising if the level of public 'bad' which is the outcome of the political process is higher under a non-egalitarian profit distribution system than under the more egalitarian alternative.

The general point is that negative externalities are associated with a high degree of concentration of company ownership in socialist or in capitalist economies, if the political process is also strongly influenced by the wealthy (in socialist countries, the *nomenklatura*-controlled central government). A more egalitarian way of distributing profits may help to reduce these externalities.

Managerial motivation and managerial discipline with a view to maximising the value of the firm are key issues in any system. It is true that, unlike private entrepreneurs, the salaried managers of public enterprises (or indeed of their capitalist counterparts) have not much of a stake in the firm and stand to gain less by good performance. They may therefore be more lukewarm in their pursuit of the rules of the game. The harsh reality of the market may be tempered by the exigencies of political accountability which put financial liability in the shade, and there is always the built-in safety net of the 'soft budget constraint' and the Western phenomenon of 'appropriation of free cash-flows' to see them through.

Finance theorists concerned with the agency problem in corporate capitalism – for example, Alchian and Demsetz (1972) and Jensen and Meckling (1976) – claim that the primary disciplining of managers comes through the capital market and the managerial labour market (both inside and outside the firm) or, in countries where capital markets are less developed, by the banks, as demonstrated in Steinherr and Huveneers (1992). In principle, there is no reason why market socialism could not reproduce the managerial labour market, provided a manager's reputation and future wages stand or fall with the performance of the firm he or she manages. It takes time and considerable depoliticised institution-building, but not necessarily a capitalist property system to nurture a corporate culture of competitive bidding in the market for professional managers. Socialism, in all its variants – including the Yugoslav labour-management system – has no institution like the stock market or independent banks acting as lenders, shareholders and proxy-voters, to provide permanent assessment of managerial performance. The threat of corporate takeover (along with stock options, which have generated considerable wealth to top executives) is supposed, in theory, to keep managers honest and the firm efficient, and thus to resolve the innate conflict of interest between risk-bearers and risk-managers. Empirical evidence fails, however, to provide strong support for this.

The financial discipline of corporate takeover tends to be a drawn-out and wasteful process. Jensen (1989) notes that in the United States, takeover and leveraged buy-out premiums average 50 per cent above market price, which goes to show how much value corporate managers can destroy before they face a serious threat of disturbance. Even the takeover process contains a basic asymmetry of information: managers are better informed about the source of a firm's problems than are outside buyers. As Stiglitz (1985) suggests, takeovers are like buying 'used firms', and are subject, as such, to Akerlof's 'lemons principle'. And, as the post-mergers and acquisitions euphoria since 1989 reveals, many takeovers were not even value-enhancing, but fell victim to the winner's curse, damaging employees and small investors alike. Nor should we forget that companies in some countries of continental Europe (such as France or Germany) have not needed corporate raids to perform well up to the mark (Steinherr and Huveneers 1992).

Bardhan and Roemer (1992) for their part propose a design for corporate control in a market socialist economy with the twin aim of solving the managerial incentive problem while maintaining a roughly egalitarian distribution of total profits generated by the economy. Their proposal relies on banks rather than the state to monitor firms and echoes the key role assigned to banks as described in Chapter 9. The firm, in this scenario, is a joint-stock company in which some shares are owned by employees, with a major block of shares owned by other public firms (including their employees) in the same financial group, together with the main investment bank and its subsidiaries.[2] The share-owning workers in one firm will be motivated to prod other firms in the group to maximise profits and have some leverage in doing so. Some shares will be owned by companies outside the group: other financial institutions, pension funds, local governments, and so on. The firm will also borrow from its house bank, which may at times organise loan consortia for the firm.[3] The main bank's primary role may be what Diamond (1984) has dubbed 'delegated monitoring', in which it keeps other investors and lenders informed of the affiliated firm's credibility. All this, of course, only applies to large firms. Depending on who owns the banks – the state, mutual funds, individual shareholders – the proposed design could be regarded as socialist ownership (the state owns the banks) or capitalism of the German or Japanese type (final owners are large numbers of individuals) Although there is still some room for concern about the efficiency of a system in which the banks are publicly owned (who monitors the monitors?), the efficiency of a bank-based system is quite remarkable when the banks are privately owned.[4]

Bardhan and Roemer (1992) favour state ownership of banks and argue that soft budget problems are less serious in a market-based society where government plays a less dominant role than in socialist countries and where incentives, penalties and accountability are much more developed. They may well be right, but there is little empirical evidence to put their claims to the test. Italy and France, two countries with long-standing and extensive state ownership of banks, have come to the conclusion that, for efficiency's sake, they have to privatise banks.

By contrast, the issue of workers' involvement in corporate management, either as shareholders or in a cooperative set-up of labour management, should not be dismissed out of hand. Workers' participation is compatible with the scenario outlined above and, if the circumstances are right, workers' management could actually be an optimal design for small and medium-sized enterprises. That is why in Chapter 12 particular care is taken to analyse the Yugoslav experience in light of the theory of worker management.[5]

Notes

1. As Vickers and Yarrow (1988) note in their survey of the evidence on ownership and efficiency, in competitive industries, competition rather than ownership *per se* is the key to efficiency, even in cases where private ownership seems to have the edge.
2. When lenders are also important equity holders, credit-rationing and other onerous terms of lending may be largely avoided, and more risk-taking encouraged. See Steinherr and Huveneers (1992) for an analysis of the owner-lender role in Germany.
3. This proposal was, in fact, elaborated for application in East Germany by Gros and Steinherr (1990). See also Chapter 9.
4. See Steinherr and Huveneers (1993) for empirical results.
5. Labour management in Yugoslavia has been studied in great detail with mixed results. A recent study on producer cooperatives in Poland by Jones (1992) presents strong evidence that workers in Soviet-type economies are responsive to economic incentives. The study suggests, also drawing on evidence in both East and West European firms, that employee ownership could credibly play a greater role than is the case at present or than is being considered.

CHAPTER NINE

Financial sector reforms

Yes, 'n' how many years can some people exist
Before they're allowed to be free
Yes, 'n' how many times can a man turn his head
Pretending he just doesn't see?
The answer, my friend, is blowin' in the wind.

(Bob Dylan)

Chapter 8 analysed the difficulties of privatising and restructuring state-owned enterprises (SOEs). In this chapter we develop the necessary reforms of the financial sector (see Steinherr 1993). A reasonably well-functioning financial sector is of central importance not only for privatisation and subsequent corporate control, but also for effective monetary management, financing of the public sector deficit and hence for stabilisation.

Virtually all of the issues discussed in this chapter are controversial in the theory of banking and finance. This suggests that theoretical reasoning needs to be enriched with the precise historical context to settle the issues. We argue that the context of reforming countries lifts much of the theoretical controversy, so that the desired reforms are not 'blowin' in the wind' – although the outcome, at least in the countries of the FSU, may still be.

Given the scope of the constraints to be confronted by reforms and the urgency for workable financial intermediation, any reform plan needs to focus on a system that is able to assure the basics of financial intermediation satisfactorily. In view of the only emerging institutional structure of a market economy and the uncertainties surrounding transition to a stable and democratic political environment, we suggest that rules should be preferred to discretionary decision-making wherever possible.

The system needs to be simple, robust and susceptible to gain credibility over time. The major tasks are collection of savings, lending and investing and participation in the payments system. The three main ingredients are a basic legal and regulatory framework, bank supervision and a workable solution to the corporate governance problem of banks and corporations. The latter is the crux of the privatisation process and of the reform of the financial sector. The analysis which follows deals with these objectives, bearing in mind the constraints enumerated above.

Section 1 discusses the setting up of the Central Bank (CB) and its scope of activity. The context of reforming economies (REs) very strongly suggests that the optimal institutional design of the CB is to anchor in the constitution its political independence, its scope of activities and of targets, and the ordering of policy targets.

Section 2 analyses the specific context faced by banks in RE and stresses the need for cutting the traditional relationships between banks and the state, on the one hand, and banks and large SOEs, who are used to treating banks as a self-service, on the other.

Section 3 then discusses several possible strategies for enterprise reforms and amelioration of the health of the banking sector and urges privatisation of the better banks and closure or activity constraints for the other banks.

Section 4 argues that, to ameliorate the governance problem and because it will take a long time to create an efficient capital market, REs should opt for the universal banking system. Multi-tier banking should also be a prominent feature: according to balance sheet quality, banks should have access to different licences.

Section 5 provides some ideas for developing an efficient securities market over time and Section 6 summarises the policy conclusions.

1. Setting up a central bank and defining its functions

There is wide consensus on the need to separate commercial from central banking. Separate central banks (CBs) have already been created in most REs.[1] This is as far as consensus goes and thus not far enough. Opinions diverge considerably on two main issues: first, the political accountability and the incentive structure of the CB. Second, the scope of CB responsibilities and their ordering.

Even in developed market economies the case for a fully independent CB is not water-tight and the empirical evidence is inconclusive.[2] Some observers point out that the Central Bank of Russia – which is independent from government and accountable to parliament – is not a show-case for CB independency.

However, under appropriate institutional design, a compelling case can be made for CB independence, particularly in REs. The problem in many of these countries is that neither in government nor in parliament is there enough stability, competence and detachment of particularist interests to provide a basis for stability-oriented monetary policy. The Russian example does not prove that a CB under governmental tutelage would have worked better. Governments are still too involved with the management (or at least ownership) of SOEs so the temptation to use credit policy for bailing out operations is too great for price stability-oriented monetary policy.

Of course, much the same may be true of parliamentary tutelage during reform years. For this reason it is important to:[3]

- appoint a CB council of independent experts for quite long periods of time;
- assure a politically acceptable regional representation in the CB council;
- make sure that managers are in actual fact professionally competent;
- provide performance-related incentives to CB managers;[4]
- define basic objectives and limits for CB operations in the constitution, to back up CB operations under adverse circumstances.

The constitutional anchoring of CB objectives is of particular importance. It should be much easier to agree on an abstract basis on the scope of CB activity (say, inflation control, bank supervision) and to define a target (price stability) for the indefinite future, than in a concrete situation marred by unemployment, collapsing firms and politicians making a lot of noise. This is a concrete application of the rules-based approach to be advocated in REs. Also the criticism that an independent CB lacks democratic controllability becomes void when a CB executes constitutional targets and is accountable to parliament for execution of that task.

In general, a CB has several distinct objectives which need to be defined:

1. The main task is the pursuit of a macroeconomic target: the price level. This requires an adequate expansion of CB money, controlled by the CB under flexible exchange rates. This can also be achieved indirectly by fixing the value of domestic currency relative to that of another country which successfully pursues a stabilisation policy, as was argued in Chapter 7. For small REs an exchange rate policy is likely to be an acceptable option, whilst countries like Russia may wish to pursue a national credit target. Hence the CB still has discretionary powers about how to fulfil the targets imposed by rules.
2. Cyclical stabilisation of real economic activity is also often seen as another macroeconomic objective of CB policy, if only of secondary priority,[5] as this is known to be difficult to achieve systematically and may hinder full realisation of the primary goal of price level stabilisation.
3. A third objective of CB policy is a microeconomic one: the prevention of system-wide liquidity squeezes and associated money market disorders and financial crises. Emphasis on this objective is based on the notion that financial disorder and crisis interfere with the ability of banks to perform their economic functions of organising an efficient allocation of capital and smooth operation of the payments system. Therefore, it is seen as one of the duties of CBs to prevent such states from occurring.

The microeconomic role of a CB is particularly relevant in the present context of REs where potentially viable enterprises suffer from lack of financial resources and where private banks are not sufficiently capitalised (and experienced) to separate the wheat from the chaff. Banks may easily run into serious difficulties with the old inherited loans and the new loans. The question then is whether the CB should act as supervisor and as lender of last resort (LLR), and under what conditions.[6]

That an LLR is required is beyond dispute. Not so evident is the question whether the CB should combine both the macroeconomic and the microeconomic functions. The main argument for divorcing the monetary from the bank regulatory function is that the combination of both might lead to conflicts of interest. This conflict could arise in several ways. The most important is that interest rates are held down because of concern about the health of the banking system, when purely monetary considerations would require higher rates.

In the context of REs this objection lacks the weight it carries in developed economies. But, even then, the pros and cons are balanced according to a careful study by Goodhart and Schoenmaker (1993). The most decisive argument in favour of CB involvement is that CB support will be needed for developing a reliable payments system in REs. To the extent that a CB would need to support a participant in difficulty, it assumes the risks and effectively becomes the implicit guarantor of the system.

A further argument against separation is that resources for efficient institution building in RE are extremely scarce. Moreover, the concern of too powerful a CB turns into a distinct advantage in any RE where daily popular and interest-group opposition to stern policies is widespread and where the CB needs to withstand assaults by populist governments or parliaments. This context pleads, therefore, for assigning the bank supervisory and regulatory authorities to the CB.

THE ROLES OF A LENDER OF LAST RESORT

Typically, CBs stand ready to provide help when individual banks, or the banking system as a whole, experience temporary liquidity problems. In this, one should clearly distinguish between routine operations of the discount window for normal monetary policy purposes, often with formalised access (for example, to meet seasonal variations in liquidity demand), and emergency type measures for troubled banks made on a more discretionary basis. It is the latter which is controversial.

In Western economies, the view is taken that such help should only be given to banks which are temporarily illiquid but solvent (and therefore fit for long-run survival). This immediately raises the question why basically sound banks should need help to begin with. With highly developed financial credit markets, a solvent bank should always find it possible to obtain credit from the private markets. Therefore, one philosophy is that the CB should never be concerned about the fate of individual banks, but only about the banking system as a whole. That is, it should see its duty as maintaining an adequate volume of liquidity for the system as a whole, but should leave the distribution and redistribution of funds to the private markets.

However, in REs where markets are far from complete, basically sound banks may find it difficult or impossible to obtain sufficient credit from the market when experiencing a temporary liquidity shortage. Therefore, CB assistance in REs should take the form of help to individual banks experiencing temporary liquidity problems when these problems endanger their survival (and possibly that of other banks and the banking system, too). In Eastern European circumstances, an LLR facility is a response of the authorities to the imperfections of the credit markets.

The very nature of bank deposit contracts implies the possible occurrence of liquidity shocks (sudden liquidity demands which exceed the bank's liquidity reserves). See, for example, Diamond and Dybvig (1983) or Baltensperger and Dermine (1987). In the unstable financial environment of the transition period in REs, volatility in inflationary expectations may also create serious volatility in demand deposits.

Such liquidity shocks create a problem for the bank facing them, because of the illiquid character of the bank's assets (in REs assets are particularly illiquid). The forced and sudden sale of such assets in response to a liquidity shock can thus be very costly to a bank. The alternative response of borrowing on the private market also involves potentially high costs (high borrowing rates) and, in any case, is not available in REs.

The role of the LLR is to prevent social costs of liquidity squeezes and failures of banks to meet their liquidity obligations. The major danger and cost has to be seen in connection with the potential for contagion and system-wide crises resulting in a breakdown of the payments system and the allocative function of financial markets. A market failure can occur because a cooperative solution among depositors is difficult to enforce. Collectively, there is no incentive to run, but, individually, there is the incentive to be first in line to collect the deposit at full value.

At the root of all this lies an information imperfection (information asymmetry between bank and bank customer). The customer (depositor) can only imperfectly judge the quality of bank assets and thus the bank's ability to honour its commitments. For the same reason, he or she can only imperfectly judge why other depositors and depositors at other banks withdraw their funds and it is therefore customary to rely on the CB.

A major beneficiary of the LLR would be the payments system. In REs payments systems are extremely under-developed for technological reasons (no computerised carrier system such as SWIFT is available) and for the lack of financial transactions. In advanced Western economies most transaction volume derives from foreign exchange and securities trading. In REs such transactions are still minor as these markets do not yet exist and the role of the payments system is confined to settling inter-firm payments. Priority for the payments system in these countries is therefore reliability and not so much maximum efficiency. Intra-day exposure is also less of a concern than in Western economies where intra-day open positions regularly shoot up to high multiples (20–30 times) of the capital of a bank. But even with much lower exposures, the low average credit standing and high variance of credit standing of banks in REs generate systemic risk. To minimise that risk we recommend adopting gross settlement (that is, no netting which may entail unwinding of operations) without intra-day credit lines.[7] This means that each payment needs to be settled by drawing down reserves with the CB.

It also requires banks to keep unremunerated reserves with the CB. The fact that such reserves are not remunerated reflects the insurance premium for the CB's guarantees. At the same time reserves fulfil a useful macroeconomic function for regulating the money supply, particularly as long as deep securities markets are not available for open market operations.

CONDITIONS FOR GRANTING LLR

The availability of LLR protects banks and the banking system, as well as bank customers, from certain risks they would have to face without such a facility.

As is the case with any protection or insurance scheme (such as deposit insurance), this creates the danger of adverse effects on the behaviour of the insured agents (adverse incentives, moral hazard). Availability of LLR induces a bank to accept a greater risk of illiquidity than otherwise, as the costs it will have to bear in case of illiquidity will be less. It is therefore important to find ways of institutionalising the LLR support in such a way that adverse incentives are constrained as much as possible.

The more liberal these conditions, the greater the danger of adverse incentive effects. It is clear, however, that it is not possible to completely eliminate adverse incentives without denying emergency help altogether. Moral hazard is part of the cost of an LLR scheme (as it is part of the cost of any kind of insurance), and must be accepted as such. A meaningful question cannot be how to avoid moral hazard completely, but rather how to minimise it for a given level of protection, and how to find the optimal combination of protection and adverse incentive costs. In order to contain an impending crisis, a CB must grant LLR, but if it grants help too liberally, it increases the probability of future crises (see Baltensperger 1993).

Although, on a conceptual basis, liquidity and solvency can be distinguished neatly, it is difficult, in practice, to separate them completely. In practice, the public perception of a 'liquidity problem' usually means that some doubts exist about the bank's solvency too. In fact, some relation between the two states cannot be denied. Unwise liquidity management implies the risk of corresponding adjustment costs which can threaten the solvency of an institution. Conversely, solvency problems, by inducing precautionary withdrawals, may quickly generate a liquidity problem, at least in the case of non-insured deposits. If this spreads to other banks, threatening the stability of the banking system as a whole, this is a matter of obvious concern to the CB, even under the most conservative view of its role as an LLR (Bagehot 1873).

Limited coverage offered by deposit insurance schemes and fears of contagious runs resulting from this, may also be a reason why lenders of last resort (CBs) also step in in the case of insolvent banks and provide not just liquidity help but, effectively, public guarantees and even subsidisation. The dangers resulting from such a policy suggest that CBs should be conservative in this respect. Realistically, however, it must be seen that this danger cannot be avoided, particularly in REs. Whilst for illiquidity problems CB lending is the appropriate tool, it would clearly be unable to deal efficiently with insolvency. The latter usually results from incompetent management or fraud, and shows up as an insufficient capital base and debauched assets. CBs should act as coordinator of a rescue mission to replace management and provide fresh capital. Typically this is done through a merger or takeover by another bank or with government intervention. For an up-to-date survey, see Goodhart and Schoenmaker (1993).

Another very important and much discussed aspect of LLR is whether it should be made available according to a clear, explicitly stated commitment by the CB, or whether availability should remain vague and subject to the discretion of the CB.

A great deal of research suggests that the CB should announce the availability of LLR without ambiguity. CBs, on the other hand, typically stress the need for ambiguity and vagueness. The latter argument, of course, is based on the idea of avoiding an excessive degree of adverse incentives and erosion of market discipline. The former argument, on the other hand, is rationalised by the desire to achieve the highest possible degree of stability and confidence in the financial system.

Opponents of vagueness argue in essence that a policy of imprecision and ambiguity weakens the stabilising properties of LLR schemes, by weakening market confidence in the financial system, while at the same time not helping to increase market discipline. The latter statement is based on the idea that market participants (banks and depositors) attempt to figure out the probable behaviour of the CB as LLR. It is argued that they will easily perceive that the CB will always provide help to large banks in a state of distress, since spillover and confidence costs are very large in the case of failure of such a bank ('too big to fail'). Therefore, it is argued, ambiguity and vagueness have little credibility.

Although this may be an over-statement, there is an obvious credibility problem here. From a theoretical point of view, such a policy can probably only be time-consistent in a long-run 'repeated-game' context. But one could claim that even if the policy is not credible, the same situation as with a policy of explicit commitment emerges and nothing worse. In light of the particular conditions in REs, it appears, however, safer to opt for explicit, institutionalised commitments, embodied in the CB constitution.

It should also be remembered that the basic problem underlying all the difficulties discussed here is one of information imperfection and asymmetry between banks and depositors. More disclosure of information by banks could go a long way towards improving the situation and reducing the source of the need for LLR. Sound banks should have an interest in informing their customers of the quality of their assets and the safety of their products. Information disclosure alone will not totally solve the problem and do away with the need for LLR, but it can contribute towards a state where the need for reliance on LLR, and the costs associated with it, are less than is the case otherwise. This consideration is the starting point for the multi-tier system proposed in Section 4.

BANK SUPERVISION

The functions of supervisor and of LLR are not easily separated. The institution providing the LLR role is required to supervise banks to prevent failures and, if it cannot do that, to be able to intervene promptly.[8]

Supervision stretches over many issues: granting of bank licences according to criteria of ownership (can industry own banks?), of management (minimum professional standards) and of capital (minimum capital requirements); granting permission to acquire or merge with another bank; carrying out controls to prevent fraud (a very difficult assignment, but also a very important one given the situation in REs); and controlling management of the bank according to supervisory guidelines and legal contracts. We set aside these more detailed functions and focus on two key regulatory issues: asset-liability management and protection of depositors.

Given the inherited problematic loan book (even after reform measures to deal with bad loans) and the highly uncertain economic context in REs, banks are faced with extremely high risk. This situation is made worse by the lack of experienced bank management and the lack of well-established bank–customer relationships on the basis of market-enforced performance.

Standard measures to enforce prudential behaviour and a spreading of risk comprise setting of limits to loans granted to an individual customer and an economic sector in relation to own funds. A reasonable guideline is provided, for example, by Western national banking laws and regulations and the EC directive on credit exposure.

A more flexible approach, but not a very satisfactory one from a risk diversification point of view, is the solvency ratio of the EC or of the Basle agreement (Cooke ratio). Classifying borrowers into three categories (government, banks and others) with a corresponding risk weighting of 0, 20 per cent and 100 per cent, banks have to back up their risk-weighted assets with 8 per cent of own funds.[9] (A definition of own funds is in the EC solvency directive and the Basle Agreement.) An adaptation of the Cooke ratio for REs is suggested in Box 9.1.

A third approach – and all three approaches could be combined – would consist in creating a multi-tier banking system, as suggested in Section 4.

Box 9.1 A solvency ratio for reforming economies

Adoption of the Cooke definition of risk-weighted assets would surely be undesirable in REs for at least three reasons, in addition to the fact that diversification is ignored. First, given the less stable institutional situation in REs and the highly uncertain medium-term outlook, maturity of claims needs to be considered even more mandatory than in Western economies. Second, long-term bank debt should not be treated as a lower risk than short-term corporate debt. Third, a zero weight of government debt would discriminate against privatisation. To correct these shortcomings, the following definition of risk-weighted assets (*RWA*) is proposed:

$$RWA = 0.2(G+B_s) + (B_l+P_s) + 1.5P_l \qquad [1]$$

where G stands for credit to government, B for banks and P for non-banks (including SOEs); s and l refer to short-term debt (say, less than one year) and long-term debt respectively.* Only banks with bank licences A and B (see Section 4) would be considered as part of banks. Risk diversification could be brought into the picture either separately (specification of maximum exposures to individual clients and sectors of economic activity) or by making the capital coefficient α a function of diversification:

$$K = \alpha RWA \qquad [2]$$

where α is 8 per cent in the Cooke ratio and K is the required minimum capital. α could be modulated according to a bank's diversification, measured by deviations from exposure criteria which are not absolute bounds but guidelines for optimal diversification and hence for low α (for example, according to shares of each sector in GDP corrected for activity volatility).

A second ratio to be satisfied is:

$$E = \beta RWA \qquad [3]$$

where E is equity (e.g. upper-tier capital) and $\beta < \alpha$.

* The weights would be scaled down to the unit-interval and offset by a higher capital/*RWA* ratio. This is not done in Equation [1] to retain some Cooke ratio parameters. Equity participations would receive maximum risk-weight up to certain ceilings (as in the EC directives) beyond which the capital backing rises gradually to reach 100 per cent.

Table 9.1 illustrates capital adequacy for selected REs. For the aggregate banking sector the Cooke ratio is surpassed everywhere. However, this is no longer the case when adjustments are made for under-provisioning of problem loans and when the ratios of Box 9.1 are used to compute risk-weighted assets.

As for market risk it would be desirable to impose the same capital requirement on duration-weighted asset-liability imbalances, that is, on 'open positions'. For the computational procedure see, for example, Kaufman (1984) and Gilibert and Girard (1988). Such a measure seems even more necessary in REs than in developed economies as interest rate volatility is greater and management capacity scarce.

TABLE 9.1 Capital adequacy in Central European banking systems

	1988	1990	1991
CSFR (Kcs bn)			
1. Capital (K)	17	85	79
2. Capital (E)	–	30	15
3. Risk-adjusted assets (I)	593	581	726
4. Risk-adjusted assets (II)	–	–	924
5. Ratio (%) (1)/(3)	2.9	14.6	10.9
6. Ratio (%) (2)/(3)	–	5.2	2.1
7. Ratio (%) (2)/(4)	–	–	1.6
HUNGARY (fl.bn)			
1. Capital (K)	52	112	161
2. Capital (E)	-	70	120
3. Risk-adjusted assets (I)	687	961	1 037
4. Risk-adjusted assets (II)	–	–	1 337
5. Ratio (%) (1)/(3)	7.6	11.6	15.5
6. Ratio (%) (2)/(3)	–	7.3	11.6
7. Ratio (%) (2)/(4)	–	–	8.0
POLAND (zloty bn)			
1. Capital (K)	137	15 030	22 336
2. Capital (E)	–	0	0
3. Risk-adjusted assets (I)	26 844	190 910	256 952
4. Risk-adjusted assets (II)	–	–	318 004
5. Ratio (%) (1)/(3)	0.5	7.9	8.7
6. Ratio (%) (2)/(3)	–	0	0
7. Ratio (%) (1)/(4)	–	–	7.0
ROMANIA (lei bn)			
1. Capital (K)	–	26	293
2. Capital (E)	–	0	0
3. Risk-adjusted assets (I)	–	692	1 966
4. Risk-adjusted assets (II)	–	–	2 556
5. Ratio (%) (1)/(3)	–	3.8	14.9
6. Ratio (%) (2)/(3)	–	0	0
7. Ratio (%)(1)/(4)	–	–	11.4

Source: IFS, April 1993; Institute of International Finance various Country Updates; CSFB (1992); own information collected.

Notes: Risk-adjusted assets (I) follow the Cooke rules: foreign assets receive a 20% weight, claims on public sector enterprises receive a 100% weight. Risk-adjusted assets (II) follow equation (1) in Box 9.1. Classification of claims as short and long-term is based on only partial information. Capital (K) is as reported in balance sheets. Capital (E) is obtained by deducting from (K) an estimate of underprovisioning for problem loans on the basis of various sources of information. The 'proper' provisioning is computed as follows: 20% for loans with possible future non-performance; 50% for doubtful loans; 100% for bad loans. Notice that inter-bank loans cancel out in the aggregate data. When equity is zero then for line 7 the ratio (1)/(4) rather than (2)/(4) is computed. All results should be taken as illustrative only.

As for liabilities, it seems unavoidable in the risky context of REs to set up a deposit insurance scheme. This cannot be self-organised – as in some European countries – and would require official support. A strong case can be made that the CB provides this insurance as it is the supervisor and LLR. To minimise the moral hazard two steps are to be recommended. First, to limit the amount of insurance to a level commensurate with the savings of average income earners (the orphans and widows argument). In the RE that could mean US$ 5,000 or even less. Second, only a share (e.g. 80 per cent) of any deposit should be insured. And, as argued in Section 4, not all banks would obtain deposit insurance at the same premium; some might not receive it at all.[10]

2. Initial conditions for banking

Socialist countries may have missed the opportunity of starting with a clean slate through currency reform when they plumped for a market-based economy, as bank claims on SOEs and SOE debt cancel out in the integrated public sector accounts. Debt claims could have been cancelled without any difficulty for the banks, and, indeed, the value of deposits would have found its counterpart in claims on the government for an amount decided by the terms of the currency reform.[11]

But because this road of radical currency reform was not taken anywhere but in East Germany, the former socialist countries now suffer from serious sectoral imbalances. Banks hold large amounts of non-performing assets[12] and now that reforms are under way, and many firms have already gone independent or private, it is too late for a general currency reform. And quite obviously, a currency reform by itself would not have contributed anything to the corporate governance problem. To see what can be done, one needs to start from the conditions as they actually exist in the East European countries.

Any proposal for financial sector reform in RE needs to deal with the following constraints:

- the massive size of bad loans on the banks' balance sheets;
- the potentially very serious conflicts of interest of managers of state banks, captives of large debtors and of moral hazard problems in view of future privatisation;
- the under-developed infrastructure and incentives for collection of savings;
- the need to attract foreign capital as a complement to national savings and as a circuit for transferring know-how;
- the under-developed human capital, technological infrastructure and accounting framework;
- the absence of securities markets.

Once government ceases its extensive regulation of resource allocation, an alternative regulator must be found and appropriate institutions created. At least initially this is the role of banks as intermediaries between savers and investors, as monitors of corporate performance and consequently as guardians of a hard budget constraint.

The transition from the socialist regime to a system of bank financing entailed first a separation of central and commercial banking operations (two-tier banking) and the creation of a number of commercial banks from the rib of the single state bank. The creation of independent banks was also authorised but these do not as yet play an important role. And since the break-up of the old monobank was accomplished along tested territorial branch lines, there is relatively little competition among existing financial institutions.

Meanwhile, however, the most important obstacle to the transformation of existing banks into genuine banking institutions is that, superficial reforms notwithstanding, the existing banks have taken over the *modus operandi* of their predecessors. Instead of monitoring corporate performance, their vulnerable loan book turned them into an instrument of the SOEs' strategy of resistance to significant departures from the *status quo* (Corricelli and Thorne 1992).

The 'new' commercial banks, being often in fact nothing other than the old regional branches of the state monobank in new guise, have developed over the years a relationship of mutual dependence with the large SOEs which they had been financing under the old regime and continued to finance under the new. Bank managers were 'captured' and felt equally threatened by the new regime. In some countries the new banks, furthermore, are part-owned by the enterprises to which they are lending. This has created an additional communality of interest and pressure to finance regardless of ultimate solvency and give more weight to maintaining production and employment.

The new banks lack expertise in credit evaluation under market conditions and tend to favour borrowers with fixed assets as collateral. They largely ignore earning potential for lack of evaluation and proper accounting techniques. This in turn results in privileging the same large enterprises as before liberalisation and starving new businesses of funds regardless of their credit-worthiness on a present value basis.

Any recapitalisation of banks is likely to be problematic and no clearly optimal approach seems to exist. Existing banks are in a difficult position to be able to resist the pressure of SOEs to maintain the *status quo*, even if their books were to be cleaned up at the expense of the budget. The very act of cleaning up might even create the expectation of future bail-outs, and it would require a very profound institutional change to embed it in a legal framework that would credibly pre-commit the state to no repetitions.[13] A law of this kind would have to modify the whole incentive and decision-making structure of the economic units in the present state sector and has little chance of seeing the light of day. Creation of an independent CB, as proposed in Section 1, would however help in limiting the government's resources for bailing out SOEs and banks and the CB could be legally barred from support operations.

One possible solution lies in recapitalising only those banks that can be privatised. This would change the incentive structure of the bank managers, and give them a fresh start. The problem, however, is that effective privatisation of the existing state banks is no easy matter either, and it is not clear whether it is worth the trouble and the expense. Many banks are very likely to have negative value and the amounts it would take for the state to pay off their liabilities could be so enormous that the state could probably capitalise an entirely new banking system with these funds. Frydman *et al.* (1992) argue that this course should be seriously considered.

3. Strategies for bank loan restructuring

The major problem besetting banks and SOEs in REs is the inherited structure of claims which are to a large extent illiquid or, even in the medium run, irrecoverable.

The major task is, therefore, to clean up the banks' balance sheets, which also implies a solution for the debt of non-banks. A great variety of approaches is available, each approach with its own implications on the future role and structure of banks which will be discussed in Section 4. Real world lessons about reforms of a bankrupt banking sector in a variety of countries are usefully surveyed in EBRD (1992).

From the outset it seems evident that a legalistic (or public) approach cannot be retained in REs. Such an approach relies on bankruptcy laws and leaves the decisions to the competent courts. If the bad loan problem only affected a small number of SOEs and banks it might be useful, but not when a large number of SOEs and virtually all the banks are bankrupt according to a strict interpretation of their situation.

Furthermore, in REs the legal system is still changing and inexperienced with bankruptcy procedures; assets are mostly non-redeployable; markets are too thin for selling off assets and, during the transition recession, prices tend to under-shoot. Bankruptcy procedures are therefore to be relegated to a minor role for some time to come and non-legalistic solutions need to be found.

With a broad brush one may distinguish between approaches that restructure the firm's balance sheet (internal approaches) and those that take assets or liabilities out of the firm (external approaches).

Internal approaches include recapitalisation by shareholders or an external agency, separating and managing bad loans from the rest of the bank's assets ('loan hospital'), debt-for-debt exchanges ('workouts') replacing existing credit by new ones that are different in maturity structure or conditions, and debt–equity swaps.

External approaches hive bad loans off the bank's balance sheet by swapping bad loans for government bonds ('asset carve-out'), selling loans at their market value if a secondary market exists or can get started, selling loans to a specialised government agency or selling the loans to a subsidiary of the bank to mark an institutional separation and thereby create a 'good' bank and a 'bad' bank subsidiary. An extensive discussion of the pros and cons of all these approaches is available in EBRD (1992).

In the context of REs the scope for internal approaches (except for debt–equity swaps) is certainly limited, so that external approaches will be required.

In recent literature four proposals for designing financial sector reforms which contain elements of the internal and external approaches have received particular interest:[14] across-the-board recapitalisation of banks; debt–equity swaps restructuring as an instrument for enterprise reform and privatisation; debt restructuring, enterprise privatisation and creation of private financial institutions; and postponing bank reform after enterprise restructuring.

These proposals see the optimal trade-off being achieved by:

- hiving all loans (rather than only bad loans which are difficult to identify) to SOEs off banks' balance sheets before privatisation.[15] Banks would receive Treasury bills in compensation. One drawback of this proposal is that there are three sources of cash outflow for the government. First, the interest payments on the Treasury bonds. Second, the principal payment, if bonds are not perpetuals. Third, the flow of subsidies for loss-making enterprises that remain state-owned (Begg and Portes 1992);
- swapping debt for equity so that banks would be called upon to play a central role in privatisation and corporate governance. The debt workout option should

only be offered to enterprises that submit reorganisation proposals acceptable to the senior creditor who, otherwise, could invoke foreclosure on the enterprise assets. Reorganisation proposals could come from new investors contributing with cash, above all from foreign banks, or from incumbent management without cash injection[16] (van Wijnbergen 1992);

- transferring bad loans to newly established investment funds and matching them by transfers of deposits of the same nominal amounts. Recapitalisation needs of banks would decrease correspondingly. The funds would carry out both investment bank and commercial bank activities. They would represent the core of a new banking system based on private ownership and would compete with existing banks (Frydman *et al.* 1992);
- prohibiting banks from lending to 'liberalised' firms during the transition period. The idea behind this proposal is that moral hazard problems are overwhelming during transition. If 'liberalised' firms – both state-owned and private – have access to bank credit, financial discipline cannot be enforced and there will be over-borrowing leading to a crisis of the banking system. Only after a few years, when prices have been stabilised and a new tax system is in place, should commercial banks begin lending. Initially, there should be only short-term lending, according to the 'Real Bills Doctrine' (McKinnon 1991).

The following five fundamental considerations emerge both from these theoretical contributions and from field work:[17]

1. A path of rapid and sustained growth cannot be achieved by forcing firms to self-finance, bar in exceptional circumstances such as those prevailing in China. McKinnon's proposal therefore appears as only rarely practicable. Moreover, historical evidence suggests that external finance plays an important role in REs.[18] The shift to a market economy sharply increases external credit needs to finance trade imbalances and temporary structural deficits.
2. 'Cleaning' the books of the existing banks is an important and urgent measure as banks continue to maintain insolvent SOEs in life. At present, much, and, in some countries, most of the total debt has been accumulated after liberalisation. Ideally, all debt should be cancelled. Such a comprehensive reform would have been easy during the early stages of liberalisation. The advantage of such a *tabula rasa* would have been twofold. First, a neat and clear fresh start. Second, the bad debts need not have been distinguished from the good and a very difficult, costly and time-consuming task could have been avoided.
3. The socialisation of debts could imply significant fiscal costs, depending on how much 'netting' can be achieved.[19] Most of the former socialist countries are over-burdened with debt and have sharply compressed spending on infrastructures and social safety nets. Cost-effectiveness is therefore a key consideration in choosing schemes to 'clean' the books.
4. Existing state-owned banks are ill-suited to monitoring enterprises. Banks in these economies lack the necessary skills and their links with SOEs are often more of a burden than an information advantage. The size of these banks and the state ownership are conducive to collusive behaviour with inefficient SOEs. In the end, the government will be forced to step in and bail out banks and firms.

5. Therefore, new, private financial institutions are badly needed. A more competitive environment, access to foreign expertise and access to foreign capital markets are indeed key elements for developing a financial system that works with a reasonable level of efficiency. Rather than recapitalising all existing banks, the most promising should be turned into joint-ventures or recapitalised in cooperation with Western banks.

4. A model for East European banking

The question of the optimal configuration of financial markets in Eastern Europe is both a theoretical and an empirical one. The empirical evidence stretches from the more market-based systems of the United States and the United Kingdom, on the one hand, to the more bank-based systems in the German-speaking countries and Japan.[20] Eastern European countries should not and could not take over any existing system part and parcel, but should build their financial framework by properly adapting an existing Western framework. One concrete proposal of a system designed for the special conditions in REs is made by Szegö (1993). This section discusses the choice of a suitable framework for adoption and the desirable adaptation.

The American model is clearly inappropriate for Eastern Europe at its present stage of development.[21] The political, economic and organisational prerequisites for an efficient capital market exceed by far what seems possible in East European countries.

The existence of a reasonably efficient, ordinary banking system that collects short-term deposits, handles transfers of funds, furnishes working capital to small and medium-sized businesses and is sufficiently well capitalised to cover ordinary banking risks, such as those embedded in loan portfolios, is what emerging economies need the most. At a low level of development at least, the banking versus markets debate misses the point. These are not alternatives: banking needs to precede markets. Present banking arrangements in most East European countries fail in one or more of these aspects, leading to a substantial circulation of funds outside the formal banking system at wide spreads and high risk.

Until such banking conditions can be met, East European countries will be disappointed in the results of both their capital market fund raising and privatisation efforts. They will also be unable to advance to the point where a choice between competing banking–industry models can reasonably be made. The first priority, therefore, should be to establish a reasonably efficient banking system.

This cannot possibly be accomplished overnight. In the meantime, the basic banking systems of the East European countries need to be reconfigured and fortified as much as possible along West European lines, with strong relationships and monitoring links between banks and industry. Where financial transparency is low and information costs are high, 'insider' status on the part of responsible external monitors is virtually mandatory in order to achieve a viable structure of corporate governance that is in the national interest.

In the process the banks urgently need to be privatised and recapitalised so that they can start off in a condition of financial viability. Once a reasonably satisfactory banking system is in place, the choice of models becomes relevant. The choice is most likely to be, therefore, between the broad-based German universal banking model and the narrow-based Japanese model.

UNIVERSAL BANKING

The Japanese system can sustain high leverage within the banking system and thereby finance rapid growth – something all the East European countries need badly. The financial crisis in Japan in the early 1990s and the previous stock market bubble do, however, illustrate the risks involved.

The German system has the advantage of being better known in Eastern Europe and of being the 'neighbour's system'. It is, however, biased toward less leverage because the funds employed go into a wider variety of less well-supervised investments in the debts and securities of client companies. See Fig. 9.1 below. On the other hand, the German system is more adaptable to changes in the future, and less exposed to the risk of collapse. Also its conservative bias may not be undesirable in the riskier context of REs.

In REs, by having both debt and equity stakes in non-financial enterprises, German-type banks would be in a strong position to force restructuring of enterprises, using both traditional lending sanctions as well as board-level influence. It is arguable

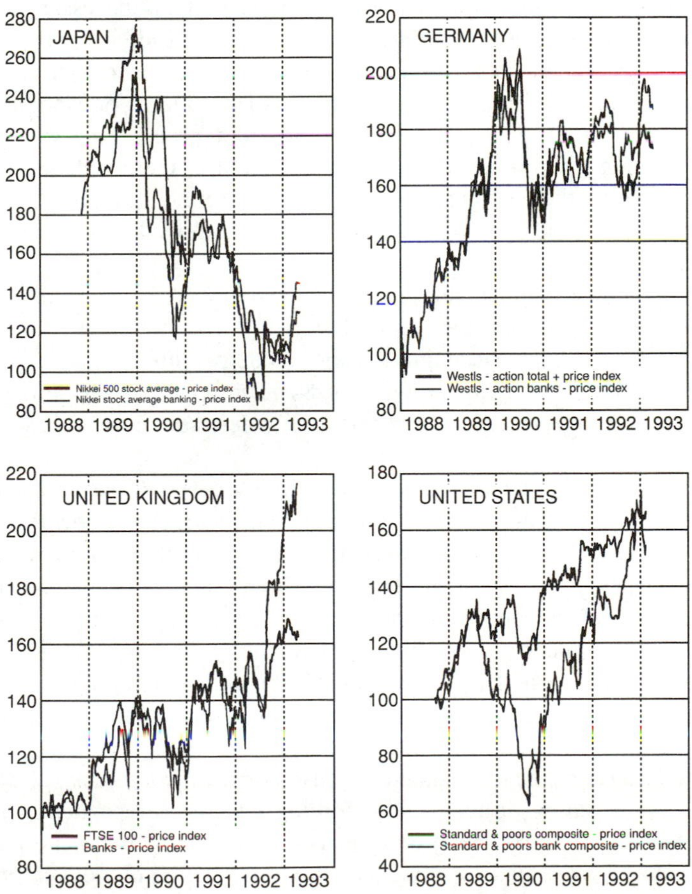

FIG 9.1 Stock markets: bank and general price indexes: 1988 = 100 (28 May 1993)
Source: Datastream

whether ordinary control functions exercised either by creditors or by external shareholders are sufficiently up to the task of unprecedented economic transformations. Indeed, it may be argued that effective privatisations in the absence of a viable equity market *can only* be carried out in the presence of strong, universal-type bank linkages.

To be sure, these benefits of the German approach would have to be weighed against the risk that the East European financial systems would become highly concentrated – with all financial services provided by a small number of universal banks.[22] It is therefore also important to maintain markets contestable in the emerging banking structures in Eastern Europe. Rather than relying only on legislative means, it is preferable to retain gates open to foreign bank entries.

The most important soft spot of universal banking is the potential conflict of interest and the abuse of inside information. For an extensive comparison across different banking structures, see Steinherr and Huveneers (1992, 1993).

Both problems are not unique to universal banks, but are potentially more pronounced. Inside information is an economic advantage that forms the basis of a long-term relationship between bank and client, that makes a long-term commitment possible and allows a more precise pricing of risk. It is the necessary condition for banking *tout court* as opposed to *ad hoc* deals. Abuse of inside information is difficult to prevent – even with segmented banking. What is needed to reduce this problem is supervision and legal punishment, as is the case under US law, for example.

If one wishes banks to play a role in the privatisation process, in swapping loans for shares, in assisting the process of corporate governance, then banks need that inside information whether they are universal or not. Because equity holdings and a seat on the company's board improve information, the universal bank is better equipped than others for such tasks.

But some potential conflicts are unique to universal banks. A bank as lender and shareholder may prefer a customer with a less risky strategy to make sure that it recuperates its loans rather than accepting a riskier strategy with a higher expected rate of return in excess of the risk premium (Aoki 1984). But this bias, which may be socially undesirable in mature economies, might be highly desirable in REs, beset by all sorts of risks.

Universal banking is both unavoidable and highly desirable in the context of REs. Unavoidable because, as argued in Section 3, it is difficult to see how the overhang of bad debt could be solved without involving banks themselves through equity swaps and increased participation in the governance of non-financial firms. The need for universal banks derives not only from practical considerations (who else could assure governance?), or temporary constraints (unavailability of a functioning capital market), but also from more basic and general theoretical arguments. For example, Dewatripont and Tirole (1993) show with a principal–agent model that (1) managers should be rewarded by low interference from outsiders when performing well. During times of good performance they should increase borrowing; and that (2) control needs to shift to lenders during difficult times, forcing owners to recapitalise the firm and preventing the firm from gambling on resurrection by restraining its new borrowings. When a firm has a large number of lenders, there may be an obvious information and incentive problem. It would therefore be better to have a major debt-holder who has access to information and incentives to monitor the firm to appropriate a large share of the gains.

If the firm is a non-bank, the obvious solution is universal banking as the universal bank typically acts as 'house-bank' (i.e. dominant debt-holder) and has maximal access to information. It plays a role of active shareholder during good times (even infusing a conservative bias into the firm's finances, as the first priority of the bank is to make sure that its credits are repaid) and of active debt-holder during bad times (to recapitalise the borrower).

When banks play a major role in governance of non-banks, governance of banks becomes a key issue. It would be unwise to rely on the disciplining role of a capital market which will remain in its infancy for some time. A necessary condition would be strict accounting and reporting requirements to make monitoring by shareholders more effective and including clear provisioning rules for problem loans. The main governance function then falls on shareholders and their board of directors. Because the assets of universal banks represent a diversified portfolio (see Fig. 9.1) they should attract investments by pension and investment funds which cannot build up the same diversification as long as stock markets are under-developed. However, because universal banks' corporate governance concerns a significant share of the economy, special precautions are necessary and warranted. For example, the state could retain a minority share and a board seat; a board seat could be reserved for a union representative and another for the Central Bank;[23] pension and investment funds could receive regulatory incentives to invest in banks and thereby gain board seats. Finally, one directorship could be reserved for a foreign auditing firm having no other relationship with the bank.

SEGMENTATION OF BANKING

The Dewatripont-Tirole analysis can be applied to banks as well. A large part of bank debt is represented by deposits and a dominant debt-holder is unavailable. Therefore, other solutions of governance need to be found for banks. One solution is to split up the bank, as discussed below; the other is external supervision and regulation.

Regulation of bank activity in theory could concentrate either on liabilities or on assets. Deposit insurance and LLR would be sufficient to protect depositors and deal with runs. But because failure is most often the result of corrupt or incompetent management, regulation of the asset side aims to reduce the risk of failure. In practice, regulation deals both with assets and liabilities.

One very effective way to regulate liabilities and assets *indirectly* is to 'split up' banking activity. Szegö (1993) proposes multi-tier banking along the lines of Bryan (1988) and Steinherr and Gilibert (1989/90) to deal with the thorny issues of moral hazard and adverse selection. That is, he proposes a legal and institutional separation of deposit, loan and investment banking. Only deposit banks would collect demand deposits and invest exclusively in government paper and high quality certificates of deposit (CDs) issued by other-type banks. Loan banks would be financed through equity, securities and time deposits and investment banks would not have access to a deposit base. This split up would make deposit insurance and lending regulation largely superfluous.

Whilst the 'split-up' bank appears to be a very attractive option in developed economies (Steinherr and Gilibert 1989/90), there is concern about its usefulness in REs. In particular, a well functioning capital market – not only for government securities but also for corporate issues – needs to exist to make the model work. Deposit banks would need liquid short-term government securities and liquid money market instruments to be able to manage their assets efficiently. Loan and investment banks would need CD and long-term bond markets of sufficient liquidity to manage their liabilities.

We also believe that different classes of bank licences should be issued. But we see greater merit in a criterion directly measuring 'quality' rather than an activity measure correlated with risk exposure. The three tiers proposed are:[24]

- Licence A for top-of-the-range banks as measured by their risk-weighted capital ratio and satisfaction of credit exposure norms.
- Licence B for banks satisfying a lower echelon of the same criteria. They would pay higher deposit insurance premiums and may be barred from participation in the payments system, or would be required to hold larger minimum reserves.
- Licence C for banks falling below the criteria set for Licence B. Deposits at such banks would not be insured, lender of last resort facilities would not be available and therefore participation in the payments system would not be possible. Debt of C banks would receive the same risk-weighting as for non-banks.

This proposal has the disadvantage of not making asset allocation rules and deposit insurance superfluous and also requires acceptance of the universal bank structure. But some very clear advantages also emerge from this tiering of bank licences which (by law) would need to be visibly exposed.

First, it would provide flexibility for the coexistence of differently structured and managed banks. Depositors could opt for riskier or safer deposits – and be remunerated differently – according to their preferences or portfolio needs.

Second, the activity scope of banks would not be constrained by regulations. Of course, if a bank wishes to minimise risk it would, in fact, become a deposit bank. To operate like a universal bank with a substantial share of equity holdings of private corporations, and to enjoy Class A privileges would require a sound capital base. Perhaps no bank could achieve that in a hard-hit RE. Then, *de facto*, there would be a split between safe banks, equivalent essentially to deposit banks, and universal banks, corresponding to low-tier investment banks.

Third, the moral hazard problem would be seriously scaled down by forming more uniform classes. Tier A banks would attach importance to not losing their status and lower-tier banks would try to be upgraded. The risk of the lender of last resort is substantially reduced by not covering Class C banks and depositors would request a risk premium for uninsured deposits at lower-tier banks. Failure of a Class C bank would not generate a run on the overall banking system.

5. Building up securities markets

As argued in Steinherr and Huveneers (1992), securities markets are under-developed in countries where universal banking is firmly implanted, as one is a substitute for the other. It is therefore important to support from the start the development of securities markets with appropriate policies.

Privatisation of SOEs and a workable solution for corporate governance, such as proposed above, will already contribute to the development of the stock-market, although more is required to ensure efficiency and rapid growth. Here we shall focus instead on debt markets.

A fixed income securities market is helpful and even necessary in the RE. Once the CB can no longer finance the government deficit, it needs to be financed through the debt market. Similarly, the different debt workouts, swaps and debt sales will require and contribute to the development of securities markets. Banks will play a key role in this in order to be able to restructure their asset books.

Debt markets would also offer an alternative for the allocation of savings to deposits and facilitate convergence to a competitive pricing structure of loans and deposits.

We see particular merit in using perpetuals[25] for loan swaps against Treasury bonds. The advantages would be to (1) reduce the Treasury's financing outflows to payment of interest rates; (2) create an interest rate below the current one because the perpetual rate would reflect much lower real rates after transition, whilst during transition real interest rates are likely to over-shoot and reach record levels; and (3) create a large, liquid market as perpetuals are by definition fungible and thus command a single price.[26]

The only possible risk of issuing perpetuals is that, if the government is not credible in its reform plans, then markets will not expect a return to low real rates for a long time to come. If reforms nevertheless succeed against expectations, then the government would be stuck with a perpetual issued at a very high rate. In a global sense this should not matter as it would be financed by high taxes, but the distributional consequences may not be desirable. To avoid such a lock-in, perpetuals could be augmented with a call option that would limit the potential gain of bond-holders.

6. Conclusions

The following reform package emerges from this analysis:

1. *Create an independent central bank*: Independence, scope of activity and macroeconomic targets to be pursued by the CB should be enshrined in the constitution to protect the CB from day-to-day politics and provide effective independence. In addition to pursuing a price level target, the CB should act as lender of last resort (in particular to the payments system) and should be in charge of bank supervision. The payments system should above all be robust. This can be achieved by gross settlement without intra-day credit lines, and exacting admission conditions.
2. *Implement strong bank regulation and supervision*: A strong bank regulation and supervision should define the framework for the operation of banks and for the development of the future financial system. Because it is the experience of most countries that this takes time, it would be most effective to adopt and adapt foreign regulation. Particularly well-suited for this purpose is the recently elaborated European banking regulatory framework.
   As a major tool for bank supervision, a definition of risk-weighted assets is proposed that differs significantly from the Cooke definition to reflect the specific context in REs. The CB should be in charge of bank supervision and should act

as LLR on the basis of pre-announced conditions. Also deposit-insurance is to be made available for upper-tier banks (see point 3).

3. *Create a multi-tier banking system*: To minimise moral hazard issues it is proposed to create a multi-tier banking system (e.g. three classes apart from the CB). The first tier would comprise banks satisfying the highest standards of prudential regulation in terms of capitalisation and asset quality. They would pay lower premiums for deposit insurance, face lower minimum CB reserve holdings and pay lower rediscount rates than second-tier banks. Third tier banks would not benefit from official deposit insurance and rediscount facilities. They would not pay deposit insurance premiums and would not be admitted to the payments system and their debt would fall into the risk class of corporate debt. Tier membership would have to be announced visibly at every cashier's desk and on every bank document.
4. *Improve corporate governance*: Due to the absence of a well-functioning capital market and the present pre-eminence of the state as shareholder, efficient corporate governance requires specific solutions and, probably, a lot of time.
   The better structured banks should be privatised, preferably with foreign partners. Activities of banks that cannot be privatised should be curtailed. See also point 5. An important role will be played by banks. Another key role could be played by investment funds in corporate governance, besides attracting domestic and foreign capital. They would get involved in enterprise privatisation and would be useful in monitoring enterprises. Over time, they could in this way grow into modern investment banks and contribute to the development of a non-banking financial sector.
5. *Universal banking*: Because, for efficiency, securities markets require highly stable political institutions, sophisticated legal systems and commitment to market economies, they can only be observed in a few of the most developed societies. The issue of a securities market versus banking approach is therefore a mute one in which REs can only have banking-based financial intermediation. At any rate, and independently of theoretical arguments, there is a universal trend toward universal banking. Advising REs otherwise would be slightly anachronistic. Once such banks exist on a privatised basis, they are likely to assume a key role in the governance of corporations from 'the cradle to the grave' (Gerschenkron 1962).
6. *Remove privatised banks' bad loans and an equal amount of government deposits and compensate with Treasury bonds (perpetuals)*: Because of the segmentation between deposit banks and lending banks inherited from the old regime, most state-owned commercial banks hold either government liabilities or central bank refinance credit. This simplifies the removal of banks' bad loans. If these liabilities are not sufficient to match bad loans, long-term bonds will be issued as compensatory items. These bonds would ideally be perpetuals.
   To overcome the illiquidity of their loan portfolio, banks should be allowed to auction off their loans – individually or in repackaged form – and, to minimise moral hazard, a share of the loss (but not the totality) would be offset by an allocation of government bonds.
7. *Debt–equity swaps*: An effective way of ensuring survival and privatisation of firms – profitable after some workouts – is an options-augmented debt–equity

swap scheme. Such an option scheme would contribute to turning banks into universal banks. With appropriate option schemes bankers would control a firm only until it regains financial health.

8. *The problem of inter-enterprise arrears and creditor ranking*: Arrears need to be netted and a secondary market needs to be created for loans as a way of making them liquid and allowing a public evaluation of the credit-worthiness of the issuer.
9. *Develop a liquid government securities market*: It would be preferable to enshrine in the constitution that the CB cannot finance the public sector borrowing requirement. Any deficits would then need to be financed through banks or direct, securitised borrowing from the market. To create maximum liquidity it would be advisable to create *perpetuals* – which by definition are fungible – for replacement of bad loans on banks' balance sheets, with a possible call option. In addition it would be necessary to create short-term notes.
Existence of an efficient and liquid market for government securities is important not only for financing the public sector deficit, but also for individuals (to offer alternatives to deposits) and banks (for treasury operations and benchmark pricing).

Notes

1. For a description of reforms accomplished in Eastern Europe, at least on paper, see Corricelli and Thorne (1992).
2. Alesina and Summers (1991) conclude from a study of 16 OECD countries that monetary discipline associated with central bank independence reduces the level and variability of inflation, but has neither large benefits nor costs in terms of real macroeconomic performance.
3. For details see the Treaty of Maastricht.
4. The 1990 Act of the Reserve Bank of New Zealand is a useful reference. See Nicholl and Archer (1992).
5. In Russia the situation in 1992–93 has been unique in that the Central Bank has tried to prop up production and employment with soft monetary policies, while the government has urged the bank to concern itself with stabilising the currency. This choice – corresponding to an unstable policy mix according to Mundell's optimal assignment problem – appears not to be the result of CB independence, but of CB dependence on parliamentary pressure.
6. There exist, of course, obvious links between price stability and the need for LLRs. Financial disruptions and crises are frequently linked to an unstable monetary environment in general and to instability of inflation and interest rates in particular. Sharp fluctuations in the level of interest rates imply corresponding changes in the valuation of existing assets, including the assets of banks and other financial firms. The risk of changes in asset values is one of the major risks banks are facing. It is clear that a policy aimed at inflation and price level stability, which avoids the necessity of pronounced disinflation efforts and related adjustment crises and interest rate volatility to the largest possible extent, is at the same time a policy which contributes towards a minimisation of the need for LLR assistance and all the problems and costs associated with it.
7. See also the BIS Lamfalussy Report (1990).
8. In already developed financial economies it may, however, be desirable to further split the supervisory and LLR roles to reduce conflicts of interest. As argued by Dewatripont and

Tirole (1992), if a regulated bank experiences difficulties, this is a sign of probably insufficient supervision. LLR or other actions may then be retarded to avoid revelation of incompetence, either by gambling on resurrection if the time horizon of the agency is sufficiently long, or, otherwise, passing the buck.

9. As banks in REs frequently have non-performing loans, it might be necessary to provide rules and instructions for making provisions for doubtful loans and writing down partially and fully non-performing loans.
10. In the United States, deposit insurance premiums paid to the Federal Deposit Insurance Corporation range from 0.23 to 0.31 bp p.a. according to capitalisation of bank. For details see Szegö (1993).
11. Currency reform as a way of dealing efficiently with all outstanding debt is discussed in Chapter 7.
12. For example, Sarcinelli (1992) claims that 25–60 per cent of the loan portfolios of seven of the nine Polish commercial banks are sub-standard and similar problems are reported in other Eastern European countries. In view of later privatisation and of macroeconomic shares, this situation is likely to deteriorate further.
13. This is essentially the reason for spelling out the CB's LLR interventions in the constitution. To solve the problem in hand, it would, however, also be necessary to bind the government's hands constitutionally.
14. Begg and Portes (1992), van Wijnbergen (1992), Frydman *et al.* (1992) and McKinnon (1991).
15. Earlier discussions of the problems are contained in Gros and Steinherr (1991a), Brainard (1991), Calvo and Frenkel (1991a).
16. Van Wijnbergen proposes a call option scheme for dealing with the possible conflicts between senior and junior creditors. The objective of the call option scheme is to convert all the debt into equity and grant control of the enterprise to the senior creditors, which presumably are the government and the state-owned banks. The call options would be granted to junior creditors, managers and workers. For example, suppose the firm owes to government (the most senior creditor for tax arrears) 100 and to banks 200, the government would receive 100 shares of equity swapped against senior debt. Banks would receive a call option on these shares at an exercise price of $1 per share. They would exercise this call if the value of the firm without any debt exceeded the value of the original claim by government. This way privatisation would be assured for firms with positive net worth, after putting aside junior debt. Managers and workers would also receive call options on shares at an exercise price of $3. They would exercise these if the net value of the firm were positive after all debts had been paid off.
17. A similar synthesis is reached by Corricelli and Thorne (1992).
18. Heavy reliance on foreign finance means that a significant share of domestic investment – up to one-third – is provided by foreign sources for extended periods of time. However, there is no historic evidence of foreign capital financing *predominantly* the growth process. See Gerschenkron (1962) and Chapter 15.
19. If all public sector is netted out, then the counterpart is the holding of deposits by households. If all enterprise debt was cancelled and replaced by government bonds (as it should because the government was owner of these firms), then the amount of bonds so created would be at most equal to the outstanding money supply (M3). If that was equal to 60 per cent of GDP then, at a real interest rate of 3 per cent, the annual debt service would amount to roughly 2 per cent of GDP. The real cost of the debt service could fall below that level if only bad debt were replaced by bonds (assuming that bad debts can be identified) and that not all enterprise debt was non-performing. On the other hand, there is a considerable risk of faulty netting so that more than the net debt may have to be bailed out.
20. A comparison between the three banking systems can be found in Smith and Walter

(1993). For a critical evaluation of universal banking in highly developed countries, see Steinherr and Huveneers (1992). Their sceptical views do not pertain, however, to the context of reforming East European countries. Empirical evidence of the contribution of universal banks to growth is contained in Steinherr and Huveneers (1993).

21. Steinherr and Huveneers (1993) set out a detailed comparison of banking systems with market-based systems.
22. At the present time quite the opposite prevails: too many inefficient, under-capitalised banks exist. Nor is there any evidence of excessive market power of universal banks in Western economies. For example, the market share of the five largest banks in Germany falls below 15 per cent. See Steinherr and Huveneers (1992).
23. This would add to the information of the Central Bank as supervisory authority and commit the Central Bank more strongly.
24. Recent US regulations adopt the same approach. See US Treasury (1991).
25. A perpetual is a security that promises, say, to pay every period (e.g. monthly) one dollar (crown, ruble, etc.) forever. Each day a price will be set for such a contract by supply and demand. New issues can therefore be added without constraints on contract specifications, which are time-independent.
26. In Slovenia, for example, the government issued 30-year maturity bonds (already a good approximation of a perpetual without the fungibility advantage) at rates very substantially below short-term rates.

References to Part II

Alchian, A. and **Demsetz, H.** (1972) Production, information costs and economic organisation, *American Economic Review*, December.

Alesina, A. and **Summers, L.H.** (1991) *Central bank independence and macro-economic performance: some comparative evidence,* Harvard University, draft.

Aoki, M. (ed.) (1984) *The Economic Analysis of the Japanese Firm*, North Holland, New York.

Arrow, K.J. (1987) Rationality of self and others in an economic system, in Hogarth, R.M. and Rider, M.W. (eds) *Rational Choice: The Contrast Between Economics and Psychology*, University of Chicago Press, Chicago.

Bagehot, W. (1873) *Lombard Street*, London: Kegan, Paul & Co.

Baltensperger, E. (1993) Monetary policy and the lender of last resort function, paper presented at the conference *Prudential Regulation, Supervision and Monetary Policy*, Bocconi University, February.

Baltensperger, E. and **Dermine, J.** (1987) Banking deregulation in Europe, *Economic Policy*, April, 63–109.

Bardhan, P. and **Roemer, J.E.** (1992) Market socialism: a case for rejuvenation, *Journal of Economic Perspectives*, Summer.

Becker, G. (1983) A theory of competition among pressure groups for political influence, *Quarterly Journal of Economics*, August.

Begg, D. and **Portes, R.** (1992) Enterprise debt and economic transformation: financial restructuring of the state sector in central and eastern europe, *CEPR Discussion Paper* No. 695.

Bennett, J. and **Dixon, H.D.** (1993) Macroeconomic equilibrium and reform in a transitional economy, *CEPR Discussion Paper*, No. 758, January.

Berg, A. and **Sachs, J.** (1992) Structural adjustment and international trade in Eastern Europe: the case of Poland, *Economic Policy*, **14**, p. 117–73.

BIS (1990) *Report of the Committee on Interbank Netting Schemes of the Central Banks of the Group of Ten Countries* (the Lamfalussy Report), Basle, November.

Bisignano, J. (1992) Banking competition, regulation and the philosophy of financial development: a search for first principles, in Fingleton, J.A. and Schoenmaker, D. (eds) *The Internationalisation of Capital Markets and the Regulatory Response*, Graham & Trotman, London, pp. 69–102.

Blanchard, O., Dornbusch, R., Krugman, P., Layard, R. and **Summers, L.** (1990) *Reform in Eastern Europe*. Report of the WIDER World Economy Group, MIT Press, Cambridge, Massachusettts.

Blanchard, O. and **Layard, R.** (1990) Economic change in Poland, Center for Research into Communist Economies, Boston, Massachusetts, July.

Blejer, M., **Burton, D.**, **Dunaway, S.** and **Szapary, G.** (1991) China: economic reform and macroeconomic management, *IMF Occasional Paper* No.76.

Bofinger, P. (1990) A multilateral payments union for Eastern Europe?, mimeo IMF, June.

Brainard, L.J. (1991) Reform in Eastern Europe: creating a capital market, in O'Brien, R. and Hewin, S. (eds) *Finance and the International Economy, 4, The AMEX Review Prize Essays,* Oxford University Press for the Amex Bank Review, pp. 7–22, Oxford.

Brus, W. (1972) *The Market in a Socialist Economy,* Routledge and Kegan Paul, London.

Brus, W. (1973) *The Economics and Politics of Socialism: Collected Essays*, Routledge and Kegan Paul, London.

Bryan, L. (1988) *Breaking up the Bank*, Dow Jones-Irwin, New York.

Calvo, G.A. (1991) Financial aspects of socialist economies: from inflation to reform, in Corbo *et al.* (eds) *Reforming Central and Eastern European Economies*, World Bank, Washington, DC.

Calvo, G.A. and **Coricelli, F.** (1993a) Output collapse in Eastern Europe, *IMF Staff Papers*, March, pp. 32–52.

Calvo, G.A. and **Coricelli, F.** (1993b) Inter-enterprise arrears in economies in transition, paper presented at the international conference *Output Decline in Eastern Europe – Prospects for Recovery?*, November 18–20, IIASA, Laxenberg, Austria.

Calvo, G.A. and **Frenkel, J.A.** (1991a) Credit markets, credibility and economic transformation, *Journal of Economic Perspectives,* **5** (4), pp. 139–48.

Calvo, G. and **Frenkel, J.** (1991b) From centrally planned to market economies: the road from CPE to PCPE, *IMF Staff Papers*, 38, June.

Clifton, E.V. and **Khan, M.S.** (1993) Interenterprise arrears in transforming economies, *IMF Staff Papers* 40 (3), September.

Coase, R.H. (1937) The nature of the firm, *Economica*, **4**.

Corbo, V. (1992) Economic transformation in Latin America, *European Economic Review*, April.

Corbo, V., **Coricelli, F.** and **Bossak, J.** (eds) (1991) *Reforming Central and Eastern European Economies: Initial Results and Challenges*, The World Bank, Washington DC.

Coricelli, F. and **Thorne, A.** (1992) Creating financial markets in economies in transition, World Bank, Washington, DC., draft.

Decaluwe, B. and **Steinherr, A.** (1976) A portfolio balance model for the two-tier exchange market, *Economica*, May.

Dewatripont, M. and **Roland, G.** (1991) The virtues of gradualism and legitimacy in the transition to a market economy, mimeo, University of Brussels.

Dewatripont, M. and **Tirole, J.** (1993) Efficient governance structure: implications for banking regulation, in Mayer, C. and Vives, X. (eds) *Capital Markets and Financial Intermediation* , Cambridge University Press, Cambridge.

Diamond, D. (1984) Financial intermediation and delegated monitoring, *Review of Economic Studies*, July.

Diamond, D. and **Dybvig, P.** (1983) Bank runs, deposit insurance and liquidity, *Journal of Political Economy*, **91**, pp. 401–19.

Dixit, A. (1989), Entry and exit decisions under fluctuating exchange rates, *Journal of Political Economy*, **97**.

Dixit, A.K. and **Stiglitz, J.E.** (1977) Monopolistic competition and optimum product diversity, *American Economic Review*, **67**.

Dornbusch, R. (1990) *Problems of European Monetary Unification,* paper prepared for conference on European Financial Integration, CEPR/IMI, Rome.

Dornbusch R., **Sturzenegger F.** and **Wolf, H.** (1990) Hyperinflations: sources and stabilization, *Brookings Papers on Economic Activity.*

Dornbusch, R. and **Wolf, H.** (1990) Monetary overhang and reforms in the 1940s, NBER Working Paper 3456, National Bureau of Economic Research, Cambridge, Massachusetts.

Duchene, G. and **Gros, D.** (1994) *Cases of Output Decline in Reforming Economies*, Centre for European Policy Studies, Brussels.

EBRD (1992) *Banking Sector and Enterprise Restructuring in Eastern Europe*, EBRD, London.

The Economist (1992) The Titan Stirs, 28 November.

Eckaus, R.S. (1990) Some lessons from development economics for Southern and Eastern Europe, MIT, Cambridge, Massachussetts, draft.

Edwards, S. (1991) *Stabilisation and Liberalisation Policies in Eastern Europe: Lessons from Latin America*, University of California, Los Angeles.

Edwards, S. and **Teitel, S.** (1986) Introduction to growth, reform and adjustment: Latin America's trade and macroeconomic policies in the 1970s and 1980s, *Economic Development and Cultural Change*, **34**, April.

Emerson, M. *et al.* (1988) The economics of 1992, *European Economy*, **35**.

Fama, E. (1980) Agency problems and the theory of the firm, *Journal of Political Economy*, April.

Feige, E. (1990) A message to Gorbachev: redistribute the wealth, *Challenge*, **33**, May-June.

Fischer, S. (1982) Seigniorage and the case for a national money, *Journal of Political Economy,* 90(2), pp. 295–313.

Fischer, S. (1992) Stabilisation and economic reform in Russia, *Brookings Papers on Economic Activity*, No 7, pp. 77–111.

Fischer, S. and **Gelb, A.** (1990) Issues in socialist economy reform, World Bank PRE Working Paper WPS565, World Bank, Washington, DC.

Fischer, S. and **Gelb, A.** (1991) The process of socialist economic transformation, *Journal of Economic Perspectives*, Fall.

Frydman, R. and **Rapaczynski, A.** (1991) Markets and institutions in large-scale privatisation: an approach to economic and social transformation in Eastern Europe, in Corbo V., F. Coricelli and J. Bossak (eds.) *Reforming Central and Eastern European Economies*, World Bank, Washington, DC.

Frydman, R., **Phelps, E.J.**, **Rapaczynski, A.** and **Shleifer A.** (1992), Notes on the banking reform in Eastern Europe, mimeo.

Gerschenkron, A. (1962) *Economic Backwardness in Historical Perspective: A Book of Essays*, Harvard University Press, Cambridge, Massachusetts.

Gilibert, P.L. and **Girard, J.** (1988) Uses of duration: A survey article, *EIB Papers*, No.5.

Giovannini, A. and **de Melo, M.** (1993) Government revenue from financial repression, *American Economic Review*, **103**, pp. 953–63.

Goodhart, Ch. and **Schoenmaker, D.** (1993) Institutional separation between supervisory and monetary agencies, London School of Economics, draft.

Gros, D. (1988) Dual exchange rates in the presence of incomplete market separation: long run ineffectiveness and implications for monetary policy, *IMF Staff Papers*, **535**, (3), pp. 437–60.

Gros, D. (1991) A Soviet payments union?, Centre for European Policy Studies Working Paper, Brussels.

Gros, D. and **Gonciarz, G.** (1994) A note on the trade potential of Central and Eastern Europe, Centre for European Policy Studies (CEPS), Brussels, November.

Gros, D. and **Jones, E.** (1991) Price reform and energy markets in the Soviet Union and Central Europe, CEPS Working Documents, No. 57, August.

Gros, D. and **Steinherr, A.** (1990) Currency union and economic reform in the GDR: a comprehensive one-step approach, CEPS Working Document No.49, Centre for European Policy Studies, Brussels.

Gros, D. and **Steinherr, A.** (1991a) *From Centrally Planned to Market Economies*, Brassey's for CEPS, London.

Gros, D. and **Steinherr, A.** (1991b) Economic reform in the Soviet Union: pas-de-deux between disintegration and macroeconomic destabilisation, *Princeton Studies in International Finance*, **71**, November.

Gros, D. and **Steinherr, A.** (1991c) Macroeconomic management in the new Germany: implications for the EMS and EMU, in Heisenberg, (ed) *German Unification in European Perspective*, Brassey's for CEPS, London, pp. 165–88.

Gros, D. and **Vandille, G.** (1994) Seigniorage in the transition, Centre for European Policy Studies (CEPS), Brussels.

Grossman, S. and **Hart, O.** (1980) Takeover bids, the free-rider problem, and the theory of the corporation, *The Bell Journal of Economics*, **II**, Spring.

Harrold, P. (1992) *China's Reform Experience to Date*, World Bank Discussion Papers, No.180, World Bank, Washington, DC.

Hayek, F.A. (1978) *Denationalisation of Money*, Institute of Economic Affairs, London.

Horiuchi, A. (1989) Informational properties of the Japanese financial system, *Japan and the World Economy*, July.

Huber, E., **Rueschemeyer, D.** and **Stephens, J.D.** (1993) The impact of economic development on democracy, *Journal of Economic Perspectives*, Summer.

Hughes, G. and **Hare, P.** (1992) Industrial policy and restructuring in Eastern Europe, *CEPR Discussion Paper*, No.653, London, March.

Jefferson, G., **Rawski, T.** and **Zheng, Y.** (1992) Growth, efficiency and convergence in China's state and collective industry, *Economic Development and Cultural Change*.

Jensen, M.C. (1988) Takeovers: their cause and consequences, *The Journal of Economic Perspectives*, **2**, (1), pp. 21–48.

Jensen, M.C. (1989) Eclipse of the public corporation, *Harvard Business Review*, September-October.

Jensen, M.C. and **Meckling, W.H.** (1976) Theory of the firm: managerial behaviour, agency costs and ownership structure, *Journal of Financial Economics*, October.

Jones, D.C. (1992) The productivity effects of employee ownership within command economies: evidence from Poland, Clinton, N.Y. Hamilton College, draft.

Kaplan, J.J. and **Schleiminger, G.** (1989) *The European Payments Union: Financial Diplomacy in the 1950s*, Clarendon Press, Oxford.

Kaufman, G.G. (1984) Measuring and managing interest rate risk: a primer, *Economic Perspectives*, Federal Reserve Bank of Chicago, Jan.-Feb.

Kay, J. and **Vickers, J.** (1988) Regulatory reform in Britain, *Economic Policy*, **7**.

Kenen, P. (1990) Transitional arrangements for trade and payments among the CMEA countries, IMF, August.

Koen, V. and **Phillips, S.** (1993) Price liberalisation in Russia, IMF Occasional Papers, No. 104, WAshington, DC, June.

Kornai, J. (1986) The soft budget constraint, *Kyklos*, **39** (1), pp. 3–30.

Kornai, J. (1990) The affinity between ownership forms and coordination mechanisms: the common experience of reform in socialist countries, *Journal of Economic Perspectives*, **4**, Summer.

Kostrzewa, W., **Nunnenkamp, P.** and **Schmeiding, H.** (1989) A Marshall Plan for middle and Eastern Europe?, *Kiel Working Papers*, No.403, December.

Kumar, M.S. (1984) *Growth, Acquisition and Investment*, Cambridge University Press, Cambridge.

Landes, D.S. (1968) *The Unbound Prometheus: Technological Change and Industrial Development in Western Europe from 1750 to the Present*, Cambridge University Press, Cambridge.

Lange, O. (1937) On the economic theory of Socialism, *Review of Economic Studies*, Parts I and II.

Larre, B. and **Torres, R.** (1991) Is convergence a spontaneous process? The experience of Spain, Portugal and Greece, *OECD Economic Studies*, No.16.

Lerner, A.P. (1939) The symmetry between import and export taxes, *Economica*, 3, pp. 306–13.

Lipton, D. (1990) Privatization in Eastern Europe: the case of Poland, *Brookings Papers on Economic Activity*, **2**, The Brookings Institution, Washington.

Lipton, D. and **Sachs, J.** (1990) Creating a market economy in Eastern Europe: the case of Poland, *Brookings Papers on Economic Activity*,: **I**, The Brookings Institution, Washington, DC.

McKinnon, R.I. (1991) *The Order of Economic Liberalisation: Financial Control in the Transition to a Market Economy*, John Hopkins University Press, Baltimore, Maryland.

Mathieson, D. and **Rojas-Suarez, L.** (1993) Liberalisation of the capital account, *IMF Occasional Papers*, No.103.

Murrell, P. (1991) Can neoclassical economics underpin the reform of centrally planned economies?, *The Journal of Economic Perspectives*, **4**.

Naughton, B. (1992) Implications of the state monopoly over industry and its relaxation, *Modern China*, January.

Newbery, D.M. (1991a) Sequencing the transition, *CEPR Discussion Paper Series*, No.575, August.

Newbery, D.M. (1991b) Reform in Hungary: sequencing and privatisation, *European Economic Review*, **35**.

Nicholl, P.W.E. and **Archer, D.J.** (1992) An announced downward path for inflation, in O'Brien, R., *The AMEX Bank Review Prize Essays*, Oxford University Press, Oxford, pp. 116–127.

North, D.C. (1990) *Institutions, Institutional Change and Economic Performance*, Cambridge University Press, Cambridge.

North, D.C. and **Thomas, R.P.** (1973) *The Rise of the Western World: A New Economic History*, Cambridge University Press, Cambridge.

Nove, A. and **Nuti, D.M.** (1972) *Socialist Economics: Selected Readings*, Penguin, London.

Nuti, D.M. (1988) Perestroika: transition from central planning to market socialism, *Economic Policy*, **7**.

Oi, W.Y. (1961) The desirability of price instability under perfect competition, *Econometrica*, **29**.

Olson, M. (1982) *The Rise and Decline of Nations*, Yale University Press, New Haven, Connecticut.

Olson, M. (1991) Autocracy, democracy and property, in Zeckhauser, R.J. (ed) *Strategy and Choice*, MIT Press, Cambridge, Massachusetts.

Olson, M. (1993) Dictatorship, democracy and development, *American Political Science Review*, September.

Osband, K. (1989) *Economic Crisis in a Reforming Socialist Economy*, The Rand Corporation, Santa Monica, California.

Pinto, B., **Belka, M.** and **Krajewski, S.** (1993) Transforming state enterprises in Poland: evidence on adjustment by manufacturing firms, *Brookings Papers on Economic Activity*, pp. 213–62.

Portes, R. and **Winter, D.** (1978) The demand for money and for consumption goods in centrally planned economies, *Review of Economics and Statistics*, **60**.

Przeworski, A. and **Limongi, F.** (1993) Political regimes and economic growth, *Journal of Economic Perspectives*, **7** (3), pp. 51–70.

Roemer, J.E. (1991) Would economic democracy decrease the amount of public bads?, University of California at Davis, Department of Economics, Working Paper.

Rostowski, J. (1993) The inter-enterprise debt explosion in the former Soviet Union: causes, consequence, cures, *Centre for Economic Performance, Discussion Paper* No.142.

Russian Economic Trends (1993) Centre for Economic Reform, Government of the Russian Federation, Whurr Publishers, London.

Sachs, J. (1991) Comparing economic reform in Latin America and Eastern Europe, Hicks Lecture, Oxford University, March.

Sachs, J. (1993) *Poland's Jump to the Market*, MIT Press, London.

Sarcinelli, M. (1992) Eastern Europe and the financial sector: where are they going?, *Banca Nazionale del Lavoro Quarterly Review*, December, pp. 463–92.

Schaffer, M.E. (1990) Les entreprises publiques en Pologne: impôts, subventions et politique de concurrence, *Economie Européenne*, **43**.

Schumpeter, J.A. (1942) *Capitalism, Socialism, and Democracy*, Harper, New York.

Sertel, M.R. and **Steinherr, A.** (1984) Information, incentives and the design of efficient institutions, *Zeitschrift für die Gesamte Staatswissenschaft*.

Shleifer, A. and **Vishny, R.** (1986) Large shareholders and corporate control, *Journal of Political Economy*, **94**, June.

Sinn, G. and **Sinn, H.-W.** (1991) *Kaltstart*, J.C.B. Mohr (Paul Siebeck), Tübingen.

Smith, R.C. and **Walter, I.** (1993) Banking industry linkages: models for Eastern European economic restructuring, in Fair, D. and Raymond, A.J. (eds) *The New*

Europe: Evolving Economic and Financial Systems in East and West, Kluwer Academic Publ., Dordrecht, pp. 41–60.

Steinherr, A. (1993) An innovatory package for financial sector reforms in Eastern European countries, *Journal of Banking and Finance*, pp. 1033–57.

Steinherr, A. and **Gilibert, P.L.** (1989/1990) Regulating the EC financial sector beyond 1991, *The Journal of International Securities Markets*, Winter 1989 (Part I) pp. 351–61 and Spring 1990 (Part II), pp. 81–90.

Steinherr, A. and **Gilibert, P.L.** (1993) Six proposals in search of financial sector reform in Eastern Europe, European Investment Bank, Luxembourg.

Steinherr, A. and **Huveneers, C.** (1992) Universal banking in the integrated European market place, in Steinherr, A. (ed) *The New European Financial Market Place*, Longman, London, pp. 49–67.

Steinherr, A. and **Huveneers, C.** (1993) On the performance of differently regulated financial institutions: some empirical evidence, *Journal of Banking and Finance*, **18**, pp. 271–306.

Steinherr, A. and **Perée, E.** (1992) Prometheus unbound: policy proposals for restructuring in Eastern Europe, in Siebert, A. (ed) *The Transformation of Socialist Economies*, Kiel.

Stiglitz, J.E. (1985) Credit markets and the control of capital, *Journal of Money, Credit and Banking*, May.

Stiglitz, J.E. (1987) The causes and consequences of the dependence of quality on price, *Journal of Economic Literature,* **25**.

Stiglitz, J.E. (1990) Whither socialism? Perspectives for the economics of information, Wicksell Lectures, Stockholm, May.

Szegö, G.P. (1993) Financial regulation and multi-tier financial intermediation systems in Eastern Europe, in R.D. Ecclesai and S. Zenios (eds) *Operation Research Models of Quantitative Finance*, Physica Verlag, Heidelberg, pp. 36–64.

Tanzi, V. (ed) (1992) *Fiscal Policies in Economies-in-Transition*, IMF, Washington, DC.

Tirole, J. (1991) Privatization in Eastern Europe: incentives and the economics of transition (draft), Massachusetts Institute of Technology, Cambridge, Massachusetts.

Triffin, R. (1957) *Europe and the Money Muddle from Bilateralism to Near-Convertibility 1947-1956*, Yale University Press, New Haven, Connecticut.

United Nations, Economic Commission for Europe (1992) *Economic Survey of Europe in 1991–1992*, UN, New York.

US Department of the Treasury (1991) *Modernizing the Financial System: Recommendations for Safer, More Competitive Banks*, Washington, DC., 5 February.

Vanek, J. (1970) *The General Theory of Labour-Managed Economies*, Cornell University Press, Ithaca, New York.

Van Long, N. and **Siebert, H.** (1991) A model of the socialist firm in transition to a market economy, Institut für Weltwirtschaft, *Kiel Working Paper* No.479, Kiel.

Van Wijnbergen, S. (1992) Economic aspects of enterprise reform in Eastern Europe, in O'Brien, R. (ed) *The AMEX Bank Review Prize Essays*, Oxford University Press, Oxford, pp. 32–45.

Vickers, J. and **Yarrow, G.** (1988) *Privatisation – An Economic Analysis*, MIT Press, Cambridge, Massachusetts.

Wiles, P. (1977) *Economic Institutions Compared*, John Wiley, New York.

PART THREE

REFORMS IN CENTRAL EUROPE

Introduction

After the description of socialist economic organisation and performance in Part I and the mainly conceptual discussion of the reform problems in Part II, the remainder of the book concentrates on the concrete situation in reforming countries. The reforms already carried out are evaluated and compared, as are the problems still to be solved.

Part III focuses on Central Europe and leaves the former Soviet Union (FSU) to Part IV because the size and nature of the problems in the FSU are incommensurable with those in Central Europe. But even in Central Europe the starting conditions are vastly different and can be regrouped into three or four different categories. East Germany is clearly apart from the rest because it has ceased to be an independent country, receives full financial and institutional support from the former West Germany and *de facto* has become a member of the European Community. This was expected to make the reconstruction of East Germany much easier and faster than that of neighbouring Eastern countries. Yet, quite to the contrary, industrial production in East Germany has fallen by some 60 per cent against some 20 per cent in the Czech and Slovak Federal Republics (CSFR), Hungary and Poland. What is the reason for this reversal of initial expectations? Is currency union the culprit? Or was wage convergence unavoidable under any scenario, and the main factor of the collapse of East German industry? Or could it be that whilst collapse was more pronounced there than elsewhere it is only a matter of speed of adjustment? This would imply that East Germany has already reached the bottom and will achieve a competitive structure and full employment sooner than other countries that have not yet freed prices and eliminated redundancies and might have to accept a longer period of under-utilisation of production factors.

Currency union spared East Germany a macroeconomic destabilisation and the need for a stabilisation policy. East Germany does not have macroeconomic problems, it only has microeconomic ones: how to produce efficiently for the home and for the world markets. As will become apparent in Chapter 10, this is not a simple problem.

In Chapter 11 we discuss the problems of the CSFR, Hungary and Poland together. Although they have much to differentiate them, they also share a number of central characteristics. Culturally, they were part of or close to the Austrian Empire until World War I. Politically, they all attempted to break away from Soviet domination and preserved reservations about the communist model. And they are committed to democratic principles, much more than their eastern and southern neighbours. Their relative income levels, past growth rates, levels of education and health all put them in the group of middle-income countries. Their political and economic crisis came in the wake of increasing maladjustment of the whole ex-Soviet bloc to the changing world growth and trade environment. In that respect the adjustment and structural reform problem of Eastern Europe would seem to be akin to that of the other middle-income countries, such as Brazil, Mexico, or Israel; these countries had enjoyed long periods of growth and relative price stability in the past, but in the course of the 1970s and 1980s they underwent severe structural crises. The delayed effects of some of these same shocks (e.g. energy and raw material prices) are only now being felt in Eastern Europe. The difference, however, is not only one of timing or of degree. In all of Eastern Europe it is the whole political and economic framework that has collapsed.

In Hungary, the 1956 uprising presaged the long period of modest economic reforms that started with the introduction of the New Economic Mechanism of 1968. These reforms evoked the suspicion of ideological autonomy and of liberalised prices and trade and, perhaps most importantly, exposure to the capitalist concepts of price signalling and management decision-making. In addition, Hungary had even built some of the institutions more typical of market economies – a two-tier banking system, for instance. But the enormity of the task of overturning central planning, withdrawing from state intervention, and privatising the means of production should not be underestimated even in this case. Hungary's starting conditions for wholesale reform, moreover, were complicated by a legacy of high foreign debt and stubborn inflationary expectations, stemming from two decades of stop–go policies.

Poland, by far the most populous of the three countries, was something of an oddity because it had maintained a large private agricultural sector under socialism, but had never dared to venture into reforms to the extent that Hungary and, briefly, Czechoslovakia did. A severe economic crisis in the late 1970s and early 1980s resulted in labour unrest and the formation of the Solidarity labour union, and eventually culminated in the imposition of martial law in December 1981. Under martial law, as shown by Darnton (1993), the Polish economy went into deep anaesthesia from which it woke up at the end of the decade only to find that there had been no operation. The ruling elite had to enter into a power-sharing agreement with Solidarity in July 1989 and the government that came into office in September confronted Poland's worsening economic crisis, by then including hyperinflation, with a comprehensive reform package introduced in January 1990. For a detailed description of the Polish reform programme, see Sachs (1993) and Calvo and Coricelli (1992).

The CSFR had experimented with reform in the Prague Spring of 1968, but the Soviet invasion had put a decisive end to this and the country had reverted to textbook-style orthodox central planning. There was virtually no private economic activity to speak of. With little open political polarisation, and reflecting a long tradition of conservative financial policies, Czechoslovakia reached the late 1980s with by far the most favourable macroeconomic conditions in Central and Eastern Europe: inflation – even including hidden inflation – below 5 per cent annually, a strong balance of payments, and low external debt. The waning of Soviet influence brought on the 'velvet revolution' of November 1989, and the year 1990 was devoted to some early reform measures and to seeking a consensus on the modalities of economic transformation. The key elements of the CSFR's programme were introduced in January 1991.[1]

As for their political future, they all see it in EC membership by or before the end of the century and have already obtained association status. They form the so-called 'Visegrad triangle', named after Visegrad in Hungary, where a treaty was signed in February 1991 to seek 'total integration into the European political, economic and legislative order'. Economically, all three have already succeeded in stabilising their economies to some extent, have started to liberalise prices and to privatise. Despite very different macroeconomic policies, output contraction in all three countries is about the same. Can this be explained?

We do not extend the discussion to the southern neighbours, Bulgaria and Romania. Their problems are not very different, although the starting point is one of lesser development. It is not the objective of this book to be encyclopaedic, but instead we try to understand the issues involved, interpret the evolution observed and indicate what actions could be usefully adopted. As, in addition, data on these two countries are even more opaque than those of the three Central European countries, we shall only comment on them in passing.

Bulgaria and Romania – together with the CSFR – were the most rigidly centralised economies in the region. While Hungary and Poland experimented with enterprise autonomy, limited price liberalisation and private ownership before the beginning of large-scale reform, these three countries remained wedded to rigid central planning more or less until the end. The three countries differed significantly, however, in their degree of adherence to financial discipline during the years of central planning. At one extreme was the CSFR, with low foreign debt and relatively few shortages. At the other was Bulgaria with high foreign debt and significant shortages. In Romania the economy was able to generate – with considerable hardship – external surpluses sufficient to eliminate its foreign debt, but significant internal imbalances were nonetheless apparent.

Bulgaria was the country with the greatest dependency on trade with the CMEA region and also the country that suffered the largest reduction in output after CMEA trade collapsed. In 1990 CMEA exports represented 34 per cent of Bulgaria's GDP, 25 per cent of the CSFR's, 16 per cent of Hungary's and 14 per cent of Poland's (Bruno 1992: Table 1).

Yugoslavia, by contrast, merits separate analysis. Yugoslavia is not a country any more, and it does not belong geographically to Central Europe. But at least parts of what used to be Yugoslavia belong culturally and historically to the *Mitteleuropa* that used to be centred on Austria. And, economically, the northern part of former Yugoslavia definitely has more in common with the classic three Central European states: its relatively high level of income and development, its historic reservations about a Soviet-dominated communist camp and its search for alternatives.

What differentiates Yugoslavia from the Visegrad triangle is, however, more important, interesting and (unfortunately) tragic. First, Yugoslavia managed to leave the socialist camp without joining the Western one. It could not, therefore, enjoy the benefits of regional trade preferences as provided by the EC, nor those of the CMEA. Second, Yugoslavia was to develop its own brand of socialism, paying more attention to decentralisation and participation by workers in decision-making. What is striking is that, although Yugoslavia's growth was remarkable until the mid-1960s, at the end of the road Yugoslavia shares all the same problems of the other Socialist countries: destabilisation, demotivation and low or even negative growth. See Table III.1.

In one important aspect it is even worse off and resembles more closely the FSU. Yugoslavia was pasted together from bits that did not fit properly, neither politically nor economically. The present disintegration, dramatic and regrettable as it is in human terms, is not economically nonsensical. Chapter 12 evaluates the overall economic performance, assesses the labour management experience and investigates whether Yugoslavia had what it takes to form a monetary and economic union.

TABLE III.1 Relative growth performance (average annual percentage change of GDP)

	1952–60	1960–70	1970–80	1952–80	1980–90
Yugoslavia	8.1	5.4	5.8	6.3	–0.3
Hungary	4.6	5.5	6.2	5.5	1.3
Czechoslovakia	4.9	3.5	4.7	4.3	1.4
Poland	4.6	6.0	8.7	6.6	0.0
USSR	6.1	7.4	6.1	6.6	2.3
Spain	3.6	7.3	3.5	4.9	2.8
Portugal	4.3	6.8	2.4	4.5	2.9
Greece	6.5	7.5	4.8	6.2	1.6

Sources: OECD, Historical Statistics and Economic Outlook and World Bank, World Tables
Note: Net Material Product Growth for Czechoslovakia 1970–1990 and USSR 1980–1990
GSP for Yugoslavia 1980–1990

The growth performance shown in Table III.1 needs to be judged on the basis of the analysis in chapter 3. At this point we want to recall some basic points that need to be taken into account when judging the first post-reform years described below: until 1980 all socialist countries recorded very respectable growth rates of output. The ranking varies somewhat from decade to decade. As shown in the first three columns: Poland was the slowest during the 1950s but the fastest during the 1980s. But the average growth rates, 1952–80, shown in the fourth column, are higher for the socialist countries than for capitalist countries such as Spain and Portugal. It is only during the last period, 1980–90, that the capitalist countries have maintained a higher growth rate. It is useful to compare Spain and Poland. In 1952 these two countries had about the same income *per capita.* During the next 40 years the recorded growth rates of Poland were on average higher than those of Spain (6.6% for Poland versus 4.9% for Spain). But when the Polish economy was opened to the world market, it turned out that Poland was not richer than Spain. On the contrary! The world market evaluated the Polish GDP *per capita* at about US $2000, whereas that of Spain was worth over $10 000. The discovery that socialist economies produced large amounts of goods that were worth very little on the world market was the main reason for the problems arising after German unification, to which we now turn.

Note

1. The breakdown of the fragile consensus that underlay this programme, together with a rise of nationalist tensions, played a part in the division of the country on 1 January 1993 into its constituent Czech and Slovak Republics.

CHAPTER TEN

German unification: an extreme example of a big bang reform

Man hat Wirklichkeit gewonnen und Traum verloren.

Robert Musil, *Der Mann ohne Eigenschaften*

East Germany used to be considered the model economy of the socialist bloc. Yet, after unification, little of that economy seemed worth preserving. But the East Germans seemed to be luckier than their Eastern neighbours as reforms and reconstruction could count on West Germany's support, a support unavailable to any other former socialist country. Overnight, unification provided the framework and the institutions needed to operate as a market economy and gave access to the financial and managerial resources of West Germany. East Germany thus obtained the necessary legal framework at the stroke of a pen when the unification treaty came into effect on 3 October 1990. Moreover, monetary union (1 July 1990) brought an untrammelled price system, a stable and convertible currency and an efficient capital market. Privatisation also started quickly under the management of the Treuhand Agency (THA).

Seen against this backdrop, which combined conditions ideal for a big bang reform and very considerable financial support, East Germany's subsequent vicissitudes appear incomprehensible to many. The question we need to answer is, was whatever went wrong the result of avoidable policy errors? Or is the collapse of the East German economy a normal consequence of a big bang reform that should have been anticipated from the outset? Most observers will acknowledge that the difficulties of reforming the economy in the East may have been underestimated, but they all have their own theories as to the policy errors that may have been made. Whilst exaggerated illusions may have been lost, this chapter shows that the East German experience has been a lesson for greater realism, and not a demonstration against the big bang.

A prime candidate for first place on the miscalculations front is, for many, the German government's decision to start the integration process with monetary union on 1 July 1990. Prior to that move, most German economists had been in favour of fixed or flexible exchange rates between the two German currencies which, it was argued, would have given policy-makers more room for manoeuvre and enabled them to keep the two labour markets separate to ensure that wages stayed in tune with the respective productivity levels in the East and the West (Hoffman 1990, Sachverständigenrat 1990, Schlesinger 1990). Runner-up for chief culprit is not currency union *per se*, but the conversion rate chosen which – as also argued by the Bundesbank – was simply set too high. Section 1 comes out against that view.

It was felt by the Bundesbank and by others that currency union could endanger West Germany's inflation record. Equally, reconstruction in the East needs to be financed. Both these facts have repercussions for the external value of the Deutsch-Mark (DM). What is not clear is which direction they will take! Higher inflation would weaken the DM in the long run and put its EMS anchor role into question, while reallocation of West German resources to the East would seem to require, according to most economists and at least in the short run, a revaluation. Section 2 sheds light on that question.

As soon as the open-border policy was implemented it became imperative from a political point of view to stem the flow of westbound Eastern emigrants. Ways had to be found to make it attractive to stay in East Germany. The lure of a brighter future in itself was hardly enough. It was decided to extend West German social security legislation and benefits to all East Germans and to achieve rapid wage convergence. The more radical alternative of redistributing former socialist state property to all East Germans without further ado was rejected. Section 3 explains why that was a mistake.

Section 4 then discusses the task of the Treuhand Agency to restructure and privatise East German State property. It argues that the difficulties and cost of that approach were mounting over time in step with the alignment of real wage costs on those of West Germany and that experience so far does not suggest that a 'model' approach has been found worthy of being used elsewhere in Eastern Europe.

Financially, the cost of integration has mushroomed with much worse unemployment increases than had been anticipated. Total unemployment in East Germany in 1992 stood at more than twice the level reached at the nadir of the Great Depression in the 1930s. The long-term consequences are analysed in Section 5. We end with some proposals for improving the unemployment situation in East Germany in Section 6.

The analysis in this chapter focuses on the period 1990–92, the years of rapidly falling production following unification. East German production reached its lowest level in 1992 and growth started to resume in 1993.

1. Currency union

Setting aside the advice of the Bundesbank and the views of most economists, the German government decided to make currency union the starting point of unification. In taking that decision, the historical lesson imparted by the 1948 currency reform – and which is widely regarded as the cornerstone of the post-war economic 'miracle' – proved decisive.[1]

The decision to introduce the Deutsch-Mark in the former GDR can be defended on economic grounds, even if the prime motive was political. We argued in the winter of 1989/90 that monetary union would have two main advantages: it would create overnight an efficient capital market that would facilitate international trade and domestic investment, and it would replace the need for a comprehensive price reform (Gros and Steinherr 1990a). This indeed is what has happened.

CURRENCY UNION CREATES AN INSTANT CAPITAL MARKET

Theoretical considerations suggested as early as 1989/90 (see also Chapter 9) – and the experience in other reforming countries has confirmed – that the most difficult part of the transformation process is to create an efficient capital market that can assess investment projects and provide financing to existing and new firms. This was fully achieved by currency union. Firms in the East, many of which are new and small, now have access to the federal banking system. Introducing the DM was thus equivalent to immediately creating an efficient capital market, which would otherwise have taken some time to develop. The experiences of other reforming countries discussed below, shows that the lack of well-functioning capital markets was a key obstacle to quick recovery. The West German banking system that 'conquered' the territory of the GDR is providing the bulk of financing for new firms. Moreover, foreign financing of investments is particularly sensitive to a stable monetary framework in the absence of restrictions on capital movements. If the former GDR had retained the Ost Mark it would have had to maintain some capital controls (as in all Central and Eastern European countries), but with the DM as the common currency all capital controls are gone and the financing of trade is no longer a problem. The large current account deficits which East Germany is running (and could be expected in 1990) became invisible (like those of, say, Bavaria in the West) and can, in principle, be financed by private capital without any difficulty. (For political reasons a large share is, however, financed by official transfers.) With two currencies the current account deficits would have been highly visible, and probably always a cause for concern of policy-makers and therefore a source of expectation of exchange rate changes.

The only alternative that would have allowed the new *Länder* to abolish capital controls immediately would have been to adopt a flexible exchange rate for the Ost Mark. This solution would have had the advantage that the exchange rate would have been established in the market and could therefore have reacted to shocks. But given the great uncertainty surrounding the success of the transition to a market economy and eventual monetary unification, this rate might have fluctuated greatly with temporary over-shooting in the transition. The experience of other reforming socialist countries is telling in this respect. Moreover, under flexible exchange rates the monetary policy of the former GDR's Staatsbank would have been the only anchor for prices and inflationary expectations in the East. Given that it would have taken some time to build up a banking system and establish procedures of monetary control, monetary policy would have been highly uncertain, and over- and under-shooting of the exchange rate would probably have been the result. Even in the absence of political considerations, therefore, flexible exchange rates would not have been a viable alternative to the adoption of the DM as a common currency for a reunited Germany.

CURRENCY UNION MAKES PRICE REFORM SUPERFLUOUS

Introducing the DM in the new *Länder* (coupled with the elimination of restrictions on trade) had the additional advantage of being equivalent to a comprehensive price reform. Prices needed to be freed anyway, but without the price system of the West prices might have taken longer to find their equilibrium level. By experience the reforms that have the most immediate effects are the freeing of the price system and *Gewerbefreiheit*, that is, the freedom to set up a business. What happened after 1990 confirmed what experience in other post-socialist countries suggested anyway, namely that it takes time to privatise. The former state-owned enterprises (SOEs) therefore continued to account for the bulk of industrial output for some time. Since these firms were in many cases local monopolists they might have used their power when setting new prices. With the DM as the common currency, and with open borders, that became impossible.

As predicted, not all prices went immediately to the West German level. Even after the introduction of the DM the prices for non-tradables, that is, personal services and real estate, continue to be lower in the East, but are converging towards West German levels over time.

Before July 1990 it was often argued that the elimination of subsidies would raise price levels, according to some estimates by as much as 30 per cent, and that this would imply a cut in real wages. However, this prediction was never appealing from a theoretical point of view since the savings from the elimination of subsidies can be used to lower taxes and increase direct income transfers. Price reform and the elimination of subsidies should therefore lead to a redistribution of income, but should have little effect on the average level of real incomes. Events immediately following currency union have shown that on the contrary, price levels in the former GDR have fallen if one compares June 1990 to December 1990. In principle it does not make much sense to compare the Ost-Mark price level of June 1990 with the DM price level later. But since wages and rents were converted at 1:1 one can argue that without any reforms the old Ost Mark prices of 30 June 1990 should have been the same as the new DM prices of 1 July 1990. The fact that the price level did not change much between June and July (and July and December) shows that the elimination of subsidies (and some indirect taxes) did not lead to a jump in prices.

A fixed exchange rate between two separate currencies would have had a similar effect of equalising prices. But the link would not have been as strong, since the exchange rate might be changed over time and this would allow inflationary pressures to develop in the East, especially since at the outset a tight monetary policy would have been difficult to implement.

The main economic argument against the introduction of the DM in the former GDR was and is that it would make it difficult to change the real exchange rate if it was too high, because wages cannot be reduced in nominal terms.[2] However, the danger of an overvaluation would not have been avoided even in the absence of monetary union since the newly reformed trade unions would probably have ‘seen through’ the effects of a devaluation of the Mark and adjusted their wage demands accordingly. This will be discussed further.

CURRENCY UNION AND THE CHOICE OF CONVERSION RATE

In order to implement currency union it is necessary to specify the rates at which current payments and stocks of financial assets are to be converted. Many have argued that the conversion rate for current payments (wages) was politically imposed and represented an overvaluation. In 1990 we argued that converting wages at much less than 1:1 would have the main effect of leading to inflation without solving the former GDR’s competitive position because Eastern wages were about one-third of the Western level and if that discrepancy had persisted a large flow of emigration to the West would have been set in motion. This might have been a necessary adjustment from an economic point of view, but it would have been politically unacceptable (Gros and Steinherr 1990a). Subsequent events have borne out the view that the conversion rate for current payments would anyway hold only for ‘a logical second’. In July 1990 wages increased and the further (substantial) wage increases that have taken place in the ensuing years show that the conversion of wages at less than 1:1 would have anyway been 'corrected' immediately. The initial conversion rate for wages was therefore irrelevant.

There is also indirect empirical evidence in support of this view. If the main reason for East German loss of competitiveness had been an overvalued exchange rate in 1990, then one would expect to see rising unemployment and falling wages. This is the standard adjustment in countries with fixed exchange rates. In East Germany, rising unemployment was, however, accompanied by rising wages in nominal and real terms.

Moreover, and quite regrettably, the objective not only of the labour unions but also of the federal government is rapid convergence of wages in the two parts of Germany. It is this objective rather than monetary union and its terms that has been the reason behind the overvaluation of East German workers.

One of the most contentious aspects of the introduction of the DM in the territory of the former GDR was the rate at which financial assets, especially the savings deposits of East German citizens, were to be converted from Ost-Mark into Deutsch-Mark.[3] The Bundesbank proposed converting financial assets at 2:1 while providing all East German citizens with a lump sum called *Kopfgeld*.[4] Was this justified? The balance-sheet of the consolidated credit system of the GDR before reunification provides a convenient background for a discussion of the economic impact of the choice of conversion rate for financial assets and liabilities which turned out to be misleading for many people (Table 10.1).

Public attention focused for a time on the most important item on the asset side, that is, 'credit to firms' of 260 bn. As demonstrated in Chapter 2 with a schematic presentation of the national income accounts in socialist countries, this was not warranted since in socialist countries like the GDR there were really only two sectors, households and the government. The latter comprised firms (all government-owned) and the 'external' sector (through the government monopoly on foreign trade). The distribution of assets between the state, firms and the external sector was therefore irrelevant and arbitrary under the socialist system.

The fact that the government controlled all firms (which then were taken over by the THA) implies that from an economic point of view it is irrelevant how much firms owe to banks and at what rate this debt is to be converted. If debts had been converted at 1:1 many firms would not have been able to repay them and the government would

TABLE 10.1 Consolidated final balance-sheet of the GDR credit system (31.12.1989, in billion Ost-Mark)

Assets		Liabilities	
Credit to the domestic sector	418	Deposits	260
of which: households	23	of which: households	176
firms	260	firms	60
Claims on external sector	45	Foreign liabilities	162
Other assets	4	Cash in circulation	17
		Capital and reserves	28
Total	467	**Total**	467

have had to pay up (or would have received less in firm sales). If firms had been able to service their debt, their privatisation value would have diminished by a corresponding amount and the government would have lost in sales revenues what it received indirectly through the banks in the form of debt-service payments. The rate at which the debt of firms was converted therefore had few economic implications. It determined only what one part of the government sector had to pay the other. Converting the debt of firms at 2:1 did, however, have advantages from an accounting point of view: fewer banks and firms became technically bankrupt. From that point of view, a rate of 3:1 or 4:1 would have been preferable. As it happens, THA frequently had difficulties selling firms with an interesting product line or goods production facilities but also massive debts.[5]

In this situation the main economic impact of the choice of the rate for currency conversion came from the net creditor position of households (*vis-à-vis* the government sector), This 'exposure' of households was equal to 176 billion GDR-marks in savings deposits,[6] not the credit to the state that appears on the asset side of the balance-sheet. Conversion at 2:1 instead of 1:1 did therefore reduce the implicit transfers from the Bundesbank by about 88 billion DM (not taking into account the *Kopfgeld*). The Bundesbank's proposal therefore aroused a storm of protest in the old GDR. Yet the decision was justified on grounds other than distributional equity: it was argued that a conversion of the 176 billion mark in deposits at 1:1 (into DM) would have led to a massive 'monetary overhang', in the sense that the increase in the DM money supply would have exceeded the increase in money demand coming from the old GDR's economy. But this argument is highly questionable.

The increase in the money supply that follows from conversion at any particular rate can be mechanically calculated from the existing money stock; however, the additional demand for money is very difficult to estimate. Most of the difficulties stemmed from the fact that it was not clear what kind of 'money' was represented by the savings deposits, that is, whether or not they could be considered equivalent to 'sight' deposits (M1 in technical terms) because they could be cashed without notice. If they were to be viewed as such, then on the basis of historical ratios in West Germany, the additional demand for DM would have been only about 40 bn and conversion at 4:1 would have been appropriate. If they were to be considered 'true' savings deposits (M3 in technical terms), the additional demand for DM would then have been about 80 bn and conversion at 2:1 would have been appropriate. Finally, if they were to be considered as representing the sum of all financial assets (because no other savings instruments were available in the old GDR), households might use them partly to buy other financial assets and even at a conversion rate of 1:1 there would not have been a monetary overhang.

A concern frequently raised was that a more favourable conversion rate for savings accounts would have generated inflationary demand pressures. We did not share this concern, which hindsight demonstrates to be unfounded. The reason for not expecting important inflationary demand pressures from this source was that the larger deposits were accumulated to top up the extremely meagre pensions most East Germans had been able to expect. Even though pensions have been increased by the federal government, many pensioners will need the interest income from their savings for some time. Moreover, savers in the new *Länder* will for the first time have access to a range of alternative real and financial investments and might also wish to insure themselves against unemployment. All this increases their propensity to save, which made it highly unlikely that East German citizens would plunder their savings to go on a spending spree.

Events after unification do not indicate that there was any monetary overhang. Interest rates have risen after unification, rather than fallen as one would expect from a monetary policy that was temporarily too slack. There was no sign, either, of demand pressures in West Germany originating in savings decumulation in the new *Länder*. As argued below, the separate issue of income transfers is another matter. German unification by itself therefore appears not to have led to uncontrollable inflationary pressures.

2. The exchange rate effects of currency union

The external effect of unification was widely expected to result in a real appreciation of the DM for several mutually reinforcing reasons. Some identified the increase in aggregate demand in united Germany as a cause of rising prices for non-tradable goods and hence the real exchange rate (Artus 1991, Fitoussi and Phelps 1990). Others noted that the increase in demand in the ex-GDR would generate excess demand for West German goods and a real appreciation would be required to redirect German exports to domestic uses (Burda 1990, MacKibbin 1990). A study by the IMF (1990) saw real appreciation as a consequence of rapid growth paired with expansionary fiscal policy and restrictive monetary policy.[7] And, finally, from a longer-run perspective, it was noted that the capital–labour ratio of united Germany and hence its export potential, would fall, so that, in the long run, a depreciation would be necessary (Basevi 1990, Siebert 1991). Wyplosz (1991) is an exception: using an inter-temporal framework he concludes that the real exchange rate change is ambiguous in the short run and a real depreciation is required in the steady state because of the fall in net external assets.[8]

We hold different views about the question as to whether the DM needed to appreciate in real terms as a consequence of unification (Gros and Steinherr 1991). To put it provocatively, would anybody expect the US dollar to appreciate if the United States absorbed Cuba?

Some intuition is provided by asking the hypothetical question as to whether the DM would have appreciated (or have been revalued) in real terms within the EMS if the ex-GDR had opted for fixed exchange rates. The two phenomena with an effect on the exchange rate are the shift in the composition of demand in the ex-GDR and the transfer-induced increase in purchasing power to the ex-GDR. The real exchange rate of the DM would only require an appreciation if increased demand for imports in the new *Länder* were biased in favour of West German goods. Even then, given the small size of the GDR and the limited scope for this potential bias, the real appreciation required would be quite small. More importantly, this effect is at least partly offset by the transfer-induced reduction in real income in West Germany, reducing both the demand for tradables and for non-tradables in West Germany.[9] As the price of the latter will need to decrease to clear the market for non-tradables, the DM's real exchange rate is more likely to depreciate.

Thus, when it is recognised that, first, increased demand in the ex-GDR need not be strongly biased in favour of West German goods and against goods from the rest of the world; and that, second, the only clearly bilateral effect between the two Germanys is the transfer, then the presumption of real appreciation needed for the DM within the EMS becomes much weaker. This is what most people would have expected in the case where the ex-GDR had retained its own currency. A more rigorous demonstration is given in the Appendix to this chapter.

These results are also of relevance in other Eastern European countries with a fixed exchange rate and one did not expect the DM to appreciate within the EMS when Yugoslavia in 1990 pegged its currency to the DM, and even less so if it had received German transfer payments.

In the following, the essential assumption is that goods which were non-tradable before unification are likely to remain so for some time after unification. It will also be convenient to distinguish between the demand effects that arise in the short run and the supply effects from factor movements that might take longer to materialise.

THE SHORT TO MEDIUM RUN: DEMAND EFFECTS

Imagine an EMS composed of two countries: France and Germany. Suddenly demand goes up in one country, Germany. Part of this increase in demand falls on tradable goods, thus reducing the external surplus of Germany, while the remainder goes towards non-tradable goods (whose supply is much less elastic than that of tradables), thus requiring an increase in the relative price of German non-tradables. At given nominal wages, an increase in the relative price of German non-tradables (*vis-à-vis* French non-tradables) requires then an appreciation of the nominal exchange rate of the DM. This is the standard framework that has been used to justify the hypothesis that German unification requires a real appreciation of the DM. The crucial point in this line of reasoning is thus that, at given German wages, the exchange rate of the DM (against the French franc for example) determines the price of German goods relative to French goods.

This conventional analysis applied to unification is wrong because it does not take into account that unification has had different effects in the two parts of Germany. The key is that their real economies are completely different although they use the same currency. It is essential to distinguish between the effects unification has on the demand for non-tradable goods produced in East Germany, on the one hand, and in West Germany, on the other. The relative price of these two goods can alter through changes in wages in East Germany, relative to those in West Germany.

If the standard tradables/non-tradables model is applied to the problem in hand, and if one takes into account the differential impact of unification on West and East Germany, then the conclusion is that no real appreciation of the DM was required. A real appreciation of the DM would have been required only if the demand for West German non-tradables had gone up. This in turn can happen only if West Germans spend more. It is therefore essential to determine whether unification increased the spending of West Germans.

Although overall demand in Germany had gone up there was no reason for demand by West Germans to go up (above trend) since West Germans lend or transfer large amounts of purchasing power to East Germany. On the contrary, West Germans know that they will have to pay sooner or later for most of the debt accumulated by the government to rebuild the ex-GDR. The expectation of higher future taxes is the reason why in general private savings increase if the government deficit rises[10]. Econometric studies in IMF (1990) indicate that in the short run the increase in private savings is not equal to government dissavings, but still about 30 per cent of additional government dissavings is offset by higher private savings. In the long run the offset rises to almost 100 per cent.

There is already some evidence that this has been happening, since the savings ratio of private households in West Germany (savings relative to disposable income) has increased from 13.4 per cent in 1989 (which is also the average for 1985-89) to 14.7 per cent in 1990 and 14.5 per cent in 1991 before declining again to 13.9 per cent in 1992 and 13.3 per cent in 1993 (see Table 10.2). This implies that overall demand by West German households was not the driving force behind the initial post-unification boom in West Germany. Without an increase in overall demand by West German households there is no increase in the demand for West German non-tradables and there is therefore also no reason why the relative price of, say, French and German non-tradables should change. Hence, there is no need for a real appreciation of the DM or a realignment in the EMS.

The increase in the savings rate suggests that expectations of future taxes have been so strong that demand by households in the Western part of Germany actually fell below trend. Part of that decrease in demand is bound to fall on non-tradables, requiring a real depreciation of the DM, which could be achieved through lower German inflation and an unchanged nominal exchange rate.[11] The evidence for this view comes from the fact that inflation in West Germany has not accelerated as much as was expected, and under this hypothesis, it should fall back as household demand in the West is checked. Though German inflation has risen, it has remained below the EMS average, and with nominal exchange rates against the EMS currencies not much changed since 1989, the DM depreciated in real terms until the EMS realignments of September 1992.

The relative price of East German non-tradables (goods that cannot be traded between say Germany and France can presumably also be considered as non-tradables between East and West Germany) will of course have to change. But that relative price can change easily. Indeed, a large jump occurred through conversion at 1:1 for wages and further adjustments took place through wage increases in the territory of the GDR.

The behaviour of prices in West Germany fully bears out our analysis. There is no price index of non-tradables, but there is an index for 'services and repairs' which should account for the bulk of non-tradables. The ratio of the index for 'services and repairs' to the overall consumer price index can thus be taken as a crude approximation of the relative price of non-tradables in West Germany. As there is a productivity bias in favour of tradables, this ratio has a positive time trend which we estimated with data from 1981–1989. The results are shown in Table 10.2. The actual price ratio increased much less than its trend value during 1990–93, providing further evidence that demand for non-tradables in West Germany has not increased as a result of unification.

Another framework that is often used to argue that German unification requires a real appreciation of the DM is one in which the emphasis is on nationally differentiated goods that are tradable. In this approach there would also be a need for a real appreciation of the DM if East Germans (they are the ones who receive the additional purchasing power) have a higher propensity to spend on West German tradables than West Germans. Although East Germans, at least initially, obviously preferred imported Western goods to their own goods there is no reason why they should prefer goods from West Germany to goods from Japan or France.

The only way to bring actual data to bear on this question is to use the experience of other European economies of a size comparable to the ex-GDR (e.g. Netherlands, Belgium). These countries receive about one fourth of all their imports from the Federal Republic. Applying the same percentage to the new *Länder* implies that even if the new *Länder* run a current account deficit of DM 150 bn per annum (as they did in 1991) the additional demand for West German exportables would be only about DM 37 bn (and the reduction in the German current account surplus would be DM 113 bn).[12] The reduction in the current account surplus from DM 108 bn in 1989 to a deficit of DM 32 bn in 1991 is perfectly in line with these rough computations. (It is argued below that the adjustment is mainly brought about by an increase in imports. Table 10.2 shows that they jumped in 1991 by DM 90 bn.) These additional 'exports' of West Germany represent only about 5 per cent of the overall exports of the Federal Republic of Germany (in 1989, prior to unification, they totalled DM 640 bn) and their effective supply is not likely to require a large price change. The crude estimates presented in the next sub-section confirm this order of magnitude.

A different way of looking at the implications of German unification for the EMS is to take into account not only its effects on demand, but to use the standard Heckscher–Ohlin framework, based on factor endowments and movements.[13] The crucial point in this framework is that East Germany starts out with a much lower capital–labour ratio. This should lead to capital flows into East Germany and should also be reflected in the capital intensity of the goods traded by East Germany.[14]

TABLE 10.2 Germany: Key Data (in DM billion)*

	1989	1990	1991	1992	1993
Exports	640	660	666	671	†629
Imports	506	556	645	638	†568
Trade balance	134	105	21	33	61
Current account	108	75	−32	−34	−33
M1 (Growth rate)	6.2	29.6	3.4	10.8	8.5
M3	5.7	19.7	6.3	7.6	10.9
Private saving (% of personal income in West Germany)	13.5	14.7	14.5	13.9	13.3
Prices (1985=100)					
Overall CPI (only West Germany)	104.2	107.0	110.7	115.2	119.9
Services (only West Germany)	109.9	112.6	116.5	122.9	130.8
Services/CPI (only West Germany)	105.5	105.2	105.2	106.7	109.1
Predicted Regression Results		106.5	107.5	108.4	109.3
Services/CPI = *−1777.38 + 0.947 (year) + 0.00012*					
(t = −6.97) (t = 7.37) (P = 7.83E-05)					
R^2 *(adj.) = 0.87, F = 54.34*					

Source: Deutsche Bundesbank, monthly reports and own estimations.

* West and East Germany combined since July 1990

† break in time series due to statistical revisions

However, given that the German capital market is open to the rest of the world, most of the capital will come from the rest of the world (hence the lower external surpluses). As long as the East German economy is in the factor-price-equalisation region, movements of goods and factors can equalise prices, and, consequently, there is again no need for a change in the relative price of (West) German exports relative to its imports.

THE EFFECTS OF UNIFICATION ON GERMANY'S EXTERNAL ACCOUNTS

During the first quarter of 1991, Germany's current account went into deficit for the first time since the early 1980s, by DM 32 bn for the entire year 1991. As suggested by our rough calculations, unification thus had a profound effect on Germany's external accounts even without a real appreciation of the DM. It is, of course, impossible to determine exactly the source of the increased demand for imports in Germany; but a useful approximation can be obtained with the procedure detailed in Box 10.1.

Box 10.1 Estimation of the unification effect on imports

To assess the unification effect on the trade account we proceeded as follows:

1 Estimate the demand for imports of the Federal Republic up to 1989 (explanatory variables: real exchange rate and domestic demand).
2 Use the estimated coefficients and the available data on the determinants of (West German) imports to forecast the demand for imports for the years after unification.
3 Take the difference between the actual and the forecast values for imports and attribute this difference to unification.

The result of this procedure can be seen in Fig. A which displays the actual values of West German imports and the actual values of total German imports (available only since July 1990) as well as the forecast obtained from a simple import demand equation.* This forecast uses actual values of total domestic demand for West Germany and the actual real exchange rate of the DM.

Unification has not affected substantially the relative prices faced by West Germans (within the EMS exchange rates did not change at all, and the dollar moved down and up without any major net change between 1989 and 1991). There is therefore no reason why West Germans should change their spending on imports. The solid line in the graph displays the import demand projected for West Germany. The difference between the solid line and the actual values can therefore be imputed to imports going to East Germany, either directly or indirectly via West Germany. However, since it is irrelevant whether the imports used in the East go first through West Germany (e.g. through West German retailers) this distinction is not pursued any further.

continued

Box 10.1 *continued*

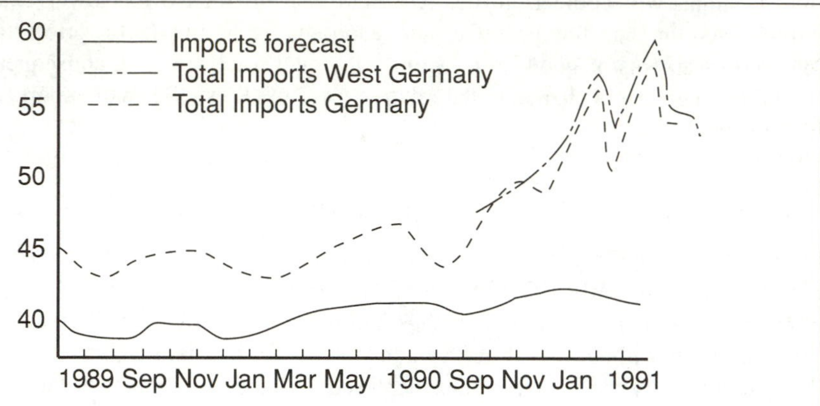

FIG A The effects of unification on German import demand

Figure A shows that the actual import values start to diverge considerably from the forecast in early 1990. By the end of that year the difference between actual and forecast West German imports reaches about 10 bn DM per month. This suggests that unification has a large effect on import demand which goes well beyond the indirect effect coming from the boom in West Germany since the latter can explain only a small part of the actual increase in imports.

It is also apparent from Fig. A that a large residual would remain even if one assumed that income in the five new *Länder* was about 10 per cent of West German income since that would increase the forecast values for imports only by about 10 per cent, from about 40 to 44 bn DM per month (income elasticity is about 1). Actual imports are, however, almost 20 per cent higher than one would expect given the past relationship between imports and domestic demand in West Germany.

* In this equation monthly import value(s) are determined by domestic nominal demand and the real exchange rate, using data from February 1979 to December 1989.

Another interesting issue that can be elucidated with this method is to what extent the increase in German imports benefits its partners in the European Community. The increase in German interest rates has forced other EMS participants to raise domestic interest rates as well. This is felt as a burden by Germany's European partners, but one should set the increase in German imports against the interest rate effect.

The beneficial effects of unification on Germany's EC partners can be estimated by applying the method of Box 10.1 to the demand for imports coming from outside the Community. This is done in Gros (1991) who finds that the residuals for non-EC imports are close to DM 4 bn on average for the last quarter of 1990 and early 1991. This suggests that about one half of the additional imports caused by unification come from outside the Community (and the other half from partner countries inside). One would have expected such a distribution anyway given that about one half of German imports come from the Community.[15]

The shift in the German import demand function has one important policy implication: it confirms our view that there is no need for an adjustment of exchange rates within the EMS (and against the dollar) to reduce the German current account surplus. See also Gros and Steinherr (1990c).

Import (and export) demand functions are certainly not the only, or even the main factors that determine the exchange rate. But our findings nevertheless support the view that the German external position can undergo large swings without requiring large exchange rate adjustments.

The large shifts of demand within united Germany require large shifts of relative prices within Germany. These are possible (at least in one direction) since, due to the exceptional circumstances, wages can move independently in the two regions of the German monetary union. The need for a change in the relative price of goods produced in one part of Germany (the western part) relative to the price of goods in the rest of Europe will be minor.

3. Privatisation: the initial options

In Chapter 8 it was argued that private ownership as such neither guarantees economic efficiency nor is it socially desirable *per se*. More important is the specification of property rights and their enforceability. In former socialist countries two further considerations are crucial: the speed with which ownership rights are distributed and the social acceptability of their distribution in the initial stages.

Germany opted for an approach in which ownership of close to 8,000 firms and *Kombinate* (large multi-enterprise groups) was transferred to a holding company (the Treuhand Agency) whose task consisted of selling them off on the proviso that 'excessive' unemployment should be avoided. The THA therefore pursued the dual objective to restructure before privatisation.

Historic examples of ownership structure can usefully be grouped into four stylised classes: a 'colonial' regime where assets are predominantly owned by foreigners; state or 'social' ownership, as was the case in the old GDR; direct ownership by residents and non-residents, as has been the case in West Germany; or indirect ownership through intermediaries such as unit trusts to whom investment choices and managerial control are entrusted. An effort has been made by the THA to attract investors in West Germany and other countries with the aim of arranging shareholdings, joint ventures or takeovers. As there is very little scope for sell-outs to East German residents, the approach came uncomfortably close to a 'colonial' system which is deeply resented by East Germans.

A further issue which had not been tackled head-on was raised by the implicit social contract of the old GDR. Presumably social ownership of the means of production meant that the state managed productive assets but that these belonged to the people. Even if one rejects this concept, it may not be wise to dismiss the substance of such a social contract completely. Of course, against initial expectations, the THA ended up with a net loss covered by the Bonn government, which in addition provides financial transfers to German citizens in the East. But the latter will not hold extensive ownership of the territory's productive assets and are not able to value transfers as a compensation for the region's sell-out.

On the operational side, the THA had great difficulty in making rapid headway towards privatisation. It had been a Herculean task to evaluate 8,000 firms in an environment characterised by profound structural change. Either the job was to be done somewhat superficially or it would take a very long time. Neither option appeared attractive. We therefore strongly believe that an alternative solution should have been given serious consideration.[16] This would have consisted in distributing ownership of the capital stock (state-owned houses and productive assets) to citizens, as discussed in Chapter 8.

To begin with, the ownership of housing could have been transferred to occupants. Rents could have continued to be paid for, say, 10 years and they would be considered as instalments towards the acquisition price. They could have been indexed to average wage rates and therefore risen only in line with purchasing power. Houses could have been bought and sold but ownership rights would have to be forfeited in the event of emigration. Instead of following this simple and socially attractive approach, public sector housing is now to be sold.[17] If something better than a shambles is to be sold some DM 50 bn – DM 300 bn need to be invested first. As this expenditure was not included in the initial budget provisions, funding is still uncertain. Had this property simply been given away – in its run-down state – there is reason to believe that the occupant-owners would have used some of their under-employed time to renovate their homes.

Second, the same system could have been applied to the agricultural sector, with co-operatives (*Genossenschaften*) free to split up or stay together.

Third, individual and small firms could have been turned over to their present managers and workers, who would have continued to pay taxes and rents to acquire the buildings.

Fourth, most of the Kombinate, or holding companies, now in the THA portfolio would have been turned into joint-stock companies. Some would have been sold to non-East German residents when technological modernisation, economies of scale or the acquisition of marketing and management skills could not be achieved in any other way. For the remainder, each Kombinat would have issued a number of shares equal to the number of citizens with voting rights. Each citizen would have received one share in each Kombinat and hence a highly diversified portfolio of the economy of the former GDR. The value of these shares need not have been known *a priori*: they would have been distributed freely. In this way collective ownership would have acquired a concrete meaning if only at the end of the socialist experience. Such shares would be tradable. Their current book value might not amount to much, but after restructuring the present value of future earnings could be a multiple for at least some of them. Therefore there is an incentive for holding on to them.

With such widespread share-ownership, all citizens of the former GDR would overnight have become 'capitalists', an objective actively pursued in West Germany – without, however, complete success. Few people invested in stocks in the late 1940s but those who did have never regretted it, nor would they have regretted staying where they were.

4. The Treuhand approach to privatisation

The THA was a state agency founded in March 1990 when the Modrow government was still in power. Originally, the THA was inadequately staffed (600 employees) for its historically unprecedented task of transforming a formerly centrally planned economy into a free market economy. By the end of October 1991 its staff had increased to about 3,000. The THA was assigned an initial stock of 7,894 enterprises, that increased to close to 13,000 after many of the large conglomerates had been split up into smaller units. This split-up was a step in the right direction as synergies were low in most Kombinate. For theoretic back-up and some empirical evidence, see Aghion *et al.* (1994).

Progress on privatisation was slow to start with. One of the main impediments was the legal decision in the Unification Treaty to favour restitution in kind over monetary compensation. The absence of any clearly defined ownership status hindered the privatisation process and inhibited new investments. The THA could not dispose of assets as long as it had not been elucidated who would put in a legitimate claim on the assets. The government addressed the issue again and abolished the absolute priority of return of expropriated property over compensation.[18]

The THA's chief mission was to restructure and privatise East German firms or, if this was not feasible, to close them down. In effect therefore, it was responsible for the most important aspect of unification. Although the importance of its task was generally accepted, opinions have varied as to the THA's strategy, the speed of the process and, closely related to this, the importance of restructuring first and privatising later. As to the latter, the much debated question was whether the THA could optimally redesign firms or whether that decision already needed to emerge from competitive forces.

One avowed goal was to complete the privatisation process rapidly. Even that goal did not remain unchallenged. The main arguments against rapid privatisation were that it would lead to lower sales revenues owing to the large supply shock[19] and to mass unemployment given both that the new private owners would be loath to keep on the supernumerary workforce and that restructuring starts in earnest after privatisation. High unemployment in East Germany is for a large part the harvest of low productivity, and privatisation merely brings to the surface the widespread inefficiency which for years was kept in the dark through subsidies and price distortions. But the question remains whether a slower pace in selling off industrial assets, or an altogether different approach, would not have mitigated the sharp fall in employment.

Arguments in favour of restructuring prior to privatisation include the difficulty of selling off large conglomerates. It is likewise argued that they need to be split up in order to create a competitive market structure. Neither argument is convincing. If a conglomerate is not profitable, then disintegration would take place via the market. A 'raider' would observe that the value of the sum of parts exceeds the value of the conglomerate and buy it, break it up and sell the parts. International competition and anti-trust law will do the rest. So the only vindication for maintaining the state in an active role is not market failure but the legitimate political resolve to control and cushion the social repercussions of the restructuring process.

Thus privatisation in East Germany was designed as a two-stage process. In the first stage, enterprises were spun off conglomerates and transformed into corporations with the legal form either of a joint-stock company or of a limited liability company. This step was completed on 1 July 1991, when all firms which had not yet been so transformed were commercialised by law. Supervisory boards were set up during that first stage, providing a vital channel for the transfer of management know-how. By the end of October 1991 about 3,600 business people from the West sat on such supervisory boards as shareholder representatives, and those with experience of Western business methods made up 91 per cent of chair people.

The next step was to establish opening balance-sheets in DM for these companies. Difficulties arose in evaluating the assets due to distortions in the product markets and to the lack of operative markets for financial assets of East German firms. Liabilities included old debts that were not related to firms' performance in the past but were rather the result of political decisions. Since the firms often had higher liquidation values (real estate) than on-going valuation, case-by-case assessment of the balance-sheets and of the potential viability of firms was a necessity. Adjustments had to be made for the liabilities incurred under the old regime (writing-off of the *Altkredite*) in order to provide the minimum equity needed to give potentially profitable enterprises a chance of survival.

When all these time-consuming preparations had been completed, the actual selling could start. By and large, the THA opted for inviting public offers. Bidders were asked to produce a future business scheme complete with investment plans and information on the number of employees to be kept on the payroll. The THA then entered into negotiation with the bidders who, if agreement was reached, had to guarantee a certain level of investment and employment. In general, bidding was open to a large group of potential investors both domestic and foreign, individual and corporate.

After some initial foot-dragging, the privatisation process in East Germany gained momentum in the second half of 1991 and achieved substantial results. Employment in state-owned enterprises assigned to the privatisation agency has fallen significantly. By September 1994 about 100,000 out of an initial 4.05 million people were still working in 350 THA enterprises that had not yet been sold, of which 21 enterprises are large companies with more than 1,000 employees. And by 1995 the THA had been closed.

Most enterprises have been sold to investors from West Germany and only about 850 passed into foreign hands. Management buy-outs (MBOs) have also played a considerable role, especially in the case of companies with fewer than 500 employees. In support of MBOs, the THA pushed through an initiative to promote small and medium-sized enterprises (Initiative Mittelstand) and also promoted management buy-ins (MBIs) in order to attract managers with restructuring expertise.

The privatisation process gained speed after a slow start as teething problems were overcome and a better-oiled organisational structure emerged, yet an abiding difficulty was that of the 'leftover' companies. For some time the question was much debated: what would THA do with companies that simply could not find a buyer? The danger of an expensive and inefficient subsidy policy for the preservation of obsolete industries was clearly seen. The agency had little option but to close such firms or else provide financial support, usually in the form of bank credit, which means that when all is said and done the federal government is liable for the debts. Since opposition to liquidation was strong in East Germany and particularly in the affected 'company towns', the THA was exposed to strong political pressure and had to delay inevitable decisions or even to preserve inefficient structures. But the THA resisted this political pressure to some extent and by September 1994 had closed down 3 600 firms and over 8,000 were privatised. Purchasers provided job guarantees for 1.5 million jobs and for investments of over DM 200 bn.[20] Sales revenues to the THA amounted to DM 65 bn (by September 1994).

To summarise the pros and cons of the THA approach it is useful to have at least an order of magnitude of the costs involved. Much of this cost is contained in the THA opening account statements presented in October 1992. This statement is summarised in Table 10.3. The delay in establishing an integrated statement is understandable considering the great size of the task entrusted to it. And indeed the margin of error is probably quite considerable, no matter how much care was taken by the THA.

At first sight the bottom line result is shocking: the entire net worth of the former GDR is negative and put at DM 209 bn.[21] Conceptually, it is not immediately obvious how one can arrive at a negative net worth for an economy that produced enough to give its citizens an average *per capita* income roughly equal to that of Spain.

Several reasons can be given to explain that negative net worth. First, as argued in Chapter 2, socialist economies paid very little heed to negative environmental impact. Certain plots on industrial sites can only be sold under (West) German law if cleaned up or suitably restored first.

Second, many firms produced negative value-added if assessed at undistorted prices. These firms have become worthless, as have those whose products cannot weather Western competition almost at any price (the Trabant epitomises this case).

Third, since the federal government refused to cancel enterprise liabilities, soft loans were transformed into hard loans. The THA took over enterprises inclusive of their debts and guaranteed reimbursement. Those who gained in the end were the East German banks, whose loan portfolios were rehabilitated so that they became attractive take-over prospects for West German banks. Bank liabilities to depositors were converted into DM either at a rate of 1:1 or at 2:1, whereas assets were mostly converted at 2:1. But they were compensated for that loss so that the banking system faced no difficulties.

Fourth, most enterprises were under-capitalised as net worth played no significant role in the socialist system. The THA took over their debts and recognised compensation claims arising from the currency reform, so that the total initial infusion of capital amounted to DM 55 bn. Even with this infusion the initial net value of all THA enterprises amounted to only DM 78.9 bn.

The opening statement recognises that additional outlays are necessary to sell firms, some even at negative prices. First of all, loss-making enterprises require financial support until they are sold or closed. Provisions for restructuring and disposing of the assets were put at DM 215 bn, much more than the enterprises are worth. In addition, the THA provided for various legal obligations amounting to DM 51 bn.

DM 45 bn were earmarked for the closure and disposal of enterprises. That was over-optimistic, as the quality of the THA portfolio declined rapidly and as strong regional impacts were already fuelling massive political opposition to closures or lay-offs. In late 1992 the federal government revised its initial objective of either privatising or closing down enterprises in East Germany. Yielding to social pressure, it was agreed to preserve 'core' enterprises in state-backed industrial holdings, if they could not be privatised until the end of 1994 but stood a good chance of survival after restructuring. Surely, this was the beginning of political concessions whose outcome risked the fate of the Italian IRI.

The THA wound up its operations at the end of 1994 with a total debt in excess of DM 270 bn. Its successor institutions act as public sector caretakers, like the IRI in Italy, with all the protracted inefficiencies and high costs this entails. In this sense the

THA record is incomplete as some of the most difficult cases were left unsettled and require continued state support. However, privatisation and closures have reduced the portfolio of loss-making firms to a level that is manageable.

5. Reconstruction and its cost

The most striking feature in the restructuring process in East Germany has been the sharp decline in production and employment, a decline far more pronounced than in other former socialist countries which have not opted for a big bang. By way of partial compensation East Germany has been spared the monetary instability that has beset other countries on the road to reform. For comparison, see Chapters 11 and 14.

Yet the fact that production has fallen more drastically in East Germany than elsewhere is not in itself evidence that the 'cold turkey' approach used in Germany is bad. See Box 10.2. After all, the East German economy may be expected to complete its overhaul and to re-equip itself both more thoroughly and more speedily than other countries which adopted a more gradual course.

TABLE 10.3 Opening balance-sheet of THA for 1 July 1990

Assets	Mill.DM	Liabilities	Mill. DM	Mill. DM
A. Assets transferred through unification treaty and Treuhand law		**A. Provisions**		
I. Corporate shares	78,909	I. Restructuring provisions		215,296
II. Mining	1,387	1. financing costs to rebuild net worth	30,573	
III. Agriculture and forestry	16,063	2. privatisation	121,082	
IV. Other	5,772	3. closures	44,723	
V. Claims on Treuhand enterprises	11,844	4. transfer to communal ownership and reprivatisation	18,918	
		II. Provisions for ownership claims		12,981
		III. Provisions for value compensation clause		14,950
		IV. Provisions for interest guarantees		17,535
		V. Other		6,504
B. Other assets of Treuhand	256	**B. Liabilities**		
		I. Bank liabilities		39,893
		1. old liabilities	38,493	
		2. other	1,400	
		II. Liabilities to Treuhand enterprises		16,363
C. Negative net worth	209,291			
Total	323,533	**Total**		323,522

Box 10.2 The welfare implications of the speed of reform

Conceptually, and neglecting other arguments in the social welfare function such as inflation, the objective of liberalisation and reform is to minimise the integral over time of the difference between potential output (at the level of Western productivity) and actual output less service on external debt and transfers received, all properly discounted. Figure A illustrates the conceptual framework.

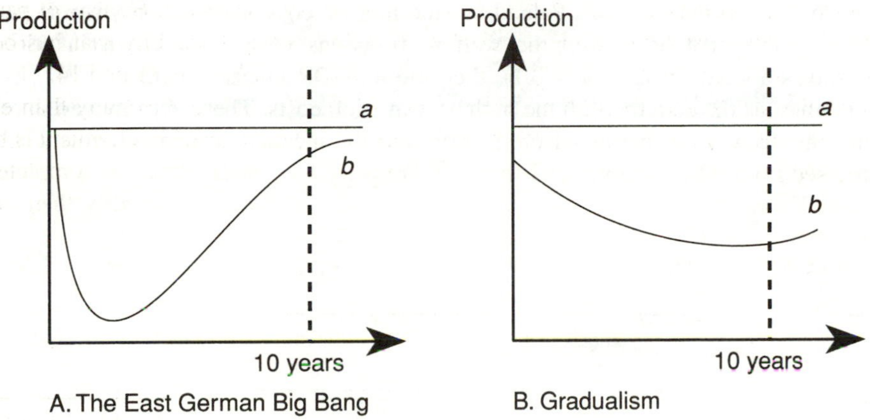

FIG A Social cost of big bang v. gradual reform

The relevant social cost in East Germany as compared to more gradual reforms is very high at the beginning but hopefully lower in the long run. It is augmented by more rapid debt accumulation (not shown in the graph). Whether the discounted integral of the surface between the base-line projection ('full employment') of curve *a* and the actual path *b* is smaller or larger for a big bang approach as compared to a more gradual approach remains to be seen over time. In addition, the base-line itself is likely to be higher if reforms are tackled more robustly than when they are more gradual.

To gain an order of magnitude of the welfare loss caused by the reform process, inclusive of monetary instability, this loss is computed with a social welfare function of the form:

$$U = \sum_t (1/(1+r))^t U_t \qquad [1]$$

where $$Ut = -1/2\,[(\log R_t/R_{89})^2 + \phi\,(\log P_t/P_t - 1)^2\,] \qquad [2]$$

U is the present value in 1989 of the welfare losses caused by reforms in the form of temporary reductions in real activity (R) and consumer price inflation ($P_t/P_t - 1$). The period chosen, 1990–93, covers the most costly years and neglects the future gains to be realised. U is therefore closer to the cost of transition than the discounted welfare gains of reforms. The discount factor retained is

continued

Box 10.2 *continued*

r = 0.05. The yearly welfare cost is given by equation [2] which takes into account real activity and inflation weighted by the factor ϕ. For real activity the decline from the 1989 level is taken for each year; for inflation the annual inflation rate. Results are reproduced in Table A below for two values of ϕ and three measures of real activity: fall in GDP, fall in industrial production and increase in unemployment.

The results suggest that during 1990–93 the cost of transition has been highest in Poland and the ex-GDR. Poland has the highest cost of transition when inflation is weighted heavily in the welfare functions (ϕ = 1.4). When inflation receives a small weight (ϕ = 0.1), then the ex-GDR emerges with two activity variables as the country with the highest transition costs. These activity variables are the decrease in industrial production and the increase in unemployment, as revised from official figures in Table 10.6 below.

TABLE A Welfare losses in five countries

	Hungary	Czech Republic	Slovak Republic	Poland	ex-GDR
ϕ = 0.1,					
R = GDP	−0.013	−0.012	−0.011	−0.047	−0.037
R = Industrial Production	−0.025	−0.033	−0.038	−0.083	−0.299
R = Unemployment	−0.0053	−0.002	−0.006	−0.043	−0.006 off. −0.056 rev.
ϕ = 1.4,					
R = GDP	−0.039	−0.037	−0.041	−0.536	−0.041
R = Industrial production	−0.051	−0.058	−0.069	−0.572	−0.302
R = Unemployment	−0.032	−0.027	−0.037	−0.532	−0.009 off. −0.060 rev.

To obtain orders of magnitude for the convergence problem, Table 10.4 provides a synopsis of the national income accounts for East Germany in 1991, that is, when the new institutional framework was already in place and restructuring had already advanced the 'destruction phase' but without much progress in 'reconstruction' and in 1993. The share of East German GNP (7.4 per cent) in total German GNP in 1991 is only one-third of the share of the labour force (19.7 per cent), suggesting a productivity level one third of the West German level. The share of domestic absorption is close to 13 per cent, nearly double the share of GNP, thanks to transfers received. East German private consumption is only a little less than GNP so that transfers pay for public sector consumption and gross investment. Not a meagre deal. The structure of production is also markedly different. The public sector is twice as important in the East as in the West, while services and manufacturing are proportionately less important. Manufacturing bears the brunt of the restructuring effort, whereas services were under-developed during the years of socialism.

TABLE 10.4 National income accounts for East Germany in 1991 and 1993 (in 1991 prices)

	1991	1993	1991	1993
	(billion DM)		% of Germany	
GNP by source				
Agriculture	7.1	7.8	17.1	17.7
Manufacturing	76.3	91.9	7.1	9.1
Commerce and transport	29.9	34.2	7.2	8.1
Other services	45.9	56.1	5.5	6.1
Public sector, housing	44.2	47.7	12.8	12.1
Other	5.6	5.8	–	-
GNP	214.0	243.5	7.4	8.5
GNP by use				
Private consumption	179.6	202.3	11.0	12.0
Public sector consumption	87.7	92.6	15.3	16.1
Gross investment	92.1	134.2	14.2	20.6
of which: - Equipment	41.8	48.8	13.7	19.0
- Buildings	50.3	85.4	14.4	21.6
External balance	−152.3	−199.2	–	–
Domestic absorption	360.0	429.1	–	–
Gross wage incomes	157.7	202.5	12.0	14.1

Source: Jahresgutachten 1993/94

Turning to the uses of GNP, it is striking to note the more than proportional and rising share of public sector consumption and the rapid rise of the investment share. Overall investment was over 60% of GNP and investment in equipment amounted to over 20% of GNP. Both ratios are about three times higher than in the old *Länder*. This is the key for the rapid growh the ex-GDR area is now experiencing. East Germany is clearly set on a path calculated to make living conditions more agreeable than would have been the case without external support, and on a path of all-out investment effort and convergent productivity levels.

EMPLOYMENT AND PRODUCTION: AN UNPRECEDENTED DECLINE

Following economic and monetary union between the two Germanys, industrial production and GDP in the East collapsed when the Eastern industry was exposed overnight to Western competition after years of isolation. Part of the collapse occurred in the first half of 1990 in anticipation of the opening-up of trade and the freedom of Eastern citizens to choose between Western and Eastern goods. It was unprecedented both in comparison with developments in Central and Eastern Europe in the period 1989–91 and with the slump in German industrial production during the Great Depression of the 1930s (Tullio *et al.* 1994). Industrial production in East Germany fell by 28 per cent in 1990 and by a further 30 per cent in 1991. By comparison, the fall in industrial production in Poland, Czechoslovakia and Hungary during this period was only about 25 per cent.

Most pronounced was the decline in the production of investment goods (from 100 in 1990 to 48 in 1992), a sector in which the East German industry, like its West German counterpart, had been highly specialised. A prime reason for that decline was the collapse of CMEA exports. Total exports fell by 56 per cent during 1990–91 alone (see Table 10.5), and three quarters of that drop were due to the decline in CMEA trade. That means that about one third of the fall in industrial production was caused by the decline in export demand and two thirds by the shift in domestic demand away from home-produced to foreign products.

Table 10.5 summarises the changes in East Germany's foreign trade. The first column gives the overall external deficit, including trade with West Germany. The total external deficit in 1993 was close to DM 200 bn or 80 per cent of GNP – a proportion unknown for independent countries which face an external borrowing constraint. This is clearly one of the advantages of currency union.

As the new *Länder* have maintained a trade surplus with respect to the rest of the world (DM 3.2 bn in 1994, which is small in relation to the overall deficit of DM 200 bn), the deficit with the old FRG is in fact even higher than the overall deficit. Clearly the old FRG alone finances all the current account deficit of the new *Länder*.

Also noteworthy is the fact that trade with the countries of the European Union (other than West Germany) has remained stable. This is very different from the experience of other former socialist economies (see Chapter 16) which have more than replaced lost CMEA trade with massive increases in trade with the European Union.

The collapse of production in East Germany in 1989-91 is unprecedented by peacetime standards, both in scope and in speed. The industrial production index reached its nadir in the course of 1991 and levelled out in 1992,[22] before climbing back in 1993. GNP growth, by contrast, picked up in 1992 (9.7 per cent), suffered only little during the slump year 1993 (6.5 per cent) and increased sharply in 1994 (9 per cent).

Despite the rebound in GNP, unemployment remained at record levels in 1992 and 1993. Official unemployment increased from 11.7 per cent in 1991 to 15.3 per cent in 1992. These figures exclude a large number of part-time workers, workers temporarily subsidised under government programmes (*Arbeitsbeschaffungsmaßnahmen*) and retraining schemes. If these workers are taken into account, the rate of unemployment rose to about 27 per cent in 1991 and 29 per cent in 1992 (Table 10.6).

So, while the official rate of unemployment peaked at about the same levels as during the Great Depression (see Table 10.6), the true unemployment rate reached its nadir at about twice the official level, extensive emigration to West Germany and a spate of early retirements notwithstanding. (In addition between 1990 and 1994 the labour force declined from close to 10 million to 7.8 million.)[23] Despite more

Table 10.5 Exports and imports of the new *Länder* (in DM bn)

	Total foreign trade				EU countries			Former socialist economies		
	External deficit*	Exports	Imports	Trade balance	Exports	Imports	Trade balance	Exports	Imports	Trade balance
1990	-	38.1	22.9	15.2	2.9	2.7	0.2	29.8	14.9	14.9
1991	−152.3	17.5	10.9	6.6	3.0	2.3	0.7	11.4	6.1	5.3
1992	−190.0	13.8	9.6	4.2	3.2	2.5	0.7	7.2	4.6	2.6
1993	−199.0	11.9	8.7	3.2	1.9	2.6	−0.7	6.2	3.9	2.3

Source: Jahresgutachten 1994/95

* Current account deficit, including the deficit with West Germany

generous unemployment subsidies, widespread unemployment – which falls disproportionately on young entrants to the job market – measured against the high hopes raised by reunification has triggered despair and bitterness. The ugly right-wing violence that is staining Germany's post-unification image and straining foreign observers' tolerance may find at least a partial explanation in this fact.

As was argued above, unification rapidly endowed East Germany with Western institutions. All in all, this was a considerable advantage, but, as illustrated by the high share of public sector consumption of GDP, these institutional transfers may also represent high costs. Some of the institutional exports of the ex-FRG are better suited to a mature, rich Western economy and are totally inappropriate for the developing East. It is very unlikely that certain Asian countries would have grown into the tigers they have if they had adopted German labour laws and regulation and had been run by the German bureaucracy.

But arguably the biggest problem has been the political promise of a rapid convergence of living standards. The sharp rise in real wages in the East was to a significant extent to blame for this development on the Eastern labour market. Gross nominal wages in industry rose from 35 per cent of West German levels in July 1990 to 60 per cent by the end of 1992 and 70 per cent in 1993.

The increase in nominal wages is only one side of the coin. Producers are concerned with real wage costs, that is, gross nominal wages deflated by producers' prices, while workers are eager to increase their real wage income, that is, net wages deflated by consumer prices. The remarkable fact in East Germany is that consumer prices have increased by more than 30 per cent between 1990 and 1992, so that gross real wage income has grown by some 40 per cent (but also wage taxation has increased). Producers had to face higher nominal wages *and* rapidly falling prices for their products (on average by about 40 per cent since unification). The real wage cost has therefore more than tripled between 1990 and 1992.

TABLE 10.6 Employment and the unemployment rate in East and West Germany: 1989–92 (as a percentage of the labour force) and in Germany: 1928–32 (annual averages)

	East Germany			West Germany		Germany	
	Employment (millions)	Official unemployment (%)	Total unemployment*	Employment (millions)	Unemployment	Unemployment 1929–32**	
1989	9.7	n.a.	n.a.	27.6	7.6	1929	5.8
1990	8.9	7.3	n.a.	28.5	6.9	1930	9.7
1991	7.3	11.7	26.9	29.0	6.1	1931	14.3
1992	6.5	15.3	28.9	29.1	6.5	1932	17.6
1993	6.3	15.9	23.6	28.7	8.1		
1994	6.2	14.6	21.7	28.3	9.4		

Source: Jahresgutachten 1993 und 1994 des Sachverständigenrats

* Includes short-time workers, workers temporarily subsidised by the government (*Arbeitsbeschaffungsmaßnahmen*) and workers involved in retraining programmes

** Source: Institut für Konjunkturforschung, *Konjunkturstatistisches Handbuch, 1933* and Sommariva and Tullio (1987)

In order to understand the damaging and unfortunate effects on employment and industrial production of real wage trends in the East, several factors must be borne in mind. First, in post-war West Germany the government has traditionally not interfered with wage bargaining, which it largely considers to be a private matter between workers and company representatives. However, by fixing a quick return to wage parity between East and West Germany as a key policy objective, government has given the wrong signal and seriously interfered with the wage bargaining process. The Bundesbank had made it known that it disagreed. And it was right to do so.[24] Second, wage negotiations in the East have not been comparable to wage negotiations in a market economy, where owners-entrepreneurs have an interest in defending profit margins and their company's value. Corporate governance and hard budget constraints only become operative after privatisation. Third, members of West German trade unions were seconded to the 'inexperienced' trade unions in the East while they were also on the board of the then state-owned enterprises, so that they were to a great extent 'bargaining' with themselves. Fourth, trade unions in the West had and still have a vested interest in a rapid increase in Eastern wages in order to protect real wages and employment in the West. The same vested interest can be attributed to West German industry whose prime objective is and was the conquest of maximum market shares in the East.

Curiously enough, the federal government (like West German taxpayers and East German unemployed) has fallen victim to its own 'soft budget constraint'. Most jobs in the East have been at risk. If unemployment benefits are positively related to wages prior to dismissal, workers have an incentive to press for higher wages even if this increases the likelihood of bankruptcy or accelerates closure. Moreover, if THA has no firm budget constraint and can increase subsidies as losses mount, it has little incentive to resist aggressive wage claims. All the less so when rapid wage convergence is applauded by government.

To be sure, a high wage differential between East and West Germany could have caused a massive outflow of workers from the East. However, the survey conducted by Akerlof *et al.* (1991) suggests that unemployment is at least as important a factor in triggering emigration as a wide wage differential. Then again, it is not the actual wage differential that causes emigration but rather the expected wage differential (over a number of years) corrected for expected capital gains that workers in the East could have cashed in if a different privatisation policy had been pursued. Such a different policy could have entailed some distribution of shares to residents in the East, as discussed in Section 3.

It is clear that the faster real wages in East Germany are adjusted to those obtaining in West Germany, the larger will be the annual volume of real investment required to bring labour productivity in the East in line with the higher real wage. The criticism that wages in the East were pulled up too fast must be judged against the scheduled official and private investment effort in the years to come. We shall see that the investment effort is very substantial indeed, but unlikely to be sufficient for a rapid convergence of real GNP per capita. It now even appears that the high cost in unemployment might rise over time rather than turn out to be a short-run, necessary evil.

The speed of adjustment of real wages in the East by itself is unlikely to have much effect on investment (as contrasted to the final level of the capital–output ratio), as long as real wages are expected to converge on Western levels in the years to come.[25]

By the time a new project is implemented, convergence will already have taken substantial strides. Investors motivated by low labour costs will choose other locations in Eastern Europe or Asia, not East Germany. East Germany's attraction for investors is totally different: the availability of a disciplined and highly skilled labour force, a tried-and-tested West German institutional framework (with all its faults), expected administrative and infrastructure support, and a rich consumer market (the European Union and for non-tradables a market in the making). The last argument suggests that investors are attracted by the production of non-tradables, such as catering, financial services and the like. And indeed, we find that the most impressive investments have been made in the non-tradable goods sector.

Labour market policies provide important financial support to the unemployed. The total cost of labour market support policies amounted to over DM 29 bn in 1991 and rose to DM 43 bn in 1992. Support of the unemployed (the 'passive' policies or unemployment 'subsidies') represented two thirds of these costs in 1991. The increase in outlays in 1992 entirely benefited the 'active' policies (job creation, education, rehabilitation, vocational training). How effective these policies are remains to be seen. In 1992/93, average productivity in manufacturing in the East was around 30 per cent of West German levels and labour costs in many sectors (e.g. construction) approached those of the United States. But in 1994 increases slowed down and average productivity rose to over 40 per cent of the West German level (with a range from 20 per cent to 86 per cent over industrial sectors). Western trade unions, which have been steadily losing members in their home territory, were quick to recruit in the East, where they won considerable benefits for their new members. Basic wage deals, guaranteeing pay parity with the West by 1995–97, depending on the sector, have been struck in many important industries. How, under those conditions, two million new jobs can be created in the East remains a mystery. Not to be excluded is the prospect of an eastern Germany resembling the Italian Mezzogiorno in everything but the sunny weather.

Although the speed of real wage adjustments in the East may have only little effect on investment, the excess over productivity growth does of course depress the profitability of existing firms and in so doing increases the required transfers from West Germany. High real wages generate higher transfers through various channels. One is the bigger losses of firms financed by the THA; another is rising unemployment resulting from more firms being closed down or from increasing lay-offs; and finally, as unemployment benefits are pegged to wages, they automatically rise as wages go up. A solution is proposed in Section 6.

TRANSFER PAYMENTS: AMOUNTS NEVER SEEN BEFORE

In exploring the comparison with the Italian Mezzogiorno we first look at total transfers to East Germany by the federal government during 1991–93, and then assess the volume of both public and private real investment flows to the East in those years. We then compare these figures with net transfers and investment by the Italian government in the Mezzogiorno to see if there is a lesson to be drawn from that. To some, the 'Mezzogiorno syndrome'[26] is haunting the chosen German policy approach.

Net transfers amounted to DM 128 bn in 1991, to DM 145 bn in 1992, and to DM 176 bn in 1993.[27] These transfers represent 65 per cent of East Germany's GNP in 1991, 65.5 per cent in 1992 and 76.5 per cent in 1993. Even allowing for the fact that GNP in the East has been depressed, these figures are nothing less than extraordinary for sheer size. By way of comparison, net official transfers from the Centre-North to the South of Italy, excluding interest payments on the public debt, amounted to around 31 per cent of Mezzogiorno GDP in 1988 (Micossi and Tullio 1992).[28] The bulk of net transfers from West to East Germany comes from the federal government, the remainder from the *Länder*, the unity fund and others.

By the year 2000 the average income in East Germany is expected to reach 80 per cent of West Germany's. However, *per capita* GNP will only reach 58 per cent of West Germany's, according to the computations of the Institut der Deutschen Wirtschaft, Cologne, and the difference would be due to transfers.[29] Transfers until the year 2000 would then accumulate to DM 1,700 bn.

The government investment support has significantly contributed to the rapid rise in gross fixed capital formation (GFCF) in the East from DM 92 bn in 1991 to DM 156 bn in 1994, or from 43 per cent of GNP to 60 per cent of GNP. Two-thirds of GFCF is, however, in buildings and only one-third in equipment. But, even so, *net* productive investments have become extraordinarily high, as amortisation in East Germany represents only 20–25 per cent of GFCF, compared to 60–70 per cent in West Germany. In fact, in 1994 net investments in the new *Länder* are projected at DM 125 bn, equal to two-thirds of West Germany's net investments of DM 186 bn. On a *per capita* basis, net investments in the East in 1994 are three times the level in West Germany. If this trend is maintained, convergence of productivity levels will be achieved rapidly.

To assess the contribution of government support for investments in the East we disaggregate transfers into current transfers and investment expenditures. Spending on infrastructure and private investment subsidies amounted to DM 45 bn in 1991 (about 20 per cent of Eastern GNP or 50 per cent of GFCF) and to DM 55 bn in 1992 (see Deutsche Bundesbank, *Monatsbericht*, March 1992). In 1993 the public sector (including Bundesbahn and Bundespost) invested close to DM 40 bn and a similar amount in 1994. Subsidised funding for regional development amounted in 1993 and 1994 to over DM 30 bn (not including special amortisation provisions and investment subsidies for medium-sized enterprises).[30]

These data compare with public investment expenditures in the Italian Mezzogiorno of only 8 per cent of GDP in 1988. (However, this excludes large investments by government-controlled enterprises, see Micossi and Tullio 1992.) The GFCF–GDP ratio has always been higher in Southern Italy than in the Centre-North (but much lower than the ratio for East Germany). Yet despite that, per capita GDP in the South has been falling behind since 1975 rather than catching up (from just over 60 per cent in 1975 to about 52 per cent in 1988). There is obviously a major problem with the quality of investment choice and spending by government-controlled enterprises in the South and private investment may be distorted by over-generous investment subsidies. In addition, it may be that official investment figures contain a component which has nothing to do with real productive investment: they may be swollen by payments to corrupt government and party officials and organised crime.

Clearly, the Italian example is not one to follow and the rapid rise of net investment in East Germany supports a much more optimistic view. Such a view is further supported by the fact that economic rather than predominantly political returns are looked for in investment – a fact also borne out by the more market-based privatisation policy pursued in Germany – and scant evidence of investment expenditures in Germany being used to finance political parties or organised crime.[31] But the German and EU Court of Auditors both reported very lax financial controls, in 1994–95, over the huge sums involved, citing wholly inappropriate investment projects and unaccounted losses of funds. One-third of expenditure appears to have escaped accounting control, and more than one-tenth cannot be accounted for.

FINANCING RECONSTRUCTION: UNBALANCING GOVERNMENT FINANCES

Turning now to the repercussions of the financing effort on the West German economy, our first stop must be government finances. Table 10.7 shows the sharp rise in public sector debt, including specialised funds (Fonds 'Deutsche Einheit', 'Kreditabwicklungsfonds', EPR-Sondervermögen, Lastenausgleichsfond), the post offices, railways and THA. Overall borrowing was DM 160 bn in 1991 (5.7 per cent of GNP), increasing to DM 207 bn in 1992 (6.6 per cent of GNP). This means that government finances have substantially worsened since 1989, when the West German general government budget deficit (excluding the off-budget items) was only 1.1 per cent of GDP. The West German government's borrowing requirement since 1992 has come close in absolute value to the general government budget deficit of Italy.

Undoubtedly, the higher budget deficit and the uncertainty as to how it will develop, in conjunction with the Bundesbank's determination to control inflation, have led in the past to a substantial increase in real interest rates, particularly at the short end of the market. There can be no question but that this increase has crowded out some private investment both in West and East Germany. Yet as the interest rate elasticity of investment functions is on the low side, this effect is likely to remain marginal. A greater cause for concern is the low proportion of transfers targeted for investment, despite the overall sharp increase in investment outlays.

TABLE 10.7 The consequences of reunification on public sector indebtedness 1989–93, billion DM

	1989	1990	1991	1992	1993
Public debt					
Federal State	490.5	542	586	612	685
Länder and local communities	431.3	453	490	544	604
ERP funds	7.1	10	16	24	28
German unification fund	–	20	51	75	88
Credit settlement fund	–	28	27	92	101
Total	928.9	1,053	1,170	1,345	1,509
Treuhand, postal services, railways	110.3	134	159	251	331
Total					
As a percentage of GNP	1,039.2	1,187	1,329	1,596	1,840
of ex.FRG	46.2	48.5	49.8	56.6	64.7

Source: Bundesbank, monthly reports

THROUGH A LOOKING-GLASS, DARKLY: THE PROSPECTS FOR GROWTH

Before venturing an educated guess concerning the growth prospects for the Eastern part of Germany in the next 10 years or so, it may be useful to look at the recovery of *per capita* GDP in West Germany after World War II. It is instructive to compare the trend *per capita* GDP in West Germany (calculated by applying to real *per capita* GDP in the whole of Germany in 1938 the average annual geometric growth rate recorded from 1880 to 1938, i.e. 1.742 per cent per annum) with the actual real *per capita* GDP from 1948 to 1969. The gap between actual real *per capita* GDP and trend GDP was 40.9 per cent in 1948, caused by wartime destruction, the loss of territories with higher *per capita* GDP, the dislocation of production in the aftermath of war and the monetary disorders of 1945–48. Actual *per capita* GDP exceeded trend GDP for the first time in 1965. Discounting the chaotic years of 1945–47, this simple extrapolation suggests that it took West German real *per capita* GDP almost 20 years to recover from the effects of the war.[32]

In the case of post-Wall East Germany (and using the labour force as the denominator rather than the population as a whole), the gap with respect to West German GDP was 73 per cent in 1991, much wider than the gap in West Germany in 1948. Catching-up theories of economic growth suggest that the wider the gap with respect to the technologically advanced country, the faster catching up can be. With regard to East Germany there are additional reasons for supposing that catching up may be even faster than in West Germany after the war. To begin with, the investment effort now under way (and described above) is far more substantial than it was in West Germany in the years following 1948.[33] Closely related to this point is the fact that East Germany is a relatively small area in relation to the Western part of the country and that the federal government is firmly committed to fast recovery in the East. Otherwise the observed ratios of investment to GDP could never have been achieved. As to capital availability, there is far more capital about in the world now than there was in the 1950s. West Germany, by running down its huge current account surplus, is using the net foreign assets accumulated in previous years. Furthermore, household savings in the East are on the increase and by 1992 they approached 12 per cent or nearly West German levels. It cannot be excluded that household savings will continue to rise as East German residents' stock of wealth is quite low and as employment prospects will remain highly uncertain for several years yet.

The human capital available in East Germany is very high, since the socialist government made education one of its primary objectives. According to Krakowski *et al.* (1992), 10.7 per cent of the East German labour force have university training as compared to 11.6 per cent in West Germany, and only 10.2 per cent have no professional training as compared to 21.1 per cent in West Germany. The East German elite may nevertheless be less productive in a market economy, as over 50 per cent of university graduates were employed in the administration. Although up-to-date technical skills may be lacking where skilled labour is concerned, these can be rapidly acquired with a sound educational grounding. Attitudes may prove more of a problem, as people are required to revert to performance-driven behaviour.[34]

The very scale of emigration from East to West to date will actually help to speed up the catching-up process in terms of GNP *per capita*. This 'safety valve' was not widely available to Germans after World War II, when immigration was not encouraged politically, as all of Europe was in a shambles and unemployment was very high everywhere.

All things considered, therefore, we do not expect catching up to last much more than 10–15 years,[35] if 60–70 per cent of Western *per capita* GNP were an acceptable level.[36] This is also assuming that the government's investment effort continues on about the same scale until the year 2000 and that private investment will gradually take the lead.

Finally, we wish to be very clear on one key point. It is often argued that the terms of the currency union were excessively generous and that the high volume of transfers to East Germany is the price to pay. Implicit or explicit in this view are two further judgements. One is that East Germans received a first gift with currency union and a second one in the form of transfers. The other spins a tale of drastic cuts in the competitive position of the East German economy following currency union and maintains that transfers are needed to keep it alive.

This is plain nonsense. In Section 1 we argued that wage convergence would have occurred anyway, currency union or no, given the institutional integration of labour markets and the government's promises. Furthermore, the overall terms of unification represented no less than spoliation of the East Germans. The only assets East Germans received were some DM 100 bn on their bank accounts. This is close to DM 6,000 a head. In fact, as we argued in Section 3, it would have been fair to treat them as owners of the land, buildings and industries in East Germany. The net worth of these real assets is clearly in excess of DM 6,000 *per capita.*

Another way to ascertain this fact is to use the GNP produced after unification (i.e. after the output shock) and capitalise it. In 1991, East German GNP was DM 193 bn (see Table 10.4). For a capital–output ratio of 2.5, which is average value for industrial countries, the value of the capital stock (neglecting non-economically used land) would be close to DM 500 bn, or five times what East Germans received.

Finally, it needs to be stressed that Germany successfully accommodated net immigration flows of over one million a year during 1989–92, mostly from Eastern Europe. Given the scale of the immigration flow, coupled with the fact that it is proving much more difficult to rebuild East Germany than anticipated, the social unrest and violence which have erupted become much more understandable. However, because immigration pressure is unlikely to diminish – about three million ethnic Germans are expected to return home in the next 10 years[37] – with the painful restructuring process in the FSU and in some parts of Eastern Europe, a deep-seated change in German immigration policy is called for. Germany needs to become more selective in admitting immigrants and its welcome policy of social assistance needs to be scaled down. Likewise it should be prepared to integrate its immigrants more easily and help them take their place in the dynamic section of Germany society.

6. High cost, high risk: can the Mezzogiorno outcome be averted?

Much went wrong in German unification, despite an excellent start. Currency union and its terms were the only reasonable option, but things quickly turned sour afterwards. Rapid wage convergence as championed by the federal government and the unions proved a killer; unemployment and transfers soared. Privatisation by THA progressed swiftly but grew increasingly laborious as enterprise profitability was caught in the scissors movement of rising wages and falling producer prices; the maintenance of production lines increasingly required subsidies and unemployment soared to historic levels. Instead of saving resources elsewhere – subsidies in West Germany by the federal government alone amounted to DM 135 bn in 1991, not counting contributions to the EC budget which help to subsidise agriculture – and trying to cash in a higher peace dividend, the federal government increased taxes in a small way and borrowings in a big way. The Bundesbank felt forced to increase interest rates, which made the financing of Eastern reconstruction even more onerous. Is there still a chance for a 'New Frontier' scenario, a view supported by the massive investment efforts under way and by Siebert (1991) and many others, or is East Germany doomed to become Germany's Mezzogiorno (Hughes Hallett and Ma 1994)?

THE MOST DISTORTED MARKET IS THE LABOUR MARKET

What can be done? To advocate a greater savings effort would be pertinent but trivial. Two solutions stand out, however, as more important. The first is to privatise the housing stock by adopting the give-away approach outlined in Chapter 8. This would help preserve much-needed budget resources which now need to be poured into housing and could help to alleviate the need for direct income subsidies. The other is to deal more effectively with the unemployment problem and the subsidisation of consumption and unemployment.

We argued in Section 1 that currency union established overnight an integrated market for goods and capital. These markets are not without imperfections, in particular owing to the subsidies provided, but these market failures pale in comparison to the situation on the labour market. Excessive growth of real wage costs has created record unemployment, which in turn has necessitated a host of policies to keep the damage at bay, such as support for the unemployed, subsidies to keep unprofitable operations on the road and subsidies to investment.

A question of key importance for policy is whether the excessive real wage growth is due to market failures and if so, what might be the optimal policy response. Clearly, the political ambition to provide East Germans with decent living conditions might call for income support policies but not for employment-destroying increases in real wages. Equally, the political aim of making East Germans stay put has called for a policy to make it more attractive for East Germans to stay where they are but not to the point of distorting factor prices and employment opportunities. Free distribution of assets, as argued in Chapter 8, would have been such a non-distortionary policy. Real wage growth decidedly is not. Likewise, the union-backed wage convergence motivated by the desire to protect West German 'insiders' is creating inefficiencies by forgoing gains from trade and by imposing lower employment on East Germans.

There is, therefore, considerable evidence that it was policy which induced serious market failures (see also the detailed discussion in Begg and Portes 1992). In an ideal world this should not have happened. But since it is unlikely that these policies will be reversed, it makes more sense to ask whether there is no way of doing better.

A case for wage subsidies to correct labour market failures was made by Akerlof *et al.* (1991) and Begg and Portes (1992) and Steinherr and Perée (1991). Akerlof *et al.*, as far back as 1991, proposed a labour cost subsidy of 50 per cent, arguing that only 14 conglomerates employing 8.2 per cent of the East German industrial labour force were viable. We also believe that a policy acting directly on the most serious market failures is the best choice. Market failures exist in labour markets and not in capital markets. What is subsidised, however, is mainly investment and unemployment.

THE CASE FOR WAGE SUBSIDIES

From an efficiency point of view, it may seem counter-productive to subsidise employment. We argued, however, that a large part of unemployment in East Germany is due to excessive wage costs. Forgone output and work-utility, in addition to the psychological hardship and lack of human capital formation on the job for young job seekers, represent costs of such magnitude that one could easily pardon some efficiency losses associated with any employment policy. However, if excessive wages are a major reason for unemployment, then a corrective subsidy would be justified even on efficiency grounds.

Unfortunately, the instinct of policy-makers traditionally favours investment subsidies. This is odd, as capital in East Germany is certainly not overpriced, unlike labour. Of course, with clay-clay technology it does not matter which factor is being subsidised and general production subsidies would do just as well. With less extreme technological assumptions it is still true that demand for both factors of production is stimulated when one factor price declines. But, although there are not many general results in the area of second-best, at least one remarkable and robust result is available: an optimum subsidy ought to be geared directly to the distorted price (see Baghwati and Ramaswami 1963).

A general wage cost subsidy, such as, for example, fiscalisation of employers' social security contributions, was originally proposed by Kaldor (1936), and revamped for application in the ex-GDR by Akerlof *et al.* (1991) and Begg and Portes (1992).[38] The latter propose a universal wage subsidy of 75 per cent in the first year, 50 per cent in the second, 25 per cent in the third and zero thereafter. The great advantage of a universal subsidy is its simplicity of application untainted by moral hazard problems. Such a policy would decrease the real wage cost and the effects on labour demand would be comparable to a reduction in real wage rates. However, the disadvantage of a general subsidy is that its size would be severely limited by its high cost. To the extent that investment and hiring decisions are based on marginal costs, it may be preferable in certain circumstances to limit subsidies to job creation. For a given budgetary cost, the possible subsidy rate is then much higher. A marginal wage subsidy is, however, more difficult to administer as it relies on discrimination between old and new jobs, creates the risk of unfair competition and an incentive to transform an old job into a new one to cash in on the subsidy. One may limit the subsidy to the non-government sector, the industrial sector, or the privatised sector. For the technical analysis see Box 10.3.

If, for cost reasons, a marginal employment subsidy (MES) scheme were preferred, then it should be designed so as to minimise distortions. Among the many options for designing an MES, here is one that seems worth considering: all unemployed workers receive a tradable voucher with a fixed maturity entitling them to unemployment benefits as a percentage of their last wage. This voucher can be sold to a firm against employment or training. The firm then collects the voucher's cash flow from the unemployment insurance.[39] It will set its reservation wage at or below marginal productivity plus unemployment benefits. If the market wage exceeds marginal productivity but falls short of the reservation wage, then a deal will be made. To the extent that there is a shortage of available skills, the voucher value would then also help to finance retraining on the job.

Unemployed workers needing start-up capital to set up a firm may be allowed to sell vouchers to cash in the discounted value of its future cash streams. For an investor the voucher would equal a series of zero coupon bonds and could be an attractive financial instrument if enough liquidity could be generated.[40] As East Germany needs to build up the service industry, the scope for small-scale firms is quite large and the possibility of actually selling a voucher in the capital market would stimulate the creation of new firms. Vouchers have a maturity of, say, three to five years to bridge the worst of the restructuring phase. Their issue may be renewed, but that will depend on the situation then and is therefore *a priori* uncertain.

Not every firm can trade in vouchers. For example, trading may be restricted to private firms to accelerate privatisation. The proposal also implies that firms will prefer to hire an unemployed person rather than one already employed elsewhere. But this should not matter too much: unskilled workers, or workers in need of retraining, are plentiful in the unemployment pool and are of undifferentiated quality. Skilled workers are less likely to be in the unemployment pool and there is therefore not much unfair competition.

Box 10.3 Design of a marginal wage subsidy

Figure A summarises the economics of the proposed MES.*

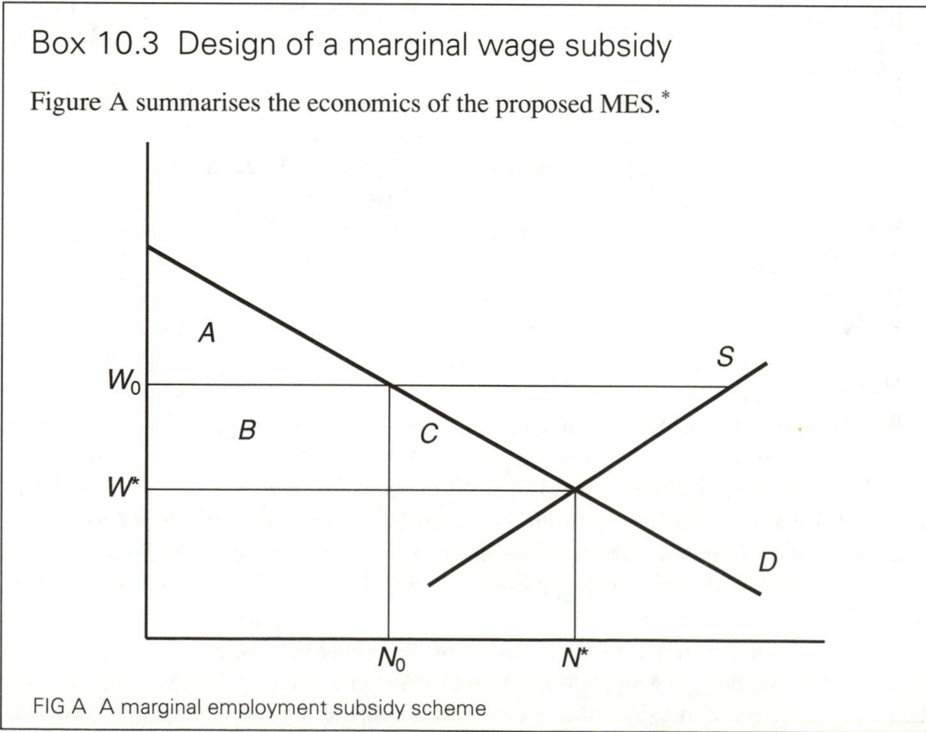

FIG A A marginal employment subsidy scheme

continued

Box 10.3 *continued*

Suppose that the initial employment, N_o , is below full employment, N^*, and the real wage, W_o , is above the full employment wage, W^*. A reduction in wages to W^* is resisted by employed workers and would increase the producer surplus by area B plus area C. If employment above N_o enjoys a subsidy equal to $W_0 - W^*$, then firms would pay W^* for $N^* - N_o > 0$ and their surplus would only increase by area C. All workers would receive W_o so that they would favour this programme (the distinction between wage cost and wage income is neglected here). Financially, this programme is self-supporting if

$$\alpha W_o (N^* - N_o) \leq \beta W_o (N^* - N_o),$$

i.e. $\alpha \leq \beta$, where $\alpha = 1 - W^*/W_o$ (= excess of W_o over W^*) and β = unemployment compensation as share of W_o.

So the system would be self-financing if the excess of the actual wage over the equilibrium wage were not larger than the unemployment benefit as a share of wage costs. Unemployment benefits represent roughly 60 per cent of wage costs and, assuming that the long-run labour demand elasticity is 0.5, this implies that this scheme would finance a subsidy for 30 per cent of the labour force. Note also that if firms were sold, the government would recoup the increase in producer surplus (area C) through higher sales prices.

To prevent lay-offs for rehiring at subsidised rates, there are several possibilities: one consists of giving priority to long stays in the unemployment pool for attribution of vouchers (first-in, first-out). This would also help to cut long stays in the pool. Another would consist of making a trade possible only when the firm augments employment above a level given by, for example, a moving average (say, over three years) of its employment.

If all private firms, old or new, can obtain subsidies for job creation, they are equally treated, at least at the margin. It may, however, be necessary to impose an upper limit on the share of subsidised labour in each firm. Any remaining competitive advantage of new firms can then be regarded as a subsidy for overcoming barriers to entry.

In a survey of employment subsidies in various countries, Steinherr and Van Haeperen (1983) found that in practical experience, subsidies always fall short of having all the following desirable properties.

1. To minimise distortions, subsidies should be granted to all new job creations. In practice, they are often limited to particular industries, regions, or job categories. They therefore only compensate for an existing, relative disadvantage and tend to produce substitutions without a major effect on overall employment.
2. To compensate for uncertainty (generated by stabilisation and restructuring), the subsidy may have to be substantial in size.

continued

Box 10.3 *continued*

3. A subsidy granted for a short period of time (one year or so) will, at best, induce some inter-temporal substitution without additional employment creation over time.

To make new investments worthwhile, firms have to be able to rely on more favourable wage costs for extended periods of time. In Chiarella and Steinherr (1982), the probability of a discontinuation of the programme is initially zero and increases over time. More pragmatically, discontinuation beyond an initial period of several years could be made contingent on labour market conditions, as mentioned above.

* The theoretical aspects, using an optimal control approach, are worked out in Chiarella and Steinherr (1982).

As with any policy designed to alleviate unemployment, this one, too, risks generating increased wage pressure. It might therefore be necessary to reduce this moral hazard problem and to reach an agreement with labour unions before an employment subsidy programme is launched. This agreement would, for example, commit unions to limiting their wage demands in line with (or below) labour productivity increases during the life of the subsidy programmes. On such a basis, all economic activities would be able to plan for the future on the basis of a constrained and roughly predictable wage evolution.

If the MES turned out to be too complicated for application, then the general wage subsidy should be used. Either one would clearly be better than not doing anything or massively subsidising investment. If an employment subsidy was introduced, then subsidies to maintain production and the investment subsidies should be scrapped.

If no radical alternative is adopted[41] to improve the situation in East Germany – through give-away privatisation of the housing stock and a wage subsidy to replace the existing subsidies on the *Gießkannenprinzip* – then there is still a risk of the Mezzogiorno phenomenon in East Germany. In judging this risk, the point made in Chapter 15 that a sustained growth process needs to be based on own rather than external resources needs to be borne in mind. One cannot impose on another country or region a growth path financed predominantly from external funds. This historic constant has too often been ignored in developing countries, in the Mezzogiorno and now in East Germany.

7. Conclusions

German unification is a laboratory case of historic significance for the merging of two societies of very different economic structures and income levels. The Federal Republic opted for a 'big-bang' solution whose stage was set by currency union, privatisation through a state-holding company and income transfers never seen before in history. It is still too early to judge this approach definitively, but several lessons have emerged.

First, currency union was the right decision. It introduced a price reform overnight and opened Eastern Germany to the world capital markets. This chapter has shown that currency union (and the 1:1 conversion rate) by itself should not be held responsible for two problems – high unemployment in Eastern Germany and the turmoils of the European Monetary System in 1992–93 – as is often claimed. High unemployment is the result of an economic structure that needed to be radically changed. Rapid wage convergence certainly did not help but convergence would have occurred anyway under any initial conversion rate as the policy goal of unification demanded by East Germans and supported by West German unions was a convergence of standards of living.

We have also shown that the common argument that currency unification should have necessarily led to a real revaluation of the DM is unconvincing. If anything there should have been a real devaluation of the DM, both in the short and the long term, albeit of a modest dimension. Therefore, what happened to the EMS in 1992–93 was not the result of German unification, but of real misalignments accumulated during 1987–92 and the restrictive monetary policy of the Bundesbank in response to currency unification.

Second, privatisation of the East German economy was entrusted to a state agency with the constraints of a five-year time horizon to finish the job and of paying close attention to employment preservation. The Treuhand Agency completed its task successfully, though it resulted in a sell-out to investors outside Eastern Germany and in a substantial cost to West German tax-payers as the net value of the East German economy turned out close to a *negative* DM 300 bn. We argue in this chapter that an alternative was available, namely to give away to East German citizens the housing stock, rural property, small enterprises and part of the claims on conglomerates. This would also have lessened the need for income transfers.

Third, East Germany is being rebuilt with massive transfers to speed up the convergence of industrial structure. A substantial part of the transfers serves, however, to finance the convergence of living standards. As the Italian experience suggests, such a policy contains substantial risks: transfer fatigue in the taxed population, reduced performance incentives in the assisted population and substantial scope for misuse. All of these signs are also visible in Germany.

A more promising approach would have been to subsidise employment creation to tackle directly the most serious problem of transforming East Germany's economic structure. Indeed, in 1992 unemployment in East Germany exceeded the level reached in Germany during the Great Depression, when official data are adjusted to take into account hidden unemployment. And, despite significant reductions, unemployment remains uncomfortably high in the new Länder.

Will East Germany end up as a 'Mezzogiorno' problem, or will it replicate the US 'new frontier' success? It is too early to tell but most likely the ultimate outcome will be somewhere in between. Some researchers claim that convergence will take a very long time, possibly 35 to 50 years. We think this is too pessimistic and expect about half that time scale. Our main reason for optimism is the massive investment that has taken place in East Germany. As of 1994/95 gross investment per capita was higher in the East than in the West and net investment was several times higher. If this can be maintained East Germany will soon emerge with the most up-to-date capital stock in Europe.

A crisis is always an occasion for change for the better. Germany, under pressure of financing unification, may be able to reduce traditional subsidies, eliminate the excess of the welfare state and thereby create a more flexible environment with greater entrepreneurial incentives. Musil might have said:

> Ein großes Ereignis ist im Entstehen. Aber man hat es nicht gemerkt. (A great event is emerging. But no one has noticed it.)
>
> (*Der Mann ohne Eigenschaften*)

Notes

1. Just how firmly Germans believed in this currency reform is amply illustrated by the following quote from a prominent left-wing politician: 'Die Währungsreform setzt somit nichts voraus, sondern ist selbst die Voraussetzung von allem. Sie muß schnellstens, unbürokratisch und unter Zurückstellung des äußerst komplizierten Kriegslastenausgleichs durchgeführt werden' (Currency reform is not dependent on other measures. Rather it is the precondition for anything else. It needs to be carried out immediately, unbureaucratically and before settlement of the extremely complex compensation of losses caused by the war.) (Leonard Mikisch 1948).
2. This effect is also considered the main potential cost of European monetary union.
3. This section is based on Gros and Steinherr (1990b).
4. The amount finally agreed varied between 2,000 and 6,000 Mark depending on age classes.
5. Dornbusch and Wolf (1992) consider the failure to start off with a clean slate by cancelling enterprise debt as an important mistake.
6. The exact exposure of households is 176 billion plus 17 billion cash minus 23 billion of real-estate credit.
7. This study is correct in its predictions but it attributes appreciation not to currency union and reconstruction per se but to the predicted policy mix. Independently of that, it is interesting to assess the exchange rate effects of integration *per se*.
8. Hughes Hallett and Ma (1994), using the IMF's Multimod multi-country model, conclude '. . . . as a result of unification the DM appreciates and then depreciates more than it otherwise would have done'. The medium-term depreciation by 1997–98 would be stronger than the initial appreciation.
9. If East Germans have the same marginal rate to save and spend on West German and on non-German goods as do West Germans (assumptions which seem close to reality), then the intra-German transfer has no external effect other than via non-tradable goods prices. See Dornbusch (1980: Chapter 3). The massive net transfer of DM 64 billion in 1990, DM 128 billion in 1991 and DM 145 bn in 1992 (see section 5 below) contributed therefore to a real depreciation of the Deutsch-Mark.
10. This argument does not mean that in the case of Germany 'full Ricardian equivalence' applies and that therefore all future taxes are immediately taken into account by consumers. All it implies is that in the present special circumstances the German public is very well aware of the burden on the public finances that will come over the next years. This public awareness, coupled with higher interest rates, should dampen expenditure in West Germany.
11. That is, the West German CPI should increase less. However, the weighted average of the East and West German CPI can be expected to show a much higher inflation rate since wages in East Germany should increase at a faster rate than wages in the West.

12. These crude calculations do not take into account the import content of West German exports into the GDR, which has been estimated to be as high as 40 per cent, implying that each DM of exports from West to East Germany reduces the current account surplus by 0.4 DM. However, preliminary calculations suggest that this effect is more or less offset by the fact that exports from the rest of the Community (and EFTA) contain imports from the FRG.
13. The demand side story takes place implicitly at given factor endowments.
14. Perfect, or instantaneous, mobility of both factors would, of course, lead to instant equalisation of the capital–labour ratio. However, since movements of both factors involve adjustment costs the capital–labour ratio will not be equalised immediately.
15. According to estimates in *American Express Bank Review* (October 1991), the greatest increases in exports due to German import demand in 1990 and 1991 were achieved by the Benelux countries, Austria and Denmark. The contribution of these additional exports to GDP growth has been in excess of 3 per cent of GDP for the Benelux countries, whereas countries in Southern Europe benefited much less.
16. This view is also shared by Dornbusch and Wolf (1992): 'In both the treatment of property rights and the cancellation of debts, the Germans' unwillingness to look forward and let bygones be bygones was a grave mistake.'
17. Some Easterners believed in communist ideology and joined youth brigades and the like to help in building up infrastructure, including housing. They are likely to feel bitter about offers to purchase their homes at reformed prices.
18. Gesetz zur Beseitigung von Hemmnissen bei der Privatisierung von Unternehmen und zur Förderung von Investitionen vom 15.3.1991.
19. Sinn and Sinn (1991) argue that in a once-and-for-all auction of all THA assets the clearing price could approach zero under conditions of imperfect information.
20. Investment and employment pledges turned out to be valueless in the economic downturn of 1993. Frequently the new owners request additional financial support from the THA to compensate for adverse conditions. Fraud has also turned out to be a problem. Some deals about to be closed fell through after demand forecasts were revised. One example is Daimler-Benz's decision to put plans for a DM 1.5 bn truck plant on ice because of higher production costs than initially forecast and because of a downward revision of demand. Other, more labour-intensive activities are earmarked for Central European countries where labour costs are much lower than in East Germany.
21. In 1989, Hans Modrow, the last communist leader of the GDR, put his country's net worth at DM 1.5 trillion. In 1990, his CDU successor, Lothar de Maizière, revised this estimate to the lower value of DM 880 billion. After unification, Detlev Rohwedder, the first head of the THA, gave an estimate of DM 600 billion for the assets on his books. In 1991 he had to admit that assets and liabilities would balance each other. The opening balance sheet net worth of the THA of minus DM 209 billion still falls short of the net worth of minus DM 270 billion in September 1994.
22. Some sectors started to bounce back in 1991, for instance, the construction industry recorded a sharp increase in its order books in the second half of 1991. By mid-1992 production in this industry was 10 per cent up on two years earlier. Orders more than doubled. As a result of excess demand in this non-traded-goods-producing sector, prices nearly doubled from 1989 levels whereas industrial producer prices declined by some 40 per cent. This exemplifies the relative price adjustment in East Germany. The sharp increase of non-traded goods prices relative to traded goods prices is a measure of the revaluation of the DM for East Germans.
23. Arguably, any such comparison between production and employment cutbacks in the ex-GDR following unification and other historic periods needs to be qualified. The Great Depression was chiefly caused by shrinking demand, whereas the problem in the ex-GDR

is one of fundamental structural change. In this respect a comparison with reconstruction after World War II is closer to the mark yet still not directly comparable. After World War II the economy had to rebuild its capital stock but it did not have to catch up with a 20–30-year technological headstart, nor did it have to adjust to an entirely new institutional and motivational set-up. On the positive side, Marshall aid for West Germany amounted to much less than the current transfers to East Germany.

24. The Bundesbank has at times in the post-war period indirectly pursued income policies by threatening interest rate increases if wage negotiations should have a negative impact on inflation, or by postponing interest rate cuts until wage negotiations had been completed. After unification, the Bundesbank increased interest rates and made a reversal of its policy contingent on a reduction in the federal fiscal deficit, and on moderation of wage increases in both parts of Germany.
25. We think it useful to separate two issues: the level of Western wages and the speed of convergence. To an investor it makes little difference whether convergence is realised in five or in seven years. What matters is the convergence goal and the level of wages in West Germany. That wages matter for investment and employment is illustrated by the comparison of the years 1973–82 and 1983–92 (in parentheses) in West Germany in average annual growth rates: unit labour costs 5.5 (2.1), investment 0.4 (5.3), capital–output ratio 4.1 (1.7), employment –0.5 (1.0). Source: Institut der Deutschen Wirtschaft March 1992.
26. This expression is used by various authors concerned by the risk that all the public money poured into East Germany may fail to produce rapid convergence and make East Germany permanently dependent on Western support. In fact, the risk is even greater. Here is our definition of the Mezzogiorno syndrome:
    1. Integration of a less developed region ('the South') with a more developed region ('the North') under the institutional set-up of the latter, thereby imposing an alien cultural and political pattern;
    2. Development of the South with government funds and subsidised investments by the corporations of the North, creating a feeling of dependency in the South;
    3. Lack of convergence, permanent dependency on Northern subsidies and South to North emigration;
    4. Gradual widening of the South's influence in the country's political and administrative system, perpetuating North to South transfers and 'infecting' the North's political culture;
    5. Decline of economic performance of the North due to the fiscal drag of the South and decreasing political support in the North of the South-infected political system.

    Characteristics 1–3 are also characteristics of colonialism. Characteristics 4 and 5 distinguish the 'Mezzogiorno syndrome' from colonialism.
27. Source: Deutsche Bank Research, 'Deutschland-Themen', 15.12.1993 and Bulletin 10.10.94.
28. However, net imports of goods and services were substantially less, averaging 20.8 per cent of GDP in 1970–74 and 19 per cent of GDP from 1975–87. This means that the Mezzogiorno used part of the proceeds from government transfers to export capital to the Centre-North or to the rest of the world. In 1988 this export of capital from the proceeds of government transfers amounted to about 12 per cent in Mezzogiorno GDP. See Micossi and Tullio (1992). The analysis below shows that this perverse effect is not likely to occur in East Germany.
29. These results are obtained with the assumption that GNP grows in West Germany by 2 per cent p.a. and in East Germany by 10 per cent p.a. It is further assumed that by the year 2000 East German *per capita* income should reach 80 per cent of West German levels.
30. At present, investments are eligible for subsidies of up to 35 per cent in the form of direct subsidies and tax rebates. In addition, they may obtain concessionary loans and accelerated

depreciation allowances. In the autumn of 1992, the federal government set aside DM 10 bn reserved for subsidies to indigenous East German investors of up to 20 per cent of investment cost. The maximum amount is DM 1 million, so that this facility favours small and medium-sized enterprises. Sometimes increased state intervention is defended by pointing to the successful restructuring of the Ruhr economy. But after 30 years of government-assisted restructuring and more than DM 50 bn in direct subsidies (not counting indirect subsidies through higher coal and electricity prices), the Ruhr economy to this very day cannot survive without continued subsidising at a current rate of DM 10 bn a year.

31. Some other features of the 'Mezzogiorno syndrome' however may not emerge until later and may invalidate much of this optimistic assessment. In particular, the new *Länder* may forge a formidable coalition to campaign for transfers. This indeed is a well-known feature of the Mezzogiorno problem: polling turnout in the South is significantly higher than in the North; the South achieves a common front across the political spectrum in order to press for transfers, and the number of Southerners in the country's political and administrative bodies is well in excess of their share in total population. The close tie between economic prosperity and political pressure fosters clientele relationships rather than the pursuit of national welfare. In this respect it is a matter of concern that union membership in East Germany, with 51 per cent of total employment, largely exceeds the 32 per cent of West Germany, according to Burda and Funke (1991). Moving the German capital to Berlin in the heart of what was the GDR may also be more than just a symbolic gesture. It may create a concrete problem very much akin to that created by the transfer of the Italian capital from Turin to Rome, via Florence.
32. These results can be found in Sommariva and Tullio (1987) using a 16 equation model of the German economy and simulating it from 1936. Borchardt (1985) reaches similar conclusions.
33. The GFCF–GNP ratio in West Germany was less than 30 per cent in the 1950s and 1960s, compared to the present 60 per cent in the new *Länder*.
34. Before World War II the East had a solid industrial base; indeed, the ex-GDR had a higher *per capita* GDP in 1936 than the Western part of Germany. See Abelshauser (1983).
35. Eastern GDP per unit of the labour force would have to grow at 10.5 per cent p.a. for 13 years in order to catch up completely with West German levels, projected to grow at 1.6 per cent p.a. See Sachverständigenrat (1991).
36. Hughes Hallett and Ma (1994) simulate East Germany's convergence with the IMF's Multimod multi-country model and conclude: 'Convergence is likely to take a long time (perhaps 30–40 years). It is likely to remain incomplete, implying continuing fiscal support and a Mezzogiorno problem in the East.'
37. It is not obvious to a rationalist – or to a humanitarian for that matter – why Germany treats ethnic Germans who emigrated centuries ago differently from other potential immigrants. To be sure, the line has to be drawn somewhere. Language would be one criterion but it should not be the only one. Other skills may be just as important or indeed more so for an immigrant to become a well-integrated member of the new home country.
38. Drèze, Malinvaud *et al.* (1994) propose a wage subsidy with the aim of reducing unemployment in the European Union. As unemployment is highly concentrated on low skills, they propose to eliminate social security contributions (roughly 40 per cent of wage costs on average in the EU) entirely on the lowest wages and progressively less along the wage scale.
39. When the firm subsequently reduces employment, it has to return a corresponding number of vouchers until its stock is exhausted.
40. Vouchers are claims on a state agency and therefore offer low credit risk. They can easily be securitised by a financial intermediary like mortgage-backed securities.
41. What Germany perhaps needs most is a less legalistic and more pragmatic approach.

Courts are in charge to judge GDR regime offenders, the rights of asylum seekers and property claims in the GDR. A more cumbersome, economically damaging and politically explosive solution is hardly imaginable – at least on the part of non-Germans.

APPENDIX: An inter-temporal equilibrium model for German unification

Consider the following model:

$$b = y_T\,(x_W, x_E, \tilde{x}; \gamma) - c_T\,(x_W, x_E, \tilde{x}, b; \beta) \qquad [1]$$

$$b + 1/r\ \tilde{b}/(1+r) = 0 \qquad [2]$$

$$e_N^W = c_N^W\,(x_W, \tilde{x}, (1\text{-}s_W)\,(y^W - t), b) - y_N^W\,(x_W, \tilde{x}) \qquad [3]$$

$$e_N^E = c_N^E\,(x_E, \tilde{x}, (1 - s_E)\,(y^E + t), b) - y_N^E\,(x_E, \tilde{x}) \qquad [4]$$

$$\tilde{e}_N = c_N\,(x_E, x_W, \tilde{x}, (1 - s)\,\tilde{y}, \tilde{b}) - y_n\,(x_E, x_W, \tilde{x}) \qquad [5]$$

and $\frac{\delta^e N}{\delta\tilde{x}} > 0,\ \frac{\delta^e N}{\delta\tilde{x}} < 0\ \frac{\delta^{\tilde{e}} N}{\delta\tilde{x}} < 0\ \frac{\delta^{\tilde{e}} N}{\delta\tilde{x}} > 0,$

$\frac{\delta^e T}{\delta\tilde{x}} < 0,\ \frac{\delta^e T}{\delta\tilde{x}} > 0.$

where:

E,W	are indices for East and West Germany respectively
N, T	are indices for non-tradable and tradable goods, respectively
~	indicates second period variables
$b > 0$	is the trade account surplus
y	is supply
c	is demand
e	is excess demand
y	is income
x	is the real exchange rate, i.e., $x = P_T / P_N$
s	is the savings rate
r	is the interest rate
T	is a transfer from West to East Germany
γ, β	are shift parameters

All variables are defined *per capita*. Hence unification lowers the *per capita* supply and demand of goods in integrated Germany. Because we treat non-tradables in East and West Germany separately, this fact is only relevant for tradable goods. The reduction in *per capita* supply is larger than the reduction in *per capita* aggregate demand (due to the transfer and the fact that savings behaviour is not very different so that $s_W \cong s_E$). Hence, unification tends to create excess demand for tradables, that is, a trade deficit.

There are, in fact, two first period real exchange rates: the W-rate and the E-rate;

and a unique second period real exchange rate. Equation [5] assumes that in the second period factor and goods markets are integrated so that wages, and hence non-tradable goods' prices, are the same in both parts of Germany. Thus, when reconstruction is achieved there is only one (integrated) market for non-tradables. Likewise, income and savings behaviour is then the same across Germany.

For a given income, Equations [3] and [4], on the one hand, and Equation [5], on the other, determine the first and second period real exchange rates. In $(x, \tilde{x})$-space of Fig. 10.A.1 the equilibrium schedules for the non-tradable goods markets in both periods are positively sloped if present and future consumption are substitutes. The slope for first period consumption equilibrium is steeper than for second period consumption because of classic stability conditions.

The model needs to be solved simultaneously; but for exposition it is convenient to proceed as if it were recursive. Equations [3], [4] and [5] determine present and future exchange rates. Then Equation [1] determines the first period trade account deficit and Equation [2] the second period equilibrium trade account.

How does unification perturb the equilibrium of Fig. 10.A.1? As we are interested in the real exchange rate of the DM, the analysis focuses on West Germany. This is the only question of interest as, due to the substantial room for price convergence in East Germany, the real exchange rate in the East can only appreciate. That is, whatever happens to the nominal DM exchange rate, it will never depreciate at a rate commensurate with price increases in East Germany.

From Equation [3] it is clear that the transfer payment reduces disposable income in West Germany and thus the N^W curve shifts to the right. Inspection of Equation [5] reveals that the $\tilde{N}$-curve only shifts if $(1-s)\tilde{y}$ is changed. With unchanged technology *per capita* product in the East should reach the West German level after reconstruction. However, as during reconstruction foreign debt accumulates which needs to be serviced later, steady-state income is lower. Hence $\tilde{N}$ shifts upwards. Both shifts are reinforced by the wealth effects induced by the first period trade deficit ($b < o$). The outcome is depicted in Fig. 10.A.2:

Thus, as equilibrium moves from A to B, the real exchange rate depreciates both

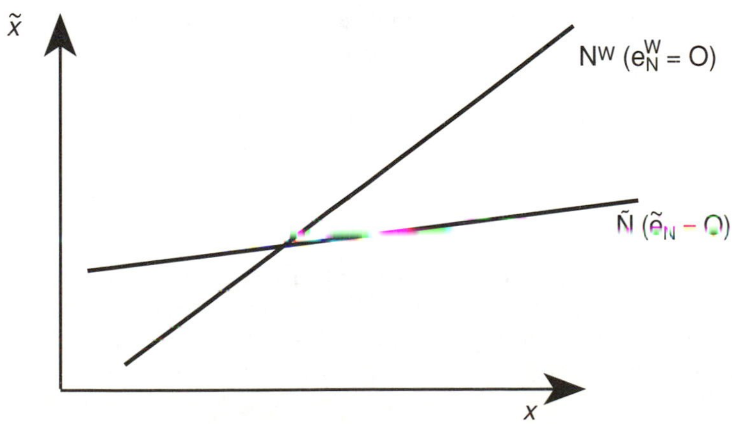

FIG 10.A.1 Real exchange rate equilibria in both periods

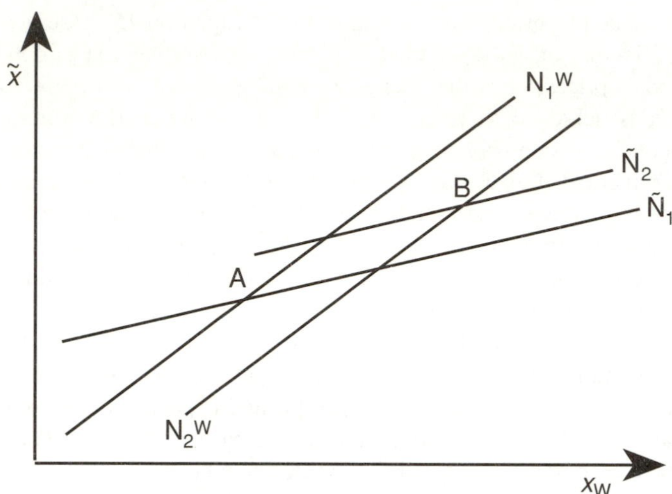

FIG 10.A.2 The effect of transfers on present and future real exchange rates

during the first and second period. (In contrast, East Germany's real exchange rate first appreciates and only depreciates in the second period.)

What could prevent the occurrence of these results, a depreciation of the real exchange rate in both the short and the long run? The transfer for reconstruction would have to be over-compensated by either a real income increase (a Keynesian reduction in West German unemployment due to higher demand from East Germany giving West Germany an advantage in comparison with other EMS countries) or a fall in the West German savings rate to offset the transfer. The second effect is unlikely, whilst the first needs to be assessed empirically.

From these results it is obvious that, whatever happens to first period exchange rates, in the second period the trade account has to achieve a surplus to pay for the first period deficit. A lower *per capita* income and a depreciated second period real exchange rate achieve this.

By contrast, the exchange rate effects on the first period trade account are ambiguous: a depreciation during the first period tends to reduce the deficit, which may, however, be offset by an even stronger second period depreciation, inducing inter-temporal substitution for present consumption of tradables.

How is the external inter-temporal equilibrium condition [2] to be met in period 2? Writing the equilibrium condition explicitly, one obtains:

$$\tilde{b} = -(1+r)b = \tilde{y}_T(x) - \tilde{c}_T(\tilde{x}, \tilde{y} - rb, \tilde{b}) \qquad [6]$$

If the second period trade surplus $\tilde{b}$ were higher than the value satisfying [6], foreign claims would accumulate and consumption of both tradables and non-tradables would increase. The real appreciation needed to clear the market for non-tradables and the reduced trade surplus due to higher demand for tradables would reduce $\tilde{b}$ until it reached the level in [6].

CHAPTER ELEVEN

Beyond stabilisation: the economic transformation of Czechoslovakia, Hungary and Poland*

Per correr miglior acque alza le vele omai la navicella del mio ingegno che lascia dietro a sé mar sí crudelee; canterò di quel secondo regno dove l'umano spirito si purga e di salire al ciel diventa degno.

Dante, *La Divina Commedia, Purgatorio*, I, 1–6

All European transition economies faced the same daunting task of profoundly restructuring their productive bases, while dealing at the same time with a number of sharply destabilising influences, ranging from the monetary overhangs left behind by previous regimes to the collapse of traditional trading arrangements. Hungary, Poland, and the Czech and Slovak Federal Republic (CSFR) – now its two successor states, the Czech and Slovak Republics – were also faced with this same challenge.[1] What sets them apart, this chapter argues, is that they have by now largely achieved the all-important first goal of stabilisation, and have moved into a second stage of transition.

This second stage, 'beyond stabilisation', involves less tractable, and unprecedented, problems. While it is relatively easy to get price signals right by liberalising prices and trade, this has not by itself proved sufficient to generate the restructuring of productive capacities and the investment necessary for growth. This chapter examines how the governments of the Central European countries, having achieved some degree of macroeconomic balance, are now focusing on improving the allocation of resources. This goal encompasses all three of the economy's key sectors: producing enterprises must become more efficient in both goods and labour markets; the financial sector must channel savings to their most productive uses; and the government's demands on resources must be kept in check and its interventions introduce as few distortions as possible. A failure by any of these sectors to live up to these standards would not only weaken growth, but also endanger the very macroeconomic stability that has opened up opportunities for growth, and there is no better recipe for

* This chapter is based on a contribution by Gerd Schwartz, Mark Stone, and Tessa van der Willigen of the International Monetary Fund. They are grateful for comments and suggestions by Gérard Bélanger, Ajai Chopra, Ke-young Chu, and Howell Zee. The views and opinions expressed are strictly personal, and do not necessarily represent those of the International Monetary Fund.

destabilisation than wasting resources. Thus, while structural reform will yield few benefits in the absence of stabilisation, in turn stabilisation will achieve little without structural reform. It is this latter challenge that the Central European countries are the first to confront head on.

The convergence of Hungary, Poland, and the CSFR on this similar point in the process of reform could hardly have been predicted. Both their histories as planned economies and their policies under their new governments show considerable variations.

Although the three countries experimented with partial reforms to varying degrees during the 1980s – a significant amount in Hungary, rather little in the other two – all faced tremendous shocks, related to both domestic and external developments, around the turn of the decade. To the extent that they were controlled, prices and trade were liberalised at the stroke of a pen in Poland and the CSFR, and over the course of several years in Hungary. Enterprises, although not privatised immediately, were subjected to an 'unleashing shock' and freed to pursue their own profit opportunities. At the same time, both export markets and pricing structures changed radically, with the breakdown of the CMEA trading system and the economic collapse of the then Soviet Union. These developments brought clear risks both for inflation and the balance of payments, which all three countries attempted to control by means of tight fiscal and monetary policies, tax-based incomes policies, and exchange rate policies. The various approaches to stabilisation are set out in detail in the Appendix.

One of the most visible developments that resulted from this configuration of shocks and policies in the early 1990s was a steep decline in output. The size of the decline in output has been disputed (see Berg and Sachs 1992 and Sachs 1993) on the grounds that the official statistics do not reflect the growth of the emerging private sector. However, nobody disputes that there has been a substantial decline in the output of the 'measurable' industrial sector. In each of the three Central European countries the magnitude of this decline has sometimes been blamed on the very stabilisation policies that set these countries apart. But if anything, the magnitude of their output decline appears to have been slightly smaller than in other European economies in transition (Table 11.1). Still, one of the more surprising features of the output declines has been that they have hit all European transition economies in rather similar fashion, even though starting positions and policies during the transition were significantly different (Borensztein *et al.* 1993, Calvo and Coricelli 1992). Kornai (1993) has pointed out that output has fallen with 'shock-therapy' in Poland, and it has fallen with 'gradualism' in Hungary; it has fallen in countries with high external debt, like Bulgaria, Hungary, and Poland, and it has fallen in countries with moderate or no external debt, like the CSFR and Romania.[2]

It is in other indicators that differences between the Central European countries and other European economies in transition are most apparent. Inflation in all of Central Europe remains substantially higher than is now common in industrial countries, and there remains work to be done on this front. But, as shown in Table 11.2, in Poland and Hungary inflation is down significantly from its earlier highs, and in the CSFR, which had much more favourable conditions to begin with, it never really took off (the large rise in the price level in 1991 being a one-off jump). In 1993, inflation ranged between 20 per cent and 35 per cent in the Central European countries, and between 70 per cent and over 1,000 per cent in other European transition economies. In 1994 inflation came down in virtually all transition countries.

TABLE 11.1 Real GDP growth (in per cent)

	1989	1990	1991	1992	1993	1994	1995 (proj.)	1996 (proj.)
Czech Republic	4.5	−1.2	−14.2	−6.6	−0.3	3.0	4.0	5.0
Slovak Republic	1.2	−2.5	−11.2	−6.1	−4.1	3.5	4.0	5.0
Hungary	0.7	-3.5	−11.9	−4.5	−1.0	2.5	0.5	1.0
Poland	0.2	−11.6	−7.6	2.6	4.0	4.0	5.0	5.0
Albania	9.8	−10.0	−27.7	−9.7	11.0			
Bulgaria	−1.9	−9.1	−11.7	−5.6	−4.2	1.0	2.0	2.0
Romania	−5.8	−7.4	−15.1	−13.6	1.0	1.0	1.5	2.0
Russia	2.0	−2.0	−15.0	−19.0	−12.0	−15.0	−7.0	0.0

Source: BIS Annual Report, 1994 and OECD World Economic Outlook for 1994 and further, No.56. December 1994

TABLE 11.2 CPI inflation (in per cent)

	1989	1990	1991	1992	1993	1994	1995 (proj.)	1996 (proj.)
Czech Republic	1.4	9.7	56.7	11.1	20.8	11.0	9.0	7.0
Slovak Republic	1.2	10.4	61.2	10.0	23.2	16.0	12.0	8.0
Hungary	17.0	28.9	35.0	23.0	22.5	20.0	17.0	12.0
Poland	251.1	585.8	70.3	43.0	35.3	30.0	23.0	18.0
Albania	0.0	0.0	35.5	226.0	85.2			
Bulgaria	5.6	23.8	339.0	91.3	72.8	120.0	60.0	30.0
Romania	0.9	5.1	166.1	210.3	256.0	130.0	45.0	35.0
Russia	2.4	5.6	160.0	1534.0	912.0	250.0	125.0	42.0

Source: BIS Annual Report, 1994 and OECD World Economic Outlook for 1994 and further, No.56. December 1994

Also, balances of payments have remained surprisingly strong in Hungary, Poland, and the CSFR, again especially in comparison with the other European transition economies. In 1992, the three countries had current accounts that were in balance or surplus, while significant deficits were recorded in Albania, Bulgaria, and Romania. While in 1993 and 1994, the Central European countries (except the Czech Republic) had markedly weaker current accounts, they were still much stronger than the ones recorded elsewhere.

Of course, continued vigilance over fiscal, monetary, and exchange rate policies is required in all Visegrad countries to keep demand from outstripping supply. But it is becoming more and more evident that this is the easy part. Efficiency in resource allocation is crucial both to the maintenance of domestic and external stability, and to the goal of 'catching up' with Western Europe. Although centrally planned economies clearly over-invested, and new investments should be considerably more productive than the old ones, there is no doubt that present levels of investment are inadequate to

TABLE 11.3 Convertible currency account balance (in per cent of GDP)

	1989	1990	1991	1992	1993	1994 (proj.)	1995 (proj.)	1996 (proj.)
Czech Republic	0.8	-3.5	1.6	0.7	1.9	3.7	2.4	1.2
Slovak Republic	0.8	−8.1	4.0	1.0	−2.6	−1.4	−1.4	−1.1
Hungary	−4.9	0.4	1.0	1.3	−4.4	−4.3	−3.5	−3.1
Poland	−2.7	1.1	−2.5	−2.8	−3.3	−1.8	−2.0	−2.6
Albania	−2.1	-5.8	−27.6	−66.5	−46.5			
Bulgaria	−6.9	−13.2	−5.2	−9.7	−10.6	−9.7	−5.9	−5.2
Romania	13.1	-7.9	−4.7	−9.3	−5.9	−3.4	−2.4	−1.0

Source: IMF (1994) and own estimations based on OECD Secretariat estimates and projections OECD World Economic Outlook for 1994 and further, No.56. December 1994

the task, which is nothing less than the radical restructuring of productive capacity. The conventional wisdom of minimising state intervention and privatising as quickly as possible has been a useful touchstone for governments preoccupied with immediate stabilisation problems, endlessly lobbied by state-owned enterprises (SOEs) used to the old systems of intervention, and often themselves unschooled in the ways of market economies. But beyond this there lurk much more complex problems. It is these problems this chapter seeks to address.

It is impossible to privatise whole economies overnight, so that economic performance will continue to depend heavily on the newly emerging private sector and on SOEs. Governments have attempted to create favourable conditions for the former, and to influence the latter by improving their governance, and, most difficult, by closing down unprofitable firms. Section 2 examines these reform efforts. Enterprises' behaviour in labour markets is particularly important, given both the havoc myopic firms can wreak in this area, and the potentially explosive social implications of unemployment; Section 3 discusses policies in this area.

Enterprises need resources both for working capital and, crucially, for new investment. Unexpectedly high savings of the household sector in the early years of reform opened up special opportunities in this regard, but to a large extent these opportunities have gone unused. Banks remain by far the largest players in the financial systems of Central Europe, but still suffer from a number of handicaps inherited from the planning system – inadequate governance, insufficient capital, weak loan portfolios, and a weak system of supervision. Section 4 examines these issues.

To some extent, banks have been freed from having to make difficult lending decisions by the availability of a superlatively attractive asset – loans to the government. Considerable progress has been made in tax reform, but structural changes in the economies and the resulting difficulties in collecting taxes have put a major dent in revenues. At the same time, some types of government expenditure, notably subsidies, have been cut sharply, but increased demands on social safety nets and rising interest burdens, in part reflecting inevitable reallocations of liabilities, have offset these to some extent. Section 5 addresses these issues, and points to some possible areas for further fiscal reform. Section 6 concludes.

1. The enterprise sector

Enterprise sector reform in economies in transition has two main elements: economic liberalisation and industrial restructuring. Getting relative prices right (the goal of liberalisation) was achieved fairly quickly by lifting price controls and adjusting the exchange rate. In contrast, industrial restructuring refers to the arduous and prolonged tasks of structural reform that are needed to improve enterprise efficiency. To a large extent, improvements in enterprise efficiency rest on being able to impose hard budget constraints on enterprises: reducing subsidies, limiting the extent of tax arrears and tax evasion, controlling inter-enterprise credit and inter-enterprise arrears, bringing about rational credit allocation by commercial banks, and minimising the exposure of enterprises to moral hazard. Clearly, industrial restructuring is a much more complex task than liberalisation.

A key aspect of the various liberalisation measures was that they limited the monopoly power of state-owned enterprises in domestic markets and forced these enterprises to produce goods that were actually in demand (Sachs 1993 emphasises this point as well). As a result, shortages, a central element of the socialist economy, soon disappeared. While many domestic enterprises were able to adjust to broad-scale foreign competition, the imported new price structures threatened to make much of the existing production non-viable. Still, the effects of liberalisation on enterprises in Hungary, Poland, and the CSFR were less dramatic than in East Germany (see Chapter 10). Monetary union meant that East German enterprises were subjected to the full extent of competition with West German enterprises from one day to the next, which forced enterprises to adjust or perish. But political union also fuelled real wage expectations that were out of line with productivity developments. In contrast to East Germany, the CSFR, Hungary, and Poland retained the exchange rate as a key policy instrument and tried to control wage developments via an active incomes policy.

All three countries carried out major exchange rate depreciations, which implied a decision on the profitability of enterprises producing tradable goods at the onset of reform. The Czech Republic has since been toughest on its enterprises, maintaining a fixed exchange rate against a basket of currencies since December 1990, and expecting – apparently credibly – firms to keep their costs in line with this; Slovakia has, since the dissolution of the federation, followed broadly the same policy, with a one-off adjustment in the exchange rate in July 1993. Poland, which at the outset of reform intended to follow a strategy similar to the Czechoslovak one, later softened its policy to a pre-announced crawling peg; Hungary generally makes periodic devaluations. While in all these cases real effective exchange rates have shown a tendency to appreciate, the currency together with some remaining tariff and non-tariff barriers, has somewhat shielded enterprises from the full force of foreign competition, and offered them a chance to adjust rather more gradually.

Economic liberalisation did not change the fact that many enterprises in the CSFR, Hungary, and Poland were operating in the wrong sectors because industrial structures had not undergone much change in over 40 years. The structure of production was bound to change only slowly even under the best set of circumstances, but the problem of enterprise reform and transformation has proved to be more challenging than expected. Initial reform measures focused on levelling the playing field for state-owned enterprises (SOEs) and the private sector, devising new legal frameworks for enterprise operations, and introducing modern systems of enterprise taxation. Reform also meant starting to privatise and restructure SOEs, including banks, and drastically scaling down producer subsidies from levels that were highly distortionary and had become unsustainable in the light of the new budgetary realities. Still, governments were generally ill-prepared for the rapid growth of private sector activity, and particularly the mushrooming of micro-enterprises that has accompanied the transition. As a result, the private sector generally went from being repressed and over-regulated to being totally free and little checked.

ENTERPRISE SECTOR GROWTH

Some six years into the transition, the most striking feature of the enterprise sectors of Central Europe is the dynamic growth of the private sector (Table 11.4), which has gone some way toward offsetting the sharp contraction of state-owned industry. More than half of all value added is now produced by the private sector in all three countries.

The growth of the private sector has been unevenly distributed; it has been most vigorous in small-scale enterprises and in those sectors that had previously been under-developed, particularly services. In Poland in 1992 (three years after the big bang), for example, the private sector's share in employment was 72 per cent in construction and over 90 per cent in trade, but only 41 per cent in industry and 23 per cent in transport. In the Czech Republic in 1992, the private sector's share in value added was 66 per cent in retail trade and 46 per cent in construction, but less than 15 per cent in industry. But even in sectors where the share of the private sector remains low, it is expanding rapidly: in Polish industry in 1992, the output of the private sector increased by 32 per cent, while that of the socialised sector declined by 5 per cent.

The expansion of the private sector was not at the beginning primarily driven by privatisation, but by new firms, implying that state ownership can be expected to continue being important for quite some time. Although here the crucial question – how much of the inherited productive structure is viable under the new circumstances – remains open, strands of an answer are beginning to appear.

First, within the state-owned sector there has been a considerable difference in enterprise performance, even within a given industry. Success stories are emerging in most sectors in the three countries, attesting to the potential for developing a diversified

TABLE 11.4 Private sector share of GDP during 1989-94 (in per cent)

	CSFR	Hungary	Poland
Share of GDP:			
1989	<5	≃16	28–30
1992	16–20	≃39	≃45
1994	60	55	55

Source: National authorities of the CSFR, Hungary and Poland, and calculations by the authors, EBRD Transition Report, October 1994.

manufacturing base, and suggesting that SOEs should not be written off. Based on evidence from Poland, for example, Pinto *et al.* (1993) and Wyznikiewicz *et al.* (1993) conclude that managerial performance is a key determinant in the success of SOEs, and that managers in successful firms have tended to stress changes in the product mix, increase efficiency in the use of materials and energy, maintain labour productivity, and show restraint in setting wages and borrowing from banks. This result is encouraging as it suggests that significant parts of the SOE sector may become viable, even after only a few years into the transition.

Second, while the emergence of success stories in all sectors is good news, it has gone hand-in-hand with a stronger polarisation among enterprises, at least during the initial years of transition: as some SOEs have become financially sound, others have grown much weaker, and in the aggregate there has been stagnation. Thus, in Poland, for example, the overall financial situation of enterprises continued to deteriorate in 1992 in all major sectors of the economy, with the gross profit rate falling from 7.7 per cent in 1991 to 6.1 per cent in 1992. Similarly, the number of enterprises reporting losses also increased significantly over the same period, and loss-makers could be found in virtually all sectors. While in 1993 gross profits recovered slightly, gross losses of enterprises still amounted to 40–50 per cent of gross profits throughout the year. The increased level of gross losses during 1990–92 seems neither related to increases in unit labour costs – gains in labour productivity more than offset increases in real product wages in 1992 – nor attributable to higher costs of borrowing. While it may be argued that part of the decline in profitability in 1992 is due to higher energy costs, higher import prices, and the continued determination of different Polish administrations to impose a hard budget constraint, it may also be true that managers have just become more adept in hiding profits. Whatever the reasons, a stagnating financial situation for enterprises spells bad news for any economy, but it is particularly bad for economies in transition, where restructuring and sustainable growth cannot be brought about without significant increases in investment.

Thus both good and bad news has emerged from the remaining SOE sector. A key challenge now confronting governments is how to ensure that SOEs are able to exploit the new opportunities that have opened up and turn themselves into success stories, and in so doing improve the financial health of the sector as a whole. At the same time, of course, further improvements in the policy framework for the emerging new private sector, which has already done much to strengthen economic performance, could yield great dividends. The following sub-sections examine the various instruments that governments can bring to bear in these areas.

STATE-OWNED ENTERPRISES DURING THE TRANSITION

Since it takes time to privatise, there is a pressing need for improvements in efficiency of SOEs, which accounted for most industrial activity in transition economies (and still do in some). However, the breakdown of central planning seemed to have opened the door for much abuse, and there was a danger that SOEs would become decapitalising, myopic firms that pay out everything in wages, and then approach the government for a bail-out. Fears of decapitalisation arose primarily because of unclear property rights: after the loss of central control the state became an absentee owner, and managers and/or workers assumed significant power over their enterprises. While it is unclear whether myopic behaviour was the norm, the worst fears of decapitalisation clearly did not materialise. However, abuses of power did occur, more commonly in Hungary and Poland than in the CSFR. For example, enterprises on the brink of bankruptcy in Poland often granted high wage increases because unemployment benefits were linked to the recipient's last wage. The relatively few abuses of power that occurred in the CSFR reflected a more efficient and honest administration, the absence of self-management experiments as in Hungary, and the less severe pressures of worker participation relative to Poland.

But what did governments do to improve SOE operations? All three countries tackled the need to harden SOE budget constraints. This was done through regulatory action, limits on explicit government guarantees, and reductions in enterprise subsidies. All this helped to enforce enterprise discipline, even though increases in inter-enterprise arrears initially softened these constraints to some extent. Furthermore, while all three countries generally levelled the playing field for SOEs and private sector enterprises, some special policies were applied to SOEs. In Poland and the CSFR this involved, for example, maintaining a tax-based incomes policy (TIP) for SOEs, which took the form of taxing SOE wage increases that exceeded a certain norm (see Section 3 below), and, in Poland, also compelling SOEs, via dividend requirements, to produce a return on the stock of state-owned assets.

However, improving the external environment of SOEs was only half the battle; improving corporate governance was the other half. In most cases, this problem was tackled initially by constructing 'halfway houses' where SOEs were 'commercialised', that is, subjected to the regular commercial code, transformed into joint stock or limited liability companies, and put under the control of an independent board of executive directors.

In Hungary SOEs were required to be commercialised by mid-1993, and property rights were redefined to make the State Property Agency the sole owner of all SOEs. SOEs were given a board of directors, required to produce properly audited balance sheets, and independent advisers were brought in to help with the preparations for privatisation. More recently, the Hungarian government created a separate supervisory board, the State Asset Management Corporation, that oversees the activities of those commercialised enterprises that will remain state-owned for the foreseeable future. In Poland, the process of commercialisation was similar to that in Hungary, except that in Hungary commercialisation was independent of the intent to privatise, while in Poland it was and still is one possible step on the way to privatisation, and is only carried out at the request of the enterprise. As a result, most SOEs in Poland were not commercialised and remain under the control of individual ministries. The Polish privatisation agency concentrated much of its efforts on profitable SOEs while leaving the problem of unprofitable SOEs to be resolved by the ministries. In the CSFR the issue of halfway houses was less pressing since ownership rights for a large number of enterprises were transferred to the private sector through mass voucher privatisation. Still, although SOEs were turned into joint stock companies and their shares handed over to the National Property Funds as a step to privatisation, the latter took no active interest in enterprise governance, and managers were essentially left to their own devices.

Bruno (1992) has argued that halfway houses are generally inevitable, unless one is willing to take the line that what cannot be privatised instantaneously had better be junked immediately. Evidence from Poland suggests that commercialisation is generally superior to the self-governance structure that currently exists in the majority of SOEs, which is characterised by dominance of the Workers' Council and seen as being in conflict with long-term restructuring and profit maximisation considerations (Pinto *et al.* 1992). However, the experiences of the three Central European countries do not allow for strong conclusions about the universal benefits of halfway houses. At least on the surface, the enterprise sector in Hungary, where firms are commercialised, does not seem significantly better off than that in Poland, where commercialisation has been confined to a minority of enterprises. Also, halfway houses *per se* do little to expose SOEs to a uniformly hard budget constraint (Kopits 1991) or to guard against decapitalisation by SOE managers (Bruno 1992), particularly when expertise on the board of directors is lacking. The recent empirical finding that managers in Polish SOEs acted as an important source of change (Pinto *et al.* 1992) may cause governments to feel more comfortable with the slow speed of privatisation and give an expanded role to commercialisation, but eventually more far-reaching decisions have to be made.

PRIVATISATION

The key rationale for privatisation, probably the most important element of structural policies, is to improve efficiency. However, when industries are highly monopolised, privatisation *per se*, without industrial restructuring and demonopolisation, is unlikely to improve efficiency. Privatisation without efficiency gains has few advantages, particularly since it cannot be expected to improve the fiscal situation. Since industrial restructuring and demonopolisation are costly in political terms, efficiency gains may need to be obtained at the expense of privatisation proceeds. In addition, privatisation has become part of a broader debate on distributional issues, which has compelled policy-makers to address a variety of privatisation policy objectives that may or may not be compatible with improving efficiency and, hence, the fiscal position. This has contributed to a situation where actual privatisation programmes are characterised by a multitude of objectives, including privatising the economy in the shortest possible time, maximising proceeds, selecting the 'right' buyers, safeguarding employment, and obtaining investment guarantees.

Notwithstanding the multitude of programmes and objectives, privatisation results have often fallen short of expectations, not only with respect to privatisation proceeds. In Poland, for example, by the end of 1993 (four years after the big bang), there had only been a handful of public flotations, 99 sales to strategic investors, and 693 worker buy-outs, amounting to a transfer of 200,000 jobs from the state to the private sector at a time when the private sector had created 3.5 million new jobs; 6,500 enterprises remained state-owned.

All this may just indicate that expectations were exaggerated to begin with. Clearly, not all objectives – speed, proceeds, ownership, employment, and new investment can be achieved simultaneously, and, in practice, trade offs and compromises are inevitable. The range of possibilities is usually constrained by the availability of domestic financing: budgetary considerations are a severe constraint when domestic financial markets are embryonic, when foreign financing is unavailable, and when inflationary financing is to be avoided.

How were these general trade offs addressed in the three countries considered here? While, on the surface, privatisation policies have differed significantly in the CSFR, Hungary, and Poland (see Chapter 8 in this volume for details of the various schemes), the commonalities of privatisation policies in all transition economies are in fact striking (Schwartz and Silva Lopes 1993). In all three countries the set of SOEs was sub-divided, and separate and specific privatisation goals were defined for each group of enterprises. In general, the more objectives have to be addressed, and the more special interest groups have to be satisfied, the more compartmentalised privatisation schemes become in practice. As a result, privatisation schemes usually comprise numerous different programmes where, for example, new owners are carefully selected for some enterprises, prices are maximised for others, a strict time frame is pursued for yet another group, and investment guarantees or employment are safeguarded in yet a further group.

Having many different objectives, all three countries used a broad mix of policy tools that included special programmes for small enterprise privatisation, enterprise liquidation schemes with asset sale or auction, leasing arrangements for state assets, management/employee buy-outs/buy-ins, direct sales either via trade sale or a public share offering to foreign or domestic investors, restitution to previous owners, and, except for Hungary, mass privatisation. While the different tools and techniques have often created a maze that has allowed insiders to exploit the process for their personal gain, they have also helped to tailor privatisation schemes to the needs of particular groups of potential buyers. Privatisation has been most successful in the retail trade and service sector, and least successful in industry. One reason for this is that retail trade and service enterprises tend to be relatively small in size, which makes them affordable to a relatively large number of people, and raises few of the rather complex problems of corporate governance that have beset privatisation of large enterprises and heavy industries, where prospects for privatisation are often remote.

CORPORATE CONTROL AND GOVERNANCE

It is impossible to privatise an economy overnight. It also may not be desirable since efficiency is unlikely to be enhanced by a simple transfer of ownership, particularly when markets are highly monopolistic and when systems of supervision, control, and taxation are still being developed. Indeed, failing to regulate and supervise the enterprise sector after it is freed from central control may lead to reductions in overall efficiency during the transition process. For the long term, the crucial issue is the form of corporate control that will replace the old system.

In general, there are two basic models of corporate control: the *outsider model*, applied in the United Kingdom and the United States; and the *insider model*, applied in most of Western Europe and in Japan. The outsider model is characterised by (1) dispersed ownership and separation of ownership from control; (2) few incentives for outside investors to participate in corporate control and, hence, weak commitments of outside investors to long-term strategies of firms; and (3) friendly and hostile takeovers, and frequent market entrance and exit. In contrast, the insider model is characterised by (1) concentrated ownership and association of ownership and control; (2) corporate control exercised by the major shareholders with outside interventions being limited to periods of clear financial failure; and (3) absence of takeovers, and infrequent market entrance and exit (Corbett and Mayer 1991).

The design of the future system of corporate control will clearly depend on government regulation; for example, whether strict limits on owning enterprise shares will be applied for specific types of investors. Policy-makers in the three countries seem not to have thought through these issues in a comprehensive manner, and, as a result, have not made an explicit decision on the system of corporate control for the private sector, often even providing conflicting signals about the future system of corporate control. For example, governments usually support the idea of universal banking – often a sign of systems that tend towards the insider model – but at the same time they have sometimes imposed limits to institutional ownership, as in the case of the CSFR, which imposed a cap of 20 per cent on the total stock of a firm that can be held by a single investment privatisation fund (IPF). In general, a failure to provide clear guidelines on the system of corporate control creates a vacuum that may invite abuse and, eventually, may slow the pace of transition.

While the available literature on corporate control has often favoured an insider system for economies in transition – in part, perhaps, since the capital markets that are needed for frequent market entrance and exit under the outsider system are not yet sufficiently developed – a major problem of the insider model is that it creates various risks of moral hazard. One particular problem is that shareholders, banks in particular, may easily come under pressure to extend credit to enterprises they own independent of the usual criteria of credit-worthiness. While the development of a full-blown system of corporate control for the private sector depends to some extent on progress with privatisation, the general direction of this development should not be left to chance.

BANKRUPTCY

An important step for improving corporate control and a prerequisite for economic reform is the creation of enforceable property rights. As pointed out by Mizsei (1993), this not only presupposes progress with privatisation of state assets and the creation of a strong private sector, but also the security of payment enforcement – hence the possibility of resort to an effective bankruptcy process. In addition, effective bankruptcy laws sort out the enterprise sector into viable enterprises, non-viable enterprises that are unable to cover even variable operating costs, and enterprises that may be viable after financial restructuring. Highly indebted firms that can operate profitably can be handled by so-called 'bad debt workouts', which will be discussed below. Firms unable to cover variable operating expenses require more drastic decisions, even though implications for budgets, banks, and employment may be severe in the short run. In these cases bankruptcy proceedings are required to obtain a speedy decision on whether a firm is to be liquidated, ensure that assets of distressed firms are disposed of in a socially efficient manner, and prevent possible major adverse long-run consequences for state budgets.

In general, bankruptcy laws need to: (1) make a credible threat of loss of control to incumbent management; (2) establish mechanisms, such as mandatory competitive bidding, that maximise the asset value of firms undergoing bankruptcy proceedings; (3) minimise the likelihood that bankruptcy proceedings are initiated when enterprises are illiquid rather than fundamentally insolvent; (4) avoid 'Chapter 11'-type procrastination while protecting the interests of both junior and senior creditors. Bankruptcy reform has proceeded at a slow pace, reflecting both the onerous budgetary and social consequences and the unfamiliarity of governments with bankruptcy, which was virtually non-existent in the command economy. In addition, existing Western systems have their own shortcomings, and would probably not work adequately in economies in transition because their procedures are not geared towards situations where the entire economy is undergoing rapid structural change. For example, US Chapter 7 regulations and the UK receivership system have often been criticised for their piecemeal approach, while US Chapter 11 reorganisations are generally recognised as being administratively inefficient and costly (Aghion *et al.*, 1992). Unable to adopt a Western system off the shelf, Central European countries have attempted to create their own systems. Did they succeed?

Hungary has probably the most advanced bankruptcy law in Central and Eastern Europe. The bankruptcy law that went into effect in January 1992 aimed at having a simple trigger mechanism for invoking the law and carrying out a swift restructuring or liquidation process. Accordingly, the law called for various rules to be applied very mechanically, and firms with obligations more than 90 days overdue were required to place themselves in bankruptcy proceedings. As a result, during 1992 and 1993 over 3,000 enterprises, employing more than 8 per cent of the labour force, entered into bankruptcy proceedings. The strict stipulations helped to control inter-enterprise arrears, and also made explicit the extent of the burden of structural adjustment that falls on the banking sector. However, the strict mechanical requirement for declaring bankruptcy also created a backlog of court cases that to some degree undermined the law's credibility. Changes in the bankruptcy law in 1993 that lifted the requirement for unanimous creditor approval of settlements greatly speeded up the pace of settlements, which at the end of 1993 were split about evenly between liquidations and restructurings. The fear that mass bankruptcies could induce a domino effect where some enterprises are forced to enter into bankruptcy proceedings simply because their upstream suppliers or downstream buyers close down appears to have abated.

Poland has separate bankruptcy provisions for SOEs and private firms, which evolved from two bankruptcy acts that date back to 1934, and the act on state-owned enterprises that dates back to 1981 and has been amended at various times. Neither of these has been applied rigorously. For example, failure to pay the dividend requirement that was levied on SOE assets until mid-1994 was formally a trigger for starting bankruptcy proceedings. In practice, creditors, including the government, have been reluctant to invoke bankruptcy proceedings and usually have waited for SOEs to decide on whether they needed to seek legal protection (Berg and Blanchard 1992), which, however, is unlikely to happen if creditors are not pursuing them. Formally, bankruptcy settlement proposals need approval by a court appointed trustee, the bankruptcy court, and creditors who represent at least two-thirds of the firm's debt obligations. Aghion *et al.* (1992) have criticised this procedure for suffering from the same deficiencies as US Chapter 7 proceedings mentioned above. While at the end of 1992 Poland adopted several new procedures that were intended to speed up financial restructuring of highly insolvent enterprises, slow progress on bankruptcy proceedings continues to hamper efficiency gains.

In the CSFR, a bankruptcy law was introduced in 1991, under which the ministry in charge of a specific enterprise could initiate bankruptcy proceedings; a number of liquidations of smaller enterprises took place under this law. More comprehensive bankruptcy legislation became effective in the two successor republics in the first half of 1993. These laws allow creditors to instigate bankruptcy proceedings, but grant companies at least a three-month protection period against creditors. This is intended to give enterprises an opportunity, in co-operation with their creditors, to consolidate their finances, and thus protect companies that are solvent but illiquid; it should also reduce the case load of the courts. It is expected that companies and banks would share the cost of restructuring (in some cases, perhaps, with government guarantees). It is too early to judge whether these laws will be effective, but strict implementation may finally reveal the true financial position of Czech and Slovak enterprises.

The cases of Hungary, Poland, and the CSFR clearly show the importance of modern bankruptcy laws. In general, where bankruptcy laws are deficient, as in Poland, financial restructuring of enterprises has lagged behind, and foreign and domestic investments have often been hesitant in coming forward. But the case of Hungary suggests that there is a trade-off between the credibility established by a strict law and the delays ensuing from an over-extended administrative capacity. Ultimately, a delicate balance has to be struck between what is desirable from an economic point of view and what is feasible from an administrative perspective.

FOREIGN INVESTMENT

Foreign investments, and more generally increased capital inflows from abroad, may help to ease the transition. They are particularly important since domestic financial markets are still embryonic, and because they offer important externalities, including access to new markets and to foreign know-how, technology, and management, but also snowball effects where major foreign investments in a certain industry may result in a number of domestic or foreign spin-off investments in related industries (e.g. Fiat's investment in FSM in Poland, Volkswagen's in Skoda in the Czech Republic, which both generated significant investments by component manufacturers). While the benefits are clear, Poland, Hungary, and the CSFR took different approaches to foreign investment.

During 1990–92, the stock of foreign direct investment (FDI) in Eastern Europe rose from US$ 2.3 billion to US$ 11 billion. Hungary has been most successful, with cumulative flows in 1991–92 amounting to over US$ 4 billion, followed by the Czech Republic with close to US$ 2 billion, and Poland with about US$ 1.5 billion; in the Slovak Republic cumulative FDI was below US$ 0.5 billion during 1991–92. Thus, during 1991-92, Hungary alone attracted as much foreign capital as Poland and the CSFR together (Table 11.5). Everywhere total investment commitments by far exceeded actual investments. In Poland, for example, total commitments during 1989–92 amounted to US$ 4.0 billion, with the largest commitment, amounting to US$ 1.8 billion, made by Fiat which purchased a controlling interest in the FSM car manufacturer.

Hungary's success in attracting foreign investment, on a *per capita* basis five times more than in Poland and the CFSR, can be attributed to the country's traditional openness to foreigners, and to the integration of foreigners, including foreign accounting and management consulting firms, into the privatisation process. By the end of 1992, enterprises with foreign participation accounted for at least 18 per cent of the total number of Hungarian enterprises. The CSFR too made a point of its openness to foreign investment. In contrast, Poland had a slow start in attracting foreign investment. While generally inviting foreign investments it implemented various restrictive requirements, like, for example, a stipulation that explicit approval by the Agency of

TABLE 11.5 Foreign investment in selected central and Eastern European countries (as of end-June 1992)

	No. of registrations	Foreign statutory capital (millions US$)	Average size of participation (thousands US$)
CSFR	4 800	1 519.0	316.5
– Czech Republic	–	1 321.5	–
– Slovak Republic	–	197.5	–
Hungary	11 196	2 993.7	267.4
Poland	8 988	832.3	92.6
Romania	13 432	386.9	28.8
Bulgaria	1 100	290.0	263.6
Baltic States	1 849	325.0	175.8

Source: East European Statistics Service (January 1993) and calculations by the authors.

Foreign Investment is needed if share participation by foreigners in privatised companies exceeds 10 per cent. In addition, various Polish officials, including the President, have gone on record with sometimes xenophobic comments about foreigners. All this may have contributed to the relatively small average size of foreign participations in Poland (Table 11.5). Of all Central and Eastern European countries, excluding the former Soviet Union, Poland has by far the largest domestic market, but foreign investment can be expected to pick up significantly only to the extent that the general investment environment shows improvements.

2. Incomes policy, employment and unemployment

INCOMES POLICY

Conventional wisdom for economies in transition holds that an explicit incomes policy is essential, mainly because full-fledged macroeconomic equilibrating mechanisms take time to develop (see e.g. Commander 1992). Both Poland and the CSFR had a tax-based incomes policy (TIP) in effect as a regulatory device for the initial reform period; Hungary eliminated its explicit TIP at the end of 1991 in the hope that SOEs would show financial responsibility. In general, TIPs took the form of taxing SOEs for paying wage increases above a certain wage norm, where the wage norm was defined either in terms of average wages or in terms of the wage bill.

In Poland, which had such an 'excess wage tax' (EWT) in effect, in one form or another, since the early 1980s, the wage norm was first defined in terms of the total wage bill, but from January 1991 it was defined in terms of average wages. Owing in part to a design fault whereby breaching the norm in one year guaranteed a more relaxed norm the following year, the instrument, instead of being a regulatory device with an optimal revenue yield of zero, became a revenue raiser: EWT revenues amounted to over 3 per cent of GDP in 1991, about 1.5 per cent of GDP in 1992, and less than 1 per cent of GDP in 1993.

The CSFR also applied a tax on wage increases above a norm, but wage agreements were also negotiated in a tripartite council consisting of representatives of employers, employees, and the government, and through 1992 wages mostly remained well below the norm. Moreover, the enforcement of EWT appears to have been very patchy. Abolition of the EWT in the Czech Republic in 1993 coincided with rather rapid growth of wages, and the EWT was reimposed in the latter part of the year. In Slovakia too, the EWT was abolished in 1993, but real wages remained subdued. Nevertheless, concerned that enterprises in a weak financial position were giving away too much in wages, the Slovak authorities reintroduced EWT in 1994 for enterprises that were making losses or whose profits were declining.

In Hungary, incomes policy has not been a major issue, perhaps owing to a tradition of manager responsibility and autonomy. When the EWT was abolished at the end of 1991, it was replaced by tripartite discussions, that, together with government wage setting for public sector employees, were expected to act as a guideline for the economy.

Contrary to conventional wisdom, it can be argued (Tait 1993) that TIPs, at least in the form of EWTs, are not desirable for a variety of reasons. When TIPs try to modify corporate behaviour they are generally a second best approach to a symptom (high wage increases) rather than the problem (lack of competition or soft budget constraints). This holds regardless of the design of TIPs, for example, whether they are applied to average wages or the wage bill. TIPs in the form of an EWT on average wages are probably more distortionary because they discourage enterprises from dismissing any worker who has a below average wage (because it raises the average wage per employee) or from rewarding exceptional productivity (because it raises both the wage bill and the average wage). However, while a forceful argument can be made for not retaining EWTs for an extended period of time, their abolition in the Czech and Slovak Republics in 1993 appears to have been premature; in Poland, too, the strong wage increases registered during the last quarter of 1993 were, at least in part, attributed to expectations that the instrument was to be eliminated in April 1994.

In gauging the success of TIPs it could be pointed out that, while the proportion of non-wage income in total income has increased significantly, real wages displayed a remarkable flexibility in all three countries. In Poland, real wages in the socialised sector declined by 18 per cent during 1989–91. In 1992, the average real after-tax wage in six key sectors of the Polish economy was about 6 per cent below the 1991 level, and in January 1993 it was still over 5.5 per cent below the January 1992 level. In Hungary, average real wages dropped by 5.5 per cent during 1989–92, with a cumulative decrease of about 10 per cent during 1989–91 and an increase of about 5 per cent in 1992. Even stronger were the decreases in the CSFR, where real wages in industry declined by a cumulative 25 per cent during 1990–92, with a cumulative decrease of about 30 per cent during 1990–91, and an increase of 7 per cent in 1992. Even after the abolition of EWT and a further increase in real wages in the Czech Republic in 1993, by an estimated 5 per cent, real wages were still well below their pre-reform level.

There is little evidence, though, that the observed real wage declines were the result of EWT. In Poland, for example, evidence presented by Pinto *et al.* (1993) suggests that EWT did not prevent profitable SOEs from paying higher wages and expanding. Overall, profitable SOEs had the highest EWT liabilities and actually paid the tax, while unprofitable SOEs had lower EWT liabilities and ran up tax arrears. In the

CSFR, where wages remained well below the norm, there existed a broad social consensus on the necessity of real wage declines, and in any event it is not clear that the EWT was properly enforced. However, it may be argued that the EWT helped to signal to the population that the government intended to bring about these declines, and that free riders would not be tolerated. In general, though, TIPs do not seem to have been instrumental in bringing about the real wage declines, although, at least in the case of the CSFR, they may have helped to reinforce an existing social consensus.

EMPLOYMENT AND UNEMPLOYMENT

Labour market issues are highly sensitive in all economies in transition. The absence of explicit unemployment under socialism reflected both an ideological emphasis on the role of labour in society, and the official view that unemployment, like poverty, was a distinguishing feature of capitalism (Atkinson and Micklewright 1992). While, to some extent, liberal disability benefits functioned as an outlet for reducing high labour market participation rates, under socialism, the constitution guaranteed the right to work, and there was a close connection between social rights and participation in the labour market. At the same time, there was virtually no connection between productivity and wages, and, to some degree, wages had the function of a universal social benefit for every labour market participant. This resulted in high labour market participation rates, and implicitly changed the constitutional right to work into a right to receive a wage income.

All this changed drastically with the introduction of the reform and transformation programmes. The resulting increases in unemployment seemed dramatic. In Poland, the number of registered unemployed increased from 56,000 in January 1990 to 2.5 million by the end of 1992, and rose further to 2.9 million by the end of 1993, making 15.7 per cent of the labour force unemployed. The number of registered unemployed in Hungary rose from 1.9 per cent of the labour force in December 1990 to a peak of 13.6 per cent in February 1993. A combination of newly created jobs and the termination of some benefits reduced the unemployment rate to 12.6 per cent by December 1993. In the CSFR unemployment only began to become significant in 1991, with the acceleration of economic reform. Recorded unemployment was still less than 1 per cent of the labour force at the end of 1990, but increased rapidly to 7.1 per cent by January 1992 before falling back during the first half of 1992, reflecting in part a reduction in incentives to register as unemployed, but also rapid growth of the small private sector. By the end of 1992, registered unemployment in the CSFR amounted to 5.1 per cent. These averages mask substantial differences between the Czech and the Slovak Republics, which persisted in 1993: at the end of 1993, unemployment in the Czech Republic amounted to 3.5 per cent of the labour force, while in the Slovak Republic it amounted to 14.4 per cent.

The emergence of substantial open unemployment is not necessarily undesirable if it reflects adjustment. It is not clear, however, that this was really the case. In Poland, for example, the increase in unemployment may largely be attributed to the overall output decline and was not only confined to workers in socialised industry. In addition, although neither can be measured with confidence given the dynamic growth of the private sector, employment declines appear to have lagged behind output declines. Thus labour productivity has generally fallen, and unit labour costs (ULC) have fallen much less than real wages. During 1990-92 ULC in industry declined by 11 per cent in the CSFR (with a small increase in 1990, a strong decline in 1991, and an increase in 1992), and declined only slightly in Poland (with a drastic fall in 1990, an almost equally drastic increase in 1991, and a moderate decline in 1992). Over the same period, the collapse of the CMEA caused the terms of trade to shift sharply against Central Europe, and it is not clear that these rather small declines in unit labour costs were sufficient to accommodate the increased costs of inputs. Thus, much labour shedding may remain to be done in established industries even at the present wage levels – let alone if real wages should rise.

Much of the near-term developments in Eastern and Central European labour markets will depend upon new job creation. For example, new job creation in the private sector appears to explain much of the unemployment differences that exist between the Czech and Slovak Republics, particularly since output in state-owned industries has behaved rather similarly. However, labour mobility, both between regions and sectors, will be crucial if new job creation is to reduce unemployment levels rather than merely create bottlenecks in the labour market. Mismatches between the supply and demand of skills and/or spatial mismatches between workers and jobs appear to have been important in Poland in the early phases of the transition: Coricelli and Revenga (1992) find that the increase in unemployment did not seem to reduce vacancies. Worse, more recent evidence by Maret and Schwartz (1993) suggests that the extent of the mismatch may not have reduced over time. Such a lack of labour market flexibility, which also appears to be a problem in the CSFR and in Hungary, may to a large degree be attributed to severe housing shortages; to the extent that these continue, active labour market measures, like retraining and public works schemes, may remain largely ineffective.

3. Financial sector reform and the macroeconomy

Changing the behaviour of production enterprises in goods and labour markets is but one piece in the puzzle of transition. Equally crucial is ensuring that financial systems efficiently channel household savings to their most efficient uses in production. The infrastructure underlying a modern financial system will have to be constructed from scratch in a setting which is still dominated by the legacy of the command economy. The hangovers from the old one-tier banking system include the lack, on the part of bankers and supervisors, of the forward-looking perspective required for the efficient exchange of money today in exchange for a promise to pay tomorrow. In addition, bank recapitalisation, necessitated by provisioning against bad enterprise debt, will be effective only if banks are given the incentives to make proper use of the new resources.

Household savings have increased of late in the Central European countries. But in Hungary and Poland banks are providing the bulk of financing for the burgeoning government deficits, and, in all three countries, banks are keeping the remaining assets either in liquid form, or are allocating funds in ways that do not always enhance the transition process. This section examines the emerging patterns of financial savings and investment, and what governments have done and can still do in their attempts to foster greater efficiency in financial intermediation.

BREAK-UP OF ONE-TIER BANKING SYSTEMS AND LEGAL REFORM

The first step in reforming banking systems was invariably to break up the old monobanks, but the decades of existence of the latter continue to influence and constrain financial systems. The passive role of the one-tier banking system in the command economy meant that the myriad of personal, technical, supervisory, and even cultural complexities of the modern financial system simply did not exist. Because the elements of bank infrastructure cannot be easily imported, they are now being developed from scratch. The situation for the non-financial sector is different: at least on the production side, the requirements for efficient operation are the same after the advent of transition as before.

The command economy banking system served as a conduit for the monetary flows that offset imbalances arising in the goods markets, which were themselves determined by the central plan. The separation of enterprise and household financial flows was a key feature. Households settled transactions by cash and most financial savings were in the form of deposits at savings banks. Transactions between enterprises were cleared through the monobank. Periodic government appropriation of SOE deposits, which were illiquid, promoted excessive investment financed by retained earnings and by bank credit. The passive role played by banks in the command economy precluded development of the credit evaluation skills necessary for success in a market economy, nor was there a need for developing the expertise and legal framework for bank supervision and bank governance. Finally, banks accumulated claims on the large SOEs whose decisions were determined more by political influence and bargaining skills than by market signals. The consequences of these credit misallocations are only now coming to the fore.

The institutional structures of the financial system under the centrally planned economy were quite similar in all three countries. The monobank performed most commercial and central banking functions, one or more national savings banks with extensive branch networks collected household deposits and generally lent to households, a foreign trade bank handled international transactions, and an investment or development bank made long-term structural loans. The ways in which the one-tier banking systems were broken up were also comparable in the three countries, with the important exception of the modalities of bank governance, which will be addressed below. The commercial banking operations of the monobanks were transmuted into new large banks organised by region in Poland, by republic in the CSFR, and essentially by market in Hungary. Interest rate deregulation began, and households and enterprises were free to transact with the bank of their choice. Restrictions on foreign exchange deposits were relaxed. New laws established bank supervision and regulation responsibilities with the central banks in Poland and the CSFR, and with a new agency in Hungary. Foreign bank involvement was allowed in all three countries leading to the establishment of numerous, but small, joint venture banks.

BANKING SYSTEM SOURCES AND USES OF FUNDS

Not only are commercial banks continuing to dominate the financial sphere in transition economies, owing to the lack of non-bank financial assets, but their importance has been enhanced by the unexpected increase in household savings that now appears to be characteristic of the transition process. So far banks have not been effectively intermediating the surge in deposits. In Poland and Hungary banks appear to be buying government securities and building liquidity rather than pushing ahead the transition by lending to enterprises. This sub-section examines the reasons behind the surge in household savings to the banking sector, one of the surprises of the transition, and reviews what banks are doing with their new-found liquidity. Before moving on to the specifics, a review of overall monetary conditions is in order.

Volatile macroeconomic developments, overall structural changes and the evolution of new instruments has made formulation of monetary policy in transition economies singularly challenging. Central banks had to deal with external and domestic shocks, sterilise foreign capital inflows, and work with monetary instruments whose relationship with the aggregates was obscured by shifts in money demand. Furthermore, direct credit ceilings on commercial banks – the surefire tool used to control credit in the early stages – were distortionary, and central banks quickly realised the importance of indirect means of control. Thin government security markets and the lack of balanced central bank government security portfolios complicated the implementation of open market operations. However, the fight against inflation was facilitated by appreciating real exchange rates and by the declines in economic activity.

In general, monetary authorities, recognising the importance of immediately building credibility at the start of reform, and fearing the lack of market incentives to discipline credit market behaviour, maintained tight credit conditions. This was relatively easy in the CSFR, which enjoyed low rates of inflation and money growth in 1990. Hungary consistently maintained tight policies, in part due to the need to offset foreign capital inflows and reduce inflation.

Declines in money velocity during the transition period are perhaps the most important monetary development during the transition (Table 11.6). The fall in inflation in Hungary and Poland probably induced higher holdings of financial assets, resulted in the substitution of domestic currency for foreign currency deposits in Poland since 1990 and in Hungary during 1992, and together with interest rate deregulation, pushed up real rates of return. Household deposits account for much of the increase in broad money, although in the CSFR and to a lesser degree in Hungary, enterprise deposits have accelerated following an explosion in the number of enterprises, each requiring a minimum level of operating liquidity. With such large swings in money demand it would have been impossible to stabilise prices, using only money supply targets. The choice to use a fixed exchange rate as the anchor for prices appears justified in this light.

The changes in personal savings behaviour unique to the transition process are tantalisingly difficult to quantify, but crucial to understanding the changing pattern of inter-sectoral flows of funds. Household financial savings as a share of disposable income in Hungary rose from 6 per cent during 1989-90 to 14 per cent during 1991-92, although the build-up of savings slowed during 1993 as households increased consumption, and deposit rates declined. In the CSFR money incomes less expenditures increased to 7 per cent of income in 1991-92, from about zero in 1990. Velocity increased during the year of price liberalisation as the monetary overhang was eliminated, but the declines in velocity in 1992 show that households then accumulated savings at a faster rate than nominal GDP growth.

The increase in household balances has been prompted by changes associated with the transition. The prospect of unemployment in the transforming economy has introduced a new motive for precautionary savings. There appears to be a newly developing cohort of wealthier households with higher propensities to save. The cessation of subsidised mortgage loans means that families must save to finance housing purchases. The scarcity of bank credit for the vibrant small enterprise sector is necessitating financing out of own savings, which are maintained primarily as deposits in the banking system. Finally, declining rates of inflation have increased the expected real value of financial assets.

Today, as before the break-up of the one-tier banking system, most household savings are held at the numerous branches of the national savings banks. It has generally not been worthwhile for the large commercial banks or joint venture banks to pay the substantial fixed costs to establish a retail branch system, which, in any case, would take some time to attract a large share of personal savings. Instead, the large commercial banks still access personal savings from the national savings banks by tapping the inter-bank markets.

In contrast to domestic savings, declines in net bank borrowing from abroad have drained resources from the banking system. Net foreign liabilities have been sharply reduced in Poland and Hungary, which began the transition with high levels of indebtedness. The CSFR began with positive claims on the rest of the world, which increased after 1990.

The opening of foreign markets and the decontrol of consumer prices has provided existing and new enterprises with a plethora of projects with favourable returns, which, owing to the lack of equity and corporate bond markets and especially for those enterprises that cannot access foreign funding, must be financed with bank loans. However, credit flows to enterprises have dwindled in Hungary and Poland as a share of the total change in credit, and, furthermore, some of the increase in bank loans appears to be in the form of capitalisation of interest payments to traditional customers. This reflects a host of factors, many shared with developed economies.

Loan demand in all three countries has been reduced by the downturn in economic activity, and, in Hungary, by the onset of widespread bankruptcy following the new law. On the bank side, commercial loan repayments are perceived as risky, collateral is difficult to value and sell, credit evaluation capabilities are under-developed, and the risk weighing of assets under the new capital requirements provide incentives to banks to purchase government paper, which is needed by governments to finance burgeoning deficits. In Poland the importance of directed credits, a large share of which is capitalised interest and at preferential terms, has slowed the development of standard enterprise loan practices. Uncertainties related to the advent of the bankruptcy law in Hungary in 1992 stifled new lending, led to a classification of a large share of

TABLE 11.6 Change in money velocity (in per cent)*

	1989	1990	1991	1992
CSFR	−3.0	2.3	10.0	−24.1
Hungary	10.1	0.8	−15.5	−15.1
Poland	2.0	117.4	−20.3	−6.3

Source: Central banks of Hungary, Poland and the CSFR, and calculations by the authors.

* Money calculated as geometric average of five quarterly observations.

enterprise loans by the end of the year, and ultimately resulted in a decline in nominal bank credit to enterprises within the year.

Fiscal austerity in the CSFR freed more bank assets for lending to enterprises compared to Hungary and Poland. Moreover banks appear to have been supportive of the emerging private sector. Admittedly shaky data suggest that the total share of outstanding credit loaned to the private sector increased from 1 per cent in 1990 to 20 per cent by the end of 1992.

Although in transition economies, as elsewhere, it is impossible to identify clearly the various components of credit declines, it is clear that in Poland and, especially, Hungary high real enterprise credit rates (deflated by the PPI) are dampening lending activity. By the end of 1992 the lag in the downward adjustment of enterprise credit rates in Hungary, following the decline in inflation since mid-1991, had brought the real cost of credit to enterprises in excess of 15 per cent. The wide bank interest rate spreads that are thwarting enterprise lending are symptomatic of a shortfall of bank capital, as well as a host of other inter-locked structural problems.

STRUCTURAL REFORM OF THE BANKING SYSTEM

The need to construct a new banking infrastructure from the ground up makes bank reform even more complicated than reform of the non-financial sector. Structural bank reform will not be completed until bank governance provides bank managers with the incentives to operate banks efficiently. The systemic risk associated with bank deposits and the benefits of efficient credit allocation for the entire economy mean that the supervision and regulation of banks is especially important, but difficult to initiate and develop. The appropriate level of bank risk taking and the allocation of bank assets to risky credit requires the proper amount of bank capital. The privatisation of banks is, of course, the logical conclusion of reforming the banking sector. These key issues of reform are reviewed in turn.

Governance

Unlike non-financial enterprises, banks did not exist as separate entities prior to the advent of reform. The historical centralisation of the various banking functions in the monobank has inhibited the development of appropriate bank governance, as has the inevitably slower pace of commercialisation and privatisation for banks, which have been the target of special government policies.

Ownership of the large banks in Hungary was assumed first by the State Property Agency in 1990, then by the State Holding Company in late 1992. The change to prudent management based on market principles has been slowed by the lack of expertise of agency personnel and of bank directors. In the CSFR, ownership of bank shares passed to the National Property Funds in a step toward privatisation, but the operations of the banks were controlled by their management.

Banks in Poland have been commercialised, and are subject to supervision by the Ministry of Finance. Also, twinning relationships with foreign banks have been arranged. The Ministry of Finance has addressed the lack of market incentives by giving stock options to bank executives to be exercised upon privatisation. This may be a relatively inexpensive way to reap some of the benefits of private ownership, particularly as progress on bank privatisation has been visible ever since the process started in 1993, and since it is to be completed in the foreseeable future.

Recapitalisation and loan consolidation

Most of the large banks are saddled with minimal or negative capital according to internationally accepted accounting standards (IAS), which, in turn, has contributed to the slow-down in bank lending. Because banks are only now recognising the magnitude of bad enterprise debt – much of which is left over from the command economy – sooner or later governments will have to provide new capital if banks are to intermediate properly. In addition, as part of their goal of integration with Western Europe, Hungary, Poland and the CSFR have committed themselves to meeting the Bank of International Settlements risk-weighted capital adequacy ratios.

The choice of how much to provide for bank recapitalisation is based on weighing the government financing costs against the costs to borrowers and lenders of the very wide interest rate spreads needed to shore up bank capital (Fig. 11.1). Recapitalisation schemes should be designed so that banks are not given the incentive to alter their reserving policy, or expect future recapitalisations (the moral hazard problem). In order to ensure that recapitalisation is a one-off 'stock adjustment' that fosters bank lending, the 'flow' problems of governance and supervision must be addressed, and recapitalisation should be implemented as quickly as possible.

Effective bank recapitalisation also requires working out bad bank loans, and concomitantly borrower restructuring. The contenders for a lead role in working out bad loans are emerging market players, a centralised government institution, or the banks themselves. The conditions required for a free-market-based solution, including reliable and available information, proper regulation, and expertise, are simply not present in transition economies. A centralised loan workout institution would be encumbered by the same handicaps as the central planner. The familiarity of banks

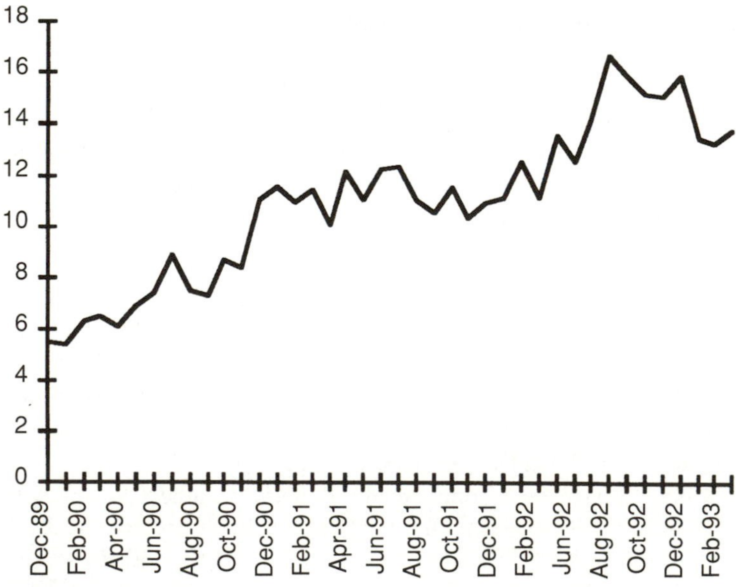

FIG 11.1 Hungary: Commercial bank interest rate spread. Rate on one year or less enterprise credit less one-month deposit rate
Source: National bank of Hungary

with the borrowers and the concentration of expertise, however limited by Western standards, means that banks, under the appropriate supervision, are best suited to work out the bad loans. The workout of bank loans, in turn, is inextricably linked to enterprise reform: banks must be given incentives to restructure the loans of viable enterprises and participate in the shut-down of insolvent enterprises only.

All three countries have taken important steps toward recapitalisation and loan consolidation. A bank recapitalisation plan that is being implemented in Poland will increase capital to asset ratios of large banks to 12 per cent or more. The capital injections are largely financed by a domestic bond issue amounting to 1.5 per cent of GDP, and the Polish government is making headway in persuading Western governments to make part of the US$1 billion stabilisation fund, created for the zloty in 1990 and not drawn on since, available for enterprise restructuring, including bank restructuring. In the meantime, the Ministry of Finance also mandated the establishment of workout units in all large banks, which are to engage in comprehensive borrower restructuring, rather than loan workouts only.

The CSFR addressed the problem of bad debt of commercial banks in several steps. First, in early 1991, it transferred a portion of bank loans to a newly established institution, the Consolidation Bank. In late 1992, commercial banks sold at a discount an additional, though much smaller, chunk of debt to the Consolidation Bank. On its liability side, the Consolidation Bank took over from the commercial banks savings bank deposits and central bank financing. Losses will likely be covered by privatisation receipts although, so far, the Consolidation Bank has experienced much lower default rates than had originally been expected. In addition, in 1991, the National Property Funds (the recipients of privatisation proceeds) issued bonds equivalent to some 5 per cent of GDP, which were used in part for a straight recapitalisation of the banks, and in part to substitute for loans that were written off by the banks. The latter part was intended specifically to support financial restructuring of enterprises that were thought to be viable, but were over-burdened with debt. Finally, since the beginning of reform, the commercial banks have made significant provisions against bad loans.

In Hungary the magnitude of requisite bank recapitalisation has been exposed by the relatively strict bankruptcy law. The decrease in profit taxes paid by banks from 3 per cent of GDP in 1991 to 0 per cent in 1992, reflecting a legal change allowing for provisioning against pre-tax income, can be viewed as a reallocation of resources from the government. Following a limited exchange of bonds for loans made prior to 1987, the government gave banks the opportunity to swap bonds for loans classified bad during 1990–92 under a 1992 scheme. However, the effectiveness of the stunningly complex operation was limited by the small amount of total net capital provided as well as by the differential impact on capital adequacy across individual banks. Banks were further recapitalised by the government at the end of 1993.

If bank recapitalisation narrows the spread between bank deposits and lending rates, then the burden of reconstituting the bank sector is shifted from savers and borrowers to the government. The entire economy will benefit as long as the advantages of enhanced intermediation exceed the costs associated with interest payments on government recapitalisation bonds. It remains to be seen to what degree the uncovering of bad bank debts in the future may lead to wider spreads, and further recapitalisations.

Supervision

Bank recapitalisation will not be effective without the proper supervisory and regulatory capabilities to gauge the health of bank balance sheets, ensure proper bank management, and monitor short-term balance sheet developments. As with bank governance, the development of bank supervision and regulation is being slowed by the need to build the personnel, technical and institutional capabilities from the ground up.

Tracking bank balance sheets, particularly the quality of loans and bank liquidity, requires first that bank financial statements be properly formulated and easily available to regulators. Legal requirements and the prospect of privatisation have motivated most large banks in Hungary, Poland and the CSFR to move toward reporting financial statements according to IAS, which requires non-mechanical criteria for classifying bad loans, provisioning against problematic bank equity holdings, and provisioning against accrued interest payments recorded as income. Proper supervision requires that banks provide supervisors with easy access to financial information, and that the appropriate computer systems be established by both banks and their regulators. Finally, as in fully developed market economies, banks should undergo regular and unscheduled on-site examinations by supervisory personnel.

For the practitioner, bank supervision is an inexact science, or perhaps an art, requiring years of experience and guidance to gain the expertise required to anticipate upcoming problems. The dearth of bank examiners in transition economies means that bank supervision is an especially fruitful area of technical assistance. Another constraint on the development and retention of bank supervisory personnel is the disparity between public and private sector salaries. As long as banks are government-owned the establishment of proper supervision is linked with ownership and governance issues. In this respect, the inevitable delays in the implementation of full-fledged supervisory capabilities may mean that the slower pace of bank privatisation relative to other enterprises may not be disadvantageous. Indeed, problems of monitoring and control unique to financial institutions may make private owners reluctant to invest in a banking system that lacks the advantages of complete supervision.

Privatisation

A large number of joint venture banks have already been established in Hungary, Poland, and the Czech and Slovak Republics, in many cases with the involvement of major United States and European institutions. However, the strategic focus of the joint venture banks on banking services rather than intermediation, and their as yet small share of total bank assets, mean that they may not play a major role in developing the efficient channelling of household savings to enterprise borrowers.

Private ownership of a share of banks sufficient to provide management with market-based incentives may be an attainable medium-term goal. The familiarity of the government-owned foreign trade banks makes them candidates for early equity ownership by foreigners. The smaller of the two foreign trade banks in the CSFR is already majority owned by foreigners. In addition, majority holdings in the large commercial banks in each CSFR republic were sold under the first wave of the voucher scheme and investment privatisation funds acquired large blocks of bank shares. The effect of this change in ownership on bank governance remains to be seen, but is likely to be positive – as long as supervision (of both banks and investment funds) is well enough developed to prevent abuses of power by the new owners. Two Polish state banks had been sold by early 1994, but, particularly in the case of second privatisation, of the Silesian Bank (Bank Slaski), the sale was surrounded by much controversy and precipitated the resignation of the finance minister.

Although Bank Slaski is one of the largest and healthiest Polish state banks it failed to attract any major commercial interest by the tender deadline of end of October 1993, and the Polish Finance Ministry persuaded the Dutch-based ING bank to take a 25.9 per cent stake at an attractive price. When Bank Slaski shares were first traded on the Warsaw stock exchange in early 1994, prices rocketed to 13.5 times their subscription value, leading to accusations that officials had seriously misjudged the market, thereby permitting profiteering and depriving the Treasury of significant proceeds. The setting of asset sale prices by governments for banks, or for any other enterprise, is especially problematic in the context of a surging stock market. While the Bank Slaski incident may be used by opponents of privatisation to slow down progress, ultimately there are no viable alternatives to full and timely privatisation.

NON-BANK FINANCING FOR ENTERPRISES

The impediments to the development of banks into the role of sophisticated lenders to enterprises lead naturally to consideration of non-bank sources of financing. The advantages of direct enterprise investment over bank lending as a source of enterprise financing that have been cited include improved governance, diversification of investor risk, and a vehicle for foreign direct investment (Calvo and Kumar 1993). To what degree can domestic stock and bond markets channel household savings to enterprises, and what is the role of foreign investors and lenders?

Before this review of financial markets, an alternative source of financing that has been tapped by loss-making firms in economies with weak governance and regulation should be considered. Although inter-enterprise arrears were the subject of considerable attention in Hungary, Poland, and the CSFR early on in the reform process, the recent evidence indicates that the involuntary extension of credit from one firm to another is now less of a concern. Although the decline during 1992 in 'involuntary inter-enterprise lending' of firms for which the National Bank of Hungary refuses to rediscount bills of exchange largely reflects the new bankruptcy law, rather than a fundamental return to profitability, the problem is now being addressed head on. Inter-enterprise arrears in Poland and the CSFR appear to have stabilised. In general the alleviation of inter-enterprise arrears may reflect the overall tightening of enterprise budget constraints, particularly the incentives for the credit-supplying firms to maintain clean balance sheets, as well as credible government policies concerning the bail-out of highly indebted enterprises.

The money and government bond markets were the first capital markets to emerge in Hungary, Poland, and the CSFR. Inter-bank markets have been channelling funds from the savings banks to commercial and other banks in Hungary, Poland, and the CSFR, and the experience gained by the participants and regulators in this, the first financial market, is important. Successful sales of Hungarian government bonds directly to the public, thus circumventing the banking system, have resulted in a fairly active government security market, which, ironically in light of the potential for crowding out, is institutionally paving the way for corporate bond and equity markets by familiarising households and enterprises with the workings of a financial market. In the CSFR a government bond market was introduced in early 1992. Finally, a small number of firms in Hungary and the CSFR have issued broker-guaranteed commercial paper.

Nevertheless, in the medium term, the macroeconomic impact of intermediation via domestic capital markets will be limited for the same fundamental reason that constrains the maturation of banks: such markets essentially did not exist until just a few years ago. The recent birth of corporate bond and equity markets in the transition economies means that in this respect they lag behind developing countries such as Mexico and India, even though Hungary, Poland and the CSFR enjoy higher *per capita* income and education levels. The growth of the corporate bond and stock markets is particularly limited by the need for reliable financial statements and experienced enterprise management, for the lack of collateral and indirect involvement of equity holders makes them even less inclined than banks to invest their funds without easily accessible information.

The time needed to make households feel comfortable transferring personal savings from savings bank deposits to stocks and bonds will further delay the growth of non-bank capital markets, although as income disparities widen savings are becoming concentrated in a smaller, and presumably more well-informed, group of households. The availability of technical assistance in the form of personal expertise and computer resources means operational considerations will not constrain the development of liquid bond and stock markets. Already, stock exchanges in transition economies have sufficient computer capacity and employees to manage much higher volume.

In Hungary, capitalisation of enterprises traded on the Budapest Stock Exchange, which was re-established in 1990, amounted to only 2 per cent of GDP in 1992, although trading volume and value accelerated rapidly late in 1993. Less then 50 companies are traded, and foreign involvement is limited to a small number of mutual funds. In the CSFR, shares of more than 300 companies involved in the privatisation schemes are, eventually, expected to be traded in the new stock exchanges in Prague and Bratislava, and many more in over-the-counter markets that use the sophisticated computer technology put in place for voucher privatisation. The investment privatisation funds that control around three-quarters of the voucher-bought shares are expected to play a key role, and, if effectively supervised, may serve as a new, and potentially important, intermediary in the transition economy.

In Poland, volume traded in the stock exchange established in Warsaw in 1991 has been increasing rapidly: during January 1993 to late January 1994 the turnover index grew from 1,040 to more than 18,000, capitalisation grew from US$ 240 million to US$ 2.8 billion (c. 3% of GDP), and price–earnings ratios climbed from 3.8 to over 35. To a large extent, the amazing growth of the Warsaw stock exchange reflects excess demand that was brought about by low interest rates, lack of alternative investment possibilities, and high expectations. Unlike the Czech and Hungarian markets, where the majority of shares are held by foreigners, foreign investors own only 25–30 per cent of Polish shares and account for only 10 per cent of the trade volume. The halving of share prices in 1994 showed that part of this boom was not sustainable.

In Hungary, more than any other transforming economy, the dearth of domestic equity investment is to some degree, as reviewed in Section 2, being offset by an influx of foreign investment, and, beginning in 1992, by direct enterprise borrowing from abroad. The externalities associated with direct investment, which are to a large degree irreversible, are an important advantage to political and economic stability.

Direct enterprise foreign borrowing which is not government guaranteed is an increasingly important source of financing for large profitable companies.

Studies of developed economies, however, conclude that banks are an important source of financing, second only to retained earnings, and that, in particular, small enterprises rely on bank loans (Mayer 1989). Thus, by accelerating bank reform governments would speed up the provision of credit to the growing small firms unable to obtain credit elsewhere, thus accelerating the pace of transformation.

WHAT NEEDS TO BE DONE?

The emerging set of financial sector issues, and their consequences for the economy as a whole, leads to consideration of how to accelerate the bank reform process, and how developments in the financial sector are, and will be, shaping growth.

First, the financial sector reforms that cost the least, but take the longest time to implement, need to be expedited. The quality of banking supervision and regulation can be quickly speeded up with the aid of foreign expertise alone. Since bank privatisation will in most cases be a lengthy process, it is imperative that bank governance ensures open and timely reporting of financial information and provides management with the proper incentives, preferably market-based. Without these reforms, bank recapitalisation will be less effective in promoting bank lending, and, because of the moral hazard problem, will entail greater costs to the government.

Bank recapitalisation and loan workouts are both more costly, and, because banks, governments and enterprises are involved, significantly more complicated. Here, an effective bankruptcy law provides the benefits of forcing enterprises to expose the amounts of bad bank (and other) debts, and requires that the government decide how much resources to provide for bank recapitalisation. The fiscal costs of recapitalising banks to at least the minimum levels of IAS can be viewed as recognition of unrecognised public sector losses. The workout of bad bank loans is the most complex problem of all. The absence of the conditions for emerging new capital markets, and bank familiarity with enterprise borrowers, point to the advantages of the banks themselves working out the loans, whether or not they maintain the loans as liabilities. Any excess of the social rate of return on successful bank workouts of enterprises over the rate of return to the banks themselves, resulting from the avoidance of employment and tax costs from the shut-down of viable but illiquid enterprises, would imply a role for government incentives, and certainly for an influx of foreign expertise.

The pace of financial reform will shape which enterprises will drive the transformation process. Foreign financing will be available for joint venture firms, and for the largest profitable enterprises, which, eventually, will be able to tap domestic equity and bond markets. The costs of developing the infrastructure for small business lending suggest that this fast growing portion of the private sector will to an important extent be owner financed in the foreseeable future, even if the pace of financial reform accelerates. Most worrying are the funding prospects of the medium-sized domestically owned firms, which are shut out of international and domestic capital markets and too large for owner financing, but will not gain access to bank financing without further reform.

4. Fiscal policy

Of course, enterprises and banks can only use resources that the government does not pre-empt, or that it does not at least compete for from a position of considerable strength. Fiscal imbalances in the Central European countries have widened with a sharp fall in revenues, the emergence of unemployment and wider income dispersion, and the reduction of the political – though not economic – scope for expenditure cuts after the initial effort to cut subsidies. And yet, as was stressed above, stabilisation efforts ultimately proved broadly successful, with inflation falling and with balances of payments righting themselves. The issue of whether there has been significant crowding-out of non-government investment is less easily addressed; however, it seems clear that firms' appetite for investment has so far been greatly curtailed in the wake of the uncertainties brought on by large-scale reform and the prospect of speedy privatisation.

Although the three countries differed greatly in their access to foreign financing, a key to the apparent paradox of stabilisation in the midst of widening deficits lies in the rise in private savings discussed in Section 4 above.[3] As money remains by far the most important financial asset and instrument of saving in all the Central European countries, this was manifested not so much through direct lending to the government but through a growing demand for broad money, intermediated to the government by a banking system that was only too happy to find such a safe haven for its resources.

But the fact that it has thus far been possible to finance these deficits without too many ill-effects is no guarantee that it will be possible to do so in the future. Private savings are notoriously volatile, and it is conceivable that they will fall just as unexpectedly as they rose. Certainly some of the factors responsible for the increase must be waning: financial savings have been rebuilt, and uncertainty is gradually being reduced. But even more fundamentally, investment will have to rise. As well as putting into place all the other prerequisites for a take-off of investment, discussed in Sections 2–4 above, governments will have to make room for it in the economy's financial accounts. For Hungary and Poland, in particular, this unambiguously means cutting fiscal deficits.

Lasting growth also requires fundamental fiscal adjustment to reduce state intervention in the economy and give greater elbowroom to private initiative. This means reducing the size of government, which typically loomed very large (Fig. 11.2), raising revenues in a less distortionary fashion, and improving the expenditure mix.

There are both striking parallels and interesting differences in the ways the three Central European countries tackled the twin problems of curtailing fiscal imbalances and reducing state intervention, and in the results of their efforts. In all three countries, the share of government revenue in GDP fell considerably (Table 11.7); this development was most spectacular in the CSFR, where government revenue was cut by almost 18 percentage points of GDP from its peak in 1989. At the same time, the share of expenditures in GDP remained fairly stable in Hungary and Poland, while it was cut enormously in the CSFR. On both fronts, the CSFR's peculiarities reflect in part its former reliance on cross-subsidisation between enterprises, which raised both revenues and expenditures.[4] But in all three countries (though less so in the CSFR than elsewhere), strong early fiscal performances were followed by growing deficits.[5]

In 1992, the deficits of the general governments (excluding privatisation proceeds) reached over 8 per cent of GDP in Hungary, 6 per cent of GDP in Poland, and over 3

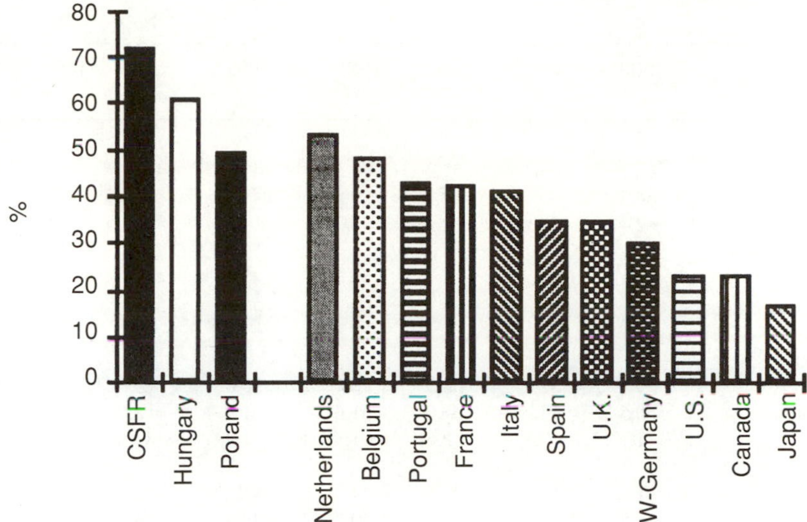

FIG 11.2 Expenditures/GDP in 1989

Source: IMF, International Financial Statistics

per cent of GDP in the CSFR. Of course, the measurement of fiscal positions is not an exact science. Table 11.7 does not purport to correct for a number of well-known difficulties in measuring fiscal magnitudes, but one needs to be aware of these problems in assessing the official fiscal accounts.

For a start, there is the problem of measuring real interest payments when inflation is reflected in high nominal interest rates, so that a part of domestic interest payments goes to offset the inflationary erosion of principal and can therefore be interpreted as amortisation. 'Netting out' this part of interest payments produces what has sometimes been called the 'operational' deficit (Blejer and Cheasty 1991), which can be significantly lower than the nominal deficit when inflation is high.

There is also the issue of contingent liabilities. These can be explicit or implicit. In the CSFR (and in Slovakia in particular), an explosion of government guarantees on bank loans to enterprises – to amounts equivalent to 2 per cent of GDP a year in 1991–92 – has been a particular problem, and has undoubtedly taken some of the strain that would otherwise have been reflected directly in the state budget. Notably, all the Central European countries have by now moved to impose limits on the amount of explicit guarantees that can be issued. Implicit guarantees, such as those that are often assumed to cover bank lending to loss-making enterprises, are more difficult to contain. In either case, excluding contingent liabilities from expenditure and fiscal balance data means underestimating both future pressures on expenditures and the role of government in the allocation of resources in the economy.

But there are still more complicated accounting problems in transition economies. Because the state was so recently dismembered into its constituent government, bank, and enterprise parts, large blocks of assets and liabilities tend to get reshuffled in the early years of the transition. Privatisation and government involvement in the problem of the banking system's bad debt are the most visible manifestations of this

TABLE 11.7 General government operations 1989–93* (in per cent GDP)

	1989	1990	1991	1992	1993	1994 (est.)	1995 †	1996 †
CSFR**								
Revenue	62.1	60.2	52.2	49.5	49.9	46.0		
Expenditure	64.5	60.1	54.2	52.8	48.5	46.0		
Balance	−2.4	0.1	−2.0	−3.3	1.4	0	0	0
Slovak Republic								
Revenue				50.7	48.0	44.0		
Expenditure				63.8	55.5	50.0		
Balance				−13.1	−7.5	−6.0	−4.0	−3.0
Hungary								
Revenue	59.2	57.7	54.5	56.1	56.0	n.a.		
Expenditure	60.5	57.2	57.0	61.6	61.9	n.a.		
Balance	−1.3	0.5	−2.5	−5.5	−5.9	−8.0	−6.0	−5.0
Poland***								
Revenue	41.4	42.9	41.5	44.0	45.5	n.a.		
Expenditure	48.8	39.8	48.0	50.7	48.4	n.a.		
Balance	−7.4	3.1	−6.5	−6.7	−2.9	−4.0	−3.5	−2.5
For comparison:								
Russia††								
Revenue	41.0				33.8			
Expenditure	49.5				41.8			
Balance	−8.5			−18.8	−8.0	−12.0	−9.0	−7.0

Sources: EBRD Transition Report, October 1994, and own computations.

* Excluding privatisation proceeds (except for Hungary, where small amounts are included in revenue). See other caveats in text.

** Before 1992 data are for CSFR. From 1992 onwards CSFR data are for the Czech Republic only.

*** Polish data are on a domestic commitment basis, i.e. foreign interest payments are recorded on a cash basis. Data for 1992 include, for the first time, the departmental enterprises of the local authorities, which had revenues of 1.7 per cent of GDP, expenditures of 2.4 per cent of GDP, and a deficit of 0.7 per cent of GDP.

† Projections for 1995 and 1996 and for Poland also for 1994 are from OECD Economic Outlook, No.56, December 1994

†† The data for Russia stemming from EBRD are consistent with those from OECD. However, both sources are clearly inconsistent with RET. For further explanations, see Chapter 14.

reshuffling. The IMF's Government Finance Statistics (GFS) methodology (IMF 1986) recommends that, depending on their exact nature, privatisation proceeds be treated either as capital revenue or as negative net lending. However, a case can be made that privatisation sales strain capital markets in much the same way as do sales of securities, so that if the proceeds are spent (rather than deposited in government accounts) crowding out may result just as with deficit spending. And an even stronger case can be made that, since a sale of assets by itself reduces the government's net worth, the proceeds should be viewed as reducing government debt (even if not actually earmarked for this purpose) (see e.g. Cheasty 1992): the loss of future earnings from enterprises that are being privatised is conceptually similar to the servicing burden of additional debt. The latter arguments suggest that privatisation proceeds should be viewed as financing, and this is why they are excluded from revenues in Table 11.7. An even trickier complication relates to the clean-up of bad loans. As described in Section 4, as long as the necessary steps are also taken to strengthen bank supervision and governance, this is probably a prerequisite for preventing, over the longer term, a further souring of bank portfolios and the ensuing even greater pressures on the fiscal position. All the Central European countries have instituted clean-up operations involving direct replacement of bad loans with government debt. But in all cases, though to different extents, banks are also making provision against bad debts inherited from the old regime, and as a result are paying less in profits tax. The stock adjustments involved in the former type of operation – though not, in principle, the ensuing debt-servicing burden – are often excluded from fiscal accounts, and this treatment is appropriate to the extent that no resource flows are involved: all that happens is a reassignment of a stock of debt from one debtor to another. But the results of the latter type of operation – clean-up through making provision against bad loans – are much the same, and yet these are inevitably reflected in budget outputs. In Hungary, where this procedure is highest, the impact on the budget has been estimated at over 2 per cent of GDP in 1992.

Accounting problems aside, the trend of worsening deficits is clear. It raises questions both for other reforming countries that may follow in Central Europe's footsteps, and for these countries' own prospects over the next few years.

REVENUES

The tax systems inherited from the planning era were not compatible with the new market economies that the CSFR, Hungary, and Poland were moving towards (see e.g. Gandhi and Mihaljek 1992). However, the three countries sequenced their tax reforms very differently. Hungary moved fastest, with a thorough overhaul of the tax system in 1988. Poland brought in a modern tax system in phases, reforming profits tax in 1989, personal income taxes in 1992, and indirect taxes in mid-1993. The CSFR limited itself to tinkering with the old system between 1990 and 1992, and then introduced – by then in the two successor countries – a wholesale tax reform overnight on 1 January 1993. In contrast to the differences in timing, however, the overall aims of tax reform in the three countries were strikingly similar, reflecting the common model of tax systems under central planning. Four broad objectives stand out.[6]

First, private economic activity, which was set to mushroom as the state sector both contracted and transformed itself, had to be subjected to tax. In the CSFR, where most forms of private economic activity had previously been illegal, this meant making some legal provision for such taxation early on, by introducing a 'citizen's income tax' to capture personal incomes other than wages. More generally, the administration of taxes had to be strengthened, as commercialised SOEs and new private firms could be expected to find it both easier and more attractive to evade taxes than did the old state sector. The institution-building of tax administration would necessarily take time; but it was also possible to write the laws in such a way that administration would be simplified (see e.g. Tanzi 1993, who recommends that, at least during the transition, simplicity should be the guiding norm). Thus there have been attempts to structure income taxes in particularly simple ways, even at the cost of other objectives of tax reform: scheduled taxation of personal income, for instance, distortionary as it is, presents major administrative advantages. In some cases, though, these attempts at simplification run aground on political compromises: the Polish personal income tax, for example, is significantly more complex than necessary.

Second, playing fields had to be levelled in two ways. Most basically, the tax authorities' discretion, as manifested in particular in the arbitrary confiscation of enterprise profits, had to be eliminated – although, of course, only privatisation can entirely remove the temptation to substitute confiscation for sound tax policies, by relieving government of its blurred role as, simultaneously, tax collector and owner. In addition, it was necessary to abolish legally enshrined discrimination between the private and public sectors, and within these sectors. The various forms and rates of taxation of profits had to be unified; these had been instruments of preferential treatment of favoured industries, and of penalisation of the private sector in those countries where some private activity existed. Personal incomes had to be subjected to similar taxation; previously wages, the most 'dignified' type of income, had typically been subject to much less heavy tax than other incomes. The hundreds of different rates of turnover tax had initially to be reduced to as few as possible, and, as soon as preparations could be completed, cascading turnover taxes themselves were replaced with VATs.[7] The bases of indirect taxes had to be broadened, in particular to capture services – an endeavour much eased by the introduction of VATs. Baroque systems of foreign trade levies, which introduced varying wedges between import and export prices and their domestic equivalents, had to be eliminated.[8] As with the pursuit of simplicity, attempts to minimise distortions have not always succeeded. VATs, for instance, still have multiple and highly dispersed rates, as governments have tried to pursue distributional objectives as well as efficiency ones through the indirect tax structure. Income taxes too have sometimes had their bases narrowed; in Poland, for instance, no less than 36 types of personal income are exempt.

Third, to different extents in the different countries, the overall burden of taxation had to be reduced, so that individuals and especially firms would play a greater role, and the government a smaller role, in deciding what to do with their resources. Profits tax rates in particular had to be reduced; in the CSFR, the worst offender in this respect, these had been as high as 85 per cent, and had been supplemented by further levies on profits, which raised no less than 6 per cent of GDP in 1989. More generally, depreciation allowances had to be made more generous – these too had functioned as an instrument of profit extraction by governments – and provisions had to be introduced allowing for, or prolonging the period of, loss carry-over.

Finally, tax systems had to take into account the fact that the more or less uniform personal incomes of the previous era would rapidly become more differentiated. In the old systems for taxation of personal incomes and especially wages, rates had generally been flat, with adjustments for the number of dependants, disability, and so on. With increased inequality, a strong case for progressive rates of personal income tax, even at the cost of some complication, appeared for the first time.

All these features are standard elements in the tax designer's tool kit. At the same time, though, reforming economies are different from fully fledged market economies, and the tax system can be used, in second-best fashion, to try to correct some of the problems inherent in these differences. Hence, Poland maintained its dividend requirement on SOEs into 1994. Hence, all three countries continued, at least in the early stage of reform, the taxes on excessive wage growth inherited from the planning era (see Section 3 above); although this tax is there for purposes of regulation, it can raise substantial revenue, particularly if it is misdesigned as it was in the Polish case. Hence, both the CSFR (in late 1990) and Poland (in late 1992) imposed temporary import surcharges. Again, while the primary aim of this instrument is to protect the balance of payments in very uncertain times, it can help the fiscal position in the transition period, and this is one of the reasons why these countries have favoured surcharges over the alternative of more exchange rate depreciation (together with the fact that it is easier and less disruptive to eliminate an explicitly temporary surcharge than to undo a temporarily 'excessive' depreciation).

Tax reform, and the necessary lowering of tax burdens, played a part in the declines in revenues witnessed in all three Central European countries: between 1988 and 1992, revenues declined more steeply than GDP, and GDP itself fell sharply. But various other factors also played crucial roles.

A number of changes in the structure of these economies – some desirable, others less so – conspired to reduce revenues. Some of these changes are not peculiar to economies in transition. The very same fall in consumption that allowed higher fiscal deficits to be financed, and which increases the room for the sought-after take-off of investment, squeezed government revenues to the extent that these rely on consumption taxes. At the same time, the recession made people poorer, and consumption shifted toward more basic goods, which, for political reasons, long continued to be tax exempt or subject to lower rates. Finally, especially in Poland, falling inflation brought with it reduced revenues from seigniorage (which in all three countries accrued mostly to the budgets in the form of transfers of central bank profits).

But the structure of these economies changed in other ways too, that are more peculiar to economies in transition. With so much economic activity still taking place in the state sector, the evolution of the financial position of SOEs has a major impact on government revenues. In Poland and the CSFR, in the year of the biggest price shock (1990 and 1991 respectively), enterprise profits were artificially inflated by the revaluation of inventories, and, as there was little or no inflation adjustment in the profits tax, much of these paper profits were transferred to the government.

This development, however, was clearly of only passing interest. Of more lasting concern was the behaviour of wages. Various authors have argued that the fiscal crisis in Central Europe, and in Poland in particular, has been due to an excessive reliance on profits taxes and to a 'gobbling-up' of profits by myopic self-managed enterprises (see e.g. de Crombrugghe 1993). Section 3 above has argued that this gobbling-up is a somewhat exaggerated stylised fact. Moreover, the disappearing profits theory of fiscal trouble requires a higher tax burden on profits than on wages. By contrast, in Poland in 1991, the tax on Zl 100 of profit was Zl 40, while the tax on Zl 100 paid out in labour costs was at least Zl 45.[9] As a result, if an enterprise had shifted Zl 100 from profits to labour costs, total taxes owed to the government would actually have gone up. Similarly, in Hungary, the tax burden on profits was 40 per cent, and on labour costs 43 per cent.[10] Only in the CSFR was the standard tax take on profits, at 55 per cent, higher than that on wages, at 47 per cent;[11] even here, however, the difference was not enormous. It would seem that the immediate fiscal impact of the division of GDP between profits and wages is not very large – although over the longer term lower profits will, of course, endanger the fiscal position indirectly through their impact on investment and growth.

More importantly, even as SOEs were changing their behaviour, private enterprises were accounting for more and more of the economy, and in various ways, in their enthusiasm for this type of activity, governments had made sure that the tax burden on it was relatively light. In the CSFR, for instance, the service sector and the self-employed were subject to lower effective rates of pay-roll tax. And in all three countries, tax holidays and other forms of tax relief for private activity were initially given very liberally.

But the laws can go only so far; they need to be abided by as well. Twin problems have become apparent in this connection. On the one hand, large amounts of arrears have accumulated, particularly in the SOE sector; as of early 1993, they were estimated at 2.5 per cent of GDP in Poland and over 3 per cent of GDP in Hungary. In part these arrears are symptomatic of a lack of profitability: in the CSFR in 1992, for instance, anecdotal evidence suggests that pay-roll and turnover taxes – the two taxes Czechoslovak enterprises had to pay whether they were profitable or not – were the most important categories of tax arrears. But the pattern of arrears also suggests that, in some cases, politically and socially powerful enterprises are exerting leverage over the government: in Poland, one third of all arrears are in excess wage tax, suggesting enterprises have simply chosen to make 'better' use of their funds than to pay taxes. In not a few cases, this leverage ultimately translates into forgiveness of the taxes owed.

The tax liabilities of the emerging private sector, on the other hand, tend to be more difficult to monitor, and in this case, avoidance and evasion are more important than arrears. SOEs too have become more motivated to minimise their tax liability, and more adept at hiding profits. In many ways the old tax laws invited avoidance: to give just one example, there were typically no safeguards against transfer pricing between related agents in the old turnover tax laws. But even the new tax laws cannot counter evasion without a major strengthening of tax administration. There are too many new tax-payers who may or may not choose to register, too rapid an increase in the number of returns (in Hungary, for instance, the number of registered business tax payers more than tripled in just over two years from the end of 1988), and too little track record of decisive action by the tax authorities. All the Central European countries have embarked on the process of hiring more tax administrators, training them, creating more appropriate and coordinated structures of tax administration, computerising record systems, resolving unforeseen administrative problems in newly rewritten legislation, and visibly enforcing the laws (the latter most notably in Poland with the creation of a 'fiscal police'). But none of this can be done overnight.

Notwithstanding all this progress, there remain a number of challenges on the revenue side. Tax and contribution rates remain on the high side (particularly for social security contributions), and should move down over the medium term. Flaws in the tax reforms need to be addressed, and this should raise revenues in itself: bases need to be broadened, exemptions and special treatments in profits and income taxes minimised, the dispersion of indirect tax rates reduced (along the lines of the recent example of Hungary, where the zero VAT rate, estimated to apply to no less than 40 per cent of consumer expenditure, was virtually abolished in 1993), and inconsistencies corrected. More use could be made of user charges, which were virtually non-existent under the old regime and are still minimal. Social security contributions, which currently function entirely as taxes, could be fashioned more into true contributions, in order to minimise disincentive effects. And last but by no means least, tax administration needs to be considerably strengthened.

EXPENDITURES

Just as inherited tax systems had to be changed, so the inherited expenditure mix was inappropriate for the new market conditions. Like other centrally planned economies, Hungary, Poland, and especially the CSFR spent very large amounts on explicit subsidies (an estimated 14, 13, and 25 per cent of GDP respectively in 1989), and this proved a fertile ground for spending cuts; indeed, it is mainly a reduction in this extraordinarily large amount of subsidies (including the elimination of cross-subsidisation) that is behind the tremendous cuts in overall expenditure achieved in the CSFR (Table 11.7). In tandem with the reform of enterprise taxation, it was generally fairly easy to reduce the subsidies to ordinary productive enterprises, which were the counterpart to the punitive taxation of their more profitable enterprises. While it took a little longer to phase out other subsidies on goods, all of these countries have by now virtually eliminated them. Subsidies to the powerful agricultural sector are an exception in the CSFR and Hungary, and seem to be staging a comeback in Poland (in the form of new subsidies on fuel for agriculture), where their reduction has led to a strong backlash.

A number of subsidies on services proved more politically sensitive and remain a burden on the budgets. Transport (particularly passenger transport) and especially housing and household energy use are the main culprits here. Heating was traditionally provided – often piped in from huge heating 'factories' – to many households at once, and the absence of individual meters or controls has made large tariff increases difficult. Housing continues to benefit from subsidies in two main ways. In cases where housing is owned by the state there are still cash subsidies to rents. Where housing belongs to individuals or cooperatives various means are used to lighten the owners' debt service burden, including for instance subsidies to reduce the interest rate on housing loans, or outright takeovers of obligations (such as the Polish takeover of the bank debt of housing cooperatives).

Of course, subsidy accounting is a very imperfect science. While recorded cash subsidies have by now shrunk to about 5–6 per cent of GDP, levels not uncommon in developed market economies, there remains a worry that various subsidies that take the form of transactions with banks may not have been properly identified as such. Moreover, implicit subsidies, difficult to quantify as they are, remain a problem. Forgiving tax liabilities is one example of such implicit subsidies. So are procurement subsidies (purchasing goods and services above market prices) and regulatory subsidies (altering market prices and access). While such subsidies are probably still quantitatively important, there is no doubt that they too are much reduced from their earlier levels.

Social benefits absorbed a large share of government spending, and with a very different focus from the one common in market economies.[12] Far from being a safety net, social benefits in the planned economy supplemented everyone's wages.[13] And the public's expectations of universality die hard: even the Czechoslovak government, the most outspokenly market-oriented of the three, provided universal income support in compensation for the removal of retail subsidies on food in 1990.

Nevertheless, it was soon understood that reform meant both creating new safeguards against new dangers – unemployment – and better targeting benefits to those in need. While most countries already had some form of income protection for those who were temporarily without a job, unemployment benefits proper were typically only introduced at the outset of the reforms. In many ways, they were initially made too generous: they were available for too long a period (over a year in Hungary, and without duration limit in Poland), with too high a replacement ratio (usually 65–70 per cent for the first few months); with too lax eligibility requirements; and, in the CSFR and Poland, even without a ceiling. All the countries have made progress toward correcting some or all of these excesses. All have shortened the duration of benefits; the CSFR has reduced replacement ratios and brought in a ceiling, and Poland has even introduced a flat-rate benefit unrelated to the individual's previous wage.

Universal child benefits, sometimes amounting to as much as 12–15 per cent of average wages per child, were an important candidate for real cuts in all three countries. While there has been much discussion of possible means-testing, the administrative difficulties with such an approach in economies in transition are even more daunting than in industrial countries. And subjecting family allowances to income tax, another option that is being considered, may actually be regressive given the inverse correlation between income and family size (see Jarvis and Micklewright 1992). Nevertheless, it is clear that these countries cannot afford the generous child benefit systems they inherited, and all have refrained from adjusting child benefits fully for inflation; the CSFR (from the outset of the transition) and Poland (from early 1992) did not even raise them in nominal terms.

Neither can state budgets of transition economies afford the responsibilities planning-era governments usually had for sick pay, as a result of which enterprises have never had much incentive to check up on their employees, and indeed now, in a period of high unemployment, have every incentive to collude with their employees to declare them sick rather than redundant. In Hungary, some responsibility for sick pay was shifted to enterprises in the early 1990s, but this covered only the first 10 days of illness; in the Czech and Slovak Republics, the entire responsibility for sick pay remains with the government. In Poland, where sick pay in SOEs but not in private enterprises has long been largely the responsibility of the employer, the current policy task is to make the private sector responsible for paying for sick leave as well.

By far the biggest share of social benefits, however, went to pensions – for old people and the disabled. In the absence of employer-provided schemes, essentially all income flows to pensioners pass through general government accounts, boosting revenues and expenditures. The inherited pension systems suffer from several problems. First, eligibility for a pension was usually defined generously. Only in Poland was the official retirement age, at 65 for men and 60 for women, comparable to those in Western Europe; in Hungary and the CSFR, it was 60 for men and 53–57 for women. Moreover, in all three countries, there were numerous job-specific early retirement provisions, and liberal disability provisions that typically defined disability as 'damaged health' rather than 'inability to work'. As a result, average retirement ages were several years lower than statutory ones; in Poland, the average actual retirement age in 1990 was 57–58 (Hambor 1992). Second, there was often no retirement test under the former system, so that it was possible to work virtually full-time without forfeiting, or in some cases even reducing, one's right to a pension. Both liberal provisions for early retirement and the virtual absence of retirement tests have contributed to a sharp increase in numbers of pensioners during the reform period: the Polish average retirement age, for instance, appears by now to have fallen further to 55–56 (Maret and

Schwartz 1993). Third, pension calculations typically used as a base only a very short earnings period (1–5 years) – not much of a problem when wages were government-set and relatively uniform, but an invitation to employer–employee collusion once enterprises acquired more power over individual wages. In addition, there were numerous occupation-specific pension top-ups that brought actual pension payments out of line with actuarial considerations.

All the Central European countries have attempted to lighten their pension load, while protecting pensioners from poverty. Typically they have done this through less-than-full inflation indexation of pensions above the minimum. Although when real wages are declining it is appropriate that pensioners share some of this burden, in practice cost-of-living adjustments (COLAs) – particularly in Poland, where inflation has been highest – have sometimes been haphazard and excessively slow. Clearly, more fundamental reform is needed to contain the costs of the pension systems. This should focus on raising statutory retirement ages where necessary, improving the pension formula, abolishing job-specific top-ups, lengthening the averaging period for calculating the pension base, introducing stricter retirement tests, and improving COLA mechanisms (Maret and Schwartz 1993).

Overall, and despite some attempts at targeting, social safety net expenditures (including pensions, unemployment benefits, and social assistance) have become very hard to compress to sustainable levels. Transfers to households are estimated to have risen by several percentage points of GDP in all three countries since 1989 – most notably by close to 10 points of GDP in Poland.

So-called government consumption expenditures have been subject to cuts, though often in an untargeted, across-the-board fashion: budgeting procedures and expenditure control are still not up to the standards common in the West. The government wage bill has been a particular target. Civil service salaries have been held back in the face of inflation, with predictable consequences in the form of a brain drain to the private sector; and the employment cuts that most observers agree should be possible have proved much more difficult to engineer, and indeed have led to strikes in Poland. All the countries also, inevitably, let the axe fall on capital expenditure. In the short term this may not be too costly; after all, there was considerable over-investment in the era of central planning, and in the early stages of reform it is not always clear what investments are appropriate. But the strategy cannot be sustained for too long, and places a heavy burden on future budgets.

Further containment of expenditure is essential if the twin goals of deficit and tax reduction are to be met. The task, however, will be complicated by a number of adverse developments. First, debt, and hence the interest burden, is rising everywhere with the fiscal deficits and with operations to clean up the banking system.[14] Second, unemployment is likely to rise further before it begins to fall, as labour-hoarding is reduced; and widening income distribution is likely to increase other demands on the social safety net. Third, over the longer haul, demography will act against these governments, with ageing populations and rising dependency ratios.

In the meantime, the easiest cuts have already been made, and the public's expectations regarding the level of social and other services have not adjusted to budgetary realities. The discussion of expenditures above has pinpointed some of the areas in which savings could still be realised. Whether this will prove politically feasible remains to be seen; but it will have to be if the hard-won stabilisation gains of the last few years are to be preserved and the much-sought take-off of investment is to occur.

5. Conclusions

For the four most advanced economies in transition the breakthrough to 'beyond stabilisation' presents a set of unique policy problems, which will determine both the pace of growth and the durability of the stabilisation success. The interplay of structural and macroeconomic problems across the different sectors of the economy makes the formulation of policy particularly onerous, especially since these economies are pioneers in facing the challenges of systemic transformation to the market.

The CSFR, Hungary, and Poland eliminated the command-imposed distortions forced upon their economies with price and trade liberalisation and financial stabilisation of unprecedented magnitudes. The goal was to create economies that follow market signals. Governments are now facing the challenge of identifying and controlling the market signals that determine the pace and efficacy of economic resurrection. Although significant shares of state assets, in particular small enterprises, have been sold off, the desire to achieve multiple and contradictory goals has slowed the pace of privatisation in most of Central Europe. Overall, privatisation appears to be facilitated by involving foreign firms, who in addition to capital provide technological expertise and access to foreign markets. The mixed performances of SOEs, which will control large shares of economic resources in the medium term, has made it imperative that governments set up incentives for proper enterprise governance.

The many enterprises that are simply no longer viable in a market economy will have to obey the hardest budget constraint of all: bankruptcy. Bankruptcy laws must provide for the termination of non-viable firms with minimum social cost, while promoting the restructuring of profitable enterprises. Another vital advantage of an effective bankruptcy process is the exposure of the magnitude of hidden liabilities incurred prior to the transformation process.

Structural and financial policies have been woven together by the shifting of these unfunded enterprise and household liabilities onto the books of the government. The people who worked in over-staffed enterprises during the days of the command economy are beginning to be laid off as part of the rationalisation of enterprises, and are imposing new fiscal burdens, partly because of over-generous severance pay and unemployment benefits. Recognition of the overhang of bad enterprise debt is swallowing up bank capital, which, in turn through lower profits and recapitalisation, transfers the burden on to the government. Similarly, some of the growing stock of enterprise and household tax arrears will eventually have to be recognised.

The assumption of previously hidden liabilities by government budgets, however, is not the only reason for the recent increase in fiscal financing needs. Ironically, the rapid transition to the market, and particularly the downturn in SOE output combined with the dynamic growth of new, usually small, private enterprises, have temporarily weakened the revenue collection capacity of the government. Governments will have to collect their fair share from these private sector firms without impairing their contribution to growth. The ease of tax avoidance during the development of new tax systems has necessitated stopgap measures such as various surcharges, and increases of tax rates have sometimes substituted for broadening the tax base. Governments must move away from these temporary measures by tightening the tax net, broadening the tax base, and promoting growth through removing tax distortions.

Deficit reduction will be necessary in most countries if investment is to reach the levels needed for these countries to 'catch up' with Western Europe in the medium term. Even if the marginal returns on investment are particularly high now and even if there is substantial unused capacity, the experience of other countries that achieved prolonged rates of real GDP growth indicate that a substantial build-up of investment from the levels now prevailing (20–22 per cent of GDP) will be needed.

Making the resources available, of course, does not guarantee that they will be invested, much less invested efficiently. Privatisation and other measures to reform SOEs and create a supportive framework for the new private sector are essential in this respect. So is financial sector reform, which alone can ensure that resources are channelled to the most productive uses. The time needed to develop non-bank capital markets, in particular direct household financing of government deficits and enterprise investment through bond and equity financing, means that banks will be likely to continue to provide the bulk of government and enterprise financing.

Some of the problems that need to be addressed in bank reform are similar to those that plague other enterprises: the governance of banks needs to be improved, ultimately through privatisation; in the meantime 'halfway house' arrangements may be particularly important for banks. But credit allocation will not function efficiently without effective bank supervision or without an appropriate level of bank capital. The legacy of the command economy is especially onerous here, impeding as it did the development both of sound bank portfolios and of the banking skills required in a market economy.

In summary, Hungary, Poland, and the CSFR have successfully stabilised their economies and have implemented many of the crucial economic reforms needed for a successful transition. In order to sustain the pace of transformation, they must now make the appropriate fiscal adjustments to pay the costs incurred by the command economy without crowding out investment. At the same time, enterprise and bank reform must continue to ensure that private savings get to the growing firms that will help to determine the pace of economic integration with Western Europe.

Notes

1. For ease of reference this chapter will use the term 'Central Europe' to refer to these three, now four, countries. When statements apply equally to the former CSFR and its successor republics, the term 'CSFR' is used.
2. See Chu and Schwartz (1993) for a brief review of the literature on the output decline in European transition economies.
3. The three countries also differed greatly in their potential for implicit financing through seigniorage but, as noted above, institutional arrangements were such that seigniorage was largely reflected in revenues.
4. This involved confiscating enterprise profits and channelling them to loss-making enterprises as subsidies (see below).
5. The Polish deficit exceeded 7 per cent of GDP as early as 1989, but this was due mainly to high inflation: not only because of collection lags, but also because various nominal

magnitudes (e.g. the penalty interest rate on tax arrears, and specific tax rates) were adjusted slowly.

6. Not all these objectives were successfully pursued in the first attempts at tax reform; Hungary, in particular, improved its new taxes significantly over the years.
7. Turnover taxes had typically been set as the difference between controlled wholesale and retail prices, so that, in theory, there could be as many rates as there were commodities. Reducing the number of rates was thus, for administrative reasons, a virtual necessity when prices were liberalised, just as price liberalisation itself was necessary for indirect taxes to be passed through to consumers rather than being absorbed by enterprises.
8. Hungary provides an interesting example of an attempt to level the playing field in this latter respect even in the centrally planned era: foreign trade levies were used to offset the pricing distortions prevalent in CMEA trade, and bring domestic prices in line with world market prices.
9. Social security contributions amounted to 45 per cent of wages, equivalent to 31 per cent of total labour costs (wages plus social security contributions); in addition, in the lowest income tax bracket, personal income tax was payable at 20 per cent of wages, equivalent to 14 per cent of labour costs.
10. Social security contributions were 55 per cent of wages, and income taxes 12 per cent in the lowest bracket.
11. Payroll taxes were 50 per cent of wages and income taxes 20 per cent.
12. In all these countries (Poland even before the reform, Hungary from 1989, the Czech and Slovak Republics from 1993), all or most social benefits are provided by funds separate from the state budget. In all cases, however, the state budget is the guarantor, and indeed the separation is of mainly administrative importance.
13. For an overview of social security benefits in these economies in the early stages of reform see Kopits (1992).
14. The latter, of course, to the extent that they involve only truly 'bad' debt, merely shift an interest burden that was quasi-fiscal (when banks bore the burden of non-payment by enterprises) onto the fiscal accounts.

Appendix: Stabilisation and reform plans 1989–92*

The first comprehensive and innovative programme for stabilisation and reform was the Polish ('Balcerowicz') plan of 1 January 1990.[1] It included broad price and trade liberalisation, nominal anchoring of the programme to money wages and the nominal exchange rate, targeting the real money supply and real interest rates, monetary and fiscal austerity, large devaluations and internal convertibility, extreme fiscal pressure on the state sector, taxes on excess wage increases and, in the longer run, privatisation and capacity restructuring. The Polish stabilisation plan has provided a prototype for other transitional countries: in 1990–91 similar plans were introduced in Romania (1 September 1990), Czechoslovakia (1 January 1991) and Bulgaria (1 February 1991). The Balcerowicz plan envisaged the following steps:

1. Instantaneous price liberalisation of 90 per cent of transactions and a reduction of government subsidies (from 17 per cent of national income in 1989 to 4 per cent in 1991); initially some budgetary support was retained for coal, electricity, gas,

* Based on Nuti (1993) and Sachs (1993)

state housing rents, heating and hot water, transport and telecommunications, and pharmaceuticals.

2. A balanced state budget for 1990, accompanied by a restrictive monetary policy aimed at restoring a positive real interest rate; interest rates were raised on old as well as new credit contracts. State enterprises' assets were revalued on average by a factor of 14 (and again in 1991), at rates differing by type of assets but uniform throughout the economy, with a uniform capital tax levied on revalued state assets. Average turnover tax was raised from 10 to 20 per cent.
3. Wage policy: money wages were set on the basis of an expected monthly rate of inflation of 45 per cent in January, with maximum wage guidelines indexed to prices at a monthly prefixed rate for 1990: 20 per cent of price inflation in January, 30 per cent in February to April, 60 per cent for the rest of the year except for June (when energy prices would be raised) when wage indexation was at 100 per cent. A tax on wage increases over these guide-lines was levied (the *popiwek*), at progressive rates of between 200 to 500 per cent of excess wages, exclusively on enterprises with state majority capital.
4. Unilateral suspension of debt service from 1 January 1990, soon followed by formal rescheduling of foreign debt, with interest and debt amortisation due in 1990 postponed to 1991; large-scale debt relief was granted by official creditors in April 1991.
5. Zloty convertibility for residents and for current account transactions; following the devaluations of 22 and 28 December, on 1 January 1990 a further devaluation of the zloty by 31.6 per cent lifted the US dollar to 9,500 zlotys, that is, practically to the year-end free market rate (the black market for foreign exchange had been legalised since March 1989). Domestic enterprises could buy freely at this rate to finance current imports; households could buy dollars for current purposes (i.e. not to invest in foreign assets) from licensed foreign exchange 'counters', at a floating rate which was maintained very close to the official rate. A US$ 1 bn loan was made available by the G-24 to support convertibility, in addition to US$ 700 mn IMF standby, US$ 300 mn structural adjustment loan from the World Bank (plus additional project loans totalling US$ 780 mn in 1990) and a substantial package of aid and loans from the EIB, the European Community, its member states and other members of the G-24. The rate of exchange was maintained until mid-May 1991, when the zloty was devalued by 17.4 per cent and linked to a basket of currencies instead of the dollar; in October a crawling peg regime was introduced, with a maximum monthly devaluation of 1.8 per cent.
6. Trade liberalisation, with a new tariff system whose average rate was 12 per cent, followed for most goods by a tariff reduction to 5 per cent (April) or outright suspension (July); the elimination of export quotas (in January and in October 1990) except for coal and a small number of items (though 20 commodities were still subject to licences at the end of 1991), and automatic authorisation to trade internationally for all registered firms whether state or private.
7. Implementation of further institutional reform in the direction of a private market economy, including the development of banking and credit institutions, competition, privatisation and the introduction of financial markets, accompanied by capacity restructuring in the medium term. A spate of new legislation was introduced in 1990–91 to implement this part of the programme. Following extensive

debates on privatisation, a new law was adopted in June 1991; small-scale privatisation (housing, retail and catering establishments, land) was to be followed by large scale privatisation of state enterprises; however, this side of the programme was delayed mostly because of the technical difficulties of implementing mass privatisation. This was to take place through the free distribution to the whole adult population of entitlements to certificates in foreign-managed investment funds, but their establishment was postponed to late 1992; there were also delays due to the complexities of property restitution to old owners (so-called 're-privatisation', first introduced by Germany).

Table 11.A.1 summarises the main features of the Polish plan and the main differences with respect to the plans subsequently adopted by other countries.

Romania adopted a more gradual price liberalisation in three stages, beginning on 15 November 1990, 1 April and 1 July 1991; price increases were subject to three months' advance notice to be given to central authorities. The nominal anchor was fixed as a 15 per cent increase of the nominal money supply. A special fund financed out of a 10 per cent tax on enterprise profits was set up for the purpose of liquidating inter-enterprise arrears (400 bn Leu). There were no provisions for wages policy. Convertibility was supposed to be introduced on 27 September 1991 but was postponed in the absence of a government and implemented on 11 November under a 'managed float' regime.

Table 11.A.1 Stabilisation and Reform Programmes in Central-Eastern Europe

Feature	Yugoslavia	Poland	Romania	CSFR	Bulgaria
Start	1.12.89	1.1.90	1.8.90	1.1.91	1.2.91
Price liberalisation	instant 90%	instant 90%	3 stages	instant 85%	gradual
Subsidy reduction 1989/91	yes	17.4 – 4%	partial	16.1 – 4.6%	16.7 – 3%
Fiscal squeeze	temporary	yes	no	yes	limited
Monetary restraint	temporary	yes	no	yes	limited
Currency devaluation	yes	yes	yes	yes	yes
Foreign trade liberalisation	extensive	extensive	very limited	extensive	very limited
Internal convertibility for firms	yes; aborted	yes	end-1991	yes; delayed	yes
Internal convertibility for households	yes; aborted	yes	no	no	no
Wages policy	yes; ignored	fiscal	no	yes	yes
Small-scale privatisation	yes	yes	yes	yes	yes
Sale of state enterprises	some	some	mostly land	slow	slow
Property restitution	no	yes	yes	yes	yes
Mass privatisation through vouchers	no	delayed	delayed	delayed	delayed
Capacity restructuring	no	little	no	little	no
Real anchoring		M,r		M,r	
Nominal anchoring	W,i	W,e		W,e	M

Source: Nuti (1993)

Note: M=money, r=real interest rates, W=wages, i=nominal interest rate, e=exchange rate

In 1990 the CSFR, ahead of the stabilisation plan, took preparatory measures that in Poland had followed the plan, such as major legislative changes, price increases, tax convertibility granted to enterprises, excluding households; even for enterprises access to foreign currency was subject in practice to considerable delays. Small-scale privatisation proceeded fast, but large-scale privatisation, much more reliant on free distribution of assets to the population, has been greatly delayed. Inter-republican conflicts between the Czech and the Slovak Republics have characterised the CSFR experience, with the creation of duplicate ministries and agencies at the federal and the republican level, and the difficulties of coordinating stabilisation and reform. Inter-republican conflict, though not as sharp as in the Soviet Union/CIS, the Russian Federation or Yugoslavia, has been a brake on transition progress.

The Bulgarian plan was perhaps the one closest to the Polish prototype, but with more gradual trade liberalisation, nominal anchoring to the money supply, slower privatisation of state assets (even small-scale, except for land, where quick progress was made). The lower real wage reached after price liberalisation was stabilised and strongly indexed, unlike the Polish real wage guideline which was indexed much more weakly but was referred to the pre-stabilisation level.

Note

1. Yugoslavia's stabilisation plan of 1 December 1989 was much less comprehensive as Yugoslavia already enjoyed a more decentralised economy. At any rate it was quickly aborted by republican disputes.

CHAPTER TWELVE

Yugoslavia: is economics pleading against disintegration?*

Take a jar and fill it with coins. Now auction off the jar in your neighbourhood tavern, offering to pay the winning bidder in bills. Chances are very high that the following results will be obtained: 1. The average bid will be significantly less than the value of the coins (bidders are risk-averse). 2. The winning bid will exceed the value of the jar (as estimates of the unknown content of the jar vary substantially). This demonstration will simultaneously provide the funding for your evening's entertainment and enlighten the patrons of the tavern about the perils of the 'winner's curse'.

Adapted from H. Thaler, *The Winner's Curse*, 1992

Yugoslavia was pasted together in the aftermath of World War I and became a socialist federation after World War II. In this putting together, economic considerations played only a trivial role compared to geographical, ethnic and power considerations. After 70 years of togetherness, and in particular, after 45 years of experimenting with its own brand of socialism – the one with the human face which turned its back on the Stalinist version, we might ask ourselves the question whether or not Yugoslavia managed to construct an organic, tightly knit economic space. The question is of obvious relevance now that the country is imploding, and it is worth finding out whether the richer former republics are economically better off in independence and whether the poorer republics will suffer from their breakaway. Or, to put it differently, and looking back with the detachment which behoves an economist, was the success in creating and maintaining the Yugoslav Federation for 45 years, with its own brand of socialism and its own microstructure, not in fact a winner's curse?

To understand the difficulties Yugoslavs have had in maintaining their country and in integrating their economy the fact cannot be ignored that there was no economic and historic rationale for creating the country in the first place. In this respect Yugoslavia shares much with the Soviet Union whose break-up is discussed in the next chapter.

Like other Central and South-East European States, Yugoslavia emerged from the collapse of the Ottoman and Austro-Hungarian empires. Of all the successor states of the Austro-Hungarian and Ottoman empires, Yugoslavia – which was not given that name until 1929 – was one of the poorest and one of the most heterogeneous in every sense – ethnic, religious and, what concerns us most, economic.

* This chapter draws on Ottolenghi and Steinherr (1993)

The notion of gathering together all the Slavs of the South (which is what the word Yugoslavia means) was, however, spawned a century earlier. The French Revolution and the awakening of national consciousness during the Napoleonic years gave rise to the 'Great Project' of the Serbs and the 'Illyrian Movement' of the Croats. Both aimed at an independent state comprising the Slavs of the South but they differed substantially over just about everything else. In 1830 Serbia became an autonomous region within the Ottoman empire.

The Congress of Berlin in 1878 granted Serbia and Montenegro full independence and recognised the occupation of Bosnia-Herzegovina by Austria-Hungary to which Slovenia and Croatia already belonged. After having gained its independence, Serbia multiplied its efforts to achieve a larger space assembling the Slavs in a state independent of Ottoman and Austro-Hungarian domination. The Balkan wars (1912–13) succeeded in pushing back the Ottoman empire. The next step of getting rid of the Austro-Hungarians was achieved after World War I – a war that was not caused by the southern Slavs but was at least sparked by the assassination of Archduke Franz-Ferdinand on 28 June 1914 in Sarajevo.

The outcome of World War I opened the door to the creation of the much longed-for nation-states. The three empires with strong interests in the Balkans (the Austro-Hungarian, Ottoman and Russian empires) had all disappeared from the scene, and the nations themselves were largely left to take their own decisions. On 20 July 1917 the Serbian government in exile announced, in Corfu, the creation of an 'independent state of Serbs, Croatians and Slovenes under a constitutional and parliamentary monarchy'. On 29 October 1918 a national council including the Serb Svetozar Pribecivic, the Croat Ante Pavelic and the Slovene Anton Korosec decided on the formation of a national government. Bosnia-Herzegovina and Vojvodina also joined up and on 1 December 1918 the United Kingdom of Serbs, Croatians and Slovenes was proclaimed by Crown Prince Alexander.

The Peace Conference of Versailles defined the official frontiers of that new state. The political borders however could not be made to match the ethnic ones. Within the newly hatched kingdom only Slovenia had a relatively homogeneous indigenous population. All other regions were mixed bags of various ethnic and religious groups. Likewise, the political and economic traditions varied widely. The regions which had been part of the Austro-Hungarian empire were not that different from other parts of 'Mitteleuropa' and already possessed a nascent industry (Slovenia, Croatia, Vojvodina). Serbia and Montenegro were less developed and more feudal. Bosnia-Herzegovina, Macedonia and the Kosovo were marked by centuries of Ottoman domination and the – partly Muslim – population was mainly agricultural, poor and backward.

It was not long before the orthodox Serbs forged ahead with the centralisation of political power. In 1929 King Alexander abolished the Constitution of 1921 and dissolved parliament in the teeth of violent protest in Slovenia and Croatia. The exiled Croatian leader Ante Pavelic started a terrorist organisation, Ustacha, whose goal was to win independence for the Croats. The conflict between Serbs and Croatians was further fuelled by the attempt to establish the Orthodox Church throughout the country's territory and by the assassination of King Alexander I by a member of Ustacha on 9 October 1934 in Marseilles. All in all, it proved impossible to achieve togetherness during the inter-war years.

When World War II broke out Yugoslavia was already deeply divided and Croatia had obtained a more autonomous status in 1939. Resistance against both the German troops and the Ustachi initially regrouped round two axes: the Chetniks – a Serbian guerilla organisation which has recently become infamous – and, a little later, the communist 'partisans' under the Croatian Josip Broz or 'Tito'. In close alliance with Moscow, Tito and his partisans simultaneously fought the Germans, the Ustachi and the Chetniks.

Tito quickly moved from military leadership to political command. In November 1943, after the Italian capitulation, the second congress of the Anti-Fascist Council of National Liberation, in which all Yugoslav people were represented, nominated Tito president of the provisional government and Marshal of Yugoslavia. In 1945 the monarchy was abolished and Tito became prime minister of the government of national unity.

Yugoslavia's departure from the Stalinist line was the result of Marshal Tito's quest for independence. Tito's strong personality and war fame succeeded in stitching Yugoslavia together after the war and putting a temporary end to the intestine divisions and civil strife between Croats and Serbs. While Stalin was mostly faced with backstage politicians in other East European countries, in Tito he met a man of exceptional will-power and not a few ambitions of his own.

Not content with his remarkable achievement in keeping Yugoslavia on the map, Tito made a bid for Trieste in Italy, for South Carinthia in Austria and for part of Greek Macedonia. He also campaigned for Balkan federalism, and the first tangible result of this was a federal agreement between Bulgaria and Yugoslavia. Albania came under his spell and was ready to join that federation.

In an attempt to take control, Stalin called for a tripartite conference on 10 February 1948 at which the creation of the new federation was to be officially announced. But while he found the Bulgarians more understanding and docile to his bidding, Tito rejected the proposal out of hand. The Kominform issued a joint declaration condemning 'the appalling, despotic and terrorist nature of the Tito regime – deviating into revisionism, anti-Soviet and anti-Communist values'. The need to overthrow 'Tito and his gang' was expressly spelled out.[1]

In July 1948, the 5th Congress of the Yugoslav Communist Party sternly denounced the Soviet accusations. This declaration consummated the schism between Yugoslavia and the rest of the socialist camp. Diplomatic relations between the USSR and Yugoslavia were severed on 25 October 1949 and Tito was tagged as a 'Hitler-Trotskyite agent-enemy'.

The implications of this development in economic terms were dire, to put it mildly. All agreements with the East European bloc were cancelled and Yugoslavia found itself facing a virtual trade embargo. Not being part of the Western camp and hence debarred from Marshall Plan aid, and shunned and rejected by the socialist camp, Yugoslavia was forced into a quasi-autarchic development programme. Poor, with just a little industry in the north, no natural resources, and no political sponsor to dispense financial largesse, Yugoslavia started out in post-war conditions more grim than anywhere else.

The controversy between Stalin and Tito could not be resolved during Stalin's lifetime. After Stalin's death, however, Khrushchev, Bulganin and Mikoyan went to Belgrade in 1955 to voice their regrets at this unfortunate situation. Tito obtained satisfaction on all fronts and was not even compelled to rejoin the various East European institutions. Yugoslavia therefore maintained its neutral position and even received sizeable economic assistance from the USSR into the bargain.

Yugoslavia is an important case-study because of the very specific features that made it unique. First, after World War II it was always a relatively independent country, keeping its distance from bloc alignments. Second, it experimented with socialist reforms in a way unrivalled in any other socialist country. And finally, thanks to strong leadership, it pieced together a country with regional differences in economic structure and development, in history and in socio-religious spread of population only comparable to the Soviet Union.

In reviewing the growth of the federation and the differences among republics, it is striking to note that there was a period ending in the mid-1960s during which growth in Yugoslavia was higher than in other socialist countries and, in fact, among the highest in Europe. But income disparities among the republics remained extraordinarily high. And as in other socialist countries, there is more than a suggestion that the Yugoslav economy became increasingly devitalised and prostrate.

This can be explained in several ways, and the explanations are linked rather than competing. The first is the argument that macroeconomic management was unable to break the mould of socialist pathological patterns and repeated the errors observable in other East European countries. This is investigated in Section 1.

The second, and popular presumption in the West is that socialism, whatever its facial expression, is a social body which does not work. This aspect is examined in Section 2. We conclude that the innovatory microeconomic structure of labour management could not perform in a macroeconomic environment of social ownership of capital, social planning and restricted freedom of enterprise in what was basically a planned economy.

Section 3 then examines the hypothesis that the different parts of Yugoslavia were ill-suited to come together in a federation. Some of its component parts, with the same macroeconomic socialist organisation and self-management at enterprise level, would have done better had they been left to go it alone instead of being pressed into the Yugoslav Federation. Similar conclusions are reached for the Soviet Union in Chapter 13. *Prima facie*, this seems to contradict the arguments that are usually used to support greater integration within the European Union, for example: the gains from the Single Market created in 1992 were estimated (in Emerson *et al.* 1988) and were found to be substantial. However, such a comparison overlooks the differences between regional integration within a small unit (Yugoslavia), that is only partially open to the rest of the world, and integration in a much larger unit (the EU), that is much more open to the rest of the world.

This conclusion is further supported by the fact that the north-western republics are in an economic sense natural allies of the European Community. Trade and monetary arrangements with the Community would be an attractive alternative to past federal structures. This analysis is pursued in Chapter 16.

1. Macroeconomic performance and policies

A GENERAL OVERVIEW

The aim of this section is not to analyse in detail all major macroeconomic developments that occurred in Yugoslavia during the period under review. It is rather to present a few stylised facts to help explain how the interaction of macroeconomic policies and 'market socialism' led to the emergence of substantial imbalances that may well have contributed to the decline in growth and the ultimate break-up of the country.

A cursory inspection of Yugoslavia's economic statistics suggests that the last four decades can be roughly divided into two distinct periods: a protracted episode of growth and development from the beginning of the 1950s until the end of the 1970s, followed by a decade of stagnation, repeated balance-of-payments crises and hyperinflation.[2] With hindsight, the discussion of Yugoslavia's growth performance[3] presented here differs in tone from earlier descriptions. For example, Horvath (1971) interpreted growth in the Yugoslav economy between 1954 and 1967 as follows: 'Self-government accelerated the growth of output and technical progress beyond anything known before, while preserving fast employment expansion'. However, a mere nine years later, Sapir (1980) sub-titled his study: 'Whatever happened to the Yugoslav miracle?'. Whether the initial spurt in growth was due to self-management, as claimed by Horvath, or due to catching up, remains therefore an unanswered question.

Between 1952, when the institutional framework of Yugoslav 'market socialism' came into being, and 1980, the growth of real GDP and GDP *per capita* averaged respectively 6.7 per cent and 5.6 per cent. GDP growth was particularly buoyant between 1956 and 1964, averaging nearly 9 per cent a year. In the course of the ensuing 20 years the rate of output growth declined, remaining quite steady in spite of marked cyclical fluctuations. At 6.2 per cent per year it stood well above the OECD (4 per cent) and EC (3.7 per cent) averages.

In the 1950s Yugoslavia was by far the best performer in the group of socialist countries. Although its growth record was less impressive in the 1960s and 1970s, it still managed to grow faster than Western European countries. By contrast, in the 1980s Yugoslavia recorded the worst growth performance together with Poland, also a top performer in times past. As shown in Table 12.1, rapid growth was accompanied by substantial diversification of output structure, with a sharp downturn in the share of agriculture and an equally large increase of that of the services.

A characteristic feature of the Yugoslav economy until the end of the 1970s was the very high rate of investment, which fluctuated around 30 per cent of GDP. Unemployment stood at very low levels until the early 1980s owing to widespread migration between the early 1960s and mid-1970s. By 1973 the number of Yugoslav workers abroad was about 1.2 million, compared with a domestic labour force of 8 million in that same year.

Until the mid-1960s, high rates of investment went hand-in-hand with high savings rates, but as a result of a change in policy orientation (see below), savings rates declined thereafter, which put pressure on the balance of payments. Although this development, compounded by external shocks in the 1970s, led to periodic foreign payments difficulties alternating with bouts of stabilisation, the country's growth performance average suffered no adverse effects. Imbalances between savings and

TABLE 12.1 Sectoral GDP shares in Yugoslavia at factor cost (at current prices, per cent)

	1952	1960	1970	1980	1988
Agriculture	23.5	24.0	17.8	12.1	11.2
Industry and mining	39.1	36.4	28.9	31.2	42.9
Construction	7.8	6.9	12.5	10.0	6.2
Electricity, gas, water	1.0	1.8	3.1	2.7	2.2
Services	28.6	30.9	37.7	44.0	37.5
GDP	100.0	100.0	100.0	100.0	100.0

Sources: Federal Institute of Statistics, OECD and World Bank estimates

investment were at first covered mostly by remittances of Yugoslav workers who had emigrated in large numbers starting in the mid-1960s, and, from the mid-1970s onwards, by recourse to external borrowing.

At the same time, Yugoslavia became gradually more integrated into the world economy, although dependence on foreign trade remained well below that of smaller OECD economies and some socialist countries. The single most apparent weakness of the Yugoslav economy during this period was its high and accelerating rate of inflation. Measured by the implicit GDP deflator, inflation averaged 12.7 per cent in the 1960s and 18.8 per cent in the 1970s.

Economic performance in the 1980s was in stark contrast with previous experience. The deterioration of the balance of payments that occurred in conjunction with the second oil shock and associated problems with foreign debt servicing forced the authorities to adopt stabilisation policies aimed at redirecting resources from domestic demand towards net exports. However, they had considerable trouble staying on course and the whole decade was one of stop–go management. Nevertheless, the objective of restoring credit-worthiness was achieved, with current account surpluses accruing between 1983 and 1989 with the exception of 1987. This turn-around was primarily the result of administrative controls on imports. Because of the high import content of investment, capital formation plummeted (by about 5 per cent a year) and GDP stagnated throughout the decade, despite a positive contribution from export growth. To make things worse, inflation accelerated sharply during the 1980s and all attempts to keep it under control failed. A determined effort to tackle the problem in 1990 met with initial success, but hyperinflation reappeared on the horizon in the months preceding the outbreak of the civil war.

While performance during the two periods summarily described here varied greatly, this did not reflect a substantial change in underlying economic mechanisms. It was, rather, a case of fundamental weaknesses that had accumulated steadily since the inception of the system of 'market socialism' finally working their way to the surface. External shocks played an important role in this process, further magnified by mounting conflicts of interest between the regions which stood in the way of effective implementation of corrective measures. The next sub-section details the failure of the system during the 1980s, a failure that was common to all socialist countries.

THE CRISIS OF THE 1980s AND ATTEMPTS TO STABILISE THE ECONOMY

The basic mechanisms at work did not fundamentally change in the course of the 1980s. What did change, with pervasive effects on the country's performance, was that there was no longer any foreign funding available to finance current account deficits. This constraint emerged clearly at the end of 1982 when Yugoslavia found it was no longer able to honour its debt service obligations. The policy emphasis then for the first time switched to stabilisation and recognised the need to shift resources to net exports for a protracted period in order to service accumulated foreign debt. The policy framework was set out in a Long-Term Stabilisation Programme (LTSP) which was adopted by the Federal Assembly in 1983. The LTSP recognised not only the need to adopt traditional stabilisation policies but also to improve resource allocation procedures through broad reliance on market forces and by enforcing financial discipline. Numerous reforms were attempted but, in practice, resistance to bearing the costs of adjustment, particularly at a regional level, prevented their effective implementation.[4] Failure to come to grips with the perverse mechanisms at work in the economy impaired, or even nullified, the effective impact of policies, which often also relied on inadequate tools. While foreign equilibrium was achieved, it was accompanied by stagnation and relentlessly accelerating inflation – from about 32 per cent in 1982 to over 1200 per cent in 1989. If anything, the process of adjusting foreign accounts was accompanied by increasing inefficiency, highlighted by the marked rise in the ICOR (incremental capital–output ratio) for the economy overall, from 5.6 in the 1970s to nearly 20 in the 1980s. Furthermore, shielded from financial discipline, enterprises continued to recruit labour in spite of prolonged stagnation, at least until 1987. As a result, productivity growth was markedly negative.[5]

The stabilisation efforts made since 1983 – again with stop–go episodes, but as a whole these spanned much longer periods than during the 1970s – relied in principle on restrictive fiscal and monetary policies, devaluation of the real exchange rate[6] and price and income policies. Indeed, with the exception of a dash for growth attempted in 1986–87 following a marked improvement in the balance of payments, the policy orientation was invariably restrictive in intent if not always in outcome. Some policy instruments were, by their very design, inadequate for the purpose of demand management. Nowhere was this more evident than in the case of fiscal policy. Ironically, this was because public administrations at all echelons of government were constitutionally debarred from borrowing to finance expenditure. Spending was therefore constrained by revenues and budgets were by and large balanced. However, while government could not incur deficits, enterprises in which regional and local administrations had a stake suffered no such constraints in their debt accumulation ('soft budget' constraints). Compared with other economies, the roles were significant.

Tight monetary policy was supposed to be the lynchpin of stabilisation. In practice, however, it was nothing if not accommodating and at times very expansionary. Throughout most of the 1980s real interest rates remained negative and were differentiated for different activities. Only briefly, between the beginning of 1988 and mid-1989, did they achieve positive, and sometimes very high, levels. Even so, this was not a deliberate act of policy, but rather the result of high and variable rates of inflation. Although negative real interest rates continued to have an adverse impact on resource allocation and led to over-accumulation, interest rates were not used as an instrument to regulate credit expansion. The central bank resorted instead to reserve requirements and credit ceilings on bank lending.

Had restrictive monetary policies been allowed to run their full course as part of a regime of financial discipline, credit rationing would have entailed the closure of many loss-making enterprises. It would also have led to extensive losses for banks with large exposures to these enterprises. Faced with increasing demand for distress lending, banks disregarded credit ceilings. The central bank for its part was unable to make banks comply with its policy and eventually accommodated credit expansion.

The control of monetary aggregates was also made difficult by a peculiar feature of the Yugoslav banking system. A large proportion of bank deposits (between 40 per cent and 50 per cent) was denominated in foreign currencies. These deposits developed rapidly in the 1970s as a result of earnings from tourism and emigrants' remittances, as they were correctly perceived as a convenient hedge against inflation. With the local currency depreciating continuously in the 1980s, this led to automatic increases in the money supply. Indeed, as the exchange risk was borne by the central bank, the result was similar to an increase in the government deficit financed by money creation. While this effect varied according to the rate of dinar depreciation, it was considerable at all times. In 1988, for example, the quasi-fiscal deficit arising from foreign exchange losses was estimated at 5 per cent of GSP. A further factor that reduced the effectiveness of policy was the rapid growth of inter-enterprise credits, the share of which in enterprise borrowing rose substantially in the course of the decade.

Income policies were particularly ineffectual in the 1980s.[7] Indeed, their very design is likely to have imparted further inflationary bias. Various partial and temporary price freezes were adopted by the federal government. These, however proved difficult to enforce at the local level and were invariably followed by large stepwise increases that accelerated inflationary momentum. Since price and wage freezes were often selective, they reinforced price–price and wage–wage spirals once they were lifted as firms attempted to re-establish profit margins or even to increase them in expectation of future controls. Furthermore, wage guidelines were usually expressed in real terms. In the absence of a nominal anchor, firms operating in a non-competitive environment had an incentive to raise their output prices rather than squeeze nominal wages.

While exports did grow in volume in the period following adoption of the LTSP, on the whole they lagged behind export market growth. The aggregate growth of exports conceals two very different trends for convertible currency trade and non-convertible currency trade. The volume of non-convertible currency exports, mainly to COMECON countries, fell dramatically after 1985, reflecting both impending recession in these countries and the impact of policies to redirect exports to convertible-currency areas to help service foreign debt. Exports in convertible currencies on the other hand rose considerably in volume terms during the same period, but gains in market shares in the OECD area were modest at best. As a result of these shifts in export direction, the share of exports to OECD countries rose from 28 per cent in 1982 to nearly 55 per cent in 1989, while that of exports to COMECON countries fell from 51 per cent to 34 per cent during the same period. About 40 per cent of imports and exports were accounted for by trade with the EC in 1989.

In late 1989, the federal government of Prime Minister Ante Markovic drafted an economic programme to pull the economy out of the quicksands. The centrepiece of this programme was the transition to a market economy. A top priority was the reduction of hyperinflation which by mid-1990 had been cut to less than 100 per cent from over 1,200 per cent in 1989. The dinar was pegged to the Deutsch-Mark and interest rates were freed. However, the policy met with massive resistance as industrial production slumped by close to 20 per cent in 1990 and as over one quarter of the country's 28,000 enterprises went into insolvency. Almost 2,000 enterprises were in fact bankrupt and over half of those were located in Serbia.

The Markovic reform programme was halted by the secession of Croatia and Slovenia and the ensuing internecine strife.

2. State planning and workers' management[8]

The Yugoslav version of socialism was markedly different from that in other socialist countries in Europe. The resulting social system acted as a unique laboratory where trial and error replaced the theoretical blueprint, the objective being to better the Stalin experience or indeed its promises for the future. Tito succeeded in obtaining independent status for his country, which opened the door to some Western financial, economic and political support. He used this freedom to experiment with institutional alternatives. Starting in 1948, Yugoslavia gradually abandoned its rigid command system and by 1952 the basis for social ownership and self-management was in place. The role of markets increased over time and although state intervention remained all-embracing, after the reforms of 1965 many features of a market system were introduced. These included a relatively liberalised trade regime and a realistic unified exchange rate, decentralisation of most production decisions to enterprises and banks and some freedom for markets in setting prices.

What set Yugoslav 'market socialism' apart was the system of workers' or labour management of firms (LMF),[9] with 'social' rather than state ownership of the means of production. This system was continually adapted over time in an effort to increase efficiency and reduce income disparities among skill classes, industries and regions. The system regressed markedly after the reforms embodied in the new constitution of 1974. This delegated the bulk of economic intervention from central government to the republics and installed a system of 'bargaining' between political and economic actors for the allocation of labour and capital. Economic problems – production inefficiencies, inflation, external deficits – mounted during the 1970s. The lack of financial discipline in firms, banks and at various levels of government fuelled inflation and rendered resource allocation even more arbitrary, while the efficiency of LMF grew increasingly doubtful.

Box 12.1 A reminder of theory

Rather than proceed on the basis of strong belief in the superiority of capitalist organisation, we find it interesting to look more carefully at the Yugoslav experience with labour management. Early theoretical work suggested that such an

continued

Box 12.1 *continued*

economy has attractive incentive features in a partial equilibrium context (Ward 1958, Domar 1966) and that it could duplicate the general equilibrium allocative efficiency of the capitalist economy (Drèze 1976), However, this general equilibrium approach neglected risk and incomplete markets and the information and incentive issues related to entry and exit. They were considered essential in Vanek's work (1970), but not fully formalised. Incentive and information problems are treated in Sertel (1982), Sertel and Steinherr (1984) and Steinherr and Thisse (1979), among others. This research shows that no general case can be made in favour of higher capitalist efficiency and that a labour-managed economy can be as efficient and, in certain circumstances, even more efficient. A synthesis of these arguments is provided in the Appendix to this chapter.

Before describing how worker management was organised in Yugoslavia and how it performed, it may be useful to outline the main theoretical requirements for an efficient design of labour management. For efficiency, the firm needs to be free in its decisions concerning internal organisation, choice of technology and product mix. While labour involvement in decision-making can enhance productivity, it can also produce red tape and obstruction. The optimal level and type of participation varies depending on the size of the organisation and the nature of the decisions to be taken (Blumberg 1969).

The greatest difficulty, and the most important design issue, concerns the organisation of factor markets. To avoid misallocation, capital needs to be priced competitively. However, a competitive rental rate is not sufficient and needs to be complemented by a market for partnership rights (Sertel 1982). If no such market exists, then members of a successful, high-income firm will tend to restrict entry (the insider–outsider conflict) and thereby generate non-efficient income differentials across firms or sectors. If, in addition, property rights are not transferable then a bias would be created in favour of current income and against future income (to be generated by current investment). See Meade (1972), Vanek (1970) and Furubotn and Pejovich (1970).

Similarly, labour markets need to be free of administrative intervention. Labour mobility is even more important in a labour-managed economy than in a capitalist economy to balance average labour income differentials, create new enterprises and run down inefficient ones. With a market for partnership rights, the creation of new firms should be relatively easy as most new firms even in the West start out in life as partnerships; closure of an LMF on the other hand may be more difficult. One compensation is that flexible average income makes it easier to ride out difficult phases in the business cycle. If average income is not administratively influenced, the LMF should do better in times of recession.

With a non-increasing returns to scale technology one would expect labour-managed firms to be smaller than capitalist firms because they maximise expected average income, not profits, and because the incentive and information advantages of a participative design are clearly more important to small firms. This should contribute to easier entry and more competitive market conditions.

So much for the theory. Box 12.1 and the Appendix to this chapter provide the analytical framework and the results of the theory of the LMF. The practical question is, however: how was the Yugoslav system designed and how did it perform?

Because there was no blueprint available for the Yugoslav model of socialism and for the organisation of LMF, institutional design followed a hit-and-miss, trial-and-error trajectory. Frequent institutional changes introduced considerable uncertainty and friction, but how much and how important is hard to assess. Detailed descriptions of the institutional setting can be found elsewhere (see Wachtel 1973, Estrin 1983), so we can confine ourselves to a short overview.

SOCIAL OWNERSHIP AND LABOUR MANAGEMENT

The Yugoslav system of social ownership and labour management can be viewed as one in which labour employed capital, instead of a system in which capital employed labour. Most enterprises were socially owned, rather than privately or state-owned. Ownership rights were theoretically vested in all citizens who delegated authority for managing socially owned property to autonomous enterprises and the representative institutions of their employees – the workers' councils and management boards.

Management of socially owned property in Yugoslavia was placed in the hands of the workers' representative bodies. At the base of the pyramidal organisational structure of the Yugoslav enterprise was the 'working collective', made up of all the employees in an enterprise. At the apex of the pyramid was the director of the enterprise; in between were the workers' council and the management board. By 1988 some 65 per cent of the labour force was employed in the 'social' sector and 34 per cent in the private sector (primarily small-scale agriculture: the share of the private sector in industrial output was negligible). It needs to be noted, however, that social ownership was effectively a form of non-ownership; workers in an enterprise were permitted to make accumulation decisions and to appropriate the surplus normally allocated to owners, but they were not permitted to sell their assets or in any way run them down in order to increase their incomes. This represents a major principal–agent problem for which no satisfactory solution was ever found. Moral hazard is extremely serious and can only be reduced by re-instituting individual property rights as in Sertel (1982) and Sertel and Steinherr (1984).

The free determination of labour income was never allowed to materialise. Several organisations did intervene to define a floor on wage incomes and sought to reduce income differentials across firms and sectors. As shown in studies such as Vanek and Jovicic (1975) and Estrin and Svejnar (1985), they were unsuccessful in this and may even have contributed to more, not less, income variance. The most important organisations which intervened in investment decisions and in the process of income determination were the trade unions, the League of Communists, the communes and the local and regional economic chambers.

The role of *trade unions* in socialist societies has always been a perplexing one. The basic contradiction lies in having an institution that represents workers' interests when all of society is supposedly controlled by the workers. The contradiction was particularly blatant in Yugoslav society, organised on the principle of workers' management. Why have another organisation representing the workers? A typical answer is provided by Marinovíc and Simíc (1970) who argue that the trade union is the 'basic organisation of the working class in implementing and promoting self-management'.

Perhaps the most significant way in which the *League of Communists* influenced enterprise affairs was by appointing party members to important managerial posts in the enterprise. The director of the enterprise, the president of the trade union branch and other leading officials were usually members of the League. Zupanov and Tannenbaum (1968) argued that the 'influence of managers . . . reflects, to some extent, the influence of the party'. However, over time the influence of the League declined dramatically.

The basic local government body in Yugoslavia was the *commune*. It was the immediate point of intersection between broader societal interests and specific enterprise interests. The commune performed some important economic functions. It frequently provided investment funds for the start-up of new firms and the expansion of existing ones. It subsidised whichever enterprise it deemed to be especially important for communal growth; it was the guarantor of minimum wages and of company debt. If an enterprise was unable to pay its employees a wage at least equal to the statutory minimum wage, the commune made up the difference. Likewise, if a firm went into bankruptcy, its creditors could seek payment from the commune in which the enterprise was located (Ward 1958). Because enterprises relied so heavily on the commune for investment funds, they were potentially subject to substantial commune influence on their affairs.

During the 1960s firms were encouraged to join *economic chambers* – associations of enterprises organised locally and regionally at industry branch level. The Chambers aimed at providing 'joint activities for the advancement of production, trade in commodities and the provision of different services', an objective defined by law. In practice, they fulfilled this legal mandate in a variety of ways. They had some formal power in the realm of price administration, and they tried to influence global enterprise policy. They transmitted national economic policy guidelines to local firms and sought to bring them into line with national policy imperatives.

In 1989, a new Law of Enterprise was passed which eliminated many of the compulsory features of labour management, such as the divisional split of firms, and legalised firms with a variety of property rights. Steps were even taken to legalise a market for participation rights but, unfortunately, the political firmament clouded over and slowed down the development of that market.

MARKET SOCIALISM

The second important principle guiding the Yugoslav social system was market socialism – the conjunction of social ownership of the means of production with markets to guide the allocation of resources in the economy. Markets for allocating resources at the micro-level coexisted with social ownership and a planning mechanism to achieve macroeconomic objectives. This made the Yugoslav economy the closest approximation to the classic model of a market-socialist economy as developed by Oskar Lange in the 1930s.

After 1952, Soviet-style central planning was replaced by a form of target planning. Annual plans were adopted for the rate of investment in the economy, part of investment allocation, the rate of development of different regions, and the macro-balance in the economy. In addition to this general emphasis on national planning, there was also a strengthening of local and regional planning. Republics and local communities were permitted to write their own plans dealing with local and regional economic problems. Detailed output targets were no longer handed down to enterprises; instead, firms were in principle granted autonomy over most input and output decisions. In practice, however, government bodies retained an effective degree of control over investment decisions as they were the major source of investment finance. During this period, firms had some measure of freedom in determining labour incomes.

The role of planning in the Yugoslav economy was watered down still further in the years from 1965 to 1971-74. The annual plans were abolished and replaced by medium- and long-range plans. These established the broad lines of Yugoslav economic development – including long-run target rates for growth, major new investment projects, investment in social overheads, and so on. Firms became much freer in their investment and output decisions when enterprise-owned banks replaced state funds as the major source of finance. Markets were used more extensively to allocate resources at the micro level, although price controls and other forms of administrative intermediation remained unchanged. The market approach reached its zenith around 1970. A definite retreat from market principles was incorporated in the Constitution of 1974, introducing a contractual bargaining system.

Until the mid-1960s investment decisions and international trade were for the most part planned centrally, and the bulk of firms' net income was taxed away in order to finance the very high investment share (averaging 34 per cent of gross material product in the 1950s), primarily through the budget. Even so, the rate of enterprise self-financing did rise during this period, from less than 10 per cent in 1953 to 38 per cent by 1964, and self-management bodies had some authority over pay structures, employment decisions, welfare issues and, towards the very end of this period, wages.

Reforms in 1965 led to a significant freeing of domestic prices and trade, and the formation of an autonomous, albeit socially owned, banking sector to replace the state's central investment funds. Newly created banks were awarded the balance of state assets and required to fill the gap in the supply of investment funds left by the withdrawal of the state. The share of taxes and deductions in enterprise net income was reduced to less than 40 per cent and the share of banks as an investment source rose from an average 3 per cent in 1960–63 to more than 50 per cent in 1970. The share financed by enterprises also declined, from 37 per cent to 33 per cent, while the state's share contracted from 60 per cent to 16 per cent. At the same time as the functions of the state increasingly devolved to firms and banks, the residual activities of the government began to be decentralised from federal to republic and even local (communal) government level.

The 1974 reforms were largely inspired by communist fears of loss of control over the economy as implied by 'market socialism'. By this time, and in contrast to other socialist countries, only a minority of Yugoslav managers were members of the party *nomenklatura*. The disintegration of the enterprise into its component Basic Organisations of Associated Labour (BOALs) was accompanied by an attempt to improve national economic coordination by means of consultative committees, loosely ordered under an indicative planning umbrella. This meant that the mediation of economic decisions through markets was, to a considerable extent, replaced by inter-BOAL negotiation and bargaining among enterprises, industry and regional consultative councils, which were channels for political intervention. While the authorities had no discretionary authority to enforce their views as they would have had in a conventional central planning system, agreements among BOALs were in principle legally binding. In practice, voluntary agreements proved incoherent and hard to enforce. Ben-Ner and Neuberger (1990) argue that the collusive rather than competitive nature of the system helped to engineer its downfall by the early 1980s; the system was to all intents and purposes abandoned by 1982, but the attendant framework for widespread collusion and political intervention survived.

The increasing incoherence of economic decision-making was accentuated by changes in the status of banks in the mid-1960s, which were effectively transformed into organisations controlled by their founders, typically BOALs and local authorities. These banks supported their local client base regardless of opportunities in other parts of the country. Loss-making BOALs were rarely bankrupted and the industrial sector typically reacted to a credit squeeze by an involuntary expansion of inter-firm credit (see Knight 1985).

During the 1970s and the 1980s a high proportion of Yugoslav industry was persistently loss-making. The authorities were always loath to permit firms to go bankrupt for fear of large-scale unemployment. It has been calculated that, even during the relatively successful 1970s, between 10 per cent and 30 per cent of the labour force in the social sector were employed in loss-making firms (see Tyson 1980). Administrative measures were used to stave off bankruptcy, primarily direct budgetary support at various levels of government, or unsecured bank overdraft facilities, so that the state acted as lender of last resort to enterprises. *De facto*, therefore, Yugoslav self-managed firms operated with the same 'soft budget constraints' as their counterparts in centrally planned economies, though the system differed in other respects.

DECLINING GROWTH: WAS LABOUR MANAGEMENT THE MAIN CULPRIT?

With labour management, as with any system, there is a gap between theory and real life experience. Above we argued that Yugoslav markets were never free of planning and intervention by the different echelons of political authority. Equally serious was the faulty design of the LMF.

The theory of labour management offers several predictions, most of which cannot be confirmed by the Yugoslav experience. The theory predicts that employment should be more stable and so it was, for reasons both of internal organisation and external employment policies. Greater incentives and better productivity performance, as observed in LMF in Western economies, may have been present in the 1950s and 1960s, but they succumbed to later reforms (Mencinger 1986; Sapir 1980).

One of the theory's predictions, that LMF are on average smaller so that competitive conditions are more easily preserved, is wide off the mark. Reliable data on enterprise size distribution and market structure are limited to the pre-1974 period because the definition of the 'enterprise' was altered by the 1974 reforms. It would seem, however, that the fragmentation of the national product market into its republican or even more local components increased after 1974 and monopoly power in the relevant market places therefore rose (Sacks 1983).

Estrin and Petrin (1990) show that in 1954 only 12 per cent of enterprises employed fewer than 125 workers and by 1973 this had declined to 4 per cent. This compares with an average of 30 per cent for the OECD countries in the mid-1970s. On the other hand, by 1973, 57 per cent of Yugoslav industrial enterprises employed more than 1,000 workers, compared with 35 per cent in the OECD countries around that time. This remarkable size distribution is testimony to the survival of the planners' bias for large enterprises.

In 1959 more than half of Yugoslavia's industrial sectors displayed concentration ratios (the share of the four largest firms in national sales) in excess of 75 per cent and none recorded concentration ratios of less than 25 per cent. The regional fragmentation of the Yugoslav economy suggests that even these figures understate actual market monopoly power at the republican or local level. In later periods levels of concentration did drift downwards in some sectors, but not in all.

In an efficient market, identical production factors would be remunerated in different locations and enterprises with comparable incomes. A striking feature of the Yugoslav system was the disparity in labour incomes across firms, sectors and regions. This suggests that there was no nationwide integrated labour market. Moreover, the large inter-firm wage differentials reveal that capital allocation and pricing were causing problems and that labour mobility was insufficient to equalise these differences. Tyson (1980) argues that inter-regional labour migration was very low and totally unrelated to unemployment and income differentials among the republics. Estrin and Svejnar (1985) estimated wage determination in Yugoslavia and found that dispersions in corporate profitability were passed on to worker earnings through the income determination proper to self-management. Labour and product market rigidities and immobilities (the insider–outsider problem) were sufficiently pronounced to prevent eradication of the resulting marginal product differences. In addition, workers were also able to appropriate monopoly rents engendered by non-competitive product markets and cheap use of capital assets.

The failure of the labour market in equalising marginal products of labour[10] was clearly the result of a combination of factors: the under-development of the labour market, to which the non-existence of a partnership market contributed significantly, regional labour immobility and the fact that with labour management there are no exogenous parametric wages.

However, socialist principles and worker-controlled income distribution accounted for smaller income differentials within firms across skill and responsibility categories than in Western economies. While attractive from an egalitarian point of view, this resulted in lower investment in human capital and hence lower skill dispersion.

As for the supply elasticity of LMF, the Yugoslav experience reveals no 'perverse' behaviour (Horvath 1986), as suggested by Ward (1958) and Domar (1966) and refuted by Sertel (1982) and Steinherr and Thisse (1979) (see the Appendix). However, supply elasticity was lower than in Western economies, thereby contributing to greater overall stability throughout the business cycle.

The lack of responsibility at managerial level or of the worker councils inside the firm and indeed of other influential actors outside the firm (banks, communes, party, trade unions), caused major misallocations without corrections. The ultimate penalty, market exit, was itself inoperative due to the alliance of outside interests with the firms' workforce. Market entry, important for innovation and to compensate for lower supply elasticities, was also remarkably low. Presumably the gains from setting up a company were insufficient in the absence of a market for participation rights.

The combination of lack of property rights and hence lack of incentives for setting up new firms, and the lack of motivation to expand employment within existing firms owing to the insider–outsider problem, slowed down growth even when external conditions were positive. Add to this the 'Furubotn–Pejovich effect' (see below) and it becomes obvious that labour management contributed significantly to the slow-down of growth.

Furthermore, such incentives as were provided by LMF were likewise not sustained. Estrin *et al.* (1987) have found that in Western LMF workers are indeed motivated to perform and participate more actively in the flow of information, resulting in productivity increases. The internal structure of Yugoslav firms was not markedly different from those of profit-maximising firms, contrary to theoretical expectations (Steinherr 1977; Williamson 1980), but labour productivity growth and overall efficiency declined over time (Mencinger 1986).

Appropriation of surplus by workers' income (the 'Furubotn–Pejovich effect') reduced investment, yet investment levels remained high. Political concern resulted in an overall policy of cheap funds, most of the time at negative real rates of interest, and in specific intervention in the allocation of funds. These outside influences on the investment decision were reinforced by a feature peculiar to the LMF which is that it operates optimally with greater capital intensity. (For an explanation, see the Appendix.) Capital–labour ratios tended therefore to fall out of step with the level of development in Yugoslavia. Rising unemployment, declining capital productivity and a very steep increase in ICORs[11] were the price. A number of important and unfortunate consequences flowed from this.

First, with capital–labour ratios out of line with factor endowments in Yugoslavia, industry employed too much capital and too little labour, slowing down the transfer of labour from agriculture and forcing a large share of labour into emigration. Output and employment growth were curtailed. Moreover, sectoral specialisation fell prey to serious distortions.

Second, socialist priorities emphasised employment stability and labour management further aggravated employment rigidity (see Appendix). As a result, inter-sectoral and regional migration was less than in market economies[12] (see Estrin 1983).

Third, the overall socialist design militated in favour of large company size, far in excess of that observed in comparable market economies. The natural advantage of labour-managed firms resides in restricted size but this never really came off. The non-competitive industrial structure, largely protected from foreign competition, generated monopoly returns which, together with under-priced capital, resulted in great inefficiency and rents that were largely appropriated by workers, and gave rise to highly differentiated incomes across sectors.

3. The country that never was

To ensure a better balance between the regions, the 1946 Constitution provided for some regional autonomy. Six republics and two autonomous provinces were created respecting their historic frontiers. Inevitably and unfortunately, it was impossible also to heed ethnic frontiers, so that the ethnic problem remained unsolved. Montenegro, Macedonia and Bosnia-Herzegovina became republics. The first two were recognised as nationalities while the latter came into being in order to stave off a Serbo-Croatian dispute since the territory would have made Serbia preponderant. By the same token and to safeguard dominant minorities' interests, Vojvodina and Kosovo were turned into autonomous provinces within Serbian borders.

Although the republics were granted greater powers under the 1966 economic reforms, ethnic and economic tensions nevertheless persisted and indeed increased, both between the different republics and within their own borders. Slovenia grew increasingly reluctant to pay for the development of other parts of the country. Nationalistic preoccupations and even protectionism resurged in trade among the republics, so that another constitutional change had to be made.

The 1974 Constitution made the republics fully autonomous in all decisions that could be devolved from central government. Experience has now shown that even that was not enough, as certain key policy areas had perforce to remain at federal level short of full independence being granted. This included defence – and most of the defence industry was located in Serbia with over 60 per cent of high-ranking officers being Serbs – and monetary policy. As argued below, it would have been preferable to allow individual republics to opt for their own currency. But more likely than not even that step, had it been taken – and of course it could have helped the richer republics to avoid hyperinflation in their own currency during the late 1980s – would have proved insufficient. As it was, the richer republics were forced, through the federal budget and their permanent current account surplus, to finance both the Serbian-dominated army, which was a potential threat to themselves, and the development of the poorer republics.

Tito's charisma and skill in arbitrating differences among the republics prevented an explosion of nationalist pretensions. His death on 4 May 1981 opened the gates to increased confrontation between, to lapse into Eurospeak, two concepts of subsidiarity. The Serbs campaigned for stronger centralised federal institutions answering to communist principles and including central planning, while Slovenia and Croatia took the opposite view of maximum decentralisation with more liberal economic management closer to market principles.

As demonstrated below, the economic decline of the 1980s placed the conflicting interests of the different republics into sharp relief. The economic crisis was decidedly not the actual cause of the ultimate disintegration but it was a strong accelerating factor. The real cause was undoubtedly that Yugoslavia was never a country in the sense that it formed a harmonious community with a widely shared set of values. It was served by the circumstantial chance of having a generally approved leader in the historic figure of Tito and the fleeting illusion of having found a unifying ideology in communism. When the leader and the ideological illusions died, the old naked facts of inherent conflict were all that was left.

REGIONAL DEVELOPMENT

The Yugoslav Federation that took shape after World War II was, from the outset, an amalgam of regions which, for historical reasons, displayed greatly varying levels of economic development. Although most republics were at the time predominantly agrarian societies,[13] Slovenia and Croatia and, to a lesser extent, Serbia and Vojvodina, had already built up an industrial and commercial base. On the other hand,

Bosnia, Montenegro, Macedonia and especially Kosovo were much more backward and organised around subsistence agriculture. The time trend of regional disparities in *per capita* income is depicted in Table 12.2.

It is obvious that the gap between developed regions (DRs) and less developed regions (LDRs) widened over time. In 1952, average income per head in the richest republic (Slovenia) was about four times that of the poorest (Kosovo). By 1989, the ratio had doubled. By comparison with EC countries, regional disparities in Yugoslavia were very large (see Table 12.3). And the widening of the gap between DRs and LDRs is also substantial compared with other countries in Europe which have experienced serious regional problems[14]. The coefficient of variation of regional GDP per head increased steadily in Yugoslavia and by 1989 it stood at twice the highest value in the EC. Two distinct periods can be identified with regard to the relative performance of output growth in DRs and LDRs. Between 1952 and 1965, output growth in the former was much faster than in the LDRs. Since then, growth rates have been roughly the same in both sets of regions, the widening gap in *per capita* income being accounted for by faster population growth in the LDRs. Population growth since the beginning of the 1950s averaged 0.7 per cent and 1.7 per cent a year in DRs and LDRs respectively (with a peak of 2.5 per cent in Kosovo), leading to speedier growth of the labour force in LDRs. Output growth in LDRs was never sufficient to absorb new entrants in the labour market so that unemployment rates in LDRs were consistently higher. By way of illustration, in 1989 the unemployment rate in Slovenia was 2.7 per cent; in other DRs it varied between 6 per cent and 10 per cent; but in LDRs it ranged from 14 per cent in Bosnia to 25 per cent in Kosovo.

On the eve of the outbreak of civil war LDRs made up about 40 per cent of the country's 23.5 million population, but represented only 23 per cent of output. Average income per head in DRs fell far short of the average of Western European countries with the lowest *per capita* income. Only Slovenia had an income *per capita* above that of Greece and Portugal. On the other hand, *per capita* income in LDRs was comparable to that of middle-income developing countries and that of Kosovo with, say, Egypt or Morocco.

TABLE 12.2 Real GDP *per capita*, 1972 prices (Yugoslavia = 100)

	1952	1965	1974	1980	1989
Developed Regions					
Slovenia	182	184	200	198	198
Croatia	121	121	126	127	127
Serbia	103	96	97	98	103
Vojvodina	90	112	116	113	118
Less Developed Regions					
Montenegro	88	76	68	79	73
Bosnia-Herzegovina	96	72	66	66	68
Macedonia	71	67	68	67	66
Kosovo	47	35	32	28	25
Max/Min	3.9	5.3	6.3	7.1	7.9
Coefficient of variation (%)	38.0	44.0	50.0	50.0	51.0

Source: Federal Institute of Statistics

TABLE 12.3 Regional disparities in GDP *per capita*, 1988, in standards of purchasing power

	Max/Min	Coefficient of variation (%)
Yugoslavia	7.90	51.0
Italy	2.34	26.0
Greece	1.69	10.0
Portugal	1.66	23.0
Spain	2.23	17.0
Belgium	1.61	15.0
Germany	1.93	13.0
United Kingdom	1.63	15.0
France	2.15	26.0
Netherlands	2.69	19.0

Source: Eurostat

Faced from the outset with wide regional disparities, the federal authorities adopted as a priority policy goal the accelerated development of LDRs. The major tool used to this end was a substantial transfer of resources from DRs to LDRs. Prior to 1965 these were almost exclusively budgetary transfers aimed at both providing infrastructure and financing business investment. From 1965 onwards federal budgetary transfers to republican authorities were earmarked for the provision of infrastructure and social services. They were supplemented by transfers channelled through the Federal Fund for Accelerated Development (FAD) whose chief aim was to assist business investment. The FAD was financed by a levy on enterprises in DRs. It provided funds to republican authorities who in turn made them available to banks with guidelines for their allocation at subsidised interest rates. By and large, budgetary and FAD transfers amounted to some 1 per cent and 2 per cent of national gross material product (GMP) respectively and to about 10 per cent of the GMP of LDRs (see Table 12.4). FAD transfers alone financed on average between 20 per cent and 30 per cent of investment in LDRs, rising to nearly 50 per cent in Kosovo.

In addition to these transfers, LDRs benefited from capital transfers both from abroad and from DRs. Between the early 1970s and the mid-1980s, LDRs ran trade deficits with the rest of the world, as did DRs.[15] Since then, however, LDRs seem to have experienced a reversal of capital flows with the rest of the world. By way of comparison, LDRs in Italy benefited from continuous capital inflows from the rest of the

TABLE 12.4 Transfers to LDRs as a percentage of GMP*

	1974	1980
Bosnia Herzegovina	5.1	6.1
Montenegro	12.9	13.5
Macedonia	7.4	8.4
Kosovo	34.5	40.7
Total LDRs	9.3	10.7

Source: Federal Institute of Social Planning

* Budgetary transfers and Fund for Accelerated Development combined

world throughout that period (see Table 12.5). As pointed out in Section 1, negative real interest rates turned these flows and inter-regional deficits into income transfers. This point needs to be emphasised when we compare regional disequilibria in Yugoslavia with regional imbalances in market economies. For example, LDRs in Italy also receive substantial fiscal transfers and run current account deficits with the rest of the world (about 21 per cent of regional GDP in 1989) and with the rest of the domestic economy. While these deficits are much larger than in Yugoslavia, there is no question of transfers as they are remunerated at market interest rates. What these very large deficits do suggest is a more complete division of labour and integration in the national economy.

It is interesting to analyse the factors of growth in LDRs in Yugoslavia against this backcloth to see whether they can explain why the LDRs failed to close the income gap with the DRs.[16] A first important feature is that capital–labour ratios were always higher in LDRs than in DRs from the moment the regional development policy was implemented in the early 1950s. Part of the difference was attributable to the structure of industrial output, which put strong emphasis on the development of basic industries. But ICORs were also higher in non-industrial sectors. As a result of this trend, the capital–output ratio in LDRs was higher than in DRs from the mid-1960s. Second, also around this time, capital started growing faster than output in most LDR sectors. This means that marginal productivity was on the wane and productivity below average. The implication of falling marginal productivity of capital is that ever-increasing amounts of capital are needed to sustain a given rate of output growth.

Furthermore, capital stock in LDRs grew faster than employment, which led to a constant increase in the capital–labour ratio to levels above those in DRs. But despite a

TABLE 12.5 Trade balances of republics as a percentage of GSP

	1971			1983			1989		
	Exports	Imports	Trade balance	Exports	Imports	Trade balance	Exports	Imports	Trade balance
Developed Regions									
Slovenia	17.4	31.8	−14.4	41.9	45.0	−3.1	22.9	21.3	1.6
Croatia	15.6	22.8	−7.2	25.5	29.8	−4.3	15.7	21.9	−6.2
Vojvodina	10.9	11.1	−0.2	22.7	33.4	−10.7	15.5	20.6	−5.1
Serbia	15.0	20.2	−7.8	31.4	33.0	−1.6	18.3	19.1	−0.8
Less Developed Regions									
Bosnia-Herzegovina	12.9	20.5	−7.6	32.3	37.0	−4.7	25.1	21.6	3.5
Montenegro	8.6	21.1	−12.5	24.6	22.9	1.7	16.9	11.3	5.6
Macedonia	13.7	28.1	−14.4	26.6	41.4	−14.8	17.4	22.2	−4.8
Kosovo	7.7	9.6	−1.9	22.6	29.0	−6.4	12.4	12.2	0.2
Italy*									
Developed regions			5.4			3.9			6.1**
Less developed regions			−17.4			−16.6			−20.9**

Source: Federal Institute of Statistics for Yugoslavia; Istituto Centrale di Statistica for Italy

* Current account surplus or deficit as a percentage of GDP ** 1988

higher ratio of fixed assets per worker, labour productivity was lower than in DRs. Hence total factor productivity trailed behind that in DRs between 1965 and 1980. Its relative contribution to growth was also less than in the rest of the country.[17] And in the course of the 1980s, when it became negative for the country as a whole,the LDRs again fared worse than the others.

A first question that arises is, why did LDRs opt for capital-intensive methods of production given that labour was in relatively abundant supply? We have already seen in Section 2 that there were strong biases in the system that provided an incentive to maximise the capital–labour ratio (absence of rental cost of capital or negative interest rates). After 1965 the republican governments were given a considerable degree of autonomy in shaping the structure of incentives in their respective regions. There appears to have been a clear tendency for republican governments heavily to promote capital formation through subsidised funding at rates which were even more negative in real terms than in DRs, reinforced by fiscal incentives. But it would be a mistake to identify this policy as underlying the stronger bias towards capital intensity in LDRs. Once real interest rates are zero, the demand for credit grows considerably. To understand the phenomenon of higher capital intensity in the poorer regions, we need to look more carefully at the credit allocation mechanism. Competition for funds was obviously more pronounced and more widely distributed in the richer than in the poorer regions. The same is true for the allocation of equity. This seems to be confirmed by the degree of concentration in industry (see Table 12.6).

The second question we need to address is why total factor productivity was lower in LDRs. Here again, it is difficult to provide a comprehensive answer. An analysis based on disaggregated data (World Bank 1982) suggests that for the country as a whole, the limited gains in total factor productivity that did occur were attributable much more to gains in technical efficiency (as firms moved to the best available practice) than to technological progress. In LDRs technical efficiency gains were well below the national average and declines occurred in a number of industrial and

TABLE 12.6 Size structure of industry by region, Yugoslavia 1974 (percentage of total manufacturing employment)

	Small firms*	Very large firms**
Developed Regions		
Slovenia	10.4	16.1
Croatia	12.8	14.1
Vojvodina	15.4	9.3
Less Developed Regions		
Serbia	8.4	23.0
Bosnia-Herzegovina	5.7	22.7
Montenegro	15.5	5.2
Macedonia	9.6	23.4
Kosovo	6.2	31.8

Source: Federal Institute of Statistics
* Less than 125 employees
** More than 1,000 employees

non-industrial sectors. As a result the proportion of firms attaining the levels of technical efficiency achieved in DRs sustained a steady downtrend from 1965.

The tendency towards autarkic regional development may explain why LDR investment efficiency deteriorated. As pointed out above, the republican authorities gained considerable independence in regional planning after 1965. They not only had a considerable say in the allocation of financial resources, they were also influential in shaping the overall investment strategies of their respective regions. Almost without exception, republican authorities set out to create an integrated productive system at home, without bothering to ask themselves whether this made sense at the national level or not. For example, all republics openly attempted to build up their basic industries in the belief that this was an essential point of departure for future industrialisation. From there the next step was to boost vertical integration within each republic. Not only were investment plans at the republican level designed to achieve this goal, but inter-republic trade was curtailed with informal barriers so as to encourage firms to buy inputs and sell their output as much as possible within their own republic.

The result was a duplication of productive capacity and failure to reap the benefits of economies of scale. The national market was *de facto* split up into republican units with little, and declining, inter-regional trade. Indeed, by the beginning of the 1980s the share of inter-regional trade in output was considerably less than trade between most European countries (OECD 1984: 48–49). The fragmentation of the national market was likewise manifest in the wide differences in prices for the same products in different republics – sometimes involving a factor of two or more – as a result of local monopolies (OECD 1990: 44–46).

Turning now to the pattern of trade between republics and with the rest of the world, Table 12.7 suggests that, given the low and declining level of regional integration, LDRs were, on average, more open to inter-regional trade than DRs (about 29 per cent and 20 per cent of their respective GDP in 1987). This can probably be explained by the relatively small size and limited productive base of the LDR group. On the other hand, and with the exception of Kosovo, there does not seem to be a significant difference in the exposure of the two groups to foreign trade. DRs, however, tend to be more exposed to foreign trade than to trade among themselves. For Slovenia, and possibly Croatia, foreign trade is more important than trade with DRs and LDRs combined.[18]

Table 12.7 also suggests that DRs, with the partial exception of Serbia, seem to conduct most of their inter-regional trade among themselves. Although trade between DRs and LDRs represents only a small part of the transactions conducted by the former group, for the latter on the other hand it is much more important than trade within the LDR group. Disaggregated data (not shown in Table 12.7) suggest an interesting picture. LDR trade with DRs is heavily concentrated on Serbia, with the exception of Bosnia-Herzegovina. Indeed, Serbia is the only region which seems to be relatively integrated with all other republics.

To sum up, despite protracted efforts spanning nearly four decades, regional disparities and lack of regional integration proved to be intractable problems. The autarkic orientation of the republican authorities did not foster efficient use of the sizable capital inflows into LDRs, so that output growth remained well below potential, given the growth of inputs. The picture that emerges is one of a set of insulated regions with a very low degree and uneven spread of integration.

TABLE 12.7 Structure of exchanges in Yugoslavia by region* (percentage of GDP, 1987)

	Intra-regional trade	Trade with DRs	Trade with LDRs	Foreign Trade
Developed regions				
Slovenia	59.7	13.5	4.8	22.0
Croatia	66.9	13.0	4.6	15.5
Vojvodina	59.4	19.3	4.7	16.6
Serbia	61.0	12.7	7.1	19.2
Less developed regions				
Bosnia-Herzegovina	50.9	27.0	3.6	18.5
Montenegro	52.4	22.1	9.4	16.1
Macedonia	58.5	17.6	4.2	19.7
Kosovo	57.3	22.2	8.7	11.8

Source: Estimates based on Federal Institute of Statistics data
* As trade flows are measured on the basis of sales, whereas GDP is a value-added concept, trade shares are artificially high

WAS THE FEDERATION AN 'OPTIMAL' ECONOMIC UNION?

When countries are born or break up, economic factors may play a role, but they are overshadowed more often than not by political, social and nationalistic considerations. The disintegration of the Soviet Union (see Chapter 13) and the break-up of the Yugoslav Federation are stark reminders of this. Nevertheless, this section aims to assess whether there was, or indeed still is, a case for economic and monetary union between the former six republics of Yugoslavia regardless of the political configuration which emerges from the hostilities that erupted in 1991. The question is indeed relevant because if there is a case for economic and monetary union, there would be costs to be borne if the republics were after all to go their own separate ways, over and above the already substantial war damage. It would then make sense for the sovereign successor states to retain a suitably defined form of economic community. This is all the more evident since elsewhere in Europe, the EC is attracting membership precisely because there are benefits to be reaped from a larger integrated economic area.

The basic criteria for evaluating the potential trade diversion of a customs union (that is, the propensity to trade with insiders rather than with outsiders entirely because of tariffs or other barriers on 'outsider' trade) are the size of the customs union, the level of protection, the degree of specialisation and the distance from other sources of supply. On all these counts Yugoslavia was never anything but a trade-diverting community: the country is small in terms of GDP and therefore needs more open trade with the rest of the world. For example, the Netherlands exports 58 per cent of its GDP as compared to 25–30 per cent for Yugoslavia. Although hard to measure, the combination of import tariffs, quotas and administrative allocation of foreign exchange represented formidable protection for domestic producers. As a result, the Yugoslav economy, like other socialist economies, never made the grade in achieving the full scale of specialisation in line with comparative advantage. Finally, Yugoslavia is geographically close to highly developed markets both inside and outside the European Community. Hence distance is not a consideration for autonomy.

An idea of what kind of trade structure could have been produced by a market-based approach is obtained by using a gravity approach. In this approach, which is to be explained and used extensively in the next chapter, trade is regarded as depending on the size of the domestic economy and of foreign markets, on the level of development, on distance, on neighbourhood and on various 'club' memberships. Using this approach, and forcing the overall trade shares to remain invariable, Havrylyshyn and Pritchett (1991) obtain the results shown in Table 12.8.

Table 12.8 suggests that with neutral trade policies Yugoslavia would conduct over 70 per cent of its trade with Western Europe, or three times the actual level of trade in the early 80s. By contrast, trade with Eastern Europe and the Middle East would be drastically reduced if fundamentals were respected. The bottom line of these considerations is that for Slovenia or Croatia there is no point in staying in a Yugoslav customs union. An association with the European Community is clearly a preferable alternative.

While this is a long-term view, one might wonder whether the short-term adjustment costs would not be excessive. We think not. Over time, as noted above, intra-Yugoslav trade has diminished steadily, while the trade of these two former republics with the rest of the world has increased. Both also showed flexibility in re-directing their exports during the 1980s from CMEA countries to the OECD. On the import side they are already trading extensively with the EC, which provides a large share of investment and intermediate goods. Finally, the hostilities that broke out in 1991 have brought internal trade virtually to a halt.

WAS THE FEDERATION AN OPTIMAL CURRENCY AREA?

Slovenia and Croatia have already created their own currencies (the tolar and the Croat dinar). Is this a wise choice or would it not have been preferable, even for now-sovereign former republics, to hold on to the Yugoslav dinar?

The literature on optimal currency areas argues that the main advantage of having a national currency is that the exchange rate is used to adjust to nationally differentiated shocks (and it assumes that exchange rate adjustments are not offset by price adjustments: workers will accept a cut in real wages if it is brought about by a devaluation, but not otherwise). Otherwise wages would have to adjust to such shocks flexibly, or labour would need to move from recession-stricken areas to high-employment areas. A more modern argument points to the ability to choose a 'monetary constitution', including an anchor to the most appropriate foreign currency. These

TABLE 12.8 Export and import shares of Yugoslavia (Actual 1980–84 and potential)

	Western Europe		Eastern Europe		North Africa/ Middle East	
	Actual	Predicted	Actual	Predicted	Actual	Predicted
Imports	54.7	73.2	24.4	10.9	14.4	2.2
Exports	25.5	74.8	49.6	16.3	–	–

Source: Havrylyshyn and Pritchett (1991)

potential advantages of a separate currency have to be weighed against the gains to be had from optimal economic integration as induced by a common currency. Introduction of separate currencies would, of course, create barriers to inter-republic trade by increasing transaction costs. How high these costs will be depends on the extent of inter-republic trade.

As shown above, 40 years of federalism have deepened the structural differences between republics. Hence it seems obvious that a fixed exchange rate regime (or a single currency) is not desirable for such a heterogeneous group of republics. The best way of dealing with republic-specific shocks is surely through exchange rate adjustments rather than price and wage adjustments alone. We have also seen that there was little incentive for capital mobility (except fiscal transfers) across republican frontiers. Furthermore, there is some indication that labour mobility within the country was also very limited. While external migration peaked at some 800,000 in the 1960s, total internal migration was less than 50,000 a year or 0.2 per cent of the population. Nevertheless, a single currency might have been justified if labour income relative to productivity had been sufficiently flexible to enhance the LDRs' competitive position and so absorb unemployment. But this was not the case. And after the political split-up there will be no more fiscal transfers. Hence, without capital mobility, labour mobility, labour income mobility, and fiscal transfers, Yugoslavia lacks the economic base for a single currency area. Adjustment at republican level requires wage flexibility and this is liable to increase with separate currencies.

Furthermore, the Federation was unable to deliver a freely convertible currency with stable purchasing power. Hence, Yugoslavs shifted massively into foreign currency holdings that had to be tolerated (and at times were even encouraged) by the authorities. And there is no telling at this point whether the ability to create a stable Yugoslav currency will emerge in the foreseeable future.

Of course, no former republic of Yugoslavia is large enough, in economic terms, or endowed with a sufficiently diversified economy, to form an 'optimal' monetary area by itself. But Slovenia's northern neighbour has shown how one deals with such a problem. Austria has chosen to hook the Schilling to the DM and so join the DM area with all the stability and international acceptability this entails. This may be too much for a country like Slovenia, in the short run. So Slovenia initially opted for a flexible exchange rate, but, as the effects of the war wear off, the Tolar has been kept close to the DM.

Choices are less clear-cut for the rest of the Federation. In the past, Yugoslavia's high and variable level of price inflation stemmed from a lack of political support in the republics for a common monetary policy. The central institutions never had the power to control the money supply and set limits on credit expansion in the Federation. For example, had the central bank decided that credit expansion was to be limited to a given percentage, and had local banks in each republic then increased credits beyond that ceiling, it would have required one republic (say, Serbia) to offset the cumulated excess of all the others. And Serbia was simply not large enough to bear the burden of responsibility for such external contingencies without paying a heavy price.

There is reason to doubt that what remains of Yugoslavia will be able to manage a common currency, which requires a strong central bank with effective control of the money supply throughout the territory.

Box 12.2 What happened with disintegration?

Economic disintegration accompanied by civil war aborted the 1990 stabilisation programme, relegated the old dinar to Serbia and Montenegro, and led to the introduction of four new republican currencies: the tolar in Slovenia in October 1991; the Croatian dinar (CDR) in December 1991 (which at the time was expected to be followed soon by a convertible Croatian kruna); the Macedonian denar, which replaced the Yugoslav dinar in April 1992; while Bosnia and Herzegovina initially used both the Yugoslav and the Croatian dinar, but decided to introduce their own currency in August 1992 (see Uvalic 1992). Territorial conquest and occupation has been accompanied by imposition of the occupant's currency.

The Slovene tolar is the only successful, convertible currency in ex-Yugoslavia (see Mencinger (1992), Pleskovic and Sachs (1992). The conversion was well prepared, with fiscal reforms intended to minimise the monetisation of budget deficits, the unification and liberalisation of foreign exchange markets, and efficient logistic arrangements for a speedy conversion. The options of a currency board and of a parallel circulation with the Yugoslav dinar were rejected as Slovenia did not have the reserves necessary for a board and wished to cut exposure to Yugoslav hyperinflation. In October 1991 parliament declared the tolar the sole legal tender in Slovenia; borders were closed to prevent an inflow of Yugoslav dinars and banks were closed for three days; most of the conversion was completed in the first 36 hours. All contracts and bank accounts were converted into tolars at par, with a US$500 per person limit on cash. The dinars collected were held for later negotiations with the rest of Yugoslavia. The exchange rate was floated (multiple rates survived until mid-1992 when they were unified). Inflation was rapidly brought under control, from a peak of 21.5 per cent in the month of conversion to 1.2 per cent in August 1992, while the dinar continued to hyperinflate and moved from parity to 5 dinars per tolar in the autumn of 1992. Foreign reserves were built up from zero*.

A sharp reduction of inter-republic trade followed monetary disintegration in ex-Yugoslavia, with cascade adverse effects on consumption and income, though it is impossible to distinguish between the effects of monetary developments and those of civil war.

Economic and monetary disintegration allowed not only differing exchange rate regimes and inflation performances (ranging from Slovene convertibility to runaway inflation in Serbia), but also vast differences in the nature and pace of reform. The former distinctive feature of the Yugoslav model – workers' self management – was virtually eliminated in Croatia, redefined in Slovenia, maintained in Serbia and Macedonia, suspended by war in Bosnia and Herzegovina. Reform of the ownership regime also differed: with mass privatisation in Slovenia, commercial sales in Croatia, retention of state ownership in Serbia, inconclusive debates in Macedonia and low priority in Bosnia and Herzegovina (Nuti 1993).

* Our preferred option of pegging to the DM, Ecu or Austrian Schilling was not retained for fear of rapidly running out of scarce exchange reserves and because of not knowing the correct level for the peg. Whether a very thin exchange market is a better guide remains a question to be answered. It is, however, a fact that sizable foreign exchange holdings by Slovenes across the border with Austria provide large amounts for speculation.

4. Conclusions

Yugoslavia's overall performance since the inception of self-management and market socialism in the early 1950s can scarcely be considered a showpiece of sustained growth and development. If indeed there ever was a 'Yugoslav economic miracle', in terms of exceptional growth in income, then it was confined roughly to the decade running from the mid-1950s to the mid-1960s, when the economy was expanding at over 9 per cent a year. But although not ten a penny, 'miracles' were not in short supply in the aftermath of World War II. The examples of Italy, Germany, Israel, Japan and the socialist countries in Europe are cases in point.

Why did the Yugoslav experience end in disaster? After all, the country's economic system did differ considerably from that of other socialist economies, and in promising ways. The answer to that question may be culled from an analysis of the inherent weaknesses of the system from a threefold perspective: that of the microeconomic setting and self-management in particular, of macroeconomic policies and of regional disparities.

Our analysis suggests that the Yugoslav experience is not an indictment of a self-managed economy. There were fundamental flaws in the design of the system as it was applied in Yugoslavia. To begin with, because of negative real interest rates and, since 1965, the virtual abolition of capital tax, firms did not face a positive rental cost of capital, with obvious effects on resource allocation. Second, there was no market for partnership property rights. This hampered labour mobility and the creation of new firms and introduced a bias towards distributing firms' surpluses to labour income rather than reinvestment. At the same time, there was a tendency towards over-investment owing to the 'soft budget' constraint arising from virtually unlimited access to credit from banks which were owned by the firms themselves. Finally, while self-management works best in small firms, the policy orientation explicitly favoured the creation and development of large enterprises.

There were other serious shortcomings in the microeconomic setting. While Yugoslavia actually began to liberalise back in the 1960s, administrative intervention remained widespread in the form of price controls, trade restrictions and interference at republican level in investment decisions. Furthermore, reliance on market signals was diluted by the 1974 Constitution when 'negotiation' was given prominence in economic decision-making. But probably the most fundamental weakness, as in other socialist countries, was the lack of financial discipline, as the soft budget constraint was compounded by the virtual absence of the bankruptcy option for loss-making firms.

These microeconomic weaknesses were exacerbated by faulty macroeconomic management and lack of proper policy instruments. Until the emergence of balance-of-payments crises in the early 1980s, the macroeconomic policy stance was almost invariably expansionary. Until the first oil shock, the foreign constraint emerged only occasionally thanks to considerable aid flows on concessional terms, earnings from tourism and substantial remittances from emigrant workers. Between 1974 and 1982, the authorities continued to adopt expansionary policies, but they did have recourse to foreign credit at commercial terms. When, in 1982, it was no longer possible to service the foreign debt, the authorities found themselves in a corner: they needed to foster stabilisation but lacked the appropriate policy instruments to do so.

The inefficiencies at the micro- and macroeconomic level were partly rooted in the failure of regional development policies. The main regional policy instrument was capital transfers, in the shape of budgetary grants or trade deficits run up by the less developed regions with the developed regions and the rest of the world. These transfers were sizable at all times, but regional income disparities, far from contracting, actually increased substantially during the last four decades. The resources put at the less developed regions' disposal were used inefficiently as each republican government attempted to establish industrial self-sufficiency by encouraging vertical integration and discouraging links with other republics. As a result there was little interaction between republics, and opportunities for exploiting comparative advantage and economies of scale were inevitably lost.

The more general lesson of the Yugoslav experience is quite clear and of considerable importance to reforms in other Eastern European countries. First, no microeconomic reform can be successful unless markets are properly organised, in particular the market for property rights. A great deal of economy-wide institution-building is a must. Second, there may be alternatives at the microeconomic level for the capitalist organisation of enterprise. The Yugoslav experience is neither a convincing illustration that labour management does not work (because the requisite markets were lacking) nor is it proof that it does. What it does demonstrate are the institutional errors that must be avoided for any microstructure, in particular labour management, to work. Moreover, the macro-environment must be stable. Negative interest rates discourage savings and lead to a waste of scarce capital.

Notes

1. Whether Stalin learned that technique from the Russian patriarch's anathema against communists is not clear. But all religions seem to need the weapon of glorious exclusion.
2. Some authors draw finer distinctions. For example, Mencinger (1986) distinguishes four periods: the period of a Soviet-type economic system (1945–52), that of a mixed administrative self-managed market economy (1953–62), the period of a labour-managed market economy (1963–73),and the period of the 'contractual' economy (since 1974).
3. Various measures of output growth are used in this section (GDP, GSP, etc) depending on availability of data.
4. In what follows, therefore, these attempted reforms are not addressed, as they have no relevance for the analysis.
5. Note that total factor productivity growth, already low in previous periods, was actually negative in the 1980s. See Bazler-Madzar (1988).
6. Although a depreciation of the real exchange rate was sought during most of the decade, it was allowed to appreciate at times in the hope of restraining inflation.
7. Theoretical considerations backed by empirical experience suggest that incomes policies are effective only if used in conjunction with spending cuts. Consider the success of the Israeli anti-inflation plan of 1985–86 as compared to the failure of the Cruzado and Austral plans in Brazil and Argentina respectively. For a description, see Bruno *et. al.* (1988). While Yugoslavia scored modestly in the 1970s in restraining demand in conjunction with incomes policies because, being applied only for brief periods, this did not threaten the survival of firms, we have seen that in the 1980s protracted destabilisation was made possible by financial indiscipline.
8. This section draws on Wachtel (1973) and the survey by Estrin (1983).

9. We use the terms self-management, worker management and labour management interchangeably.
10. It should be borne in mind that in market economies too, there are considerable wage differentials across industries even when other factors (skill, environmental quality, etc.). are controlled. Krueger and Summers (1988) show that in 1984 wage differentials across US industries were +38 per cent for petroleum, +24 per cent for mining and automobiles, -15 per cent for education. The weighted standard deviation of the differential is 15 per cent. Several explanations have been offered, none of which are fully convincing: the fair-wage model by Akerlof (1982), shirking, turnover and adverse selection models.
11. During the 1950s an average investment share of about 25–30 per cent brought an average GDP growth of close to 10 per cent (ICOR=(I/Q)/(dQ/Q) $\cong$ 2.5). With equally high investment shares in the 1980s, GDP remained virtually stagnant so that ICORs became very large.
12. One of the reasons was that it was illegal for a worker to bid for entry into high-earning firms at lower rates of pay.
13. In the late 1940s two-thirds of the population lived off the land and agriculture accounted for about one-third of the country's global output.
14. For example, the ratio of *per capita* income in the two extreme regions in Italy (Valle d'Aosta and Calabria) increased by only 12 per cent between 1970 and 1984 and the coefficient of variation for all regions was approximately stable during that period.
15. A more appropriate measure would be the balance on goods and non-factor services, which is not available on a regional basis. Note also that since a large proportion of Yugoslav emigrant workers came from LDRs, these regions probably benefited more than DRs from workers' remittances.
16. This analysis of the factors of growth draws extensively on World Bank (1982) and Bazler-Madzar (1988).
17. Total factor productivity accounted for 28 per cent of growth in Vojvodina, 22 per cent in Slovenia, 20 per cent in Croatia, 14 per cent in Serbia and Macedonia, 18 per cent in Bosnia, 10 per cent in Montenegro and 5 per cent in Kosovo.
18. In Table 12.7 the ratio of foreign trade to GDP does not include earnings from tourism. Croatia accounted for some 80 per cent of Yugoslavia's tourism earnings, equal to nearly 10 per cent of the republic's GDP.

Appendix: Some theory for labour-managed firms

In theory, the performance of capitalist firms is close to perfection and so upholds the institutions of capitalism. But of course, what matters is how it works in practice and there the record is less than perfect. Externalities and income distribution are the two factors which give the most cause for concern in capitalist societies.

While theory is not all, it does at least provide a benchmark for building the requisite institutions and it furnishes the conditions which the system needs in order to function, less than sufficient though they may be. For example, if labour management could be shown to be inferior to capitalism in theory, then there would be scant hope of doing better in practice.

We shall take as the benchmark the capitalist firm and describe its equilibrium behaviour. We then repeat the exercise with a labour-managed firm (LMF) and show that there are, indeed, problems as long as there is no market for property rights. Using the term 'rehabilitated labour-managed firm' (RLMF) to describe an LMF whose workers have transferable ownership rights, we show that the RLMF is at least equal and in some ways superior to its capitalist counterpart.

We consider a competitive economy in which both capitalistic and workers' enterprises may operate, and we look at a small industry of (still smaller) price-taking firms all confronted with the same technology and tastes. The output of a typical firm in this industry is given as a positive and quasi-concave, increasing function

$$Y = F(K, L)$$

of K and L, where K stands for the input of capital goods and

$$L = \sum_{i=1}^{m} x_i$$

for the total labour input of the workers, $i = 1, \ldots, m$, in the firm, the ith worker contributing $x_i > 0$ of effort or labour. (For the marginal product F_K decreasing in K and F_L decreasing in L.) People in this economy all have the same preferences between income y, measured in the units of Y, and effort (or labour) x, as represented by the utility function

$$u = y - E(x),$$

where E is a positive and strictly convex, increasing real-valued function representing the disutility of effort with $E'(0) = E(0) = 0$. The *price* of output is denoted by p, the *rental* on capital goods by r, and the *wage* on L by w.

THE CAPITALIST FIRM

The capitalistic prototype in this industry is interested in maximising the firm's profit

$$P = pY - rK - wL,$$

the first-order conditions for which, in the 'long run' where K is adjustable, subject to the prices p, r and w, are the usual

$$pF_K = r \qquad [1]$$

and

$$pF_L = w \qquad [2]$$

The typical worker in this firm, receiving an income

$$y = wx$$

as a wage-taker, maximises u by setting the marginal disutility of effort at

$$E' = w \qquad [3]$$

Equation [3] determines x equal to some positive $\underline{x}$, and thus u. Equations [1] and [2] determine the long-run profit-maximising levels $\underline{K}$ and $\underline{L}$ of K *and* L, respectively, facing the prices p, r and w. Thus, the long-run *size* $\underline{m}$ of the typical capitalistic enterprise in this industry facing the prices mentioned, as measured in terms of workers employed, is determined as

$$\underline{m} = \underline{L} / \underline{x}$$

THE LABOUR-MANAGED FIRM

For the LMF in the industry, we assume that its m (identical) members share alike in both the toils and fruits of their labour. Thus,

$$x = L / m$$

is the typical worker-partner's contribution of effort, and

$$y = V/m$$

is the income of such a member from the enterprise, where

$$V = pY - rK$$

stands for the value added by labour in the firm. The typical worker-partner's utility then becomes

$$u = V/ m - E(L/m),$$

and the typical workers' enterprise of size m maximises this function. In the 'long run', where K is variable, the first-order conditions for this maximisation give

$$pF_K = r \qquad [4]$$

and

$$pF_L = E' \qquad [5]$$

We see immediately that [4] duplicates [1] above and that if the workers' enterprise were the same size $m = \underline{m}$ as the typical capitalistic enterprise, its members would be contributing the same effort $x = \underline{x}$, thus using the same inputs $K = \underline{K}$ and $L = \underline{L}$ and producing the same output $Y = F = F(K,L)$, but that the incomes of the members of the workers' enterprises would be augmented, in comparison with their working colleagues in the capitalistic sector, by a fraction $^1/_{\underline{m}}$ of the non-negative profit earned by the typical capitalistic firm, leaving the worker-partners just so much better off than their colleagues in the capitalist sector.

Graphically, the short-run equilibrium of capitalist and of labour-managed firms can be depicted as in Fig. 12.A.1.

The LMF maximises average income and therefore sets employment at level L_{LM}, below the level L_P of the profit-maximising capitalist firm which drives labour until marginal labour product is equal to the exogenous wage w. Over time, labour would move from capitalist firms to LMFs, or investments would be attracted into the capitalist sector by risk-free profits to make y and w equal.

One peculiarity of the equilibrium for the LMF has attracted much attention. For example, if the exogenous output price rises or interest rates fall, then it can be shown that the optimal level of the LMF's output and employment contracts, whereas in the profit-maximising firm output and employment expand (see Ward 1958).

This 'perverse' result has become famous and has raised doubts about the soundness of labour management. Among other things, it has been used to explain the high

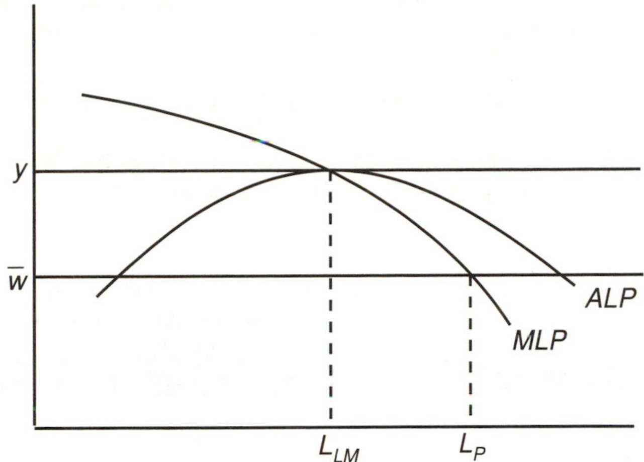

FIG 12.A.1 Short-run equilibrium: capitalist firms and LMFs

capital–labour ratios in Yugoslav enterprises coupled with large income differentials across firms and high unemployment.

For an intuitive understanding of this problem between insiders and outsiders, consider an optimal level of employment at point L_{LM} in Fig. 12.A.1. Any additional members of the firm would provide two benefits: they would bring in the value of their marginal productivity (PF_L) and would assume a share of the capital cost (rK). However, they wish to receive their share of the output value, namely PF/L. At L_{LM} the revenue-enhancing effects of their partnership are just equal to the loss occasioned by sharing with an additional member. Suppose now that r increases with K constant. Now the sharing of the burden becomes more valuable so that the balance tips in favour of a new member joining the firm. For the same reason, an increase of the price of output makes it optimal to lower employment. It is now easy to see what happens when there are negative costs of capital and accelerating inflation: the optimal employment level shrinks drastically.

This model treats price increases and decreases symmetrically. In fact, the LMF is more likely to react differently to incentives for employment reductions as compared to increases once the incentives are properly specified.

The 'perverse' behaviour of the LMF is basically due to imcomplete specification of the property rights structure of workers. For example, it is not clear on what grounds workers are dismissed from the LMF. To avoid arbitrary property rights Steinherr and Thisse (1979) consider the cases where such workers are drawn at random or, alternatively, need to be compensated for the differential income loss ($y - \bar{w}$). With such clearly defined rights to membership in an LMF, the 'perverse' behaviour is reduced but not eliminated. That is, workers are not dismissed any longer when output prices increase but no additional workers are hired. The problem is that new entrants enjoy the superior performance of the firm as a windfall gain.

All such troubles and perversities disappear when property rights are fully specified for incumbent and new workers (Sertel 1982) in the form of tradable membership rights in the LMF. To prove this we have to specify the demand and supply function for membership rights that characterise the rehabilitated LMF (RLMF).

THE REHABILITATED LABOUR-MANAGED FIRM

Denoting the utility of a typical member in an LMF of size *m* by *u(m)*, workers in the capitalistic sector are willing to pay a *demand price* of up to

$$D(m) = u(m) - \underline{u}$$

of this income to quit their present job and join the workers' enterprise. On the other hand, a new member joining the workers' enterprise would cause each current member a loss of $-du/dm$, so the workers' enterprise would admit marginal applicants to worker-partnership only as long as they are willing to forgo at least the *supply price* of

$$S(m) = -m \frac{du}{dm}$$

in units of their income upon joining. The workers' enterprise achieves its long-run equilibrium size only when the market for its worker-partnership deeds is equilibrated, that is, only when $D(m) = S(m)$. This equilibrium condition amounts to

$$p(F-rK)/m - E(x)-\underline{u} = -m \frac{du}{dm}$$

and this can be shown to simplify to

$$pF_L x - E(x) = \underline{u}.$$

Recalling Equations [1]–[3] we see that this is satisfied precisely when the workers' enterprise is of size

$$m = \underline{m},$$

in which case the workers in RLMF each contribute the same effort input $x = \underline{x}$ as their colleagues in the capitalistic sector, employing the same level $K = \underline{K}$ of capital goods and producing the same output as the capitalistic counterpart of their enterprise. In this long-run equilibrium position, of course, the members of the typical RLMF enjoy an average utility

$$u = \underline{u} + \underline{P}/\underline{m},$$

exceeding that of their working colleagues in the capitalistic sector by an amount just equal to the long-run profit per worker in the capitalistic sector.

Sertel (1982) then shows that the RLMF reacts to exogenous changes exactly like the capitalist firm. The RLMF therefore increases its size, its labour input, its output and its supply of output to the market, in its 'short-run' response to an increase in the relative price of its output, all in perfectly standard and economically sensible fashion.

A second critique of LMF goes back to work by Furubotn and Pejovich (1970) and argues that labour-managed firms are doomed by their very design to a chronic shortage of investment funds.

There are two main features of this critique. The first is that workers without property rights will always prefer to cash in a surplus rather than to re-invest it in the firm. This problem disappears in the RLMF. The other concern is that the labour-managed firm is virtually cut off from external sources of credit and investment, so that investment in the firm is restricted to retained earnings. Such a strict inaccessibility of capital markets is, of course, a severe handicap for any kind of firm. The question is why LMFs need be particularly prone to being boycotted by financiers.

Certainly, by definition an LMF self-imposes a constraint on the means it can utilise to secure external finance. It cannot issue voting stock to non-workers, since this would mean extending the roster of voters affecting management beyond that of workers, thus violating the principle of total sovereignty of the workers in the running of the enterprise. This leaves open to the LMF, however, all sorts of non-voting stock and bonds as means of obtaining external finance. But this observation invokes two further questions. One concerns the relative importance of the taboo for a workers' enterprise on voting stock issued to non-workers. The other question is whether outsiders are going to be willing to finance the operations of a workers' enterprise in whose management they will have no say.

Drèze (1976) argues that there is something of a 'moral hazard problem' in an outsider financing a workers' enterprise when certain forms of uncertainty prevail. If business is sufficiently bad in a particular year, the firm may prefer to go bankrupt than to undertake heroic measures in order to satisfy creditors. And, what is more, a risk premium which the creditors may wish to exact for this reason, may tend to worsen things, effectively triggering the bankruptcy declaration of their debtor in years which are not so lean.

The practical solution to such problems seems to lie in designing forms of contract which can cope with the intricacies of the situation at hand. A key element in the design of such contracts is the priority ranking of various creditors at bankruptcy of the debtor workers' enterprise. Just as labour may usefully occupy first priority for a defaulting capitalist firm, 'capital' (external financiers) may do the same for a defaulting workers' enterprise. (See Inselbarg and Sertel 1979 for some relevant analysis under alternative priority schemes.) Actually, for the case where the uncertainty applying to the value of output is independently observable in the form of, say, the price of output, Sertel and Steinherr (1984) have presented a simple form of contract, between a workers' enterprise and its creditors, which efficiently solves the resource allocation problem by what mocks a parity guarantee, that is, a guarantee on relative prices. The generally wise idea of farming out risk to proper insurance markets continues to demand further research and creative contract design to find practical solutions to the problems encountered by Drèze (1976).

References to Part III

Abelshauser, W. (1983) *Wirtschaftsgeschichte der Bundesrepublik Deutschland* (1945–1989), Suhrkamp, Frankfurt.

Aghion, P., Blanchard, O. and **Burgen, R.** (1994) The behaviour of state firms in Eastern Europe, pre-privatisation, *European Economic Review*, June.

Aghion, P., Hart, O. and **Moore, J.** (1992) The economics of bankruptcy reform, paper presented at the National Bureau of Economic Research (NBER) Conference on Transition in Eastern Europe, Cambridge MA, February 26–29.

Akerlof, G.A. (1982) Labour contracts as partial gift exchange, *Quarterly Journal of Economics*, 87, pp. 543–69.

Akerlof, G., Rose, A., Yellen, J. and **Hessenius, H.** (1991) East Germany in from the cold: the economic aftermath of currency union, *Brookings Papers on Economic Activity*, No. 1, The Brookings Institution, Washington, DC.

Artus, P. (1991) Réunification allemande, dynamique et contraintes: un cadre d'analyse, Caisse des dépôts et consignation, Paris, January.

Atkinson, A.B. and **Micklewright, J.** (1992) *Economic Transformation in Eastern Europe and the Distribution of Income*, Cambridge University Press, Cambridge.

Baghwati, J.N. and **Ramaswami, V.K.** (1963) Domestic distortions, tariffs and the theory of optimum subsidy, *Journal of Political Economy*.

Basevi, G. (1990) Some implications of the development of Eastern Europe for the European Economic and Monetary Union, unpublished manuscript, University of Bologna, Bologna.

Bazler-Madzar, M. (1988) Regional differentiation of development level and efficiency of growth, *Economic Analysis and Workers' Management*, **XXII** (4).

Begg, D. and **Portes, R.** (1992) Eastern Germany since unification: wage subsidies remain a better way, *CEPR Discussion Paper* No. 730.

Ben-Ner, A. and **Neuberger, E.** (1990) The feasibility of planned market systems: the Yugoslav visible hand and negotiated planning, *Journal of Comparative Economics*, **14** (4).

Berg, A. and **Blanchard, O.** (1992) Stabilization and transition; Poland 1990–1991, paper presented at the NBER Conference on Transition in Eastern Europe, Cambridge, MA, February 26–29.

Berg, A. and **Sachs, J.** (1992) Structural adjustment and international trade in Eastern Europe: the case of Poland, *Economic Policy*, **14**, pp. 117–73.

Blejer, M. I. and **Cheasty, A.** (1991) The measurement of fiscal deficits: analytical and methodological issues, *Journal of Economic Literature*, **29**(4) pp. 1644–78.

Blumberg, P. (1969) *Industrial Democracy: The Sociology of Participation*, Schockan Books, New York.

Borchardt, K. (1985) Nach dem Wunder: über die wirtschaftliche Entwicklung der Bundesrepublik, *Merkur*, **1**, p. 35–45.

Borensztein, E., Demekas, D.G. and **Ostry, J.D.** (1993) An empirical analysis of the output declines in three Eastern European countries, *IMF Staff Papers*, **40** (1) pp. 1–31.

Bruno, M. *et al.* (eds) (1988) *Inflation Stabilisation*, MIT Press, Cambridge, Massachusetts.

Bruno, M. (1992) Stabilization and reform in Eastern Europe, *IMF Staff Papers*, **39** (4) pp. 741–77.

Burda, M. (1990) Les conséquences de l'union économique et monétaire de l'Allemagne, in Fitoussi, J.P (ed.) *A l'Est en Europe*, Presses de la Fondation Nationale des Sciences Politiques, Paris.

Burda, M and **Funke, M.** (1991) German trade unions after unification – third degree wage disassociating monopolists?, *INSEAD*, manuscript.

Calvo, G. and **Coricelli, F.** (1992) Stabilizing a previously centrally planned economy: Poland 1990, *Economic Policy*, **14**, pp. 175–226.

Calvo, G. and **Coricelli, F.** (1993) Output collapse in Eastern Europe, *IMF Staff Papers*, **40**, (1), pp. 32–52.

Calvo, G. and **Kumar, M.** (1993) Financial markets and intermediation, Part I of Financial sector reforms and exchange arrangements in Eastern Europe, *IMF Occasional Paper*, No. 102, International Monetary Fund, Washington DC, February.

Cheasty, A. (1992) Financing fiscal deficits, in Tanzi, V. (ed) *Fiscal Policies in Economies in Transition*, International Monetary Fund, Washington DC, pp. 37–66.

Chiarella, C. and **Steinherr, A.** (1982) Marginal unemployment subsidies: an effective policy to generate employment, Commission of the European Communities, *Economic Papers*, No.9, Brussels.

Chu, K. and **Schwartz, G.** (1993) Output decline and government expenditures in European transition economies, paper presented at the conference Output Decline in Eastern Europe – Prospects for Recovery? in Laxenberg (Austria), November 18–20.

Commander, S. (1992) Inflation and transition to a market economy: an overview, *The World Bank Economic Review*, **6**, (1), pp. 3–12.

Corbett, J. and **Mayer, C.** (1991) Financial reform in Eastern Europe: progress with the wrong model, *Oxford Review of Economic Policy*, **7**, (4), pp. 57–75.

Coricelli, F. and **Revenga, A.** (1992) Wages and unemployment in Poland: recent developments and policy issues, in Coricelli, F. and Revenga, A. (eds), *Wage Policy During the Transition to a Market Economy: Poland 1990–91*, World Bank Discussion Paper No. 158, The World Bank, Washington DC, July.

Darnton, J. (1993) Poland revisited, *New York Times*, March 17, pp. A1 and A8.

de Crombrugghe, A. (1993) The Polish government budget – stabilization and sustainability, paper presented at the Institute for EastWest Studies (IEWS) Conference on Public Finance in the Process of Transition in East-Central Europe, Prague: IEWS, February 19–21.

Domar, E. (1966) The Soviet collective farm as a producer cooperative, *American Economic Review*, 734–57.

Dornbush, R. (1980) Employment, the trade balance and relative prices, in Dornbusch, R. *Open Economy Macroeconomics,* Basic Books, New York.

Dornbush, R. and **Wolf, H.** (1992) Economic transition in Eastern Germany, *Brookings Papers on Economic Activity*, No. 1, The Brookings Institution, Washington, D.C.

Drèze, J.H. (1976) Some theory of labour management and participation, *Econometrica*, **44**.

Drèze, J.H., Malinvaud, E. *et al.* (1994) Growth and employment: the scope for a European initiative, *European Economy*, Reports and Studies, 1.

Emerson, M. *et al.* (1988) The economics of 1992, *European Economy*, **35**.

Estrin, S. (1983) *Self-Management: Economic Theory and Yugoslav Practice*, Cambridge University Press, Cambridge.

Estrin, S., Jones, D. and **Svejnar, J.E.** (1987) The productivity effects of workers' participation, *Journal of Comparative Economics*, **11**, pp. 40–61.

Estrin, S. and **Petrin, T.** (1990) Patterns of entry, exit and merger in Yugoslavia, in **Geroski, P.** and **Schwalbach, J.** (eds), *Entry and Market Contestability: An International Comparison*, Blackwell, Oxford.

Estrin, S. and **Svejnar, J.E.** (1985) Explanation of earnings in Yugoslavia – the capital and labour school compared, *Economic Analysis*, **1**.

Fitoussi, J.P. and **Phelps, E.S.** (1990) Global effects of East European rebuilding and the adequacy of Western saving: an issue for the 1990s, *Rivista di Politica Economica,* December.

Furubotn, E.C. and **Pejovich, S.** (1970) Property rights and the behaviour of the firm in a socialist state: the example of Yugoslavia, *Zeitschrift für Nationalökonomie*, **30**.

Gandhi, V. and **Mihaljek, D.** (1992) Scope for reform of socialist tax systems, in Tanzi, V. (ed.) *Fiscal Policies in Economies in Transition*, International Monetary Fund, Washington DC, pp. 142–65.

Gros, D. (1991) The effects of unification on the German current account, manuscript, Centre for European Policy Studies (CEPS), Brussels May.

Gros, D. and **Steinherr, A.** (1990a) Currency union and economic reform in the GDR: a comprehensive one-step approach, in German Unification in European Perspective, *Centre for European Policy Studies Working Document* No. 49, March.

Gros, D. and **Steinherr, A.** (1990b) A German compromise that makes economic sense, *Financial Times*, 21 May.

Gros, D. and **Steinherr, A.** (1990c) Relax, GEMU poses no problems for EMU, *The Wall Street Journal*, 23 July.

Gros, D. and **Steinherr, A.** (1991) Einigkeit macht stark – the deutsche mark also?, in O'Brien, R. (ed.) *Finance and the International Economy:5*, Oxford University Press, Oxford.

Hambor, J. (1992) Issues in Eastern European social security reform, Research Paper, No. 9201, U.S. Treasury Department, Washington DC, June.

Havrylyshyn, O. and **Pritchett, L.** (1991) European trade patterns after the transition, World Bank Working Paper WPS 748, World Bank, Washington, DC.

Hoffmann, L. (1990) Wider die ökonomische Vernunft, *Frankfurter Allgemeine Zeitung*, 10 February.

Horvath, B. (1971) Yugoslav economic policy in the post-war period, *American Economic Review*, May.

Horvath, B. (1986) Farewell to the Illyrian firm, *Economic Analysis*, **1**.

Hughes Hallett, A.J. and **Ma, Y.** (1994) Real adjustment in a union of incompletely converged economies: an example from East and West Germany, *European Economic Review*, 38, pp. 1731–61.

Inselbarg, I. and **Sertel, M.R.** (1979) The workers' enterprise under uncertainty in a mixed economy, *Economic Analysis*, **13**.

International Monetary Fund (1990) German unification: economic issues, *Occasional Paper*, International Monetary Fund, Washington DC.

Jarvis, S.J. and **Micklewright, J.** (1992) The targeting of family allowance in Hungary, paper presented at the World Bank Conference on Public Expenditures and the Poor: Incidence and Targeting, The World Bank, Washington, DC, June 17–19.

Kaldor, N. (1936) Wage subsidies, a remedy for unemployment, *Journal of Political Economy*, December

Knight, P.T. (1985) Financial discipline and structural adjustment in Yugoslavia: rehabilitation and bankruptcy of loss-making enterprises, *Economic Analysis*, **1**.

Kopits, G. (1991) Fiscal reform in European economies in transition, IMF Working Paper No. WP/91/43, International Monetary Fund, Washington, DC, April.

Kopits, G. (1992) Social security, in Tanzi, V. (ed.) *Fiscal Policies in Economies in Transition*, International Monetary Fund, Washington DC, pp. 291–311.

Kornai, J. (1993) Transformational recession – a general phenomenon examined through the example of Hungary's development, Discussion Paper No.1, Collegium Budapest, Institute for Advanced Study, Budapest, June.

Krakowski, M., Lan, D. and **Turx, A.** (1992) Die Standortqualität Ostdeutschlands, *Wirtschaftsdienst*, October.

Krueger, A.B. and **Summers, L.H.** (1988) Efficiency wages and the inter-industry wage structure, *Econometrica*, **56**, pp. 259–93.

Lange, O. (1937) On the economic theory of socialism, *Review of Economic Studies* (Parts I and II).

Lipton, D. and **Sachs, J.** (1990) Creating a market economy in Eastern Europe: the case of Poland, *Brooking Papers on Economic Activity*, No.1, The Brookings Institution, Washington, DC.

McDonald, D. and **Thumann, G.** (1990) Investment needs in East Germany, in Lipschitz, L. and McDonald, D. (eds) German unification: economic issues, International Monetary Fund Occasional Papers, No.75, December, pp. 71–77.

MacKibbin, W. (1990) Some global macroeconomic implications of German unification, *Brookings Discussion Papers in International Economics*, No.81, The Brookings Institution, Washington, DC.

Maret, X. and **Schwartz, G.** (1993) Poland: The social safety net during the transition, IMF Working Paper No. WP/93/42, International Monetary Fund, Washington DC, May.

Marinovíc, M. and **Simíc, Z.** (1970) *The Yugoslav Trade Unions*, Radnica Stampa, Belgrade.

Mayer, C. (1989) Myths of the West: lessons from developed countries for development finance, World Bank Working Paper, WPS 301, The World Bank, Washington DC, November.

Meade, J.E. (1972) The theory of labour-managed firms and of profit-sharing, *Economic Journal*, **82**, pp. 402–28.

Mencinger, J. (1986) The Yugoslav economic systems and their efficiency, *Economic Analysis*, 31–39.

Mencinger, J. (1992) How to create a currency? The experience of Slovenia, Austrian National Bank, Vienna.

Micossi, S. and **Tullio, G.** (1992) Equilibri di bilancio, distorsioni economiche e performance di lungo periodo dell'economia italiana, *Rivista di Politica Economica*, **82**, July.

Mizsei, K. (1993) *Bankruptcy and the Post-Communist Economies of East Central Europe*, Institute for EastWest Studies, New York.

Nuti, D.M. (1993) Monetary disintegration: ex-Yugoslavia, ex-CSFR and ex-USSR, Annual Meeting of the Austrian Economic Association, Graz, April.

Oakeshot, R. (1978) *The Case for Workers' Co-ops*, Routledge and Kegan Paul, London.

Obradovic, J. and **Dunn, W.** (eds) (1979) *Workers' Self-Management and Organisational Power in Yugoslavia*, University of Pittsburgh, Center for International Studies.

OECD (1984, 1988, 1990) Yugoslavia, *Economic Surveys*, OECD, Paris.

OECD (1992) *Reforming the Economies of Central and Eastern Europe,* OECD, Paris.

Ottolenghi, D. and **Steinherr, A.** (1993) Yugoslavia: was it a winner's curse?, *Economics of Transition*, **1** (2).

Pinto, B., Belka, M. and **Krajewski, S.** (1992) Microeconomics of transformation in Poland, World Bank Working Paper, WPS 982, The World Bank, Washington DC, September.

Pinto, B., Belka, M. and **Krajewski, S.** (1993) Transforming state enterprises in Poland, World Bank Working Paper, WPS 1101, The World Bank, Washington DC, February.

PlanEcon (1990) How big are the Soviet and East European economies?, Report, No.6(52), December 28, pp. 1–18.

Pleskovic, B. and **Sachs, J.** (1992) *Currency Reform in Slovenia: The Tolar Standing Tall*, World Bank, Washington, DC.

Prasmkor, J., Svejnar, J. and **Klinedinst, M.** (1992) Structural adjustment policies and productive efficiency of socialist enterprises, *European Economic Review*, **36**.

Romer, P.M. (1986) Increasing returns and long-run growth, *Journal of Political Economy* **94**(5), pp. 1002–37.

Rothschild, M. and **Stiglitz, J.** (1976) Equilibrium in competitive insurance markets: an essay on the economics of imperfect information, *Quarterly Journal of Economics*, **90**: pp. 629–49.

Sachs, J. (1993) *Poland's Jump to the Market Economy*, MIT Press, Cambridge, Massachusetts.

Sachverständigenrat (1990) Bedenken der Sachverständigen gegen Währungsunion, *Frankfurter Allgemeine Zeitung*, 10 February.

Sachverständigenrat (1991, 1992) *Jahresgutachten*, Government Printing Office, Bonn.

Sacks, S. (1983) *Self-Management and Efficiency: Large Corporations in Yugoslavia*, Allen and Unwin, London.

Sapir, A. (1980) Economic growth and factor substitution: whatever happened to the Yugoslav miracle?, *Economic Journal*, **90**, pp. 294–313.

Schlesinger, H. (1990) Mit sofortiger Währungsunion lassen sich die wirklichen Probleme nicht beheben, *Handelsblatt*, 24 January.

Schwartz, G. and **Silva Lopes, P.** (1993) Privatization: expectations, trade offs, and results, *Finance and Development*, **30** (2), pp. 14–17.

Sertel, M.R. (1982) *Workers and Incentives*, North Holland, Amsterdam.

Sertel, M.R. and **Steinherr, A.** (1984) Information, incentives and the design of efficient institutions, *Zeitschrift für die Gesamte Staatswissenschaft.*

Siebert, H. (1990) The economic integration of Germany, *Kiel Institute of World Economics Working Document* No. 160, May.

Siebert, H. (1991) German unification: the economics of transition, *Economic Policy*, **13**, pp. 287–340.

Sinn, G. and **Sinn, H.W.** (1991) *Kaltstart*, J.-L.B. Mohr, Tübingen.

Sirc, L. (1979) *The Yugoslav Economic System and its Performance in the 1970s*, Institute for International Studies, University of California, Berkeley.

Sommariva, A. and **Tullio, G.** (1987) *German Macroeconomic History 1880–1979: A Study of the Effects of Economic Policy on Inflation, Currency Depreciation and Growth*, Macmillan, London.

Steinherr, A. (1977) On the efficiency of profit-sharing and labour participation, *Bell Journal of Economics.*

Steinherr, A. and **Perée, E.** (1991) Prometheus unbound: policy proposals for restructuring in Eastern Europe, in Siebert, H. (ed.) *The Transformation of Socialist Economics*, J.C.B. Mohr, Tübingen.

Steinherr, A. and **Thisse, J.F.** (1979) Is there a negatively sloped supply curve in the labour-managed firm?, *Economic Analysis*, **43**, (1–2).

Steinherr, A. and **van Haeperen, B.** (1983) Approche pragmatique pour une politique de plein emploi: les subventions à la création d'emplois, Commission of the European Communities, Economic Papers, No.22, Brussels.

Tait, A. (1993) The continuing false fascination of tax-based income policies (TIPs), Topical Seminar Note, TN/93/4, Fiscal Affairs Department, International Monetary Fund, Washington DC, May.

Tullio, G., Steinherr, A. and **Buscher, H.** (1994) German wage and price inflation after unification, in De Grauwe, P., Micossi, S. and Tullio, G. (eds) *Inflation and Wage Behaviour in the EMS*, Oxford University Press, Oxford.

Tyson, L. (1980) *The Yugoslav Economic System and its Performance in the 1970s*, Institute for International Studies, University of California, Berkeley.

Uvalic, M. (1992) *Yugoslavia: the Economic Costs of Disintegration*, European University Institute, Florence.

Vanek, J. (1970) *The General Theory of Labor-Managed Economies*, Cornell University Press, Ithaca, New York.

Vanek, J. and **Jovicic, M.** (1975) The capital market and income distribution in Yugoslavia: a theoretical and empirical analysis, *Quarterly Journal of Economics*, **89**, pp. 432–43.

Wachtel, H. (1973) *Workers' Management and Workers' Wages in Yugoslavia*, Cornell University Press, Ithaca, New York.

Ward, B. (1958) The firm in Illyria: market syndicalism, *American Economic Review*, **68**, pp. 566–689.

Williamson, O.E. (1980) The organisation of work: a comparative institutional assessment, *Journal of Economic Behaviour and Organisation.*

World Bank (1982) *Yugoslavia: Adjustment Policies and Development Perspectives*, World Bank, Washington DC.

World Bank (1991) *World Development Report 1991,* Oxford.

Wyplosz, C. (1991) On the real exchange rate effect of German unification, *Weltwirtschaftliches Archiv.*

Wyznikiewicz, B., Pinto, B. and **Grabowski, M.** (1993) Coping with capitalism – the new Polish entrepreneurs, Discussion Paper, No. 18, International Finance Corporation, Washington DC, June.

Zupanov, Z. and **Tannenbaum, A.S.** (1968) The distribution of control in some Yugoslav industrial organisations as perceived by members, in Tannenbaum, A.S. (ed) *Control in Organisations*, McGraw-Hill, New York.

PART FOUR

THE FORMER SOVIET UNION

Introduction

Events since 1989 have shown that the reforms have been less successful the further one goes east. While the Central European countries have put the first phase of reforms behind them, as analysed in Part III, most countries in the Former Soviet Union (FSU) still have to undertake some of the basic reform steps outlined in Part II. The main reason for this difference in behaviour is that the Central Europeans had 'only' to return to Europe. And their populations and politicians decided that they would do whatever was needed to achieve this goal. The newly independent states in the FSU area are in a different situation for obvious historical reasons. Each of these states would merit a separate analysis, but we concentrate on the most important one, namely Russia. Developments in Russia will affect all of Europe for better or for worse, whereas the developments in the other successor states of the FSU matter only to the extent that they provoke a reaction by Russia. As an aside we note that we do not consider the Baltic countries to be part of the FSU. They had an autonomous culture under the czars and were incorporated into the Soviet empire only after having tasted freedom and relative prosperity during the inter-war years.

In relating events after the fall of the Soviet Union we therefore concentrate on two aspects that are discussed in the next two chapters separately: the economic consequences of rapid disintegration and the crucial initial reform period in Russia.

The first basic fact of the FSU is its sudden disintegration despite the very intensive internal trade links. We do not pretend to offer any insights into why the political elites in most former Soviet republics (including Russia) suddenly chose to go for independence. The main factor behind this political development was certainly a reawakening of national feelings. On top of that came the unwillingness of the Union government under Gorbachev to consider radical economic reforms. We leave these political factors aside and concentrate on the economic aspects of the disintegration of this huge unified economic area that took place in 1991–2.

It is difficult to analyse the disintegration of the FSU dispassionately because opinions, inside and outside the FSU, about this issue tend to one of two extremes. One school of thought (prevalent among the radical reformers in Russia and some of their Western advisers) maintained that the economic links between the former Soviet republics were artificially created by central planners. The newly independent states should have introduced national currencies immediately in 1992 and terminated all preferential trade arrangements among them. The opposite extreme (prevalent among

Western official institutions until the end of 1992), argued that the former Soviet republics were so tightly integrated that they should have stayed together in the economic sphere even after they became politically independent.

The analysis of this chapter suggests that both extremes were wrong and that serious policy mistakes were made during the transition. If the transition had been managed carefully, taking into account both the trade structures inherited and their likely future evolution, the economic costs of the collapse of the FSU could have been mitigated. The virtual break-down of intra-CIS trade could have been avoided, and even Russia's output decline could have been less severe.

We first show that, once reforms had started, it did not make sense to keep the former Soviet republics together in an economic and monetary union, as was often suggested in 1991–92. But we also do not agree that the FSU really had, during its last years of existence, 'the worst monetary constitution one can imagine'. In a similar vein we also argue that the strange ruble zone that survived until late 1993 cannot be considered a cause of inflation in Russia and elsewhere, as has often been argued.

We argue that the transition to separate currencies should have been managed more carefully with the aid of a multilateral clearing system. A treaty to that effect was actually signed, ratified and . . . never implemented. An opportunity missed!

While the disintegration of the FSU is a *fait accompli* and irreversible despite the periodic attempt by some Russian policy-makers to resurrect some imperial system through bilateral agreement, or through the Commonwealth of Independent States (CIS), the fate of reforms in Russia has not been totally decided yet. The experience of reforms in Russia is a sobering tale.

We do not pretend to give a complete picture of the Russian economy. This would be impossible, not only because the situation continues to change rapidly, but mainly because in Russia few things are really as they appear at first sight. Hence we concentrate on three specific issues that came up during the crucial initial reform efforts in 1992–93 to illustrate this general point. The three issues more closely examined are price liberalisation, trade liberalisation and the link between fiscal policy and macroeconomic stabilisation.

We argue that price liberalisation was unavoidable, but the most important part of it, namely the liberalisation of energy prices, never happened. Trade policy, the showpiece of the reformers because of the liberalisation of imports, was, and remains today, actually a disaster area. Initially there were huge import subsidies and, all throughout the period under consideration, large export restrictions. This combination was deadly for Russian trade, which shrank, instead of expanding by 50 per cent as in the Central European countries. Inflation, which was brought partly under control only after two years, was probably due to a large fiscal deficit, but this cannot be proven because the official numbers are close to meaningless.

We then turn to the eternal question 'Who lost Russia?'. Where did the billions of dollars go? (Or did they never arrive?) Our analysis shows that the Russian government could have used the substantial foreign aid it did receive to stabilise the economy if it had conducted a completely different foreign trade policy. However, given the disastrous trade policy followed by Russia, most of the aid that was actually delivered in 1992–92 reduced welfare in Russia. Stabilisation could also have been achieved with a different kind of foreign assistance. Both sides thus contributed to this failure.

The general lesson we draw from all this is that in the case of Russia most things are different from what they appear to be at first sight and a number of widespread preconceptions do not stand up to closer analysis. This also applies to the privatisation process. On paper close to 100 per cent of Russian industry outside the military–industrial complex has been privatised. However, the behaviour of management has not changed noticeably for most enterprises. We suspect that this will continue to be the case and that large swings in policy that are reported periodically in the Western press do not correspond to reality. Over the first few years there has been only very limited, but nevertheless tangible, progress towards a market economy. One should not expect much more from Russia, but also not much less.

CHAPTER THIRTEEN

The disintegration of the Soviet Union

The one absolute certain way of bringing this nation to ruin, of preventing all possibility of its continuing to be a nation at all, would be to permit it to become a tangle of squabbling nationalities.

Theodore Roosevelt (1915)

This chapter analyses the economic aspects of the disintegration of the Former Soviet Union (FSU). Opinions about this tend to one of two extremes. One maintains that the economic links between the former Soviet republics were artificially created by central planners. The intensity of inter-republican trade should therefore not be of consideration for policy-makers in the newly independent states who should have introduced national currencies immediately in 1992. The opposite extreme (and one that was prevalent among Western official institutions until 1991–92), argued that the former Soviet republics were so tightly integrated that they should have stayed together in the economic sphere even after they became politically independent.

The analysis of this chapter suggests that both extremes were wrong and that serious policy mistakes were made during the transition. If the transition had been managed carefully, taking into account both the trade structures inherited and their likely future evolution, the economic costs of the collapse of the FSU could have been mitigated. The virtual break-down of intra-CIS trade could have been avoided and even Russia's output decline could have been less severe.

Section 1 opens with a brief description of the starting point, namely the high degree of integration and the massive transfers from Russia that were implicit in the old pricing system. However, a closer look in Section 2 at inter-republican trade within the FSU leads to two apparently conflicting conclusions. If one accepts the limited degree of openness of the FSU to the rest of the world, inter-republican trade had a structure similar to that of trade among market economies. However, the level of inter-republican trade was clearly much above what one would expect if trade with the rest of the world were to be opened. This suggests that while inter-republican trade had its own logic under the old system, it was condemned to become marginal in the long run.

Section 3 shows that, once reforms had started, it did not make sense to keep the former Soviet republics together in an economic and monetary union as was often suggested in 1991–92. Section 4 then turns to the monetary aspects and asks whether the FSU really had during its last years of existence 'the worst monetary constitution one can imagine'? It also shows that the strange ruble zone that survived until late 1993 cannot be considered a cause of inflation, as has often been argued. Section 5 turns to a missed opportunity, namely that of the multilateral clearing system that had been agreed to among 10 CIS states, but was never implemented. Section 6 presents conclusions.

1. The starting point

This section sets the stage for the subsequent discussion by providing a brief analysis of the last years of the Soviet Union and some basic facts about the former Soviet republics and their economic relations. The reader who is already familiar with this background is invited to go directly to Section 2.

THE CENTRE VANISHES

The former Soviet Union was a centralised state in which all power came from one structure, namely the Communist Party. Formally speaking, however, the Union was a federal structure based on the 15 constituent republics. The population that lived in the different republics maintained a separate identity in terms of language and culture throughout the Soviet period.

We are concerned here with the economic aspects of the process of disintegration. Most of this chapter is devoted to an analysis of the events that followed the dissolution of the Soviet Union. In this section, we discuss in particular the interplay between disintegration and economic reform during the years that preceded the onset of serious reforms in Russia at the beginning of 1992.

The formal dissolution of the Soviet Union in late 1991 was only the final act of a gradual process that had started much earlier and that evolved differently from one republic to another. One common feature, however, was that the republican structures, which had hitherto been practically irrelevant, were suddenly filled with life through the initiatives of the local population and political elites. This process first occurred in the Baltic and Caucasus states where there still existed the memory of a separate statehood. Subsequently, however, it spread to most other republics, including Russia.

As the policy of *Glasnost* advanced, the republican structures became more active and, starting in 1989–90, they felt strong enough to deal with economic reform, which constituted after all the central issue of that period. The two processes of disintegration and economic reform thus became intertwined.

Even a brief look at the history of attempted reforms in the former Soviet Union shows there was no shortage of plans. In 1990 alone, no less than four major reform programmes were discussed at the highest political level. Despite some differences in emphasis, they all agreed on three goals: a market economy, stabilisation of the economy and the need to maintain an economic and monetary union for the territory of the Soviet Union.

However, none of these programmes could be implemented because of the 'war of laws' that was being waged at the same time. One republic after the other passed a declaration of sovereignty stating that its laws took precedence over Union laws, whereas the Union government insisted that Union law took precedence. Since at that stage the Union government under Gorbachev did not want, or perhaps rather did not dare, to use force, the reforms could be implemented only after agreement on a new Union Treaty had been reached that would define the respective powers of the republics and the Union. An agreement was reached in May 1991, but when it was about to be put into force the attempted August putsch set in motion a chain of events that led within four months to the demise of the Soviet Union.

The increasing regional disintegration was thus the main reason why the reform plans of 1990 and 1991 were not implemented. Moreover, the loss of control of the Union government over the budgets of the republics was an important factor for the large public sector deficit that destabilised the Soviet economy. Many Western observers and the Union government argued therefore that a disintegration of the Soviet Union into a number of independent economic units that competed against each other should have been avoided even in the face of the demands for total independence advanced by some republics as early as 1990.

The paralysis of economic policy because of the war of laws was certainly damaging for the reform process. However, this does not imply that a centralised approach to economic reform would necessarily have been superior to competition in reform (see Gros and Steinherr 1991 for details).

In economic terms the fundamental point is that any sub-unit that is part of a larger area with distorted prices can gain by implementing reforms on its own and allowing its inhabitants to trade freely at 'true' market prices. It was often alleged in 1990–91 that price reform had to be implemented at the union level because otherwise differences in prices would lead consumers to buy where the goods are cheapest.

For example, if any republic had implemented a complete price reform (a partial reform might not be beneficial because of 'second best' considerations), abolishing all subsidies and taxes, its price structure would have been different from that of the rest of the Union. Residents of other republics would then certainly have come to 'plunder' shops for those goods that had become cheaper in that particular republic. However, this 'plunder' would have been desirable since all these goods would have been sold at their marginal cost of production, and an increase in demand can only lead to an increase in the surplus of domestic producers. Given the Soviet habit of taxing many consumer goods viewed as 'luxury', in practice the producers of a large range of consumer goods would have benefited. Similarly, consumers of the republic that initiated a reform in isolation would have gained by buying goods such as bread and other staple commodities in the rest of the Union at the old subsidized prices.

However, all this 'arbitrage' is the essence of a market economy and should thus not have been viewed as a cost, but a gain in efficiency. Moreover, price reform would also have acted on the supply side. Entrepreneurs in a republic that was the first to implement fundamental reforms would therefore gain by being able to satisfy a pent-up demand for diversified products coming from the entire union area. While a reaction in supply is not immediate (as the subsequent experience of the reform process showed) any supply response would have only increased the benefits from reform.

In an uncoordinated reform process those republics that are slow to reform thus lose because residents of the republic that initiates reforms on its own then buy more union goods that are priced below cost elsewhere. This has the advantage that it is an incentive to implement reforms in the remainder of the Union as well.

Competition in reform would thus have had advantages. The real problem with an uncoordinated reform process would have been a political one. The response to unilateral price reform in some republics turned out to be border controls to suppress commodity arbitrage. These border controls contributed to the collapse of intra-FSU trade and were in themselves costly. However, the task of an enlightened Union government would have been to maintain open borders and thus allow competitive pressures to act at least within the borders of the union.

The reaction to the price reform undertaken unilaterally by Russia in January of 1992 shows that the economic mechanism was very powerful. The other smaller republics could not really contemplate closing their borders to Russia and not following its lead. This sort of competition in reform should have been allowed early on. China offers an example of regional structures that compete in reforms in which each province emulates the most successful, and usually most open, provinces to improve the standard of living of the local population (see Qian and Roland 1994).

In the area of macroeconomics, however, competition can be dangerous because negative externalities can arise quite easily. This is apparent in the monetary sphere: it is not possible to have one currency and several competing central banks. Each central bank has an incentive to create as much money as possible because the inflationary consequences are borne by everyone whereas the benefits remain with the home country.

This was the central problem during the Soviet Union's last year of existence. It is discussed at some length below (Section 4), since it was at the root of the developments in 1992–93. In the monetary sphere, it is thus clear that competition within one currency area is dangerous.

In the fiscal area, a similar danger existed. Indeed, a central aspect of the power struggle between the Union and the republics concerned the distribution of expenditure and taxes. Despite the formal federal structure of the FSU, there was no organised fiscal decentralisation. Only the Union was empowered to levy taxes, but in practice the source of public sector revenues (enterprises and wage taxes) fell increasingly under the control of the republican authorities. The latter were obviously tempted to keep the revenues for themselves while holding the Union government responsible for the payment of subsidies and the provision of public goods. The result was a growing deficit of the Union government whereas the republican budgets remained balanced until 1991, when all controls were lifted. The deficit of the Union government was, of course, not unavoidable. If the Union government had given macroeconomic stabilisation the priority, it could have slashed subsidies and balanced the budget. However, Gorbachev either did not realise this or felt that he was politically too weak to do this. Qian and Roland (1994) show that a well-organised fiscal decentralisation can actually be beneficial as long as there is a clear will at the centre to stabilise.

We therefore conclude that competition in economic reform would have been beneficial, but that a poorly defined macroeconomic system in which different levels of power compete can lead to a disaster. The Soviet Union was in the worst of all worlds during its last years of existence: no competition in reform, but macroeconomic destabilisation.

Was this unavoidable? If Gorbachev had wanted to create a market economy, he should have allowed the republics much greater freedom early on in structural reforms (elimination of price controls, privatisation, etc.), in exchange for stricter controls on the macroeconomic side. As this fundamental choice was not made, the reform process never got off the ground in 1990–91, and the macroeconomic destabilisation that had occurred in the meantime made the structural reforms that started in the newly independent states in early 1992 much more difficult.

ECONOMIC RELATIONS AMONG THE SOVIET REPUBLICS

As long as the FSU was one country, it was only natural that the constituent parts of this economic space were tightly integrated. The high degree of integration became important only when the local population, acting through the republican structures, asked first for more autonomy and finally total independence. The desire for independence was in most cases politically motivated, especially in the case of the Baltics, but this conflict between political aspirations for full independence contrasted initially with the existence of a common economic space.

Just how tightly the 15 republics were integrated is shown in Table 13.1. For the smaller ones, trade with other republics accounted for one-half of output and even for Russia, inter-republican trade was more than twice as important as international trade. Moreover, as most trade had gone through Moscow, the smaller republics traded often four and sometimes six times as intensively with the rest of the FSU as with the outside world. This extraordinary degree of integration was the reason why it was often argued that the republics could not survive on their own.

Another reason why it was often argued that most republics had an interest in staying in the Soviet Union was that the Soviet pricing system implied very large transfers

TABLE 13.1 Soviet republics: trade with the Union and the rest of the world in 1988

	Trade as a per cent of GNP*			
	Total	Domestic	Foreign	Population (millions)
USSR Total	30	21	8	284.5
Russia	22	13	9	146.5
Ukraine	34	27	7	51.4
Belorussia	52	45	7	10.1
Uzbekistan	40	34	5	19.6
Kazakhstan	34	29	4	16.5
Kirghizia	46	40	5	4.2
Tadzhikistan	44	38	6	5.0
Turkmenistan	42	38	4	3.5
Armenia	54	48	5	3.5
Georgia	44	38	5	5.3
Azerbaijan	41	35	5	6.9
Lithuania	55	47	7	3.7
Moldova	52	46	6	4.2
Latvia	54	47	7	2.7
Estonia	59	50	8	1.6

Source: *Statistical Year Book of the Soviet Union*, 1990
Note: Table uses 1988 data
* Assuming the same GNP–NMP ratio as for the USSR as a whole

from the producers of under-priced raw materials (mainly Russia) to the producers of over-priced manufactured goods. Table 13.2 shows the actual trade balance of individual republics and the trade balance they would have had if energy had been priced at world market levels. This table shows that the smaller industrialised republics received an implicit subsidy of about 10 to 20 per cent of the value of their production (NMP). For the central Asian states, this implicit subsidy came on top of direct transfers from the Union budget.

It was already clear, even before the Soviet Union was dissolved, that the old pattern of inter-republican trade and subsidies within the former Soviet Union could not be sustained in the emerging new environment of 15 independent states with market-based economies, and 15 different currencies. It was also clear then that most republics would in the long run dramatically increase their trade with the rest of the world.

The following section quantifies the shift towards world trade that can be expected in the long run and estimates to what extent the inter-republican trade pattern under the old system was similar to what one would expect from the experience of market economies.

TABLE 13.2 Soviet republics: inter-republican trade account in 1988

	Trade Account as a % of NMP	
	At world prices*	Only energy at world prices**
Russia	6.5	3.5
Ukraine	−3.5	−3.7
Belorussia	1.9	7.3
Uzbekistan	−24.2	−20.7
Kazakhstan	−23.2	−22.3
Kirghizia	−18.4	−14.1
Tadzhikistan	−31.8	−26.9
Turkmenistan	−3.7	8.4
Armenia	−3.2	6.0
Georgia	−16.1	2.1
Azerbaijan	10.2	20.8
Lithuania	−35.4	−19.5
Moldova	−20.1	4.0
Latvia	−24.1	−8.9
Estonia	−28.2	−9.7

Source: Bofinger and Gros 1992

* Trade account adjusted for total world import prices means that trade was evaluated at world market prices. In practice this means that the values of trade of all branches were adjusted by a conversion factor equal to world import price/inter-republican price.

** Trade account with only energy evaluated at world prices.

2. Trade patterns: past and future

EXPLAINING PAST INTER-REPUBLICAN TRADE PATTERNS

All of the former republics, with the possible exception of Russia, are fairly open economies. It is therefore vital for them to have an idea of how their foreign trade will evolve in the future. Most Western economists and most of the new policy-makers agree that in the long run there has to be a radical reorientation in trade, away from inter-republican trade and towards more trade with the West.

As shown in Table 13.1, under the old regime inter-republican trade was several times larger than international trade (i.e. trade with the former COMECON area and the West together). It was already clear before the FSU collapsed that this had to change. It never has been, however, and to some extent it still is not, a straightforward exercise to determine the size and the speed of the change. The main purpose of this section is thus to quantify the extent to which trade with the West (and in particular with the European Community) can be expected to grow relative to inter-republican trade.

The approach used here is the standard so-called 'gravity equation' which starts from the idea that the amount of bilateral trade between two countries is determined by their size and the distance between them. The larger the two countries, in terms of income and population, the more trade there should be between them. The greater the distance, the less trade one should observe. Box 13.1 provides a more detailed description of the gravity approach.

The existing estimates of this gravity approach show that it efficiently explains trade patterns among market economies. The three variables mentioned so far (income, population and distance) together with dummy variables for other factors (such as whether or not the two countries have a common frontier, participate in a preferential trade agreement or share a common language) usually explain well over one-half of the overall variance of the geographical distribution of trade. A typical finding is also that the elasticity of trade with respect to income exceeds one.

Gros and Dautrebande (1992b) follow this approach using data about the matrix of bilateral trade between all the 15 former republics. They explain the amount of bilateral trade (of all possible 210 combinations) as a function of the NMP of the two partners, the distance between them (and their areas as a further proxy variable for distance). These variables explain over 90 per cent of the variability in the geographical distribution of inter-republican trade. Moreover, the parameter estimates for the elasticities of trade with respect to income and distance are quite similar to the ones found in other studies of the gravity approach which always used data from market economies. This is surprising since it implies that the Soviet planning system led to a geographical distribution of trade that is similar to the one typical for market economies.

Box 13.1. The Gravity Model

The gravity model explains the geographical distribution of the bilateral trade of a given country (or region) with its different trading partners. It is usually estimated on cross section data referring to a single year or average of several years.

continued

Box 13.1 *continued*

The model describes the trade flow, say exports, from a particular country *i* to another country *j*. Exports from country *i* are assumed to depend on national income in *i* (as proxy variable for the supply of exportables) and national income in *j* (as proxy variable for the demand for *i*'s exportables in country *j*).

Per capita output is sometimes also used to take into account the idea that, as income increases the share of tradables, overall income should increase; that is, for a given overall income, a country with a higher income *per capita* should trade more intensively (have more exports and imports) than a poorer country. Similar arguments apply if one estimates the distribution of imports: national income of the home country represents demand, and national income of the foreign country represents supply.

Most of the other variables used in the estimation of the gravity approach reflect transport costs and other obstacles to trade. The most obvious factor here is distance, which should have a negative effect on trade. The area of the importing or exporting country should also have a negative effect because it stands for the transport cost from the hinterland to the economic centre. A related variable is adjacency, that is, the presence (or absence) of a common border which should affect trade positively.

The equation estimated here is therefore :

$$
\begin{aligned}
\text{Ln (exports from } i \text{ to } j) = \; & a \times \ln(\text{distance between } i \text{ and } j) \\
& + b \times (\text{adjacency: dummy}) \\
& + c \times \ln(\text{NMP of } i) \\
& + d \times \ln(\text{NMP of } j) \\
& + e \times \ln(\textit{per capita} \text{ NMP of } i) \\
& + f \times \ln(\textit{per capita} \text{ NMP of } j) \\
& + g \times \ln(\text{area of } i) \\
& + h \times \ln(\text{area of } j)
\end{aligned}
$$

The same equation was estimated for imports of country *i* from country *j*. Data for the complete 15 × 15 matrix of inter-republican trade for 1987 (the most recent year available) was then used to estimate this type of equation. See Gros and Dautrebande (1992b) for details.

A comparison with the results for market economies is even more revealing of the good fit of the gravity approach for intra-FSU trade. This is done in Table 13.3 below which compares our results for inter-republican exports to three other widely known estimates: Aitken (1973), Havrylyshyn and Pritchett (H&P) (1991), and Wang and Winters (W&W) (1991).[1]

The basic message of this table is that the intra-FSU trade is explained remarkably well by the gravity approach. First of all, the fit of the inter-republican equation is better than that of the two recent estimates, H&P and W&W. Only the estimate for Europe in the 1960s has a better standard error, but its adjusted R^2 is still lower. While one should not put too much emphasis on these indicators of the overall fit, it is clear that the economic variables used here explain the distribution of inter-republican trade remarkably well.

TABLE 13.3 Estimates of inter-republican trade compared to studies of market economies

Explanatory Variables	Inter republican trade	H&P, 21 Middle-income LDCs	W&W, 76 Market economies	Aitken, 12 European countries
constant	−10.48 (−7.9)	−9.54 (−5.7)	−12.49 (34.2)	1.07
ln(dist *ij*)	−0.39 (−6.3)	−1.56 (−16.4)	−0.75 (22.3)	−0.35 (2.74)
border	0.59 (3.1)	1.15 (4.0)	0.78 (3.3)	0.89 (4.41)
ln(GDP *i*)	1.01 (19.1)	0.86 (13.7)	0.79	0.72
ln(GDP/pop *i*)	0.32 (2.7)	1.05 (5.5)	0.38	0.33
ln(area *i*)	−0.11 (−3.0)	−0.01 (−0.2)		
ln(GDP *j*)	0.69 (13.2)	0.93 (23.3)	0.80	0.54
ln(GDP/pop *j*)	−0.06 (−0.5)	0.22 (3.3)	0.22	0.15
ln(area *j*)	0.16 (4.4)	−0.18 (−6.5)		
Other variables				
trade integration dummies:				
Linder effect		0.08 (0.9)		
R^2	0.92		0.7	0.87
S.E.	0.47	1.67		0.22
Observations	210	420	4320	132

A comparison of the point estimates of the different coefficients for the main explanatory variables also reveals more similarities than differences,[2] which suggests that the distribution of inter-republican trade was governed by similar considerations.[3]

Given that the gravity equation performs so well for inter-republican trade (in some respect better than for trade among market economies), the size of the parameter that shows the relationship between trade and distance becomes the key to the argument that intra-FSU trade was not driven by the market and should hence disappear as soon as possible. The implicit argument has often been that the planners set up enterprises in remote areas without any regard for transaction costs.

Table 13.3 shows for inter-republican trade an elasticity of trade with respect to distance of around 0.4, which is close to those found for European market economies[4] (i.e. Aitken 1973, who finds 0.35), but this does not necessarily indicate that Soviet planners took transport costs adequately into account. Given the logarithmic formulation, this question cannot really be answered on the basis of the coefficients of the gravity equations.[5] If transport costs were on average twice as high in the FSU as in Europe, this would just show up in the constant.

Another, very simple piece of evidence, however, suggests that transport costs were not excessive: in the FSU about 6 per cent of national income (NMP) was devoted to the sector 'Transport and communications'. This is almost exactly equal to the share of this sector in the European economy (measured by gross value added). Since one could argue that given the distorted pricing system in the Soviet Union, NMP shares cannot really be compared to shares in value added at market prices in the West, one can compare shares of employment. However, the share of total employment in this sector in the FSU was also similar to that of the EU as shown in Table 13.4.[6]

TABLE 13.4 The importance of transport and communications

Share of transport and communications in:	FSU (1985)	European Union (1987)
NMP (Gross value added)	6.1	6.5
Employment	7.2	6.2

Source: IMF (1991), Lipton and Sachs (1992) and Eurostat, *National accounts, detailed tables by branches*

ESTIMATING THE SHIFT IN TRADE

Turning to the future, the approach used here is again quite simple. It starts by using parameter estimates from the studies on the geographical distribution of international trade of market economies already mentioned above. The results from the estimations of the old intra-Soviet Union trade are not used here, because it might be objected that this would perpetuate Soviet trade patterns. This objection would in fact be without basis because the parameter estimates are similar. Hence it does not really matter which set of parameter estimates one uses. A prediction of the future distribution of trade of a given former Soviet republic, say Ukraine, can then be obtained by multiplying these parameter estimates with the actual values of the income and the population of Ukraine (and those of all its potential trading partners) and the distances between Ukraine and its trading partners. (See Box 13.2 for details.)

This exercise yields estimates of the shift in the direction of trade that the former Soviet republics will experience in the long run. The same method is also used in Baldwin (1994), Wang and Winters (1991) and Havrylyshyn and Pritchett (1991) to predict the future trade patterns of the Central European countries.

To apply this approach to the former republics thus only requires data about income, population and distances. The latter two variables can be measured easily, but to guess the income *per capita* of the former republics in the long run is more difficult. We assumed that Russia has a *per capita* income of $2,500. This is somewhat above the actual value for 1993–94 and, given the continuing decline in production, should not be far from the actual value for the end of this decade. The results would not be affected even if Russia were to grow by 30 per cent more than assumed here because this would still leave Russia's GDP below one-tenth that of the EU. See Box 13.2 for more details.

Table 13.5 summarises the outcome of this exercise. The main result is that most of the international trade of the former republics will be with the West and not with other former republics. The reason for this is that in gravity equations the most important determinant of the distribution of trade is income. The income of the entire former Soviet Union (all the former republics together) is less than one-fifth that of the European Community or the United States. This size effect is not offset by a strong distance effect for the western former republics for which trade with the EC (or the EEA of the EC and EFTA combined) will thus become several times as important as trade with the other former republics.

Given its large market size and relative proximity, the EC emerges thus as the dominant trading partner of all former republics. The United States is further away than the EC and its market is slightly smaller; it is therefore not surprising that it trades much less with the former republics.[7]

Table 13.5 presents the predicted percentage distribution of the overall international trade for the average of all former republics, indicated by the FSU and Russia separately, using the mean of the predictions that one obtains based on the parameter estimates of the three studies mentioned above. Gros and Dautrebande (1992b) show that the predictions one obtains from each of these three different studies are very similar.[8]

Box 13.2 Predicting future trade flows

We use here the parameter estimates of three estimates of the gravity model for market economies. Two represent recent work with data from the 1980s and the third is a classic study referring to Europe in the 1960s. As will be shown below, however, all three sets of parameter estimates yield to quite similar predictions for the future trade pattern of the former republics. The three studies used are the same ones already used above as comparators for the analysis of the past inter-republican trade pattern: Wang and Winters (1991), Havrylyshyn and Pritchett (1991) and Aitken (1973). See Table 13.3 above for the parameter estimates obtained by these studies.

To form predictions about the future trade patterns of the former republics, we now need to combine the parameter estimates with the independent variables which are distance, population and some economic data. The former do not change a lot over time. The only economic input needed to calculate the future trade of the former republics is national income (GDP). Estimates of the income of the former Soviet Union were always unreliable and the experience with Central Europe has shown that most Western estimates (especially those made by the CIA) were on the high side. We therefore use a low estimate of $2,500 for the entire Soviet Union, which should be a reasonable minimum as argued in Gros and Steinherr (1991). This figure is also close to, but still above, the GDP per capita of Russia in 1994, the third full year with a market economy. Since the *per capita* income in Russia is, according to official Soviet figures for 1987, approximately equal to the average for the entire old Soviet Union, we assumed that Russia has a GDP *per capita* of $2,500. GDP *per capita* for all the other former republics was then calculated by multiplying the $2,500 with the ratio NMP *per capita* of the republic concerned over NMP *per capita* of Russia. Multiplying the *per capita* figures by population then yields the total GDP for each republic.

As before, the distance between two regions is calculated as the straight line distance between the two economic centres (usually the capital) of the regions. The adjacency dummy equals 2 if the two countries share a common border; otherwise, it equals 1.

continued

Box 13.2 *continued*

In the case of Russia, it is difficult to maintain the assumption that the capital is the main economic centre for trade. In other words, the distance between Alma Ata and Moscow might not be the relevant factor to use to predict trade between Russia and Kazakhstan since Kazakhstan would naturally trade more with western Siberia than with the Moscow region. Moreover, for the trade between Japan and Russia, the distance between Vladivostok and Tokyo should be more relevant than the distance between Moscow and Tokyo. Russia was therefore divided into six regions with the following centres: former Leningrad, Moscow, Volgograd, former Sverdlovsk, Novosibirsk and Vladivostok. Each region was assigned a total income equal to its share in the total population of Russia.

Using the parameter estimates of Table 13.3 above, we then calculate the potential exports of the former Soviet republics (14 countries plus the 6 regions of Russia) to the other republics and to eight other countries or regions: the EC, Scandinavia, Japan, Germany, United States, Central Europe (Czechoslovakia, Hungary, Poland, Romania, Bulgaria, Yugoslavia), China and India. These countries and regions accounted for 89 per cent of Soviet exports in 1989.

A number of authors have used the gravity equation to predict not only trade shares, but also the actual level of trade (e.g. in billions of US$). However, it has not been recognised that the figures for the predicted exports are strongly influenced by the constant in the estimation of the three studies used here. This constant is usually not precisely estimated; it represents the joint effect of all the factors that affect trade (exports) proportionally and does not affect distribution. In Havrylyshyn and Pritchett, the standard error surrounding the point estimate of the constant exceeds 1.5; this implies that even a one standard error band of confidence around the predictions for the absolute values is plus or minus 3. Since this is in logarithmic terms, this implies that the upper bound is 20 times as large as the lower bound. The predictions for the trade flows in absolute dollar terms are therefore not reliable.

We therefore concentrate here on the *relative distribution* of the predicted exports in percentage terms over the main economic regions taken into account.

Table 13.5 shows that the gravity model predicts that the share of trade with the other former republics will have to drop dramatically. In the past the ratio of international trade to inter-republican trade was 1:4. Table 13.3 suggests that in the future this ratio might be the other way round, that is, closer to 4:1. The mean of the three predictions is that the (average) former republic will conduct only 13.3 per cent of its trade with the other former republics; this corresponds actually to a ratio of inter-republican trade to trade with the rest of the world of 5:1. Since the average former republic will only conduct 7.3 per cent of its trade with Russia it is unlikely that in the long run Russia will continue to be able to dominate its neighbours in economic terms as it does at present.

The share of the EC (plus Scandinavia) is always estimated at around 50 per cent and that of the six countries of Central Europe considered here is between 6 and 8 per

TABLE 13.5 Predicted trade patterns of former republics

% of Total Trade with:	EC+ Scandinavia	Japan	US	FSU	Central Europe	Russia
USSR	45.6	17.4	12.2	15.3	7.4	7.3
Russia	45.9	24.9	13.7	7.5	5.4	–

cent for the average of all former republics and between 4 and 7.5 per cent for Russia. The collapse of trade with Central Europe that has already taken place is thus unlikely to be reversed in the future, and the EC emerges as the dominant trading partner for Russia and most of the other former republics.

Overall these results confirm the widely accepted notion that 'gravity' will reorient the trade of the former republics radically towards the West. A large part of the adjustment has already taken place in the most reformist countries. In Estonia, where the most radical reforms were implemented, trade with the EU plus Scandinavia now accounts for two-thirds of all trade, whereas in 1987 all non-FSU trade accounted for only 16 per cent of the total as shown in Table 13.1. In the case of Russia the ratio of trade with the EU to trade with the FSU is now about 2:1 where it used to be 1:2 in 1987. It needs hardly to be emphasized that this reorientation of trade does not call for any specific policy actions. But it should lead policy makers in the CIS to pay more attention to their trade relations with the EU.

3. Should the FSU or the CIS form an economic and monetary union?

Economic integration can bring large economic benefits. For the European Community, economic arguments have been one of the main motors of the integration process (see Commission of the European Communities, 1988 and 1990a). Do the same arguments apply to the former Soviet Union and justify the attempts to preserve or create a 'Soviet' economic space encompassing the CIS? We discuss this issue separately for monetary and trade matters.

A 'SOVIET CUSTOMS UNION'?

Exports and imports within the CIS are now subject to a variety of restrictions. In 1992–93 most of them were in the form of quantitative limitations instead of tariffs since many of the peripheral CIS countries were much slower in their reform effort than Russia. This has now (1994–95) changed; trade is now subject 'only' to ordinary tariffs, contradictory VAT rules and – this is the most serious part – the whim of customs officials. All barriers to trade have economic costs and these trade restrictions certainly contributed to the decline in inter-republican trade that has intensified the disruption of production. A policy of free trade pursued by all former republics unilaterally represents the optimal scenario from a general point of view. While this was politically impossible, an acceptable 'second best' alternative might have been to keep the CIS together in a customs union. Should the CIS countries form a customs union?

The standard analysis of customs unions shows that the benefits from joining a customs union are primarily a function of (1) the degree of protectionism practised by the union, (2) the size of the union, and (3) the regional distribution of trade.

1. If the external trade policy of a potential CIS customs union were close to free trade all member states should participate since they would then have virtually free trade with the entire world. However, this is not a likely outcome because Russia would certainly dominate any customs union and has already switched to a restrictive policy on hard currency imports as the ruble has strengthened. The smaller CIS countries are much more likely to keep a liberal trade policy stance on their own because in most cases they do not have domestic products to protect. The other CIS members would therefore be better off conducting their own liberal commercial policy: inside a CIS customs union they would import more high-cost products from the other republics (so-called 'trade diversion').
2. The size of the customs union is also an important factor because the larger the customs union the more likely it is that it contains the lowest cost producers of most goods. Therefore this aspect does not favour a potential CIS customs union because, in economic terms, the former Soviet Union is quite small. As mentioned above, the value of the output produced by all 15 former republics is less than one-fifth that of the EU.
3. The most fundamental reason for believing that the FSU is not an attractive trading block is that in the long run inter-republican trade will drastically decline in importance, as documented above. It does not make sense to create a customs union with a group of countries that do not trade intensively with each other.

In a sense, a CIS customs union would be similar to the number of customs unions (and other preferential trading areas) between the poorer countries of Latin America. These regional agreements have never really worked for the same reason: trade among the members is usually only a small fraction of overall trade. In the case of the CIS one has to add some practical problems that have impeded the implementation of the numerous treaties and agreements to create a customs union in the CIS that have been concluded over the last years. A first issue that was never really resolved centred around the decision-making mechanism for setting the tariffs for the union. Russia was not really ready to subordinate its own tariff structure to majority voting in some sort of customs council and the other CIS states were not willing to abdicate the determination of their external tariff policy entirely to Russia. Ensuring a proper redistribution of the tariff proceeds also turned out to be difficult to organize.

Finally, Russia insisted, until 1994, that any free trade or customs union agreement in the CIS should exclude export tariffs. The background to this curious demand for asymmetry was that Russia wanted to keep domestic energy prices low through export tariffs on oil and gas, but was not willing to let Russian oil producers supply the other CIS countries with large amounts of oil and gas at a fraction of the world market price.

These political difficulties came on top of the fact that sectoral interests were determining trade policy more and more in Russia and pushing it in a direction that was too different from that of the other CIS countries. This is why a customs union was not created despite a treaty to this effect that had been signed and ratified in due form.

THE FORMER SOVIET UNION AS AN OPTIMAL CURRENCY AREA?

Would the CIS countries benefit economically from having a common currency (see Emerson *et al.* 1992)? The 'optimal currency area' literature says that countries should form a monetary union if (1) they trade intensively among themselves, (2) asymmetric shocks will be minor, (3) the monetary union will deliver price stability and (4) a national fiscal policy cannot threaten the common monetary policy stance. These points are discussed in a medium-run perspective to put the specific problems that dominated the events of 1992–93 into a broader framework.

Trade links

The first criterion in deciding whether or not a country should be part of a monetary union is the importance of trade within the potential currency area. It was shown above that in the past trade links were very intense, but that the future should bring a completely different trade pattern. The likely reorientation of trade illustrated above is thus a first argument against a Soviet monetary union.

One might argue that the Baltic states (and some other smaller CIS countries) are too small to be viable currency areas on their own. What should they do? Section 2 above already showed that there should be a redirection of trade. For the Baltics one can be more specific. Once they are integrated into the world economy, their geographical trade patterns are likely to resemble that of Finland today. In that case they would gain more from joining the emerging European Economic and Monetary Union (EMU) than from remaining in the ruble area. Estonia has already effectively done this through the currency board arrangement that links its currency to the DM.

For the larger republics, inter-republican trade was less important in relation to output (see Table 13.1 above, for Ukraine it was under 30 per cent, comparable to the ratio for France, which has approximately the same population) so that the economic argument against a separate national currency is weaker. The larger republics may therefore represent viable currency areas of their own.

Asymmetric shocks

The main advantage of a separate currency is that exchange-rate changes can facilitate the adjustment to nationally differentiated shocks. The classic argument goes like this: imagine a country that is hit by an adverse shock to its balance of payments and that would need a real depreciation in order to restore external balance. If the country is part of a monetary union, the only way this real depreciation can be achieved is by a fall in domestic wages and prices (relative to those in the rest of the currency area). In the face of an external shock, the exchange rate is a useful adjustment tool because a fall in wages and prices is often difficult to achieve and always takes some time, whereas the exchange rate can be moved instantaneously.

In the case of the former Soviet Union, this argument is particularly relevant for several reasons. In the short run, the reform process in itself already provides a source for large regionally differentiated shocks because price reform (especially energy price reform) leads to large changes in relative prices and therefore an important redistribution of income given the high degree of specialisation of many republics and regions. For example, wages in Ukraine fell to less than one third of the Russian level in real terms even after Ukraine achieved the same level of stabilisation as Russia in 1994.

Given that Ukraine imports most of its energy the direction of movement in relative wages was not surprising, but the extraordinary size would have been difficult to predict given that under the Soviet regime wages were at about the same level. Belarus experienced a similar real depreciation. Figure 13.2 in Section 4 provides more evidence on the evolution of relative wages in the CIS. Moreover, the overall reform process proceeded at different speeds in the different former republics.

In the longer run, one large source of asymmetric shocks will remain. Because the value of the Russian ruble will be determined by world market prices for oil and gas, the ruble will become essentially a 'petro' currency. Given that Russia (together with Kazakhstan and Azerbaijan) accounts for most energy exports of the former Soviet Union, changes in the world market prices for oil would thus constitute a major source of asymmetric shocks.

Price stability

The most important consideration concerning a monetary union is that a common currency also implies a common inflation rate. This could be achieved through maintaining the ruble as a common currency or through an EMS type of fixed exchange-rate system with the ruble providing the anchor like the DM in the EMS. Can a link to the ruble assure price stability in either case? This has clearly not been the case so far and it is not likely that in the future the ruble will be a very stable currency. However, there is also little reason to believe that national currencies will be more (or less) stable than the Russian ruble, so that this argument seems to cut both ways. Except for the Baltics and Kirgistan all former republics adopted even more inflationary policies than Russia when they were forced to introduce their own currencies. Again one has to consider all the options. For the Western former republics an alternative that could provide some price stability would be a link to the Ecu. In the short run this was too tight a policy constraint for most former republics, but in the long run the Ecu, which by then would be the single currency of the enlarged Community, should provide a stable anchor.

Financing budget deficits

The decisive factor that destroyed all attempts to maintain the ruble as the common currency was, however, different from the optimal currency area-type considerations discussed so far. In these economies in transition, the government can finance deficits only by printing money, since in the early years of the reform process markets for public debt instruments simply did not exist. A common currency therefore implies also a common fiscal policy, at least during the transition period. There were enormous differences in the degree to which different governments were willing and able to withstand the multiple pressures for social safety nets and subsidies to uncompetitive industries. At one extreme one finds Estonia, where a balanced budget was seen as crucial for the survival of the country, and at the other end would be Ukraine where a weak government tried to spend its way out of the structural problems.

The sharp difference between the short and the long run that has come up repeatedly in this section suggests one conclusion. Even under the best of circumstances, most of the former republics would anyway sooner or later have found that it was in their interest to establish a national currency (and perhaps link it to the Ecu). The real question is therefore how the disintegration of the ruble zone should have been organised.

The optimal solution would have been a stable and convertible ruble to serve for some time as a common currency. As soon as the banking systems in the other CIS member countries had developed enough to allow for normal international banking relationships these countries should have introduced their own national currencies one by one: currencies that would also have been convertible and stable. However, this did not happen. The ruble was semi-stabilised only after two years and in the meantime trade among CIS countries collapsed as the normal payment channels were disrupted. The following section analyses what actually happened and why it did not conform to this prescription.

4. The 'worst monetary constitution one can imagine'?

The seeds for the dissolution of the (Soviet) ruble zone were already sown some time before the dissolution of the Soviet Union. The ruble zone started to crumble once the Central Bank of the Soviet Union (called Gosbank) started to lose control over its head offices located in the 15 republics.

The Gosbank of the Union was organised, like all institutions of the Soviet Union, formally along federal lines. There were thus head offices in all 15 republics. As long as the party controlled everything, this did not really matter, but things changed when, gradually during 1991, the Union Gosbank lost control over its republican branches. When the different republics declared their sovereignty, the head offices of the Gosbank became 'central' banks on their own, that were supposed to be free of control from the Union.

There were thus 15 'independent' central banks,[9] with the self-declared authority to create money in one currency area. This situation was not tenable because each 'national central' bank had an incentive to give its clientele (state-owned enterprises, republican governments) as much credit as possible. The consequences in terms of greater inflationary pressures would be borne by the entire Union. There was thus a clear free-rider problem, which was most acute in the case of the smaller republics. For example, if the central bank of a republic that initially accounts for 5 per cent of the total credit supply (and 5 per cent of the total income of the FSU) doubles the credit of its own government, total Union credit increases only by 5 per cent. A small republic could thus assume that even huge rates of domestic credit expansion would have virtually no inflationary consequences for itself. This is why it was often said that in 1991 the Soviet Union had 'the worst monetary constitution one can imagine'.[10] As will be shown below, however, the Union authorities could have controlled the situation as long as they controlled the printing presses.

At the end of 1991, the Soviet Union ceased to exist.[11] But all the national central banks that emerged from the republican head offices of the Gosbank continued to give credit in rubles (implicitly Soviet republics). But, despite a very serious cash shortage, they dared not print additional 'Soviet' rubles and all printing presses were located in Russia (see Box 13.3 for the story of bank note designs in Russia). The Baltic republics and Ukraine announced immediately that they would introduce their own currency as quickly as possible. In fact this did not happen right away: Estonia started the process in late June 1992 and Ukraine followed only in November. However, these countries started right away to print substitute rubles (so-called coupons).

Box 13.3 From Soviet to Russian banknotes

Soviet bank notes carried inscriptions in all the 14 official languages of the FSU. In the course of 1992 the Russian mint began to substitute the old 'Soviet' designs on banknotes. In a first step the translation of the face value (1, 3, 5, etc. rubles) in all 14 official languages of the FSU was suppressed, the only 'language' used on banknotes was Russian. But until mid-1992 these banknotes still carried the heading 'the State Bank of the USSR' and conserved the old 'Soviet' symbols. The next step came with ruble notes without 'Soviet' symbols (i.e. without Lenin's face and the hammer and sickle) that bore the mark 'issued by the Central Bank of Russia'. These banknotes circulated for some time in the 11 former Soviet republics that did not introduce a national currency until the end of 1993 despite the fact that they are clearly 'Russian' and not 'Soviet' or 'CIS'. The old Soviet cash was gradually taken out of circulation in 1992–93 as the old, lower denomination, banknotes became useless because of inflation. The final step came when the Central Bank of Russia (CBR) announced, in July of 1993, that all the pre-1992 banknotes would no longer be accepted in Russia after September and that Russia would no longer deliver any cash to the other republics unless they sign a treaty to subordinate their monetary and fiscal policies to that of Russia. This completed the creation of the 'Russian' ruble (see Box 13.4).

In the meantime most of the former Soviet republics were thus in the strange situation that they still used the 'Soviet' ruble and their central banks continued to grant credit in rubles. Thus, the free-rider problem continued in 1992. The main change with respect to 1991 was that after price liberalisation, excessive credit expansion could (and did) show up quickly in higher prices. In a sense the free-rider problem became even more acute than before since the states that intended to introduce their own currency anyway had no concern at all for a stable purchasing power of the ruble.

The situation was different for Russia. Since Russia considered itself to be the successor state to the dissolved USSR, it wanted to keep the ruble. Gaidar's government pledged to stabilise the economy with a tight monetary and fiscal policy in Russia. It recognised quickly, however, that it could never succeed if the central banks of the other countries from the FSU could continue to issue credit in rubles. One solution would have been a monetary reform, that is, simply to introduce officially a Russian ruble. However, this path was not used for political reasons.

The problem for Russian policy-makers was therefore how to isolate Russia from the perceived inflationary impact of ruble credits originating from other countries in the CIS. (Below we show that in reality there was no threat.) The solution adopted was to impose controls on cross-border movements of bank accounts.[12] The CBR decreed that all bank transfers to and from other former Soviet republics would have to pass through special correspondent accounts held by its headquarters in Moscow. The idea underlying this move was simple: if the CBR could ensure that there were no *net* movements of funds between Russia and the other former Soviet republics, credit emission in these countries could no longer affect the money supply in Russia. In this way Russia would be able to stabilise the ruble. In effect this measure was equivalent to the introduction of a Russian non-cash ruble.

The correspondent account system was imposed by the Central Bank of Russia over the space of six months (January-July 1992). Transfers to and from the Baltics were immediately controlled starting in January 1992. But for the rest of the FSU, the system really started working after 1 July 1992. Before that date, all payments from CIS countries were automatically credited in the Russian banking system and the CBR was informed only *ex-post facto* of the balance of outgoing and incoming payments. Box 13.4 provides a chronology of the evolution of the correspondent system and the dissolution of the ruble zone.

Box 13.4. Chronology of the dissolution of the ruble zone

1992:

January	All former republics still use the (Soviet) ruble, correspondent account system created but, except for Baltics, all payments from other former republics are automatically credited in Russia.
May	Agreement on the creation of a joint Central Bank council for the CIS (never implemented).
June	Estonia is the first former republic to introduce national currency (Kroon); agrees to return old Soviet rubles to Russia.
July	Limits on balance on correspondent accounts introduced by Russia after a large Russian surplus has been accumulated and Ukraine decides on a huge credit emission. To facilitate introduction of the new system overdrafts in the form of 'technical credits' are given.
September	Agreement on the creation of an Interstate Bank at Bishkek (Kyrgystan). Negotiations on details start.
Aug.-Nov.	Technical credits exhausted, the Central Bank of Russia (CBR) blocks correspondent accounts and processes payments from other former republics on a selective basis.
November	Ukraine formally delinks 'coupons' from ruble.

1993:

January	Agreement on Interstate Bank signed (not implemented).
Jan–June	Credits on the correspondent accounts in principle no longer available from the CBR. Other countries can run a deficit only if the Russian government provides explicit government to government credits. Existing credit balances are transformed into official debt and indexed on the dollar.
July	The CBR decides suddenly to withdraw all old 'Soviet' (i.e. pre-1992) bank notes from circulation by September and announces that it will deliver new bank notes only to those former republics that subordinate their monetary and fiscal policy totally to that of

continued

Box 13.4 *continued*

	Russia by signing an agreement on a monetary union. Many CIS countries initially declare their intention to join the monetary union.
Sept–Nov	End of ruble zone. When the other CIS countries see the fine print on the monetary union proposal all decide to introduce a national currency.

The correspondent account system worked as follows: imagine that an enterprise in Ukraine wished to pay an enterprise in Russia for a delivery of oil. It would send a 'payment order' to its local bank which in turn transmitted the corresponding transfer order to the National Bank of Ukraine. In Kiev all transfer orders towards Russia (i.e. requests to transfer funds to pay for imports from Russia) were collected and sent periodically in large sacks to the 'international computing centre' in Moscow. This organisation, part of the CBR, also collected all the payment orders coming from Russian enterprises that wanted to pay for Russian imports. All payments from Ukraine (i.e. Ukrainian imports from Russia) were booked on the liability side of the correspondent account of Ukraine, and Russian imports from Ukraine were put on the asset side. The net payments were supposed to be balanced over time.

In theory the nature of the correspondent accounts system changed radically in July 1992 when the Central Bank of Russia decreed that the correspondent account would have to balance. However, the Central Bank of Russia gave each CIS country, including Ukraine, a line of credit at the start of the new system (1 July 1992) to allow them time to adjust. In principle, each republic thus knew the maximum amount of debt it could accumulate and should thus have taken measures to reduce its deficit when it came close to its limit. However, the limits were not taken seriously because the other CIS states hoped that they could obtain additional credits once the initial one had been exhausted. They counted on the pressure of Russian exporters that would ask the CBR to pay (sometimes for deliveries already made). In some cases policy-makers did not comprehend why the Russians should be allowed to block a payment order that had been properly filled in and sent to Moscow. This explains why the initial credit lines were used up quite quickly. Ukraine had from the beginning a negative balance (or deficit) so that its debt towards Russia was growing all the time. Within two or three months, many former Soviet republics had already reached their limit. At that point the CBR started to get tough. For each republic that had exhausted the credit line, it processed each day only an amount of payments for imports of that republic equal to the amount of the payment orders for exports coming from the republic concerned.

There is considerable anecdotal evidence that the deficits of Ukraine, for example, did not reflect an excess of Ukrainian imports over its exports to Russia, but capital flight from Ukraine where interest rates were even lower than in Russia despite even stronger inflationary pressures. However, this cannot be verified since no reliable customs data for the trade between Russia and Ukraine exists for this period.

THE RUBLE ZONE IN 1992–93: A RECIPE FOR INFLATION OR A DISCIPLINARY DEVICE?

There were nine CIS countries that kept the ruble (a 'generic' ruble as opposed to a well-defined national ruble or the Russian ruble) as their currency during 1992 and most of 1993. However, this 'ruble zone' was not a unified currency area. Households in these countries used Russian banknotes[13] but domestic transactions in non-cash form were denominated in rubles (without any specification) and transfers through bank accounts to and from Russia were subject to a variety of regulations and delays. All official non-cash payments between Russia and the other CIS countries had to go through the so-called 'correspondent accounts' between the CBR and the other national central banks, as explained above.

Since the official correspondent accounts were often blocked (see below), it was very difficult for enterprises outside Russia to pay their Russian suppliers even if they were in principle ready to pay a premium. This was one of the reasons why during 1992–93 commercial banks were again allowed (gradually) to have direct correspondent accounts with commercial banks in other countries. These only semi-regulated transactions between commercial banks developed into an informal market for 'national' rubles, that is, rubles in bank accounts in any one of these countries. The rubles outside Russia were usually worth less than the Russian ruble, that is, in a bank account in Russia. In this sense, the CIS countries that used the ruble in 1992–93 had already 'quasi' national currencies.

This ill-defined situation satisfied neither the Russian government nor the other CIS states. The Russian political system was itself divided. Some political forces, notably in the conservative parliament, wanted to save at least part of the former empire. In that view, the preservation of a unified ruble zone was an indispensable part of that strategy. The more reformist elements of the government however, preferred a clean solution. They demanded that the other CIS countries either introduce their own currencies or give up all their monetary independence.

The other CIS countries were constantly torn between two considerations: on the one hand they wanted to have an independent monetary policy; but, on the other, they also wanted to reap the advantages of staying in the ruble zone. These advantages were important because as a part of the ruble zone they could in principle have a slice of the cheap credit distributed by the Central Bank of Russia. Moreover, at least in 1992–93, the Russian government linked the price of oil to the currency issue. Countries within the ruble zone were charged a price in rubles that was close to the domestic Russian price. Other countries had, in principle, to pay the world market price, which was about two to five times higher. Given that imports of oil accounted for a very large proportion of their national income,[14] the second point was the crucial one.

During the first half of 1992, international efforts to help Russia concentrated on a ruble stabilisation fund of potentially $6 billion. It was widely perceived, however, that it would not be possible to stabilise the ruble unless a clear arrangement for the ruble zone was found. In early 1992, the other CIS countries were not willing to introduce national currencies for the motives mentioned above. Under pressure from the IMF[15] and the Russian government most CIS countries thus signed in May 1992 an agreement on a joint central bank council that would determine credit expansion for the entire area and take decisions on all relevant monetary policy instruments (interest rates, minimum reserves, foreign exchange interventions, etc.). However, that agreement was never implemented. That there was never any intention to do so becomes clear from the fact that one article stipulated that the decisions of the joint central bank council would be binding only on those members that agreed to be bound.

The key issue that made an agreement on a joint central bank impossible was the voting power to be attributed to each state in the decision-making instance of the common central bank. Russia insisted for obvious reasons on a formula that linked voting power to size or economic strength. The CIS states were not willing to give up even a small part of their sovereignty, so recently acquired, and insisted on the principle 'one state, one vote'.

The failure of the joint central bank project was one of the reasons for the introduction of the limits on the correspondent accounts between central banks in July 1992. However, as Russia continued to deliver oil at below world market prices and extend credit to the ruble zone states during 1992 and early 1993, the CIS states in Central Asia and Belarus succeeded for a while in having their cake and eating it too.

Let us now return to the question of whether the existence of a 'quasi-ruble zone' made it impossible to stabilise the (Russian) ruble. As mentioned above, the IMF and the Russian government took the position that the introduction of a real national currency in the other CIS countries was a pre-condition for an effective stabilisation programme for the (Russian) ruble.

In contrast, we argue that the use of the ruble by other countries cannot really have been an obstacle for the stabilisation of the Russian ruble. On the contrary, the ruble zone was rather a 'disciplinary device' for the other CIS countries, forcing them to subordinate their national monetary policies to that of the CBR, because the other CIS countries were constrained by the Russian monopoly on ruble bank notes and by the fact that since July 1992, inter-state credit had been limited.

The proposition that control over the printing press allowed Russia to guarantee price stability follows immediately, if one accepts the view that the price level can be controlled as long as there is a well defined demand for cash in real terms (see Fama 1990). This argument simply says that if the government determines the nominal quantity of any good for which there is a well defined demand in real terms, it also determines indirectly the price level.

However, one can also make the argument in terms of the more conventional premise that the price level is determined by the supply of 'money'. The latter is usually defined as the sum of cash and deposits with the *domestic* banking system. Through the usual system of requested reserves, the central bank can ensure that the domestic banking system can expand its deposit base (if and) only if the central bank increases the monetary base. Control over the monetary base thus implies control over inflation. This is the standard framework used in macroeconomic textbooks (see e.g. Dornbusch and Fischer 1981).

To argue that the ruble zone cannot have been a major source of inflation in Russia, one can also show that it was comparable to a currency board. However, it was a special currency arrangement because of the separation between the cash and the non-cash circuits. These two aspects are now discussed in turn.

THE USE OF THE RUBLE AS A CURRENCY BOARD ARRANGEMENT

In most respects the relationship between the ruble zone countries and Russia was not much different from that of Estonia[16] *vis-à-vis* Germany. Estonia opted for a currency board arrangement when it introduced a national currency. Estonian Kroons could from the start be exchanged at a rate of 8:1 against DM. Belarus (formerly Bellorussia) was a good example of a ruble zone country. It issued banknotes, the so-called 'hares', that were perfect substitutes for Russian rubles at the rate of 10:1.[17]

The Central Banks of Estonia and Belarus were in principle free to grant as much credit to their national economic agents (government or private sector) as they wanted. These credits could have been denominated in rubles, Kroon or theoretically even DM. The argument that ruble credits granted by the Central Bank of Belarus created inflation in Russia must ultimately rest on the idea that ruble credits originating from the Central Bank of Belarus led to an increase in the monetary base in Russia. The same should hold true for DM credits issued by the Central Bank of Estonia. However, nobody would seriously maintain that when the Central Bank of Estonia issued credits German monetary policy or, more precisely, the assets and liabilities of the Bundesbank would be affected. The following step-by-step analysis shows why this is the case.

Imagine that the Central Bank of Estonia gives credits in DM (the equivalent of the Central Bank of Belarus issuing credits in rubles). As long as these credits are given only to Estonian enterprises and banks there will obviously be no impact on money supply (and demand) in Germany. But Estonian economic agents might use the credit they thus obtained to buy goods and services in Germany. The German exporter, however, probably wants to be paid with something that can be used to pay for the costs in Germany. The Estonian importer cannot pay in cash, but can only give the German exporter a claim in DM on the Estonian Central Bank. The German exporter will then ask the Estonian Central Bank to provide DM funds through a bank account in Germany. The Estonian Central Bank can do this only if it has foreign exchange reserves. In this case the Estonian Central Bank can thus extend credit only to the extent that it has foreign exchange reserves, that is, if it follows the rules of the currency board.[18]

Box 13.5 Cash versus Non-cash

Up to this point, we have shown that operations of other CIS countries should have no impact on the money supply in Russia. This is indeed the case for fully fledged market economies in which all agents can exchange unlimited amounts of cash into non-cash on a 1:1 basis, as in Estonia after the introduction of the Kroon. However, this was not the case in the CIS in 1992–93. This separation of the cash and non-cash circuits played a central role in giving national central banks outside Russia some room for manoeuvre. The dual standard of cash and non-cash should, in principle, have been eliminated with the radical reforms undertaken by the Russian government in early 1992. However, in contrast to other reforming countries in Central Europe, this did not happen in Russia.

As mentioned above, non-cash payments between Russia and the other CIS countries had to go through so-called 'correspondent' accounts between the CBR and other national central banks.[19] However, from July 1992 the CBR has tended

continued

Box 13.5 *continued*

to block payments through these accounts whenever the partner country in question had a deficit that exceeded certain limits. The currency board type mechanism described in the previous section, which relies entirely on bank transfers, therefore does not work in the CIS. Would cash transactions be a substitute?

In most CIS countries until 1994 it was difficult to convert non-cash into cash. This was crucial for inter-state transactions as well. If it had been possible to exchange unlimited amounts of local non-cash into cash, enterprises (and households) could just have converted their local bank accounts into cash and sent the cash by plane to Moscow (or somewhere else in Russia) to pay their Russian suppliers.[20] In this case 'excess' credit creation by other CIS countries would have had to be covered by reserves of (Russian) cash. However, these countries did not have substantial reserves of (Russian) cash since most of them received only enough cash from Russia to keep their local economies supplied with enough currency to effect transactions.

The separation of the cash and non-cash circuits outside Russia was thus necessary to safeguard some independence for the national central banks. As shown above, any national central bank that guaranteed to exchange its liabilities at 1:1 into (Russian) rubles (in the form of banknotes) would *de facto* become a mere currency board. But how much autonomy did the separation between cash and non-cash give national central banks in Central Asia and the Caucasus?

The crucial point here is that the separation of the two monetary circuits was (and even more now, is) not perfect.[21] The explicit and implicit restrictions on the conversion of non-cash into cash varied from country to country so that it is difficult to make generalisations. However, there were some restrictions in all countries and cash traded at a premium over non-cash most of the time.

How can this premium arise? Imagine that a local central bank issues too much credit (by definition in non-cash form). If this credit is given to enterprises to pay wages, the central bank cannot really refuse to hand out the same amount in cash almost immediately since in most CIS countries enterprises have the 'right' to demand cash to pay their workers. The local central bank will thus not be able to engineer a local credit expansion to pay wages if it does not have enough Russian cash. In this respect it has to behave like a currency board or it will not be able to provide enterprises with enough cash to pay wages, and cash will then become more valuable than non-cash.

Of course, it is possible that the credit from the local central bank is given to enterprises for payment to other enterprises, so that the local central bank does not have to hand out any cash right away. However, either the credit ends up being used to pay wages or to pay for imports. In the latter case the national central bank will be asked to provide either dollars (for hard currency imports) or, if the additional imports come from Russia, more payment orders will be sent to the Central Bank of Russia (CBR) which, once a certain limit has been attained, will not accept them. Once the bilateral correspondent account with the CBR is

continued

Box 13.5 *continued*

blocked, the local authorities will have to ration imports.[22] This implies that within the country where the credit expansion took place the (perhaps implicit) premium of cash over non-cash will increase because enterprises will demand more cash to make payments to Russia.

The premium of cash over non-cash should thus be an indicator of the degree to which credit expansion outside Russia has been larger than in Russia. Anecdotal evidence suggests that this premium has rarely exceeded 30 to 50 per cent. The exchange rate for cash rubles on which more systematic data is available never deviated more than about 10–15 per cent from the rate in Moscow. This partial evidence suggests that in 1992–93 the national central banks in other former Soviet republics did not really try to have an independent monetary policy. The common cash ruble has thus probably imposed some discipline on the non-Russian ruble zone countries during this period.

The analogy between the currency board of Estonia (using the DM) and that of Belarus (using the ruble in 1992–93) is not perfect because the Estonians knew that they would never obtain any credit from the Bundesbank if they were to run a deficit on their external accounts. Belarus did receive substantial credits from Russia and was thus able to cover its large deficits. However, this policy was not inherent in the ruble zone arrangement; it constituted a deliberate policy choice of the Russian government. If the Russian government (and the CBR) had simply refused to give any credits to the other CIS countries (for example in the context of a tough ruble stabilization programme) there could have been no inflationary impact coming from the other ruble zone countries. In reality the Russian government chose to extend large credits, domestically and towards some CIS countries, but this does not imply that the ruble zone arrangement *per se* was inflationary.

THE EVIDENCE

The view that the use of a common ruble in a number of CIS states was inflationary and destabilised monetary policy in Russia must imply that monetary policy in the other CIS states was even more expansionary than in Russia. This can be checked by looking at the monetary aggregates in the CIS relative to those for Russia. The only aggregate for which one can obtain a comparable series is M3. Figure 13.1 therefore shows the ratio CIS–Russia for M3. Since Ukraine left the ruble zone earlier than the others and since Ukraine already had a parallel currency in the form of coupons in 1992, Fig. 13.1 shows two lines: one is the ratio of Ukrainian M3 to Russian M3, the other is the ratio of the sum of the M3s of all the other CIS states that used the ruble to Russian M3. Even a superficial look at the data suggests that the policies in the rest of the CIS (excluding Ukraine) cannot have been more expansionary than in Russia since the ratio actually declines somewhat in 1992. Only in late 1993, when the ruble zone was dissolved, did most CIS states embark on a really inflationary policy. Ukraine is different since in this case the inflationary path had already started by the end of 1992,

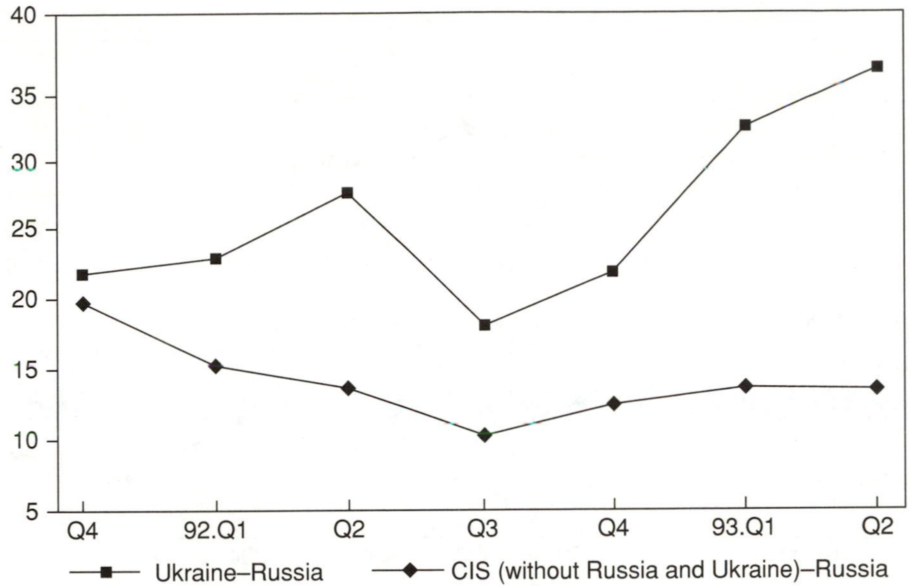

FIG 13.1 Money supply in the CIS (relative shares of the republics in overall money supply)
Source: Own calculations based on IFS, Supplement on the countries of the FSU, Supplement series no. 16
Note: The expansion of Ukrainian money supply starts with the approval of the Karbovanets as sole legal tender on 12.11.92

but even in this case there is no evidence that in early 1992 Ukrainian monetary policy was clearly worse than that of Russia.

Another way to test the hypothesis that the other CIS states had a highly inflationary policy on the back of the common ruble is to look at the behaviour of wages. If policies in the rest of the CIS had been too expansionary, wages should have risen relative to those in Russia. However, this was also clearly not the case as shown in Fig. 13.2 which again shows two lines. One shows wages in Ukraine as a percentage of those in Russia and the other shows the (unweighted) average wage in the rest of the CIS, again as a percentage of wages in Russia. Since wages in the rest of the CIS were already lower than in Russia before the reforms started, one should compare the 1992 and 1993 data with the data from the end of 1991. However, even on this basis, one cannot see a tendency of wages in the CIS to increase relative to those of Russia. By the end of 1991, wages in the CIS (without Ukraine) were about two thirds of Russian wages. By mid-1993, they had fallen to about one half. It is interesting to note that the process of wage dispersion had started much earlier. In 1985 wages in the eight Soviet republics considered here (Armenia, Azerbaijan, Belarus, Kazakhstan, Kyrgystan, Moldova, Tadzhikistan, Uzbekistan) stood at 93 per cent of the Russian level, by 1990 they were at 84 per cent and by the last quarter of 1991 they had fallen to 70 per cent. This development might have been one additional reason for the increasing dissatisfaction with the 'Union' during that period.

The Ukrainian data shows some slight increase in 1992 relative to the baseline at the end of 1991, but it is so small, about 10 per cent, that it cannot have had a strong

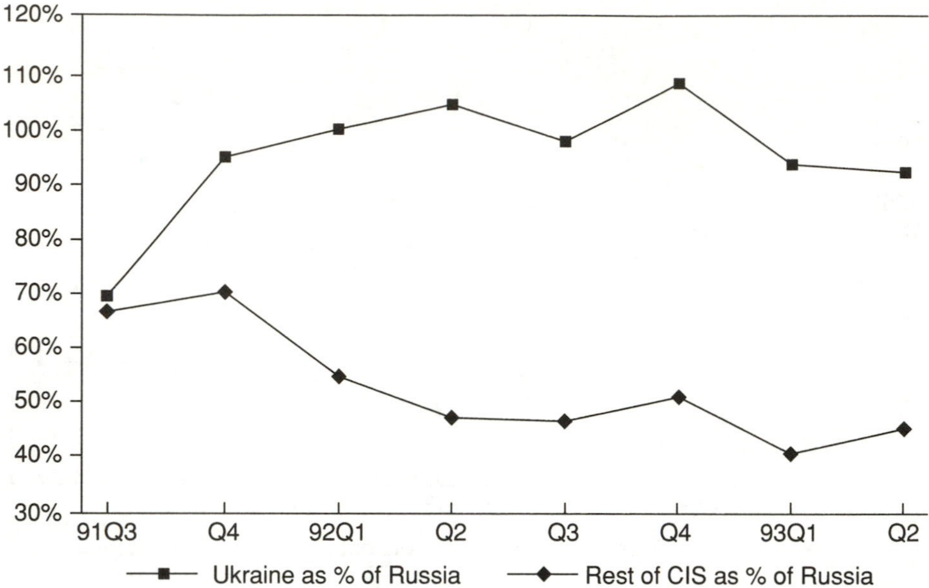

FIG 13.2 Wages and inflation (a comparison of nominal wages in the CIS)

impact. The really inflationary policies in Ukraine come much later. But the fact that Ukrainian wages (in karbovanetz) reached 200 per cent of the Russian level is completely irrelevant for Russian monetary policy since it came one year after the formal break with the ruble in the third quarter of 1992.

The data on money supplies and wages are, of course, the outcome of a general equilibrium game under the rules explained above. However, the argument made here is that this game should lead to the result found here: a roughly similar rate of monetary expansion because of the currency board-like nature of the ruble zone. Given that the linkages were not perfect, one would expect monetary expansion to be somewhat *higher* outside Russia if these countries had been more inflationary. However, the opposite is true; monetary expansion was somewhat *lower* outside Russia.

There is thus no compelling evidence that the other CIS states that used the common ruble pursued a more inflationary policy than in Russia and thus created additional inflation there. The badly defined ruble zone that existed in 1992–93 cannot be held responsible for inflation in Russia during that period.

However, the ruble zone, as long as it lasted, certainly exerted a disciplinary effect on the peripheral countries. This can be seen from Fig. 13.3 and 13.4 which show the evolution of six of the new national currencies against the ruble during 1993–94. Figure 13.3 shows the ruble exchange rate of the three Western former Soviet republics: Belarus (ruble), Ukraine (karbovanets) and Moldova (lei). It is apparent that all three of these currencies started to depreciate against the ruble (itself not a very hard currency even during the temporary stabilisation of 1993) as soon as they were created. The (Belorussian) ruble started out at 1:1, but reached over 25 to the

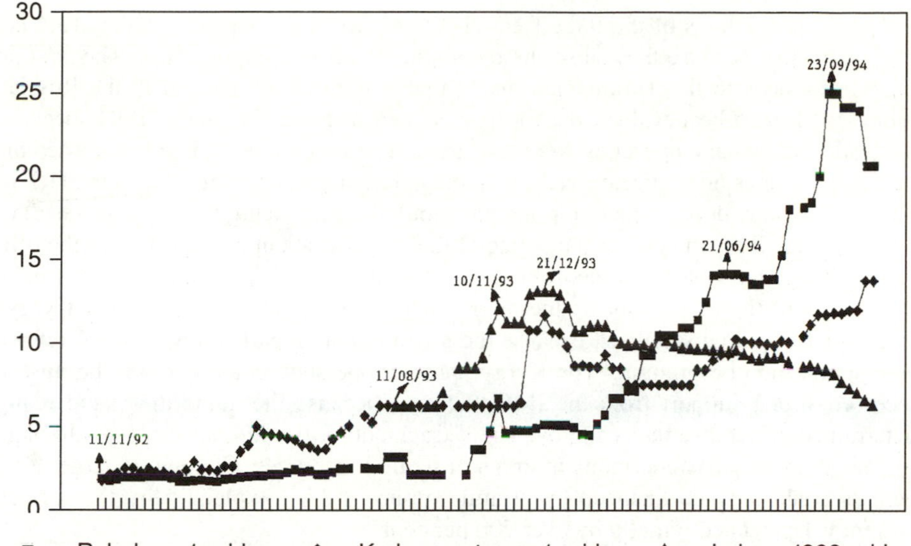

FIG 13.3 Currencies of Belarus, Ukraine and Moldova (11.11.92–21.10.94)
Source: Own calculations based on Finansovye Izvestia

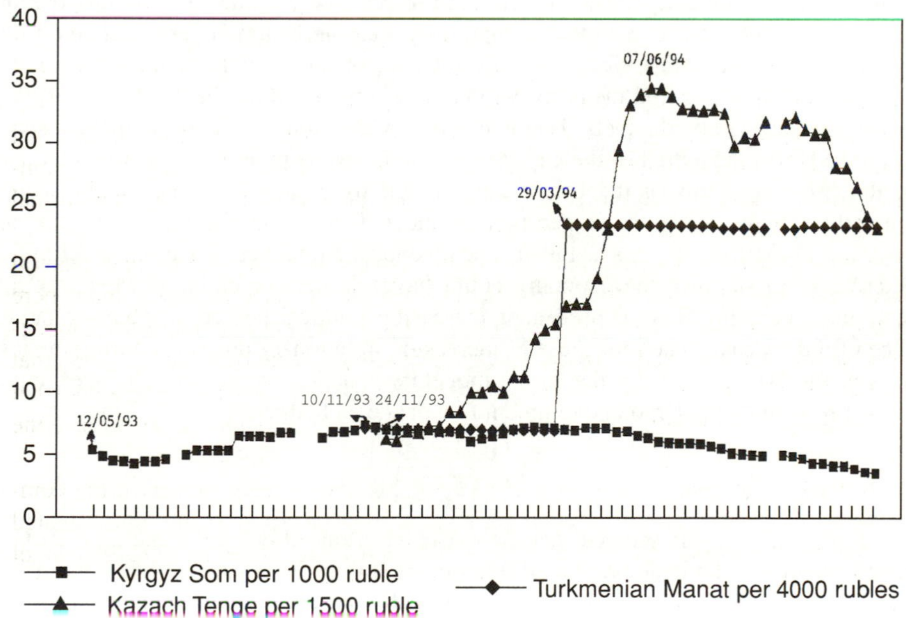

FIG 13.4 Currencies of Central-Asiatic republics of the FSU (12.5.93–21.10.94)
Source: Own calculations based on Finansovye Izvestia

(Russian) ruble late in 1994; the Ukrainian karbovanet also started off at 1:1 and fell to over 10. These two currencies thus depreciated by 2,500 and 1,000 per cent, respectively (always *vis-à-vis* the Russian ruble). The Moldavian lei did marginally better with a depreciation over this period of 'only' about 500 per cent.

The exchange rates of the three Central Asian currencies depicted in Fig. 13.4 are also instructive because they show three completely different approaches. The straight line corresponds to the Turkmenian manat that was officially pegged to the Russian ruble, but had to be devalued by 500 per cent in one step in March 1994, because domestic inflationary pressures were too great. The continuing straight line after the depreciation does not indicate a radical stabilisation programme, but shows the lack of reforms in that country, which in principle should be very rich given its huge reserves of natural gas. The official exchange rate of the manat is about as important as the official exchange rates of the Soviet ruble under the old regime. The almost stable line at the bottom of the picture shows the market-determined exchange rate of the Kyrgyz som which could be stabilised because the government embarked on a radical reform and stabilisation programme. The Kyrgyz programme succeeded, not only because it received strong support from the IMF, but also because the authorities were really determined to stabilise the economy. The Kasach authorities did not succeed, although this large country has enormous reserves of natural resources. Continuing large fiscal deficits could only be financed by printing money, which explains why the Kasach currency depreciated initially by over 700 per cent.

The theoretical argument that the ruble zone was really more a currency board for the other CIS countries applies *a fortiori* also to the situation that existed during the last days of the Soviet Union. The only difference was that the Union government controlled, at least until early 1991, the printing presses and was thus in a similar position to Russia in 1992–93. It was often thought then that the Union government could not stabilise the Soviet ruble since it could not control the republican branches of the Gosbank that had declared themselves to be independent central banks. However, this is also contradicted by the facts. The main cause of destabilisation during the last years of the FSU was the deficit of the Union, not deficits of the republics. It is true that part of the fiscal problems of the Union government were caused by the republics that withheld revenues. But the larger part of the deficit of the Union came from an *increase* in expenditure, not a fall in tax revenues. Moreover, a Union government determined to stabilise the economy could have slashed expenditure whenever the republics (including Russia) used their increasing political powers to obtain a larger slice of the tax cake. The root cause of increasing inflationary pressures during the last days of the SU was thus not the 'worst monetary constitution one can imagine', but a lack of resolve by the Union government to balance its budget.

IMPLICATIONS

The foregoing analysis showed that the existence of an ill-defined ruble zone cannot have been one of the major causes of inflation in Russia. This implies that, contrary to what was argued all throughout 1992 by the IMF and others (e.g. Sachs 1994b), the creation of true national currencies in all CIS countries was not a pre-condition for stabilisation in Russia and should thus not have been regarded as a pre-condition for granting the ruble stabilisation fund that was much discussed in 1992-93, but never disbursed.

Another implication of this analysis is that even in 1991, the Union government under Gorbachev could have stabilised the (Soviet) ruble if it had maintained strict control over the printing presses, which would have been possible if it had balanced the Union budget.

We now turn to the missed opportunity of 1992–93 namely, the failed attempt to create a multilateral clearing system to offset the bilateralism of the correspondent accounts.

5. An opportunity missed: the Interstate Bank

The system of bilateral correspondent accounts incited each participant to aim for a bilateral balance, since it was not possible to offset a surplus with one country against a deficit with another country. This section describes the damage done by the bilateralism and the attempt to overcome it through the creation of a multilateral payments mechanism incorporated in the Interstate Bank.

THE GAINS FROM MULTILATERALISM

How important was the absence of multilateral clearing in the CIS? This is a difficult question to answer because one has to compare two hypothetical situations: full multilateralism versus strict bilateral balancing as implicit in the correspondent account system.

It is not possible to say what level of trade would have taken place in 1992–93 if all payment relations had been on a multilateral basis. However, an indication of the orders of magnitude can be obtained from the data on inter-republican trade flows in the FSU.[23] For example, the correlation coefficient between the balances calculated on the 1987 data and the actual outcome during the first quarter of 1993 is 0.8, if one values the 1987 trade flows at world market prices.

One way to assess the impact of bilateralism is to assume that all CIS countries want to achieve a precise balance in all their bilateral relationships and that the supply of exports is given in the short run. Under this hypothesis the amount of trade is determined mechanically by the lower value of either exports or imports. A second approach, used in Kaplan and Schleiminger (1989) to assess the European Payment Union (EPU), just compares the sum of the absolute value of the bilateral balances to the sum of the overall, multilateral balances. Both approaches are pursued in Box 13.6.

Box 13.6 Quantifying the losses from bilateralism

a. The effects of strict bilateral balancing

If one imposes a strict bilateral balancing requirement, one also eliminates the structural deficit of the rest of the CIS *vis-à-vis* Russia. However, this deficit was anyway not sustainable. Its elimination should thus not be regarded as a consequence of bilateral balancing, but rather as an unavoidable adjustment process.

One way to eliminate the influence of the structural surplus of Russia is just to eliminate Russia from the trade matrix. If this is done, strict bilateral balancing implies that trade (among the 10 remaining CIS countries) goes down by about

continued

Box 13.6 *continued*

30 per cent. This is still about 4 per cent of the combined NMP of this group of 10 states. This result is interesting since it shows that the potential gain from a multilateral payments mechanism that does not involve Russia would still be substantial. But in this case the benefits for Russia are, by definition, equal to zero.

Another way to eliminate the influence of the Russian structural surplus is to assume that Russia has an overall balance with the other 10 countries and that this balance is achieved through a reduction in Russian exports that is the same in proportional terms for all surpluses. One can then compare the hypothetical strict bilateral balancing to this other hypothetical situation which requires only overall balancing (for Russia). This yields the result that strict bilateral balancing reduces trade by about 20 billion rubles, about 3.3 per cent of the overall NMP of the CIS. However, the gains are very unevenly distributed: for Russia the gain is only 1.5 per cent of NMP, for the other 10 CIS countries the gain is, on average, 6.5 per cent of NMP.

b. Overall imbalances versus bilateral imbalances

This approach just looks at the sum of the (absolute value of the) imbalances in trade. Under bilateralism the bilateral imbalances 'matter' while under multilateralism only the overall (or multilateral balance) 'matters'. 'Matters' in this context means that deficits have to be financed so that the imbalances determine the need for reserves. If one uses this approach, there is no longer a problem with the Russian surplus since one looks only at the difference between the two sums which does not imply anything for the overall Russian position. Using the same data source as above this yields the following result: the sum of the absolute value of the bilateral imbalances was 83.6 billion rubles while the sum of the multilateral imbalances was 65.9 billion rubles. The ratio of these two numbers is about 1.3 and the difference is equivalent to about 3 per cent of the combined NMP of the CIS. In this case one cannot distribute the gains between Russia and the rest of the CIS.

The two approaches pursued in Box 13.6 suggest that the Interstate Bank (IB) would have made it much easier to sustain a volume of trade that is worth 4 per cent of the NMP of the 'peripheral' CIS members and about 3 per cent on average for the entire CIS, including Russia, using the second approach. Russia would have gained much less in relative terms; about 1.5 per cent of GDP using the first approach. In relative terms this result is not surprising since Russia has a surplus with most CIS countries. Of course, these numbers just indicate an order of magnitude. In 1992–93 both the nominator (trade) and the denominator (NMP) had contracted strongly in real terms for other reasons. It is thus difficult to know what would have been the situation if an efficient multilateral clearing system had existed then.

Are these potential 'gains' large? Under ordinary circumstances a gain of several percentage points of GDP would be considered very large. For example, the gains expected from the internal market programme of the EC are of a similar order of magnitude. However, the CIS countries are not in ordinary circumstances. The transition process and policy errors have already caused output to drop by more than 20 per cent. The bilateral nature of the system that emerged in 1992–93 can thus not have been responsible for most of the output decline that actually occurred and the creation of a multilateral system would not be sufficient to reverse the decline. But eliminating one fourth or one fifth of the overall decline would be a substantial contribution.

Another way to measure the potential importance of a multilateral mechanism for the CIS, relative to the European experience, is to look at the experience of the EPU that was created after World War II in Europe. The EPU is the standard by which all plans to create a payments union for Eastern Europe have been measured (see Eichengreen 1993 and Gros 1993). Most analysis of the EPU emphasises one important difference which is that the EPU covered a large proportion of world trade as all European countries (plus their overseas dependencies) participated in the system. It is thus in a certain sense unfair to use the EPU as a yardstick. However, the result is still interesting. For the first year of its operations, 1950–51, the clearing under the EPU, that is, the difference between the sum of the bilateral and the multilateral imbalances, was equivalent to about 1 per cent of the GDP of EPU member countries at that time, much less than the potential for the CIS identified so far. The reduction in trade that would come with strict bilateral balancing (relative to unrestricted multilateral trade) would be about 20 per cent, the same as for the CIS.

The estimates of the gain from multilateralism presented here are based on past intra-FSU trade data. As shown above this trade will diminish sharply in the long run. The results based on 1987 data thus overstate the importance of intra-FSU trade in the long run and some adjustment towards the long run has already taken place by now. The real question is, however, whether this adjustment takes place gradually within an environment in which firms choose to shift their exports in response to market forces, or whether entire markets are suddenly cut off by the lack of a multilateral payment system. Even if one assumes that the shift away from the old trade patterns would anyway have led ‘naturally’ to a reduction of intra-FSU trade by 50 per cent (within one year!), the potential contribution of a multilateral clearing system would still have been significant. In terms of percent of GDP, this could have been even more important than the EPU.

Box 13.7 Intra-CIS trade and the causes of decline

What were the main factors behind the large decline in (recorded) output? It has often been argued that it is due first of all to the fall in military procurement and the overall investment rate. The one factor that should determine whether in a given sector output should decline is the rate of profitability at world prices.

Input–output data from Russia (on a sectorally disaggregated basis) were used to determine the sectoral impact of these factors. The dependent variable used was the index of output in 1992 as a fraction of the output of 1990 for 54 ‘branches’ for which a representative product was available. In other tests, somewhat different proxy variables for the output decline were used: for example, the

continued

Box 13.7 *continued*

ratio 1992/91, 1993/92, etc., for the same panel of industries/products. All the results were broadly similar.

The mean of the dependent variable was 0.747, which implies that the average output decline was about 25 per cent over this period (1990–92). The standard deviation was rather high, 0.125. This implies that one can just barely reject the hypothesis that the average was due to chance.

The values of the independent variables were calculated using the 1987 input–output (I-0) table of the Soviet Union. The variables tested in a first run were:

(1) The share of direct and indirect oil inputs in a unit of output of each branch.
(2) The share of output of each branch going directly or indirectly to military ends.
(3) The share of output of each branch going directly or indirectly to investment needs.
(4) The share of value added in gross output, both indicators calculated in world 1988 prices, for each branch.
(5) The share of imported inputs.
(6) The share of gross output going directly and indirectly to other republics.

The basic statistics (average and standard deviation across sectors) for these variables were the following (in 1991):

	(1)	(2)	(3)	(4)	(5)	(6)
Aver.	0.19	0.04	0.3	0.13	0.06	0.18
Std.dev.	0.22	0.05	0.29	0.63	0.15	0.12

With all the six variables used as explanatory factors, the results from an ordinary cross section regression were: adj. $R^2 = 0.209$ and the point estimates were:

Variable	Coefficient	Standard Error	t
Constant	0.760	0.120	
(1)	0.156	0.094	
(2)	0.665	0.371	
(3)	−0.037	0.063	
(4)	0.080	0.035	>2
(5)	0.018	0.118	
(6)	−0.395	0.154	>2

The constant, that is, the 'unexplained' average decline of output, is equal to 24 per cent (compared to the actual average decline of 25 per cent).

The overall explanatory power of the six variables used here is rather low as

continued

Box 13.7 *continued*

evidenced by the low R^2. This already implies that these six variables account for only about one fifth of the overall variability of the output decline across sectors.

The only significant coefficients are for variables (4) (share of value added at world prices) and (6) (inter-republican trade). Different tests with a subset of independent variables confirm this result.

Since the average starting level of variable (6) was 0.18, the coefficient of 3.6 implies that a drop of inter-republican trade of 50 per cent should lead to a fall in output of about 3 per cent ($0.18 \times 0.5 \times 0.36$). Inter-republican trade thus contributed significantly to the overall decline in output in Russia.

One might note that one of the strongest presuppositions of most economists is that the increase in profitability should be a major determinant of output. Again this does not emerge at all. If one regresses the output decline only on the increase in value added (comparing the value added at domestic prices to the value added at world market prices) one obtains an R^2 of 0.014 (and, of course, a coefficient with a t statistic below 1). Combining the increase in value added with the other two important variables that emerge from the results shown above does not change anything: the inter-republican trade is still significant with the same coefficient as shown above and the increase in value added has a t statistic below 1.

There is, however, some evidence based on recent data which suggests that the estimates based on 1987 data perhaps under-estimate the economic costs of the breakdown of intra-CIS trade. This evidence starts from an analysis of the causes of the output decline. There is still great controversy about this topic, but a simple analysis of the output decline across a number of Russian industries suggests that the decline in intra-FSU trade had a significant impact on the output decline. As shown above in Box 13.7, Duchêne and Gros (1994) regress the output decline in a number of products/sectors of the Russian economy against a number of sectoral indicators, such as the share of oil input, the share of output going to the military, the increase in profitability resulting from a switch to world market prices, to name just the most important. Most of these indicators are not significantly correlated with the decline in output in 1990–92. However, there is one indicator that shows a robust and significant relationship: the share of gross output going to other republics. The estimated coefficient is about 0.35 to 0.39. Since in 1990, 18 per cent on average of output went to the rest of the FSU, it implies that a reduction in intra-FSU trade of 50 per cent could explain a fall in output in Russia of about 3 per cent. The actual decline in intra-FSU trade was probably much larger, but this is impossible to document. While this is only a fraction of the overall drop in output in Russia, it is still a substantial cost that might have been avoided or mitigated. For the other FSU countries the cost must have been much higher since their economies depended much more on intra-FSU trade. Not all of this decline was due to bilateralism, but since the Interstate Bank described below would also have improved the intra-CIS payments system in general, it should have helped to avoid a considerable part of this decline in trade.

Box 13.8 The Interstate Bank

The bilateralism of the official correspondent account system was the background to the negotiations for the creation of a multilateral clearing system that was initiated by the Bishkek CIS summit of October 1992.

At the Minsk CIS summit of 22 January 1993, the heads of state and governments signed an agreement on the creation of the 'Interstate Bank' (IB). The main function of this bank was planned to be the management of a multilateral clearing and settlement system for the 10 (possibly 11) founding member states.

The multilateral clearing system foreseen by the Minsk Agreement would have used the (Russian) ruble as the unit of account. The actual clearing would have been done daily on the basis of the international payment orders transmitted to the IB by the central bank of the importing country. The IB would then have established (on the basis of a summary document sent by the participating central banks) each day the net deficit or surplus of each country *vis-à-vis* the entire system. On the basis of this daily balance (a flow), a 'cumulative position' was to be calculated as the sum of the past daily balances (plus interest on past cumulative positions).

An important aspect of the system was that there was a limit on the cumulative deficit, or debtor position, a country could accumulate. The limit for the cumulative (debtor) position was set equal to one month of export receipts (i.e. the imports from the country concerned that are declared to the IB by the other member countries). Settlement of the cumulative balances should have occurred every second week. Debtor countries could at first use their credit line (up to one month of export receipts) to settle. Once they had exhausted their credit line they had to find Russian rubles, or offer the creditor payment in hard currency.

The highest decision-making body of the Interstate Bank was to be a board with one representative from each founding member state. Decisions were to be taken with a 75 per cent majority with weighted voting. Russia had 50 per cent of all votes and the weights of the other CIS states were to be proportional to their intra-FSU trade in 1990.

THE INTERSTATE BANK

The treaty on the creation of the Interstate Bank was signed in January 1993. This institution was planned to run a multilateral payments system for the CIS (see Box 13.8 for details). It would thus have overcome the bilateralism of the correspondent accounts with the positive effects mentioned above.

However, the IB never started to operate.[24] What were the reasons for this failure to implement an agreement that promised sizable economic gain? There are two main reasons that should be kept in mind because they have implications for future efforts to arrange cooperation between CIS states.

The first symptomatic reason for the failure of the IB project was a typical collective action problem: no particular CIS state had an incentive to take the initiative (and possibly incur some political costs) to push for the creation of the IB because most of the benefits would anyway accrue to all the other states. The (narrowly defined) self-interest of Russia was anyway not served by the creation of a multilateral system because the power of Russia could be brought to bear much more effectively on a bilateral basis.

The second symptomatic reason for the failure of the IB project lies in the nature of the public service in Russia and elsewhere in the CIS. Lower and middle level officials do not always carry out decisions at the top, especially if these decisions run counter to their own interests. This lack of discipline, coupled with a pervasive corruption, was actually the main reason for the overall failure of stabilisation in Russia. The creation of the IB would have severely limited the discretionary power of some officials at the CBR to decide which transfers to other CIS states should go through. This is the main reason why the CBR in particular showed little interest in setting up the IB.

Finally there was, and still is, a deep-seated tendency in many CIS countries to wait for Russia to take the initiative. However, Russia never took the necessary steps to set up the Interstate Bank because the political motive was also not very strong since Russian leaders felt, correctly, that Russia did not need such an institution since it ran a surplus with all CIS countries. Finally, there was considerable opposition from some of the radical reformers[25] in the Russian government against any official payments mechanism. The basic reason for this opposition was that the IB would lead to more pressure on Russia to extend cheap credit. This was basically a political judgement since the charter of the IB explicitly excluded any further credit. The overall argument was that convertibility is the first best, and attainable immediately, so that there was no need to discuss anything else.

An additional reason why the IB was not created is that it has proven extremely difficult to create any type of public institution in Russia. Given that the gain for Russia would have been small, a weak opposition was sufficient to stop all the practical steps that were needed to set up the IB.

6. Conclusions

In some ways, the story of the dissolution of the FSU is one of missed opportunities. When the Soviet Union still existed, the adoption of strict macroeconomic policies at the Union level, combined with a substantial devolution of powers to the republics to foster competition in economic reforms, would have allowed the reforms to start much earlier and would have diminished the transitional costs.

The main reason why these opportunities were missed is that extreme and simplistic positions determined the debate about economic relations among the FSU states. On the one side, it was argued that the currency separation should have been faster because the ill-defined ruble zone that existed in 1992–93 was inflationary and that the collapse of intra-FSU trade was desirable because that trade had not been driven by the market. On the other, it was argued that because of the high degree of integration of the economies of the former Soviet republics, a common currency should be maintained to preserve the existing trade links.

These two extreme positions do not stand up to close analysis. While the level of inter-republican trade was clearly excessive it did have its own logic. It is therefore not surprising that the collapse of this trade contributed to the decline of production even in Russia. The problems of the disorganised ruble zone of 1992–93 came mainly from inconsistencies in Russia's policies. One cannot argue that expansionary policies in the other CIS states undermined Russia's attempt to stabilise when wage increases and rates of monetary expansion were lower outside Russia.

The economic analysis thus reveals that the separation was inevitable; attempts to maintain an economic and monetary union were doomed from the start. However, the speed with which the existing trade links were disrupted made the process of separation very costly for all the countries that were once Soviet republics.

Notes

1. Aitken (1973) uses annual data for a sample of seven EFTA and the five original EC countries (Belgium-Luxembourg counts as one for this purpose). His results do not vary from year to year; we compare ours with his 1967 results. H&P have two different samples with the data averaged over 1980–82. We use their results for a group of 21 countries for the comparison below. W&W have the largest sample, 76 countries, and also average their data (over 1984–86).
   These comparators used roughly the same explanatory variables; however, in some cases income and population were only used separately, not in the combination income and income per capita (i.e. income/population). We decided therefore to rearrange the coefficients to make them comparable. Whenever we did this we do not report the t-statistics as they are no longer applicable. The overall fit of the equation and the coefficient estimates of the other variables are obviously not affected by this procedure.
2. An anomaly appears in the coefficients of area, which should have a negative sign because they represent transport costs within the country. For the home country, *i*, our coefficient is consistent with this presupposition (and the findings of the comparators), but for the partner region, *j*, we find a significant positive sign. This is puzzling.
3. The most important explanatory variable is always income. For the elasticity of trade with respect to the income of the home country (country *i*) our coefficients are similar to those obtained for market economies.
   However, the coefficients regarding the influence of *per capita* output reveal some important differences: while we have a similar result to W&W (around 0.3), H&P find a value of 1 for the home country *i*. For the partner country *j*, the comparators find a significant coefficient, equal to 0.22 in H&P and W&W and 0.15 in Aitken, whereas we find a negative sign; but our coefficient is not significant.
4. The other two studies find a much higher elasticity: H&P find (1.56) and W&W find (0.75). However the difference between our results and the two recent estimates could be due to the fact that the latter include a number of maritime distances. This is not the case in inter-republican trade and in the sample of European countries used by Aitken most trade is also via land (or river).
5. It would have been interesting to estimate not only the elasticity but also the absolute impact of distance on trade; however, with the logarithmic formulation this is not possible. Estimates using the raw data (not their natural logarithms) did not work well, this is why it is preferable to stick to the logarithmic formulation despite this drawback. (See Gros and Dautrebande 1992b for details.)
   An anomaly appears in the estimated influence of area. The results suggest that trade decreases with the area of the home country *i*, but increases with the area of the partner country *j*.The same remark applies to the adjacency dummy where our estimates are lower

than in the comparators 1.15 in H&P, 0.78 in W&W and 0.89 in Aitken, but 0.59 in our estimation; however, the difference here is not very large in relative terms.

6. In 1987 the sum of the value added of inland transport services, maritime and direct transport services, auxiliary transport services plus communication services was 201.9 bn ecu, compared to a total value added (GDP) of 3,320 bn ECU. These same sectors employed 6,353 million workers out of a total European workforce of 106.5 million.
7. It is worth emphasizing that this approach deals only with the *geographical distribution of the volume* of trade. It has nothing to say about the product composition of trade, nor about bilateral (or even overall) balances.
8. The main difference between the predictions based on different sets of parameters comes in the distribution among the 'Western' countries, i.e. mainly the EC and the US (and to some extent Japan). This is a consequence of the large difference in the estimates for the impact of distance on trade which is three times stronger in H&P than in Aitken. This is why the share of the US in the exports of Russia is only 4.3 per cent if one uses the parameter estimates of H&P but 20.2 per cent if one uses the parameter estimates of Aitken. The parameter estimates of H&P put such a premium on distance that Japan, which is close to one part of Russia, is predicted to take a share of Russia's exports (34.8 per cent) that is eight times that of the US. However, these discrepancies concerning the role of the US and Japan in the foreign trade of the former republics do not change the fundamental results that the main OECD economies will be the decisive export markets for all former republics. Moreover, Wang and Winters (1992) and Havrylyshyn and Pritchett (1991) arrive at similar results for the trade of the entire Soviet Union.
9. Initially these so-called central banks consisted of little more than a president with a secretary. Even in Ukraine, the largest republic after Russia, the headquarters of the NBU numbered only a dozen employees in February 1992.
10. This dictum is commonly attributed to Stanley Fisher.
11. After the attempted August 1991 coup, a treaty on an economic and monetary union to be composed of 12 former republics was concluded and signed by some at Alma Ata. This treaty was never implemented and became irrelevant when the CIS was created in December 1991. The economist Gregory Yavlinsky who had been nominated Prime Minister of the Union after the failed putsch was then succeeded, as Prime Minister of Russia, by a proponent of the 'Russia first' approach,Yegor Gaidar.
12. Controls on the movements of bank accounts (i.e. non-cash in the Soviet terminology) are in principle not sufficient, since the other CIS countries could print substitute rubles (in the form of coupons, etc.); not that ruble banknotes could come back to Russia, but this effect had to be limited. Once all ruble notes had concentrated on Russia there could be no further inflationary effect for Russia from the printing of coupons and other ruble substitutes in other countries of the FSU. Since the cash that was held outside Russia at the beginning of 1992 accounted probably for more than 50 per cent of the total 'Soviet cash', substitute rubles could be responsible for, at most, a doubling of the cash component of the monetary base in Russia. Viewed against the almost tenfold increase of cash (in Russia) during 1992 this effect could never have been the main cause of inflation. Moreover, later events showed that Soviet rubles were held in considerable quantities outside Russia.
13. Or local substitutes, e.g. 'Manats' in Azerbaijan, both at a fixed rate of 10:1.
14. For many CIS countries the value of the oil imported from Russia would have been larger than their entire GDP if world market prices had been applied.
15. Representatives of the IMF have repeatedly denied that they put any pressure on the other CIS countries. They maintain that the IMF had only asked them to choose between a common central bank and a national currency. However, from the point of view of the Central Asian countries it was out of the question to introduce a national currency in 1992. This is

why the position of the IMF was perceived as being pressure to sign an agreement on a joint central bank.

16. The discussion here ignores certain peculiarities of the Estonian arrangement which imply that it does not really represent a full-fledged currency board.
17. The fact that in Estonia the rate is 8:1 (instead of 10, or 1:1) is irrelevant here. The analysis would also not be affected if the Estonians were to print 'Deutsch-Mark' instead of Kroons on their Estonian banknotes. The Central Bank of Belarus cannot print any Russian ruble banknotes, nor can the Central Bank of Estonia print any DM banknotes.
18. In case the German exporter does not insist on being paid immediately (or if a German bank is willing to provide an export credit) Germany exports capital. However, in this case the fact that the Estonian central bank issues credits in DM (as opposed to Kroons) is irrelevant. German economic agents will extend this credit anyway only if they expect that they will be repaid in the future. An inflationary impact in Germany could arise only if the Bundesbank provided an implicit bail-out guarantee for German banks that lend to foreigners in DM, so that the German monetary base increases automatically when there is a default by foreign borrowers. Of course, if German banks extended credits at highly negative real interest rates the German authorities would intervene and try to stop these gifts to foreigners. However, this is a different question which has nothing to do with the control of inflation in Germany.
19. The system of correspondent accounts also introduced a new problem since it worked on a bilateral basis.
20. Straight cash deals between enterprises are forbidden in Russia. But the cash could have been deposited into a Russian bank account first.
21. The picture is complicated by the fact that even inside Russia cash and non-cash could not be exchanged freely at 1:1 in 1992.
22. Usually this rationing did not use market prices. Only Belarus created an auction market for the right to have access to the Russian banking system; the rate initially fluctuated around 1.2 to 1.4 local units for one Russian ruble.
23. Gros (1993) shows that the only data available, which dates from 1987, is probably still a useful guide for 1992–93.
24. The reason for the initial delays was that the fate of the ISB was linked to that of the ruble zone. Although the clearing mechanism of the Interstate Bank had been designed carefully so that it could work as efficiently with separate national currencies as under a ruble zone, some people argued that as long as the reconstitution of a (possibly smaller) ruble zone remained on the agenda, the ISB should not be set up. This argument was no longer tenable after Russia had introduced its own separate banknotes in August 1993, and after the ruble zone was effectively removed from the political agenda because the offer to create a 'new type ruble zone' had been rejected by all countries (except Belarus and Tadzhikistan). The ISB could then be envisaged to solve part of the problems created by the disappearance of the ruble zone coupled with the limited convertibility of the new currencies and the lack of an efficient payments system.
25. And one of their Western advisors. Most of the middle-level opponents of the IB remained when the 'flagship' reformers abandoned all government duties in early 1994.

CHAPTER FOURTEEN

Russia 1992–93: pas de deux between destabilisation and reform

The economic system of Russia has undergone such rapid changes that it is impossible to obtain a precise and accurate account of it. . . . Almost everything one can say about the country is true and false at the same time.

J.M. Keynes (1925)

The dictum by Keynes applies again today. Developments in Russia have been the focus of attention in the West, because of the strategic importance and the military potential of this vast country, but the judgements on the effectiveness of the Russian reforms that come from international institutions, academics and the press range across the entire spectrum from very positive to extremely pessimistic. As of the end of 1994, the critics could point to official statistics that show a cumulative drop in recorded output and of the measured real wage of about 40 per cent (compared to the end of 1991) and a continuing large fiscal deficit. The optimists could emphasise that measured output in the state sector should fall to make room for the private sector, that the boom in the private sector does not show up in the official statistics and that the drop in measured real wages is only a statistical artifact. Moreover, they point to the fact that most of the industrial workforce has been privatised and that the ruble was stabilised until October 1994.

It is thus not easy to provide an overall judgement of the reforms in Russia as already anticipated by Keynes 70 years ago. Hence, this chapter does not pretend to provide a comprehensive overview of developments in Russia since the reforms were initiated in early 1992. Instead, it concentrates on the most salient features of the reform process in Russia, often comparing them to what happened in Central Europe in order to find some general features that can help in understanding how the Russian economy works in general and hence where it will be going in the future.

After describing the developments that led to the reform process in 1992, the chapter analyses the consequences of the 'big bang' price liberalisation that was introduced in January 1992. The main conclusion here is that the very large size of the jump, which was politically costly for the reformers, could have been anticipated. Moreover, the benefits of price liberalisation were not apparent as quickly as in other reforming economies because local and regional price controls persisted for some time and there was no immediate reaction from the supply side because of the desolate state of the agricultural sector.

The liberalisation of foreign trade, discussed in Section 3, was another area where it should have been possible to achieve liberalisation quickly. A closer look shows, however, that substantial distortions remained at least until the end of 1993. Their budgetary effects contributed, perhaps decisively, to the initial destabilisation that is discussed in Section 4.

The common thread that emerges from this analysis is the large discrepancy between appearances and reality. Official programmes also seem often to have little to do with the actions of the Russian government. Combined with the virtual absence of market institutions and enforcement mechanisms for private sector contracts, one can begin to see why the reform process has had only partial success so far.

Before presenting its conclusions, the chapter touches briefly on the unavoidable question of 'who lost Russia?'. If the real question is why stabilisation was not achieved in 1992–93 despite large official aid flows, the answer has two parts: Russia is to blame because given the massive subsidies to imports, most of the aid that was actually delivered, namely trade credits, actually had a negative impact. Thus more of that sort of aid would have made matters worse. However, even given the (wrong) policies pursued by Russia, the right sort of aid, namely direct subsidies to the budget, could have increased the chances of achieving stabilisation. It takes two to tango (meaning, in this case, to produce a failure): more aid for the reformers would have been desirable, but if the reformers had been smarter in using the aid that was available, they could have achieved stabilisation at a much earlier date.

This chapter concentrates only on developments in Russia. The complex problems arising from the dissolution of the economic space of the former Soviet Union (FSU) were discussed separately in Chapter 13.

The reader should be warned from the outset that any accurate analysis of the Russian economy is made extremely difficult by the absence of reliable statistical data. Prices (foreign exchange rates, commodity prices, etc.) can be measured without great difficulties and are regularly recorded in the Russian business press. But serious problems arise for variables that require calculations and adjustments or are based on data from many different sources. The problems are most severe when the official data are politically sensitive. Two good examples are estimates of national income and the budget deficit. The latter is officially given for 1992 at 3.5 per cent (of revised GDP), whereas unofficial estimates are four to six times higher and the very high inflation tax revenues (see below) suggest that it must certainly have been above 10 per cent, and possibly close to 20 per cent. Estimates of national income are always subject to some uncertainty. But Russia's exceeds internationally accepted norms. The original data for GDP in 1992 were revised upwards by 50 per cent (from 14 to 20 trillion rubles) during that year. At the end of 1993, the GDP estimate was then revised downwards to 18 trillion rubles. The first revision reduced the estimated fall in GDP for 1992 (relative to 1991), and the second revision (in late 1993) reduced the fall in GDP for 1993 (relative to 1992). Both revisions were politically expedient. In OECD countries revisions of 1 per cent are extremely rare.

1. Setting the stage

This section provides a brief description of the political developments that led to the late start of the reform process in 1992. The reader who is already familiar with this background is invited to skip ahead to Section 2.

The Russian state in its present form is young, since it emerged only in December of 1991 from the ruins of the Soviet Union. The beginning of the reforms in January 1992 thus coincided with the creation of a new state. The main reason reforms started so late was that Mikhail Gorbachev persisted in his belief that socialism was superior to capitalism. As long as Gorbachev was the head of the Soviet Union (as First Party Secretary of the CPSU and later as President of the Soviet Union), no real reforms were possible.

The movement towards reforms acquired momentum only when Boris Yeltsin, then only President of the RSFSR (Russian Soviet Federated Socialist Republic), acquired more effective power than the Union government under Gorbachev by standing up publicly to the attempted putsch in August of 1991. Immediately after the failed putsch, it still seemed that it would be possible to keep the Soviet Union together at least as an economic and monetary union. That would have implied that reforms would have to take place at the Union level. In the last three months of 1991, however, the Union government rapidly lost most of its influence and the republics became the only real power centres. Moreover, most republics were not willing to contemplate radical reforms, whereas the leadership of the Russian republic, which had inherited most of the reformist elements of the Union government, was determined to act as quickly as possible. Nevertheless, the Russian government did not really have the legal and political means to proceed on its own as long as the Soviet Union continued to exist. The creation of the Commonwealth of Independent States (CIS) and the dissolution of the Soviet Union in December of 1991 finally gave Russia the possibility to start real reforms.

When the Gaidar government came to power in Russia at the end of 1991, it proposed to implement a package of radical reform and stabilisation measures. The intention then was certainly to effect a 'big bang' in Russia, even if these words might not have been used. Two years later, the leading reformers (Deputy Prime Minister Yegor Gaidar and Finance Minister Boris Fyodorov) left government and explained to the Western press that Russia's problem was not that it had undergone shock therapy, but that, on the contrary, there had been no shock at all (and by implication, no therapy). What went wrong? The remainder of this chapter describes what actually happened in 1992-93. We leave it to the judgement of the reader whether or not one can label the events of 1992 a 'big bang'.

BACKGROUND: FAILED REFORM PLANS IN THE LAST YEARS OF THE SOVIET UNION

January 1992 certainly opened with a 'big bang' in the form of 300 per cent price rises in the first days of that month. This indicated that a very serious disequilibrium had been accumulated during the previous regime. In order to understand why it had come to that point, it is useful to consider briefly the last years of the Soviet period.

The 'big bang' that was supposed to take place in Russia in January of 1992 came after a long period during which a number of competing reform plans had been discussed, but nothing much had been done. Indeed, reform projects enjoyed a long tradition in the Soviet economy. The system of central planning never worked satisfactorily, even to the standards of its creators, and was therefore overhauled from time to time – since World War II, in 1957, 1965, and 1975. On top of that, the currency was changed in 1947 and 1961. None of these reforms, however, was supposed to change the nature of the system. Similarly, the various partial (and mini-) reforms attempted between 1985 and 1989 were also directed at increasing the efficiency of the existing system of central planning.

The partial and piecemeal reforms up to 1989 undermined the central planning system. This led to a deterioration of the economic situation because the plan could no longer be fully enforced and most of the non-state economic activities thrived on the distorted pricing system still in use. The 1987 law that gave enterprises a modest degree of financial autonomy can be viewed as the end of the strict planning period because enterprises could now evade constraints imposed from the 'centre' by initiating their own operations. This law loosened financial discipline and was thus the beginning of a considerable acceleration in the growth of the monetary overhang as documented in Section 2 below. But this law also increased the incentive to export to the West, which initiated a shift in the export structure of the FSU that predates the collapse of the CMEA. Section 3 below shows that the shift in exports towards Western markets was already well advanced by 1991, so that the (partial) trade liberalisation of 1992 did not have a strong effect on trade patterns.

The general weakening of central control led in 1989–90 to the widespread admission that the entire system of central planning had to be abandoned. During the summer of 1990, three competing comprehensive reform plans for the transition to a market economy were presented to the Supreme Soviet of the Union, which was to adopt the necessary legislation. The Supreme Soviet, however, refused to approve any of the three plans. Instead, it gave President Gorbachev broad emergency powers and authorised him to present a plan of his own. The compromise plan presented by the president, called 'Basic Guidelines for the Stabilisation of the National Economy and the Transition to a Market Economy', was then approved by a large majority on 19 October 1990.

The president's guidelines, which were more general and political than the other three plans, became the official programme of the Union government, but their implementation was checked by the constitutional crisis that developed between the Union and the republics.[1] The economic situation continued to deteriorate. Prices had to be increased and a clumsy attempt by the Ryshkov government in April of 1991 to confiscate large denomination notes was a complete failure. In May 1991, the Union government then again presented a vague outline of a reform plan, concentrating on macroeconomic stabilisation.

The four major plans that dominated the discussion in 1990–91 all agreed on three final goals: a market economy, stabilisation, and the preservation of the Soviet Union as a unified economic space. Furthermore, all of these plans contained most of the necessary elements outlined in Part II.[2]

None of these programmes could be implemented, however, as long as President Gorbachev did not really believe in a market economy. Moreover, even timid reform measures were impossible as long as there persisted the 'war of laws', under which each republic passed a declaration of sovereignty stating that its laws would take precedence over Union law, whereas the Union government insisted that Union law would take precedence. The implementation of reforms would have required an agreement (in effect, a new Union treaty) that defined the powers of the republics and the Union. Such an agreement was reached in May of 1991, but the aborted coup of

August of that year set in motion a chain of events that led to the dissolution of the Soviet Union.

Towards the end of 1991, it became clear that only the nascent Russian state would be able to implement reforms. The Russian President Yeltsin then created a government with a group of economists, led by Yegor Gaidar, that was charged with the elaboration and implementation of a comprehensive reform plan. Since this new team was installed only late in 1991, and since the political environment was changing quickly, it is not surprising that the plan was elaborated in detail only after its major element, namely price reform, had already been implemented. However, given that the deterioration of the economy accelerated with the overall breakdown of authority, the Russian government did not really have a choice.

2. Price liberalisation with a 'big bang'

The liberalisation of prices that occurred in early 1992 was thus unavoidable given the accelerating loss of control of the government, rather than a deliberate choice that could have been avoided. The most outstanding feature of price liberalisation in Russia is the size of the jump in the price level that occurred almost instantaneously. At the end of January 1992, the consumer price level was almost three times higher than at the end of December 1991 (an increase of 280 per cent). Industrial producer prices increased by 100 percentage points more. But even if one is only concerned with consumer prices, the Russian experience is extreme when compared to that of other reforming economies.

It is difficult to decide whether the entire impact of price reform should come within the first month or whether it takes longer for the monetary overhang to be eliminated. Table 14.1 shows what happened during the first month and the first quarter after price reform or price liberalisation. The table shows the percentage increase in both prices and money (cash in circulation) to segregate the impact of price reform from that of an expansionary monetary policy which might also have had an influence on prices. It is apparent that for the first month, the increase in money is so small compared to that of

TABLE 14.1 Price liberalisation

Country/ (month of price reform)	Present increase in the PPI after price reform during the first:	
	month	quarter
FSU (4/91)	52 (7.3)	71 (21.7)
Russia (1/92)	296 (13.6)	518 (42.9)
Poland (8/89)	40	N.A.
Poland (10/89)	55 (18.3)	124 (63.4)
Poland (1/90)	80 (12.4)	115 (91.5)
Czechoslovakia (1/91)	26	41
Bulgaria (1/91)	123	N.A.

Source: Koen and Phillips (1993) and IMF, *International Financial Statistics*, various issues
Note: The figures inside the parentheses represent the percentage increase in money over the same period, where money is defined as cash in circulation

the price level that one can neglect its impact. However, after one quarter, the potential influence of monetary policy, while still small in most cases, can no longer be neglected.

Table 14.1 presents data for three distinct periods in Poland, two of which were a combination of partial price liberalisation and administrative price increases under the last Communist government. These episodes represent a key to understanding what happened in Russia, as argued below.[3]

Table 14.1 shows clearly that Russia had by far the highest price jump among the group of four economies with rapid price liberalisation.[4] The second highest increase was about 120 per cent in Bulgaria. By contrast, in Poland it was 'only' 80 per cent during the first month of final price liberalisation in January of 1990, which is usually considered to be the Polish 'big bang'. If one considers the first quarter following price liberalisation, the difference is even larger: in Russia, prices increased by 518 per cent, almost five times more than in Poland where the increase during the first three months of 1990 was 115 per cent.

The extent of the price increase in Russia surprised most observers, although by the end of 1991, the ratio of free to controlled prices had reached multiples of five (Koen and Phillips 1993). For example, the IMF had calculated before the reforms took place that a jump in the price level of around 50 per cent would be sufficient to eliminate the monetary overhang (see IMF 1991 and Cottarelli and Blejer 1992). These calculations were based on an estimate of the difference between actual money holdings and the money demand one could expect once prices had been liberalised. Why was this estimate so far off the mark?

One explanation that has been put forward by Russian economists is that the government gave the wrong signal by increasing energy prices administratively between three and fivefold in January 1992. The authorities, of course, did not intend to signal with this move the likely size of the average increase in prices. Rather, they wished to achieve a more realistic *relative* price for energy. The argument that the Russian government gave the wrong signal implies that the actual increase in consumer prices that took place in January had really overshot the equilibrium and that prices should have decreased in the following months. However, this was not the case, as consumer prices increased by more than 30 per cent in February and March, and inflation continued at double digit rates until July 1992.

A closer examination of the historical data shows that the size of the jump in prices could have been expected to a large extent. However, most observers and advisors did not use this data[5] from the 1960s and 1970s and failed to analyse the Polish experience carefully enough.

The evidence for the thesis that a very large price increase had to be expected in Russia because a huge monetary overhang had been accumulated since the 1960s and 1970s is presented in Fig. 14.1 which shows the evolution of the velocity of money (measured by the ratio of cash to monthly income) in the FSU since 1961. It is apparent from this figure that there was a strong trend. 1961 is a convenient base year because at that date a sort of currency reform took place. Soviet citizens started off the period (in 1961) holding about 50 per cent of their monthly income in cash (not surprising given that they were paid twice a month). However, over time the Soviet government brought more cash into circulation than would have been justified by the increase in nominal income. By the early 1970s, cash holdings (relative to income)

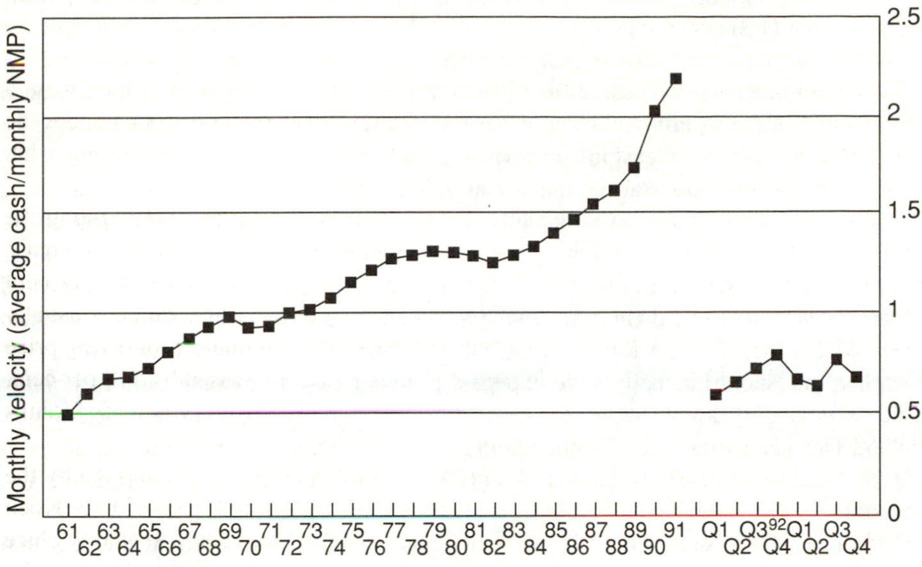

FIG 14.1 Long-term evolution of velocity in the FSU

had already doubled. Some of these additional cash holdings might have been voluntary since this period also saw an increase in real incomes[6] which is usually accompanied by an increase in the real demand for money. Between 1970 and 1985, cash holdings relative to income rose by over 50 per cent, this time against a background of rather slow growth. However, the steepest increases came later, after the start of *perestroika* in 1985, and with declining real incomes. From the perspective of 1991, one thus had to expect that the elimination of the monetary overhang would require more than a price increase of 50 per cent (which would have brought velocity to about the level of 1985). Indeed the actual adjustment brought velocity back to the value it had started from in the early 1960s.[7]

Any comparison over such a long period that involves two different regimes is, of course, always difficult. However, since the way cash was used and paid out to workers did not change much over time and since it was not affected by the reforms, it is possible to compare the two periods in this respect.

There are also some other reasons why the size of the price increase should have been anticipated. A careful look at the Polish experience would also have suggested the need for a very large price rise in Russia. The jump in prices on 1 January 1990 in Poland was much smaller, but it was not sufficiently appreciated that a large part of the monetary overhang had already been eliminated in Poland under the Communist regime during 1989. In Poland the total increase in prices over the five-month period that starts with the partial price liberalisation in August 1989, and ends just before the final price liberalisation in January of 1990, was 400 per cent, whereas the increase in the money supply during the same period was 123 per cent; the real money had thus already been halved. By contrast, the price increase of about 120 per cent in the FSU between April and December 1991, before the price liberalisation of 1992, did not really dent the monetary overhang since the money supply had increased by about the same amount (110 per cent).

The *Solidarnosc* government thus inherited a much better starting position than the Gaidar team in Russia because a large part of the monetary overhang had already been eliminated.[8] This explains why the price increase in January 1990 turned out to be 'moderate' in Poland, at least in comparison with Russia.

Moreover, if one looks at the numerical values of the velocity of money, one sees that the experience of Russia is actually not that different from Poland's. Indeed, in both countries velocity measured by the cash–monthly GDP ratio went to about 1/2 after price liberalisation. In the case of Russia a value of about 1/2 was to be expected because wages were paid (in cash) twice a month. The cash supply should thus turn over twice a month or 24 times a year. Given that in Poland many wages were paid monthly, one should actually have expected a higher cash to income ratio in Poland. Since one already knew before the price reforms started in Russia that velocity in Poland had gone to about 1/2, one should thus have expected, if anything, an even higher increase in prices in Russia, if only this simple element had been taken into account.

This brief discussion concerning velocity has not taken into account the fact that money demand depends on expected inflation. In Russia, inflation turned out to be very high in 1992 (on average about 20 per cent per month, excluding January), whereas in Poland it averaged less than 5 per cent per month in the 11 months after February 1990. One could therefore argue that the high velocity of circulation in Russia came about because the Russian population correctly anticipated this much higher inflation. This argument is not convincing, however, because it overlooks the fact that after January 1992, velocity was apparently not affected substantially by the large swings in inflation that took place in Russia in 1992–93.

The much larger than expected price increase in Russia deserved some careful analysis because it was not just an embarrassment for economists; it also constituted a severe setback for all the other reform measures that were planned for 1992. The extreme and sudden increase in prices gave a lot of ammunition to the conservative opponents of Yeltsin who came to dominate the Russian parliament which then effectively blocked many reforms until the crisis of September-October 1993.[9]

THE POLITICAL ECONOMY OF PRICE LIBERALISATION IN RUSSIA

Three years after the fact, it does not seem very interesting to look at the effect of price liberalisation, which was, in retrospect, unavoidable. However, the perceived impact of price liberalisation during the first months of the reform programme was very important in determining the political environment in which subsequent steps were to be taken. In Russia, the effects of price liberalisation created a political environment that was not favourable to strong additional reform measures.

Price liberalisation might have been more popular if it at least had the virtue of immediately ending all shortages. Here again, the experience of Russia is different from that of Poland. In Russia, the availability of goods increased greatly with price liberalisation, but not to the same extent as in Poland where the millions of individual farmers who were already engaged in producing food started almost immediately to sell their output directly to city dwellers. Since Russian agriculture had been much more thoroughly collectivised, no similar diffuse supply of food existed. This is one explanation why in Russia intermittent shortages of some staple commodities (e.g. sugar) continued throughout 1992. Another explanation is that as late as June 1992, over 40 Russian cities had municipal price controls for at least some food products (see Koen and Phillips 1993). Over time, the authorities realised that these price controls were unenforceable in the new environment, and most of the shortages disappeared in the course of 1993, but the full benefits of price liberalisation (and the liberalisation of commerce) were not immediately apparent in Russia.

The delayed effectiveness of price liberalisation on the availability of goods was thus a transitory problem, but in politics even half a year can be a very long time. A more serious and permanent issue was the perceived fall in living standards. Part of the popular discontent with the reformers was undoubtedly due to the fact that as consumer prices rose almost threefold in January of 1992, measured real wages were cut to about one-third of their end of 1991 level. The anti-reformist camp obviously seized this apparent fall in real wages as the best proof that the reforms were 'misguided' or 'hasty'. In other countries, notably Poland, similar arguments had also been used, but the size of the price increase in Russia meant that, given that wages did not rise along with prices in January of 1992, *measured* real wages also fell by much more in Russia than in other reforming economies.

On impact (i.e. comparing December 1991 to January 1992), measured real wages fell in Russia to about one-third of their previous level, more than in Poland where measured real wages fell to about one-half and in Czechoslovakia where they fell by only about 20 per cent. However, it is by now generally accepted that these reductions in real wages were mostly a statistical artifact since in the last years, sometimes months, of the socialist system workers obtained large increases in nominal wages for which they were not able to buy anything more since production was already declining. This had been particularly pronounced during the last days of the Soviet Union.

It is thus clear that one cannot compare wages deflated by the price level immediately before and after price reforms. A more appropriate comparison would use a base year in which shortages were minimal. Koen and Phillips (1993) argue that 1987 represents a good base year. If one thus compares real wages in 1992 to their level in 1987 the result is quite different. In Russia, real wages stabilised after an initial strong dip at about 20 per cent below the measured 1987 level. Most of the huge cuts in measured real wages that one finds by looking at the first months thus disappear if one uses a more appropriate base period.

The drop in real wages in Russia, using 1987 as the base period, was similar to the one that occurred in the Central European countries. However, this should be viewed as an anomaly because in principle one could have expected a stronger recovery of real wages in Russia than in other transforming countries because with the dissolution of COMECON, the price of energy deliveries to Central Europe went to the world market level and, with the dissolution of the Soviet Union, Russia no longer had to subsidise the other republics with cheap energy and raw materials. The latter did not happen immediately, but a process started in 1992 and by the end of 1993 most former Soviet republics were charged world market prices for energy deliveries (although most 'paid' only in arrears). Russia thus reaped a considerable terms of trade gain. By contrast, the Central European countries had to accept a terms of trade loss. Hence real wages should have been able to increase during 1992 and 1993 in Russia; however, if anything, there has been a moderate decline.

There is another difference between Russia and the other reforming countries which would suggest, at first sight at least, that real wages should have recovered more quickly in Russia. The Russian government did not really have an income policy whereas, in most reforming countries, the government recognised that they had to discourage state-owned enterprises from granting excessive wage increases. In Poland, for example, wage payments in excess of a certain ceiling were taxed by up to 400 per cent, in the sense that the enterprise had to pay over four times the net salary to the government (see Sachs 1993). In Russia, the only penalty for higher wage increases was that enterprises could not add the wage bill above four times the minimum wage to their costs for the computation of the profit tax. Given a profit tax rate of about 30 per cent, this was not a strong deterrent. After a while, as the minimum wage was not increased along with inflation, the average wage was higher than four times the minimum wage so that this tax had to be paid on more than half of the entire wage bill.

However, it would be wrong to link the evolution of real wages to the absence of an effective income policy. At the beginning of the reforms, there were no capitalists who could be squeezed. Real wages (after tax) therefore had to follow overall production. As wages increased, Russian enterprises were in the end compensated because the government subsidised them through cheap credit in 1992 and 1993. The result was much higher inflation, and thus households, including workers, had to pay for the subsidies that financed their wages through the inflation tax.[10] This illustrates a general principle: as long as the government still owns the industrial sector and thus provides directly or indirectly over 90 per cent of all employment, it can give with one hand (higher wages) and take away with the other hand (higher explicit taxes or a higher inflation tax).

PRICE LIBERALISATION . . . BUT WHAT ELSE?

Price reform is an indispensable element of any reform programme, and the liberalisation of prices in Russia had an enormous impact in the medium to long run. However, price reform, while necessary, is not enough on its own to create a stable market economy. In Russia, as in many other transition countries, price reform came early because it can be achieved by the stroke of a pen; but the other elements, which comprised the entire reform programme that was the basis for the Gaidar government in early 1992, were not implemented as planned. This applies in particular to the two tasks that require concrete and sustained action by the government, namely stabilisation and privatisation. It is exactly in these areas that the Russian reform programme failed to make much progress in 1992. This failure is not a reflection of a lack of good will on the part of the government forced to spend most of 1992 and 1993 in battle with the Central Bank of Russia and an increasingly hostile parliament. Rather, the root cause must be sought in the lack of an appropriate legal framework and supporting institutions.

The entire legal structure for a market economy did not exist in Russia. In Central Europe, large parts of the pre-war legal system had survived, at least on the books, and provided these countries with an acceptable starting point. In Russia nothing similar existed. From this point of view, one had thus to expect that it had to take more time to create the legal infrastructure of a market economy. Moreover, the conservative Supreme Soviet slowed down the efforts of the reformist government and President Yeltsin.

The incompleteness of the Russian reforms in 1992 can be illustrated through some concrete examples:

1. The development of a new private sector and the privatisation process were held up for some time by the continuing uncertainty about the question whether private land ownership was to be permitted.
2. The distinction between cash and non-cash money, clearly a relict of the Soviet period, was maintained until 1993. Until then firms could convert their bank accounts into cash only for certain approved purposes (chiefly to pay wages). *De facto* the distinction between cash and non-cash could not be maintained tightly since after a while specialised 'financial services' firms developed that offered to convert cash into non-cash and vice versa. This example shows how incomplete reforms favour the emergence of a semi-legal sector.
3. 'Soft budget constraints' continued *de facto* for large state-owned enterprises which in early 1992 initially simply stopped paying each other and were later bailed out by the Central Bank of Russia.
4. Privatisation had a very slow start in 1992. Whereas in Poland, small-scale privatisation (shops and artisans) had been privatised within half a year, in Russia it took one year to privatise less than 20 per cent of all small enterprises. Even at the end of 1993, less than one third of all small firms had been privatised.

   Large-scale privatisation got under way only in 1993. But once it had begun, it proceeded very quickly and was officially complete by July 1994. At this point it is not yet possible to say whether the transfer of ownership titles to managers and workers that was the essence of privatisation in Russia in 1993–94 will lead to large-scale restructuring and adjustment.

The incompleteness of the reforms (in 1992) illustrated can go some way towards explaining why 1992 cannot really be considered a 'big bang'. That there had been no shock therapy in Russia was actually one of the main criticisms of the departing finance minister Fjodorov in early 1994. However, at the time of his departure, most of the points noted above had been taken care of and this probably saved the reform movement (but not the political fortunes of its most visible exponents).

One could argue that it was simply not possible to create a working market infrastructure in Russia in 1992–93. However, the government made one mistake that could have been avoided, namely it failed to increase energy prices close to world market levels. Wholesale (e.g. for crude oil and gas) and retail (e.g. for electricity and petrol) prices of energy were only a fraction (between 20 and 50 per cent) of the world market level until well into 1993 (see below). As will be shown, one can argue that the failure to increase energy prices was the main reason why the foreign trade liberalisation had only limited effects and why stabilisation was delayed by two years. These two issues are discussed separately below, but before turning to them it is useful to provide a brief illustration of the importance of energy for the Russian economy.

Energy and raw materials (chiefly minerals) continue to provide two-thirds of

Russian exports. One could even argue that energy was *the* Russian economy in 1992. During 1992 the energy consumption in Russia (790 million tonnes oil equivalent) would have been worth (on world markets) about $80 billion[11] or almost exactly equal to the value of the entire Russian GDP of that year (if evaluated at market exchange rates and after the various adjustments mentioned above). This shows that in 1992 the economy was still so distorted that the rest of the Russian economy contributed very little to the international market value of Russian output. Even if one assumes that one-half of energy consumed was used up (directly or indirectly) in energy production, the rest of Russian industry did not produce a lot of value added. From this point of view, it is no surprise that stabilisation and the real appreciation of the ruble (which increased the market value of Russian GDP to $300 billion in 1994) came roughly in parallel with the gradual increase of real energy prices.

3. External liberalisation

LIBERALISATION OF INTERNATIONAL TRADE

Full external liberalisation can in principle be achieved by the stroke of a pen. However, this was not the case in Russia in 1992. In most evaluations of the Russian reforms, it is stressed that imports were almost completely liberalised, in the sense that in January 1992 quantitative restrictions were abolished and only in July a flat import tariff of 5 per cent was levied.[12] The problem with the policy on imports was not trade barriers, but in a sense the opposite, namely the huge budgetary subsidies given to state trading organisations that paid only a fraction of the world market price for their imports. During the first quarter of 1992, these subsidies accounted for 25 per cent of GDP (see Sachs 1994b: Table 2); over the entire year, they amounted still to over 10 per cent of GDP. As shown in Box 14.1 (see also Gros 1994a), the distortions caused by these subsidies led to welfare losses of possibly up to 10 per cent of GDP. Fortunately, import subsidies had already been reduced considerably during 1992 (to 15 per cent of GDP during the last quarter) and completely phased out in 1993 (Konovalov 1994).

Box 14.1 The welfare cost of import subsidies

The starting point is a conventional constant elasticity demand function for imports. Supply is not considered here because many imported goods do not really have close substitutes that are manufactured in Russia, and because it is difficult to make conjectures about the elasticity of supply of the raw materials that Russia exports. However, the omission of supply implies that the following calculations provide a *lower limit* for the welfare losses.

Demand is thus given by:

$$P = AQ^{-\beta} \qquad \beta > 0 \qquad [1]$$

continued

Box 14.1 *continued*

No specific assumption about β needs to be made at this point. Since consumption of imports fell substantially when the subsidies were reduced in 1993, the elasticity should be substantial.

The starting point for all welfare calculations is the consumer surplus (CS), which is given by:

$$CS = A \int Q^{-\beta}\, dq = A\, Q^{1-\beta}/(1-\beta) - QP \qquad [2]$$

The loss of welfare from a tariff is equal to the loss of consumer surplus (the difference between the consumer surplus under free trade and with the tariff) plus the tariff revenue. Denoting the quantity consumed under free trade by Q_{FT}, and the quantity consumed with the trade restriction (tariff or subsidy) by Q_T, and using the demand equation, the loss of consumer surplus can be written as:

$$\text{Loss of } CS \equiv CS_{FT} - CS_T = A\,[Q_{FT}^{1-\beta} - Q_T^{1-\beta}]\,/\,(1-\beta) - A\,[Q_{FT}^{1-\beta} - Q_T^{1-\beta}] \qquad [3]$$

$$= [\beta/(1-\beta)]\, A\, [Q_{FT}^{1-\beta} - Q_T^{1-\beta}]$$

The absolute values of the loss of consumer surplus are difficult to interpret unless they can be measured in an international unit or related to another measure of the Russian economy. For the following it will be easiest to measure the welfare loss as a ratio to national income, Y. The loss of consumer surplus can then be rewritten as:

$$\text{Loss of } CS/Y = [\beta/(1-\beta)]\, A\, Q_T^{1-\beta}\, [\,(Q_{FT}/Q_T)^{1-\beta} - 1]\,/\,Y \qquad [4]$$

The ratio Q_{FT}/Q_T has to be equal to $T^{1/\beta}$, where $T \equiv (1 + t)$ is one plus the *ad valorem* tariff rate of t. This term can thus be deduced from estimates of the implicit tariff.

The term $(A\, Q_T^{1-\beta}/Y)$ can be calculated from the information on the budgetary cost of the import subsidies or the potential export tax revenues. The cost of the import subsidies is given as 25 per cent of GDP. This implies $P_w\, Q_T(T-1) = 0.25\, Y$, where P_w is the world market price, which is here assumed to be given because Russia is a small economy in terms of trade flows (Russian exports and imports are about as large as those of Belgium). The domestic price is given by T times the world price ($P = P_w\, T$). Substituting in the demand curve (which implies: $A\, Q_T^{1-\beta} = P_w\, Q_T$) this leads to:

$$(A\, Q_T^{1-\beta}/Y) = 0.25\,[T/(T-1)] = 0.25\,(1+t)/t \qquad [5]$$

The welfare loss (as a proportion of national income) can then be written as:

$$\text{Welfare loss}/Y = 0.25\,\lfloor\, [\beta/(1-\beta)]\,[T/(T-1)]\,[T^{(1-\beta)/\beta} - 1] - 1] \qquad [6]$$

To obtain numbers one needs to have an estimate of T and of β.

For the case of the import subsidies T below 0.5 (corresponding to an import subsidy of over 100 per cent) should be appropriate since the value of imports (at

continued

Box 14.1 *continued*

world market prices) was more than 50 per cent of GDP in early 1992 (and the cost was about 25 per cent of GDP). Using $T = 0.5$ the terms in the square brackets on the RHS of [6] collapse to: $-[\beta/(1-\beta)]\ [2^{-(1-\beta)/\beta} - 1] + 1$. Table A below shows the value of this expression for selected values of β and the welfare loss as a proportion of GDP under the assumption that the budgetary cost of the subsidies was indeed 25 per cent of GDP:

TABLE A

β	$\beta/(1-\beta)[2^{-(1-\beta)/\beta} - 1] + 1$	Welfare cost as % of GDP
2	0.2	4.3
1.00001	0.3	7.7
0.5	0.5	12.5

These three values could be interpreted as the low elasticity case ($\beta = 2$ implies an elasticity of demand equal to one half), a medium elasticity ($\beta = 1$) and a high elasticity ($\beta = 0.5$ implies an elasticity of demand equal to two).

An interesting special case is $\beta = 0.5$ because in this case the RHS of [6] collapses to $0.25 \times (T-1)$. In this case the welfare loss is linear in T; which is in apparent contradiction to the usual convexity of the welfare loss. However, this result is due to the fact that the tariff revenue has been held constant. Equation [6] just says that (for $\beta = 0.5$) the welfare loss is linear in the tax rate that yields 25 per cent of GDP.

However, even more serious problems arose on the export side as the initially very liberal stance on imports contrasted starkly with the regime that was retained for exports of raw materials and energy which had to be controlled because domestic prices of these goods had not been liberalised. The government evidently feared that most of the large industrial enterprises would go bankrupt if they had to pay world market prices for energy and other raw material inputs. The reasons for this decision are not important for this section. What matters is that these products accounted for about 75 per cent of all Russian exports because this raises the question of whether one can still speak of trade liberalisation if most exports are subject to restrictions.

There is a basic, but not widely appreciated, theorem from international economics, the 'Lerner symmetry theorem' (Lerner 1936). This theorem states simply that an export tariff is equivalent to an import tariff. This equivalence of export and import taxes can easily be understood if one regards foreign trade as using exports to pay for imports. In the case of a domestic sales tax, it does not matter whether the tax is paid by the seller or the buyer; similarly in international trade it does not matter whether it is the Russian importer or the Russian exporter who pays the tax. The claim of the Russian government that it had the most liberal trade regime in the world was thus somewhat disingenuous.

The maintenance of restrictions on the exports side was necessitated by the price controls on energy (and other raw materials) that continued in 1992 and 1993. Although the official prices of oil, gas and electricity were increased from time to time, their dollar equivalent did not always come closer to the world market price. The ratio of domestic price to world price was thus highly variable for these goods, but the domestic price was typically only a fraction of the world market price as shown in Table 14.2, which gives the prices quoted on Russian commodity exchanges (not the official fixed prices, which were sometimes even lower) as a percentage of world prices.[13]

Since all these goods are homogeneous and easily traded internationally with low transport costs, one would expect the domestic Russian price to be close to the world market price. A value below 100 per cent indicates that export restrictions have created a wedge between the domestic and the world price. The nature of the export restrictions officially in place varied over time and was different for the commodities in Table 14.2. In some instances there were explicit export taxes and/or export quotas that could account for the price differentials; in other cases this is not possible. Instead of going through the official records of export regulations, one can simply use the proportional price differential as a crude approximation of the (*ad valorem*) export tariff that would have been equivalent to the export restrictions that were actually applied. This approximation is not exact since it neglects transport costs and exchange-rate fluctuations that make it difficult to determine the exact world price to compare to the price quoted on the Russian commodity exchanges. However, the orders of magnitude that this exercise yields are revealing.

As an aside it is interesting to note the variability of the implicit export tariff over time that is apparent from a comparison across columns. For example, the implicit tariff for petrol fuel ranged from almost 300 per cent in May 1993 ($0.26 \cong 1/(1+3)$) to about 75 per cent in September of the same year ($0.58 \cong 1/(1+0.75)$). The somewhat random dates in this table were dictated by the availability of the data.

More important than the variability over time is the global average. Given the spotty data available, it does not make sense to compute formally the mean of the ratio of domestic to world price. But it is clear it must have been below 50 per cent since most values for oil-related products are below 50 per cent. The implicit export tax on energy-related products must thus have exceeded 100 per cent most of the time. Since energy alone accounted for 50 per cent of overall exports and since for other raw materials (like aluminium, which accounted for another 25 per cent of exports) a

TABLE 14.2 Domestic prices as percentage of world prices for some raw materials

	Dec. 1992	May 1993	Sept. 1993
Crude oil	28	21	28
Heating oil	36	23	50
Diesel	34	28	55
Petrol	40	26	58
Aluminum	45	47	65

Source: *Russian Economic Trends*, 1993, **2** (3), Table 22

similar differential between domestic and world market prices existed, about 75 per cent of all exports were thus implicitly taxed at this rate. In view of the equivalence between export and import tariffs mentioned above, one can only conclude that the liberalisation of Russian trade in 1992 was partial, at best.[14]

FISCAL CONSEQUENCES OF POROUS BORDERS

It proved impossible for the Russian government to enforce the official restrictions on raw material exports. The main reason was that initially Russia did not have a customs service along its borders with other former Soviet republics. The huge difference between the domestic Russian and the world market price for oil and other raw materials meant that large gains could be made by transporting these commodities to other former republics and then re-exporting them for hard currency. On top of that one has to add the notorious corruption of the Russian civil service which was exposed to extraordinary temptations. The price difference on a simple shipment of 20 thousand litres of fuel on a single truck would be worth $2,000, several times the annual salary of a Russian customs official.

Given the illegal nature of this activity, it is hard to document in detail, but its scale can actually be documented on the basis of official statistics. Western import statistics, which are quite reliable, can be used to give an idea of the scale of the problem. EU import statistics show, for example, that raw materials and energy constituted about 70 per cent of all goods shipped from the three Baltic states and the Ukraine, although these countries do not produce significant amounts of these commodities. In 1992 the EU imported about four billion ecu of fuel products from Russia and about one billion from the Baltics and Ukraine.

These re-exports were always a highly contentious issue between Russia and the other former republics. However, it is not clear who really benefited from this 'contraband'. The intermediary agents, who bought at a low price in Russia and then sold at the world market price, might have been Russians, but were also well connected Ukrainians or Baltic citizens.

It is thus not clear whether or not the Russian economy really did lose from re-exports. It is clear, however, that the Russian government did lose an important source of revenue because of its inability to collect a significant part of the difference between the domestic price and the international price in the form of export taxes, royalties, and so on.

How much in potential government revenue was lost? This is difficult to estimate precisely since the official tariffs changed over time. However, a crude calculation can indicate the order of magnitude: in 1992 Russia exported about $20 billion worth of energy products and other raw materials. Given that the implicit export tariff was about 100 per cent, as shown above, the Russian government should have been able to collect at least $10 billion (50 per cent of export sales at world market prices) in tariff revenues from these exports. At the average 1992 exchange rate of about 250 rubles to the dollar, the loss of revenue was thus equivalent to 2.5 trillion rubles. This should be compared to total government revenues of about 5.3 trillion rubles and an official deficit of 650 billion rubles (3.3 per cent of revised GDP). The official 1992 budget deficit could thus have been easily covered from this source alone which would have increased government revenues by 50 per cent. This is, of course a very crude calculation. But it serves to indicate the order of magnitude of the problem.

Who obtained the revenues the government lost? This is also impossible to determine precisely; most went presumably to producers and agents in energy trade. A significant part was also given away directly as the government granted many exemptions to particular regions or producers.

EXPORT PERFORMANCE

'The proof of the pudding is in the eating.' The proof of a substantial liberalisation of foreign trade is the actual behaviour of exports and imports. The latter were sustained by massive subsidies in 1992 and then fell considerably in 1993–94. What about exports? All of the Central European countries increased their exports to the West by between 30 and 40 per cent in the two years following the start of serious reforms. This export boom was helped by a substantial nominal devaluation and the opening of major export markets, such as the EU. Privatisation cannot have been the main reason since most of the exports came from enterprises that were at the time still state-owned. This shows that even the managers of SOEs were not blind to the profit opportunities that arose when wages were only about $100 per month, as initially in Poland.[15]

The experience of Russia seems to have been different again. Unfortunately, however, it is very difficult to document Russian trade performance over the last years.[16] Konovalov (1994) reports that official Russian statistics actually show a collapse of exports from $80 billion in 1990 to about $40 billion in 1992. However, these numbers cannot be accepted because the most reliable source that exists, namely Western import statistics, shows totally different figures. Using this source (which has its own problems), one can at least compare the Russian experience to that of Poland on a consistent basis. This is done in Table 14.3.

TABLE 14.3 Russian and Polish exports

		Year before reform	Year of reform*	Year following reform
Russia (FSU)	Wage ($/month)	$42	$27	$62
	Exports (billions of $)			
	Total	44.5	42.4	43.0
	To OECD	28.8	28.6	21.7
	Manufactures to OECD	7.6	7.7	5.8
Poland	Wage ($/month)	$155	$108	$167
	Exports (billions of $)			
	Total	13.5	16.2	14.3
	To OECD	5.7	8.3	9.2
	Manufactures to OECD	3.2	4.9	5.9

Sources: For trade statistics: OECD, Short-term economic indicators transition economies, 2/1994 and Short-term economic statistics Commonwealth of Independent States, International Monetary Fund, Directions of Trade, various issues. The DOT data for Russia refers to the entire FSU, but Russia should account for over three-quarters of the total. For wages: OECD, Short-term economic indicators, 1/1993 and 2/1994, IFS, RET

* Year of reform for Poland is 1990, and 1992 for Russia

Although the devaluation of the ruble was even stronger than that of the zloty (and other Central European currencies), and although the average wage expressed in US dollars was even lower in Russia (below $30 per month during 1992, compared to over $100 in Poland), Russian exports to the West did not increase significantly in 1992 whereas Polish exports to the West increased by over 50 per cent. Since most of the Soviet Union's (and Russia's) exports are raw materials whose supply does not react strongly to wages and the real exchange rate, one should perhaps look at exports of manufacturing goods only. However, exports of manufactured goods from Russia also declined in 1992 and by even more than exports of raw materials. Between 1990 and 1992, exports (from the entire FSU) of machinery and equipment fell from $19.5 billion to $6.6 billion.

If one takes Russian sources, the picture would be much worse in the sense that external trade seemed to be falling sharply in 1992. Most of this reported decline, however, is probably due to an over-valuation of trade under the Soviet regime and an under-reporting of trade in 1992 due to the embryonic stage of the Russian customs service. Nevertheless, even using Western statistics that give a much rosier picture of Russian trade, one sees that trade did not expand as much as one would have expected. Moreover, the share of barter and counter-trade actually increased in 1992 to about 40 per cent for exports (and 26 per cent for imports, see Konovalov 1994), which is hardly an indication that foreign trade became more market-based.

Finally, it is often argued that a major achievement of the apparent liberalisation of foreign trade in 1992 was a redirection of trade away from the 'bad' trade with the socialist economies and LDCs that did not pay for their imports of Soviet weaponry, towards 'good' trade with Western economies based on market principles. However, if one takes a slightly longer look at the evolution of Soviet foreign trade, it turns out that this redirection of trade had already started much earlier. Figure 14.2 shows the evolution of the share of CMEA and of market economies in FSU exports. It is apparent that from 1986 (when the law on the partial financial liberalisation of enterprises mentioned above began to take effect) until 1991, the share of CMEA fell by one-half, from about 40 to 20 per cent of overall exports. During the same period, the share of market economies approximately doubled, from about 30 to 60 per cent. By 1991, the adjustment was thus complete. In a sense this should not be surprising since the CMEA had ceased to exist by then; however, it is interesting to note that in 1992 the share of CMEA countries increased slightly and that of the Western market economies fell somewhat. This is another indication that the year 1992 did not bring a radical liberalisation of foreign trade.

THE FOREIGN EXCHANGE MARKET

More progress was made on the issue of convertibility, which can also be achieved by the stroke of a pen (as long as the exchange rate is not fixed), since all that the government has to do is to allow anyone to buy or sell foreign currency without restrictions. Full current account convertibility was not permitted immediately, but in July of 1992, the various exchange rates were unified and anyone with an import contract could then participate in the increasingly frequent auctions for foreign exchange. This implied that from July 1992 onwards, the ruble was convertible for current account transactions. Given the laxity of controls, one could even argue that *de facto* convertibility

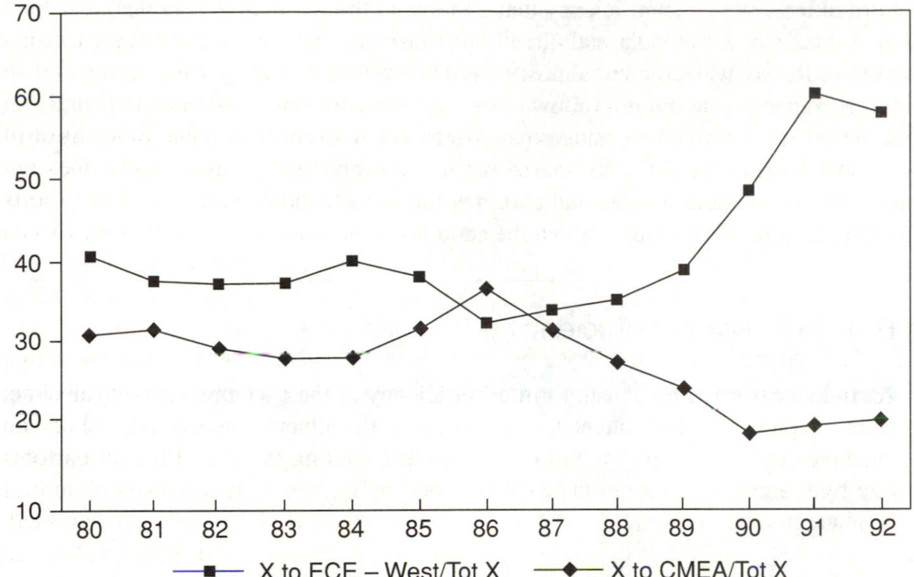

FIG 14.2 FSU's redirection of exports
Source: Own calculations based on ESE, 1993, Economic Survey for Europe in 1992–93 and IMF, DOT Yearbook 1993

also extended to capital account transactions. A large degree of capital account convertibility was officially permitted when, in the summer of 1993, non-residents were allowed to open ruble accounts which they could also use for investment purposes.

In order to make convertibility operative, a foreign exchange market must exist in which enterprises can buy and sell foreign exchange. Such a market can in principle be created quite quickly. Somebody, for example, the central bank, just regularly convenes potential buyers and sellers of foreign exchange and organises an auction mechanism to find a price at which supply and demand meet. This has been done on a regular basis in Moscow since January 1992; at first, twice a week and later, daily. A market for foreign exchange thus existed from the start of the reforms.[17] Since this currency trading was legal, there was no significant parallel 'black market'.

How did this market perform? It has often been observed that the volume of transactions that went through the official auctions was rather small when compared to recorded foreign trade. For example, in 1992, the total turnover on the Moscow Interbank Currency Exchange was about $3 billion, while in 1993 it rose to $12.1 billion (Koen and Meyermans 1994), which was, nevertheless, still much less than Russia's exports of about $40 billion. It has therefore often been argued that this market was not representative, nor 'efficient'.

Market efficiency has a precise meaning. In its so-called 'weak' forms it means that information on past prices cannot be used to make more by predicting future prices. This proposition can be tested through some basic econometric methods as explained in Box 14.2. If one applies this simple approach by just testing whether exchange rate changes are correlated on time one finds that past exchange rate changes do not contain information about future exchange rate changes.

Formal tests of market efficiency that go beyond the illustrative approach explained in Box 14.2 (see De Nicola and Gros 1994) also indicate that the foreign exchange market in Russia was efficient almost from the start. Efficiency means in this context that the exchange rate did not follow any predictable pattern in general. This indicates that the price for foreign exchange that is set by a small market must not necessarily be wrong. Moreover, preliminary tests that relate exchange rate movements to central bank intervention data suggest that currency traders would not even have been able to profit from insider information about the central banks' actions.

Box 14.2 Market efficiency

A crude measure of the (weak form of) efficiency of the exchange market (or any asset market) can be obtained by regressing the change in the (log of the) exchange rate on a constant and its own past. Denoting the log of the exchange rate by s_t and the change in the exchange rate by $ds_t = s_t - s_{t-1}$, the equation to estimate is thus:

$$ds_t = \text{constant} + ß\, ds_{t-1} + \text{disturbance} \qquad [1]$$

The constant measures the expected rate of depreciation. The coefficient on the lagged change in the exchange rate measures to what extent information on past prices can be used to make profits. Weak form efficiency implies thus only that the coefficient, ß, should not be significant and that there should be no autocorrelation in the error terms. If these conditions are not satisfied, any trader could use information on past prices to predict future exchange rates. For example, if there were a negative autocorrelation in the errors in the sense that an unexpectedly large depreciation was, on average, followed by an appreciation (a 'correction' in market jargon), any trader with access to the foreign exchange market could make profits by buying rubles whenever a large depreciation occurred and selling these rubles when the correction arrived.

The sign and significance level of the constant has no particular implications for market efficiency; it just shows to what extent the ruble depreciates on average per week. In the absence of capital controls, however, the intercept should reflect the difference between domestic and international interest rates. The magnitude of the constant can thus be used to see whether there are capital controls.

De Nicola and Gros (1994) find that the estimate of the constant varies considerably over time from close to zero to about 0.06 in mid-1992 and back to 0.04 in 1993. The estimates of ß are never significantly different from zero after early 1992. This implies that after April 1992 one cannot reject the hypothesis that the Russian foreign exchange market was efficient.

Formal tests of the ruble/$ market also show that the expected rate of depreciation of the ruble varied greatly over time. During the first months of 1992, the market seems to have believed in the initial announcements of the Gaidar government to stabilise the ruble. However, this honeymoon did not last long and by mid- to late-1992, the expected rate of depreciation was apparently as high as 6 to 7 per cent per week. Such a rate of depreciation would multiply the exchange rate by a factor of 18 (a depreciation of 1,700 per cent) in the course of one year. In early 1993, this slowed to 4 per cent per week (an annual rate of depreciation of about 800 per cent).

Since interest rates on the inter-bank market in Russia during these two years were always below 200 per cent, this suggests that there must have been capital controls in the sense that banks could not just obtain a loan in rubles and use the proceeds to invest in dollars. Capital movements of this kind were not allowed formally since access to the non-cash inter-bank dollar auctions was, until summer 1993, limited to enterprises with 'legitimate' business, that is, official trade transactions. There were no such restrictions, however, on the cash market.

The events of October 1994 also revealed, however, how official intervention can affect the performance of the foreign exchange market. During the preceding months one department of the Central Bank of Russia had been intervening with increasing amounts to keep the ruble stable at around 2,000 per US dollar. At the same time another department of the same institution was handing out increasingly large credits to some sectors of the Russian economy (agriculture, the cities in the northern regions) without fully informing anybody about this. The Ministry of Finance was also supporting the attempt to stabilise the ruble because it had not been informed about the increase in credit emission.

During the summer the people at the CBR responsible for stabilising the ruble through interventions at daily foreign exchange auctions noticed that they could no longer keep the ruble stable because their losses of foreign exchange were increasing. Hence, starting in early October, they let the ruble slip a bit every day. After it had depreciated by a cumulative 40 per cent despite continuing massive sales of dollars they decided to stop their interventions totally for some time in order to 'teach the market (and their political adversaries) a lesson'. This was done on 11/12 October and had the result that the ruble depreciated by almost 30 per cent in one day. This led to a political crisis and the almost immediate return to strong interventions at the foreign currency auctions. The (acting) minister of finance and the head of the Central Bank were asked to leave although the ruble returned to the previous level after only two days.

The ruble crisis of October 1994 consisted thus mainly of two foreign currency auctions during which the ruble was quoted at a 30 per cent lower rate than before or after. Few deals were actually concluded at this rate since the turnover was modest. All in all the 1994 ruble crisis was thus more a political than an economic one.

4. Macroeconomic destabilisation

As documented above, the reforms in Russia began with an increase in the price level of 250 per cent at the beginning of 1992. This was not the end of the story, however. Prices continued to increase at two-digit levels and the monthly average for the year excluding January was close to 20 per cent; the average for 1993 was at a similar level. Only in early 1994 did average inflation fall below the one-digit level (always on a monthly basis). What was the cause of this destabilisation?

The immediate cause of high inflation is almost everywhere the same: a large public-sector deficit that is monetised. Russia is no exception to this rule, but the way in which the deficit arose was somewhat different in the sense that the official fiscal deficit always remained moderate.

An important particularity of Russia was that the two entities that constitute the public sector, namely the government and the central bank, did not follow the same policies. The Russian government was in principle committed to stabilisation whereas the Central Bank of Russia tended to defend the interests of large state-owned enterprises and did not care about inflation, which, in the official view of the CBR, was caused by forces other than excessive rates of monetary expansion. The government was not able to control the CBR because the latter had been subordinated to parliament.

THE BUDGET

The concern of the government with inflation explains why destabilisation in Russia did not start directly with a (reported) large fiscal deficit. During the first months of 1992, the government was actually able to keep a rough balance, if one accepts the official accounts, mainly because the profits of state-owned enterprises increased tremendously after price liberalisation. This was to some extent to be expected since the Polish government had experienced a similar windfall gain during the first year of reforms. Even over a two-year period, the fiscal deficit does not seem to be huge as shown in Table 14.4. The officially reported deficit was only 4.8 per cent of GDP in 1992 and even the IMF arrives at a deficit of only 7 per cent of GDP on a cash basis (9 per cent on a commitment basis, see Sachs 1994b: Table 2). The revenues of the central government in Russia (37 per cent of GDP) were actually much higher than those of the Polish government which collected only 32.5 per cent of GDP during the first year after the reforms (Sachs 1994b: 66). The big difference that might explain the much lower inflation rate of Poland (about 4 per cent per month after price liberalisation) is that the Polish budget was officially balanced in 1990. However, the 1991 Polish deficit (4 per cent of GDP) is again equal to the official Russian figure, but inflation stayed at 4 per cent per month in Poland.

In 1992, the Russian government also spent an estimated 15 per cent of GDP on import subsidies that are not contained in the official budget. However, since these subsidies were used only for imports of goods that were paid for with Western export credits, they did not have any direct budgetary implications (the Russian import agency just received the goods for free, or at a low price and the Russian government did not have to pay anything in 1992). It would thus be easy to arrive at a deficit of 19.7 or 22 per cent of GDP, but the 15 per cent of GDP was directly financed from abroad and should thus not have contributed to the destabilisation of the Russian economy.

TABLE 14.4 The official Russian budget

As% of GDP	1992	1993
Revenue	37.8	31.5
Expenditure	42.5	36.5
Balance	−4.7 (−7.0)*	−4.0

Source: Ministry of the Economy, Republic of Russia
* IMF estimate cited in Sachs (1994b)

These deficits are not large by any standard, and it is therefore at first sight difficult to explain why inflation stayed so high in Russia.

In a certain sense it is surprising that the Russian government was able to obtain more than 30 per cent of GDP in revenues despite the high inflation rates. In many Latin American countries, high inflation rates have eroded the real value of government tax receipts because taxes are typically paid with some time lag. With inflation at about 20 per cent per month, a payment lag of one quarter would be sufficient to cut the real value of tax payments by half. However, this so-called 'Tanzi effect' did not operate in Russia because Russian enterprises had to pay their taxes (profits and VAT) in advance on the basis of expected revenues.

One is thus tempted to argue that the behaviour of inflation in early 1992 cannot be explained by a fiscal deficit since, during the first quarter, the government ran a small surplus. Moreover, credit expansion during the first half of 1992 was also moderate. During this period there was thus reason to belief that the Russian government would be able to achieve some degree of macroeconomic stabilisation. Even during this initial honeymoon, however, prices continued to increase by more than 20 per cent per month.

SOFT BUDGET CONSTRAINTS FOR ENTERPRISES?

It has often been argued that the main reason why prices could continue to increase although monetary expansion was moderate was that in early 1992 enterprises stopped paying each other and therefore needed less money and credit to finance a higher level of transactions in nominal terms. The basic argument is that enterprises were effectively creating their own money by running up massive amounts of so-called inter-enterprise arrears. However, a closer look at the situation reveals again that perception and reality do not match.

The perception in 1992–93 was that there was a serious crisis. It was widely reported in the financial press that by early summer (June-July) of 1992, the stock of these inter-enterprise arrears in Russia was close to the GDP of the first half of the year. This observation created the impression that the arrears, also called 'inter-enterprise debt' or IED, 'attained truly epic proportions' in the FSU (Rostowski 1993).

The reality, however, was somewhat different if one looks more carefully at the data. In analysing this phenomenon, one has to distinguish carefully between stocks and flows.[18] It is useful to start with an analysis of the stocks: did the stock of arrears ever reach dangerous proportions in Russia? Since it is not possible to say *a priori* what level of IED is dangerous one can answer this question only by reference to a case where IED, at least *ex post facto*, did not turn out to be a problem. Poland and the former CSFR are good examples in this respect.

Figure 14.3 therefore shows on a quarterly basis how many months of industrial production inter-enterprise arrears were worth in Russia, Poland and the former CSFR. For Russia, the series starts at the end of 1991 (equals TO, i.e. the start of reforms) when IED was worth about one month of industrial production. It then increased rapidly to a value of three in June of 1992, after which it declined continuously until it had gone back to a value of one in mid-1993. Did June 1992 represent a crisis? Fig. 14.3 also shows that in Poland IED was much more stable; it hovered between one and

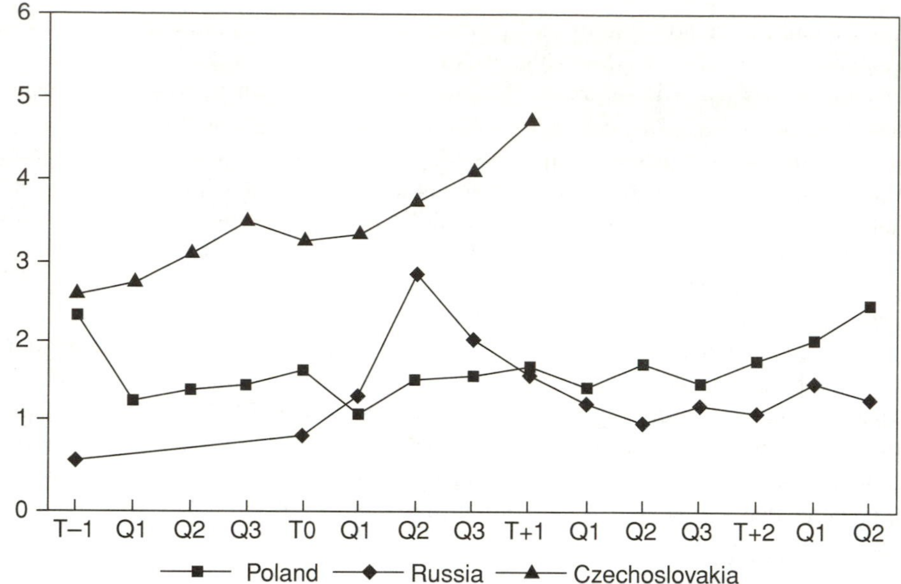

FIG 14.3 Inter-enterprise arrears. A comparison between Poland, Czechoslovakia and Russia
Source: Own estimations using Fan and Schaffer (1994, ESRC n 191), Rostowski (1993, ESRC n 142) and *Goskomstat*

two for some time after the 'big bang' of 1990 and slowly crept up to almost three in 1992 (equals year T+Z). During this period, it cannot really be said that stabilisation in Poland, which made slow but steady progress, was endangered by IED. The case of the CSFR constitutes an even stronger counter-example: in that country, IED reached a peak of over 4.5 months of industrial production by the end of 1991 (T+1, i.e. one year after the start of comprehensive reforms in the CSFR), which is 50 per cent higher than the peak reached by Russia. Even if one discounts the usual uncertainty about the underlying data (different sources give quite different values for IED), it is clear that the situation in Russia was not notably worse than in other countries.

To some extent the impression of a crisis in Russia was based on a simple conceptual error. The detailed calculations of annual GDP for industrial production based on monthly data shown here are useful to clear up a confusion that arose in 1992 when the stock of arrears in Russia as at end June 1992 was compared to the GDP that had been produced over the preceding six months. Since the price level had doubled over the same period, this was not an appropriate comparison. GDP and the value of industrial production in June were thus running at double the rate of January.

The emergence of large amounts of inter-enterprise arrears was thus a common experience of most reforming countries. To some extent this should be viewed as an equilibrium phenomenon. In developed market economies, suppliers are often willing to give their clients some time (typically three months) to pay their bills. This makes sense in an environment where suppliers know their clients well through a history of business contacts that might have evolved over some time. In these circumstances, suppliers might be in a better position to assess the credit-worthiness of their clients than are banks. This explains why in certain circumstances the supplier does not just ask the client firm to take a bank credit and pay immediately. In most Western market economies, so-called trade credit is given in a significant proportion of all transactions.

The post-socialist economies should have started off without any trade credit since enterprises, at least theoretically, did not have any discretion about their own accounts under the old regime. One would therefore expect that initially there might be a surge of trade credit until the new equilibrium level of the stock outstanding has been reached. Once the equilibrium has been established, however, there should be no new (net) creation of trade credit. New trade credit creation during a given period should just be large enough to offset the credit that is being repaid.

Turning to the build-up, that is, the flows, one could argue, however, that there was a danger in early 1992. During the short build-up phase, the second quarter of 1992, the increase in IED was close to the GDP produced during this period. During this period, only every second transaction was paid if one applies the rule of thumb that each ruble of GDP is based on two rubles of transactions. However, Fig. 14.3 also shows that the build-up of IED in Russia occurred more quickly than in Poland, but not faster than in the former CSFR in 1991.

When comparing the experience of Russia to that of the Central European countries, one has also to keep in mind that the gain from delaying payment in Russia was much higher since at an inflation rate of about 20 per cent per month the real value of a payment is halved in three months. In Czechoslovakia inflation was running at about 20 per cent per year, the gain from delaying payments was thus over 10 times smaller. This is the main reason why IED could have potentially become a problem in Russia. Another danger from a too rapid build up of IED is that the entire economy could get into a situation where nobody pays because nobody receives payments. Under these circumstances, money could lose its usual meaning. For a description of how such a 'bad' equilibrium could arise, see Sachs (1994b).

The Russian government recognised this problem and tried to introduce hard budget constraints by decreeing, in June of 1992, that deliveries should only be made after payment (system of pre-payment). Given that at that time most enterprises were still state-owned, this decree had some limited effect, as suggested by the deceleration observed in Fig. 14.3.

Uncontrolled growth of IED was thus averted in Russia. However, the impression of a crisis that had emerged in 1992 then led to the real problem, because the way in which the accumulated arrears were dealt with did not contribute to establishing hard budget constraints. The accumulated stock of arrears was cleared within Russia and the net arrears, or net debt, that remained after the clearing process in Russia were covered by credits from the CBR via the Ministry of the Economy. In a certain sense this measure just recognised reality, that is, that some enterprises had a debt towards the government (which in principle still owned them). This is just another expression of the fact that without effective bankruptcy procedures and without control over central bank lending, the Russian government was not able to force managers of state-owned enterprises to recognise a 'hard budget constraint'. The huge credits issued to cover their net debts and, even more, the credits issued by the CBR in the summer of 1992 to allow firms to pay all their bills, doomed the attempts of the government to stabilise the ruble. The arrears, which had been a potential danger for stabilisation, were thus eliminated by destabilisation.

The root cause of inflation was thus an uncontrolled credit expansion that initially served mainly to deal with a perceived IED crisis. However, enterprises were not the only beneficiaries of the huge amounts of cheap credit extended by the CBR in late 1992 and early 1993; commercial banks and CIS states also received substantial amounts of credit as shown in Table 14.5.

The sum of these credits, amounting to over 25 per cent of GDP, most of which did not go through the official budget presented above, were the root cause of inflation. The distribution is discussed below.

It is interesting to note that if one adds revenues from the official budget (37 per cent of GDP) to the estimate of the seigniorage revenues (21 per cent of GDP), one obtains an indirect estimate of total expenditures which is about 58 per cent of GDP. This is higher than the corresponding ratio for the last years of the FSU and shows how little adjustment in the size of the state sector took place in 1992.

Would it have been possible to finance this level of expenditure? An effective export tax (instead of the quotas used) could have financed most of this as illustrated above. However, this would have required a customs administration along Russia's CIS borders which simply did not exist in 1992 and early 1993. An alternative would have been to tax imports from the West in the way explained below. Simply increasing energy prices would have yielded a large revenue from the profits of state owned oil and gas producers.

SEIGNIORAGE AND FINANCIAL REPRESSION

The gap between state expenditure and revenue was, however, covered in a different way, namely by printing money. Another way of saying the same thing is that the high rates of monetary expansion that went hand in hand with the very high inflation rates gave the Russian government an extremely high seigniorage revenue. Cash in circulation increased in 1992 about 10-fold, from 184 to 1,716 billion rubles; the increase of 1,532 billion rubles was equivalent to 8.5 per cent of GDP, or close to the total revenue from all direct taxes.

On top of the seigniorage from cash holdings, the Central Bank also profited from the reserves of commercial banks that constitute the remainder of the monetary base. During 1992 the increase in the reserves held by commercial banks with the Central Bank amounted to another 2,100 billion rubles, equivalent to 13 per cent of GDP, so that the total seigniorage revenue for that year was about 21 per cent of GDP. In 1993, seigniorage remained very large: the cash component changed very little, it was equal

TABLE 14.5 Net credit of CBR (billion ruble)*

	1992		1993	
Received by:	Net Credit	as% of GDP	Net Credit	as % of GDP
Ministry of Finance	2,430	13,4%	9,571	5,9%
Commercial Banks	2,490	13,8%	6,434	3,9%
CIS	1,566	8,7%	2,582	1,6%
Enterprises	33	0,2%	108	0,1%

Source: Own calculations based on RET
* For 1993, there were no data on CBR-credit for December

to about 7.6 per cent of GDP and the total amounted to about 12 per cent of GDP. The big change with respect to 1992 was in the reserve component, which declined from over 13 per cent to 3 per cent of GDP.

These numbers should be compared to those of other high inflation countries. Fischer (1982) found that the average revenues from seigniorage over a large number of (generally high inflation) countries was about 3 per cent of GDP. Or, to take a more concrete example, one could compare Russia to Brazil in 1991. In that country the consumer price level increased by a factor of about seven between 1990 and 1991, close to the Russian value for 1992. Over the same period the increase in cash in circulation (the cash component of seigniorage) amounted to 1.6 per cent of GDP, and the increase in the overall monetary base (i.e. total seigniorage revenue) was equal to 3.7 per cent of GDP.[19] The main difference with respect to Russia is that in Latin America a (market-based) financial system has had decades to adapt to a high inflation environment whereas the Russian financial system was barely operational in 1992-93. Seignorage in Russia was nevertheless large, even if compared to other transforming economies (see Gros and Vandille 1994).

The importance of seigniorage in Russia can also be seen from the fact that the printing press turned out to be the most important source of revenues for the public sector. In 1992, seigniorage was more important than the *sum* of indirect and direct taxes obtained by the government.

Who paid the seigniorage in Russia? The simple answer is: those who held the monetary base. Since most of the cash is always held by households, they paid most of the approximately 7 per cent of GDP that came from the currency component of seigniorage. For wage earners, who represent the great majority of households, the inflation tax on cash holdings amounted probably to about 10 to 15 per cent of income, since currency holdings were about one-half of the monthly wage and inflation was running at about 20 per cent per month.[20]

The other part of seigniorage came from the 'bank-industry' complex (most banks were and still are owned and controlled by large enterprises) which holds most of the deposits subject to reserves requirements. However, Russian banks appeared to be profit minimisers in 1992 because they held over three times as much reserves in zero interest-bearing accounts with the CBR than they were required to by law. This is difficult to understand in an environment of 20 per cent inflation per month and a similar rate of depreciation of the currency. The explanation of this, at first sight extraordinary, behaviour is twofold. First, the payment system in Russia (and all over the FSU) broke down in 1992. Bank transfers often took more than a month because the documents were held up in the regional offices of the CBR. Since transfers could be executed only if the bank that was giving the order had enough funds in the accounts of the CBR, and since the timing of the actual transfer was so uncertain, banks had to keep very large funds with the CBR. Second, a large part of the credit emission of the CBR was at close to zero interest rates and although it was destined for specific enterprises the amount was parked for some time in the accounts of commercial banks with the CBR until the money was actually used. One could thus argue that these funds did not represent seigniorage in the sense that they did not constitute a source of revenue for the government. If one follows this argument, only the minimum required reserves should be counted in the seigniorage revenue which would then amount only to about 11 per cent of GDP. However, to the extent that the second explanation of the excess reserves is true, one should also correct the official data on transfers to enterprises, and hence the official budget deficit by an equivalent amount.

There is no need to make these calculations since, as mentioned above, the official fiscal deficit was anyway only about 3.5 per cent of (revised) GDP. From this point of view, one could argue that the government did not apparently receive most of the seigniorage revenue. If the government did not receive it, the CBR must have used it to extend credit, either to domestic agents or to foreigners. The latter would have implied an accumulation of huge reserves, which was not the case in 1992. The counterpart to the seigniorage was thus a huge expansion of (cheap) credit to domestic agents as shown in Table 14.5.

The main beneficiaries of the credits from the CBR (usually at very low interest rates) were the government, commercial banks and other CIS states as shown above. Even in 1993 the government obtained net credits equal to about 9 per cent of GDP – more than twice the official deficit. This is another indication that the official budget deficit numbers are close to meaningless. The main other beneficiaries were commercial banks; in 1992 they received the equivalent of 15.5 per cent of GDP. Other CIS states also received substantial support amounting to about 7 per cent of GDP in 1993.

Commercial banks in 1992 received more in credits than they held in reserves. They were thus the main beneficiaries of this situation. In theory, commercial banks should only be a conduit for these cheap credits. It is well known, however, that part of the implicit interest rate subsidies remained with the commercial bankers themselves as they had considerable leeway as to when to hand out the money. Unfortunately, it is not possible to say how much of this ended up in private pockets. It is important to keep in mind that the implicit subsidies discussed here are *in addition* to the sums received by enterprises directly in the form of interest rate subsidies from the budget.

Since commercial banks were net debtors of the CBR, they would have lost out in stabilisation (i.e. if the government had ended inflation and cheap credit at the same time). It is clear that some particular enterprises and commercial banks would lose a lot and others would gain a lot. New private enterprises with no access to cheap credit from the CBR would gain from stabilisation, whereas the heavy debtors among the large state-owned enterprises would lose. This is just one example of how destabilisation represents an obstacle for the development of an honest private sector.

The concept of seigniorage used so far measures how much revenue the government can obtain by creating its own liabilities, that is, the monetary base. This is not exactly the same as the loss of real purchasing power that is borne by the holders of money. Their loss is equal to the inflation rate times the amount of money, corrected for any interest payments they might receive. This loss is also called the inflation tax. The inflation tax goes to the issuers of the assets on which no interest is paid. The gain of the government as issuer of the monetary base was discussed above. Households thus paid a tax of about 10 to 15 per cent of income on their holdings of cash. On top of that, households paid in 1992 a capital levy on their holdings of savings deposits. At the end of 1992 (after price liberalisation), deposits with Sberbank were still worth about 8 per cent of GDP. At the end of the year they were worth only 1.4 per cent of GDP. Since practically no interest was paid on them and nothing could be withdrawn, the holders of these deposits were effectively expropriated to the tune of 6.6 per cent of GDP. Since Sberbank is owned by the government, this represents another gain of the public sector, which is not contained in the official accounts. This capital levy in effect constituted an additional source of finance for the 'commercial banks and large enterprises' complex through cheap credit.

The basic message is thus that destabilisation stifled the private sector and led to a colossal redistribution of income from households towards that small part of the population that was able to dominate the financial sector and obtain huge amounts of cheap credit.

5. Who lost Russia?

The evolution of the Russian economy was closely followed in the Western press, and in 1992-93, the G-7 economic summits devoted a lot of their time to discussion and debate on how to help Russia. From all this one could gain the impression that the Russian economy is somehow important for the global economy. This would be completely wrong, however. That Russia is important for non-economic reasons may be obvious. But it is not widely appreciated how small the Russian economy really is. Translated at market exchange rates, the entire Russian GDP of 1992 was about $80 billion, about the same as that of Denmark. During 1993 and early 1994, the ruble appreciated considerably in real terms so that the Russian GDP was running at about $300 billion in 1994. This puts Russia only in the same league as Brazil.

It is often argued that one cannot translate the Russian GDP at the market exchange rate and that one should use a purchasing power exchange rate to measure the Russian economy. This is really beside the point, since the numbers mentioned above just serve to measure the weight of Russia in the world economy; they have little to say about just how poor the Russian population is. To measure the latter, one would indeed have had to apply a purchasing power corrected exchange rate. But in order to avoid this argument one can also measure the weight of Russia by its international trade. However, even from this point of view, Russia is small: its exports (and imports) were equal to about $40 billion in 1992. In 1993, exports continued at about the same level, but imports went down to about 25 billion. This is the same order of magnitude as Brazil (or Denmark) in overall terms; but in terms of exports of manufactured goods, Russia is much smaller than either of these two countries.

In comparison to these magnitudes, the aid packages of $28 and $42 billion that were promised at the G-7 summits in 1992 and 1993 look gigantic. The 1992 package would have been close to 30 per cent of GDP and the 1993 package was larger than the total imports of Russia during that year! However, it is apparent that the total amounts announced to the press were used mainly for propaganda purposes. Grants made up only a very small part and the largest single components of the overall packages were always bilateral export credits that would have been (and in fact were) given anyway. These export credits were substantial: in 1992 they amounted to about 12 billion, about 15 per cent of GDP, or almost 40 per cent of total imports. They were thus important in sustaining Russian consumption, but they did not help the government directly. This is a general point that has been made forcefully in Lipton and Sachs (1992), Sachs (1994a).

The debate about aid to Russia becomes somewhat sterile: Western officials point to the large amount of aid actually delivered, whereas the critics point out that this was the wrong kind of aid and that the Russian government did not receive what it needed most, namely direct budgetary support. If one analyses the reasons why the assistance actually delivered was so ineffective, however, one discovers that both sides are right (and wrong).

The critics are even more right than they have argued so far since the credits to finance Russian imports probably did harm the Russian economy. However, if the Russian government had adopted different policies (taxing, instead of subsidising imports as argued below), it could have used these credits to stabilise the economy. The technical details of the standard welfare approach which implies all this are presented in Boxes 14.3 and 14.4. But the general arguments are straightforward.

Regarding the welfare from emergency credits one has to start from the realisation that credits to finance imports do not constitute a gift; they have to be repaid at some point in the future. Their value to the receiving economy lies in the access to credit markets that would otherwise not be available. The value of this access to international credit markets can be quantified in terms of the standard welfare theoretic approach. Box 14.3 shows how much the average or 'representative' consumer gains if he or she can maintain consumption of imports at a roughly constant level even if exports are temporarily low. This is another crucial point for an economic analysis of this policy: the emergency credits offered by Western governments made sense under the assumption that Russian exports would increase considerably once the reforms had had enough time to increase the efficiency of the Russian economy and thus allow exports to increase, which in turn would provide for the necessary debt service obligations. If one could not have expected that Russia would increase its exports in the future, grants would have been more appropriate and credits would not have made sense.

There was a need for official credits because private lenders were not willing to extend credits to Russia in 1992–93 (on the contrary, they even asked for reimbursement of old debts coming due). In this situation the only way to maintain imports until exports would pick up was to use official credits. Hence there was a case for official export credits on economic grounds.

Box 14.3 thus presents a model that allows one to calculate an order of magnitude for the welfare gains that a country that has been cut off from the international private capital market can expect if it obtains emergency credits from an official source. Russia was in this situation in 1992–93 and Ukraine might be in this situation at present.

Box 14.3 uses a very crude model that consists essentially of a standard utility function. Combining this model with some estimates of the parameters of the utility function then generates estimates of the welfare gain from export credits. The results of the numerical application reported in Box 14.4 indicate that the magnitude of the welfare gains depends most of all on the elasticity of inter-temporal substitution in the utility function as represented by the degree of relative risk aversion. Empirical studies from a number of different authors tend to indicate that the degree of risk aversion should be around 2. Hence one should take the column corresponding to this value. This implies that even if one assumes that half of all income is spent on imports, Western export credits amounting to over 50 per cent of all Russian imports would have increased welfare by about 4.3 per cent. If the proportion of all income going to imports is assumed to be smaller (as it is indeed in Russia) the welfare gain would be correspondingly smaller.

Box 14.3 Welfare gains from emergency credits

The following model is designed to lead to a numerical estimate of the welfare gain from the inter-temporal shift in consumption that a country can achieve if it receives emergency credits from an official source (and if the private sector would otherwise not be willing to provide any new funds.) Assume a representative agent with a standard Cobb–Douglas utility function, defined over two goods, called x (tradables) and y (non-tradables), and over two periods, indexed by the subscripts 1 and 2. Welfare over the two periods is thus given by:

$$W = [1 / (1-R)]\ \{(x_1^{\alpha} y_1^{1-\alpha})^{1-R} + A\,(x_2^{\alpha} y_2^{1-\alpha})^{1-R}\} \qquad [1]$$

where A is the time discount factor in utility ($A = 1/(1+r) \leq 1$ with r the conventional interest rate), α indicates the weight of tradables in the utility function and R is the index of relative risk aversion.

Assuming for simplicity that the production (= consumption) of non-tradables is constant over time, and equal to y, welfare can be rewritten as:

$$W = [1 / (1-R)]\ y^{(1-\alpha)(1-R)}\ \{x_1^{\alpha(1-R)} + A x_2^{\alpha(1-R)}\} \qquad [2]$$

The only part of consumption that changes over time are thus the tradables (here really importables). If the international real interest rate is equal to the rate of time preference, the desired consumption profile of tradables will be flat over time. The actual consumption profile will be flat only if Russia can borrow during the first period and pay back during the second. In this case the consumption of tradables would in both periods be equal (and the present value would be equal to the present values of export receipts). Denoting exports by e and assuming that they are exogenously given by e_1 and e_2 this implies that consumption of tradables would be equal to: $x = [(e_1 + Ae_2)/(1+A)] = (e_1 + Ae_2)(1+r)/(2+r)$ in this case. With perfect access to international capital markets (or a 'Marshall Plan' that has only emergency credits) welfare would thus be equal to:

$$W_{mp} = [1/(1-R)]\ y^{(1-\alpha)(1-R)}\ [(e_1 + Ae_2)/(1+A)]^{\alpha(1-R)}\ \{1+A\} \qquad [3]$$

If Russia does *not* have access to international capital markets, consumption of tradables is constrained each period by export capacity and welfare will be equal to:

$$W_{c.\,rat.} = [1 / (1-R)]\ y^{(1-\alpha)(1-R)}\ \{e_1^{\alpha(1-R)} + A e_2^{\alpha(1-R)}\} \qquad [4]$$

The rationale for the emergency export credits (or a Marshall Plan) must be that the short-run export capacity of Russia is much below the long-run value (and that private international capital markets do not work, possibly because of credit rationing *à la* Stiglitz and Weiss). In order to make this assumption workable it is convenient to assume that $e_1 = D\, e_2$, where D is a decline factor (the temporary decline in exports during the transition) smaller than one. For example, a value of $D = 0.5$ would mean that the long-run export capacity of Russia is two times actual 1992–93 exports. Without an increase in future export capacity there

continued

Box 14.3 *continued*

would be no reason to extend additional credits because they could not be served in the future. Welfare under the Marshall Plan or the export credits that make it possible to smooth completely the consumption of imports, can then be written as:

$$W_{mp} = [1/(1-R)]\, y^{(1-\alpha)(1-R)}\, [(e_2\,(D+A))/(1+A)]^{\alpha(1-R)}\, \{1+A\} \qquad [5]$$

Welfare without access to international capital is given by:

$$W_{c.\,rat.} = [1/(1-R)\,]\, y^{(1-\alpha)(1-R)}\, e_2^{\alpha(1-R)}\, \{D^{\alpha(1-R)} + A\} \qquad [6]$$

The welfare gain can then be calculated by taking the ratio between the two last expressions:

$$\text{Welfare gain} = [(D+A)/(1+A)]^{\alpha(1-R)}\, \{1+A\} / [D^{\alpha(1-R)} + A] \qquad [7]$$

The welfare gain in percentage terms is equal to this expression minus one, multiplied by 100. Tables A and B below show the numerical values of the welfare gain one obtains by assuming different values for α, R and D. The time discount factor, A, is always assumed to be equal to 1 (i.e. if the discount rate, r, is set equal to zero) since changes in A cannot affect the result significantly because it enters both the denominator and the numerator of equation (7). The annex to Gros (1994c) shows that this remains true even for rather low values of A.

However, the relative degree of risk aversion, R, has a very strong impact on the result. Given that the empirical literature seems to find values for R around 2, this is the central case considered here. The exact value of the share of tradables in consumption does not influence the results as strongly; a range of 0.2 to 0.5 should be appropriate. The problem here is that the Cobb–Douglas formulation is clearly inadequate since it implies constant expenditure shares, whereas in reality the share of imports in Russian GDP has varied a lot with the real exchange rate over the last two years.

Finally, the value for D could be chosen with reference to the actual credits given in 1992. In the optimum, that is, if the consumption profile of imports is smooth, consumption of imports is given by $e_2(1+D)/2$, as mentioned above. Since exports are only De_2 during the first period, this implies that the export credits have to cover the difference between actual exports and desired imports. This difference is equal to $e_2(1-D)/2D$. At the optimum the ratio of export credits to actual imports should thus be equal to: $(1-D)/(1+D)$. Russian imports in 1992 were about $36 bn, hence the ratio of Western trade credits to imports (from the West) was about 1/3. This implies that D should be set equal to one-half (if one assumes that the volume of export credits actually given was large enough to put Russia on the optimum path in terms of import consumption) since $D = 0.5$ implies that Russia's exports will double in the long run; this value anyway seems generous.

continued

Box 14.3 *continued*

TABLE A Welfare gain in % for the case $D = 0.5$

	$R = 0.90$	$R = 2$	$R = 4$
$\alpha = 0.50$	0.28	4.34	19.57
$\alpha = 0.20$	0.12	1.41	5.52

Increasing D only somewhat, say to 0.7 (which implies that exports increase 'only' by 50 per cent in the second period), reduces the welfare gains to one third, as can be seen from Table B.

TABLE B Welfare gain in % for the case $D = 0.7$

	$R = 0.90$	$R = 2$	$R = 4$
$\alpha = 0.50$	0.08	1.18	5.74
$\alpha = 0.20$	0.03	0.38	1.51

Overall this exercise suggests that the welfare gains from emergency credits to sustain the import capacity of a country that experiences a temporary decline in exports (and does not have access to private international capital markets) will in general be rather modest unless the credits cover a very large proportion of all imports, and tradables constitute a large part of consumption.

One can thus tentatively conclude that the welfare gains from the emergency credits were modest, especially if one takes into account the large amounts involved. Moreover, these small gains have to be contrasted with the large losses that arose because imports were subsidised. The crucial point in the case of Russia, however, is that the huge import subsidies of 1992 gave no incentive to the economy to economise on imports, which were thus wasted, while the government had to assume additional debt obligations. The welfare losses that resulted from this waste were probably much larger than the welfare gains calculated above. Box 14.4, which uses essentially the same models as Box 14.1, shows that given the size of the import subsidies prevalent in early 1992, the welfare loss for each dollar of export credit should have been between 9 and 25 cents. If one takes into account the bureaucratic waste and the corruption that arose in the distribution of the subsidised imports, the welfare loss might have been as high as 25 to 50 cents for each dollar of subsidised imports. Given that the export credits amounted to \$12.5 billion, the welfare loss could have been anywhere between \$1 and \$6 billion, the equivalent of 1 to 7 per cent of GDP for 1992. Causing welfare losses of this magnitude, of course, does not constitute a desirable result of foreign aid.

Box 14.4 Welfare losses from export credits

The starting point is the same conventional import demand function already used in Box 14.1 above. This demand function ($P = AQ^{-\beta}$) implies that the impact of the import subsidies on the consumer surplus is equal to:

$$\text{Change in } CS \equiv CS_{FT} - CS_T = A\,[Q_{FT}^{1-\beta} - Q_T^{1-\beta}]\,/\,(1-\beta) - A\,[Q_{FT}^{1-\beta} - Q_T^{1-\beta}] = [\beta/(1-\beta)]\,A\,[Q_{FT}^{1-\beta} - Q_T^{1-\beta}] \qquad [1]$$

The consumer surplus increases with lower prices, but this comes at the expense of higher revenues that have to be borne by the government when it services the debt. The total welfare effect of export credits given by the West is thus:

$$\text{Welfare effect} = \text{change in } CS - \text{budgetary cost of import subsidies} \qquad [2]$$

The budgetary cost of import subsidies is given, as before, by $(T-1)\,P_w\,Q_T$, where T is equal to one minus the subsidy rate. Using the demand curve (which implies: $A\,Q_T^{1-\beta}\,/\,T = P_w\,Q_T$) this leads to:

$$\text{Welfare effect} = [\beta/(1-\beta)]\,A\,[Q_{FT}^{1-\beta} - Q_T^{1-\beta}] - A\,Q_T^{1-\beta}\,(T-1)/T \qquad [3]$$

The total welfare effect per unit of export credit given (the value of the imports is $A\,Q_T^{1-\beta}\,/\,T = P_w\,Q_T$) can then be written as:

$$\text{Welfare effect / credits} = [\beta/(1-\beta)]\,T\,[T^{(1-\beta)/\beta} - 1] - (T-1) \qquad [4]$$

For the special case $\beta = 0.5$ this expression reduces to the simple result that the welfare effect is equal to $(T-1)(T-1)$. Assuming, as above, that T is equal to 0.5, which implies an import subsidy of 50 per cent (in reality imports were often sold at less than 50 per cent of the world market price), this implies that each dollar of export credits given to Russia in 1992 led to a loss of welfare of 25 cents. A lower elasticity of demand, that is, a higher value of β, gives a somewhat lower result. If β equals 2 the RHS is equal to $(-0.5) \times T \times (T^{-0.5} - 1) - (T-1)$. This can be rewritten as: $(1 - T^{0.5})^2$. With $T = 0.5$ this is approximately equal to 0.09. Both these quadratic expressions imply the usual result that the welfare loss is minimised if $T = 1$; that is, the optimal policy is free trade. This changes, however, if one takes into account two additional effects that arise in the Russian reality.

Sachs (1994a) emphasises, probably rightly, that the benefits from cheaper imports did not go to the entire population since these imports were allocated on an administrative basis. This can be captured in this model by assuming that the increase in consumer surplus resulting from the subsidised prices is only a proportion W of the consumer surplus that would be obtained without administrative allocation. This waste factor, W, would obviously be below one.

Moreover, if one argues that the Russian government needed external finance for stabilisation it must be true that the social value of an additional dollar of

continued

Box 14.4 *continued*

revenues for the government is larger than one because it allows the government to reduce taxes that would otherwise cause distortions or because it reduces the amount of money the government needs to print and hence reduces inflation.

One can thus argue that the real cost of the additional debt burden (from Western export credits) for the Russian government is more than the cost of the debt service (whose present value is equal to the credit itself) because each additional dollar in revenues that the Russian government needs to raise causes additional distortions in the Russian economy. The budgetary cost should thus be multiplied by a tax revenue cost factor, denoted here by $K = 1 + k$, where k is the social cost of the distortions caused by an additional unit of revenues for the government (through ordinary taxes or the inflation tax). The welfare impact would then be given by:

$$\text{Welfare effect / credits} = [\beta/(1-\beta)]\, T\, [T^{(1-\beta)/\beta} - 1]\, W - K\,(T - 1) \quad [5]$$

For the case of $\beta = 0.5$ this reduces to $(T - 1)(W - K)$. It is difficult to say what values for K and W would be realistic. As an illustrative example, one could assume that $W = 0.5$, which implies that due to the administrative nature of the distribution of the import subsidies only one half of the potential increase in consumer surplus is actually attained and that $K = 1.5$, which implies that each dollar of revenue to be raised by the Russian government leads to another 50 cents in collection costs. In this case the welfare cost of a dollar of export credits would increase to $(T - 1)$, or 50 cents to the dollar if one continues with the assumption that $T = 0.5$.

The value for T has so far been taken as given, but one could turn the problem round and ask what would be the optimal value of T given that the social value of the tariff revenues is K times the amount actually collected? It is clear that the answer must imply that imports should not be subsidised. This in turn implies that imports can no longer be allocated on an administrative basis so that one should no longer take into account the waste factor W. For the case $\beta = 0.5$ (and $W = 1$) the RHS of Equation [5] reduces to:

$$\text{Welfare effect / credits} = [\beta/(1-\beta)]\, T\, [T^{(1-\beta)/\beta} - 1] - K\,(T - 1) \quad [6]$$

The FOC for a maximum of this expression with respect to T is given by:

$$0 = [\beta/(1-\beta)]\,(T^{(1-\beta)/\beta} - 1) + T^{(1-\beta)/\beta} - K \quad [7]$$

For $\beta = 0.5$ this reduces to $K = 2T - 1$, which implies:

$$t^{op} = 0.5\, k \quad [8]$$

The optimal import tariff is equal to one-half of the social 'excess' cost of government revenues.

If $k = 0.5$ the optimal import tariff to finance the budget deficit is equal to 25 per cent.

One can certainly discuss the details of the calculations based on such a crude model, but the central point is quite clear: the export credits lavished on Russia in 1992 probably helped to *reduce* the welfare of the average Russian citizen. This was not the fault of the West since the cause for this unintended effect was the under-pricing of imports through massive subsidies operated by the Russian government. But this example shows that sometimes helping a severely distorted economy can have unintended negative side effects.

But why should one accept the bad policies of the Russian government? Given the need to limit inflationary monetary financing, the government should have pursued a different policy. It should have taxed imports. Taxing imports that are paid for by foreign credits should have been administratively easy since these imports had to be declared officially in order to obtain the credits. Box 14.3 shows that for reasonable parameter estimates the optimum import tariff would have been 25 per cent. Even if applied only to the imports financed by credits (i.e the $12.5 billion) this would have yielded a revenue of $3 billion, or 4 per cent of GDP. If applied to all imports, the revenue might have been double (taking into account that imports would have been lower). This would have been used to reduce the deficit to a magnitude that could have been financed with an acceptable inflation rate. A smart government could thus have used the 'wrong' type of aid efficiently to achieve early stabilisation.

These illustrative calculations show that both the West and the Russian government are to blame if the substantial assistance that was given in 1992 did not lead to stabilisation. In 1993, stabilisation could begin not only because of the impressive efforts of the new finance minister Fjodorov to cut credit emission, but also because the environment for aid changed: import subsidies had been abolished and import tariffs were gradually introduced so that the declining amounts of import credits did have a positive effect. Moreover, some limited amounts of the 'right' type of aid were slowly forthcoming.

The West also lost an opportunity in the sense that, even given the bad policies pursued by the Russian government, a moderate amount of the right aid, namely budgetary assistance to the government, could have helped to achieve stabilisation. How large should direct assistance to the government have been in order to achieve stabilisation? The proper criterion should be the level of support from the West that would have allowed the authorities to avoid creating too much money. It was argued above that the relevant part of seigniorage was worth about 2,000 billion rubles; approximately $8 billion at the average 1992 exchange rate. Buying stabilisation this way would have been more expensive in 1993 when the increase in cash in circulation was worth about $12 billion. But this would still have been less than the export credits that were given in 1992. This is not surprising: providing a country of 140 million people with international purchasing power is an expensive proposition, but providing the government with internal purchasing power to cover its deficit is cheap if the real exchange rate is low.

All in all, the story of Western financial assistance to Russia is thus one of missed opportunities on both sides.[21]

6. Conclusions

The three particular aspects of the Russian economy that have been highlighted in this chapter suggest that a closer analysis quite often reveals a significant gap between perception and reality. A closer analysis of other issues would take up too much space, but some brief considerations on three other issues suggest that one should avoid hasty judgements in other areas as well.

It is often argued that the rapid transfer of formal share ownership from the government to managers and workers achieved by mid-1994 represents a true privatisation that will lead to the necessary restructuring. Before this can be claimed, one should show carefully what incentives managers and workers face under the present circumstances. All one can say at present is that the same managers that formerly were supposed to act under the orders of the government are now the formal owners of the enterprises together with their employees.

Another example concerns the role of the ruble zone in the inflationary developments in 1992–93. It is often argued that excessive monetary expansion in other CIS countries undermined Russian attempts at stabilising the ruble. This issue was discussed in more detail in Chapter 13, where it was shown that if one looks at the data one finds that between 1 January 1992 and mid-1993, monetary aggregates expanded *less* in the other CIS countries than in Russia. Hence, one cannot really argue that the ill-defined ruble zone that existed in 1992–93 was a major source of inflation for Russia.

Yet another example concerns the output decline recorded by the official statistics. It is clear that the official statistics that miss the private sector entirely overstate the real fall in output. But the often repeated claim that the recorded output decline just reflects the necessary reduction in military expenditure and the elimination of low, or perhaps even negative, value-added activities also does not stand up to a closer analysis. As shown in Duchêne and Gros (1994) (see Chapter 13 for details), there is no correlation between the importance of military expenditure and the output decline across sectors and there is also no correlation between profitability and the output decline across sectors.

These three examples illustrate again that sweeping statements about the Russian economy are usually wrong. The three specific instances discussed in this chapter (price liberalisation, external trade and stabilisation) show that most economic policy measures are at first implemented only partially and thus contain internal contradictions. Over time, however, the initial shortcomings have been made up. In a certain sense one can therefore conclude that the 'big bang' lasted for about two years in Russia. The most serious mistake of the reformers was not to have increased energy prices and not to have eliminated import subsidies immediately.

What does all this imply for the future? The critical analysis of the reform process in 1992-93 has shown that the policies actually implemented (as opposed to the policy announced) had serious negative welfare effects. This can explain why the constituency for reforms was initially rather weak. However, since most of the errors have now been corrected, this analysis suggests a cautious optimism. The welfare gains from the elimination of import subsidies and the reduction of export controls are probably dimly perceived by the population at large and this might be the main factor why the continuation of the reforms is no longer an issue. The lesson that the continuation of reforms improves the economy and pays off politically has not been lost on the political system, which implies that one can expect for the near future a continuation of the slow, but imperfect progress that has been the hallmark of developments in Russia so far.

It seems therefore appropriate to conclude with another quote from the same noted economist cited in the opening:

> If one is to make any generalisation in present conditions, it must be this – that at a low level of efficiency the system does function and possesses elements of permanence.
>
> J.M. Keynes

Notes

1. A law establishing a two-tier banking system and an independent central bank was approved on 1 November 1990, and survived the subsequent upheavals not only in Russia, but also in most other former Soviet republics.
2. For a comparison of various reform plans, see Commission of the European Communities (1992). There were important differences between the reform plans in the emphasis given to these goals and the speed with which they were to be attained. In general, the government programmes put more emphasis on macroeconomic stabilisation than on liberalisation, and they insisted, for obvious reasons, on more powers for the Union.
   The famous '500-day programme' elaborated for the Russian government by a group under Professor Shatalin came the closest to containing all the elements of a comprehensive reform. Although 500 days would have represented a rather protracted 'big bang', this transition period must be considered as ambitious at least in retrospect, in view of the time it actually took to implement reforms in Russia and stabilise the ruble.
3. The (final) Polish price reform of January 1990 was also followed by a substantial increase in the supply of money (i.e. currency), whose magnitude was close to the increase in the price level over this period. Could one therefore argue that the increase in prices of the first quarter of 1990 just represented the usual inflation caused by excessive monetary expansion? A large part of this increase in cash might have been due to the de-dollarisation of the economy. If this is true, the increase in currency supply might have been justified by an increase in demand; and the increase in prices would be due to the overhang inherited from the past.
4. Hungary cannot be used as a basis of comparison since price reform there was too gradual. Price reform also came in several steps in Romania.
5. It was suggested to the authors that some of the historical data on money was still classified by the end of 1991.
6. A form of monetisation of the agricultural sector also took place in the sense that the employees of collective farms were no longer paid exclusively in kind.
7. The discussion of Fig. 14.1 has so far not mentioned one aspect that is not strictly comparable, namely the measurement of national income. Before 1992, the only data available refers to NMP whereas after 1992, the national income means GDP. However, this problem was taken crudely into account by multiplying NMP by the factor 1.3. It is usually assumed that the difference between NMP (which does not take into account services) and GNP is about this size. Different assumptions concerning the difference between NMP and GNP (e.g. 20 or 40 per cent) would not lead to substantially different conclusions given that the changes in velocity that came with price liberalisation are of a different order of magnitude.
8. A prominent expert on Eastern European economies is widely quoted as saying that 'the best thing the Communist government could do for Poland was to increase prices and then resign'.

9. The new parliament that was elected in December 1993 after the violent confrontation between the old Supreme Soviet and President Yeltsin, however, was not much different; this was the main reason why most of the reformers (especially Gaidar and the finance minister Fjodorov) preferred to leave government in early 1994.
10. Given that wages were paid (in cash) twice a month, the average worker in Russia must have held about one-fourth of wage income in cash. Given a monthly inflation rate of about 20 to 25 per cent this implies an inflation tax (on wages alone!) of 5 to 6.25 per cent. Actual cash holdings were about twice as high as the minimum one would expect from wage-payment patterns. The rest of the population (or excessive cash holdings by workers) thus paid the other half of the inflation tax.
11. See BP (1994); this calculation assumes a price of $100 per tonne of oil (and equivalent in other fuels). Russia did in fact obtain this price for its exports to the EU: the unit price (per ton of oil) was almost exactly equal to 100 ecu ($115), according to EU import statistics, and EU cif gas prices were $2.6 per million BTU, which corresponds to $104 per tonne of oil equivalent. These two fuels accounted for 75 per cent of Russian energy consumption in 1992.
12. The import tariff rate was later increased to 15 per cent (in September 1993), but this did not change the overall liberalisation of import trade that lasted until the ruble began to strengthen in late 1993 so that import competition became a serious threat in a number of sectors. At that point, a number of high tariffs on goods that competed with Russian products (e.g. cars) were introduced.
13. This list does not include natural gas, which cannot be traded in the same way. It is interesting to note that the price for gas deliveries to industry was 'increased' in August 1993 to 10 per cent of the West European price! See *Russian Economic Trends* (1993), 2 (3), p. 6.
14. It is also interesting to note that the domestic price of wheat (of which Russia is a net importer) stabilised at 54 per cent of the world market price after the wheat market was liberalised at the end of 1993.
15. The export boom went hand in hand with a boom of imports from the industrialised countries. As foreign financing became more widely available, imports increased by more than exports and most Central European countries developed a trade deficit. But this development has nothing to do with the overall expansion of trade generated by trade liberalisation.
16. A first problem is that no reliable statistics exist at all for Russian trade before 1992 because it was simply part of the Soviet Union's trade. A second problem is that during 1992, the Russian trade data collection system worked only partially, and many Western import statistics lumped all former republics together. Russian trade statistics for the FSU period have been reconstituted, but are extremely unreliable because they show that exports in 1990 were close to $80 billion whereas the IMF Directions of Trade Statistics show that the rest of the world declared imports from the entire FSU of only $50 billion.
17. Initially, these auctions (for US dollars only) were held on Tuesdays and Thursdays at the Moscow Interbank Currency Exchange. Later DM auctions were also introduced and auctions in other cities also started. As mentioned earlier, until 1993 a significant difference between the 'cash' and 'non-cash' markets persisted. The following uses only the data from the non-cash market; i.e. the rate for bank account transactions.
18. Moreover, it is not easy to define at what point a non-payment becomes overdue. The following analysis neglects these conceptual problems and accepts the official classification of IED.
19. Cash in circulation at the end of 1991 (3,672) minus the stock end of 1990 (989) divided by GDP (164,991). The monetary base increased to 8,166 from 1,995. (All figures in billions of cruzeiros.)
20. Under the socialist system households were forced to save because there was nothing they

could buy. With the inflation rates that followed price liberalisation, they were forced to save in order to protect their balances against inflation.

21. We do not discuss other types of aid, such as technical assistance, that are valuable but cannot be expected to have an immediate impact.

References to Part IV

Aitken, N.D. (1973) The Effect of EEC and EFTA on European trade: a temporal cross-section analysis, *American Economic Review*, **63**, (5), December, pp. 881–92.

Aslund, A. (ed.) (1994) *Economic Transformation in Russia*, Pinter, London.

Baldwin, R. (1994) Towards an Integrated Europe, CEPR, London.

Begg, D. and **Portes, R.** (1993) Enterprise debt and economic transformation: financial restructuring in Central and Eastern Europe, *European Economic Review*, (37), pp. 396–407.

Bergstrand, J.H. (1985) The gravity equation in international trade: some microeconomic foundations and empirical evidence, *The Review of Economics and Statistics*, **67**, (3) August, pp. 474–81.

Bofinger, P. and **Gros, D.** (1992) A multilateral payments union for the Commonwealth of Independent States: why and how?, *CEPR Discussion Paper* No. 654, May.

Boycko, M., Shleifer, A. and **Vishny, R.W.** (1993) Privatising Russia, *Brookings Papers on Economic Activity*, No. 2, The Brookings Institute, Washington, DC..

BP (1994) *BP Statistical Review of World Energy*, BP London.

Brada, J.C. and **Méndez, J.A.** (1985) Economic integration among developed, developing and centrally planned economies: a comparative analysis, *The Review of Economics and Statistics*, **67**, (4), pp. 549–56.

Christensen, B.V. (1994) The Russian Federation in transition External developments, Occasional Paper No. 111, International Monetary Fund, Washington, DC, February.

Commission of the European Communities (1988) The economies of 1992: an assessment of the potential economic effects of completing the internal market of the European economy, *European Economy*, No. 35, March 1988, Brussels.

Commission of the European Communities (1990a) One market, one money. An evaluation of the potential benefits and costs of forming an economic and monetary union, *European Economy*, No. 44, October 1990, Brussels.

Commission of the European Communities (1990b) Stabilisation, liberalisation and devolution: assessment of the economic situation and reform process in the Soviet Union, *European Economy*, No. 45, December 1990, Brussels.

Cottarelli, C. and **Blejer, M.I.** (1992) Forced saving and repressed inflation in the Soviet Union, 1986–90, *IMF Staff Papers*, **39**, (2), June.

De Nicola, C. and Gros, D. (1994) The efficiency of emerging foreign exchange markets: the case of the ruble/dollar rate, Centre for European Policy Studies, Brussels.

Dornbush, R. and **Fisher, S.** (1981) Macroeconomics, McGraw-Hill, Singapore.

Duchêne, G. and **Gros, D.** (1994) A comparative study of output decline in transition economies, Centre for European Policy Studies (CEPS), Brussels, June.

Eichengreen, B. (1993) A payments mechanism for the former Soviet Union : is the EPU a relevant precedent?, *CEPR Discussion Paper* No. 824, London, August.

Emerson *et al.* (1992) *One Market, One Money. An Evaluation of the Potential Benefits and Costs of Forming an Economic and Monetary Union*, Oxford University Press, Oxford.

Fama, E.F. (1990) Banking in the theory of finance, in Mayer, T. (ed.) *Monetary Theory*, International Library of Critical Writings in Economics, Gower, Aldershot.

Fan, Q. and **Schaffer, M.** (1994) Government financial transfers and enterprise adjustments in Russia, with comparisons to Central and Eastern Europe, *Economics of Transition*, **2** (2), pp. 151–88.

Fisher, S. (1982) Seigniorage and the case for a national money, *Journal of Political Economy*, **90** (2), pp. 295–313.

Giovannini, A. and **de Melo, M.** (1993) Government revenue from financial repression, *American Economic Review*, **83**, (4), pp. 953–63.

Gros, D. (1993) Bilateralism versus multilateralism in the FSU, what is the potential gain from the ISB?, manuscript, Centre for European Policy Studies (CEPS), May.

Gros, D. (1994a) Comment on 'Russian trade policy', by Konovalov, Vladimir, in Tarr, D. (ed.) *Trade in the New Independent States*, World Bank, Washington, DC.

Gros, D. (1994b) Intra-CIS Payments: The Interstate Bank Project: Its Genesis and Demise, in Tarr, D. (ed.) *Trade in the New Independent States*, World Bank, Washington, DC.

Gros, D. (1994c) Welfare gains from emergency credits, unpublished manuscript, CEPS, Brussels, September.

Gros, D. and **Dautrebande, B.** (1992a) Did Soviet planners follow the rules of the market after all?, unpublished manuscript, CEPS, Brussels, March.

Gros, D. and **Dautrebande, B.** (1992b) International trade of former republics in the long run: an analysis based on the 'gravity' approach, CEPS Working Document No. 71, Centre for European Policy Studies (CEPS), Brussels, May.

Gros, D. and **Steinherr, A.** (1991) Economic reform in the Soviet Union: pas-de-deux between disintegration and macroeconomic destabilisation, *Princeton Studies in International Finance*, No. 71, November.

Gros, D. and **Vandille, G.** (1994) Seigniorage in economies in transition, draft, Centre for European Policy Studies, Brussels, July.

Havrylyshyn, O. and **Pritchett, L.** (1991) European trade patterns after the transition, Working Paper 748, The World Bank, Washington, DC, August.

International Monetary Fund (various) *International Financial Statistics*, IMF, Washington, DC.

Kaplan, J.J. and **Schleiminger, G.** (1989) *The European Payments Union: Financial Diplomacy in the 1950s*, Oxford University Press, Oxford.

Keynes, J.M. (1992) A short view of Russia, 1972, *Essays in Persuasion*, *The Collected Writings of John Maynard Keynes*, Part IX, London and Basingstoke.

Koen, V. and **Meyermans, E.** (1994) Exchange rate determinants in Russia: 1992–93, International Monetary Fund Working Document, IMF, Washington, DC.

Koen, V. and **Phillips, S.** (1993) Price liberalisation in Russia, International Monetary Fund, Occasional Papers, No. 104, Washington, DC, June.

Konovalov, V. (1994) Russian trade policy, in Tarr, D. (ed.) *Trade in New Independent States*, World Bank, Washington, DC.

Lerner, A.P. (1936) The symmetry between import and export taxes, *Economica*, **3**, pp. 306 –13.

Linnemann, H. (1966) *An Econometric Study of International Trade Flows*, North Holland, Amsterdam.

Lipton, D. and **Sachs, J.** (1992) Prospects for Russia's economic reforms, *Brookings Papers on Economic Activity*, **2**, pp. 213–65.

Qian, Y. and **Roland, G.** (1994) Regional decentralisation and the soft budget constraint : the case of China, *CEPR Discussion Paper No. 1013,* London, September.

Rostowski, J. (1993) The inter-enterprise debt explosion in the former Soviet Union: causes, consequences, cures, *CEPR Discussion Paper No. 142,* London School of Economics, April.

Russian Economic Trends (various years) Centre for Economic Reform, Government of the Russian Federation, Whurr Publishers, London, various issues.

Sachs, J. (1993) *Poland's Jump to the Market*, MIT Press, London.

Sachs, J. (1994a) Life in the economic emergency room, in Williamson, J. (ed.) *The Political Economy of Policy Reform*, Institute for International Economics, Washington, DC, pp. 501–23.

Sachs, J. (1994b) Russia's struggle with stabilisation: conceptual issues and evidence, Paper for the Annual Bank Conference on Development Economics, Washington, DC.

Stiglitz, J. and **Weiss, A.** (1981) Credit rationing in markets with imperfect information, *The American Economic Review*, **71** (3), pp. 393–410.

Wang, Z.K. and **Winters, A.** (1991) The trading potential of Eastern Europe, *CEPR Discussion Paper No. 610,* London, November.

Williamson, J. (1993) *Economic Consequences of Soviet Disintegration*, Institute for International Economics, Washington, DC.

PART FIVE

THE NEW EUROPE FROM THE ATLANTIC TO THE URALS

GABLE
GLOBE AND MAIL
Toronto
CANADA

Cartoonists & Writers Syndicate

Introduction

It is time to conclude and reflect on the actions to be taken by the West to help rebuild Eastern European societies. Part I has helped in understanding what went wrong with the Soviet attempt to realise the Marxist dream. Part II explored the actions required to reform these economies, and identified possible pitfalls. Parts III and IV analysed different classes of countries, facing different classes of problems.

Part V focuses on what the West, and in particular Western Europe, can do to help reforms and the reconstruction of the East. Chapter 15 examines the financial needs for reconstruction of the East. It concludes that financial transfers are not the most important help that the West can provide. Certainly, financial support is helpful and at times even necessary (FSU states) to sustain political momentum for reforms, particularly at an early stage. But massive Western support is not required on a lasting basis. Much more important is access of Eastern Europe to West European markets. However, the situation in the FSU needs to be sharply distinguished from the one in Central Europe where stabilisation has already been achieved and structural reforms are progressing. In Russia and neighbouring states both stabilisation and structural reforms have stalled and even the basic design of the political and economic institutions is still fuzzy. We argue, therefore, in favour of a Marshall Plan II support of reforms justified by pure self-interest of the West.

The issues at stake are not primarily financial, but rather a new configuration of the political map of Europe. Due to its neighbourhood relationship, Western Europe is, of course, more concerned by political instability, military threats, nuclear pollution, economic misery or prosperity in Eastern Europe than are other parts of the world. In Western Europe political and not only economic reasons have been the propelling forces since the beginning of European integration, and the question therefore is whether the EU should expand towards the East, for the benefit of both the incumbent members of EU and Eastern European countries. This question is treated in the final chapter, Chapter 16.

Of course, the choice is not restricted to joining the EU or not. There may be cases where full EU membership is not desirable for at least one of the two partners, but some arrangement such as free trade is desirable.

The situation of individual countries is, naturally, very different. East Germany has already become a member of the EU after unification. The Visegrad countries and Slovenia (perhaps Croatia) are obviously much better placed for EU membership than the rest of South-Eastern Europe and the successor states of the FSU.

What should be done? We argue for a gradual and prudent eastward enlargement of the EU that needs to be accompanied by a reform of the Common Agricultural Policy to make the financial burden for the EU budget acceptable, and drastic reforms in the decision-making structure of the EU. An immediate expansion without this would benefit neither the EU nor the applicants for membership. However, not all former socialist countries should be allowed to join. In order to minimise the impact of this unavoidable seclusion, we strongly support expanding the scope for multilateral free trade by creating a European Free Trade Zone (EFTZ) from the Atlantic to the Pacific (thus englobing Russia).

CHAPTER FIFTEEN

The cost of reconstructing the East

'Cela est bien dit', répondit Candide, 'mais il faut cultiver notre jardin'.

Voltaire *Candide*, Ch. 30

What will it cost to reconstruct the formerly socialist economies and who will pay for it? This is the question that will determine the future of economic relations between the Eastern and Western parts of Europe. We do not pretend to provide a complete answer to this question, but even the very rough exercise we perform below is useful to provide an order of magnitude and to evaluate alternatives.

We are aware of the fact that capital is only one limiting factor of production in Eastern Europe. Whereas unskilled labour is in adequate, or even in excess, supply, skilled labour in some areas (e.g. managers) is scarce. It has often been observed that Eastern Europe has many engineers and other technical personnel and should thus be well-endowed with this type of human capital. However, this apparent advantage has not yet shown up in high productivity or standards of living. This chapter, therefore, focuses on the investment process and the lack of physical capital, leaving aside the question of human capital adequacy because the latter is almost impossible to measure.

This chapter is about 'gardening' and the time and resources required to obtain the desired results. Section 1 briefly discusses models of growth and their implications for capital accumulation in transition economies. Section 2 reviews published estimates of the cost of reconstruction and of the desired Western contribution, with our own assessment following on. We argue that a sustained growth path will be based mainly, but not exclusively, on capital accumulation. In the future capital productivity should increase as the amount of Western technology incorporated in new investments accumulates, rather than fall as would be predicted by a static neo-classical analysis. Section 3 asks how much external financing will be necessary and available, given domestic savings potential in Eastern Europe on the one hand and the competing investment opportunities worldwide, on the other. Section 4 discusses the case for a new Marshall Plan targeted on the successor countries of the former Soviet Union. Section 5 concludes with an outlook for the migration flows likely to be set in motion as impatience with the pace of East European catching up with West European standards of living grows. The Appendix provides information on international commitments to assist Eastern European countries.

1. Models of growth and capital accumulation

In order to be able to estimate the future investment needs of Eastern Europe, it is necessary to start with a model of growth and capital accumulation. The basic notions and models of growth were presented in Chapter 3. What follows here is an extremely condensed and simplified presentation of the capital accumulation approach.

By definition the rate of growth of GDP is equal to s/v where s is the savings rate which in a closed economy is equal to the investment rate, and v is the incremental capital–output ratio (ICOR). Different theories vary in their views of what defines s and v, that is, whether they are constants (Harrod–Domar models) or well-defined functions (neo-classical models), and whether v includes processes of key importance such as the role of human capital (e.g. managerial capacity), of technological progress hidden in physical capital, of economies of scale and the like (endogenous growth models).

In Eastern Europe, the assumption of a constant v may only be a reasonable approximation towards the end of the adjustment phase. For the transition period itself, a certain minimum level of productive capital may have to be accumulated before production can be run efficiently. As productive capital stock mounts, capital productivity should rise to a maximum and diminish thereafter. Thus, the capital–output ratio may be variable, declining sharply during the initial phase and rising slowly thereafter.[1]

Thus, the neo-classical growth model with constant returns to scale and full employment may be an adequate approximation of growth conditions in industrial countries, but is not suitable for reforming economies. The latter are likely to experience increasing returns as capital per worker increases, mainly due to the accumulation of 'social overhead capital' in the form of infrastructure investments and efficiency in market institutions. See Box 15.1.

Box 15.1 Growth with increasing returns to scale

Using a production function which permits phases of increasing, constant and diminishing returns to scale generates multiple equilibriums, as in Fig. A. below. For low values of k ($k < k^{**}$), output per worker (q) is growing at increasing returns, for higher levels of k ($k > k^{**}$) at decreasing returns. However, the lower equilibrium point at k^{**} is unstable, and k tends to fall back to zero for $k < k^{**}$. To escape such a 'poverty trap', the economy must be pushed over point k^{**} to the right. To this end, the capital stock per worker could be raised through capital transfers from abroad or via temporary savings and investment incentives. Alternatively, the production function could be shifted upwards by improving on the efficient use of production factors via economic reforms.

In the case of Eastern countries, k could be interpreted as an increasing function of time (for $k^{**} < k < k^{*}$): during the initial phases of reform, k would be low but would increase as reform progressed. In long-run equilibrium, k^{*} should be comparable to the capital intensity in industrial countries.

continued

Box 15.1 *continued*

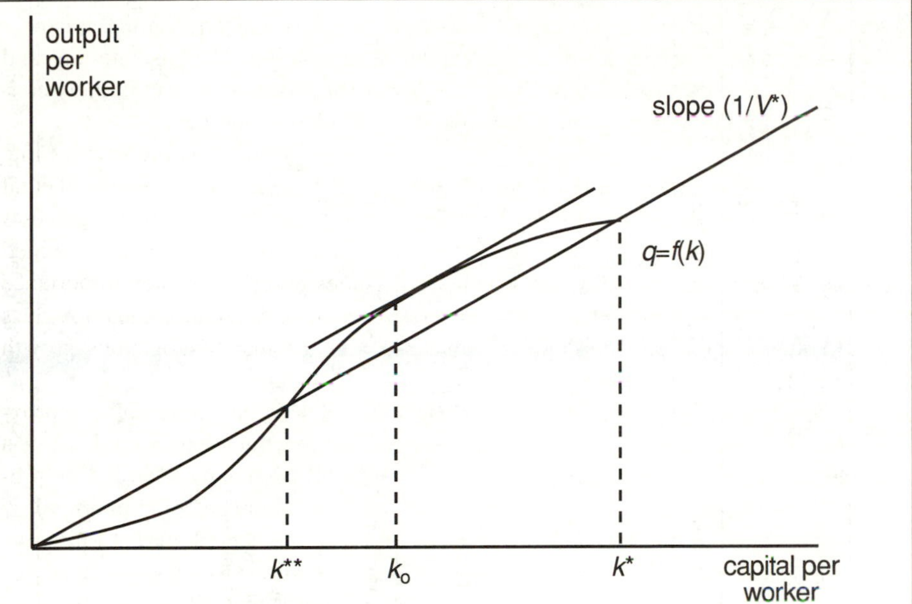

FIG A Neo-classical growth model with multiple equilibria

Corresponding to the shape of the production function, the average capital–output ratio V varies over time. At the outset, while k is small, V is rather high. As k rises but remains below k_o, V diminishes. For $k_o < k < k^*$, V rises to approach the (constant) equilibrium level V^* at k^*.

Another way of arriving at a variable V within the framework of the neo-classical model, is to rely on vintage models where V would depend on the age structure of the capital stock.

The 'new theory' of (endogenous) growth provides additional arguments in favour of increasing returns which are seen to result either from externalities or from monopolistic competition. In the first case new knowledge, produced by the research sector, increases production possibilities in other sectors and so may yield, even in competitive equilibrium, increasing aggregate returns to scale (Romer 1986, Lucas 1988). Alternatively, the price taker assumption is dropped and incomplete competition permitted: innovative entrepreneurs develop new technologies or find niches in some other way where there is little or no competition, at least for some time (Scott 1992). Both arguments have some bearing on transition economies.

What do these models imply for capital needs? In our view the basic message is 'no pain, no gain', as illustrated also by the experience of the fast growing NICs discussed below. Rapid growth requires massive investment, and although the marginal efficiency of investment should now be better than in the past, it is unlikely to be much higher than in developed market economies.

TABLE 15.1 Estimated investment needs of Eastern countries

Source	Regional coverage	Sector level	Policy target	Growth period (years)	Capital–output ratio	Value of existing capital stock	Average annual investment needs (US$ billion)	Of which annual external financing (US$ billion)
CEPR (1990)	E5	National	Doubling GDP per capita (7% p.a. average GDP growth rate)	10	2.5 (constant)	0	103 (net)	103
					4.0 (constant)	0	226 (net)	226
Fitoussi and Phelps (1990)	E5	National (excl. housing and non-marketable capital)	Average labour productivity as high as today in FRG and France	10	—	Non-zero	180 (gross) 110 (net)	Partly
McDonald and Thumann (1990)	Former GDR	National	Attaining labour productivity as in GDR	10	—	390	90–120 (net)	—
Collins and Rodrik (1991)	E7	National	Average labour productivity as in the West	10	2.5 at end of period	E5: 600 FSU: 1,700	E5: 421 (net) FSU: 1,164 (net)	Partly
			7% p.a. average GDP growth rate	10	2.5 at end of period	0	E5: 344 (net) FSU: 571 (net)	Partly
Gros and Steinherr (1991)	E3 and FSU	National	Average GDP per capita of EU in 1990	10–15	2.0 (constant)	—	E3: 126 (net) FSU: 687 (net)	Partly
Boote (1992)	E5	National	Productivity level relative to EU (implicit GDP growth 12.5% p.a.)	10	3.2 (average of country group, range from 2.6–4.0)	1,300	260 (gross)	—
Giustiniani *et al.* (1992)	E5, FSU, former GDR	National	Catching up with Western reference countries (9–10% p.a. average GDP growth rate)	14–23	—	—	—	85 (E5) 149 (FSU) 65 (former GDR)
OECD (1992)	E5	National	5% p.a. GDP per capita growth after 1995	25	Stable at current level	—	—	25

Abbreviations: E3 CSFR, Hungary, Poland E5 CSFR, Hungary, Poland, Bulgaria, Romania E7 CSFR, Hungary, Poland, Bulgaria, Romania, former Yugoslavia, former Soviet Union FSU Former Soviet Union

2. Appraisal of previous estimates of reconstruction costs

At the current stage of transformation, various future growth paths can be imagined for the Eastern European countries. Therefore, empirical estimates of capital needs differ markedly according to the particular set of assumptions employed, and can at best serve to delineate orders of magnitude. No estimate recently presented in the literature attempts a forecast of future growth. Rather, each study relies either on some sort of convergence argument or on some other references. A further key assumption relates to present efficiency levels and potential efficiency gains in former socialist countries. Most studies confine themselves to average development up to a certain point in time (usually 10 years from now). A synoptic view is provided by Table 15.1. The wide discrepancies between the various results underscore how sensitive they are to the specific assumptions concerning initial *per capita* GDP, the initial value of capital stock, the specific targets chosen, the length of the adjustment period, and the shape of the underlying production function. Box 15.2 discusses the main ingredients of some contributions.

Box 15.2 Why estimates of Eastern European capital needs differ

CEPR (1990) assume that the countries of 'Eastern Europe', excluding the former Soviet Union (FSU), Yugoslavia and East Germany, will seek to double their *per capita* GDP within 10 years, which implies an average annual rate of growth of about 7 per cent. For the required capital stock at the end of that period, a *lower limit* is derived by assuming a (constant) average capital–output ratio of 2.5. Alleging that present capital is worthless, average annual net investment needs amount to some US$ 103 bn. To arrive at an *upper limit,* the capital–output ratio is set at 4, and the initial level of aggregate GDP is assumed to be one third higher than in the lower-limit scenario. Average annual investment needs would then amount to US$ 226 bn. The study postulates that all net investments will be financed externally.

Fitoussi and Phelps (1990) model the demand for new capital in Eastern countries on a sudden increase in the world's labour force (by adding the East to the 'world') at a given capital stock. As a result, capital is reallocated to the East, real interest rates rise and real wages fall. The postulated target for the five countries considered ('E5', i.e. CSFR, Hungary, Poland, Bulgaria and Romania) after 10 years is to achieve average productivity of labour on a par with levels in Germany or France today.

Collins and Rodrik (1991) formulate a productivity target and a growth target. In the productivity approach they assume that, in a Cobb–Douglas production function, the share of capital in total income is one-third, and labour productivity in the East is at present only half of that in the West. Then, capital intensity in the

continued

Box 15.2 *continued*

West is currently eight times as high as in the East (US$ 85,900 versus US$ 10,700, respectively). Putting the average capital–output ratio in the West at 2.5, the present capital stock is estimated to be US$ 601 bn in Eastern Europe and US$ 2,265 bn in all Eastern countries. If labour productivity in Eastern countries is to attain Western levels within 10 years, capital stock would have to increase sevenfold, implying annual net investments in Eastern Europe of some US$ 420 bn (and US$ 1,600 bn if the FSU is included).

This approach assigns to capital the major explanation for observed income differentials, and leaves out of the picture the value of human capital stock and the disorganised state of the economy. The productivity approach is extremely crude, and the results are highly sensitive to the assumed labour productivity differential today (of which we know little), to the shape of the production function and to the implied target for closing that productivity gap.*

Giustiniani *et al.* (1992) match each East European country with a group of reference countries in the West regarded as relevant targets. The FRG serves as a reference country for the former GDR; Greece and Portugal for Romania and the FSU; Greece, Portugal and Spain for all others except Czechoslovakia, which obtains a high target through the inclusion of Austria in its reference set.

Assuming Cobb–Douglas technology, initial labour productivity of one-third of Western levels, and an adjustment function for the differences in labour productivity and total factor productivity, they obtain a dynamic simulation model that generates investment needs. Their results suggest that capital stock and GDP would grow in the range of 9–10 per cent, and the time required to catch up would range from 14 years for the former GDR to 23 years for Poland and the FSU. Moving on to the rather implausible assumption that savings ratios will remain at their 1989 levels – ranging from 22 per cent in the former GDR to 34 per cent in Romania – they come up with estimates of foreign financing needs. Inclusive of debt service, accumulated debt would reach a peak of US$ 4.8 trillion after 20 years and decline thereafter. Net import requirements would accumulate over 16 years at average annual amount of some US$ 300 bn (US$ 85 bn for the E5 countries, US$ 149 for the FSU and US$ 65 for the former GDR).

Some of the differences between the various estimates surveyed are due to divergent assumptions for initial *per capita* GDP. Conversions based on observed exchange rates are subject to frequent and substantial price changes. The less erratic purchasing power parities are likely to yield more realistic real income estimates. Havlik (1992) prefers a comparison based on welfare indicators which, however, refer to inputs more than to outputs and partly disregard differences in product quality. In our view, they yield implausibly high *per capita* income values. Joining issue with, for example, Gulde and Schulze-Ghattas (1992), Handler and Steinherr (1993) base their estimate (for 1990) on the PPP method used by PlanEcon (1990).

* Had it been assumed that labour productivity in the East were only one third, the capital–labour ratio would be only one-27th of the Western value.

In previous research (Gros and Steinherr 1991) we asked how much capital would be needed to bring the Central and East European economies close to average income in the European Community. Because the Central European countries are holding out for EU membership, this would seem to be a useful benchmark. More realistically, even taking into account the widely shared impatience to achieve convergence of living standards, the Central European countries will have done very well if they can match, in the next 10 years, the average standard of living enjoyed by the EU countries in 1993 (as opposed to the one probably reached by the EU at the end of the period considered).

Today it is no longer necessary to assume initial GDP levels as done in previous studies. The reforms have progressed enough to make the measured GDP data roughly comparable to Western figures (this was obviously not the case for the old data on net material product so that one can now take GDP measures in national currency and convert them at the market exchange rate. This yields figures for GDP *per capita* that are much lower than the ones used by previous studies. For example, in 1989 and 1990 the income *per capita* of Poland was usually estimated at around US$ 5,000 (at 1980 prices!) whereas the actual GDP *per capita* in 1992 and 1993, translated at market exchange rates, was about US$ 2,000 (much less than US$ 2,000 at 1980 prices!).

Early studies on capital needs were based on a data set published by Summers and Heston (1988) (and compiled with great care by independent economists and the World Bank) which gave the Central European countries a GDP up to 50 per cent higher than that of Greece or Portugal (the two poorest members of the Community). Today, at market exchange rates, the GDP *per capita* of Greece and Portugal is about two to three times higher than that of even the richer Central European countries. Where does this sudden 'impoverishment' of Central and Eastern Europe come from? It results mainly from four sources:

1. Some of the Western agencies that in the past published estimates of the income of the socialist block had an interest in estimates that pointed to strong socialist economies (CIA estimates are the best example). This 'Cold War' bias has been overcome and the old CIA estimates are now clearly obsolete.
2. Estimates of 'real' income that just deflate nominal incomes by official prices are misleading for the centrally planned economies since many goods were not readily available at the official prices. Officially measured real incomes and wages overstated the amount of goods people could really buy. This is just the mirror image of the so-called monetary overhang discussed in Part II. The correction of the monetary overhang required a jump in the price level of over 50 per cent even in a relatively stable country like Czechoslovakia (and over 250 per cent in Russia, see Chapter 14 for more details). From this point of view it is not surprising to find that 'real' income thus measured has fallen by up to one half.
3. If one translates GDP at market exchange rates the value of non-tradables (services, housing, etc.) and hence the purchasing power of income is difficult to determine. However, this problem is not specific to the transforming economies. For most poorer market economies one finds that GDP measured at purchasing power parity (PPP) exchange rates is higher (and in richer countries lower) than at market exchange rates because non-traded services are evaluated at very low wage rates, as shown in Table 15.2. For example, GNP *per capita* in Turkey and

TABLE 15.2 Comparisons of GNP per capita in US$ at market exchange rates and at PPP exchange rates in 1992

	Market exchange rates	PPP exchange rates
Market economies		
Germany	23,030	20,610
Greece	7,290	8,010
Portugal	7,450	10,120
Turkey	1,980	5,170
Reform economies		
Czech Republic	2,450	7,160
Slovak Republic	1,930	5, 620
Hungary	2,970	5,740
Poland	1,910	4,880
Russia	2,510	6,220
Romania	1,130	2,750
Bulgaria	1,330	5,130

Source: World Development Report 1994, Infrastructure for Development, World Development Indicators, The World Bank
Note: The data for reforming countries are subject to considerable margins of error. For example, most researchers give a GDP *per capita* below US$ 2,000 for Russia in 1992

Poland are similar both at market and at PPP exchange rates. However, it is not clear *a priori* how one should take this phenomenon into account. If one wants to compare how well off consumers are in different countries, one should compare income at PPP. By contrast, for comparisons of the weight of different countries in global economic relations, income should be measured at market exchange rates.

4. A further factor behind the statistical impoverishment of Central and Eastern Europe was the output decline. However, according to official data the decline in real GDP was about 20 to 30 per cent. This factor must have had only minor influence compared to the other factors mentioned.

The upshot from all this is that Central and Eastern Europe start from a much lower base than had been assumed earlier. How low is the starting level and what would be a reasonable target?

We are interested here in the question of how long it will take the formerly socialist countries in Central and Eastern Europe to come close to Western standards of living. Income should be measured at PPP exchange rates to deal with this question. However, Western capital, if needed, will not come at PPP exchange rates, hence it should be compared to GDP measured at market rates. We therefore base our calculations of the need for foreign capital on income valued at market exchange rates. But we take into account the difference between market GDP and PPP GDP when calculating the required growth rates for (partial) catch up by *not* assuming that the *market* GDP of Central and Eastern Europe has to reach, or even come close to, the average of the EU, as we would if the target were specified in PPP terms. Box 15.3 illustrates the implications of converging non-tradable goods prices (the main factor behind the differences between market exchange rates and PPP evaluations) with a comparison of GDP growth in Eastern Germany and in Central Europe.

Box 15.3 Catch up of Eastern Germany

Developments in Eastern Germany provide an interesting contrast to the scenarios developed here. The Eastern German case is different from the Central and Eastern European countries discussed in this chapter because of the huge transfers from Western Germany. These transfers (see Chapter 10) have been estimated (precise figures cannot really be established because East Germans pay taxes and social security contributions, some transfers come as direct hand-outs, others as tax incentives, etc.) to amount to far over US$ 100 bn a year on average in 1990–1993, or over US$ 6,000 *per capita* and per year. The size of these transfers can perhaps best be gauged by comparing them to total income in Central Europe: US$ 6,000 per year is twice the actual market GDP *per capita* in the former Czechoslovakia (and three times that of Poland). East Germans must certainly be materially much better off than their former fellow victims under socialism in the neighbouring countries.

A more interesting question is how much East Germans are themselves producing under the imported West German market system. The numbers are again startling: the market value of the goods produced (i.e. GDP) in the former GDR was equal to about US$ 6,500 (DM 11,600) *per capita* in 1991. By 1993 GDP *per capita* (which does not include transfers) had risen to over US$ 10,000 (DM 17,700). While this was still 'only' 40 per cent of the West German GDP *per capita* (of 1993), it was three times the Czech level and almost five times the Polish level.

It is usually assumed that the former GDR and Czechoslovakia were at a similar level of income before the reforms started in 1989. What is then the reason for this huge difference in the market value of goods produced three years after the reforms?

The huge transfers from Germany are not directly responsible since they increase only the consumption potential of East Germans and thus have no direct influence on productive capacity. The main reason for the huge difference in GDP *per capita* is that East German non-tradables are produced and evaluated at East German wages, which are much closer to the West German than to Czech or Polish ones. Transfers from West Germany have an indirect impact here since they sustain the demand for non-tradables in Eastern Germany, thus increasing their market value.

The difference between East Germany and its eastern neighbours that matters for growth (as opposed to the starting level of GDP) is the investment rate which reached over 40 per cent of East German GDP whereas it stayed at around 20 per cent in most of Central Europe. In 1993 (gross) investment *per capita* was about US$ 5,000 in East Germany (about the same level as in West Germany); but only

continued

Box 15.3 *continued*

US$ 400 in Poland and US$ 600 in the Czech Republic (in GDP *per capita* measured at market exchange rates). This is the main reason why the ratio GDP *per capita* in the ex-GDR to GDP *per capita* in CSFR has already widened from a factor of 'only' two in 1991 (US$ 6,000 in the ex-GDR versus US$ 3,000 in CSFR) to a factor of three in 1993 (US$ 10,000 versus, again, about US$ 3,000).

No directly comparable estimates of *per capita* GDP at purchasing power parity that include the former GDR and the Central European countries have been published yet. However, a simple comparison suggests that the gap between East Germany and Central Europe is large. Turkey had, in 1993, about the same GDP *per capita* evaluated at market exchange rates as Poland. In the same year the GDP *per capita* of Eastern Germany, evaluated at the purchasing power standard of the EU, was about 70 per cent higher than that of Turkey, and by implication also 70 per cent higher than that of Poland. These numbers even underestimate the gap since consumption was much higher than GDP in East Germany, hence consumption *per capita* was much more than 'only' 70 per cent above the Turkish level. East Germans are thus clearly not only much better off than their fellow victims under socialism, but they also have a much brighter future because they invest so much more. For a more detailed description of the East German story, see Chapter 10.

Table 15.3 shows the 'required' growth rates for the three main Central European countries (Czech Republic, Hungary, Poland) and Russia if the target were to reach either 50 per cent (column 3) or 100 per cent (column 4) of EU GDP *per capita* of 1993 (US$ 19,000) by the year 2008. Column (2) represents a pessimistic scenario of a 5 per cent growth, which is modest but probably realistic.

The full catch up is clearly not feasible: for Poland it would require growth rates of over 16 per cent a year, and even the Czech Republic would have to grow by 14.5 per cent each year to reach the EU level by 2008.[2] Even a much less ambitious target of 50 per cent of the EU level looks out of bounds since it requires sustained growth of 9.5 per cent and more over the next decade in all countries, except Hungary.

Column (5) reproduces GNP at PPP exchange rates in 1993 from Table 15.2. Assuming a 5 per cent growth rate this yields the results for 2008 in Column (6) which are between US$ 10,000 and US$ 13,000 *per capita* which exceeds 50 per cent of the current EU level of US$ 19,000. Experience inside the EU shows that if the market GNP *per capita* of one country is 10 per cent lower than that of another, the difference in GNP *per capita* at PPP exchange rates is only about 7 per cent.[3] If the Central European countries were to reach 50 per cent of the average of the EU level at market exchange rates they would thus be in terms of purchasing power at almost two-thirds (65 per cent). In PPP terms catching up is thus somewhat easier.

One lesson that emerges from this exercise is that full catching up will take more than one generation, even for the most advanced East European countries. This lesson has considerable bearing on the question of whether and when some of these countries can be integrated into the European Union (as discussed in the next chapter).

TABLE 15.3 Growth rates required for convergence to current EU income levels

	(1) GNP per capita 1993 (at market exchange rates)	(2) GNP per capita in 2008 at 5% growth	(3) Required rate of growth to catch up by 2008	(4) Required rate of growth to catch up to 50% by 2008	(5) GNP per capita in 1993 (at PPP exchange rates)	(6) GNP per capita in 2008 (at PPP exchange rates) at 5% growth	(7) Net capital needs per capita in 2008 (accu-mulated	(8) Savings at 20% of GNP per capita from 1993 to 2008
				in US$ in 1993				
Russia*	2 500	5 200	14.5%	9.5%	6 220	12 930	13 000	11 550
Czech Republic	2 450	5 100	14.5%	9.5%	7 160	14 890	12 750	11 325
Hungary	3 000	6 240	13.0%	8.0%	5 740	11 940	15 600	13 860
Poland	2 000	4 160	16.5%	11.0%	4 880	10 150	10 400	9 240

Source: Own calculations based on World Bank data.

* The GNP *per capita* of US$ 2,500 for Russia is the World Bank's estimate for 1993. Most observers would consider this figure as much too high. US$ 1,500–2,000 may be closer to reality, in which case the results for Poland in the table may apply to Russia.

So far we have only discussed what is 'required' if a certain target is to be hit. But a more interesting question is what would be the capital needs assuming 'reasonable' growth rates and current savings patterns. This question is addressed in Columns (7) and (8) of Table 15.3. Given the poor quality of available data and the long time horizon of the exercise (15 years), a rough-and-ready approach that yields easily interpretable results is chosen in preference to a sophisticated econometric exercise.

Column (7) of Table 15.3 exhibits the net capital needs (neglecting depreciation) for the growth paths of 5 per cent p.a. in Column (2) – the most reasonable sustained path. Net capital needs are obtained by assuming a constant incremental capital–output ratio of 2.5, which corresponds to the average capital–output ratio in the EU. This assumption neglects not only additional costs, such as depreciation, social investment and the cost of an environmental clean-up, but also ignores the potential efficiency gains from reforms through better use of existing resources. These offset one another at least partially.

To accumulate the amounts of capital shown in Column (7), a corresponding amount of domestic savings or foreign investment is required. Domestic savings ratios for the period 1985–89 range from 24 per cent (CSFR, Hungary) to 30 per cent (Poland, FSU), but they are likely to fall from their forced levels in spite of possibly safer and higher returns. So far, the declines observed have not been dramatic, as the precautionary motive for saving plays a more significant role in a market economy. Most formerly socialist countries in Europe seem to have gone for a (national) savings rate of about 20 per cent of GDP. Increased uncertainty and insufficient state provision for old age, sickness, and unemployment are bound to induce people to save in the future as well. Subtraction of Column (8) from Column (7) of Table 15.3 gives the required foreign capital imports to sustain a growth path of 5 per cent p.a. The need for foreign capital represents about 12 per cent of total investments over the entire period of 15 years. The needs range from US$ 1,160 *per capita* in Poland to US$ 1,740 in Hungary. Multiplied by the population of each country this yields a total foreign capital need of some US$ 300 bn. Over a period of 15 years this is not an unmanageable amount and clearly less than the amount advanced in the earlier studies summarised in Table 15.1. In practice more would be needed at the beginning and less towards the end of the period.

The above scenario suggests that sustained growth does not require an excessive increase in foreign debt over the period as a whole provided domestic savings can be maintained at a reasonable level. This is an important conclusion, because some of the countries concerned are already heavily indebted, and foreign private investors are still reluctant to commit themselves while the future looks so uncertain.

Foreign funds will be particularly useful early on to finance the take-off and to offset income losses generated by the shock of restructuring. This is very clearly evidenced in Poland and the FSU. Unfortunately, borrowing foreign funds is particularly difficult in the early days of a new regime, so that it is crucial to establish credibility and credit-worthiness as rapidly as possible. As long as foreign investors are not confident about a future return to stable growth with open borders, they will either not invest or invest only in projects with very short payback periods. The importance of foreign capital at the start of the growth process is increased by the fact that direct foreign investment is imperative to effect the transfer of technology and management skills and to assist in reallocating national resources.

A recurrent policy message of all the studies carried out so far (see Table 15.1) is that ambitious growth targets are achievable only if the accumulation of physical capital is accompanied by substantial efficiency gains. These will only materialise if direct foreign investment, the implementation of market-oriented legal and institutional structures continues apace.

The next section examines in more detail the validity of the assumptions retained in our approach and turns to more qualitative questions.

3. Are large financial transfers to Eastern countries the key to success?

PRIVATE INVESTMENT DEMAND

The fundamental force propelling economic reform in the formerly centrally planned economies of Eastern Europe is their people's thirst for better living standards. Whether or not the reform effort can be kept up probably depends on whether satisfactory rates of economic growth can be achieved in the not too distant future, and private investment behaviour is the key to how fast these economies can move to a sustainable path of healthy economic growth. By the same token, the behaviour of savings will determine the feasibility of high growth and fix the required level of foreign financing.

The most serious obstacle to the emergence of strong private investment demand has been the extent of uncertainty accompanying the reform process. The irreversibility of many types of capital investment makes it optimal from the individual investors' point of view to wait before committing funds to new activities, except in the case of projects which are expected to produce very high yield. This effect is likely to prove especially strong when investors are banking on much of the uncertainty evaporating within a few years, as is currently the case in Eastern Europe. Each single individual who fails to invest adds to the credibility problem and makes investment less attractive to all others, so that some of these economies are in danger of getting caught in a stagnation equilibrium. The policy message again comes through loud and clear: the reform process must proceed quickly, not least with regard to the 'rules of the game' that will govern private enterprise. In addition, there may be scope for well-designed measures to stimulate private investment today by offering temporary benefits to enterprises that undertake investment early in the reform process. In the meantime, recorded investment has plummeted. In Russia the ratio of investment to GDP was below 15 per cent in 1993, about half the value of the 1980s. In the Central European countries, where the uncertainty about the reform was much lower, the decline in investment (now at about 20 per cent of GDP) has been less severe.

As regards the short- to medium-term prospects for growth in Eastern Europe, there is no need for undue pessimism. Although it may indeed prove difficult to reach levels of investment of 30–40 per cent of GDP (as in the high growth countries) over the next few years, reasonably high rates of growth may prove to be within reach with more modest investment rates of about 20 per cent of GDP – certainly much lower than these economies have nominally generated in the past. We base this conclusion on the fact that the reform process will help to improve efficiency in the investment sphere and so contribute to a gradual, but significant, decline in incremental capital–output ratios.

DOMESTIC SAVINGS POTENTIAL

If there is to be sufficient investment, adequate levels of savings will have to be produced if unsustainable macroeconomic imbalances are to be avoided. In the previous exercise we assumed that 20 per cent of GDP will be saved during the next 10 years. In order to assess the realism of this assumption it becomes crucial to assess the savings potential in the East and to take a closer look at fears that savings will turn into a serious growth inhibitor. In this connection, the prime areas of concern will be the need to transform the methods of public sector financing and the impact of privatisation on household saving. In the short run, the availability of foreign savings – or at least its private component – is likely to depend on factors similar to those affecting private domestic investment, since both represent claims on the respective domestic economies.

Past savings of the household sector (mainly savings deposits) in most Eastern countries have been virtually wiped out by price adjustments. In the immediate aftermath of liberalisation a build-up of new household savings was held up as private citizens sought to satisfy their long-frustrated demand for consumer goods. In the short to medium term, however, substantial savings should come from all domestic sectors, both private and public.

Compared to most industrialised countries in the West, household savings never amounted to much in the former socialist countries. This was particularly true of Czechoslovakia, where households produced only some 6–7 per cent of total domestic savings in 1990. Yet as in Hungary and Poland, household savings in the CFSR have in more recent years helped to shore up the national savings rate, which dropped sharply after 1988, largely because of falls in government and enterprise savings.

Hungary presents much the same picture with an aggregate savings rate at a steady 25 per cent since the mid-1980s (24 per cent in 1991). Household savings amounted to 14 per cent in 1991, a remarkable result since at first glance soaring unemployment and shrinking household incomes seem less than ideal conditions for adding to the family deposit book.

In Poland the savings pattern since 1990 has been dominated by a recovery in household savings (20 per cent of GDP), partly offsetting a marked fall-off in government and enterprise savings well into 1992 as both tumbled from the lofty heights attained in the wake of the prolonged burst of economic recovery in the 1980s. That recovery was affected by high inflation and relative price shifts, and by 1989 inventory changes amounted to 22 per cent of GDP (11 per cent in 1990). By that time, total domestic savings had peaked at close to 30 per cent of GDP, a far cry from the deep recession in 1978–82 when domestic savings had plummeted to a mere 11.5 per cent of GDP.

The prospective sectoral breakdown of total savings may be evaluated as follows:

1. As in most fast-growing countries, *household saving* is likely to give the overall savings rate in Eastern Europe a significant shot in the arm. By and large, this process is helped along by spillover effects from a newly expanding, private enterprise sector. It will, however, be some time before its share of overall output is sufficient to make more than a modest contribution to household saving, so that a realistic assumption would be maintenance of a household savings ratio of over 6–8 per cent of GDP in the medium term.
2. The East European public authorities on the other hand will have their work cut out even if all they aim for is a return to the average 5–8 per cent of GDP *government savings* ratio recorded in the past. Reform of the tax structure may well prove imperative if they are to succeed, since pressures for more public spending are unlikely to abate and capital will have to be found to finance pressing infrastructure improvements.
3. If the government savings target is met, this leaves 5–10 per cent for the *enterprise sector* to achieve an overall 20 per cent savings rate as we assumed. A first obvious move is to cut inventories, which will find some 3–4 per cent, and a further 7–8 per cent can be produced with little effort through depreciation allowances. Swift completion of the privatisation process is crucial here, as is the emergence of sound financial markets, neither of which is a realistic proposition even in the medium term. Enterprises continuing under state control must not, therefore, be allowed to evade the 'hard budget constraint' if the 10 per cent savings target in this sector is to be achieved.

Will the recent rise in household savings be sufficiently long-lived to make a positive impact on national savings prospects? Certainly, the private sector is growing fast and yielding considerable income gains, an offshoot of which is likely to be increased household saving. In Hungary and Poland in particular, the recent upswing in the savings rate may well point to a high propensity to save in the new business sector.

Private sector savings should not be eaten up by public sector dis-savings.[4] This is why a sound fiscal policy is imperative. The ideal would be a small surplus of the government budget that is not attained at the cost of reducing public sector capital spending. However, a sound fiscal policy alone is not enough, it needs support from proper exchange rate policies and wage-setting practices. Here Eastern Europe can usefully look to examples such as Chile where fixed exchange rates and wage indexation played havoc with company profitability and savings rates in the late 1970s, or to Korea whose fate at that time was only marginally less dramatic: recovery only came after a substantial depreciation. The three Central European countries have opted for a combination of fixed but adjustable nominal exchange rates and incomes policies which keep real wages down. This does steer enterprise savings into safer waters and reduce the risk to the current external account, but in the longer run social dissatisfaction is liable to cast a shadow over the entire reform process, with the inherent risk of systemic uncertainty as evidenced in several Latin American countries.

Exactly how financial markets help in generating savings and supporting a higher rate of growth is something of an enigma. If the ratio of M2 to GDP is taken as a measure of financial depth, there seems to be a strong and positive correlation with real growth and savings. Yet countries such as China and Korea (which have a large ratio of M2 to GDP: for China it is above 100 per cent; see BIS 1994) have achieved very high growth rates, although their financial markets cannot in all honesty be said to enjoy a large measure of emancipation. The three Central European countries will probably gain more from an early reform of their banking and financial systems. Since capital resources are tight, positive real interest rates coupled with a broad range of financial assets could stimulate household saving. Likewise, the support of a sophisticated financial system will be indispensable to the privatisation of state-controlled firms. Last but not least, relatively deep capital markets will be needed to avoid monetisation of the near-term budget deficits, as argued in Chapter 9.

According to our results in Table 15.3, which in terms of foreign funding needs are on the low side in comparison with other studies, at least 12 per cent of total investment would need to be financed from foreign sources. This would represent some 2.5–3 per cent of GDP over 15 years, an order of magnitude that is not uncommon for countries 'taking off'. But what if efficiency gains are slow to materialise, errors in the allocation of investments accumulate, fiscal reforms fail to become effective in good time, and domestic savings fall short of the assumed 20 per cent of GDP? Is it reasonable to expect much higher foreign capital contributions? Box 15.4 develops some insights and provides comparative data for some Asian and European economies during their 'take-off' to assess these issues.

Box 15.4 Can sustained growth rely predominantly on foreign funding?

During the initial years of reform and reconstruction the demand for funds is likely to exceed the supply by domestic savings. Figure A illustrates the benefits of foreign funding: as is to be expected, the real world market interest rate r^* is

continued

Box 15.4 *continued*

lower than the domestic equilibrium rate r. Hence a higher level of investment ($I^*>I$) can be realised thanks to foreign funding. Of course, the country will accumulate foreign debt at the rate of $I^*–S^*$. The question is: what is a sustainable level of $(I^*–S^*)/I^*$?

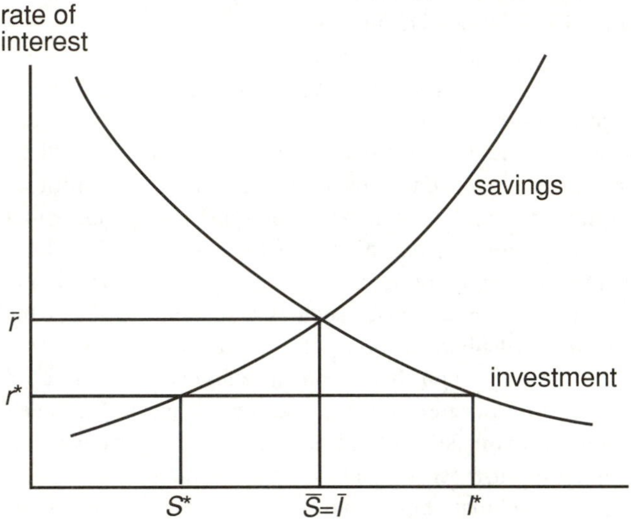

FIG A Benefits of foreign funding

To begin, it may be useful to recall the following identities:

- domestic investment + current account surplus = national savings;
- national savings – net factor payments from abroad = domestic savings;
- domestic savings = household savings + enterprise savings + public sector savings.

Table A below summarises the key macroeconomic data for selected, rapidly growing Asian economies.

Several facts emerge from a study of the table. First of all, *per capita* income and savings seem not to be correlated at all. Some of the poorest countries have savings rates comparable to or even higher than those recorded in the industrialised countries.

Second, the foreign contribution to domestic investment financing is sporadic and marginal over extended periods of time for most countries. The 5 per cent or so of GDP registered in Korea or Thailand for periods of up to a decade seem to have been the exception rather than the rule.[5]

continued

Box 15.4 *continued*

TABLE A Savings rates and related variables*

	National saving/ GDP	Current account/ GDP**	Real Growth	Per capita income US$	ICOR†
			1970s		
	in percentages, unless otherwise indicated				
				(1975)	
China	30.0	0.0	8.1	180	3.7
India	20.5	−0.3	3.2	140	6.5
Indonesia	16.7	−1.8	8.0	220	2.3
Korea	22.8	−5.2	8.2	560	3.4
Malaysia	24.0	0.3	8.0	760	3.0
Thailand	14.2	−3.3	6.8	350	2.6
			1980s		
				(1985)	
China	34.2	−0.5	8.8	310	3.9
India	21.7	−1.8	5.7	250	4.1
Indonesia	26.3	−2.4	5.3	530	5.4
Korea	29.9	0.1	9.3	2,180	3.2
Malaysia	27.6	−3.0	5.9	2,050	5.2
Thailand	21.7	−4.0	7.7	830	3.3

Sources: World Bank: World Tables, World Debt Tables and Social Indicators of Development; IMF: International Financial Statistics and World Economic Outlook; and OECD: Economic Outlook and National Accounts.

* Average ratios or growth rates for 1970-80 and 1980-90 respectively.

** Surplus

† Measured as investment/GDP ratio divided by growth of real GDP, averages for 1970-80 and 1980-90 respectively.

Third, the success of the NICs in terms of real growth is readily related to a high investment ratio and to proper balancing of investments and savings. Mann (1990) quotes the Republic of Korea as an outstanding example: initially (from 1965 to 1973) investments were largely financed by growing foreign debt; from 1973 to 1980, gross investment and savings ratios rose sharply (average share in GDP of 31 per cent and 25.7 per cent respectively); in the course of the 1980s, investments remained buoyant, while some of the external debt was repaid. Investment savings patterns were largely similar in Taiwan (Urban 1992). A strong positive correlation between investment and *per capita* income growth was also found by De Gregorio (1991) for the fastest-growing economies in Latin America.

Fourth, it is, therefore, not consistent with historical experience to argue that the countries of Eastern Europe should be provided with foreign funds much in excess of 10 per cent of GNP as we have suggested for periods of a decade or

continued

Box 15.4 *continued*

more. The reason for the high correlation between domestic investments (and growth) and savings may not be lack of available funds but rather that the capacity to invest and the capacity to obtain domestic funding require the same organisational skills. A society unable to collect taxes, unable to win the confidence of savers, unable to intermediate the flow of funds from savers to the best possible uses, is a society which may not be ready to absorb foreign funds efficiently. To put it provocatively: a society incapable of saving is also incapable of investing. Trying to shorten the process by leap-frogging this development and calling on foreign funds may be quite a waste, as is amply demonstrated in the foreign aid arena. More important than foreign capital is the ability to export and to open domestic markets. Indeed, the increasing export dependence of fast-growing countries is as spectacular as their savings ratios. The export–GDP ratio increased in Germany from 11.5 per cent in 1950 to 20.1 per cent in 1960; in Korea from 5.4 per cent in 1960 to 28 per cent in 1975; in Malaysia from 49 per cent in 1978 to 74 per cent in 1989. (Countries and periods are chosen for exceptional bouts of growth.)

To sum up, an investment ratio of 25 per cent of GDP or more, of which up to one-fifth might be financed by capital imports, looks not at all implausible, always assuming the public sector and enterprises continue to pull their weight on the savings front. But in order to foster investment-led recovery and keep dependence on foreign capital in check as the process gains momentum, the Eastern European countries still face the major hurdle of promoting a responsive private sector and ironing out glaring inefficiencies in the tax system.

If they fail this test, they will find themselves far more dependent on foreign credits than they are bargaining for in the medium term.

EXTERNAL AVAILABILITY OF FUNDS

Can annual transfers of US$ 100 bn and more to East European countries (including the countries of the FSU), on top of a transfer of similar magnitude to the ex-GDR, be financed without creating major strains on world financial markets? A basis for discussion is provided by the estimates of Collins and Rodrik (1991). They consider three scenarios: a lower-bound scenario of US$ 30 bn transfer per year to Eastern Europe, including the ex-GDR and the FSU; an intermediate scenario of US$ 55 bn; and a high-level scenario of US$ 90 bn per year.

With unchanged transfers to LDCs, these additional flows would raise real interest rates worldwide by 96 basis points (bp), 176 bp and 288 bp respectively. The sharp increases in interest rates result from the very low interest elasticity of savings and investment as estimated by these authors. Alternatively, increased transfers to the East may crowd out transfers to LDCs, at unchanged interest rates. This would decrease investment as a share of GDP in the LDCs by up to two percentage points. Of course, if interest rates were to rise, then LDC borrowing would also decline, so that transfers to Eastern Europe would be funded by adjustment both in developed and in less developed countries.

It might be informative to approach this question from another angle. Table 15.4 gives regional current account imbalances from 1990 to 1993 as estimated by the IMF.[6] The major surplus countries in the 1990s are Japan and other smaller Asian countries. For some time to come, the developing countries' deficit is expected to increase, as Africa will be unable to support itself, as Latin America is returning to positive growth, as the Middle East is suffering from a decline in oil prices in real terms and growth will benefit from better peace prospects, and as Asia is growing fast. The US current account deficit is likely to contract but not to disappear. At best, this reduction will be enough to offset the increases in the Latin American deficit. Europe's surpluses of the late 1980s have now vanished as a result of the switch in the German current account from a large surplus to a deficit. However, most estimates of future trade flows conclude that more substantial financial flows to Eastern countries will be reflected in high current account surpluses in Europe and Asia, as they step up their exports to the European East (see also Gros and Steinherr 1991).

One immediate lesson of this analysis is that surplus countries, in particular Japan, should not be induced to trim their surpluses. Furthermore, it may even become possible for amounts closer to the upper range of estimated financing needs to materialise without significant increases in world interest rates, if Western excesses and inefficiencies are scaled down.[7]

TABLE 15.4 Regional imbalances–payments balances on current account* (excluding Exceptional Financing)

	1990	1991	1992	1993
		US$ billion		
Industrial countries	−117.8	−34.2	−46.2	−5.2
United States	−90.5	−8.3	−66.4	−109.2
Japan	35.9	72.9	117.6	131.5
Germany**	45.8	−18.8	−22.1	−21.4
Other industrial countries	−109.0	−80.0	−75.3	−6.0
Developing countries excl. Eastern Europe and former USSR	−2.4	−76.6	−61.7	−103.9
Eastern Europe and former USSR	−22.4	−9.2	−2.7	10.2
Eastern Europe	−1.4	−6.8	−6.7	−5.8
Former USSR†	−21.0	−2.4	4.0	16.0
All developing countries	−24.8	−85.8	64.4	93.7
By region:				
Africa	0.7	−1.9	−4.7	−8.7
Asia	−0.4	−3.3	−6.3	−25.7
Europe	7.0	3.0	4.5	13.9
Middle East	5.1	−59.1	−20.8	−20.6
Western Hemisphere	−1.4	−16.1	−32.1	−40.9
Former USSR	−21.0	−2.4	4.0	16.1

Source: IMF International Financial Statistics
* Including official transfers
** Data through June 1990 apply to West Germany only
† Russia after 1992

The figures for Russia (FSU before 1992) suggest that the availability of external funds is sometimes of no use. If conditions for domestic investment are as bad as they were in 1992–93, private agents will prefer to export capital. The mirror image of this capital export (mostly unrecorded and hence more appropriately called capital flight) is the current account surplus of Russia during these years.

Moreover it is not clear whether more funds could really be officially channelled even into those countries that do not experience capital flight. International organisations are having difficulty spotting suitable projects for financing. Also, it is not financial constraints that are inhibiting industrial investment in Eastern Europe, but rather lack of projects of the desired quality and the overall climate of uncertainty. Many investments that are carried out are modest in scope and their purpose is mainly to keep options open.

To sum up, it is quite clear that not all the financing needs in Eastern Europe will and can be met by the West. Recent experience shows that the absorption capacity of Eastern countries is quite limited, but, that domestic savings potential remains intact. To mobilise new savings as well as foster domestic investment, economic reforms (particularly with regard to privatisation, legal and economic stability, financial intermediation) would need to continue (or rather start, in some countries). Otherwise Eastern Europeans will prefer to invest in the West.

Net foreign financing has been modest so far as mirrored by the small current account deficits of the Eastern European countries, and is likely to remain modest in the years to come. This is particularly true of foreign direct investment, which is wary of the uncertainties still bedevilling the reform process. Funding will undoubtedly accelerate once these uncertainties are reduced sufficiently to create a reliable investment climate. Eastern Europe will then become a major borrower of external funds for which, however, there will be fierce competition. Only solid projects will be able to obtain funding from private capital markets, and marginal borrowers everywhere will be crowded out. This means that East European projects will need to offer foreign investors risk-adjusted returns at least comparable to those in the developed countries.

4. A 'Marshall Plan' for the countries of the FSU?

So is official financing the solution?[8] We argue that there is not a very large need for official financing in Central Europe. The case of the countries of the former Soviet Union is, however, a very different one. These countries arguably need more official assistance than existing institutions may be able to provide. Since the analogy with the Marshall Plan has been extensively used in the public discussions about how to aid Eastern Europe, one needs to look closely at the arguments for and against.

In response to the political change in Eastern Europe, the international community was quick to set up a new institution, the EBRD, with the exclusive aim of helping reforms and reconstruction with both financial means and expertise. The European Community reacted expeditiously by establishing technical assistance through a new institutional support, PHARE and TACIS. Furthermore, it concluded 'European agreements' (EAs) with a number of Central European countries in order to facilitate and prepare those countries for future membership of the European Union. By contrast, special arrangements that had proved useful in Western European post-war reconstruction, such as the Marshall Plan and the European Payments Union (EPU), were discussed but not found worth implementing. (See the Appendix to Chapter 6 for a discussion of the West European post-war reconstruction experience.) By and large, this was the right decision for Central Europe, but Marshall aid in a payments system for trade among the successor states of the former Soviet Union (FSU), modelled on the European Payments Union, might have helped to prevent trade disruption and could have smoothed restructuring. Chapter 13 argues that the pay-off from a payments union would have been large, but trade destruction has now reached a stage (which is irreversible) where this is no longer a viable option.

Some analysts and decision makers would not dispute the risks of reform failure in the FSU and would be ready to support reforms but are convinced that financial support would be counter-productive (see Desai 1994 and Hare 1994). Sachs (1994) responds to this agnosticism by recalling that very much the same sentiments were prevalent in the United States in 1947, during the discussion of the Marshall Plan. He also reminds us of the devastating consequences of the total collapse of government authority in deep financial crisis, as in China after 1912, Russia after 1917 and Germany after 1918. Is there nothing more the West can do to prevent a repeat of history in the FSU?

In 1992 an opportunity perhaps existed to set up a Marshall Fund II with a reincarnation of the OEEC (Organisation for European Economic Cooperation, precursor to today's OECD) and a payments union modelled on the EPU. The clearing system (or payments union) would have served to prevent the disruption of supply that has bogged down the economies of the FSU countries and would have been supported by hard-currency credit lines. A concrete project without hard currency credit lines exists, but has not been implemented for lack of external support (see Gros 1993).

Marshall Plan II funds could still be used for reform programmes with strong externalities, some of which would directly benefit the West. One such use would be social support programmes to make reforms politically acceptable and socially sustainable. Strong externalities also characterise nuclear safety, security of energy supplies, restructuring of the defence industry[9] and reduction of environmental pollution. In all these cases, neighbours – and in particular Western Europe – would benefit substantially.

Marshall Plan II funds would complement existing financial interventions, which until 1994 have been modest, due to political and institutional constraints. For example, the total resources made available by the IMF are unimpressive. During 1990-94 annual average disbursements worldwide have been between SDR 5.2 and SDR 6.8 billion. The net annual flows, that is, annual disbursements less reimbursements, represented only about SDR 1 billion. The share of Eastern Europe in disbursements has, however, been increasing from about 5 per cent in 1990 to 22 per cent in (fiscal) 1993 and 55 per cent in (fiscal) 1994, mainly due to one drawing of SDR 2.2 billion by Russia.

The financial commitments of Marshall Plan II would not need to be as important as the effort made by the United States at the end of the 1940s, as measured in relation to Western GDP, to grant a similar support in terms of GDP of the FSU. Table 15.5 provides the magnitudes involved for a repeat of 'history's most successful structural adjustment programme' (De Long and Eichengreen 1993).

Between April 1948 and December 1951 the Marshall Plan transferred US$ 12.4 bn to 16 Western European countries, mostly in the form of outright grants. If this

TABLE 15.5 Marshall Plan based magnitudes of grants for the FSU

	US$ bn
Marshall Plan (1948–51)	12.4
Inflation adjusted (in 1991, US$)	65.4
Real per capita adjusted	66.8
1% of donor GDP (OECD)	544.0
2% of recipient GDP for 4 years	32.0

Source: Collins and Rodrik (1991)

amount is adjusted for inflation it would represent US$ 65 bn in current dollars – considerably more than what the FSU has been promised so far. In terms of efforts to be made by the West (say, the OECD countries), US$ 65 bn would amount to roughly one-eighth of a per cent of OECD GDP over four years. If OECD countries were to transfer 1 per cent of GDP – as provided for by the United States under the Marshall Plan – this would represent US$ 544 bn. As a share of GDP of recipient countries the Marshall Plan represented 2 per cent of the aggregate GDP of 16 Western European countries. Two per cent of FSU GDP over four years would amount to US$ 32 bn (taking a GDP of US$ 400 bn). Ratios to GDP might be misleading, however, since the funds provided by the West increase only the international purchasing power of the recipient. Since Russia's imports remain at only US$ 30–40 bn per annum, US$ 10 to 15 bn could have a very significant effect in this regard.

We would argue that a Marshall Plan II providing over the six years 1994–2000, in addition to the bilateral and multilateral support available, some US$ 30 to 70bn (or US$ 5–10bn annually) would be a low price (less than one twentieth of one per cent of OECD GDP for six years) for obtaining a better chance of maintaining peace and making sure that these countries move forward towards stable democratic societies.

The usual objections to a Marshall Plan II seem quite valid for Central Europe, but not for the FSU. These arguments rightly point out that the world has changed since the 1940s: there is an international capital market, private entrepreneurs seize opportunities with foreign direct investments and there is public sector support through multilateral institutions. Another major difference between post-war Western Europe and the FSU today is that the institutional, legal and socio-economic framework for a market economy was basically available in Western Europe but needs to be built up in the FSU. Moreover, the governments functioned, corruption was limited and laws were actually implemented. This is not the case in Russia and most of the rest of the FSU. Therefore there is a great need today in the FSU for grants but also a greater necessity to channel and monitor the use of these funds within an economy-wide framework. For that reason financial support administered either by the EBRD or by a new OEEC would be preferable to an SDR allocation, as proposed by the IMF. However, the West cannot force the FSU countries to adopt the reform measures that allow Western support to become effective. It cannot force the recalcitrant countries (mainly in the FSU) to adopt reforms, but it can strengthen the hand of the reformers by providing a clear signal that substantial aid will become available rapidly once local conditions are ripe. While this should just be common sense, it risks falling into the chicken and the egg trap: without reforms no aid, without aid no reforms. Over the last years the West has insisted on tangible success in reforms *before* any aid package could be discussed. With hindsight it is clear that this policy contributed to the partial failure of reforms and stabilisation in the FSU and particularly Russia, as described in Chapters 13 and 14 above. Given the strategic importance of Russia, this was a mistake. Even a 'long-shot' bet on stabilisation and reform in Russia would have been worthwhile (as argued passionately by Sachs 1994).

Suppose that in 1992 and 1993 the West had supported the new reform-minded government in Russia with US$ 10 bn of *grants* per year (not the support credit actually given[10]) to allow the budget deficit to be financed without the massive recourse to inflation tax that actually took place, as shown in Chapter 14. Such a policy would have been worthwhile despite the risks involved in not leading to stabilisation in Russia. The increase in military expenditure that the United States, the European countries and Japan have to contemplate as a result of the harder Russian foreign policy stance, which in turn is also a consequence of the failure of the reformists, will quickly exceed US$ 20bn. The attempt to save reforms in Russia would probably have been worthwhile even if the odds had been 1:2 or 1:3 against, but unfortunately such an audacious approach was never seriously considered.

Sweeping judgements about the generalised failure or success of reforms in Russia are usually wrong, as argued in detail in Chapter 14, but it is true that the reforms have failed from a political point of view. The Russian people have not been convinced that a market economy based on the rule of the law and a stable macroeconomic framework is in their best interests. This political failure of the market economy model in Russia will cost the Russian people and the West dearly for some time to come.

5. The alternative: labour migration

In those countries where reforms do not improve the standard of living, people will vote with their feet. From an economic point of view Eastern Europe's catching up with Western European standards of living can be viewed in the light of the conditions for factor–price equalisation, as taught in international trade courses. For factor–price equalisation to happen, or anyway to tend in that direction, at least one of the following conditions needs to be satisfied, apart from the general conditions underpinning competitive markets: free movement of goods across frontiers, free movement of capital, or free movement of labour. Because free trade and perfect mobility of production factors remain a theoretical abstraction, it would be a good thing to have as much free exchange as possible of all three, second-best considerations notwithstanding.

What, then, can be expected from factor movements, that is, migration from Eastern to Western Europe?

To begin with, the incentives are certainly there. At wage differentials of 10:1, emigration becomes an interesting alternative, even taking into account the cost of migration, which is enormous: the physical cost of selling one's assets in presumably illiquid markets for land, dwellings, household belongings and the like; the uncertain prospects at the other end; the time and effort involved in learning another language and absorbing a new culture; and the cost of setting up in the new country. The more uncertain or unpromising the returns at home, the more the perceived cost of migration goes down through the positive externalities of mass emigration and the positive welcome policy of the host country, and the more the cost-benefit analysis tilts in favour of emigration.

Most East European countries now allow their people to go where they please. If reforms in these countries fail, the pressure to emigrate will intensify. But even if reforms are successful, they are likely to generate high unemployment for some time. That would also add to the incentive to move.

Layard *et al.* (1992) estimate that Western Europe may have to cope with some 10 million would-be immigrants over the next decade – about four million from Eastern Europe and another six million from the FSU. On top of this, another three million ethnic Germans might come 'home'. Can Western Europe cope with such an influx of immigrants? The answer to that question probably depends on a host of factors, but in the meantime it should be acknowledged that Western Europe is politically unprepared for the onslaught.

During the 1960s and 1970s, about five million Southern Europeans moved north. But these two decades were blessed with much more rapid growth in the European North than is likely to occur in the decade ahead of us. Also, a considerable proportion of South–North migration was temporary, so that host countries were spared the infrastructure outlay needed to provide permanent homes for new citizens.[11]

During the 1990s there is a demographic reason for regarding immigration over the next decades as almost necessary despite reduced growth prospects. Western Europe is ageing fast. Life expectancy is rising, education retards entry into the labour market and the birth rate is below replacement levels (and declining further). As a result, the number of active members of the total population is on a sharp downtrend. Western Europe will soon be short of young workers and so lacks the tax base needed to support the non-working population in comfort. Figure 15.1 depicts the actual and forecast increases in Western Europe's labour force.

From a peak of over a million net increase a year in the labour force during the late 1970s, this increase has since fallen off to 0.4 million in 1990 and is forecast to become a decline of more than a million in the year 2025. On that basis net immigration of half a million a year or even more would appear to be a manageable and even a desirable target. But there are other factors which militate against this view.

First, as already mentioned, growth may not match the performance of the late 1980s - although this is something which only time will tell. Another imponderable is the level of training and adaptability of the migrant labour force. Third, the outrageously rigid West European labour legislation is a formidable barrier unlike anything the United States has ever seen. The United States currently accept up to 750,000 immigrants a year. Pay structure, employment protection and social security benefits are, however, far more flexible and much less costly on the other side of the Atlantic than in Europe.

Finally, Germany is a textbook example of the political problems which mass immigration can cause when there is no proper policy response. Germany has found room, of sorts, for up to a million immigrants a year since 1989. However, the social tensions sparked by high immigration flows coupled with rising unemployment were very serious indeed because of a social welfare system that discourages the newcomer from finding work rapidly. The result was that xenophobic tendencies became a major political problem.

So what ought to be done? First of all, Western Europe should assist Eastern

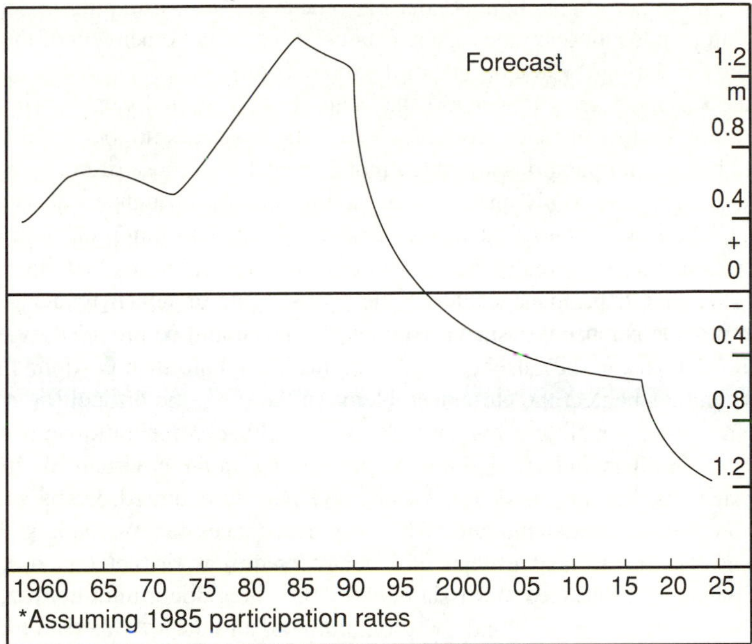

FIG 15.1 Western Europe's labour force (annual changes due to domestic demographics)
Source: Layard *et al.* (1992)

Europe, mainly through better trade arrangements (as argued in the next chapter) and then through financial back-up. Second, Western Europe should prepare itself for an influx of up to half a million East Europeans a year. To make the best of that immigration, it should be careful not to repeat the errors of the past. In particular, it should regard this immigration as permanent and absorb the new arrivals into a 'European melting-pot' rather than marginalise them as *Gastarbeiter*, German style. In doing so, West Europeans have every right to be as selective as the United States. In other words, why should not Europe put in a bid for well-trained people and discourage the unskilled immigration which West European labour markets do not need? Instead of attracting immigrants destined to swell the ranks of the unemployed by waving welcome cheques at them, Europe should spend money on promoting the integration of the best and the brightest. To invoke Voltaire, Western Europe could make good use of gardeners if they came with the right skills and if Europe's gardens were growing vigorously.

6. Conclusions

In this chapter we have evaluated the chances for Eastern European economies of early catching up with the European Union. At present the income *per capita* measured at market exchange rates is only a fraction of the EU average. But current exchange rates probably overestimate the gap. If one looks at how well people live, in terms of purchasing-power exchange rates, Central and Eastern European countries appear in a more favourable light. Under reasonable growth assumptions, Central and Eastern European countries stand a good chance of reaching 50 per cent of the average level of the EU during the first decade of the next century.

Will the sustained growth scenario that leads to this limited catch up be feasible without a large inflow of funds from the West? The answer is no, but the magnitudes suggested by our computations are much more modest than those of previous studies. If reforms proceed smoothly and national savings can be brought to 20 per cent or more of GDP, Russia (once out of its present reform doldrums) and the Visegrad countries need 'no more' than US$ 300 bn over the next 15 years or US$ 20 bn per annum. This should be manageable on the global scale at which financial markets work. To provide perspective, such a volume of funds could be provided by Germany alone if it went back to the current account surplus it had before unification.

These numbers neglect the current problems in the FSU: the difficulties in pushing market and institutional reforms through, in installing democratic institutions, in reforming the military-industrial complex, in cleaning up the environment and reducing nuclear risks. For that US$ 100 bn or more may be required, but is unlikely to come from private capital markets. This requires concessionary funding. We also showed in Chapter 13 that official emergency credits at market conditions – the dominant financial assistance to Russia in 1992–93 – is of doubtful utility to the recipient countries. We suggest a 'stand-by' programme of a Marshall Plan II to prepare for the possibilities that FSU governments change tack and create the necessary preconditions for effective external support. Although it is unlikely that this will actually happen, the West should improve the odds by clearly announcing that if the recipient countries accept the creation of a multilateral institution – a new OEEC – to control the allocation and good use of these funds and to take an active role in the reform process, then substantial grant money would be forthcoming. The greatest failure of the West has been that such a clear signal has never been given.

Finally, what might happen if these countries fail to catch up? There are major geopolitical risks and the risk of massive outward emigration. For the last century Russia has suffered from massive emigration of its most educated citizens and would suffer dramatically from a new haemorrhage. But, also, recipient countries in Western Europe do not seem to be ready to turn such an immigration wave to their advantage. The best they can do is to pick the best and accommodate skilled Eastern European immigration on a modest scale.

Notes

1. For industrial countries the average capital–output ratio ($V=K/Q$) is roughly constant in the long run, at levels somewhere between 2 and 4. Moreover, a standard economic model would suggest that marginal capital productivity steadily declines until the steady state is reached, as best projects are undertaken first. This neo-classical view underestimates, however, the importance of social organisation and economies of scale in infrastructure.
2. Since target growth assumptions are rather rough, the effects of population growth may be disregarded in the current context. Boote (1992) sets average population growth in Eastern Europe at 0.3 per cent p.a.

3. A simple cross-section OLS regression with GDP *per capita* at PPP exchange rates as the dependent variable and GDP at market rates as the independent variable yields an R2 of 0.97 and a coefficient of 0.691 (with a standard error of 0.038).
4. In the transforming economies financial markets are not efficient enough for the 'Ricardian equivalence' to hold.
5. This observation holds true even for African and Latin American countries, with very few exceptions. Very small countries like Malawi obtained more generous foreign assistance.
6. One problem with this approach is that it does not respect the summing-up constraint for current account imbalances. All large geographical areas have a deficit adding up to over $ 100 bn.
7. A case in point is Italy. Should Italy succeed in cutting its public debt from the current 100 per cent-plus of GDP to the Maastricht convergence mark of 60 per cent of GDP, savings in the region of $ 500 bn would be freed for other uses, including investment financing in Eastern Europe. Other EU countries, e.g. Belgium and Ireland, face similar adjustment problems.
8. Schulmann (1992) argues that the real crowding out will occur in official financing. As a percentage of GDP, the official development assistance (ODA) provided by the industrial countries has stagnated at 0.35 per cent for the last 30 years. There is little reason to expect this percentage to increase dramatically in the near future. Since there are more customers queuing up for ODA than ever, competition for official funds – in particular grants and soft loans – will soar in the years to come. As we move towards a world of 200 nation states (a tripling in the space of 50 years), the distribution of official aid will become even more skewed, favouring smaller political units. Paradoxically, this occurs at a time when economic units across the globe become more integrated and more dependent on one another than ever before.
9. It can be argued that the privatisation success stands and falls with privatisation of the military industrial complex (Gros and Steinherr 1991) which controls the best physical and human resources, is implanted all over the FSU typically in 'company towns', experienced the steepest falls in production and is represented by the most powerful conservative interest group, with the support of the armed forces (Davis and Dunne 1994).
10. As shown in Chapter 13, import financing provided by exporting countries in 1992–1993 resulted in a net welfare loss because the recipient country created the wrong macroeconomic framework.
11. Whether this inflow of southern Europeans was a blessing to the north is still a moot point. Some believe that it was beneficial because it helped to maintain growth. The following argument undermines this view. *Per capita* growth did not necessarily benefit from extensive growth methods. On the contrary, it can be argued that immigration slowed real wage growth in the host countries by reducing excess labour demand, thereby slowing down industrial restructuring from more labour-intensive to more capital-intensive (physical and human capital) activities. This was the conclusion reached by Steinherr and Runge (1978).

Appendix: How much external financial support is Eastern Europe receiving?

Financial support is not easy to evaluate. First, it would be helpful to have a breakdown of the data into grants, concessional loans and full-cost loans. Such a breakdown is not available on a consistent basis. Second, the most extensive information available concerns *commitments* which in some cases exceed *disbursements* by a large multiple.

Funding available for investment is, of course, only the *net transfer* equal to disbursements minus repayments (= net disbursements) minus interest payments. Just to provide an order of magnitude for these definitions, in fiscal year 1991/92 the World Bank (IBRD and IDA) made commitments of US$ 21.7 bn, gross disbursements of US$ 16.4 bn, net disbursements of US$ 6.3 bn and net transfers of *minus* US$ 1.9 bn.

Table 15.A.1 reproduces external financial support for Central and Eastern Europe and the Russian Federation. 'External financing needs' is used here as an *ex post facto* concept and simply represents the total amounts made available. For the region as a whole external funds have been increasing (except in 1994) but the evolution of the sources of funds has been very uneven. Foreign direct financing, mainly for investments, is steadily increasing whilst the lending by international financial institutions (IFIs) exhibits no clear trend. Net bilateral financing (mainly of Western exports to the region) were very dominant in 1990, 1991 and 1992, but started to decline in 1993. Other flows (mainly private capital movements) were negative in 1990, 1991 and 1992 (in large part due to loan repayments and capital flights from Russia) and became positive in 1993 (the outflows from Russia decreased sharply and capital inflows into the Visegrad countries picked up).

Within the region, Russia received more than any other country, but on a *per capita* basis much less than the Visegrad countries. Together the Visegrad countries received the largest dollar amounts.

Table 15.A.2 summarises G-24 assistance to Eastern and Central European countries up to the end of 1993. Of the countries of the FSU, only the Baltic States are included. Disbursements are not available on a comparable basis. The lion's share has been committed to the Visegrad countries, or 62 per cent of total commitments of ECU 61 bn. The European Union provided 42 per cent of total commitments, the United States a much more modest 13 per cent (less than Germany alone and without its contributions channelled through the EU budget) and international financial institutions a respectable 26 per cent.

Table 15.A.3 structures commitments according to their targets, and isolates grants. Overall, grants represent 30 per cent of commitments. Grants are most important for emergency assistance (95 per cent), debt reorganisation (76 per cent), food aid (73 per cent), and social infrastructure and services (62 per cent). The largest assistance was committed to multi-sector and general programme assistance (54 per cent of total), followed by debt reorganisation (13 per cent), economic infrastructure and services (11 per cent) and production sectors (8 per cent).

The largest commitment by type of economic activity is official export credit (22 per cent of total). As with debt reorganisation, the question is whether this is a real transfer. In Chapter 14 it was shown that Russia's welfare was actually lowered by export credits due to the maintenance of import subsidies in 1992. As to debt restructuring, there may not be a net transfer as debt is typically restructured when the debtor country refuses to pay. Restructuring is a sort of 'financial support' that the West cannot really refuse to grant.

To highlight the difference between commitments and disbursements, Table 15.A.4 focuses on the Russian Federation, admittedly an extreme, but very important, case. At the Tokyo G-7 summit meeting in July 1993 an impressive aid package of US$ 43.4 bn was promised. If this aid had been forthcoming in one year it would have represented 10 to 15 per cent of Russian GDP, estimated at about US$ 300–400 bn. The

TABLE 15.A.1 Central and Eastern European Countries and Russian Federation: External Financing, 1990–1995 (US$ bn)

	1989	1990	1991	1992	1993 (est.)	1994 (proj.)	1995 (proj.)
Region							
External financing needs*	2.7	−4.3	−4.5	7.6	21.3	16.3	23.2
Foreign direct financing	0.5	0.5	2.4	3.8	4.6	5.0	6.1
Financing by IFIs	0.0	1.1	5.5	4.2	3.3	5.7	6.6
Net bilateral financing	1.6	10.7	14.9	14.6	6.2	2.7	3.8
Other flows	0.6	−16.5	−27.2	−14.8	7.2	2.8	6.8
Czech Republic							
External financing needs	0.0	−0.4	0.3	−1.2	2.5	2.3	2.7
Foreign direct financing	0.2	0.1	0.5	1.0	0.5	0.6	0.7
Financing by IFIs	0.0	0.0	1.1	0.4	0.1	−0.5	0.1
Net bilateral financing	0.1	−0.2	0.0	0.2	−0.1	−0.2	−0.2
Other flows	−0.3	−0.3	−1.3	−2.9	2.0	2.4	2.1
Hungary							
External financing needs	1.4	−0.7	2.6	0.1	5.9	2.2	2.0
Foreign direct financing	0.2	0.3	1.5	1.5	2.2	1.5	1.5
Financing by IFIs	0.0	0.5	1.6	0.2	0.2	0.1	0.0
Net bilateral financing	−0.2	0.0	0.3	0.1	−0.1	−0.1	0.0
Other flows	1.3	−1.5	−0.8	−1.7	3.6	0.7	0.5
Poland							
External financing needs*	2.1	1.5	1.4	0.7	2.2	3.4	1.8
Foreign direct financing	0.0	0.0	0.1	0.3	0.6	0.7	0.9
Financing by IFIs	0.0	0.6	0.7	0.2	0.0	1.1	0.4
Net bilateral financing	2.4	2.0	0.7	−0.1	−0.2	−0.1	0.0
Other flows	−0.4	−1.1	−0.2	0.3	1.9	1.7	0.5
Slovak Republic							
External financing needs	0.1	0.4	1.5	−0.9	0.5	0.8	0.7
Foreign direct financing	0.1	0.1	0.1	0.1	0.1	0.1	0.2
Financing by IFIs	0.0	0.0	0.6	0.2	0.1	0.1	0.1
Net bilateral financing	0.1	−0.1	0.0	0.1	0.0	0.1	0.1
Other flows	0.0	0.5	0.8	−1.2	0.2	0.4	0.4
Russian Federation							
External financing needs	–	−7.1	−11.7	5.9	6.6	3.3	12.3
Foreign direct financing	–	0.0	0.1	0.7	0.8	1.5	2.0
Financing by IFIs	–	0.0	0.0	1.7	2.0	3.0	5.3
Net bilateral financing	–	9.2	13.1	14.1	6.0	2.7	3.5
Other flows	–	−16.3	−24.9	−10.6	−2.2	−3.8	1.6

Source: IMF, International Institute of Finance and own computations.

* Includes cost of debt buyback and debt enhancement in DDSR operations.

Note: Data for Albania, Bulgaria, Estonia, Latvia, Lithuania and Romania are not reproduced as commitments are small. For example, in 1993 they only add up to US$ 3.5 bn for these countries.

US$ 23 bn actually delivered, equal to 6-7 per cent of GDP, still looks impressive. But this is deceptive. The largest part of this went to export credits, generally at market rates of interest not tied to any particular reforms and, in fact, mainly serving export interests of the West.

Table 15.A.2 G-24 assistance commitments by recipient country 1.1.1990–31.12.1993 (ECU mn)

Recipients	Albania	Bulgaria	Czech Republic	Czecho-slovakia (90–92)	Baltic States	Hungary	Poland	Romania	Slovak Republic	Slovenia	Yugoslavia	Regional/ Unspecified	Total
Donors													
EU members	457.19	286.58	340.25	2548.65	200.16	2843.49	6739.29	1805.13	121.28	126.59	802.73	1382.90	**17688.48**
of which: Germany	52.98	105.06	220.69	1608.54	71.98	1954.34	3825.75	754.72	93.45	117.57	572.05	435.20	**9846.53**
EU Programmes	268.12	710.37	60.12	616.00	427.86	594.00	1026.46	1007.98	40.32	27.93	762.58	536.55	**6105.16**
EIB		196.00	222.00		5.00	397.00	553.00	144.00	138.00	47.00			**1702.00**
CECA							25.00					175.00	**200.00**
EU Total	725.31	1192.95	622.37	3164.65	633.02	3834.49	8343.75	2957.11	299.60	201.52	1565.31	2094.45	**25695.64**
EFTA	48.62	259.96	82.93	362.97	404.57	392.47	1765.77	240.51	43.24	60.87	132.44	1841.99	**5638.34**
Japan	17.22	76.64		224.77	59.18	723.31	1212.21	75.06				155.21	**2550.60**
United States	110.77	140.43	73.50	484.98	151.49	828.77	3964.65	250.46	15.93	2.21	519.54	1605.38	**8153.01**
G-24	1004.52	1757.74	778.98	4552.71	1273.32	6012.43	16871.72	3805.03	358.98	264.60	2227.18	5709.30	**44683.58**
EBRD	22.27	114.04	168.23		139.61	559.30	445.51	337.33	70.60	73.67		125.61	**2080.19**
World Bank	68.86	346.20	260.40	334.45	106.47	1197.54	2826.57	739.18	112.07	66.41	737.28		**6795.43**
IMF	68.49	452.63	201.65	887.25	525.33	1685.77	2346.85	727.85	73.88		468.98		**7453.52**
IFI	159.62	912.87	630.28	1221.70	771.41	3442.61	5618.93	1804.36	256.55	140.08	1206.26	125.61	**16329.14**
GRAND TOTAL	1164.14	2670.61	1409.26	5774.41	2044.73	9455.04	22490.65	5609.39	615.53	404.68	3433.44	5834.91	**61012.72**
% of total	*1.91%*	*4.38%*	*2.31%*	*9.46%*	*3.35%*	*15.50%*	*36.86%*	*9.19%*	*11.01%*	*0.66%*	*5.63%*	*9.56%*	***100.00%***

Source: G-24

TABLE 15.A.3 G-24 assistance commitments by sector 1.1.1990–31.12.1993m (ECU mn)

Assistance Types		Sector Aid		Technical Cooperation		Official Export Credit	Official Support for Private Investment	Other Unspecified	TOTAL	of which Grants
Sectors	Investment Projects	Total	of which assistance for economic reforms	Total	of which training					
Social infrastructure and services	658.57	147.37	3.3	1226.98	241.77	1.34	23.26	145.43	2202.95	1377.21
Economic infrastructure and services	4706.15	212.76	29.36	1117.04	106.33	33.40	16.94	578.40	6664.69	1845.94
Production sectors	2665.15	115.84	48.50	1442.58	91.07	361.87	252.40	200.80	5038.64	1689.97
Multi-sector	1293.41	30.35	12.34	514.00	60.96	12257.21	2063.80	2193.50	18352.27	1447.96
General programme assistance	6.90	16.80	16.60	803.56	9.36	317.90	30.03	13589.85	14765.04	1091.26
Debt reorganisation		2094.67	2094.67			106.39	2.25	6144.16	8347.47	6378.70
Food aid		607.62		0.03		370.34		1064.51	2042.50	1497.15
Emergency assistance (excluding food aid)	0.18	350.51		22.67	0.25	40.29		871.05	1284.70	1216.03
Support for private voluntary organisations		1.35		30.90	0.39		15.35	14.53	62.13	61.07
Unallocated/Unspecified	7.90	9.76		353.78	8.05	310.56	20.21	1547.47	2249.68	1666.91
TOTAL	**9338.26**	**3587.03**	**2204.80**	**5511.54**	**518.18**	**13799.30**	**2424.24**	**26349.70**	**61010.07**	**18272.20**
% of total	*15.31%*	*5.88%*	*3.61%*	*9.03%*	*0.85%*	*22.62%*	*3.97%*	*43.19%*	*100.00%*	*29.95%*

Source: G-24

TABLE 15.A.4 Russia: details of official financial assistance (US$ bn) by G-7

	1992 Announced by G-7	Delivered by G-7	Announced (Prel.)	Delivered by G-7	1993 Announced (Prel.)	1992 and 1993[a] Delivered
Bilateral creditors						
European Union[c]	11	14	10	6	21	20[b]
IMF (including stabilisation fund)	9	1	13	1.5	14	2.5
World Bank, EBRD	1.5	0	5	0.5	5	0.5
Official debt relief	2.5[d]	–	15	15(e)	15	15
Total	24	15	43	23	55	38

Reminder: *The G-7 Aid Package*

		USD bn
Bilateral governments:	– public debt rescheduling	15.0
	– export credits and guarantees	10.0
IMF	– systemic transformation facility	3.0
	– standby loan	4.1
	– currency stabilisation fund	6.0
World Bank	– World Bank loan commitments	3.4
	– import rehabilitation loans	1.1
	– oil sector loan	0.5
EBRD	– small/medium enterprise fund	0.3

Source: IMF Survey, February 1994

(a) Excludes most double-counting, i.e. amounts announced but not disbursed in 1992 and announced again in 1993. The largest of these elements is the USD 6 billion for a ruble stabilisation fund from the IMF. A small amount of double counting for the two-year total may nevertheless persist.
(b) Delivered total excludes some items in the announced packages for which reliable data are not available (e.g. technical assistance, nuclear facilities, rehabilitation, etc.)
(c) Does not include about US$ 4 billion from Germany to re-house Russian troops. These grants were not intended to be part of the announced package.
(d) This amount of interest deferral was not formally granted during 1992.
(e) Includes US$ 6.5 billion that was deferred or that went into arrears in 1992.

Also alarming is that multilateral support, as requested by the G-7, fell dismally short of objectives. In 1992 IMF, World Bank and EBRD delivered US$ 1bn of the US$ 10.5bn announced and in 1993 US$ 2bn of US$ 18bn announced. In March 1994 the IMF finally, surprisingly, made the second disbursement of the structural transformation facility (STF) when budgetary conditions had greatly deteriorated and the government supported reforms with much less enthusiasm than in 1993.

Table 15.A.5 traces the evolution of foreign debt (which does not include DFIs and grants, but includes payment arrears) since 1989. Absolute indebtedness (Panel A) has increased modestly during the transition years: by about 20 per cent for countries with high indebtedness in 1989, such as Hungary and Poland; up to 50 per cent for countries with a low foreign debt in 1989, such as Bulgaria, the Czech Republic or the Russian Federation.

Panel B relates external debt to GDP (at market exchange rates). As GDP has declined in most reforming countries, the ratio of external debt to GDP ratio has been increasing very sharply. Hungary is the only exception as GDP in US$ increased and the increase in external debt was modest. In the case of Russia the very drastic real depreciation of the ruble led to an extraordinary fall in GDP at market exchange rates in 1992, which was partly corrected in 1993. External debt–GDP ratios for countries with sharp savings in the real exchange rate – such as Bulgaria in 1991, Poland in 1990 or Russia in 1992 – are therefore to be interpreted with care.

During 1994 and 1995 the debt–GDP ratios are expected to stabilise or decline, partly as a result of declining debt (Bulgaria and Poland, see Panel A) and partly as a result of increasing GDP.

TABLE 15.A.5 Debt and Debt Service Indicators: 1989–95

A: Total convertible currency external debt (US$ bn)

	1989	1990	1991	1992	1993 (Est.)	1994 (Proj.)	1995 (Proj.)
Region	133.9	148.4	157.8	174.7	190.9	190.9	204.8
Albania	0.1	0.3	0.6	0.7	0.8	1.0	1.2
Bulgaria	9.6	11.0	12.5	13.1	13.5	11.4	11.5
Czech Republic	6.0	6.0	6.7	6.9	9.0	10.2	11.1
Slovak Republic	2.6	2.7	3.1	2.8	3.4	3.9	4.0
Baltic States	–	–	–	0.2	0.6	1.3	1.8
Hungary	20.4	21.3	22.4	21.5	24.9	26.9	28.6
Poland	40.2	48.9	48.3	48.7	48.7	38.8	39.4
Romania	1.1	1.2	2.8	4.3	5.8	7.0	8.0
Russian Federation*	54.0	57.1	61.4	76.5	84.2	90.4	99.2

B: Debt/GDP ratio, 1989–95 (converted at market rates) (US$ bn)

	1989	1990	1991	1992	1993 (Est.)	1994 (Proj.)	1995 (Proj.)
Region	9.7	11.3	16.5	65.8	51.5	37.8	35.6
Albania	3.2	14.0	55.9	100.7	86.0	66.4	66.1
Bulgaria	44.1	93.8	173.3	141.3	104.9	86.6	84.7
Czech Republic	17.2	18.9	27.5	25.3	28.7	29.0	29.2
Slovak Republic	17.1	20.3	31.2	28.4	30.9	34.4	33.7
Baltic States	–	–	–	12.9	24.8	48.7	60.3
Hungary	69.6	64.7	68.6	60.7	68.1	70.8	72.4
Poland	48.9	78.5	62.0	57.8	56.7	42.0	39.4
Romania	2.6	3.2	10.3	24.3	23.3	27.5	29.9
Russian Federation*	4.9	5.3	8.4	100.1	52.5	32.3	29.5

* 1989 figures refer to the USSR
Source: IIF and IMF

CHAPTER SIXTEEN

The new Europe: trade arrangements and expansion of the European Union

Il s'agit que la Russie évolue de telle façon qu'elle voie son avenir, non plus dans la contrainte totalitaire imposée chez elle et chez les autres, mais dans le progrès accompli en commun par des hommes et par des peuples libres. Il s'agit que les nations dont elle a fait ses satellites puissent jouer leur rôle dans une Europe renouvelée. . . . Il s'agit que les six Etats qui, espérons-le, sont en voie de réaliser la communauté économique de l'Europe occidentale parviennent à s'organiser dans le domaine politique et dans celui de la défense afin de rendre possible un nouvel équilibre de notre continent. Il s'agit que l'Europe, mère de la civilisation moderne, s'établisse de l'Atlantique à l'Oural dans la concorde et dans la coopération en vue du développement de ses immenses ressources et de manière à jouer, conjointement avec l'Amérique sa fille, le rôle qui lui revient quant au progrès de deux milliards d'hommes qui en ont terriblement besoin.

Charles De Gaulle, *Discours et Messages*, Vol IV, 1970, p. 341

The collapse of socialism in Eastern Europe has transformed the economic and political parameters of the European continent. In this chapter we discuss the economic forces and the political choices that will create the 'new' Europe.

Most of the countries west of the FSU have already made their choice: they want to join the European Union (EU). Since this is not possible immediately, they have in the meantime sought a close association with the EU in another form. Section 1 describes the existing arrangements and Section 2 provides theoretical support. Whilst an expansion of the EU to the East may be worth pursuing from an intuitive viewpoint, it soon becomes obvious that the issue is quite complex and that not every Eastern European country should become a member. Section 3 expands the discussion round the question of the optimum size of the EU. The main parameters retained for this discussion are the structure of the economies concerned, the goals of the EU and the capacity of institutions to make decisions. Not included here is the obvious key aspect of geography, which is of such importance as to merit separate treatment in Section 4.

The EU is much more than a free trade area.[1] If it were only that then the case for joining the EU rather than opting for world-wide free trade would be greatly weakened. The EU is a customs union and much more, namely an integrated single market – with free movement of capital and labour – supported by institutions that make the single market work and provide the indispensable common regulatory framework. Moreover, the EU will become a monetary union with its own central bank. How does this affect the choice of the Central European countries? In a separate appendix we discuss two sectors of importance for West and East Europe, for which political solutions need to be sought: agriculture and energy.

1. The principal European trade initiatives

The single most important trade initiative concerning the transition economies are the so-called 'European Agreements' (EAs) between the EU on the one side and the former Czechoslovakia, Hungary and Poland on the other, signed in December 1991, while EAs with Bulgaria and Romania followed one year later.[2] The Central European Free Trade Area that consists of the three (now four) Visegrad countries is only of secondary importance. The EAs were clearly critical for the Central European countries since, as Table 16.1 shows, the EU (plus Switzerland and Norway) accounts for over 60 per cent of the overall foreign trade of the three Visegrad countries (Poland, Hungary and Czechoslovakia). Trade with the enlarged EU in turn accounted for 80–90 per cent of the trade of all Central and Eastern European countries with the industrialised world, as can be seen by comparing Columns A and B. This table also shows the increase in exports by Eastern European countries to the Western world (approximated here by the OECD area) since the end of socialist rule. The growth of exports is remarkable and illustrates the speed at which structural changes took place.

The EAs (see Box 16.1 for details) aim to further the integration of the respective Eastern European economies with the EU by providing steps towards the free movement of goods, services and factors, establishing a framework for political dialogue, harmonising legislation, cooperating on science and technology, and providing for financial assistance and technical cooperation from the EU in a number of areas. The Agreements explicitly recognise the Eastern European countries' ultimate goal of joining the Community.

The EU has also concluded Partnership and Cooperation Agreements with Russia and most other Western CIS countries. However, these agreements do not go much beyond the mutual granting of 'most favoured nation' status and do not imply a significant trade liberalisation by the EU.

TABLE 16.1 Exports of countries in Central and Eastern Europe to the OECD areas by destination

	Exports to OECD (US$ millions) 1988		1992		
		A		A	B
Bulgaria	683	31.9	1 466	56.5	44.8
CSFR	4 992	34.1	7 950	64.5	60.0
Hungary	3 786	38.1	7 517	70.2	64.1
Poland	6 160	45.9	9 729	69.2	64.3
Romania	4 712	36.9	2 111	47.2	38.0
ex-USSR	21 539	51.8	29 305	60.0	51.2

Source: IMF trade statistics
A = share of OECD in total exports
B = share of EU+Switzerland and Norway (=old EEA) in total exports

Box 16.1 European Agreements

The EAs establish a (bilateral) free trade area for trade in goods between the EU and the respective partners within a period of 10 years. The provisions of the Agreements are asymmetric: the period for phasing out import restrictions is usually much shorter for the EU than for the Central and Eastern European partner. For most products the EAs provide for free entry into the EU from the start. For certain 'sensitive products' which include coal, iron and steel, some chemicals, furniture, leather goods, footwear, glass, clothing and textiles, a maximum of five years (six years for products included in the Multifiber Agreements) is stipulated in separate protocols for the elimination of tariffs and/or quotas by the EU. Steel quotas are to be eliminated immediately, while tariffs drop from 5 per cent initially to zero after five years. For other sensitive products, tariffs and quotas generally remain temporarily in place. Trade in agriculture is excluded from the proposed free trade areas: nevertheless, the agreements foresee reduced customs tariffs for a number of agricultural products, generally within a set quota, with either the tariff or the quota arrangement in most cases being improved over a five year period. Thus exports of meat, fruit, dairy goods and vegetables from the Eastern European signatory countries are allowed to rise by 10 per cent a year over five years. The sensitive items scheduled for slower liberalisation account for up to half of the 1991 exports of the partner countries, according to EC sources.

While there is disagreement over whether recourse to impartial GATT rulings in trade disputes may have become more difficult in practice for EA partners, the EAs add a consultative mechanism to the usual GATT procedures regarding contingent protection. Thus, anti-dumping action and temporary safeguards for injured industries are permitted only after a 30-day period during which the Association Council – supplied with the relevant information – can attempt to find an acceptable alternative or the exporter takes other decisions that put an end to the difficulties, for example, through price adjustments or voluntary export restraints (VERs). Countervailing duty (CVD) action is also permitted in the case of state aid to exporting industries, and both parties are to provide the information needed for the relevant calculations upon request. However, within a three-year timeframe the Association Council is to adopt EU competition rules which will then eliminate the possibility of recourse to CVDs. Lastly, the partner country (but not the EU) may, within certain limits and with a set timeframe for elimination, introduce protection for infant industries or sectors undergoing restructuring.

At the Copenhagen Summit of the EU in June 1993, the associated countries of Central and Eastern Europe were offered the perspective of EU membership upon fulfilment of a number of general economic and political conditions. Economic conditions include, among others, the 'capacity to cope with competitive pressure and market forces within the Union'. No date was set for formally revising the progress made towards meeting these criteria, but the multilateral political dialogue and consultation were institutionally strengthened. With regard to the trade component of the EAs, the decision was taken to shorten the timeframe of liberalisation of EU market access horizontally, that is, across broad product groups. This includes an accelerated reduction of customs duties on a number of industrial goods subject to GSP treatment, with the deadline for free trade set at three instead of five years from the entry into force of the Agreements.[3]

What should one think of EAs? From a general viewpoint, they are to be judged positively because they open up the Union market without insistence on reciprocity and because they prepare for ultimate membership. However, there are also shortcomings.

First, 'sensitive' goods such as agricultural products, steel products, textiles and leather products remain protected in the EU. This is a major shortcoming for Eastern European countries as they are particularly competitive in these products. However, by 1995, the end of the transition period, trade in manufacturing products had to be freed so that this was mainly a transitional pattern provided the letter and spirit of the agreements were fully observed. The EAs as such are thus generous in the long run. The political willingness of the EU to implement them fully is another issue.

Second, the Union may be seen as pursuing a 'hub-and-spoke' approach (Baldwin 1994) by negotiating free-trade arrangements bilaterally. This biases competition in favour of the Union as long as Eastern countries do not pursue free trade among themselves. It could also discourage investments in the East to serve the entire region. Although only a temporary disadvantage (until Union membership), the dynamics of locational accumulation are such that a permanent disadvantage may result from the initial situation (Krugman 1991a). Empirically, however, this argument may not be as important as it sounds. For Eastern countries the most important decision is to get access to the 'hub'; trade with other Eastern countries is not that important, as demonstrated in Section 4 below.

Third, those countries not enjoying an EA are obviously disadvantaged. And because the ultimate goal of an EA is Union membership, not all Eastern countries can obtain an EA. As we shall propose below, the Union's approach should be based on two concentric circles: one of future Union members and another which includes the rest of Eastern Europe with a free trade arrangement.

The above disadvantages of the EA have often been highlighted by economists as being potentially important. A look at the numbers is therefore useful in order to check how trade has actually developed. Table 16.1 above showed the impressive growth rates of exports to the West and the EU. Did the remaining protectionism of the EU impede an even better performance? This is a difficult question, but a tentative answer can be found by once again utilising the gravity model used in Chapter 13.

The gravity model explains the volume of trade among any pair of countries mainly on the basis of their incomes (to take into account demand and supply) and their distance (to take into account transportation costs). Brenton and Kendall (1994) estimate such a model for trade among 25 countries (the US, Canada, Japan and 22 European countries) in 1992. Their equations can account for more than 85 per cent of the variance of the over 600 bilateral trade flows within this group of 25 countries. The details of the results are presented in Box 16.2. They find, not surprisingly, that trade between EU members is about 60 per cent larger than one would expect on the basis of distance and income, but that trade between the EU and the five EFTA countries (in 1992) is about normal. These results have been confirmed by other studies as well. However, if one includes a so-called 'dummy' variable for East–West trade (i.e. trade between EU members and Central and Eastern European countries) one finds that this variable carries a significant positive coefficient. The estimated value of the 'excess East–West trade' variable is 0.23 as shown in Box 16.2. This implies that trade between the Central and Eastern European countries of this sample and the EU is about 23 per cent larger than one would expect on the basis of geography and income alone. Hence it is difficult to argue that the EU has been overly protectionist; if this had been the case overall trade should have been reduced.

The often heard counter-argument that the EU is running a trade surplus with Eastern Europe cannot invalidate this finding because this is the only way in which the EU can transfer capital to the East and thus finance part of the reconstruction as analysed in Chapter 15.

However, Box 16.2 also shows that the higher than expected East–West trade does not concern the entire EU. If one splits Germany from the EU data one finds that trade between Germany and Eastern Europe is about 100 per cent higher than one would expect on the basis of distance and income whereas the trade of the rest of the EU with the Central and Eastern European countries is 'only' about normal. This might also explain why Germany attaches so much more importance to a pro-Eastern Europe policy for the EU. Certainly, the finding that Germany has a special position does not invalidate the result that overall the EU seems to be trading intensively with Central and Eastern Europe. All in all there is no indication that the EU has been protectionist against imports from the transforming economies.

Box 16.2 Estimates of the gravity model 1992

This box presents some of the technical details of the results found by Brenton and Kendall (1994). They used 600 observations of bilateral trade flows for estimation of the following cross-section equation:

$$\ln T_{xm} = \alpha + \beta_1 \ln GDP_x + \beta_2 \ln POP_x + \beta_3 \ln GDP_m + \beta_4 \ln POP_m + \beta_5 \ln DIST_{xm} + \Sigma\gamma_k D_{kxm} + u_{xm}$$

where

T_{xm} is the value of the trade flow from country x (exporter) to country m (importer),
GDP_i is the Gross Domestic Product of country *i*, (x or m),
POP_i is the population of country *i*, (x or m),
$DIST_{xm}$ is the distance between countries x and m,
D_{kxm} are dummy variables representing the adjacency of x and m (*ADJ*) and preference relationships between x and m, and
α, β_i and γ_k are parameters to be estimated.
u_{xm} is the error term

continued

Box 16.2 *continued*

The results of an ordinary least squares regression were as shown in Table A.

Table A Estimates of the gravity model using data for 25 countries for 1992

	A	B	C
Constant	1.38 (4.80)	0.92 (2.60)	1.03 (2.97)
GDP_x	1.01 (27.75)	1.05 (25.93)	1.03 (26.11)
POP_x	−0.24 (−4.99)	−0.28 (−5.50)	−0.28 (−5.53)
GDP_m	0.89 (24.61)	0.94 (23.11)	0.92 (23.26)
POP_m	−0.14 (−2.98)	−0.19 (−3.65)	−0.19 (−3.70)
DIST	−0.64 (−16.11)	−0.61 (−14.61)	−0.60 (−14.68)
ADJ	0.75 (6.86)	0.78 (7.11)	0.74 (6.74)
EUEFTA	0.52 (5.63)	0.57 (6.02)	0.57 (6.09)
CEEC	1.38 (7.72)	1.63 (7.81)	1.60 (4.76)
EU12CEEC		0.23 (2.26)	
EU11CEEC			0.11 (1.06)
GERCEEC			1.06 (4.76)
R^2 adj	0.87	0.87	0.88
F	520.03	466.06	432.90
S.E	0.73	0.72	0.71

Source: Brenton and Kendall (1994)

The different dummy variables have the following meaning: EUEFTA: equal to one when both countries are members of either the EU or EFTA (to represent the EEA); EU12CEEC: equal to one if one of two trading partners is in the EU12 and the other one of the CEEC (Central and Eastern European countries); EU11CEEC: equal to one when one of the two trading partners is part of the EU12 except Germany and the other is one of the CEEC. GERCEEC: one for trade between Germany and the CEEC.

2. Joining the EU versus free trade with the rest of the world

The previous section showed that the EAs have virtually established free trade. So why bother joining the EU? The major economic argument against joining the EU is that free trade with the entire world is preferable to free trade restricted to a geographic area. Why then are Eastern European countries set on joining the EU and why is the EU ready to accommodate at least some of these requests? The major reason is that, as shown above, the EU accounts for 80–90 per cent of all trade with the rich part of the world[4] (and 60–70 per cent of overall trade). Free trade with the EU thus effectively means free trade with the only market that really counts for Central and Eastern European countries. However, there is an additional reason why integration with the

EU brings economic gains. The EU offers far more than free trade. It offers the elimination of border controls and a framework that ensures the durability of its free trade, backed by legal provisions and institutional support. And it goes beyond free trade, offering free movement for capital and labour, coordination of economic policies and a treaty for economic and monetary union. It also offers financial support to accelerate convergence and enhance cohesion and it operates sectoral economic policies, such as the CAP, scientific development, development aid, and so on. It would be wrong to believe that Eastern European countries seek membership mainly for the financial advantages, although we will show that they will be substantial. The policy and institutional framework of the EU offers much more than financial incentives which may have to be revised at any rate before integrating new members, as argued below.[5]

Returning to the analysis of trade arrangements, the demonstration that unrestricted free trade is better than any other arrangements is easy: no distortion (free trade with the entire world) must be better than some distortions (the external tariffs of the EU). However, it is not always true that joining a customs union is better than having some tariffs at the national level without any preferential arrangements. Both the newcomers and the incumbents might lose out if a preferential trading area, such as an FTA or a customs union, expands (see Box 16.3).

Box 16.3 The ambiguous welfare results of a free trade area

This ambiguity is most simply demonstrated in *partial equilibrium* as in Fig. A.

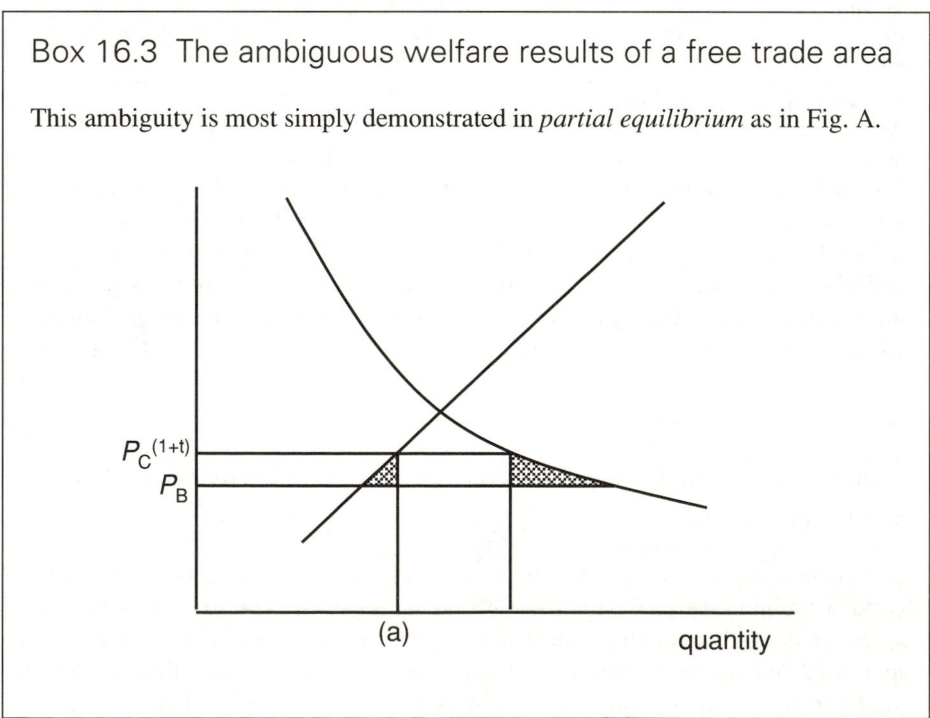

continued

Box 16.3 *continued*

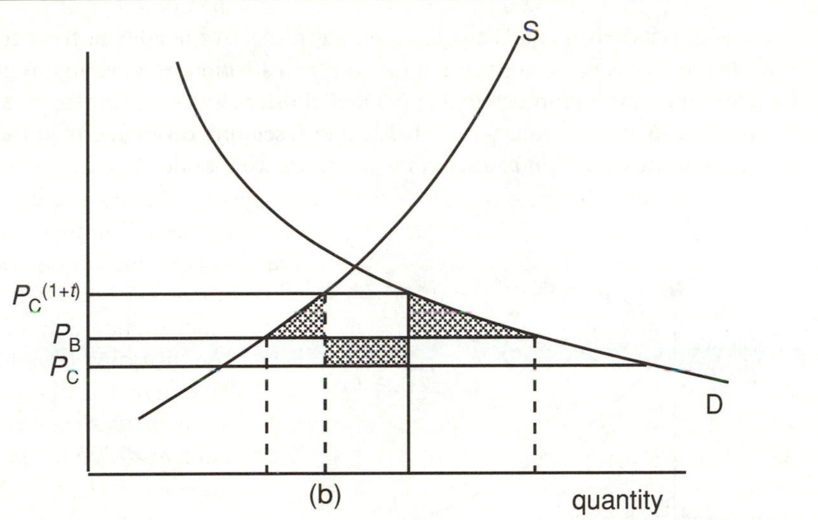

FIG A The gains from joining an FTA: partial equilibrium

Elimination of trade barriers among members of the newly formed FTA disadvantages outsiders except when the most efficient producers are inside the FTA. In this case there will only be 'trade creation', illustrated in Fig. A(a) by the expansion of trade between the two countries A and B due to the elimination of trade barriers among them. The outside world (country C) is absent from Fig. A(a) as its offer price is above P_B. The net gain comes from the consumer and producer surpluses in the form of the two shaded triangles.

Fig. A(b) illustrates 'trade diversion' which occurs when the most efficient producers are outside the FTA. When the FTA is formed, country A now buys from country B instead of country C because the price of B without a tariff is below the tariff-augmented price of C, that is $P_C(1+t)$. There are again gains – the two triangles – but also a loss – the shaded rectangle. The net result is ambiguous.

Figure B depicts the *general equilibrium* case in the simplified two-goods (denoted 1 and 2) case. If both of the prospective members of an FTA import the same good from the rest of the world, they will still do so in the FTA if outside tariffs are unchanged. With such structures of production an FTA brings no benefit, but there will also be no costs if there is no trade between them.

In the more interesting case where the partner countries import different goods, assume that country A imports good 1 and country B exports it. In Fig. B, M_1^A and E_1^B are the general equilibrium import demand curve of A and export supply curve of B respectively. The horizontal line P^C is the relative price at which C (the rest of the world) is willing to buy and sell good 1. The supply curve is horizontal as the quantities demanded by A and B are assumed to be small in relation to the size of the rest of the world.

continued

Box 16.3 *continued*

Autarky prices in A and B are given by the respective heights of their curves at their points of origin. Under free trade, the gains from trade are represented by the area under the import demand curve and above the world price for A, and that above the export supply curve and below the world price for B. Given free trade and constant costs in C, it neither gains nor loses from trade.

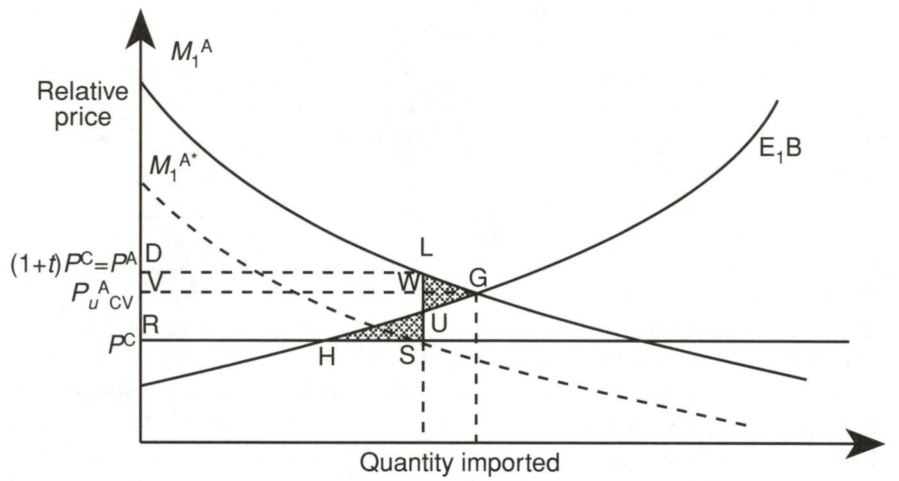

A's gain: area LGW less area RSVW; B's gain: area RHGV

FIG B The gains from joining an FTA: general equilibrium

Assume that initially A levies a non-discriminatory tariff at rate t on imports from B and C. A's import demand curve is now given by $M_1{}^{A^*}$ which lies below $M_1{}^A$ by the amount of tariff per unit. The border price facing *A* is P^C and total imports are RS. Of these, RH comes from B and HS from C. Domestic price in A is given by P^A which is the height of the import demand curve as perceived by A's residents. The gains from trade in A are given by area $M^A{}_1$LD plus tariff revenue DRSL and those in B by area RH$E^B{}_1$.

Now introduce an FTA between A and B. Imports from B are no longer subject to a tariff. As drawn, imports from C are 'diverted' to B because the supply price of C augmented by the tariff, $P^C(1+t)$, is larger than the price P^A_u at which B can just satisfy all of A's import demand The union benefits B both because its terms of trade improve and because its exports expand. The country's net gain equals area RHGV. The effect on A is ambiguous in general because on the one hand, A's terms of trade deteriorate (or equivalently it loses all tariff revenue, the area DRSL) while, on the other hand, the distortion between the domestic and

continued

Box 16.3 *continued*

(new) border price is eliminated. The country gains or loses as area LGW is larger or smaller than the rectangle RSWV. As drawn the country loses. The effect on joint welfare of A and B is also ambiguous. They benefit jointly in area LGU through larger consumer and producer surpluses. If they are larger than the higher costs that arise through production in B instead of C (the vertically shaded area, HSU), they have a net gain, but lose otherwise. As drawn, the union, as a whole, loses from the FTA.

Figure B has been drawn in such a way that an FTA between A and B eliminates the imports from C entirely. This is done to highlight the point that an FTA will generally generate both positive and negative effects and that the effect on the union's welfare is likely to be ambiguous. If B's export supply curve were redrawn so that it crosses A's solid curve to the left of point L, the FTA does not eliminate imports from C. In this case, the internal price facing A is unchanged while its terms of trade with B deteriorate by the full amount of the tariff. B's share in imports rises but total imports remain unchanged. A's welfare declines because its terms of trade with B worsen without any improvement in efficiency; B's welfare rises because its terms of trade improve and exports expand; and the union's welfare declines because over some range imports coming from B cost more than C's price and there is no gain in efficiency in A.

What factors make the gains from an FTA larger or the losses smaller? First, the higher the initial tariff in a given sector, the larger the favourable effect (area LUG) and smaller the unfavourable effect (area USH) of the FTA. Second, the lower the post-FTA tariff on extra-union countries, the less likely that the lower-priced goods of the latter will be displaced. Third, the higher the tariffs in the outside world on the partner, the larger will be the gain or the smaller the loss. In terms of Fig. B, the higher the tariff in C, the higher will be P^{C} facing A and B and the smaller will be the area HSU. Fourth, the greater the complementarity in import demands of A and B, the larger the gains from the FTA. In terms of Fig. B, the farther apart are the import demand and export supply curves of A and B, the larger will be the gains (area LGW) and the smaller the losses (area HSU).

Source: de Melo *et al.* (1993)

Theoretically the Central European countries could complement the EA (with the EU) with a policy of unilateral free trade against all other countries. In this way they could be certain that the EA does not lead to trade diversion (i.e. that they import goods from the EU that are produced with higher costs, but are cheaper than products from third countries because they are not subject to tariffs). However, it needs to be recalled that no country has ever adopted free trade with the entire world, although regional efforts abound. Some are successful, such as EEA or NAFTA (the European Economic Area compromised of EU and EFTA and the North American Free Trade Area, respectively), others are less successful, such as various past efforts in Africa and Latin America. Why do countries wish to form or join preferential trade areas despite the warning lights of theory?

One argument is that the political economy of free trade is not favourable. From a public choice point of view the interests of producers are more concentrated that those of consumers (who are the main beneficiaries) and (some) producers lose from free trade. If governmental policy is conditioned by group pressure then unilateral free trade is not the optimal public choice outcome. A PTA (of which an FTA is a special case) provides visible advantages for exporters as *quid pro quos* for higher imports and makes it more attractive for producers as a social group.

A second argument is that a PTA is a protection against the risk of more protectionist policies of trading partners in the future. And as a PTA usually regroups the most important trading partners[6] this insurance can be worth more than the loss from trade diversion. Moreover, when the most important *ex ante* trading parties are in the PTA then trade creation dominates so that there is a net gain. The additional gain of free trade with the rest of the world can then be rather marginal.

Third, PTAs may serve as building blocks rather than stumbling blocks for global free trade. When the EC was formed the average external tariff was reduced from 13 per cent in 1958 to 10.4 per cent in 1968 and 6.6 per cent after the Kennedy round.[7] Since 1958 the Community of Six has evolved into a European Economic Area comprising 18 countries and forming the largest FTA in the world with supplementary agreements allowing the free entry of goods from a large group of Mediterranean and ACP countries.

Fourth, in any PTA pressure forms to further integration beyond trade: free movement of factors of production, coordination of associated policies such as external trade policies, product standardisation and certification, and so on. But there is also a risk: the Common Agricultural Policy (CAP) is an example of a policy that negates free trade, causes massive trade diversion and was negotiated as a complement (and side-payment) to the free trade arrangement of the EU.

Finally, whilst a small country on its own has little weight in trade negotiations and cannot affect world prices, a larger block of countries can more easily defend its interests and may even turn the terms of trade to its favour.[8] This advantage has, of course, another side: it may tempt the block to become more protectionist (e.g. the concern about 'fortress Europe'). Box 16.4 reproduces the optimum tariff argument, taking into account policies that are influenced more by producer than consumer interests.

Box 16.4 Are large trading blocks protectionist?

Trading blocks are both 'trade creating' and 'trade diverting' (as shown in Box 16.3) so that the overall change in welfare is ambiguous. Independently of that, greater size brings market power which may be used for more protectionist policies. This is what the optimum tariff literature suggests.

The optimum tariff for any country or block of countries is

$$t^* = 1/(\hat{\mu} - 1)$$

where $\hat{\mu}$ is the elasticity of demand for the country's exports. Clearly, for a very small country $\hat{\mu}$ is large and t^* is close to zero. The optimum tariff increases

continued

Box 16.4 *continued*

therefore with size. However, if blocks are symmetric and therefore charge the same tariff rate, it can be shown (Krugman 1991b) that a tariff war in which each country (or block) charges the optimal tariff without taking into account the reaction of the others leads to an equilibrium in which

$$t^* = 1/(1-s)(\phi - 1)$$

where s is the share of each block's exports in the rest of the world's income and ϕ is the elasticity of substitution between any pair of products. The larger the share of each block's exports the higher will be the tariffs. The maximum t^* is reached when there are only two blocks.

If government is not maximising an unbiased social welfare function but pays more attention to the interests of producers then the optimum tariff is obtained from

$$t^*/(1+t^*) = \pi / \mu m$$

where π is the premium placed on producers' interests (the implicit weight in decision-makers' objective function), m is the ratio of imports to domestic production and μ is elasticity of import demand (equal to the rest of the world's elasticity of export demand). Therefore, the greater the weight attached to producers in a given industry, the higher will be the tariff maximising the government's objective functions. Similarly, for smaller values of μ and m: smaller elasticities of import demand need a higher tariff to reduce imports by a given amount and so do lower shares of imports (so that the tariff is effective in transferring income to producers).

The parameter π is not in an obvious way dependent on size, unlike μ, m and s. If a trading block expands the ratio of imports to domestic production, in the aggregate and industry by industry, the optimum tariff is generally reduced. One can therefore conclude on theoretic grounds that larger trading blocks tend to be more protectionist than small countries or blocks.

Sources: Krugman (1991b, 1993).

Having established the second-best economic rationale for a PTA (free global trade remaining first-best), it should be obvious that every PTA needs to be examined for its welfare potential and that not all would make economic sense.[9] Does it make sense for Eastern European countries to join the EEA (the argument for joining the EU being a separate one)? Consider first some general arguments.

As shown in Box. 16.3, the chances of gaining from joining a PTA increase (1) the higher the tariffs of the newcomer and the lower the tariffs of the PTA, (2) the larger the PTA (an FTA comprising the whole world is global free trade), and (3) the more competitive the existing (but the more complementary the potential) trade structure of the newcomer with that of the PTA.

How do these arguments work? In argument (1) one can say that the external tariffs of the EU are low, indeed lower than those of most Eastern European countries. The

EU is a very large trading area so that argument (2) also favours EU membership. The last, argument (3), is more difficult to judge since little is known about the potential trading structure of the Eastern European countries once they have joined.

How about the existing trade structure? This is analysed in detail in Box 16.5. The main result of the analysis is that the commodity structure of the exports of the former Czechoslovakia (and Slovenia) to the EU is quite similar to the commodity structure of the exports of the average EU member to its partners. The structure of exports from Hungary and Poland already differs much more from the average within the EU, and Bulgaria and Romania have completely different trade structure. The individual EU member countries that show the closest correlation with Central Europe are Portugal and, surprisingly, Italy. This suggests that at least the existing trade structures are mainly competitive, satisfying the last criterion for participation in a PTA.

The results presented in Box 16.5 are also interesting from another point of view. Joining the EU does not mean only joining a trading area. In future it will also mean joining a monetary union. As already discussed in Chapter 12 (concerning Yugoslavia) and in Chapter 13 (concerning a possible ruble zone), two countries should become a monetary union only if their trade structures are sufficiently similar to make the emergence of large asymmetric shocks unlikely. Exchange rate adjustments are a useful policy instrument if a shock hits only one country. In that case it will usually be quicker to change the exchange rate than to wait for wages and prices to adjust. Given that the EU is now already in the second stage of the EMU plan, the issue is whether a stronger degree of monetary integration is optimal for the countries in Central Europe.

The finding that the structure of trade of Central European countries with the EU is not too dissimilar from intra-EU trade implies that if there are shifts in the demand for their products, the rest of the EU will in most cases be affected in a similar way. Hence these data suggest that countries like the Czech and Slovak Republics (and Slovenia) are in a way less likely to be subject to asymmetric shocks than poorer member countries like Greece, Ireland and Portugal.

Moreover, all Central European countries are very open, so that they have a lot to gain from eliminating the barriers to trade that are implicit in the cost of exchanging currencies, hedging exposures and so on. Indeed for former Czechoslovakia (and Slovenia) trade with the EU corresponds to over 25 per cent of GDP, more than for most member countries.

We therefore conclude that the Czech and Slovak Republics (and Slovenia) should participate in the process of European monetary integration and eventually in full EMU whenever it comes. These countries can expect substantial benefits because they trade intensively with the EU and they should have to bear few costs because they should not be subject to more asymmetric shocks than most member countries.

Box 16.5 The structure of trade: the EU and Central Europe compared

The commodity structure of the trade of a given country is measured here by calculating the percentage of each product in total imports of the EU (i.e. exports of

continued

Box 16.5 *continued*

the country concerned) at the SITC 2-digit level (80 products). In order to have a measure of the similarity of this structure between any pair of countries we then compute the correlation coefficients between the commodity structures of individual member countries' imports from Union partners and imports into the Union from different countries in Central Europe (including Slovenia).

Table A shows the complete matrix of correlation coefficients (of the export shares) for trade between member countries and the Union as a whole, as well as among member countries themselves. On the central diagonal the standard deviations (STD) of the export shares inside the Union are presented to give a summary statistic of the overall concentration of exports. A low standard deviation would indicate a low concentration of exports in specific categories of goods. According to this criterion Spain, the Netherlands, Portugal and Greece have the highest commodity concentration of exports to the EU. However, there is otherwise little difference among member countries in this respect.

This table shows that the countries with a trade (export) structure closest to the European average are Germany, France, Belgium-Luxembourg, the UK, Italy and Spain. All bilateral correlation coefficients in this group of countries are above 60 %. Surprisingly the trade structure of the Netherlands and Denmark deviates (from moderately to substantially) from those of the other countries and the European average. This is *a fortiori* true for Ireland, Portugal and Greece. For the latter countries this could be expected, however, because they are much poorer and are generally judged to be at a different level of development.

TABLE A EU Correlation coefficients of export structures

STD	EU12	BLEU	FRA	GER	ITA	SPA	UK	NETH	DEN	IRE	POR	GRE
EU12	1.9											
BLEU	91	2.4										
FRA	95	87	2.0									
GER	96	89	94	2.4								
ITA	82	67	71	76	2.0							
SPA	87	89	86	86	62	3.7						
UK	85	67	78	76	67	60	1.9					
NETH	66	55	50	47	45	47	73	1.7				
DEN	36	24	27	28	39	14	13	40	2.0			
IRE	34	15	25	20	26	6	53	57	40	2.6		
POR	44	36	34	34	68	31	31	20	17	7	3.2	
GRE	18	12	11	3	44	12	9	17	8	1	71	3.7

Source: Own elaboration of EUROSTAT data. Correlation coefficients and standard deviations times 100.

How does this intra-European trade structure compare to that of Central and Eastern Europe? Table B shows the correlations between the commodity structure of the exports to the EU of the countries of Eastern Europe and the structure of total intra-EU trade, and among themselves and between the structure of each

continued

Box 16.5 *continued*

country's exports to the EU, whereas Table C presents the correlation matrix of the Eastern European countries' trade with individual EU members.

In Table B the Slovenian trade structure has the highest degree of affinity with the average intra-EU trade structure. Together with former Czechoslovakia it is ranked at the top among the Eastern European countries in terms of resemblance of its trade structure to the intra-EU one. The Czech (and the Slovenian) correlation coefficients are about as high as that for the Netherlands. However, Table B also shows that even for these two countries the correlation with the structure of the exports (to the EU) is lower than for trade with the other Eastern European countries. The latter correlation hovers around 70 per cent, and except for Bulgaria is always marginally higher than that with the EU. (The Baltics would clearly form a separate group if they were included, but the data on the commodity composition of their trade is dominated by re-exports of Russian raw materials, and is therefore not presented here.) It is interesting to note that for all Eastern countries except Romania exports to the EU are less concentrated than those of Portugal, Spain and Greece as their standard deviations (shown on the diagonal) are lower!

TABLE B Eastern European correlation coefficients

	EUR12	SLO	CZE	HUN	POL	ROM	BUL
SLO	68	3.0					
CZE	64	71	2.0				
HUN	42	73	59	2.3			
POL	34	72	66	72	2.2		
ROM	19	70	57	74	76	4.4	
BUL	21	65	57	78	79	81	2.4

Source: Own elaboration on EUROSTAT data. Correlation coefficients and standard deviations times 100.

Tables A and B together thus imply that the trade of former Czechoslovakia (and Slovenia) with the EU has a structure that is similar to that of countries like the Netherlands which are usually counted in the core of the EU.

TABLE C Eastern Europe and the EU members, correlation coefficients

	SLO	CZE	HUN	POL	ROM	BUL
BLEU	62	68	32	32	14	17
FRA	61	54	30	25	9	13
GER	65	59	30	25	8	9
ITA	78	75	64	52	50	51
SPA	60	50	23	27	4	9
UK	46	47	29	18	11	10
NET	27	29	38	22	8	14
DEN	23	19	45	21	22	16
IRE	7	6	24	−1	4	6
POR	85	61	75	67	77	78
GRE	57	42	67	69	74	82

Source: Own elaboration on EUROSTAT data. Correlation coefficients times 100.

continued

Box 16.5 *continued*

However, as Table C shows, the Slovenian trade structure is not only similar to the European average, but even more strongly correlated with the trade structure of two of the Southern EU-members, namely neighbouring Italy and especially Portugal. The latter country's trade structure bears quite a close resemblance to that of almost all the Central and Eastern European countries. This confirms the widely held notion that the Central European countries are potential competitors for the Southern Europeans and especially Portugal.

Although the degree of similarity of Slovenia's EU trade is the same as Netherlands' EU trade the direct correlation Slovenia–Netherlands is rather low. This can be explained by the fact that the resemblance of Slovenia to the EU average is caused by the importance in Slovenia's exports towards the EU of SITC-categories belonging to the category of basic manufactures (e.g. paper, textile yarn and fabrics, iron and steel) and of motor vehicles. The resemblance to Portugal comes out clearly in the importance of exports of clothing and accessories. In this sense there might be some direct competition between Central European countries and the Southern European EU members.

It has often been argued that the trade relations of Central Europe with the EU are difficult because of the high proportion of 'sensitive' exports (agriculture, steel and textiles). However, when one calculates the share of sensitive products in EU imports it becomes clear that the share of these products in EU imports from the Eastern European countries is comparable to that of EU imports from the southern EU members which range from 54 per cent (Portugal) to 60 per cent (Greece) whereas for former Czechoslovakia the share of sensitive products is 'only' 46 per cent, and for Hungary and Poland it is 51 per cent and 55 per cent, respectively.

Source: Gros and Vandille (1994), Gros and Gonciarz (1994)

What is the reason for these results from the point of view of trade theory? A by now widely accepted synthesis of the traditional comparative advantage view and the modern view of trade based on economies of scale and product differentiation suggests that there will be intense intra-industry trade between highly developed countries, simultaneously with inter-industry trade between countries with different capital–labour ratios (see Helpman and Krugman 1985). There should be little trade, however, between countries with a similar capital–labour ratio that are not developed enough to specialise in the industrial goods exchanged within the group of rich countries.[10] Thus, trade between developed countries consists of the exchange of differentiated industrial goods produced with economies of scale but similar capital intensities, whereas the trade between rich countries with high capital–labour ratios and less-developed countries with low capital–labour ratios consists of an exchange of products with different capital–labour ratios.

This view of international trade can explain why numerous attempts to create PTAs in Latin America and Africa have all failed, suggesting that regional integration among less-developed economies is not very practical. Trade between the richer Latin American countries provides a particularly useful basis for comparison with the FSU because their GDP *per capita* of around US$ 2,500 is close to that of Central and Eastern European countries. A comparison of trade flows is shown in Table 16.2.

As shown in Panel A of Table 16.2, Chile, with one of the highest GDP *per capita* in Latin America (1992: US$ 3,303) conducts only 20 per cent of its trade within the region, but 27 per cent with the EU and another 20 per cent with the United States. The bilateral trade flows between Argentina and Brazil are also interesting because the relation between these two countries is similar to that between the Ukraine and Russia in terms of population and GDP.[11] 11 per cent of Argentina's foreign trade is with Brazil, but more than 28 per cent is with the EU. Similarly, only 8 per cent of Brazilian trade is with Argentina (not shown in Table 16.2). A PTA between Argentina and Brazil is therefore not likely to yield large economic benefits. On the contrary, such a PTA might actually be detrimental because it might lead to more trade diversion than trade creation (unless the common external rate of protection is much lower than the present average of the two countries' national rate as planned with MERCOSUR).

Among groups of countries at a similar level of development (e.g. the OECD countries), the geographical distribution of trade flows is determined primarily by the gravitational factors: distance, cultural affinity, size of the different markets. Simple equations that embody these factors, as those in Box 16.2, suggest that the overwhelming factor in determining the geographical distribution of trade flows is market size, which implies that the EU is likely to become the dominant trade partner for all European countries and for the European countries of the FSU. See Section 4 below.

We have shown above that the Central European countries already sell most of their exports to the EU. For them the case is clear. However, for the FSU trade with the outside world in general and with the EU in particular was rather unimportant. Will this change? Chapter 13 showed on the basis of a gravity model that in the future the 'average' former Soviet Republic will conduct about 50 per cent of all trade with the EU. The data in Panel B of Table 16.2 on Finland, Greece and Yugoslavia confirm this by showing that trade with the EU is very important even for countries that are at its periphery. Indeed, even for a country like Finland (which was not a member of the EU in 1992), Germany alone is more important as a trading partner than the FSU. The

TABLE 16.2 Country trade with economic centres, 1992 (percentage of average imports and exports) [% of trade of country in row with country or area in column]

		Panel A		
	Brazil	Latin America	EU	United States
Argentina	13.6	28.2	28.3	15.6
Chile	7.4	19.6	26.9	19.6
		Panel B		
	Germany	USSR	EU	United States
Finland	14.4	13.1*	44.4	5.9
Greece	21.7	2.0	61.6	4.6
Yugoslavia	15.6	18.4	38.7	5.2

Source: IMF trade statistics, 1994

* Trade between Finland and USSR is now (1995) much lower.

Finnish example is particularly revealing because the Baltic Republics are in a similar position and of a similar size (Lithuania has about the same population as Finland). As the case of Greece shows, the EU market, and in particular Germany, assumes a dominant role for poorer states.

We have argued so far that the trade patterns of established market economies imply that the countries on the western edge of the FSU will in the future trade much more with Western Europe than with each other. This argument is valid only if the trade links created in the past can be changed quite quickly. Although Krugman (1991a) suggests that historical accidents may have a permanent impact on trade, it appears from recent experience (see Table 16.1) that reformed former socialist countries in Central Europe did redirect their trade flows very rapidly.

3. The optimum size of the European Union

If the EU were only a PTA then the determination of the optimal size of the EU would be relatively easy: one could argue that it should be as large as possible. And, indeed, the negotiations that led to the creation of the EEA were definitely easier than those that characterise EU expansion. Also the perspective of an EEA extending into the FSU, as argued below in Section 4, is more easily accepted at the political level than expansion of the EU. For geographical and historical reasons the Visegrad countries will become members of the EU some time towards the end of this decade or early in the next decade. But the key question remains: is this expansion in some sense desirable for the citizens of the EU? If so, where should the EU's border be drawn?

Trade theory is of little help in determining the optimal size of the EU, because the EU is much more than a PTA. A pointer is provided by the question whether the EU is ready for monetary integration. As some member sub-groups are more homogeneous than the group of all 12 members in terms of economic structure and policy preferences, a two-speed approach has been proposed, which is a way of saying that the EU is not the optimal size for EMU, or for other advances in integration. 'Widening' integration can thus be seen as an alternative to 'deepening', and was already seen in these terms by General de Gaulle.[12]

This example illustrates that for the various political economy dimensions of EU (factor mobility, social policy, CAP, structural funds, monetary integration), new members have to satisfy quite a demanding list of conditions to ensure that EU expansion is positive for the incumbents.

It would be helpful if newcomers had political preferences close to those of the EU, taking into account that membership is likely to make preferences more convergent. On that basis Austria was and Hungary will be more readily admitted than Turkey or Belarus. Furthermore, the newcomer should show evidence of an aspiration to become a member of the European family – as is the case of the Visegrad countries – and not be absorbed by internecine struggles. Moreover, to fit into the EU the whole political apparatus of the newcomer must conform to European institutions: democracy, human rights and a decentralised economic structure must be firmly established, otherwise the country could not operate within the political, legal and institutional framework of the EU.

And, finally, the level of economic development must be above a certain threshold:

first, to be able to keep pace with the speed of integration deepening; and, second, in order not to stretch the structural funds of the EU beyond acceptable levels. Countries like Greece and Portugal are probably on the borderline. They experience difficulties in following the pace of integration (single market, financial market integration, EMU) and from a financial point of view the question is how many countries can and will the net financial contributors to the EU afford?

This last question points to possible institutional and financial reforms and adaptations of the EU before expansion. Certain institutions and features lose their 'optimality' when the EU is expanding. For that reason net beneficiaries of EU funds fear the redistributive effects of expansion and are usually less supportive of expansion than are net contributors.

Apart from financial questions, the EU needs to make difficult institutional adjustments in case of further expansion. For example, in the Community of Six it was not too problematic to accept all member languages, which amounted to only four. When the EC expanded to 12 members, nine languages were certainly no longer optimal. Without a difficult choice of language(s) for the EU, any expansion is likely to generate a Tower of Babel situation.

The crucial issue is, however, money. Eastward expansion will require a radical reform of the CAP to limit the financial cost of accepting new members with an agricultural sector that could explode with current CAP prices. This issue is so important that it merits a careful analysis. Since the CAP and regional funds have the lion's share of financial transfers within the EU, we shall concentrate on these two items.

The potential candidates for membership considered here are the EFTA countries (three of which joined in 1995) and the countries in Central and Eastern Europe (west of the CIS). The latter are grouped under three headings: Visegrad (Poland, Hungary, the Czech and Slovak Republics), Balkan (Bulgaria, Romania) and Baltic (Estonia, Latvia, Lithuania).

Our results of the estimates of receipts and contributions are summarised in Table 16.3. Column (3) of Table 16.3.A shows that the EFTA3 would make a substantial net contribution to the EU budget of approximately 2.7 billion of 1992 ECU, if, in the future, the two richest EFTA countries (Switzerland and Norway) joined the EU, the effective contribution of the EFTA countries would increase to 4.5 billion of 1992 ECU.

Table 16.3.A also shows that the candidate countries from Central and Eastern Europe could count on substantial net transfers. If one assumes that these countries would receive the same *per capita* allocations from the structural funds as the poorer current members, the transfer could easily be above 12 per cent of their GDP. Thus, making the structural funds available to Eastern European countries would have a highly significant effect upon investment and growth in those countries. However, these transfers would not have a great effect upon the EU budget. Structural fund expenditures in the Visegrad countries would cost less than 0.3 per cent of EU GDP.

In addition to the structural funds, one has to consider the effect of the common agricultural policy (CAP). Here, predicting the impact of enlargement is much more difficult so that we present two scenarios. Much would depend upon how producers and consumers in Eastern Europe adjust to the new environment they face. If agricultural production does not adjust at all, one obtains the results of Table 16.3.A which

TABLE 16.3.A The budgetary effects of accession. Current agricultural production (in ECU billion unless stated otherwise)

	Structural funds (1)	FEOGA guarantee (2)	Budget Contrib's (3)	Net receipts (4)	Net rec. as % of GDP (5)	Other expend.* (6)	Budget as % of EU GDP (1992) (7)
EC12	16.32	28.36				11.60	1.20
E.Germ.	3.32	0.91	1.24	2.99	2.56	11.60	1.26
EFTA (3)	0.09	1.40	2.73	−1.24	−0.43	11.60	1.22
Visegrad (4)	12.90	3.67	1.40	15.17	11.61	11.60	1.51
Balkan (2)	6.98	1.49	0.48	7.99	17.76	11.60	1.66
Baltic (3)	1.59	4.76	0.16	6.19	41.24	11.60	1.77

TABLE 16.3.B The budgetary effects of accession in 1999 with partial adjustment in agriculture in Eastern Europe by 1999 (in ECU billion unless stated otherwise)

	Structural funds (1)	FEOGA guarantee (2)	Budget Contrib's (3)	Net receipts (4)	Net rec. as % of GDP (5)	Other expend.* (6)	Budget as % of EU GDP (1992) (7)
EC12	25.46	28.36				17.20	1.21
E.Germ.	5.46	6.78	1.56	10.68	7.31	17.20	1.39
EFTA (3)	0.14	1.40	3.41	−1.87	−0.52	17.20	1.33
Visegrad (4)	21.23	17.62	1.74	37.11	22.67	17.20	1.90
Balkan (2)	11.48	5.75	0.60	16.63	29.51	17.20	2.14
Baltic (3)	2.61	9.00	0.20	11.41	60.76	17.20	2.31

Source: Brenton and Gros (1993)

* Other expenditures are those of the EU budget not listed in columns (1) and (2)

shows that the Visegrad countries would not benefit strongly from the CAP, for the simple reason that they are currently only small exporters of agricultural products.

However, if one allows for a reaction of agricultural production and consumption to the higher prices of the current CAP, the picture changes. Table 16.3.B is therefore based upon the reasonable assumption that farmers in the potential new members should be able, by 1999, to bridge one half of the current gap in yields between East and West (in addition the structural funds are augmented by the cohesion funds in column 1). Under this assumption the accession of the Visegrad countries alone would increase the cost of the CAP by at least 60 per cent of the current levels of support. The Balkans and the Baltics would, together, add a similar amount. We therefore conclude that the CAP will have to be radically reformed on this account alone.

Admitting the Visegrad countries would cost, each year, about 15 billion ECU under the more favourable hypothesis represented in Table 16.3.A. Is this a large sum? It is large in relation to the present budget (slightly over ECU 60 billion), but it is also only about one-quarter of one per cent of the GDP of the EU. If farmers in Eastern Europe catch up partially towards the productivity levels of their Western counterparts the cost would double to about one half of one per cent of EU GDP. (If they become even more efficient the cost would increase correspondingly.) Adding the Balkans and the Baltics would again double the cost to reach one full per cent of EU GDP. These calculations show that the EU cannot afford too many efficient agricultural producers.

We have considered the budgetary impact of enlargement mainly from the point of view of the EU. Since the EFTA countries are substantial net contributors, a simultaneous northward and eastward enlargement (say, three, in the future five, EFTA plus all Visegrad countries) would have a substantial, but ultimately bearable net budgetary cost for the EU, on the condition that the CAP is reformed. Without a radical reform of the CAP the agricultural potential of Eastern Europe could lead to enormous costs for the EC budget. What does this analysis imply for the new members?

For the EFTA countries the budgetary implications, that is, the net transfer to the EC budget they have to make, is not a decisive factor since it amounts to less than one per cent of their GDP. However, the situation is radically different for the Eastern Europeans. They can expect to make at least 10 per cent of their GDP in net transfers. Membership would thus fundamentally transform the economic potential of these countries. The reason transfers from the EU have such a large impact on these countries is simply that they are so poor. As the income *per capita* in Poland is still below ECU 2,000, the structural funds alone, which should amount to approximately ECU 200 *per capita*, therefore represent a sizeable proportion of national income.

It is sometimes argued that the income *per capita* measured at market exchange rates underestimates the standard of living in these countries and that, therefore, transfers should not be based on these data. Income *per capita* in Greece and Portugal is about ECU 5,000 to ECU 6,000, two to three times higher than in Poland or even the Czech Republic. This difference is felt to exaggerate the differences in the standard of living. However, this argument misses the whole point about the impact of the transfers from the EU, which is to give the recipient country additional purchasing power at the EU level. To put it differently, in 1992 Polish imports were approximately equal to ECU 13 billion; the transfers from the structural funds would allow Poland to increase imports by over 50 per cent without exporting more. Five years' worth of structural funds would also be sufficient to wipe out Poland's external debt of ECU 35 billion.

While the impact of membership on the Eastern European countries will be fundamental, the impact on the EU will remain marginal. The overall budget would exceed the ceiling fixed at Edinburgh (1.27 per cent of GDP), but the overall cost of a joint EFTA and Eastern European enlargement would be small. As already mentioned, the EFTA countries provide a net contribution to the EC budget that could be offset against the net transfer to Eastern Europe. The other, and ultimately more important reason, is that in economic terms the Eastern European countries are so small when compared with the EU. The GDP of the EU is about 40 times larger than the combined GDP of the Visegrad countries (EU: ECU 4,675 billion, Visegrad: ECU 130 billion in 1990). This means that a transfer that is only one-quarter of one per cent of the GDP of the EC can amount to 10 per cent of the GDP of the Visegrad countries.

An expanding EU will necessarily become more diverse. Therefore it is only desirable to expand if decision-making can be made easier in other ways. One reform goal would consist in moving generally to majority voting, suitably weighted if necessary, for all day-to-day decision making.[13] Others would be reform of the political and administrative institutions of the EU (as one cannot simply add directorates to create room for additional staff from new members); redistribution of decision-making power to the European Parliament, to fill the 'democracy gap'; and a review of the role and decision-making of the Council. Some of these features are captured in a theoretical model in Box 16.6.

Box 16.6 The optimum size of a club

Clubs are associations in the pursuit of a well-defined common interest. Their optimum size is neither one individual, nor humankind (with its diverse tastes). To find the optimum size of a club, the benefits and costs of increasing membership need to be defined. In the following it is assumed that membership benefits are a *private* good and not a *public* good.

Starting from a small number of members, benefits to incumbent members will initially rise with increasing membership but eventually start to decline as congestion becomes dominant (congestion implies that not only the benefit of a new member declines, but that of existing members as well). Similarly, cost to incumbents of an additional member declines initially, but will increase eventually. Increasing marginal costs are also the result of congestion and the increasing difficulty of finding agreement among more numerous members with more heterogeneous preferences. Costs will also increase more than proportionately for the political opportunity of each additional member to express its viewpoint, independently of size.

The optimum club size (M*) is given by the equality of marginal benefits and costs of incumbents, which are the decision-makers for new admissions, as in Figure A.

Institutional changes can affect both benefits and costs. For example, replacing unanimity decision rules by majority voting will shift the marginal cost curve downward so that optimal size increases.

Assuming that the European Union of 15 members is close to the optimal level M*, or even above it, with its present institutional set-up, does this mean that Eastern Europe could not be gainfully integrated into the European Union?

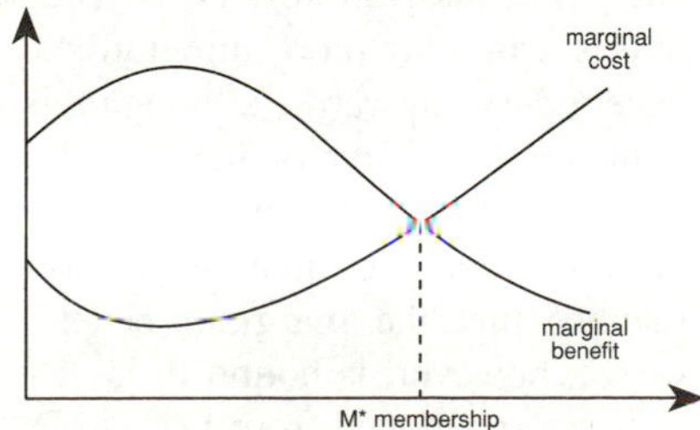

FIG A Cost and benefits to existing club members of expanding membership
Source: De Benedictis and Padoan (1994)

continued

Box 16.6 *continued*

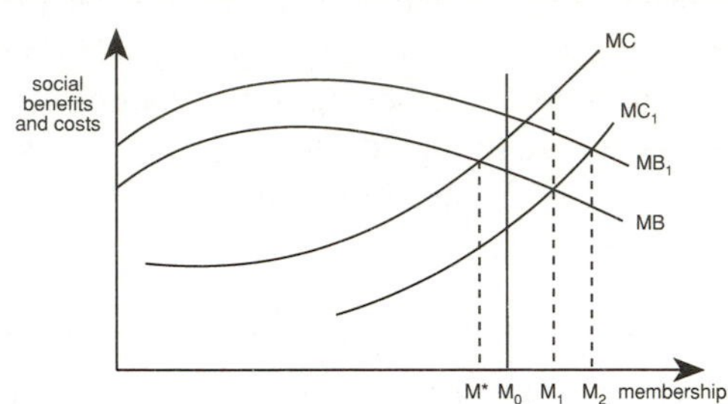

FIG B Institutional reforms of the EU as a condition for enlargement to the East

In Figure B it is assumed that the present EU of 15 members (M_0) is already larger than optimum membership M* with its present institutional arrangements. If M_0 were to the left of M* there would be scope for enlargement. If M_0 is at M* or to the right of M* then enlargement requires institutional reforms (such as majority decisions, reform of the CAP), which would be desirable even without enlargement. Enlargement to M_1 without institutional reforms would increase the welfare cost as measured by the vertical distance between MC and MB at M_0 to the one at M_1. Reforms shift the marginal cost curve MC down to MC_1. If substantial enough enlargement to M_1 would be optimal. Some of these reforms, such as CAP reforms, would not only decrease costs but would also increase benefits, shifting the MC curve to MC_1, thereby making a greater enlargement to M_2 desirable. For a given reform programme expansion of optimal membership may not be enough to accommodate all membership candidates. Only those with marginal benefit in excess of marginal cost should be admitted. To enlarge further either the countries which are refused membership reform themselves to increase the marginal gain above the marginal cost of the EU or further EU reforms are possible and are carried out. These examples illustrate that optimal enlargement depends both on policies in candidate countries *and* in the EU.

One concern about EU enlargement is that deepening integration will be made more difficult. A good example is monetary union which seems to be easier for a sub-group of EU countries, the so-called core countries, than for all EU countries. Enlargement to include structurally weaker East European countries is likely to make integration even more difficult, as depicted in Figure C.

The horizontal axis in Figure C measures the depth of integration. For the EU of 15 members the optimal depth of integration is D^*_{15}. The actual level is presumably lower at D_{15} so there is scope for more integration. Adding new members may shift the marginal benefit curve upwards, although this gain may be small, as illustrated by the gains to incumbents of a monetary union in an enlarged, as compared to the present, size of the EU. Even the new members may not gain, as illustrated by the reluctance of some EU members to join monetary union. For simplicity, Figure C assumes that the marginal benefit curve to incumbents remains unchanged. The cost, however, is bound to increase. The optimum level of depth of integration is therefore reduced from D^*_{15} to D^*_{20}. In this sense it can be argued that enlargement is likely to require a trade-off in terms of integration.

continued

Box 16.6 *continued*

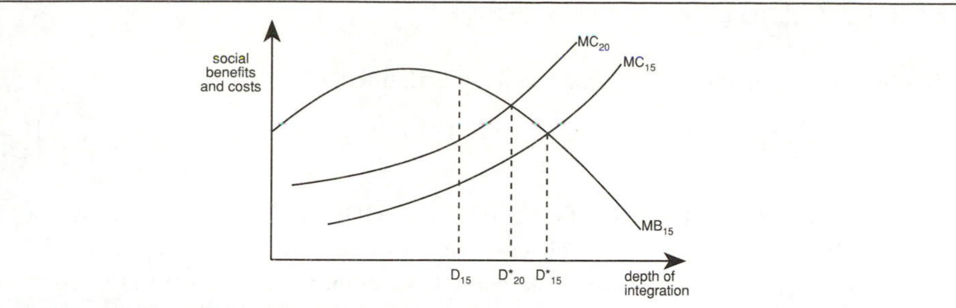

FIG C Deepening integration in an enlarged EU

Of course, D^*_{20} is not necessarily to the right of D_{15}. If it is then further gainful integration is still possible. If it is to the left of D_{15} then the current level of depth of integration would already be excessive.

In the end it is therefore the choice of Union (how deeply integrated?) and its ultimate goal (e.g. federation or confederation) that is key to the optimal size of the EU. The more ambitious the ultimate goal, the more restrictive is its optimal size. The more a potential member differs in political and economic structure and maturity, the less compelling is its membership. For the moment, the Visegrad countries and Slovenia seem to be the only ones to qualify for membership within the next decade.

4. The weight of geography

In Section 2 it was argued that the optimum number of trade blocks was either small or very large. Furthermore it was shown that global free trade is always better than free trade limited to a restricted area. These arguments, however, neglect geography. Indeed, imagine two continents with sizable inter-continental transport costs and two countries per continent which trade intensively with each other but little with the countries of the other continent in view of high transport costs. Then a PTA per continent is better than no or only one PTA and is, in fact, close to global free trade. In this section we concentrate therefore on the geographical position of Eastern European countries by again using the gravity model. We develop a gravity index (see Box 16.7) that measures the trade potential of a given country by taking the sum of the country's supply potential (its GDP) adjusted for the size of the internal market and the trade demand it can expect given its geographical position. A country that is rich and close to other rich countries will have a high index and countries that are poor or far from the centres of economic activity will have a low index (will be 'peripheral'). This gravity (or periphery) index is attractive for several reasons. Geographic proximity, size of markets, trade arrangements and cultural affinities are part of the index and matter, as demonstrated by the estimation of gravity models. The time dependent ingredients are relatively straightforward to forecast (GDP and population growth) and the unchanging geography is easy to measure.[14]

Box 16.7 The gravity index defined

The gravity or periphery index for country *j* is defined as

$$R_j = \sum_i Y_i X_i u_{ij} / d_{ij} + bY_j X_j / d_{jj} = R_j^{(1)} + R_j^{(2)} \qquad [1]$$

where Y_i is GDP in US dollars of country *i*; X_i is GDP *per capita* deflated by the highest GDP *per capita* among all countries so that $0 < X_i \leq 1$; $d_{ij} = (D_{ij})^{1/2}$ where D_{ij} is the distance between the capitals of countries *i* and *j* (in km); $d_{jj} = 1/3(Sj/\pi)^{1/2}$ where S_j is the surface in km^2. u_{ij}, a dummy variable for closeness either in a historical, cultural sense or due to trade treaties, is 1.21 for trade among the six regions of Russia to reflect the fact that they form an integrated country; 1.1 for various regional groupings and 1.0 for all other bilateral relations.

To calibrate the two factors in definition [1] the weight *b* (identical for all *j*) is used. Weight *b* is defined as:

$$b = \sum_j R_j^{(1)} / \sum_j R_j^{(2)} \qquad [2]$$

and forces globally the weight of the $R_j^{(1)}$ and $R_j^{(2)}$ to be equal.

The data used are listed in Table A below except for bilateral distances to save space. The index R_j is a measure of the trade potential of country *j* within a given set of countries. The ranking established is specific to this set and can be changed by adding or subtracting countries. For this reason computations for a variety of country groupings were carried out.

Source: Gros and Steinherr (1992)

TABLE A Raw data used for gravity index

	Area *1000 km^2	Population *1000	GDP US$ mn (1990)	Per head US$ (1990)	GDP US$ mn (2000)	Per head US$ (2000)
St.Petersburg	529	11,128	27,820	2,500	45,316	4,072
Moscow	1,530	47,339	118,348	2,500	192,776	4,072
Volgograd	589	20,810	52,025	2,500	84,743	4,072
Sverdlovsk	3,097	39,489	98,723	2,500	16,089	4,072
Novosibirsk	3,564	15,886	39,715	2,500	64,692	4,072
Vladivostok	7,767	13,289	33,233	2,500	54,116	4,072
Ukraine	604	51,700	98,489	1,905	160,427	3,103
Belarus	207	10,200	25,169	2,468	40,997	4,019
Estonia	45	1,570	3,937	2,508	6,413	4,084
Latvia	64	2,680	6,720	2,508	10,946	4,084

Table continued

continued

Box 6.7 *continued*

TABLE A *continued*

	Area *1000 km²	Population *1000	GDP US$ mn (1990)	Per head US$ (1990)	GDP US$ mn (2000)	Per head US$ (2000)
Lithuania	65	3690	8552	2318	13,930	3775
Moldavia	34	4340	7400	1705	12,053	2777
Armenia	30	3280	5568	1698	9,069	2765
Azerbaidzhan	87	7030	10,475	1490	17,062	2427
Georgia	70	5450	9796	1798	15,957	2928
Kazakhstan	2,717	16,540	25,844	1563	42,097	2545
Kyrgystan	198	4290	4805	1120	78,275	1824
Uzebekistan	447	19,900	19,900	1000	32,415	1629
Tadzhikistan	143	5110	4612	903	7,512	1470
Turkmenistan	488	3530	4518	1280	7,360	2085
Poland	313	38,200	89,388	2340	145,604	3812
Former GDR	108	16,600	149,822	9025	244,044	14,701
Czechoslovakia	128	15,700	46,500	2962	75,744	4824
Hungary	93	10,600	32,100	3028	52,288	4933
Romania	238	23,200	35,500	1530	57,826	2492
Bulgaria	111	9000	22,400	2489	36,487	4054
France	547	56,000	1,186,180	21,182	1,594,127	28,467
Benelux	75	25,132	479,679	19,086	644,648	25,651
Italy	301	57,600	1,086,104	18,856	1,459,633	25,341
United Kingdom	245	57,200	986,282	17,243	1,325,481	23,173
West Germany	249	61,990	1,498,219	24,169	2,013,481	32,481
Scandinavia	1,111	17,600	469,605	26,682	631,110	35,859
Japan	378	123,200	2,865,751	23,261	4,668,006	37,890
USA	9,373	249,970	5,423,400	21,696	8,834,147	35,341
Iran	1,648	53,900	390,502	7,245	636,087	11,801
Pakistan	804	1,104,000	39,731	360	64,718	586
Turkey	781	55,400	70,598	1,274	114,997	2,076

Table 16.4 lists the periphery index for various regional groupings. This index reveals potential geographical trade structure after reforms have resulted in the required structural changes, say by the year 2000.[15] Population is assumed to be constant; GDP growth is projected at an average of 5 per cent a year for Japan, the republics of the former Soviet Union and Central Europe to reflect catching up (see Chapter 15); all other countries are assumed to grow at 3 per cent a year Experimentation with different assumptions about GDP growth showed that the general thrust of the results reported below is robust. Russia is too large and heterogeneous to be treated as a single region with a well defined centre. For this reason Russia is split up into six regions. The fact that these regions are part of one state is reflected by a dummy variable.

The columns of Table 16.4 represent different hypothetical trading blocks. The absolute values are meaningless, but a horizontal comparison reveals the trading potential of a given country within different groupings. Comparing, for example, the value for Kazakhstan across Columns 1 and 2 shows that opening trade with Iran, Pakistan and Turkey increases the trading potential by a factor of 15.[16] In contrast, comparing Columns 1 and 7 suggests that the trading potential of the Central Asian republics is increased by a factor of 'only' about 8 through free trade with the rest of the former Soviet Union. The reason for this result is proximity, which becomes important at a similar level of income.

Comparing Columns 7 and 8 shows that free trade with Central Europe increases the trading potential of the former Soviet republics only marginally. The other way round the influence is stronger, as can be seen by comparing Column 5 with Column 8. However, it is apparent that the real increase in trading potential occurs when the formerly socialist countries open to Western Europe. Comparing Column 8 with Column 9 indicates that this leads to a 10 to 20-fold increase in the trading potential of all members of the former Soviet block. (For Central Europe separately the effect is visible in the difference between Columns 5 and 6.) This implies that the former Soviet block did not make a lot of economic sense.

TABLE 16.4 Periphery Indexes (2000)

	1	2	3	4	5	6	7	8	9	10
St. Petersburg							6	8	147	289
Moscow							9	9	140	281
Volgograd							7	8	127	270
Sverdlovsk							6	6	107	248
Novosibirsk							3	5	87	233
Vladivostok							2	3	68	308
Ukraine							9	10	161	305
Belarus							7	10	168	312
Estonia							4	8	167	310
Latvia							4	9	176	319
Lithuania							5	9	174	317
Moldavia							5	8	163	308
Armenia							4	6	121	268
Azerbaidzhan							4	6	115	263
Georgia							4	6	123	268
Kazakhstan	0.39	6					3	4	85	232
Kyrgystan	0.40	6					2	4	85	232
Uzbekistan	0.45	6					3	5	89	235
Tadzhikistan	0.46	7					3	4	88	235
Turkmenistan	0.45	10					3	5	96	245
Poland					7	192		17	201	345
Former GDR					21	277		104	342	499
Czech/Slovak Rep.					8	231		18	240	387
Hungary					6	202		15	209	356
Romania					5	162		9	166	311
Bulgaria					5	168		10	172	319

continued

TABLE 16.4 *continued*

	1	2	3	4	5	6	7	8	9	10
France			400	407		579			932	1143
Benelux			408	456		628			976	1185
Italy			307	355		544			931	1146
United Kingdom			371	417		592			949	1160
West Germany			496	578		943			1695	1974
Scandinavia				209		205			399	564
Japan										3703
USA										1359
Iran		40								230
Pakistan		6								155
Turkey		8								185

Finally, Column 10 reveals that adding the rest of the world (mainly the United States and Japan) increases the trading potential of Central European countries and most Western former republics only moderately. However, the Vladivostok region (East Siberia) would gain greatly through the influence of Japan.

As for Western Europe, the main trade potential is within the EU. Adding Scandinavia increases the trade potential less than free trade with the Central European countries or with the FSU (comparing Column 3 with Columns 6 and 9).

Comparing the values within each column reveals that the gravity centres within the FSU are Moscow and the Ukraine, whilst any westward expansion brings the Baltic states and Belarus into more central positions. As seen from Column 9, when the FSU trades openly with Western Europe, the Baltic states become the gravity centre of the ex-USSR. Most peripheral are the Central Asian republics and Siberia. Clearly the EU is the gravity centre of world trade (Column 10) and within the EU Germany is the epicentre. This is already true of West Germany in isolation and is reinforced by adding the ex-GDR (the indexes are, however, not additive).

The results in Column 9 are used in Fig. 16.1 to design the future economic map of Europe in the year 2000. The more central a country is according to the index of Column 9, the darker is its surface.[17] Siberia (not shown) would have the purest white as the most peripheral area, followed by the Central Asian republics. The area or republics closer to Western Europe gain light grey tones and black is achieved in the epicentre represented by (West) Germany.

The map in Fig. 16.1 suggests a very pronounced core-periphery pattern. What does this imply for the future development of Central and Eastern Europe? Krugman (1991a) argues that there might be a 'U' shaped relationship between transport costs and the probability of the emergence of a link between a manufacturing core and its agricultural periphery. At zero transport costs location does not matter and at very high transport costs each region will produce its own mix of food and manufacturing products and will thus gain some of the economies of scale in manufacturing. At the extremes of the 'U' no core–periphery pattern should therefore develop. However, there is an intermediate region where transport costs are positive, but just low enough to make it worthwhile to produce manufacturing goods at the core (which thus gets all

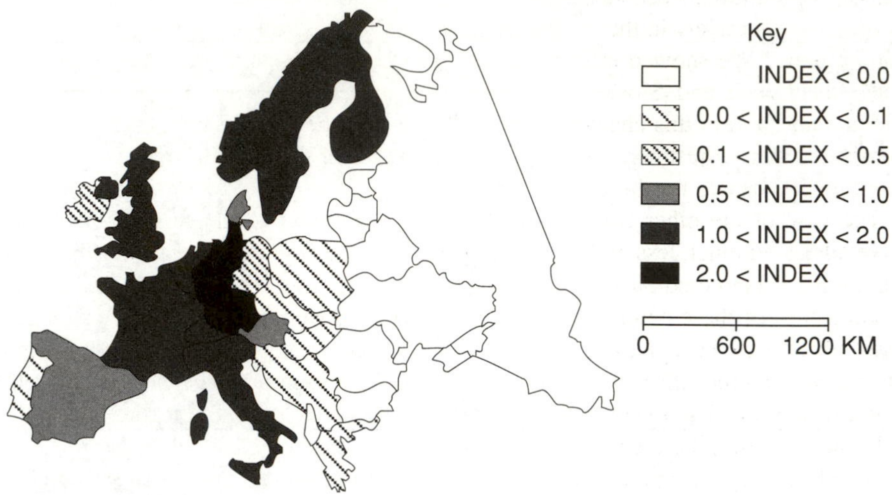

FIG 16.1 Economic centres in Europe 2000

the economies of scale) and export them to the periphery, which specialises in agriculture.

Liberally interpreted this view would suggest the following: within the EU there is a core around Germany which encompasses France, the UK and the Benelux countries and which may be extending into Southern Europe. The Central European countries which are very close to the core might benefit from the proximity of the core and may ultimately become part of it. However, the countries further away might fall into the category where transport costs are just high enough to induce manufacturing firms to locate in the core rather than in the periphery. Only the Asian regions of Russia (not shown on the map) might be sufficiently far away to make it worthwhile to locate some manufacturing activities there because transport costs are too high.

We showed in Section 1 above that the radical shift in trade patterns predicted by gravity models has already taken place in the case of the Central European countries. This implies that our map of economic centres describes today's reality and it is likely that this core–periphery pattern will persist for decades.

5. Conclusions

The analysis in this chapter suggests that in the long run most of the Central and Eastern European countries will re-orient their trade towards the EU. The Central European countries have already done so to compensate for the collapse of trade with the FSU area which has hurt them significantly.

The EU has already concluded Association or 'Europe' agreements with all countries West of the FSU (except the former Yugoslav republics) and will offer the three Baltic countries the same treatment. The EAs contain a commitment to abolish all barriers to trade in industrial goods and successive European Councils have reaffirmed the willingness of the EU to let the associated states become members when they satisfy the minimum economic and political performance that would allow them to participate effectively in the highly integrated EU that is still in the making. What else can be done? We showed in Part III that the most advanced Central European countries (the Czech and Slovak Republics, Hungary, Poland) have consolidated their initial gains, and in this chapter we have shown that they (and Slovenia) have already completed their adjustment to the new trade pattern of the new Europe. There is little more the EU can do for these countries.

The case of the other countries (including the Baltics) is different. Their reforms have advanced much less and their industrial structure is too different from that of the EU to make them credible candidates for membership in the near future. The bilateral relationships of these countries with the EU will be governed by the EAs which guarantee them free access to the EU market, but obstacles remain for trade among themselves and the CIS countries (not to speak of the former Yugoslav republics other than Slovenia) which do not even have guaranteed access to the EU market.

In the short run, these countries have great difficulties increasing their exports to the West which they so urgently need to pay for the pent-up demand of their population for Western consumer goods and Western capital goods so necessary for the modernisation of their economies. We therefore suggest that the EU should invite all Eastern European countries, including the successor countries of the FSU, to establish a multilateral European Free Trade Zone (EFTZ), stretching from the Atlantic to the Pacific.[18] The EFTZ would encompass over 700 mn consumers (and hopefully almost as many producers) and would have a number of advantages. First of all it would open the huge EU market for exports from Eastern Europe. At present EU imports of manufactured goods from that area are negligible (ECU 5 bn from Central Europe and ECU 2 bn from the FSU). The 'cost' to the EU in terms of the displacement of domestic production can thus only be minor.

Second, it would lock in outward-looking reforms as it would keep Russia and other countries of the FSU (where these reforms are still uncertain) open to Western competition which is essential for a successful and rapid transformation into market economies.

A third advantage is that this free trade zone would help to ensure that trade among Eastern European countries (including trade among countries of the FSU) is facilitated. Given the importance of inter-FSU trade, it is important that it is not cut off by artificial barriers.[19] The offer of participation in the EFTZ would be a powerful incentive for countries of the FSU to refrain from imposing trade barriers against each other as they are doing at present because they would then lose access to the largest market of the world. The EFTZ would thus overcome the 'hub and spoke' pattern inherent in the present arrangement.

Finally, direct investment in Eastern Europe and the FSU will be forthcoming only if Western entrepreneurs can be certain that they will also be able to export from there to the EU. Although the EFTZ alone would not be a sufficient condition to create substantial flows of direct investment, access to markets is certainly a necessary condition without which other efforts at stimulating flows of private capital would be ineffective.

It should be clear that what is proposed here is just a free trade area which does not imply a common external trade policy. The EFTZ would therefore be a 'building' and not a 'stumbling' block for general free trade (Lawrence 1991), like the North American Free Trade Area (NAFTA) which, one day, may cover the Americas. The

EFTZ, like the NAFTA, would not have any direct bearing on exchange rate arrangements; but it is likely to have an indirect influence on them because the heavy concentration of trade flows will also influence the exchange rate regime the Eastern European countries will choose. This is already happening now in the case of the Central European countries, all of which have given the DM a large weight in their exchange rate policy. Appearing on the horizon is thus a tripolar world in terms of trade and monetary arrangements. NAFTA will be centred on the US dollar, the EFTZ area (except possibly Russia because of its oil exports) would be tied to the ECU, and in East Asia a yen-zone is emerging (Frankel 1991).[20]

Over time this EFTZ would evolve and some parts would become members of the EU. Our analysis suggests that during the next generation only the Visegrad countries (and Slovenia) will be able to qualify for full membership, but all others should be considered for appropriate association agreements. However, the EFTZ should not evolve only in geographical terms. After the necessary reforms of the CAP it should also be extended to cover agriculture and at any time it could be enriched by a specific agreement to create an integrated energy market and provide guarantees for Western investment in the East (see Appendix).

As to enlargement of the European Union, this chapter argues that the optimal size does depend, most of all, on how successful the Union itself will be in adapting its decision-making institutions and its financial programmes. To make membership, especially membership in EMU, viable for the Central Europeans they need to converge in social, political and economic terms. History and present performance suggests that the Visegrad countries are likely to converge successfully and this makes them the best candidates for membership over the next 5–10 years.

For the others the jury is still out. Should the EU do still more for them? We showed in Chapter 15 that external support can be important (and crucial in a crisis situation like Russia 1992–93, see Chapter 14) but most of the effort has to come from the country concerned. If the political system is not able to create an environment in terms of macroeconomic stability and the rule of law that leads to the investment rate of about 20 per cent of GDP necessary for catch up, there is nothing much the West can do except damage limitation. Many Latin American countries went through 'lost decades' of this type. It is clear what this type of failure would imply: economic distress and a re-emergence of militarist nationalism. We therefore argued that it is worthwhile to invest in aid programmes even if the probability that the situation will be turned round is not high. Even a small chance to redress a potentially disastrous situation is worth a lot.

But as long as the Western, Central and Eastern European leaders do their homework another scenario is more likely : one where the European Union reforms itself, deepens its political integration and welcomes the best performing Central European countries, providing an example for the others to follow. We argued that enlargement to include countries of the FSU is not a practical proposition. But we also showed that this does not mean that nothing can be done. Free trade from the Atlantic to the Pacific and active participation in the reform of key sectors of the FSU (energy and agriculture) with a Marshall Plan II, as argued in Chapter 15, is the way to maximise the chances that reforms in the FSU succeed, following up General De Gaulle's vision. Fully aware of the risks and difficulties lying ahead, we conclude this long journey that started early this century under the banner 'socialism in one country' with some optimism that a 'New Europe' will finally emerge – a continent co-operating and prospering in peace to the benefit of its citizens.

Notes

1. A reminder of terminology: a *preferential trade area* (PTA) accords easier access to its members than to non-members; a *free trade area* (FTA) is a special PTA with no trade restrictions among members; a *customs union* is an FTA with common external tariffs (and hence also a PTA); a *common market* is a customs union with free movement of capital and labour, and an *economic union* is a common market supported by coordinated, joint or supranational policy-making in selected domains.
2. Since the Agreements cover areas beyond the Commission's competence, the EAs had to be ratified by individual EC member governments. Pending this, Interim Agreements implementing only the trade chapters of the EAs were put into effect immediately. For a critical review see Rollo (1992) and Hughes and Hare (1992).
3. The Copenhagen Summit also called upon the EU Commission to submit proposals for developing the existing trade agreements with the three Baltic states into free trade agreements, this has not been done and the Baltic States will also be able to obtain EAs.
4. This is where the threat of protectionism against Central European exports is greatest.
5. The motivation for EU expansion is not completely symmetric. The optimum size of EU is therefore treated separately in Section 3.
6. Canada exports 78 per cent of its total exports to the USA and Mexico 76 per cent before NAFTA.
7. Empirical studies conclude that 'trade creation in the EC has been substantial in absolute terms and has exceeded trade diversion several times' (Balassa 1975).
8. Even without an explicit policy regional trade integration affects the terms of trade, as shown in Box 15.1. The terms of trade gains of the initial EC of six members, originating in the manufacturing sector, were estimated to represent between 0.3 and 0.5% of GNP (Petith 1977).
9. This statement is true for any country evaluating its potential gains from joining an FTA. From a global perspective, a small or a large number of FTAs are welfare-superior to an intermediate case (Krugman 1991b). A single FTA spanning the world is equal to global free trade; a number of FTAs equal to the number of countries in the world is the *status quo*. Between these extremes there are cases where welfare may be inferior to the *status quo*.
10. Balassa and Bauwens (1988) contain extensive tests of this view. Möbius and Schumacher (1990) provide a sectoral analysis of the trade of Eastern European countries that also confirms this general view.
11. The population of the Ukraine is 55 million (vs. 30 million for Argentina), and that of Russia is 140 million (the same as Brazil).
12. General De Gaulle's famous veto to Britain joining the EEC was based, probably among others, on the belief that Britain's often insular concerns would slow down the speed and depth of integration of the EEC of Six.
13. Voting weights would need to be renegotiated to better reflect an expanded EU's coexistence of small and large members.
14. Bismarck emphasised the importance of geography 'as the only stable factor in external relations'. Of course, measurement is a different matter. Transport costs are not always strongly correlated with distances: transport from Tokyo to San Francisco is much cheaper than from one side of the Himalayas to the other. Nevertheless it is preferable to use an imperfect proxy variable than to neglect geography. Gravity models were also used by

Hamilton and Winters (1992) and Havrylyshyn and Pritchett (1991) to assess Eastern European trade potential.

15. This choice of time period is always somewhat arbitrary. Orwell chose 1984 because it seemed a safe 35 years away from his time of writing. In 1957 the former Soviet leader Khrushchev chose a horizon of 10 years to reach and overtake the US economy. We choose the year 2000 for convenience and to allow at least initial reforms to be worked out. The actual results may, of course, take longer.
16. Pakistan, Turkey and Iran have invited Azerbaidzhan, Turkmenistan, Uzbekistan, Tadzhikistan and Kyrgystan to join the Economic Co-operation Organisation (ECO), the association of the three countries formed 27 years ago without having produced an echo. Afghanistan could also become an ECO member once peace has been established there. Further east, Kazakhstan, Uzbekistan and Kyrgystan are attempting regional cooperation, including a free (at least preferential) trade area.
17. Gravity indexes were computed for all European countries, even for those not shown in Table 16.4. Indexes were regrouped into six classes which correspond to six colour shades.
18. The gravity analysis provides support for an EFTZ from the Atlantic to the Urals. Extension to the Pacific would be for political reasons. Central Asian countries might prefer to join other regional arrangements.
19. The natural decline which we predict will happen as a result of market forces is a different matter.
20. These three blocks would correspond roughly to Orwell's Oceania (as he liked to call the Americas), Eurasia and Eastasia, forecast to exist in 1984. Like him we also neglected 'the large quadrilateral with its corners at Tangier, Brazzaville, Darwin and Hong Kong'. Although Orwell gave economic relations among the three blocks an eccentric slant, his economic forecasting, if not the timing, is remarkable.

Appendix: A special framework agreement for trade in agriculture and energy?

Energy (and to some extent agriculture) deserves special treatment. In both cases the reasons lie in the political sphere, rather than in economic factors, such as the presence of externalities or natural monopolies. The declared objectives of the Common Agricultural Policy (CAP) of the EU are to prevent depopulation of rural areas, and an excessive dependency of the EU on agricultural imports which could be irreversible in cases of war or epidemics in major exporting countries. After two oil shocks, many politicians feel that a total energy dependency is perilous. Moreover, the externalities of accidents in nuclear power generation in Eastern Europe have become a major West European concern. One way of ensuring (a safe) supply is to enter into long-term contracts or even better joint production, purchasing and transporting agreements backed up politically. If one has to accept that politically motivated interventions for all these reasons are anyway likely, one may ask what could be done to ensure that the outcome makes economic sense.

The FSU countries, and in particular Russia, are also motivated to develop energy and agriculture as part of an overall Continental design. First of all, these two sectors offer major trade potential either to save or to generate the foreign exchange needed to rebuild the economy. But this potential can only be realised if there is a secure foreign market outlet. As suggested by geography, the major potential market is the EU.

Second, Eastern European countries suffer most from the threat of disruptions of food supplies or of nuclear accidents. Therefore, reforms should gain support throughout Europe. Third, only the West can supply technology, management and resources to deal with these issues in time.

AGRICULTURE

In all Eastern European countries, the effects of collective ownership and centralised planning have been most disastrous in agriculture, but the worst situation is to be found in the FSU. This is best illustrated by the fact that the Soviet Union was a net importer of agricultural products, although its arable land surface was far larger than China's, which feeds more than one billion people. What are the prospects for agriculture in the FSU countries? We concentrate on the potential rather than the expected scenario although reality will certainly fall short of the theoretical potential. In the Central European countries it is more likely that there will be a substantial (even if incomplete) recovery of agricultural productivity as assumed in the calculations of the cost of EU membership of these countries.

Collectivisation of agriculture in the Soviet Union began in the 1930s, about 20 years earlier than in Eastern Europe. The destruction of the traditional peasantry is therefore more complete and property rights have to be developed from scratch. In addition, collective farms were larger and more dominant in Soviet agriculture, so that the division of labour was more pronounced. Low pay and long distances to urban centres have made living conditions in the countryside so dismal that people with the slightest skills have left for urban centres. Hence, one major obstacle to reorganising agriculture will be the low skill level of the rural population. Western assistance in managing and equipping production, distribution and processing will make a very important contribution. The importance of these factors can be seen from the fact that highly processed food contributes a large proportion (or 10 per cent) of the total imports of all FSU countries.

In our view, some of the countries of the FSU (Russia, Ukraine, Belarus, Moldavia, the Baltic States) should be gradually able to reduce agricultural imports and become net exporters. Price liberalisation, private ownership and foreign assistance would help in moving towards this goal.

We see long-term opportunities in the excellent quality of soil in the south-western and western FSU, combined with the proximity of the European Union, the largest market in the world. Northern, Central and Southern Europe are all accessible through waterways, assuring transport costs competitive with trans-Atlantic ones. The vital question is whether the EU market for agricultural products will be opened up. We see some grounds for guarded optimism. For some key data see Table 16.A.1.

It will become very awkward for the EU to keep its agricultural markets closed to imports from Eastern Europe, for the most effective help Europe can provide is to open its markets, including its agricultural markets. Maintaining the CAP in its present form will be increasingly difficult because of the high resource cost, the political conflicts created by the dumping of European surpluses and the environmental problems caused by over-production. The reforms of the CAP approved in mid-1992 (the so-called MacSharry Plan) are a modest, but promising start. The accession of major producers (or the mere threat of accession) will bring further pressures for reforms

TABLE 16.A.1 Soviet agriculture in international comparison

	Soviet Union	China	US	Western Europe
Land area in 1988				
(1 000 ha)	2 227 200	932 691	916 660	372 487
– arable	227 700	93 345	187 881	82 422
– permanent crops	4 726	3 300	2 034	12 018
– permanent pasture	371 800	319 080	241 467	68 354
– forest and woodland	945 000	117 115	265 188	128 236
Irrigation (1 000 ha)				
– 1973	12 746	40 852	16 510	8 861
– 1988	20 782	44 938	18 102	11 501
Tractors in use in 1988				
(1 000)	2 692	876	4 670	8 573
Percentage of population in agriculture				
– 1980	20.0%	74.2%	3.5%	10.4%
– 1989	13.6%	68.2%	2.4%	7.1%
Production in 1989				
(1979–1981 = 100)				
– livestock	125.1	188.6	109.8	106.0
– cereals	127.8	129.3	93.3	117.9
Yield (kg/ha)				
– cereals	1 905	4 014	4 410	4 503
– potatoes	11 613	11 550	32 160	25 100
– cotton	2 529	2 193	1 819	2 727

Source: Food and Agriculture Organisation of the United Nations, 1989

since, as shown above, even a partial recovery of Central European agriculture could bankrupt the CAP if some of these countries are admitted. A theoretical treatment is developed in De Benedictis and Padoa (1994).

With the CAP relaxed, imports from Eastern Europe can substitute for EU production. In the longer run, it is perfectly reasonable to go a step further. Animal husbandry in the EU uses high-cost domestic (e.g. wheat) or cheap imported foodstuffs (e.g. soya beans) and causes serious environmental problems in the most efficient, and hence dense, production centres. Europe's environment is a very expensive production factor and its cost rises much faster than in the vast spaces of Eastern Europe. It would therefore be desirable to reduce animal husbandry in the EU and to transfer production to the East. Instead of exporting animal foodstuffs, Eastern Europe would then have the opportunity to export products with high value-added (meat and dairy products, for example).

A suggestive estimation of the welfare gains (as opposed to the budgetary cost at unchanged policies) derived from granting Eastern European (without the FSU) agricultural exports free access to the EU is available in Rollo and Smith (1993). They assume that 1989 export destinations remain the same and that Eastern European agricultural exports are doubled, with the additional flow being diverted to the EU. Further assumptions define the reaction of the EU. One assumption is to leave CAP unchanged. Then the increase in imports from Eastern Europe is exactly matched by an increase in (subsidised) EU exports to the rest of the world. This would leave former consumers in the EU in an unchanged position and tax-payers worse off. The alternative assumption is that EU exports to third countries remain unchanged. Then the effect of increased supply falls entirely on the EU price level.

In Table 16.A.2 the case where EU prices are allowed to change is shown in the first five lines. The last line corresponds to the case where the CAP remains unchanged. In that case EU welfare is reduced by ECU 2 bn in the form of a transfer to Eastern Europe by tax-payers in the EU. If CAP prices are lowered then EU farmers would lose ECU 3.7 bn, consumers would gain ECU 3.9 bn and tax-payers ECU 1.8 bn. The net impact on EU welfare would be a gain of ECU 2 bn, whilst Eastern Europe would gain ECU 1.9 bn. Therefore, overall, Europe would gain and EU farmers could be compensated for their loss. If there is strong resistance to Eastern European imports it must be that these compensatory payments are not perceived as really obtainable and that certain regions of the EU with dense temperate agriculture would be more than proportionally affected.

In the light of these tentative estimates, we conclude this part on an optimistic note. Eastern European agriculture has export capacity if it manages to introduce private property, to reform prices, and to secure Western support for improving food storage, processing and distribution. In addition, it needs access to European markets, and this should not prove impossible over the long term. Opening up its agricultural markets is arguably the greatest contribution Western Europe can make to Eastern European development.

ENERGY

Energy is now the most important sector of the Russian economy.[1] According to official sources, it accounted for 'only' 10.8 per cent of the total output of the FSU in 1990. But when output is evaluated at competitive market prices, the energy sector accounts for much more. At world market prices, the value of the energy output of

TABLE 16.A.2 Welfare changes of increased imports from Eastern Europe (ECU millions)

	Cereals	Sugar	White Meat	Red Meat	Milk	Oilseeds	Oils	TOTAL
Change in producer surplus	−773	−338	−599	−1283	−305	−64	−379	−3741
Change in consumer surplus	557	259	612	1250	291	186	817	3972
Change in tax payer cost	427	181	102	1019	224	0	279	1788
EC net welfare change	210	106	115	986	−238	121	717	2017
Gain to Eastern Europe	476	34	58	1040	217	0	61	1887
Memo:								
Tax-payer cost, EC prices unchanged	−504	−36	−80	−1139	−222	0	−99	−2081

Source: Rollo and Smith (1993)

Note: Negative sign indicates loss to tax-payer. Eastern Europe is defined as the five countries that have signed the 'Europe Agreements'

Russia in 1992 was equal to the value of the entire Russian GDP. In 1993, when the exchange rate moved to a more realistic level, the value of the tradable energy output (oil and gas) of Russia was still over 50 per cent of GDP.

Energy was even more important in the FSU's foreign trade, accounting for over 50 per cent of hard currency earnings and over 60 per cent of Russian exports in 1993. The FSU was the largest producer of energy (and oil) in the world and, after Saudi Arabia, the largest oil exporter. Russian oil production has declined a lot, but it remains in the top league, especially in gas where the FSU is estimated to hold 40 per cent of world reserves.

The fate of the Russian economy will depend, therefore, on whether income from energy can be sustained or even increased over the years to come. Pessimism is widespread because some of the most easily accessible oil fields are now depleted so that the cost of exploitation is rising and investment in production and transport has collapsed since 1990.

Oil production in the FSU has decreased between 1980 and 1990. Until 1990 this decrease was more than offset by the increase in natural gas production, but domestic consumption rose in line with supplies. Since 1990 natural gas production has declined marginally.

It is difficult to compare the FSU statistics with the more recent ones for Russia. But the basic factors have not changed: production, transport, and refining capacities are inefficient and grossly wasteful. Oil refineries are technologically backward and lacking hydrocracking and catalytic units. As a consequence, the share of heavy oils, which must be sold at unattractive prices, remains excessive. Finally, security aspects have stopped expansion of nuclear energy production and caused stoppages of gas transportation and resistance to further development. About one-third of the existing pipelines have polymeric insulation, reliable for 10 years but planned to be in use for 30.

As shown in Table 16.A.3, energy waste in domestic consumption remains at record levels in Russia. The ratio of energy use to GDP is about 15 times that of Western Europe and 10 times that of the United States if one evaluates Russian GDP at market rates (in early 1994 Russian GDP *per capita* was below US$ 2,000). Reducing this waste requires, first of all, moving domestic energy prices gradually to world market levels. The reaction of demand will require time since it has to be based on the installation of meters for private consumption and the re-equipping of industry.

What is the potential for energy savings in the FSU and especially Russia? The starting point is a ratio of energy consumption to (market) GDP of above 3 (tons oil equivalent per US$ 1,000) for Russia,[2] as compared to only 0.2 for Finland (a rich Nordic market economy), 0.33 for the United States (with similar climatic conditions) and 0.46 for Turkey (with a similar GDP *per capita*).

A reduction of the energy to GDP ratio by 3 per cent per year over the next 10 to 20 years should be the minimum in the light of recent OECD experience after the two oil price increases of 1973 and 1979. Between 1972 and 1989, the energy intensity of real GDP in the United States fell by 28 per cent; in the European Union, it fell from a lower level by 20 per cent. Over the same period the intensity of output with respect to oil alone fell by about 35 per cent and 40 per cent respectively.[3] These reductions were achieved in spite of the ultimately negligible energy-price increases in real terms for final energy users, because between 1972 and 1989 energy prices in the US

TABLE 16.A.3 Energy intensity*

Country	US$ (billion) GDP	Energy Consumption (tons, oil equivalent)	Energy Intensity
European reform economies			
Russia (1994)	256.82	815.2	3.17
Ukraine est.***	52.15	195.8	3.75
Czech Republic/Slovakia **	33.17	61.4	1.85
Hungary	35.21	24.2	0.69
Poland**	78.02	98.3	1.26
European market economies			
Finland	109.54	21.6	0.20
Germany	1776.92	335.1	0.19
Sweden	246.83	41.2	0.17
Turkey **	108.00	50.1	0.46
Other market economies			
Argentina	228.89	41.8	0.18
Brazil **	405.77	92.3	0.23
Canada	568.04	208.6	0.37
Japan	3670.03	451.0	0.12
United States	5950.70	1960.8	0.33

Source: Own calculations on data from IMF and BP
Notes:
* 1992 data
** 1991
*** Estimates are US$ 1,000 *per capita*

consumer price index increased by only 17 per cent over non-energy items. Therefore, in the FSU, a much more substantial increase in energy prices relative to non-energy prices (over 100 per cent), combined with a restructuring of industry (which has also contributed to energy savings in the OECD countries, but in smaller proportions[4]), should lead to at the very least comparable reductions in energy intensities, say 100 per cent over a decade.

What does this imply for Russian energy production, consumption and exports? Table 16.A.4 contains two scenarios for Russia and the FSU: scenario I assumes no price change, and hence no change in energy intensity, so that domestic demand will grow in line with GDP which we assume grows, on average, at 3 per cent p.a. over the next decade. Scenario II assumes that prices will increase by 100 per cent so that consumption will be cut by 50 per cent over one decade; this is in line with the empirical findings of a long-term price elasticity of demand equal to 0.5. For each of these two demand scenarios two production scenarios are provided. The first one assumes that energy production will continue its growth trend at minus 2.5 per cent p.a. The second simply assumes that production will be constant. If prices are really increased this assumption might turn out to be too conservative. Since production is only partially determined by the physical factors stressed by energy engineers, we concentrate on the combination of constant energy prices plus declining production and increased energy prices plus constant production. For Russia the differences between these two combinations are very large and reach their maximum in the year 2002 of almost US$ 85 billion (at 1992 prices) in annual export earning, more than twice current energy exports. In the worst case Russia would cease to be a net energy exporter around the turn of the decade. In the best case exports would almost double to US$ 72 billion. For the FSU the difference between worst and best case is even more pronounced, as high as US$ 120 billion in the year 2002.

These rough calculations show that the pricing of energy is crucial for the Russian economy (and the FSU) and its place in the world trading system. We have so far deliberately discussed only the demand for energy in aggregate terms. What form Russian energy exports will take (oil, gas or electricity) will depend largely on the behaviour of oil production and the extent to which Russia can become a reliable partner so that Western Europe is willing to increase its dependency from that source. This might require, however, an international framework, such as the European Energy Charter discussed below.

TABLE 16.A.4 A. Export potential: Russia (net energy exports in US$ billions)

	Scenario I No price change/3% growth		Scenario II 100% price increase/3% growth	
	(1)	(2)	(1)	(2)
1993	40.3	44.5	46.1	50.3
1994	34.3	42.6	45.6	53.9
1995	28.3	40.6	44.9	57.3
1996	22.4	38.6	44.1	60.3
1997	16.5	36.6	43.0	63.0
1998	10.7	34.4	41.7	65.5
1999	4.9	32.2	40.2	67.6
2000	−0.8	30.0	38.6	69.5
2001	−6.6	27.7	36.7	71.4
2002	−12.4	25.3	34.7	72.5

TABLE 16.A.4 B. Export potential: FSU(net energy exports in US$ billions)

	Scenario I No price change/3% growth		Scenario II 100% price increase/3% growth	
	(1)	(2)	(1)	(2)
1993	23.9	29.3	32.7	38.2
1994	15.7	26.5	33.0	43.8
1995	7.6	23.3	32.9	48.8
1996	−0.5	20.5	32.4	53.4
1997	−8.5	17.3	31.6	57.6
1998	−16.6	14.1	30.5	61.3
1999	−24.6	10.8	29.1	64.5
2000	−32.6	7.3	27.4	67.4
2001	−40.6	3.8	25.4	69.9
2002	−48.5	0.1	23.1	71.9

Production scenarios: (1) production declines by 2.5 per cent per annum; (2) constant production

Resources for investment in the energy sector have been declining in the 1990s. During the 1980s, the energy sector absorbed about 20 per cent of overall investments, with a net acceleration between 1985 (14 per cent) and 1988 (24 per cent). The heavy emphasis on energy investments represented a drag on resources available for investments elsewhere and mainly served to maintain wasteful energy consumption. In addition, the productivity of new investments was very low. According to several reports, even physical productivity was sometimes negative (that is, it sometimes required more than one unit of energy to increase supply to users by one unit). This huge absorption of resources without corresponding returns contributed significantly to the overall economic downturn. It will be essential in the future to reduce costs by using energy more efficiently rather than by simply increasing production. In the energy sector itself, high prices should focus investment on more efficient technology in production, transport and refining, not on expanding extraction. The largest investment, however, will be required on the user side; existing equipment must be replaced by more energy-efficient machinery.

Because reasonably rapid development and reconstruction of Russia and the FSU will not be feasible without a substantial contribution from the energy (and agricultural) sector, several important lessons emerge from this discussion.

First, major efforts must be made on both the production and consumption sides in order to generate a large surplus for energy exports. Given the technology and capital requirements, Western resources will be needed.

Second, given the exorbitant waste of energy, a rapid price reform is mandatory, as argued above. The effects on industry and consumers could be spread over several years, but all new equipment will be energy efficient if price reform is certain. If such a policy were carried out consistently, much higher gains in energy efficiency would be attainable. Given the desolate condition of Russian industry, within the next 10 years at least 50 per cent of all capital will be scrapped or replaced. With an average growth of 3 per cent p.a. or more for the next ten years, about two-thirds of the 1994 capital stock would be replaced by the year 2004 and thus be energy-efficient. The efficiency level could double, and annual net exports could rise above the levels indicated in Table 16.A.4.

Third, under any scenario, oil will play a reduced role and natural gas an expanded one. Will export markets exist for natural gas? Western Europe is for the moment well supplied (Netherlands, Norway, Algeria) with natural gas, but not so at a higher level of demand in the medium-run.[5] Any shifts to Russian gas are, however, inconceivable without political negotiations and a redesigning of the transport networks. Inspired by these requirements and the need for massive Western assistance to the Russian energy sector, the Dutch Prime Minister Ruud Lubbers launched the idea of a European Energy Charter (EECH, see Ludlow and Ross 1990). The Charter so far only represents a political statement of intent although it was signed on 17 December 1991 by EU members and 43 states including most of the states of the FSU, including Russia.

The EECH was to build a framework for energy trade and co-operation in technological and financial matters. Main principles include:

- a stable and transparent legal framework for the private energy sector, in keeping with free market principles;

- increased access to energy resources (with due respect for national sovereignty) as well as related technology;
- the development of trade in energy products, materials and equipment;
- access to transport infrastructures, especially with regard to international energy transmission networks;
- improvements in energy efficiency in general and particular attention to the restructuring of the energy sector of Central and Eastern Europe and the FSU.

The EECH thus represents a formal link between the energy systems of the EU and those of the FSU.

The EECH is an example of policy proposals taking their inspiration from Western European integration: as a sectoral approach it is inspired by the experience of the European Coal and Steel Community (ECSC). How solid is the case for EECH? Let us first survey the arguments in favour.

Starting from the historic lesson of the ECSC it is significant that the ECSC was created for both political and economic reasons. The political aim was to control Germany's iron and steel industry and thereby control the key sector for economic growth and the defence industry. Economically, the idea was to manage politically a market where economies of scale in production had given rise to production cartels. Similar motivations underlie the EECH proposal. With energy as the key industrial sector, opening up to Western influence would facilitate the restructuring of the Russian economy. At the very least, Western investments in the Russian energy sector could be facilitated by reducing sovereign and industrial risks within an integrated framework. Because energy efficiency depends on reforms embracing the whole economy (price and structural reforms), the conditions attached to Western intervention could have an economy-wide effect. The magnitude of the energy problem and its key role suggest the energy sector as an efficient focus for reforms.

It would also be possible to negotiate long-term market contracts and the development of a transport network spanning the European continent. Given the externalities and economies of scale, a planned approach such as this might be economically justifiable. This could also apply to a common management of environmental problems. The Chernobyl disaster has demonstrated that the externalities involved can affect the entire continent. Reduced nuclear-energy production in the Soviet Union might thus be financially compensated within such a framework. These are the considerations that weigh in favour of an EECH. But there are also considerable difficulties.

First, it is not yet clear with which partners such a scheme would need to be negotiated, as energy-intensive areas even inside Russia claim independence.

Second, the European scale of the project is necessary, but hardly sufficient. Most of the energy resources are located in Siberia and could also be exported to Asia. Moreover, United States oil companies have already started to invest in the FSU.

Finally, the approach would need to respect meticulously priority for market solutions, that is, to take care only of problems which the private sector cannot solve. The ECSC was a supra-national authority with a heavy *dirigiste* orientation. This would not be feasible or desirable in the EECH, which should support a market-based solution.

Notes

1. After agriculture and the military complex on the basis of official sources using actual non-market determined prices.
2. According to estimates by the International Energy Agency (1990), the Soviet Union used 1 tons oil equivalent per US$ 1,000 of GDP in 1988, as compared to 0.4 toe for OECD countries. The ratio of 2.5 is lower than our estimate of 3 in Table 16.A.3 because the Agency used a much higher GDP estimate for the Soviet Union.
3. See Economic Report of the President (1991), Commission of the European Communities (1990).
4. The inefficient use of energy is much higher in certain sectors than is suggested by overall data. Because these sectors also represent a disproportionate share of overall economic activity (larger than in the West), the savings would be particularly large (the least energy-intensive sector, services, accounted for only 27 per cent of the GDP of the FSU, as compared to over 50 per cent in the OECD countries.
5. According to current estimates (see Caddy 1993) demand for gas in Western Europe is to increase by 60% until the year 2005. At present 80–85 million tons oil equivalent remain uncontracted. This gap must be filled by seeking out new sources of supply.

References to Part V

Balassa, B. (1975) Trade creation and diversion in the European Common Market, in Balassa, B. (ed.) *European Economic Integration*, North Holland, Amsterdam.

Balassa, B. and **Bauwens, L.** (1988) *Changing Trade Patterns in Manufactured Goods: an Econometric Investigation*, North Holland, Amsterdam.

Baldwin, R.E. (1994), *Towards an Integrated Europe*, Centre for Economic Policy Research, London.

Bank for International Settlements (BIS) (1994) *Annual Report*, BIS, Basle.

Boote, A.R. (1992) *Assessing Eastern Europe's capital needs*, International Monetary Fund, Working Paper WP/92/12, February.

Brenton, P. and **Gros, D.** (1993) *The budgetary implications of EC enlargement*, Brussels, Centre for European Policy Studies, CEPS Working Document No.78, May.

Brenton, P. and **Kendall, T**. (1994) *Back to earth with the gravity model: further estimates for Eastern European countries*, Centre for European Policy Studies, Brussels, December.

Caddy, J. (1993) The export of oil and natural gas from Russia: prospects for the future, *MOCT*, No.3.

CEPR (1990) *Monitoring European Integration: The Impact of Eastern Europe*, CEPR, London.

CEPR (1992) *Is Bigger Better? The Economics of EC Enlargement*, CEPR, London.

Collins, S. and **Rodrik, D.** (1991) Eastern Europe and the Soviet Union in the world economy, Institute for International Economics: *Policy Analyses in International Economics*, No.32, May.

Commission of the European Communities (1990) Stabilisation, liberalisation and devolution: assessment of the economic situation and reform process in the Soviet Union, *European Economy*, No.45, Brussels: CEC, December.

Davis, I. and **Dunne, P.** (1994) Disarming the military, *European Brief*, **1** (5), p. 12.

De Benedictis, L. and **Padoan, P.L.** (1994) The integration of Eastern Europe into the EC: a club-theory interest groups approach, in Lombardini, S. and Padoan, P.L. (eds), *Europe Between East and South*, Kluwer Academic Publ., Dordrecht..

De Gregorio, J. (1991) *Economic growth in Latin America*, International Monetary Fund, Working Paper WP/91/71, July.

De Long, J.B. and **Eichengreen, B.** (1993) The Marshall Plan: history's most successful structural adjustment program, in Dornbusch, R., Noelling, W. and Layard,

R. (eds), *Postwar Economic Reconstruction and Lessons for the East Today*, MIT Press, Cambridge, Massachusetts.

de Melo, J. and **Panagariya, A.** (eds) (1993) *New Dimensions in Regional Integration*, Cambridge University Press, Cambridge.

de Melo, J., Panagariya, A. and **Rodrick, D.** (1993) The new regionalism: a country perspective in de Melo, J. and Panagariya, A. *New Dimensions in Regional Integration*, Cambridge University Press, Cambridge).

Desai, P. (1994) No megabucks and no miracles, *European Brief*, **1** (5), p. 8.

Economic Report of the President (1991) Government Printing Office, Washington, DC.

Fitoussi, J.P. and **Phelps, E.S.** (1990) Global effects of East European rebuilding and the adequacy of Western saving: an issue for the 1990s, *Rivista di Politica Economica*, December.

Frankel, J. (1991) Is a Yen bloc forming in Pacific Asia?, in O'Brien, R. (ed.) *Finance and the International Economy: 5*, Oxford University Press, Oxford.

Fratianni, M. and **Pattison, J.** (1982) The economics of international organisations, *Kyklos*.

Giustiniani, A.F., Papadia, F. and **Porciani, D.** (1992) Growth and catch-up in Central and Eastern Europe: macroeconomic effects on Western countries, *Princeton Essays in International Finance*, No.186, April.

Gros, D. (1993) Costs and benefits of economic and monetary union: an application to the Former Soviet Union in Masson, P.R. and Taylor, M.P. (eds) *Policy Issues in the Operation of Currency Unions*, Cambridge University Press, Cambridge, pp. 55–74.

Gros, D. and **Gonciarz, A.** (1994) A note on the trade potential of Central and Eastern Europe, manuscript, Centre for European Policy Studies (CEPS), Brussels.

Gros, D. and **Steinherr, A.** (1991) Economic reform in the Soviet Union: pas-de-deux between disintegration and macroeconomic destabilization, *Princeton Studies in International Finance*, No.71, November.

Gros, D. and **Steinherr, A.** (1992) *Redesigning economic geography after the fall of the Soviet empire*, Centre for European Policy Studies (CEPS), Brussels.

Gros, D. and **Vandille, G.** (1994) *Slovenian and European Trade Structures*, manuscript, Centre for European Policy Studies (CEPS), Brussels, and Catholic University of Leuven, December.

Gulde, A.M. and **Schulze-Ghattas, M.** (1992) *Aggregation of economic indicators across countries: exchange rate versus PPP based GDP weights*, International Monetary Fund, Working Paper WP/92/36, May.

Hamilton, C.B. and **Winters, L.A.** (1992) Opening up international trade with Eastern Europe, *Economic Policy*.

Handler, H. and **Steinherr, A.** (1993) Capital needs and investment financing in Eastern countries in: Fair, D.E. and Raymond, R.J. (1993) *The New Europe: Evolving Economic and Financial Systems in East and West*, Kluwer Academic Publ., Dordrecht.

Hare, P.G. (1994) A blank cheque could bounce, *European Brief*, **1** (5), p. 10.

Havlik, P. (1992) East–West GDP comparisons: problems, methods and results, in Richter, S. (ed.) *The Transition from Command to Market Economies in East-Central Europe*, The Vienna Institute for Comparative Economic Studies (WIIW).

Havrylyshyn, O. and **Pritchett, L.** (1991) *European trade patterns after the transition*, World Bank, WPS 748, World Bank, Washington, DC.

Helpman, E. and **Krugman, P.** (1985) *Market Structure and Foreign Trade: Increasing Returns, Imperfect Competition, and the International Economy*, MIT Press, Cambridge, Massachusetts.

Hughes, G. and **Hare, P.** (1992) Trade policy and restructuring in Eastern Europe, in Fleming, J. and Rollo, J. (eds) *Trade, Payments and Adjustment in Central and Eastern Europe*, Royal Institute of International Affairs, London.

International Energy Agency (1990) *Energy Efficiency in the USSR*, Organisation for Economic Co-operation and Development, Paris, November.

Krugman, P. (1991a) Increasing returns and economic geography, *Journal of Political Economy*, June.

Krugman, P. (1991b) *The move to free trade zones*, Federal Reserve Bank of Kansas City Review, December.

Krugman, P. (1993) Regionalism versus multilateralism: analytical notes in De Melo, J. and Panangariya, A. (eds) *New Dimension in Regional Integration*, Cambridge, University Press, Cambridge.

Lawrence, R.Z. (1991) Emerging regional arrangements: building blocks or stumbling blocks? in O'Brien, R. (ed.), *Finance and the International Economy: 5*, Oxford University Press, Oxford.

Layard, R., Blanchard, O., Dornbusch, R. and **Longman, P.** (1992) *East-West Migration: The Alternatives*, MIT Press, Cambridge, Massachusetts.

Lucas, R.E. (1988) On the mechanics of economic development, *Journal of Monetary Economics*: **22**(1), pp. 3–42.

Ludlow, P. and **Ross, H.** (1990) An energy for the future Europe, *Financial Times*, 24 October.

McDonald, D. and **Thumann, G.** (1990) Investment needs in East Germany in Lipschitz, L. and McDonald, D. (eds) German unification: economic issues, International Monetary Fund, *Occasional Papers*, No.75, December, pp. 71–77.

Mann, C.L. (1990) *Towards the next generation of newly industrialising economies: the roles for macroeconomic policy and the manufacturing sector*, Federal Reserve Board, International Finance Discussion Papers, No.376, March.

Möbius, U. and **Schumacher, D.** (1990) *Eastern Europe and the European Community: trade relations and trade policy with regard to industrial products*, Paper prepared for the Joint Canada Germany Symposium, Toronto, November.

Ochel, W. (1991) Der Kapitalbedarf Osteuropas und der Sowjetunion, *Ifo-Schnelldienst*, **31**, pp. 3–8.

OECD (1992) *Reforming the economies of Central and Eastern Europe*, OECD, Paris.

Petith, H. (1977) European integration and the terms of trade, *Economic Journal*, **87**.

PlanEcon (1990) *How big are the Soviet and East European economies?*, Report No.6(52), December 28, pp. 1–18.

Rollo, J. (1992) *Association Agreements Between the EC and CSFR, Hungary and Poland: a Half Empty Glass?*, Royal Institute of International Affairs, London.

Rollo, J. and **Smith, A.** (1993) The political economy of Eastern European trade with the European Community: why so sensitive?, *Economic Policy*, April.

Romer, P.M. (1986) Increasing returns and long-run growth, *Journal of Political Economy*, 94(5), pp.1002–37.

Sachs, J. (1994) Buying time for democracy, *European Brief*, April/May.

Sapir, A. (1992) Regional integration in Europe, *Economic Papers of the Commission of the EC*, No.94, Commission of the EC, Brussels.

Schulmann, H. (1992) How to design a capital magnet, *The International Economy*, July/August.

Scott, M.F. (1989) *A New View of Economic Growth*, Oxford University Press, Oxford.

Scott, M.F. (1992) Policy implications of 'A New View of Economic Growth', *The Economic Journal*, **102**, pp. 622–32.

Solow, R.M. (1956) A contribution to the theory of economic growth, *Quarterly Journal of Economics*, **70**(1), pp.65–94.

Steinherr, A. and **Runge, J.** (1978) The evolution of the foreign trade structure of West Germany from 1962 to 1972, *Zeitschrift für die Gesamte Staatswissenschaft*, June.

Summers, R. and **Heston, A.** (1988) A new set of international comparisons of real product and prices: estimates for 130 countries, *Review of Income and Wealth*, **34**.

Urban, W. (1992) Economic lessons for the East European countries from two newly industrialising countries in the Far East? in Richter, S. (ed.) *The Transition from Command to Market Economies in East-Central Europe*, The Vienna Institute for Comparative Economic Studies (WIIW).

World Bank (1991) *World Development Report*, Oxford University Press, Oxford.

Index